Multi-Criteria Decision Analysis in Management

Abhishek Behl
Indian Institute of Technology, Bombay, India

A volume in the Advances in Logistics, Operations, and Management Science (ALOMS) Book Series

IGI Global
DISSEMINATOR OF KNOWLEDGE

Published in the United States of America by
IGI Global
Business Science Reference (an imprint of IGI Global)
701 E. Chocolate Avenue
Hershey PA, USA 17033
Tel: 717-533-8845
Fax: 717-533-8661
E-mail: cust@igi-global.com
Web site: http://www.igi-global.com

Library of Congress Cataloging-in-Publication Data

Names: Behl, Abhishek, 1987- editor.
Title: Multi-criteria decision analysis in management / Abhishek Behl, editor.
Description: Hershey, PA : Business Science Reference, [2020] | Includes bibliographical references and index. | Summary: "This book provides insights into the rationale behind using MCDM techniques to solve decision-making problems and provides comprehensive discussions on these techniques from their inception, development, and growth to their advancements and applications"-- Provided by publisher.
Identifiers: LCCN 2019037785 (print) | LCCN 2019037786 (ebook) | ISBN 9781799822165 (h/c) | ISBN 9781799822172 (s/c) | ISBN 9781799822189 (ebook)
Subjects: LCSH: Multiple criteria decision making. | Decision making.
Classification: LCC T57.95 .M818 2020 (print) | LCC T57.95 (ebook) | DDC 658.4/03--dc23
LC record available at https://lccn.loc.gov/2019037785
LC ebook record available at https://lccn.loc.gov/2019037786

This book is published in the IGI Global book series Advances in Logistics, Operations, and Management Science (ALOMS) (ISSN: 2327-350X; eISSN: 2327-3518)

British Cataloguing in Publication Data
A Cataloguing in Publication record for this book is available from the British Library.

For electronic access to this publication, please contact: eresources@igi-global.com.

Advances in Logistics, Operations, and Management Science (ALOMS) Book Series

John Wang
Montclair State University, USA

ISSN:2327-350X
EISSN:2327-3518

Mission

Operations research and management science continue to influence business processes, administration, and management information systems, particularly in covering the application methods for decision-making processes. New case studies and applications on management science, operations management, social sciences, and other behavioral sciences have been incorporated into business and organizations real-world objectives.

The **Advances in Logistics, Operations, and Management Science** (ALOMS) Book Series provides a collection of reference publications on the current trends, applications, theories, and practices in the management science field. Providing relevant and current research, this series and its individual publications would be useful for academics, researchers, scholars, and practitioners interested in improving decision making models and business functions.

Coverage

- Computing and information technologies
- Political Science
- Finance
- Production Management
- Networks
- Services management
- Information Management
- Operations Management
- Organizational Behavior
- Risk Management

IGI Global is currently accepting manuscripts for publication within this series. To submit a proposal for a volume in this series, please contact our Acquisition Editors at Acquisitions@igi-global.com or visit: http://www.igi-global.com/publish/.

The Advances in Logistics, Operations, and Management Science (ALOMS) Book Series (ISSN 2327-350X) is published by IGI Global, 701 E. Chocolate Avenue, Hershey, PA 17033-1240, USA, www.igi-global.com. This series is composed of titles available for purchase individually; each title is edited to be contextually exclusive from any other title within the series. For pricing and ordering information please visit http://www.igi-global.com/book-series/advances-logistics-operations-management-science/37170. Postmaster: Send all address changes to above address.

Titles in this Series

For a list of additional titles in this series, please visit: www.igi-global.com/book-series

Handbook of Research on Project Management Strategies and Tools for Organizational Success
Nelson Antonio Moreno-Monsalve (Universidad EAN, Colombia) H. Mauricio Diez-Silva (Universidad EAN, Colombia) Flor Nancy Diaz-Piraquive (Universidad Catolica de Colombia, Colombia) and Rafael Ignacio Perez-Uribe (Universidad EAN, Colombia)
Business Science Reference • © 2020 • 400pp • H/C (ISBN: 9781799819349) • US $285.00

Advancing Skill Development for Business Managers in Industry 4.0 Emerging Research and Opportunities
Sara Fazzin (H-Farm College, UK)
Business Science Reference • © 2020 • 168pp • H/C (ISBN: 9781799820369) • US $185.00

Management and Inter/Intra Organizational Relationships in the Textile and Apparel Industry
Vasilica-Maria Margalina (Technical University of Ambato, Ecuador) and José M. Lavín (CESINE University Centre, Spain)
Business Science Reference • © 2020 • 427pp • H/C (ISBN: 9781799818595) • US $215.00

Neutrosophic Sets in Decision Analysis and Operations Research
Mohamed Abdel-Basset (Zagazig University, Egypt) and Florentin Smarandache (University of New Mexico, USA)
Engineering Science Reference • © 2020 • 300pp • H/C (ISBN: 9781799825555) • US $245.00

Leadership, Management, and Adoption Techniques for Digital Service Innovation
Kamaljeet Sandhu (University of New England, Australia)
Business Science Reference • © 2020 • 342pp • H/C (ISBN: 9781799827993) • US $225.00

Global Perspectives on Green Business Administration and Sustainable Supply Chain Management
Syed Abdul Rehman Khan (Tsinghua University, China)
Business Science Reference • © 2020 • 362pp • H/C (ISBN: 9781799821731) • US $225.00

Handbook of Research on the Applications of International Transportation and Logistics for World Trade
Gökçe Çiçek Ceyhun (Bursa Technical University, Turkey)
Business Science Reference • © 2020 • 578pp • H/C (ISBN: 9781799813972) • US $345.00

Informing View of Organization Strategic Perspective
Bob Travica (University of Manitoba, Canada)
Business Science Reference • © 2020 • 386pp • H/C (ISBN: 9781799827603) • US $245.00

IGI Global
DISSEMINATOR OF KNOWLEDGE

701 East Chocolate Avenue, Hershey, PA 17033, USA
Tel: 717-533-8845 x100 • Fax: 717-533-8661
E-Mail: cust@igi-global.com • www.igi-global.com

Editorial Advisory Board

Table of Contents

Preface xv

Acknowledgment xx

Chapter 1
Interpretive Structural Modeling: Background, Concepts, and Application 1
Aastha Behl, Pranveer Singh Institute of Technology, India
Abhinav Pal, Symbiosis International University, India

Chapter 2
Application of ISM in the Manufacturing Sector 28
Abhinav Pal, Symbiosis International University, India
Jisha Rajendran, Amity School of Economics, Amity University, India
Aastha Behl, Pranveer Singh Institute of Technology, India

Chapter 3
Exploring Key Success Factors of Indian Pharmaceutical Supply Chain Using Interpretive Structural Modelling 46
Anurag Mishra, Indian Institute of Technology, Bombay, India
Pankaj Dutta, Indian Institute of Technology, Bombay, India
Suruj Kakoti, Indian Institute of Technology, Bombay, India

Chapter 4
Hybrid Multi-Criteria Models: Joint Health and Safety Unit Selection on Hybrid Multi-Criteria Decision Making 62
Ömer Faruk Efe, Afyon Kocatepe University, Turkey

Chapter 5
Multi-Criteria Decision-Making Process for Decentralized Healthcare Services Assessment 85
William Alberto Cruz Castañeda, Universidade do Estado de Santa Catarina, Brazil

Chapter 6
Multicriteria Decision Support Model for Selection of Tinplate Suppliers: A Case Study in CAN Company 111
Rafaela Ribeiro Pinho, Polytechnic of Porto, Portugal
Ana Paula Lopes, Polytechnic of Porto, Portugal

Chapter 7
The Technique for Order of Preference by Similarity to Ideal Solution Method in Fuzzy Environment: Fuzzy TOPSIS Method 139
Merve Cengiz Toklu, Sakarya University, Turkey

Chapter 8
Intuitionistic Fuzzy TOPSIS Model Based on Reliability Criteria and a Dynamic Mathematical Operator for Solving MCGDM Problems 169
Daniel Osezua Aikhuele, Bells University of Technology, Nigeria

Chapter 9
Modified TOPSIS Method With Banking Case Study 189
Semra Erpolat Taşabat, Mimar Sinan Fine Art University, Turkey & Bahçeşehir University, Turkey
Tuğba Kıral Özkan, Bahçeşehir University, Turkey

Chapter 10
TOPSIS vs. VIKOR: A Case Study for Determining Development Level of Countries 225
Semra Erpolat Taşabat, Mimar Sinan Fine Art University, Turkey & Bahçeşehir University, Turkey
Tuğba Kıral Özkan, Bahçeşehir University, Turkey

Chapter 11
Entropy-Based VIKOR Method and a Case Study: An Evaluation of Websites' Technical and Popularity Performances 251
Burcu Avcı Öztürk, Bursa Uludag University, Turkey

Chapter 12
Promethee: A Tool for Multi-Criteria Decision Analysis 282
Priyam Verma, Symbiosis International University, India

Chapter 13
Fuzzy Failure Mode and Effects Analysis in a Pharmaceutical Production Process With Fuzzy PROMETHEE Method 310
Sündüz Dağ, Istanbul University, Turkey

Chapter 14
Nudge Theory and Decision Making: Enabling People to Make Better Choices 335
Vikramsinh Amarsinh Patil, Symbiosis International University, India

Chapter 15
Data Analysis on Global Stratification.. 355
Kirti Raj Bhatele, Rustamji Institute of Technology, India & BSF Academy, Gwalior, India
Stuti Singhal, Rustamji Institute of Technology, India & BSF Academy, Tekanpur, India
Muktasha R. Mithora, Rustamji Institute of Technology, India & BSF Academy, Gwalior, India
Sneha Sharma, Rustamji Institute of Technology, India & BSF Academy, Tekanpur, India

Compilation of References 379

About the Contributors 416

Index 420

Detailed Table of Contents

Preface xv

Acknowledgment xx

Chapter 1
Interpretive Structural Modeling: Background, Concepts, and Application 1
Aastha Behl, Pranveer Singh Institute of Technology, India
Abhinav Pal, Symbiosis International University, India

The chapter explains the technique of ISM (Interpretive Structural Modeling) in Multi-criteria decision Analysis (MCDA). ISM is a method to identify inter relationship among various factors pertaining to the authors' research problem. This technique starts with identification of key factors, collected through an extensive literature review of the study. The factors are validated with the help of expert opinions. A pair wise comparative analysis helps in developing a structural self-interaction matrix (SSIM). This is followed by conversion of SSIM to Reachability Matrix, partitioned into different levels. This helps in developing a diagraph, with the help of which an ISM Model is developed. It is also accompanied by MICMAC Analysis which presents a graphical picture of the driving power and dependence power of each factor considered for the study. The chapter would help in understanding the steps involved in the application of ISM technique with the help of hypothetical cases.

Chapter 2
Application of ISM in the Manufacturing Sector 28
Abhinav Pal, Symbiosis International University, India
Jisha Rajendran, Amity School of Economics, Amity University, India
Aastha Behl, Pranveer Singh Institute of Technology, India

This chapter discusses the application of Interpretive Structural Modelling (ISM) in the manufacturing sector. Authors provide a brief about ISM and its usage in the current scenario, and a comprehensive literature review that sheds light on the methodology used over the years in the application of ISM. The chapter assesses the method's advantages and disadvantages. It introduces the technique of ISM in the manufacturing sector, and discusses the applications of ISM in the manufacturing sector along the review of literature.

Chapter 3
Exploring Key Success Factors of Indian Pharmaceutical Supply Chain Using Interpretive Structural Modelling 46
Anurag Mishra, Indian Institute of Technology, Bombay, India
Pankaj Dutta, Indian Institute of Technology, Bombay, India
Suruj Kakoti, Indian Institute of Technology, Bombay, India

Indian pharmaceutical industry is witnessing enormous challenges due to varying patent laws, increasing demand, and continuous pressure from the government to provide medicines at a lower price. To overcome these challenges, there is a need for a more robust supply chain (SC) which will help in information sharing and reduce overall cost. The chapter determines the key drivers of Indian pharmaceutical SC, and draws the attention of industry, stakeholders, and top management to emphasise on these drivers to enhance the performance and profitability of SC. An interpretive structural modelling-based approach has been employed to model the pharmaceutical SC key drivers. The 16 key parameters have been identified across all major dimensions such as SC, HR, & organizational, market, technology, and reverse logistics. Further fuzzy MICMAC analysis is done to categorize based on their driving and dependence power. The factors like collaborative relationship among SC partners, quality regulations, third party logistics, and end-to-end responsive SC are found to be more important enablers.

Chapter 4
Hybrid Multi-Criteria Models: Joint Health and Safety Unit Selection on Hybrid Multi-Criteria Decision Making 62
Ömer Faruk Efe, Afyon Kocatepe University, Turkey

JHSUs should have occupational safety specialists, workplace physicians, and other health personnel to establish and provide services. To provide occupational safety services in the most effective operating environment, it is necessary to select the most appropriate JHSU. This chapter provides a hybrid model to assist the JHSU selection process. Using fuzzy logic linguistic variables makes an important contribution to decision making in uncertain environment. The hybrid model using Fuzzy AHP (Analytical Hierarchy Process) and Fuzzy TOPSIS (Technique for Similarity Sorting Preference for Ideal Solution) approaches were used in JHSU selection. The most important criterion was found to be the references of JHSU. Candidate JHSUs were evaluated on the basis of criteria with fuzzy TOPSIS. Five alternative JHSU were evaluated. Alternative 2 was found to be the most appropriate choice. A numerical example is presented to demonstrate the effectiveness of the proposed hybrid model.

Chapter 5
Multi-Criteria Decision-Making Process for Decentralized Healthcare Services Assessment 85
William Alberto Cruz Castañeda, Universidade do Estado de Santa Catarina, Brazil

Home health service, as decentralization form in many health systems, has an objective to deliver high-quality, long-term care inside the patient's home. However, management of those services is about handling a complex decision problem related with the care delivery process composed by technologies, patients, structures, and professionals. Consequently, the decision problem requires finding effective ways to involve assessment and management of several criterias to achieve continuous quality improvement. For this purpose, its useful implements structured approaches with multiple criteria decision analysis (MCDA) techniques. Nevertheless, there are many MCDA methods available and these differ not just in how they are put into practice but also in terms of fundamental theories underpinning them. Therefore, this chapter contributes with a methodological approach to establish a decision analysis for assessing home health services through MACBETH and ULOWA techniques. To demonstrate the feasibility of the methodology, a study case was applied into a homecare service.

Chapter 6
Multicriteria Decision Support Model for Selection of Tinplate Suppliers: A Case Study in CAN Company 111
Rafaela Ribeiro Pinho, Polytechnic of Porto, Portugal
Ana Paula Lopes, Polytechnic of Porto, Portugal

The evaluation and selection of suppliers has been an issue of great strategic importance over time. In this way, a structured evaluation is crucial, considering several criteria. This work reviews several multicriteria decision support methodologies explored in the literature to solve the supplier evaluation process based on CAN company specifications, strategies, and requirements. Considering the characteristics of each supplier and a set of criteria with different weights, the AHP method and the PROMETHEE method are applied to establish a ranking according to the performance in the selected criteria. In addition, to help the company make the best decision, an analysis of ranking stability is performed by varying the weights assigned to the criteria. The study and models developed were easy to apply and understand, meeting the specified objectives.

Chapter 7
The Technique for Order of Preference by Similarity to Ideal Solution Method in Fuzzy Environment: Fuzzy TOPSIS Method 139
Merve Cengiz Toklu, Sakarya University, Turkey

Decision-making process is the selection of the most appropriate one among the alternatives. Different selection criteria are considered in the decision-making process. Simultaneous assessment of different evaluation criteria may not always be possible. Multi-criteria decision-making techniques provide an easily applicable mathematical solution in this respect. Technique for Order Preference by Similarity to Ideal Solution (TOPSIS) method is one of the multi-criteria decision-making techniques. This method is used in many problems in literature and allows multiple decision makers to choose the most suitable alternative by evaluating them together with different criteria. Assessments of decision makers may include linguistic statements. In this case, the Fuzzy Logic approach can be used. In this chapter, Fuzzy TOPSIS method is explained with a detailed numerical example.

Chapter 8
Intuitionistic Fuzzy TOPSIS Model Based on Reliability Criteria and a Dynamic Mathematical Operator for Solving MCGDM Problems 169
Daniel Osezua Aikhuele, Bells University of Technology, Nigeria

This chapter proposes a model based on the IF-TOPSIS method and the DIFWGϵ operator for the evaluation of renewable power plants. The model uses five reliability-based criteria and addresses the dynamic factors associated with renewable power plant operations. The factors include: the changing energy demand and consumption, the changing environmental conditions, rapidly increasing population, social activities, and awareness. The result from the evaluation shows that the Solar power plant (S3) is the most preferred power source considering the dynamic factors associated with the plant operation, the plant location, and the reliability-based criteria used for the assessment.

Chapter 9
Modified TOPSIS Method With Banking Case Study 189
Semra Erpolat Taşabat, Mimar Sinan Fine Art University, Turkey & Bahçeşehir University, Turkey
Tuğba Kıral Özkan, Bahçeşehir University, Turkey

In this chapter, an alternative measure to Euclidean distance measurement is proposed which is used to calculate positive and negative ideal solutions in the traditional TOPSIS method. Lp Minkowski family and L1 family distance measures were used for this purpose. By taking the averages of the distance measurements in the Lq and L1 families, more general and accurate level units were tried to be obtained. Thus, it was shown that TOPSIS method can give different results according to the distance measure used. The importance of the distance measurement unit was emphasized to rank the alternatives correctly. The implementation and evaluation of the proposed method was carried out through the financial performance of the deposit bank operating in the Turkish Banking Sector. It was seen that the rankings of the alternatives changed according to the distance measurements used. By referring to the distance measurements that can be used in the TOPSIS method, it was shown that the rank of the alternatives can vary according to the preferred distance measure.

Chapter 10
TOPSIS vs. VIKOR: A Case Study for Determining Development Level of Countries 225
Semra Erpolat Taşabat, Mimar Sinan Fine Art University, Turkey & Bahçeşehir University, Turkey
Tuğba Kıral Özkan, Bahçeşehir University, Turkey

Evaluating multiple criteria and selecting and/or ranking alternatives is called Multi Criteria Decision Making (MCDM). These methods which are considered important decision-making tools for decision makers due to their multidisciplinary nature have been developed over the years. As a result, there are many MCDM methods in the literature. In this chapter, TOPSIS and VIKOR, widely used in the literature, will be discussed. The major reason for examining these two methods is that the aggregating function used by both methods is similar because VIKOR method uses linear normalization and TOPSIS method uses vector normalization. The process of the methods is shown on a data set that includes the Human Development Index (HDI) indicators, which have been developed to measure the development levels of countries as well as the unemployment indicator. It was observed that the methods yielded similar results.

Chapter 11
Entropy-Based VIKOR Method and a Case Study: An Evaluation of Websites' Technical and Popularity Performances 251
Burcu Avcı Öztürk, Bursa Uludag University, Turkey

Due to the rapid advances in Internet technology, the number of websites and the amount of information obtained from websites are increasing day by day. Internet users want to access the website and the information they need more easily and quickly. This is also the case getting news so effectiveness of newspapers' websites in terms of content and the speed at which pages are opened is also an important indicator for users. The purpose of this chapter is to investigate the technical and popularity performance of the newspapers' websites in Turkey. The study will show the applicability of an objective weight-determining method, Entropy technique, for finding the weights of criteria and VIKOR for evaluating websites' technical and popularity performance. As a result of the evaluation, the best websites were determined in terms of technique and popularity, and ranked in terms of overall performance.

Chapter 12
Promethee: A Tool for Multi-Criteria Decision Analysis 282
Priyam Verma, Symbiosis International University, India

This chapter decodes the techniques of PROMETHEE (Preference Ranking Organization Method for Enrichment Evaluation) in MCDA. Rigorous literature review will assist in deciphering and rationalising the progressions in the techniques since the inception of PROMETHEE. The chapter shall extensively review literature on PROMETHEE and shall concisely explore relevant cases. The literature shall include journal articles, research paper based on case studies and conference proceedings concentrating mainly in the discipline of management science. The chapter will untangle the essential steps that will simplify the mathematical component used in PROMETHEE I and PROMETHEE II with a hypothetical case and a practical case. In the final phase of the chapter the limitations of PROMETHEE I and II shall be accentuated.

Chapter 13
Fuzzy Failure Mode and Effects Analysis in a Pharmaceutical Production Process With Fuzzy PROMETHEE Method 310
Sündüz Dağ, Istanbul University, Turkey

Failure mode and effects analysis (FMEA) is a quality improvement technique that defines potential errors and ranks them according to their degree of effectiveness in both service and production processes. While enterprises want to produce quality products or services, they also strive to reduce the cost of quality. At this point, the FMEA method provides a proactive approach to decision makers by ensuring that the types of errors in products sent to both internal and external customers and the probability of occurrence of these errors are predicted. In recent years, the FMEA method has begun to be evaluated in the frame of fuzzy logic to obtain more effective results. In this way, results have become realistic and objective. This chapter analyzes pharmaceutical production process to define potential error types and the effect of these errors. Risk priority order of error types is determined by Fuzzy PROMETHEE Method.

Chapter 14
Nudge Theory and Decision Making: Enabling People to Make Better Choices 335
Vikramsinh Amarsinh Patil, Symbiosis International University, India

This chapter examines the theoretical underpinnings of nudge theory and makes a case for incorporating nudging into the decision-making process in corporate contexts. Nudging and more broadly behavioural economics have become buzzwords on account of the seminal work that has been done by economists and highly publicized interventions employed by governments to support national priorities. Firms are not to be left behind, however. What follows is extensive documentation of such firms that have successfully employed nudging techniques. The examples are segmented by the nudge recipient, namely - managers, employees, and consumers. Firms can guide managers to become better leaders, employees to become more productive, and consumers to stay loyal. However, nudging is not without its pitfalls. It can be used towards nefarious ends and be notoriously difficult to implement and execute. Therefore, nudges should be rigorously tested via experimentation and should be ethically sound.

Chapter 15
Data Analysis on Global Stratification 355
Kirti Raj Bhatele, Rustamji Institute of Technology, India & BSF Academy, Gwalior, India
Stuti Singhal, Rustamji Institute of Technology, India & BSF Academy, Tekanpur, India
Muktasha R. Mithora, Rustamji Institute of Technology, India & BSF Academy, Gwalior, India
Sneha Sharma, Rustamji Institute of Technology, India & BSF Academy, Tekanpur, India

This chapter will guide you through the modeling, uses, and trends in data analysis and data science. The authors focus on the importance of pictorial data in replacement of numeric data. In most situations, graphical representation of data can present the information more distinctly, informative, and in less space than the same information requires in sentence form. This chapter provides a brief knowledge about representing data to more understandable form such that any person whether layman or not can understand it without any difficulty. This chapter also deals with the software Tableau which we use to convert the table data into graphical data. This Chapter contains 11 heat maps related to the world economies and their detailed study on several different topics. It will also give light on the basics of Python Language and its various algorithm studies to compare all the world economies based on their development.

Compilation of References 379

About the Contributors 416

Index 420

Preface

"Oftentimes, the most important decisions are the most difficult to make - for, your future, and the future of the generations that come after you, hinges on the outcome of those decisions." – J. E. B. Spredemann

Multi-criteria decision making (MCDM) is a discipline that deals with decisions involving the choice of a best alternative from several potential alternatives, subject to numerous yardsticks or criteria that may be precise or ambiguous. Decision-makers at all times try to select the optimal solution when making decisions. Unfortunately, an optimal solution only exists for a single criterion; almost any decision involves some conflicts or vexation in real decision situations. A decision problem is typically a situation where an individual has alternative courses of action at his disposal and has to select one of them without a priori knowledge of which one is the best. MCDM methods are used to help individuals make their decisions according to their preferences, finding the optimal choice among the alternatives in cases where there is more than one conflicting criterion. It is not just a matter of choosing the best alternative to make a decision. Often it is necessary to prioritize all resource allocation alternatives or to combine the strengths of individual preferences to form a collective preference. Consequently, the technique consists of breaking a complex problem into its smaller components and determining value or priority to rank the alternatives in a detailed and general way to mathematically analyze the problem. MCDM's main point of departure is to try to represent frequently abstract priorities in terms of the number of specific requirements: how to quantify what are known as intangibles and combine their measurements to create an overall choice or ranking; and how to use it to make the best possible mathematical decision. It's a critical job to define the collection of alternatives. MCDM theory often differentiates between cases where the set of alternatives is explicitly defined by a finite list of alternatives (called multi-attribute decision-making) and cases where the set of alternatives is implicitly defined by a mathematical programming structure (called multi-objective optimization theory). MCDM is one of the most commonly used decision methodologies in different fields such as energy and climate, industry, economy, development, and so on. MCDM techniques and strategies enhance decision performance by producing more effective and compelling growth.

The book features contributors from a variety of disciplines, who bring in diverse perspectives and viewpoints on multiple criteria in decision-making, and actions taken from the standpoint of making effective choices.

OBJECTIVES

The book acts like a handbook for young scholars and researchers in the area of MCDM working in the applied areas of management. While, there are a lot of technically sound books available, this book holds a practical and managerial viewpoint in addressing the gaps using MCDM techniques. The book offers technical understanding on key MCDM techniques with special focus on developed case-based studies in order to make the readers understand the real application of the same in any industry specific problem. The book creates an impact on the society at large by catering to a varied audience ranging from students to managers. Another key objective of this book is to enhance the nuances of applying any MCDM techniques based on real time issues which most of the books miss out. This book, therefore, offers a comprehensive debate about why a particular MCDM technique holds better than their counterparts to address specific issues in the industry.

TARGET AUDIENCE

The primary target audience of this book includes researchers, academicians and policy makers from a variety of disciplines interested in analysing and researching MCDM. A secondary target audience consists of students and scholars pursuing advanced study in management and decision sciences.

ORGANIZATION OF THE BOOK

Chapter 1, "Interpretive Structural Modeling: Background, Concepts, and Application," authored by Aastha Behl and Abhinav Pal, primarily focuses on the technique of Interpretive Structural Modeling (ISM) in Multi-criteria Decision Analysis (MCDA). ISM is a method to identify interrelationship among various factors pertaining to the research problem. This technique starts with identification of key factors, which have been collected by developing an extensive literature review. The factors are validated with the help of the opinions of the experts. Then a pair-wise comparative analysis helps in developing a structural self-interaction matrix (SSIM). This is followed by conversion of SSIM to Reachability Matrix which is partitioned into different levels. This helps in developing a diagraph, with the help of which an ISM model is developed. It is also accompanied by MICMAC analysis which presents a graphical picture of the driving power and dependence power of each factor considered for the study. The chapter would help in understanding the steps involved in the application of ISM technique with the help of hypothetical cases.

Chapter 2, "Application of ISM in the Manufacturing Sector," authored by Abhinav Pal, Jisha Rajendran and Aastha Behl, discusses the application of Interpretive Structural Modelling (ISM) in the manufacturing sector. For this purpose, the chapter first gives a brief about ISM and its usage in the current scenario. This is followed by a comprehensive literature review that sheds light on the methodology used over the years in the application of ISM. Lastly, the chapter discusses the application of ISM in the manufacturing sector specifically and assesses the advantages and disadvantages of relying on this method.

Chapter 3, "Exploring Key Success Factors of Indian Pharmaceutical Supply Chain Using Interpretive Structural Modelling," authored by Anurag Mishra, Pankaj Dutta and Suruj Kokati, explores how Indian pharmaceutical industry is witnessing enormous challenges due to varying patent laws, increasing demand and continuous pressure from the government to provide medicines at a lower price. To overcome these challenges, there is a need for a more robust supply chain (SC) which will help in information sharing and reduce overall cost. The chapter aims to determine the key drivers of Indian pharmaceutical SC, draws the attention of industry, stakeholders and top management to emphasise on these drivers to enhance the performance and profitability of SC. An interpretive structural modelling-based approach has been employed to model the pharmaceutical SC key drivers. The sixteen key parameters have been identified across all major dimensions such as SC, HR & organizational, market, technology and reverse logistics. Further fuzzy MICMAC analysis is done to categorize based on their driving and dependence power. The factors like collaborative relationship among SC partners, quality regulations, third party logistics, end-to-end responsive SC are found to be more important enablers.

Chapter 4, "Hybrid Multi-Criteria Models: Joint Health and Safety Unit Selection on Hybrid Multi-Criteria Decision Making," authored by Ömer Faruk Efe, provides a hybrid model to evaluate the Joint Health Safety Unit (JHSU) selection process. Using fuzzy logic linguistic variables makes an important contribution to decision making in uncertain environment. The hybrid model comprising Fuzzy AHP (Analytical Hierarchy Process) and Fuzzy TOPSIS (Technique for Similarity Sorting Preference for Ideal Solution) approaches are used in JHSU selection.

Chapter 5, "Multi-Criteria Decision-Making Process for Decentralized Healthcare Services Assessment," authored by William Alberto Cruz Castañeda, discusses how home health service, as decentralization form in many health systems, has an objective to deliver high-quality long-term care inside the patient's home. However, management of those services is about handling a complex decision problem related with the care delivery process composed by technologies, patients, structures, and professionals. Consequently, the decision problem requires finding effective ways to involve assessment and management of several criteria to achieve continuous quality improvement. For this purpose, it is useful to implement structured approaches with multiple criteria decision analysis (MCDA) techniques. The aim of this chapter is to contribute with a methodological approach to establish a decision analysis for assessing home health services through MACBETH and ULOWA techniques.

Chapter 6, "Multicriteria Decision Support Model for Selection of Tinplate Suppliers: A Case Study in CAN Company," authored by Rafaela Ribeiro Pinho and Ana Paula Lopes focuses on a review of several multicriteria decision support methodologies explored in the literature to solve the supplier evaluation process based on CAN company specifications, strategies and requirements. Considering the characteristics of each supplier and a set of criteria with different weights, the AHP method and the PROMETHEE method are applied to establish a ranking according to the performance in the selected criteria. In addition, to help the company to make the best decision, an analysis of ranking stability is performed by varying the weights assigned to the criteria.

Chapter 7, "The Technique for Order of Preference by Similarity to Ideal Solution Method in Fuzzy Environment: Fuzzy TOPSIS Method," authored by Merve Cengiz Toklu discusses Technique for Order Preference by Similarity to Ideal Solution (TOPSIS) method as one of the multi-criteria decision-making techniques. This method is used in many problems in literature and allows multiple decision makers to choose the most suitable alternative by evaluating them together with different criteria. Assessments of decision makers may include linguistic statements. In this case, the Fuzzy Logic approach can be used. In this chapter, the Fuzzy TOPSIS method is explained with a detailed numerical example.

Chapter 8, "Intuitionistic Fuzzy TOPSIS Model Based on Reliability Criteria and a Dynamic Mathematical Operator for Solving MCGDM Problems," authored by Daniel Osezua Aikhuele explores a model which is based on the IF-TOPSIS method and the DIFWGϵ operator for the evaluation of renewable power plants. The model which uses five reliability-based criteria addresses the dynamic factors associated with renewable power plant operations. The factors include: the changing energy demand and consumption, the changing environmental conditions, rapidly increasing population, social activities, and awareness. The result from the evaluation shows that the Solar power plant (S3) is the most preferred power source considering the dynamic factors associated with the plant operation, the plant location and the reliability-based criteria used for the assessment.

Chapter 9, "Modified TOPSIS Method With Banking Case Study," authored by Semra Erpolat Taşabat focuses on an alternative measure to Euclidean distance measurement which is used to calculate positive and negative ideal solutions in the traditional TOPSIS method. Lp Minkowski family and L1 family distance measures are used for this purpose. By taking the averages of the distance measurements in the Lq and L1 families, more general and accurate level units are attempted to be obtained. Thus, it is shown that TOPSIS method can give different results according to the distance measure used. The importance of the distance measurement unit was emphasized in order to rank the alternatives correctly. The implementation and evaluation of the proposed method is carried out through the financial performance of the deposit bank operating in the Turkish Banking Sector. It is seen that the rankings of the alternatives changed according to the distance measurements used. By referring to the distance measurements that can be used in the TOPSIS method, it is shown that the rank of the alternatives can vary according to the preferred distance measure.

Chapter 10, "TOPSIS vs. VIKOR: A Case Study for Determining Development Level of Countries," authored by Semra Erpolat Taşabat and Tuğba Kıral Özkan, discusses TOPSIS and VIKOR, widely used in the literature. The major reason for examining these two methods is that the aggregating function used by both methods is similar; VIKOR method uses linear normalization and TOPSIS method uses vector normalization. The process of the methods is shown on a data set that includes the Human Development Index (HDI) indicators, which have been developed to measure the development levels of countries as well as the unemployment indicator. It was observed that the methods yielded similar results.

Chapter 11, "Entropy-Based VIKOR Method and a Case Study: An Evaluation of Websites' Technical and Popularity Performance," authored by Burcu Avcı Öztürk, Uludag investigates the technical and popularity performance of the newspapers' websites in Turkey. The study shows the applicability of an objective weight determining method, Entropy technique, for finding the weights of criteria and VIKOR for evaluating websites' technical and popularity performance. As a result of the evaluation, the best websites were determined in terms of technique and popularity, and ranked in terms of overall performance.

Chapter 12, "PROMETHEE: A Tool for Multi-Criteria Decision Analysis," authored by Priyam Verma, attempts to decode the techniques of PROMETHEE (Preference Ranking Organization Method for Enrichment Evaluation) in MCDA. Rigorous literature review assists in deciphering and rationalising the progressions in the techniques since the inception of PROMETHEE. The chapter extensively reviews literature on PROMETHEE and concisely explores relevant cases. The chapter untangles the essential steps that simplify the mathematical component used in PROMETHEE I and PROMETHEE II with a hypothetical case and a practical case. In the final phase of the chapter, the limitations of PROMETHEE I and II are accentuated.

Chapter 13, "Fuzzy Failure Mode and Effects Analysis in a Pharmaceutical Production Process with Fuzzy PROMETHEE Method," authored by Sündüz Dağ explores Failure Mode and Effects Analysis (FMEA) as a quality improvement technique that defines potential errors and ranks them according to their degree of effectiveness in both service and production processes. While enterprises want to produce quality products or services, they also strive to reduce the cost of quality. At this point, the FMEA method provides a proactive approach to decision makers by ensuring that the types of errors in products sent to both internal and external customers and the probability of occurrence of these errors are predicted. In recent years, the FMEA method has begun to be evaluated in the frame of fuzzy logic in order to obtain more effective results. In this way, results have become realistic and objective. A pharmaceutical production process is analyzed to define potential error types and effect of these errors and then risk priority order of error types is determined by Fuzzy PROMETHEE Method.

Chapter 14, "Nudge Theory and Decision Making: Enabling People Make Better Choices," authored by Vikramsinh Amarsinh Patil examines the theoretical underpinnings of nudge theory and makes a case for incorporating nudging into the decision-making process in corporate contexts. Nudging and more broadly behavioural economics have become buzzwords on account of the seminal work that has been done by economists and highly publicized interventions employed by governments to support national priorities. Firms are not to be left behind, however. What follows is extensive documentation of such firms that have successfully employed nudging techniques. The examples are segmented by the nudge recipient, namely - managers, employees and consumers. Firms can guide managers to become better leaders, employees to become more productive and consumers to stay loyal. However, nudging is not without its pitfalls. It can be used towards nefarious ends and be notoriously difficult to implement and execute. Therefore, nudges should be rigorously tested via experimentation and should be ethically sound.

Chapter 15, "Data Analysis on Global Stratification," authored by Kirti Raj Bhatele, Stuti Singhal, Muktasha Mithora, and Sneha Sharma, guides through the modelling, uses, and trends in data analysis and data science. The authors focus on the importance of pictorial data in replacement of numeric data. The chapter provides a brief knowledge about representing data to more understandable form. This chapter also deals with the software Tableau which is used to convert the table data into graphical data.

Abhishek Behl
Indian Institute of Technology, Bombay, India

Acknowledgment

The editor of the book would like to express their gratitude to each and everyone who directly or indirectly supported us in finalizing our idea, nurturing it and helping us finish our project. The editor would like to thank all our academic associations and researchers who have contributed in the intellectual capital of the book. An extended thanks to all the authors who worked hard in offering their time and intellect to write chapters which would serve the readers. I would also like to appreciate their hard work and diligence with which they shaped the content of the chapters.

It would not have been easy without constant support and mentoring by Dr. Rameshwar Dubey who symbolizes excellence in research and teaching. I am really thankful to him for mentoring me on this project. The project was conceptualized and discussed with Anurag Mishra and the editor would like to extend his gratitude to him for his support. I would also like to thank Indian Institute of Technology, Bombay, India for offering all the necessary support from nurturing the idea to its execution.

I would like to thank the Almighty for guiding us with mature thoughts and an ability to take right decisions for the success of the book. The support of my family remains unparalleled in any success and the same goes here as well. I would like to thank our parents, family members and friends who helped us stay motivated during the entire course of the book.

Lastly, I would like to express our gratitude to the editorial advisory board members who helped us with their timely reviews and the team of IGI who supported us constantly at every phase of the book.

Abhishek Behl
Indian Institute of Technology, Bombay, India

Chapter 1
Interpretive Structural Modeling:
Background, Concepts, and Application

Aastha Behl
Pranveer Singh Institute of Technology, India

Abhinav Pal
Symbiosis International University, India

ABSTRACT

The chapter explains the technique of ISM (Interpretive Structural Modeling) in Multi-criteria decision Analysis (MCDA). ISM is a method to identify inter relationship among various factors pertaining to the authors' research problem. This technique starts with identification of key factors, collected through an extensive literature review of the study. The factors are validated with the help of expert opinions. A pair wise comparative analysis helps in developing a structural self-interaction matrix (SSIM). This is followed by conversion of SSIM to Reachability Matrix, partitioned into different levels. This helps in developing a diagraph, with the help of which an ISM Model is developed. It is also accompanied by MICMAC Analysis which presents a graphical picture of the driving power and dependence power of each factor considered for the study. The chapter would help in understanding the steps involved in the application of ISM technique with the help of hypothetical cases.

INTRODUCTION

Interpretive structural Modeling (ISM) is a technique that provides a structure of the Model which helps in understanding the inter relationship between the factors of the study. Since there are numerous factors present in a research problem which complicates the study, this method helps in identifying the relevant factors for the study. It helps in creating a new approach to the research problem, thus helping the researchers to eliminate the unimportant factors for the study. It helps in locating the hierarchy of the factors according to its dependence and driving power. ISM is presented in the form of a model as

DOI: 10.4018/978-1-7998-2216-5.ch001

the entire structure and the interrelationship of factors are illustrated in graphs (Agarwal et al., 2007). ISM is thus a structured approach to develop a graph on the interrelationship of various factors under consideration (Faisal,2010). Specific to this paper, some hypothetical cases are used to explain the steps of application of ISM.

ISM was initially created by J.N. Warfield in 1973 as a computer aided method to understand and simplify the complex issues. This was done by developing a structure in a form of a clear understandable graph. Mathematical computer programs were used to structure the elements of the study. The model was originated as Structural Modeling (SM) in which graphics and words were used to develop a structure of the complex issue of the study in a qualitative form. It provides the researcher the ways through which the complexity of the variables can be understood by imposing a certain order to it (Sahney et al., 2008). Warfield expanded the dimensions of SM and created ISM by including the opinions of the experts as the sole basis for selection of factors for the study. The interrelationship among the factors chosen for the study was based on the pair wise contextual relationship after consulting the same with the group of experts. The judgement of the experts helps in interpreting the depth of mutual relationship of the factors for the study. This technique is used when the researchers wish to use systematic and logical approach to understand the complex issue of the problem (Ravi et al., 2005). ISM has always been a cumulative group learning process but is also used by researchers individually. It focuses on transforming unclear structuring of factors into a useful model by mapping the complex relationships. This helps in facilitating the researchers to understand the causal association among various variables and helps the managers in the decision-making process (Anantatmula and Kanungo, 2008; Yeravdekar and Behl, 2018; Behl et al., 2018). ISM also helps in structuring the compound associations of factors into a heterogeneous directly related structure. With the increasing demands of various stakeholders on improving the quality of the products, it has to be sincerely addressed from different perspectives of assessment, conceptualization and its implementation. Here, ISM plays a significant role in prioritizing the strategic issues qualitatively by proposing a hierarchal structure through categorizing of ideas by prioritizing and sequencing the same.

STEPS INVOLVED IN ISM APPROACH

Step 1: Identify the Basic Factors

The first step of ISM technique is to develop a matrix known as SSIM. For developing this matrix, the first and foremost work is to develop an extensive literature review of our study, which shall consist of all the factors relating to our Research problem affecting our study. The entire list of factors is then consulted with the experts in understanding the relationship between various factors related to the study. Delphi technique is used for interviewing the experts from various industries or academic groups who have sound knowledge about the factors which are considered for the study. The consensus of experts' opinion helps us in identifying the relationship among all the factors and eliminating those which do not possess a relationship among them. The selection of experts for the consultation could be on the basis of experience and knowledge of that study. For this various brainstorming sessions and questionnaire are done for shortlisting the pair wise contextual relationship between the factors. For getting a clear idea about this, please refer to the flow diagram (Figure 1) for constructing ISM model given below:

Figure 1. Flow diagram for preparing ISM model
Adapted by: Wu and Niu (2017)

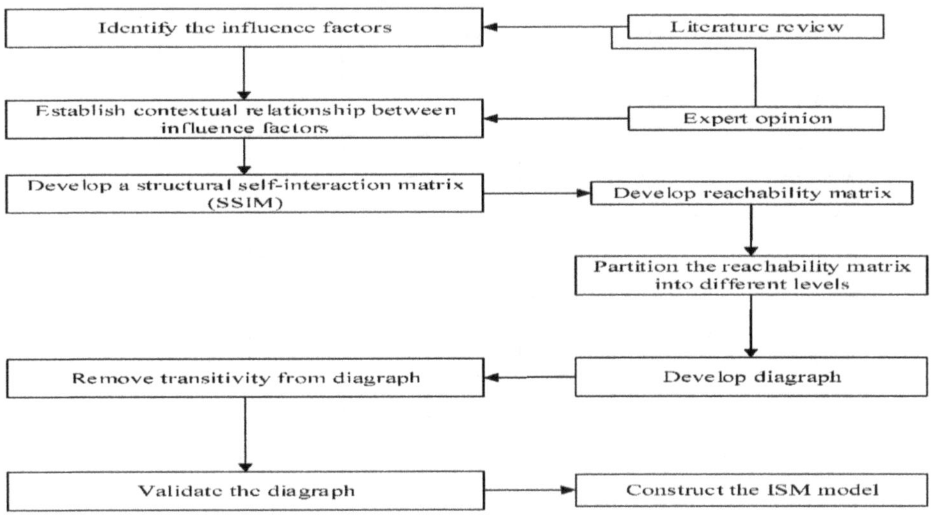

Step 2: Structural Self-Interaction Matrix (SSIM)

For understanding the relationship between the factors, it is essential to understand that 'drive to', 'leads to', 'affects', 'influences' type should be present in them. This means that one factor drives, leads, affects, or influences the other. On the basis of this, a contextual pair-wise relationship is developed.

Once this pair relationship is developed, we try to create an association between the two factors. In SSIM, we name the two factors as 'i' and 'j'. For depicting the direction of the association between the two factors (i and j), we use four symbols namely:

V: the relation from factor i to j (factor i will help to achieve j/ factor i will influence j)
A: the relation from factor j to i (factor j will help to achieve i/factor i will be influenced by factor j or factor j will influence i)
X: both i and j are related (factor i and j will help to achieve each other/ both i and j will influence each other)
O: there is no relation between i and j (both i and j are unrelated to each other)

On the basis of this, a pair wise contextual relation is derived and a SSIM matrix is developed. The consensus expert opinion is the sole basis of formation of this matrix. Once this is made, it should again be cross checked and finalized with the same experts according to their opinions.

For understanding it further, refer to the matrix given below:

In the above matrix (Table 1), we assume 10 factors as K, L, M, N, O, P, Q R, S and T. Through this, we try to understand the relationship of K with T, then K with S, then K with R and so on. All the factors written in a row are factor 'i' and factors written in columns are factor 'j'. In the first relation, if K helps to achieve T, then we would name this as 'V' and if T helps to achieve K, we would name it as 'A'. If both K and T helps in achieving each other, we would name it as 'X' and if there is no relationship between each other then we would name it as 'O'. Similarly, we would continue it with other rows and columns.

Table 1. Structural self-interaction matrix (SSIM)

Factors i	Factors j									
	T	**S**	**R**	**Q**	**P**	**O**	**N**	**M**	**L**	**K**
1. K										
2. L										
3. M										
4. N										
5. O										
6. P										
7. Q										
8. R										
9. S										
10. T										

Table 2. Table showing VAXO relation matrix

Factors i	Factors j									
	10. T	**9. S**	**8. R**	**7. Q**	**6. P**	**5. O**	**4. N**	**3. M**	**2. L**	**1. K**
1. K	O	X	O	X	X	X	A	O	A	
2. L	O	V	V	O	O	A	V	V		
3. M	V	O	V	O	O	O	V			
4. N	X	V	X	O	O	O				
5. O	V	O	V	O	O					
6. P	A	X	O	X						
7. Q	A	X	O							
8. R	X	V								
9. S	A									
10. T										

Given below (Table 2) is an assumption, which clearly shows the relation of all the variables taken in the matrix:

Step 3: Forming a Reachability Matrix and Conducting a Transitivity Check

The next step is to develop a reachability matrix from SSIM. For this we substitute the symbols of SSIM into binary numbers, i.e. we substitute the symbols 'V', 'X', 'A' and 'O' into 1s and 0s(zero). This helps us in creating an initial reachability matrix.

Following are the rules of its substitution (Table 3):

- If the entry in SSIM is 'V', then:

Table 3. Table showing rules for developing a reachability matrix

	V	A	X	O
Entry(i,j)	1	0	1	0
Entry(j,i)	0	1	1	0

  - The (i,j) entry in the reachability matrix will be '1'; and
  - The (j,i) entry in the reachability matrix will be '0'
- If the entry in SSIM is 'A', then:
  - The (i,j) entry in the reachability matrix will be '0'; and
  - The (j,i) entry in the reachability matrix will be '1'
- If the entry in SSIM is 'X', then:
  - The (i,j) entry in the reachability matrix will be '1'; and
  - The (j,i) entry in the reachability matrix will be '1'
- If the entry in SSIM is 'O', then:
  - The (i,j) entry in the reachability matrix will be '0'; and
  - The (j,i) entry in the reachability matrix will be '0'

With these rules, an initial reachability matrix is developed with 1s and 0s. This can be understood with the Table 4 and Table 5 given below. The table represents the reachability matrix created from the SSIM of Table 2:

In Table 4, we just need to flip the table and substitute all the 'V' with 1s, 'A' with 0s, 'X' with 1s, and 'O' with 0s. We would get the result as shown in Table 5:

Once we are done with completing one side of it, we need to do the other side(the colored side). In Table 5, we understood the reachability matrix created by showing the effect of factor 'i' on 'j'. The next step would be to show the effect of factor 'j' on 'i', i.e. the colored portion. For this, we would refer to

Table 4. Table showing flipped VAXO relation matrix

Factors i	Factors j									
	1.K	2.L	3.M	4.N	5. O	6. P	7.Q	8.R	9.S	10.T
1. K		A	O	A	X	X	X	O	X	O
2. L			V	V	A	O	O	V	V	O
3. M				V	O	O	O	V	O	V
4. N					O	O	O	X	V	X
5. O						O	O	V	O	V
6. P							X	O	X	A
7. Q								O	X	A
8. R									V	X
9. S										A
10. T										

Table 5. Table showing initial reachability matrix

Factors i	Factors j									
	1.K	**2.L**	**3.M**	**4.N**	**5. O**	**6. P**	**7.Q**	**8.R**	**9.S**	**10.T**
1. K		0	0	0	1	1	1	0	1	0
2. L			1	1	0	0	0	1	1	0
3. M				1	0	0	0	1	0	1
4. N					0	0	0	1	1	1
5. O						0	0	1	0	1
6. P							1	0	1	0
7. Q								0	1	0
8. R									1	1
9. S										0
10. T										

Table 4 and not Table 5. For filing in the remaining colored portion (effect of 'j' on 'i'), we would take the reverse of what we did in Table 4.

For example, if the effect of factor 'i' named as 1.K(in row) on factor 'j' named as 2.L(in column) is 'A', then the entry of (i,j) was taken as 0, whereas when we fill in the reverse effect for the entry of (j,i) of the factor 'j' named as 1.K (in column) with the factor 'i' named as 2.L(in row) as 1.

Considering one more example from Table 4, if the effect of factor 'i' named as 8.R(in row) on factor 'j' named as 9.S(in column) is 'V', then the entry of (i,j) was taken as 1, whereas when we fill in the reverse effect for the entry of (j,i) of the factor 'j' named as 8.R (in column) with the factor 'i' named as 9.S(in row), the binary number shall be taken as 0.

With this we create an initial reachability matrix, substituting the entire matrix with 1s and 0s. We can also see that the diagonal numbers in the matrix are always represented by 1s. This is shown in Table 6 below:

Following the rules of initial reachability matrix, the tabular matrix is developed. After this is done, a transitivity check is conducted. A transitivity check is a basic assumption in ISM which states that if factor 1.K is related to factor 2.L and factor 2.L is related to factor 3.M then factor 1.K would definitely be related to factor 3.M. After this check is conducted, some entries which was showing as 0s in initial reachability test would be converted and marked as 1*. It helps in eliminating those gaps which were there while collecting expert opinion about the relationship between 2 factors in SSIM. Once the transitivity check is conducted, we develop the final reachability matrix for the ISM Approach, which is shown in Table 7. The driving power is calculated by summing the rows and dependence power is calculated by summing the columns of the Final Reachability Matrix, as shown below. This means that the driving power shall consist of all the factors (of 1s) which drives other factors in the matrix, or which it can have impact on whereas the dependence power shall consist of all the factors which can be depended upon (of 1s).

Table 6. Table showing the initial reachability matrix

Factors i	Factors j									
	1	**2**	**3**	**4**	**5**	**6**	**7**	**8**	**9**	**10**
1. K	1	0	0	0	1	1	1	0	1	0
2. L	1	1	1	1	0	0	0	1	1	0
3. M	0	0	1	1	0	0	0	1	0	1
4. N	1	0	0	1	0	0	0	1	1	1
5. O	0	1	0	0	1	0	0	1	0	1
6. P	1	0	0	0	0	1	1	0	1	0
7. Q	1	0	0	0	0	1	1	0	1	0
8. R	0	0	0	1	0	0	0	1	1	1
9. S	1	0	0	0	0	1	1	0	1	0
10. T	0	0	0	1	0	1	1	1	1	1

Step 4: Developing Reachability Set and Antecedent Set

Once the Final Reachability Matrix (FRM) is developed, reachability set and antecedent set for each factor are derived (Warfield, 1974). The reachability set consists of the factor itself and other factors which it can create an impact on, whereas the antecedent set consists of the factor itself and other factors that may create an impact on it.

For understanding this, refer to Table 8.

Table 7. Table showing final reachability matrix after transitivity check

Factors i	Factors j										
	1	**2**	**3**	**4**	**5**	**6**	**7**	**8**	**9**	**10**	**Driving Power**
1. K	1	0	0	0	0	1	1	0	1	0	4
2. L	1	1	1	1	0	1*	1*	1	1	1*	9
3. M	1*	0	1	1	0	1*	1*	1	1*	1	8
4. N	1	0	0	1	0	1*	1*	1	1	1	7
5. O	1*	1	1*	1*	1	1*	1*	1	1	1	10
6. P	1	0	0	0	0	1	1	0	1	0	4
7. Q	1	0	0	0	0	1	1	0	1	0	4
8. R	1*	0	0	1	0	1*	1*	1	1	1	7
9. S	1	0	0	0	0	1	1	0	1	0	4
10. T	1*	0	0	1	0	1	1	1	1	1	7
Dependence Power	10	2	3	6	1	10	10	6	10	6	

*signifies transitivity

Table 8. Table showing reachability set, antecedent set and its intersection

Measure No.	Reachability Set	Antecedent Set	Intersection
1	1,6,7,9	1,2,3,4,5,6,7,8,9,10	1,6,7,9
2	1,2,3,4,6,7,8,9,10	2,5	2
3	1,3,4,6,7,8,9,10	2,3,5	3
4	1,4,6,7,8,9,10	2,3,4,5,8,10	4,8,10
5	1,2,3,4,5,6,7,8,9,10	5	5
6	1,6,7,9	1,2,3,4,5,6,7,8,9,10	1,6,7,9
7	1,6,7,9	1,2,3,4,5,6,7,8,9,10	1,6,7,9
8	1,4,6,7,8,9,10	2,3,4,5,8,10	4,8,10
9	1,6,7,9	1,2,3,4,5,6,7,8,9,10	1,6,7,9
10	1,4,6,7,8,9,10	2,3,4,5,8,10	4,8,10

In the above table, Reachability set consists of the measure numbers of 1s from the Driving Power of FRM (Table 7). This means all the rows showing the driving power of 1s are stated in Reachability set.

For example, if the driving power of 4.N is 7, then Reachability set shall mention all the seven 1s of the row named 4.N(1,4,6,7,8,9,10).

Similarly, Antecedent set consists of the measure numbers from the Dependence power of FRM. This means all the columns showing the dependence power of 1s are stated in Antecedent set.

For example, if the Dependence power of 8.R in the column is 6, then the Antecedent set shall mention all the six 1s of the column named 8.R (2,3,4,5,8,10).

After a table of Reachability set and Antecedent set is prepared, we find the intersection of the two sets, i.e. the common numbers between both the sets, as shown in Table 8.

Step 5: Level Partition Through Iteration

The factor which is excluded from successive iterations and is allotted top priority if the membership in Reachability set and intersection is said to be completely agreed. In other words, the numbers in Reachability set shall be same as the numbers in Intersection to award the respective iterations to them and exclude successive iterations. To understand this, Table 9 can be understood:

In the above Table 9, it is important to understand that the membership of Reachability set and intersection should be the same to classify Iteration I to them. This helps in achieving the highest level of ISM hierarchy. In Table 9, the Reachability set of measure no. 1,6,7,9 are same as their intersection and they completely agree with each other. Hence they are allotted Level I. This should be continuously done to obtain the levels of all the other factors, which are considered for the study. Once Level I is derived, we numbers 1,6,7,9 are to be completely removed from the all the parts of reachability set and then again it should be matched with the intersection as shown below in Table 10:

In the above table there are three places where the reachability set 4,8,10 matches to intersection. So we would name this Level II. Again we would continue Iteration Level III by removing the numbers 4,8,10 from the Reachability set as shown in Table 11 and continuing the same in Table 12 and 13 for finding Iteration level IV and V.

Table 9. Iteration level I

Measure No.	Reachability Set	Antecedent Set	Intersection	Iteration
1	1,6,7,9	1,2,3,4,5,6,7,8,9,10	1,6,7,9	I
2	1,2,3,4,6,7,8,9,10	2,5	2	
3	1,3,4,6,7,8,9,10	2,3,5	3	
4	1,4,6,7,8,9,10	2,3,4,5,8,10	4,8,10	
5	1,2,3,4,5,6,7,8,9,10	5	5	
6	1,6,7,9	1,2,3,4,5,6,7,8,9,10	1,6,7,9	I
7	1,6,7,9	1,2,3,4,5,6,7,8,9,10	1,6,7,9	I
8	1,4,6,7,8,9,10	2,3,4,5,8,10	4,8,10	
9	1,6,7,9	1,2,3,4,5,6,7,8,9,10	1,6,7,9	I
10	1,4,6,7,8,9,10	2,3,4,5,8,10	4,8,10	

Table 10. Iteration level II

Measure No.	Reachability Set	Antecedent Set	Intersection	Iteration
2	2,3,4,8,10	2,5	2	
3	,3,4,8,10	2,3,5	3	
4	4,8,10	2,3,4,5,8,10	4,8,10	II
5	2,3,4,5,8,10	5	5	
8	4,8,10	2,3,4,5,8,10	4,8,10	II
10	4,8,10	2,3,4,5,8,10	4,8,10	II

Table 11. Iteration level III

Measure No.	Reachability Set	Antecedent Set	Intersection	Iteration
2	2,3	2,5	2	
3	3	2,3,5	3	III
5	2,3,5	5	5	

Table 12. Iteration level IV

Measure No.	Reachability Set	Antecedent Set	Intersection	Iteration
2	2	2,5	2	IV
5	2,5	5	5	

Table 13. Iteration level V

Measure No.	Reachability Set	Antecedent Set	Intersection	Iteration
5	5	5	5	V

From the Iteration levels identified in the above Tables, we would be able to derive the factors which would make the Top hierarchy in the diagraph and designing the ISM Model.

Step 6: Framing a Conical Matrix

After we are done with deriving the Iteration levels, we develop a Conical matrix by clustering the factors as per their levels, i.e. all the factors falling in the same level are clustered to form a group and are put according to their Iteration levels. This is explained in Table 14:

The above Table clearly depicts the placements of factors according to their Iteration levels as 1,6,7,9 is placed first in both the rows and columns. This is followed by 4,8,10 and then 3,2,5. The binary numbers are then filled according to the Final Reachability Matrix formed in Table 7.

Step 7: Developing a Diagraph

From the conical matrix, we need to obtain a preliminary diagraph consisting of transitive links. The diagraph represents the factors in a form of a structure and their independence. For developing a diagraph, the highest hierarchy of Iteration level is positioned at the top, followed by Iteration level II in the next position and it continues till all the levels are achieved. The lowest level is placed at the bottom most position in the diagraph. The diagraph shows the direct relationship of the factors among themselves through an arrow at their respective levels. The arrow shows the influencing factor, as to which factor influences the other factor through the flow of direction.

Step 8: Developing the ISM Model

The ISM structure is then obtained from the diagraph. The model contains the detailed information of all the factors of the study. It depicts the inter relationship of each factor and their reachability of the hierarchy between them. The model is represented with nodes and links between the factors, representing the contextual relationship through the direction between them. This can be explained in figure 2 below:

Table 14. Table showing a conical matrix

Factors	1	6	7	9	4	8	10	3	2	5
1. K	1	1	1	1	0	0	0	0	0	0
6. P	1	1	1	1	0	0	0	0	0	0
7. Q	1	1	1	1	0	0	0	0	0	0
9. S	1	1	1	1	0	0	0	0	0	0
4. N	1	1*	1*	1	1	1	1	0	0	0
8. R	1*	1*	1*	1	1	1	1	0	0	0
10. T	1*	1	1	1	1	1	1	0	0	0
3. M	1*	1*	1*	1*	1	1	1	1	0	0
2. L	1	1*	1*	1	1	1	1*	1	1	0
5. O	1*	1*	1*	1	1*	1	1	1*	1	1

Figure 2. Figure showing the diagraph of ISM model

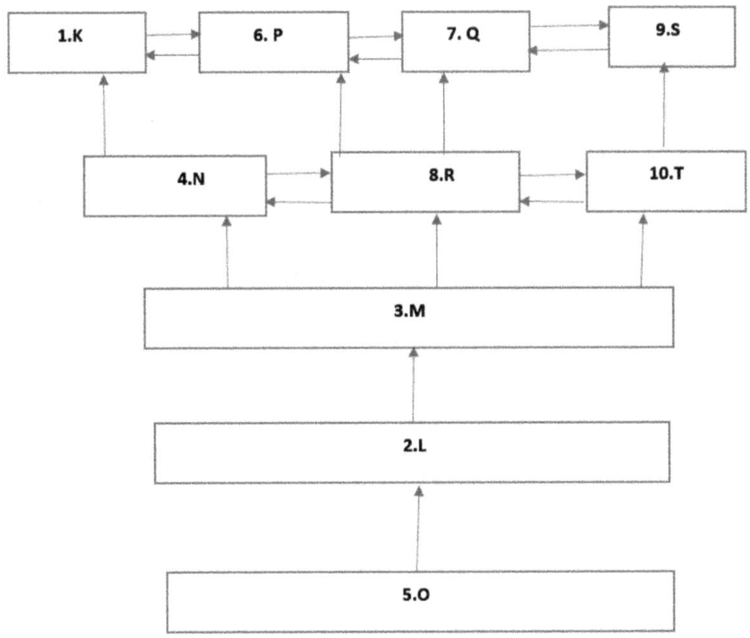

In the above figure 2 depicting the ISM Model, it should be understood that the lower most hierarchy, i.e. 5.O is dependent on itself and drives all the other 9 factors above it. Similarly, when we talk about 2.L, then 2.L is dependent on 5.O but drives all the other 8 factors above it. Then 3.M is dependent on 2.L and 5.O but drives all the other factors above it. Again 4.N, 8.R, 10.T is dependent on the factors beneath it but drives all the factors above it namely 1.K, 6.P, 7.Q and 9.S and so on. This is how a pair wise contextual relationship between the factors is derived.

Step 9: MICMAC Analysis

This is also called cross-impact matrix. MICMAC analysis is used to identify the driving power and dependence power of various factors. These driving and dependence powers are broadly classified in the four categories:

1. **Autonomous factors:** These factors have weak dependence power and weak driving power. They are relatively not connected to the system with which they have few strong links.
2. **Linkage factors:** These factors have both strong driving and dependence power. These are so interconnected and unstable that any action on the factors would leave an effect on other factors as well and also a feedback effect on itself.
3. **Dependent factors:** These factors have strong dependence power but weak driving power.
4. **Independent factors or Driver's factors:** These factors have strong driving power but weak dependence power. The factor having strong driving power is known as 'key factor'. This 'key factor' is categorised as independent factor.

Figure 3.

Notes: Cluster I: Autonomous factors; Cluster II: Dependent factors; Cluster III: Linkage factors; Cluster IV: Independent factors

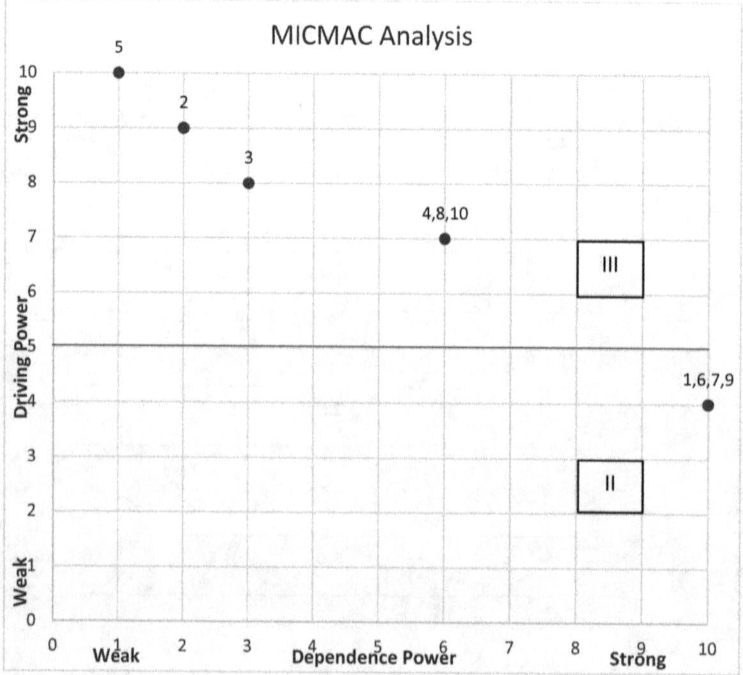

MICMAC Analysis can be explained with the figure 3 below:

The MICMAC Analysis graph shows the dependence power on the x axis and driving power on the y axis. To plot this graph, we need to refer to Table no. 7, which is the Final Reachability Matrix showing the Driving power and Dependence power of each factor.

For example, if we look at factor 1.K in Table no. 7, then it has the driving power 4 and dependence power as 10, which is plotted in the graph. It falls under Cluster II. Similarly, if we take factor 4.N whose driving power is 7 and dependence power is 6, then it falls under Cluster III and so on.

Once the plotting of all the factors is done, we get a graph showing the places of all the 10 factors. There are no factors lying in Cluster I, i.e. Autonomous factors. It means that there are no factors which has weak driving power and weak dependence power. Even if there had been factors lying in Cluster I, as Autonomous factors, we would have deleted them as they are not important for analysing the relationship between the factors. There are four factors falling in Cluster II, named as Dependent Factors. This means that factor no. 1,6,7 and 9 have weak driving power but strong dependence power. This can also be seen from the ISM model, where 1,6,7 and 9 forms the top most hierarchy and is dependent on all the factors beneath it. Then Cluster III refers to Linkage factors, which are factor no. 4,8 and 10. These factors has both strong driving factor and strong dependence power. Lastly, there is Cluster IV referred to as Independent factors which are factor no. 3,2 and 5. They have strong driving power and weak dependence power.

CASE STUDY

The process of ISM is demonstrated with the help of a case study of enablers of Corporate Social Responsibility(CSR). In the present era, the contribution of Companies in CSR activities has changed from voluntary to a mandatory legal requirement. According to Companies Act, 2013, Indian Companies are mandatorily required to contribute 2% of their profits into CSR activities. It has resulted into creating a sense of responsibility among the Companies for making contributions towards socially responsible initiatives. The existing literature depicts a picture of the enablers of CSR and this chapter would help us in understanding the contextual relationship between the enablers of CSR. However, we would randomly take any 4 enablers, so as to understand the practical example of ISM technique and thereafter develop a model for the same. Although ISM process requires an expert survey to shortlist the existing literature review about the study, we have chosen the enablers from a recent study conducted (Divesh Kumar et. all,2019). This would apparently help in understanding the process of ISM in a better way.

Step 1: Identification of Basic Factors

According to the recent expert survey conducted (Divesh Kumar et. all, 2019), eight enablers of CSR were shortlisted. In the study, 16 experts were consulted and brainstorming sessions were conducted to check the interrelationship of various enablers of the study. Many enablers were identified such as satisfaction of customers, satisfaction of employees, company's reputation, meeting Government regulations, top management commitment, better financial position, cost reduction, formal strategic planning, and organizational culture. Out of them, we randomly choose any 4 enablers to explain the process of ISM in a better way. We take satisfaction of customers, satisfaction of employees, company's reputation, meeting Government regulations as examples to explain the ISM process.

Step 2: Structural Self-Interaction Matrix (SSIM)

For understanding the relationship between the enablers (e.g. i and j), it is essential to understand that 'drive to', 'leads to', 'affects', 'influences' type should be present in them. This means that one enabler drives, leads, affects, or influences the other. On the basis of this, a contextual pair-wise relationship is developed. To find out the relationship between two enablers say 'i' and 'j', four symbols are used namely:

V= enabler i will help to achieve enabler j
A= enabler j will help to achieve enabler i
X=both the enablers i and j will help to achieve each other
O= enablers i and j are unrelated.

In Table 15, it's pretty clear in the first row that there is no relationship between satisfaction of customers and Meeting Govt. regulations (represented as 'O'), whereas satisfaction of customers would help to achieve Corporate reputation (represented as 'V') and satisfaction of employees will help to achieve satisfaction of customers as well (represented as 'A'). Similarly, in the second row, both satisfaction of employees and Govt. regulation helps to achieve each other and is represented by 'X' and satisfaction of employees will also help to achieve Corporate reputation (represented as 'V'). Lastly meeting Govt. regulations also helps in achieving Corporate reputation (represented as 'A').

Table 15. SSIM

Enablers i	Enablers j			
	4	3	2	1
1. Satisfaction of customers	O	V	A	
2. Satisfaction of employees	X	V		
3. Corporate reputation	A			
4. Meeting Govt. regulations				

However, the relationship between the enablers are identified through expert opinions, which is the basis for developing a SSIM table.

Step 3: Forming a Reachability Matrix (RM) and Conducting a Transitivity Check

The next step is to develop a reachability matrix from SSIM. For this we substitute the symbols of SSIM into binary numbers, i.e. we substitute the symbols 'V', 'X', 'A' and 'O' into 1s and 0s(zero). This helps us in creating an initial reachability matrix.

Following are the rules of RM, as discussed above:

In the above Tables 16 and 17, the VAXO table is substituted by the binary no.s 1s and 0s. As per the example, in the first row, the entry of enabler 'i' of satisfaction of customers with entry 'j' satisfaction of employees is represented with A, hence it will get the binary no. 0 (as per rules of RM in Table 16), whereas the reverse action of entry of enabler 'j' satisfaction of employees on enabler 'i' of satisfaction of customers would be binary no. 1 (as shown in Table 18, row 2, column 1). Similarly, if enabler 'i' of satisfaction of customers has O relationship with entry 'j' Meeting Govt. regulations, then it would be represented by binary no. 0, and on the reverse side of entry of enabler 'j' Meeting Govt. regulations

Table 16. Rules of RM

	V	A	X	O
Entry(i,j)	1	0	1	0
Entry(j,i)	0	1	1	0

Table 17.

Enablers i	Enablers j			
	1	2	3	4
1. Satisfaction of customers		A	V	O
2. Satisfaction of employees			V	X
3. Corporate reputation				A
4. Meeting Govt. regulations				

Table 18. Initial reachability matrix

Enablers i	Enablers j ->			
	1	2	3	4
1. Satisfaction of customers	1	0	1	0
2. Satisfaction of employees	1	1	1	1
3. Corporate reputation	0	0	1	0
4. Meeting Govt. regulations	0	1	1	1

with that of enabler 'i' of satisfaction of customers would also be binary no. 0 as per the rules of RM (as shown in Table 18, row 4, column 1). The process continues in the same way with the other enablers to attain Reachability Matrix as shown in Table 18.

After attaining the initial RM, we need to work on attaining a Final RM through the integration of transitivity process. As explained in the steps of ISM, Transitivity is a process of creating relationship with the other variables. For example, If enabler 1 and 2 are related and enabler 2 and 3 are related, then there must be relationship between 1 and 3 as well. This is shown in Table 19, where enabler 4 has a relationship with enabler 2 which is depicted by value of x42=1. Also enabler 2 has a relationship with enabler 1 shown as x21=1. Hence, there is a relationship between enabler 4 and enabler 1 for which x41 one transitivity (1*) is added.

The driving power is calculated by summing the rows and dependence power is calculated by summing the columns of the Final Reachability Matrix (FRM), as shown below. This means that the driving power shall consist of all the factors (of 1s) which drives other factors in the matrix, or which it can have impact on whereas the dependence power shall consist of all the factors which can be depended upon (of 1s).

Step 4: Developing Reachability Set and Antecedent Set

The reachability set consists of the factor itself and other factors which it can have impact on, whereas the antecedent set consists of the factor itself and other factors that may impact it. In the Table 20 given below, Reachability set consists of the measure numbers of 1s from the Driving Power of FRM (Table 19). This means all the rows showing the driving power of 1s are stated in Reachability set. Similarly, Antecedent set consists of the measure numbers from the Dependence power of FRM. This means all the columns showing the dependence power of 1s are stated in Antecedent set.

Table 19. Final reachability matrix

Factors i	Factors j				
	1	2	3	4	Driving Power
1. Satisfaction of customers	1	0	1	0	2
2. Satisfaction of employees	1	1	1	1	4
3. Corporate reputation	0	0	1	0	1
4. Meeting Govt. regulations	1*	1	1	1	4
Dependence Power	3	2	4	2	

Table 20. Intersection from reachability and antecedent set

Enablers	Reachability Set	Antecedent Set	Intersection
1. Satisfaction of customers	1,3	1,2,4	1
2. Satisfaction of employees	1,2,3,4	2,4	2,4
3. Corporate reputation	3	1,2,3,4	3
4. Meeting Govt. regulations	1,2,3,4	2,4	2,4

In the above Table 20, the reachability set of satisfaction of customers is 1,3 because 1 and 3 contains binary no. 1 as its driving power, and in the same way they have Antecedent set 1,2 and 4 because they have binary no. 1 in the dependence power. After a table of Reachability set and Antecedent set is prepared, we find the intersection of the two sets, i.e. the common numbers between both the sets.

Step 5: Level Partition Through Iteration

A factor is allotted top priority and is excluded from successive iterations if, the numbers in Reachability set shall be same as the numbers in Intersection to award the respective iterations to them and exclude successive iterations.

Since the reachability set and intersection has the same number 3 in row 3, so this is classified as Iteration Level I. We continue classifying the levels on the same basis by excluding number 3 from all the rows of reachability and antecedent set thereafter.

In Table 22, Level II is classified as the similarity of 1 in both reachability set and intersection. After this, 1 is removed from all the reachability and antecedent set. Similarly in Table 23, we allot Level III to both the enablers which show 2 and 4 as common numbers of reachability set and intersection.

From the Iteration levels identified in the above Tables, we would be able to derive the enablers which would make the Top hierarchy in the diagraph and designing the ISM Model.

Step 6: Framing a Conical Matrix

After we are done with deriving the Iteration levels, we develop a Conical matrix by clustering the factors as per their levels, i.e. all the factors falling in the same level are clustered to form a group and are put according to their Iteration levels.

Table 21. Level I

Enablers	Reachability Set	Antecedent Set	Intersection	Iteration
1. Satisfaction of customers	1,3	1,2,4	1	
2. Satisfaction of employees	1,2,3,4	2,4	2,4	
3. Corporate reputation	3	1,2,3,4	3	I
4. Meeting Govt. regulations	1,2,3,4	2,4	2,4	

Table 22. Level II

Enablers	Reachability Set	Antecedent Set	Intersection	Iteration
1. Satisfaction of customers	1	1,2,4	1	II
2. Satisfaction of employees	1,2,4	2,4	2,4	
4. Meeting Govt. regulations	1,2,4	2,4	2,4	

Table 23. Level III

Enablers	Reachability Set	Antecedent Set	Intersection	Iteration
2. Satisfaction of employees	2,4	2,4	2,4	III
4. Meeting Govt. regulations	2,4	2,4	2,4	III

Table 24. Conical matrix

Enablers	3	1	2	4
3. Corporate reputation	1	0	0	0
1. Satisfaction of customers	1	1	0	0
2. Satisfaction of employees	1	1	1	1
4. Meeting Govt. regulations	1	1	1	1

The above Table clearly depicts the placements of factors according to their Iteration levels as 3 is placed first in both the rows and columns. This is followed by 1 and then 2 and 4(Level III). The binary numbers are then filled according to the Final Reachability Matrix formed in Table 19.

Step 7: Developing a Diagraph

For developing a diagraph, the highest hierarchy of Iteration level is positioned at the top, followed by Iteration level II in the next position and it continues till all the levels are achieved. The lowest level is placed at the bottom most position in the diagraph.

Step 8: Developing the ISM Model

The ISM structure is then obtained from the diagraph. The model contains the detailed information of all the factors of the study. It depicts the inter relationship of each factor and their reachability of the hierarchy between them. The model is represented with nodes and links between the factors, representing the contextual relationship through the direction between them. This can be explained in figure 4 below:

In the above figure 4, it is clearly visible that Corporate reputation forms the top most level, which means it is dependent on all the enablers below it. Similarly, satisfaction of customers drives corporate reputation but satisfaction of employees and Meeting Government regulation is dependent on enabler 1, i.e. satisfaction of customers. In the same way, the enablers of CSR are categorized according to their

Figure 4. Figure depicting the ISM model

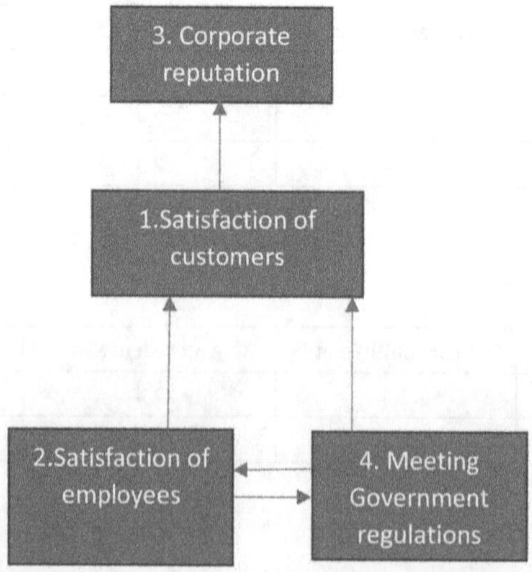

levels of their emergence into the conical matrix. The final reachability matrix demonstrates the inter-relationship among various enablers and helps in creating an ISM model by eliminating the indirect links.

Step 9: MICMAC Analysis

The purpose of MICMAC analysis is to identify the driving power and dependence power of various enablers. The MICMAC Analysis graph shows the dependence power on the x axis and driving power on the y axis. To plot this graph, we need to refer to the Final Reachability Matrix showing the Driving power and Dependence power of each factor.

1. **Autonomous factors:** These enablers have weak driving power and weak dependence power (Cluster I). There are no autonomous enablers in this example.
2. **Dependent factors:** These enablers have weak driving power but strong dependence power. Corporate reputation and satisfaction of customers have weak driving but strong dependence power (Cluster II).
3. **Linkage factors:** These enablers have both strong driving and dependence power. There are no linkage factors in this example (Cluster III).
4. **Independent factors or Driver's factors:** These enablers have strong driving power but weak dependence power. Satisfaction of employees and Meeting Government regulations have strong driving power but weak dependence power (Cluster IV).

BENEFITS OF ISM MODEL

1. It is a systematic process as it establishes a pair wise contextual relationship among all the factors selected for the study.

Figure 5. MICMAC analysis
Notes: Cluster I: Autonomous factors; Cluster II: Dependent factors; Cluster III: Linkage factors; Cluster IV: Independent factors

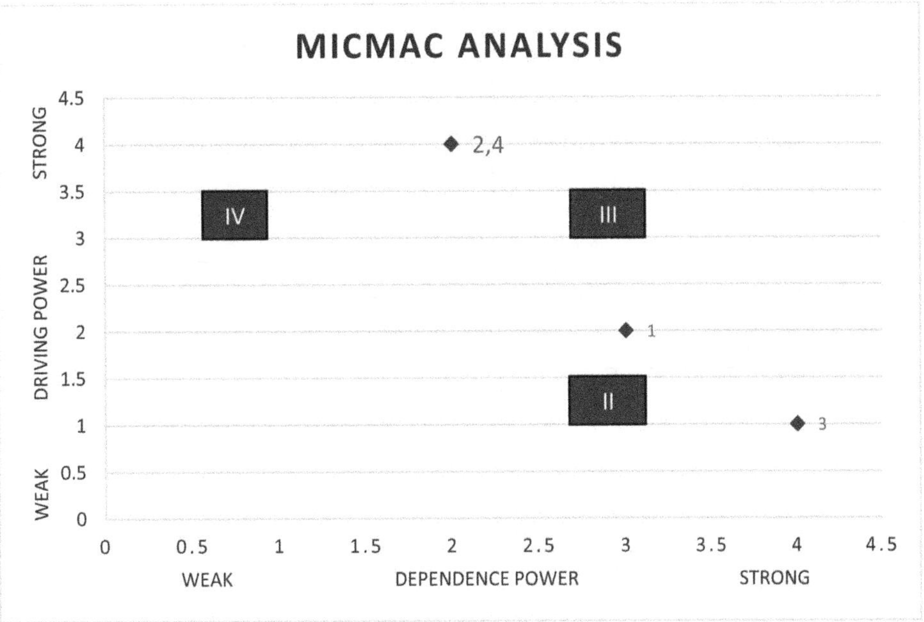

2. Experts should only have sound knowledge about the area considered for the study. No knowledge of ISM process would not affect the accuracy of the results.
3. It produces a graphical representation of the poorly articulated elements of the study.
4. It enhances the area of the study by presenting a structured model on the same.
5. It provides logical thinking and analysis on the factors considered under the study.
6. It encourages the participants to involve in developing interrelationships and links among the elements of the study.
7. It serves as a comprehensive and practical learning process.
8. It helps the managers in decision making process in different functional areas.

APPLICATION OF ISM IN DIFFERENT SECTORS

See Table 25.

CONCLUSION

It is concluded that ISM serves as a method to simplify the complex problems through a directional framework. It helps the researcher to present a hierarchal image of the factors considered for the study. It involves a series of steps initiating from identification of factors, developing interrelationships between the factors, partitioning the same into various rank orders and converting the same into a systematic structural model. This technique has been very useful in transforming the unstructured complex factors

Table 25.

Author and Year	Sector of Application
Norman et al. 1965; Waller 1980; Warfield 2003	mathematical foundations of the methodology of ISM
Warfield 1974, 1976, 1994	analysis and concepts of the ISM process
Malone 1975	uses of ISM in analysing personal values by analysing the problems faced in investment
Hawthorne and Sage 1975	planning of programs of higher education.
Hansen et al. 1979	decision support systems
Jedlicka and Meyer 1980	cross cultural studies
Mandal and Deshmukh 1994	selection of vendors.
Sharma and Sushil 1995	waste management
M.D Singh et al. 2003	engineering industries for knowledge management.
Jharkharia and Shankar 2004	mutual influence of the enablers which affects IT enablement of supply chain.
Bolanos et al. 2005	Used by executives working to improve decision making process in different functional areas.
Ravi et al. 2005	determining various logistics variables which helps in better performance of computer hardware supply chains.
Saxena et al. 2006	energy conservation policies.
Lin et al. 2006	product design
Agarwal et al. 2007	supply chain management
Singh et al 2007	implementing the knowledge management in engineering industries
Qureshi et al. 2007	determine the variables of logistics which depicts the relation between shippers and logistics service providers (LSPs) and its effect on the competitiveness and productivity of the shipper company.
Thakkar et al. 2007	comparative analysis of supply chain relationships between small and medium enterprises.
Mohammed et al. 2008	value chain management
Raj et al. 2010	understanding mutual relationship of the factors that affects the flexibility of FMS
Talib et al. 2011	relationship of various barriers to the implementation of total quality management.
Attri et al. 2012	analysis and identification of the barriers in the implementation of Total Productive Maintenance
Haleem et al. 2012	world-class manufacturing
PS Poduval et al. 2015	determing various factors of Total Productive Maintenance (TPM)
Yadav et al. 2015	Success factors of humanitarian supply chain
Poduval et al. 2015	Concept of ISM explained through barriers in implementation of Total Productive Maintenance
Sivaprakasam et al. 2015	Implementation of Green Supply Chain Management through a case study of Textile manufacturing Industry.
Behl et al. 2016	Barriers and enablers of mobile banking opportunities
Behl et al. 2016	Enablers that enhances the efficiency of the cooperatives.
Purohit et al. 2016	Enablers of Mass customisation of Indian footwear Industries
Sharma et al. 2016	Customer satisfaction in retail banking services
Thirupathi et al. 2016	Indian automotive component sector to understand various factors of manufacturing sustainably.
Sarhan et al. 2016	overview of ISM in Construction Management Research
Pravin Kumar et al. 2017	automobile manufacturing organization to fix its agility index.
Verma et al. 2018	relation between various enablers of Supply Chain Competitiveness
Liu et al. 2018	determine various factors that helps in understanding and managing safety at Subway Construction
Hughes et al. 2019	Elucidation of Information System project success factors
Behl et al. 2019	Sustainability of environmentally sound technologies

into a heterogeneous well-defined model. However, it had been used by several researchers of interdisciplinary groups along with MICMAC analysis as it has the capability of handling large problems and converting the same into an understandable structure. The model is easy to use and can be helpful to a large number of people in handling varied complex relationship of the factors of the study.

LIMITATIONS OF THE STUDY

The technique of ISM is entirely based on the opinion of experts, who helps in narrowing the variables considered for the study. If right variables are not projected from the literature review, then it may not help us in getting the right results. This requires tremendous collection of literature review, which in turn might list a large number of variables for the study. This complicates the study, which may serve as one of the limitation of this study. There may also be chances that some of the factors are overlooked or ignored in the collection data from comprehensive review of literature. This may lead to inaccurate results as there could be possibility of multiple interpretations by the researcher. The model is not verified with the experts after its completion. The role of the experts is strictly restricted till identifying the dependence power and driving power of the variables. Since none of the variables are statistically validated, it is important to test the model with the help of Structural Equation Modeling (SEM).

RECOMMENDATIONS AND FURTHER RESEARCH DIRECTIONS

The interactive relationships drawn by directed links for the variables comparatively lacks in ISM technique, which distorts the decision-making process. In that case, Total interpretative Structural Modeling(TISM) is a really helpful approach to beat these problems in decoding the directed links within the structural model of factors/variables. Since TISM interprets both nodes and links in the diagraph, it gives a better explanatory framework of the variables(Yeravdekar and Behl, 2017). Apart from TISM, various other modelling techniques can also be used such as AHP, ANP or Multi-Dimensional Scaling(MDS).

ISM is a worldwide phenomenon, which is interdisciplinary in nature. This study has explained the general steps for the implementation of ISM technique. Further studies require us to test the model to statistically verify it. The model of ISM can further be tested and statistically verified with the help of Structural Equation Modeling (SEM). It is a powerful analytical tool for methodological evaluation of models by multivariate analysis. With this, Exploratory Factor Analysis and Confirmatory factor analysis (CFA) can be used as statistical tools for placing the factor structure and verifying the variables. The model can be validated, specified and properly identified by Path Analysis using AMOS. A theoretical model based on hypothesis is specified and the raw data after cleaning is fed into the SEM software which fits the data to the specified model and provides overall model fit statistics.

ACKNOWLEDGMENT

I would like to thank the reviewing team who helped me improve the quality content of this chapter. I would also like to extend our gratitude to Guest Editors who had helped in shaping the manuscript by adding their valuable comments to it. I am also thankful to the language editors who have helped to improve the standard of writing and systematically organizing it.

REFERENCES

Agarwal, A., Shankar, R., & Tiwari, M. K. (2007). Modeling agility of supply chain. *Industrial Marketing Management, 36*(4), 443–457. doi:10.1016/j.indmarman.2005.12.004

Anantatmula, V., & Kanungo, S. (2008). Role of IT and KM in improving project management performance. *Vine, 38*(3), 357–369. doi:10.1108/03055720810904862

Anukul, M., & Deshmukh, S. G. (1994). Vendor selection using interpretive structural modelling (ISM). *International Journal of Operations & Production Management, 14*(6), 52–59. doi:10.1108/01443579410062086

Attri, R., Grover, S., Dev, N., & Kumar, D. (2013). An ISM approach for modelling the enablers in the implementation of total productive maintenance (TPM). *International Journal of System Assurance Engineering and Management, 4*(4), 313–326. doi:10.100713198-012-0088-7

Behl, A., & Pal, A. (2019). Sustainability of environmentally sound technologies using interpretive structural modelling. *International Journal of Innovation and Sustainable Development, 13*(1), 1–19. doi:10.1504/IJISD.2019.096702

Behl, A., Pal, A., & Roy, K. K. (2016). Integrated framework for governance of cooperative: An Interpretive Structural Modeling approach. *Indian Journal of Economics and Development, 4*, 2.

Behl, A., Rathi, P., & Kumar, V. A. (2018). Sustainability of the Indian auto rickshaw sector: Identification of enablers and their interrelationship using TISM. *International Journal of Services and Operations Management, 31*(2), 137–168. doi:10.1504/IJSOM.2018.094750

Behl, A., Singh, M., & Venkatesh, V. G. (2016). Enablers and barriers of mobile banking opportunities in rural India: A strategic analysis. *International Journal of Business Excellence, 10*(2), 209–239. doi:10.1504/IJBEX.2016.077999

Bolaños, R., Fontela, E., Nenclares, A., & Pastor, P. (2005). Using interpretive structural modelling in strategic decision-making groups. *Management Decision, 43*(6), 877–895. doi:10.1108/00251740510603619

Haleem, A., Sushil, Qadri, M. A., & Kumar, S. (2012). Analysis of critical success factors of world-class manufacturing practices: An application of interpretative structural modelling and interpretative ranking process. *Production Planning and Control, 23*(10-11), 722–734. doi:10.1080/09537287.2011.642134

Hansen, J. V., McKell, L. J., & Heitger, L. E. (1979). ISMS: Computer-aided analysis for design of decision-support systems. *Management Science, 25*(11), 1069–1081. doi:10.1287/mnsc.25.11.1069

Hawthorne, R. W., & Sage, A. P. (1975). On applications of interpretive structural modeling to higher education program planning. *Socio-Economic Planning Sciences*, *9*(1), 31–43. doi:10.1016/0038-0121(75)90039-7

Hughes, D. L., Rana, N. P., & Dwivedi, Y. K. (2019). Elucidation of IS project success factors: An interpretive structural modelling approach. *Annals of Operations Research*, 1–32.

Jedlicka, A. (1980). Interpretive Structural Modeling: Cross Cultural Uses.

Jharkharia, S., & Shankar, R. (2004). IT enablement of supply chains: Modeling the enablers. *International Journal of Productivity and Performance Management*, *53*(8), 700–712. doi:10.1108/17410400410569116

Kumar, D., Goyal, P., & Kumar, V. (2019). Modeling and classification of enablers of CSR in Indian firms. *Journal of Modelling in Management*, *14*(2), 456–475. doi:10.1108/JM2-07-2018-0100

Kumar, P., Singh, R. K., & Kumar, R. (2017). An integrated framework of interpretive structural modeling and graph theory matrix approach to fix the agility index of an automobile manufacturing organization. *International Journal of System Assurance Engineering and Management*, *8*(1), 342–352. doi:10.100713198-015-0350-x

Lin, M. C., Wang, C. C., & Chen, T. C. (2006). A strategy for managing customer-oriented product design. *Concurrent Engineering*, *14*(3), 231–244. doi:10.1177/1063293X06068390

Liu, P., Li, Q., Bian, J., Song, L., & Xiahou, X. (2018). Using interpretative structural modeling to identify critical success factors for safety management in subway construction: A china study. *International Journal of Environmental Research and Public Health*, *15*(7), 1359. doi:10.3390/ijerph15071359 PMID:29958438

Malone, D. W. (1975). An introduction to the application of interpretive structural modeling. *Proceedings of the IEEE*, *63*(3), 397–404. doi:10.1109/PROC.1975.9765

Mohammed, I. R., Shankar, R., & Banwet, D. K. (2008). Creating flex-lean-agile value chain by outsourcing: An ISM-based interventional roadmap. *Business Process Management Journal*, *14*(3), 338–389. doi:10.1108/14637150810876670

Nishat Faisal, M. (2010). Sustainable supply chains: A study of interaction among the enablers. *Business Process Management Journal*, *16*(3), 508–529. doi:10.1108/14637151011049476

Norman, R. Z. (1965). Structural models: An introduction to the theory of directed graphs.

Poduval, P. S., & Pramod, V. R. (2015). Interpretive Structural Modeling (ISM) and its application in analyzing factors inhibiting implementation of Total Productive Maintenance (TPM). *International Journal of Quality & Reliability Management*, *32*(3), 308–331. doi:10.1108/IJQRM-06-2013-0090

Purohit, J. K., Mittal, M. L., Mittal, S., & Sharma, M. K. (2016). Interpretive structural modeling-based framework for mass customisation enablers: An Indian footwear case. *Production Planning and Control*, *27*(9), 774–786. doi:10.1080/09537287.2016.1166275

Qureshi, M. N., Kumar, D., & Kumar, P. (2007). Modeling the logistics outsourcing relationship variables to enhance shippers' productivity and competitiveness in logistical supply chain. *International Journal of Productivity and Performance Management*, *56*(8), 689–714. doi:10.1108/17410400710833001

Raj, T., & Attri, R. (2010). Quantifying barriers to implementing total quality management (TQM). *European Journal of Industrial Engineering*, *4*(3), 308–335. doi:10.1504/EJIE.2010.033333

Ravi, V., & Shankar, R. (2005). Analysis of interactions among the barriers of reverse logistics. *Technological Forecasting and Social Change*, *72*(8), 1011–1029. doi:10.1016/j.techfore.2004.07.002

Ravi, V., Shankar, R., & Tiwari, M. K. (2005). Productivity improvement of a computer hardware supply chain. *International Journal of Productivity and Performance Management*, *54*(4), 239–255. doi:10.1108/17410400510593802

Sahney, S., Banwet, D. K., & Karunes, S. (2008). An integrated framework of indices for quality management in education: A faculty perspective. *The TQM Journal*, *20*(5), 502–519. doi:10.1108/17542730810898467

Sarhan, J. G., Hu, X., & Xia, B. (2016, December). An overview of the application of Interpretive Structural Modeling (ISM) in construction management research. In *Proceedings of the International Conference on Sustainable Built Environment SBE16* (pp. 316-319).

Saxena, J. P., Sushil, & Vrat, P. (2006). Policy and strategy formulation: An application of flexible systems methodology. GIFT Pub.

Sharma, H. D., Gupta, A. D., & Sushil. (1995). The objectives of waste management in India: A futures inquiry. *Technological Forecasting and Social Change*, *48*(3), 285–309. doi:10.1016/0040-1625(94)00066-6

Sharma, M., Tiwari, P., & Chaubey, D. S. (2016). Summarizing factors of customer experience and building a structural model using total interpretive structural modelling technology. *Global Business Review*, *17*(3), 730–741. doi:10.1177/0972150916630825

Singh, M. D., Shankar, R., Narain, R., & Agarwal, A. (2003). An interpretive structural modeling of knowledge management in engineering industries. *Journal of Advances in Management Research*, *1*(1), 28–40. doi:10.1108/97279810380000356

Singh, R. K., Garg, S. K., Deshmukh, S. G., & Kumar, M. (2007). Modelling of critical success factors for implementation of AMTs. *Journal of Modelling in Management*, *2*(3), 232–250. doi:10.1108/17465660710834444

Sivaprakasam, R., Selladurai, V., & Sasikumar, P. (2015). Implementation of interpretive structural modelling methodology as a strategic decision-making tool in a Green Supply Chain Context. *Annals of Operations Research*, *233*(1), 423–448. doi:10.100710479-013-1516-z

Talib, F., Rahman, Z., & Qureshi, M. N. (2011). Analysis of interaction among the barriers to total quality management implementation using interpretive structural modeling approach. Benchmarking. *International Journal (Toronto, Ont.)*, *18*(4), 563–587.

Thakkar, J., Deshmukh, S. G., Gupta, A. D., & Shankar, R. (2007). Development of a balanced scorecard. *International Journal of Productivity and Performance Management*.

Thirupathi, R. M., & Vinodh, S. (2016). Application of interpretive structural modelling and structural equation modelling for analysis of sustainable manufacturing factors in Indian automotive component sector. *International Journal of Production Research, 54*(22), 6661–6682. doi:10.1080/00207543.2015.1126372

Verma, A., Seth, N., & Singhal, N. (2018). Application of Interpretive Structural Modelling to establish Interrelationships among the Enablers of Supply Chain Competitiveness. *Materials Today: Proceedings, 5*(2), 4818–4823.

Waller, R. J. (1980). Contextual relations and mathematical relations in interpretive structural modeling. *IEEE Transactions on Systems, Man, and Cybernetics, 10*(3), 143–145. doi:10.1109/TSMC.1980.4308451

Warfield, J. N. (1974). *Structuring Complex Systems. Monograph No. 4.* Columbus, OH: Battelle Memorial Institute.

Warfield, J. N. (1974). Developing subsystem matrices in structural modeling. *IEEE Transactions on Systems, Man, and Cybernetics, SMC-4*(1), 74–80. doi:10.1109/TSMC.1974.5408523

Warfield, J. N. (1976). *Societal systems.* Planning, Policy, and Complexity.

Warfield, J. N. (1994). *Science of generic design: managing complexity through systems design.* Iowa State Press.

Warfield, J. N. (2003). *The mathematics of structure.* AJAR Publishing.

Wu, H., & Niu, D. (2017). Study on influence factors of electric vehicles charging station location based on ISM and FMICMAC. *Sustainability, 9*(4), 484. doi:10.3390u9040484

Yadav, D. K., & Barve, A. (2015). Analysis of critical success factors of humanitarian supply chain: An application of Interpretive Structural Modeling. *International Journal of Disaster Risk Reduction, 12*, 213–225. doi:10.1016/j.ijdrr.2015.01.008

Yeravdekar, A., & Behl, A. (2018). The unprecedented commercialisation of Indian cricket: A study using total interpretive structural modelling. *International Journal of Services and Operations Management, 31*(3), 277–302. doi:10.1504/IJSOM.2018.095558

Yeravdekar, S., & Behl, A. (2017). Benchmarking model for management education in India: A total interpretive structural modeling approach. Benchmarking. *International Journal (Toronto, Ont.), 24*(3), 666–693.

ADDITIONAL READING

Beikkhakhian, Y., Javanmardi, M., Karbasian, M., & Khayambashi, B. (2015). The application of ISM model in evaluating agile suppliers selection criteria and ranking suppliers using fuzzy TOPSIS-AHP methods. *Expert Systems with Applications, 42*(15-16), 6224–6236. doi:10.1016/j.eswa.2015.02.035

Byrne, B. M. (2013). *Structural equation modeling with EQS: Basic concepts, applications, and programming*. Routledge. doi:10.4324/9780203726532

Chang, D. Y. (1996). Applications of the extent analysis method on fuzzy AHP. *European Journal of Operational Research, 95*(3), 649–655. doi:10.1016/0377-2217(95)00300-2

Chin, W. W. (1998). The partial least squares approach to structural equation modeling. Modern methods for business research, 295(2), 295-336.

Jena, J., Sidharth, S., Thakur, L. S., Kumar Pathak, D., & Pandey, V. C. (2017). Total interpretive structural modeling (TISM): Approach and application. *Journal of Advances in Management Research, 14*(2), 162–181. doi:10.1108/JAMR-10-2016-0087

Lomax, R. G., & Schumacker, R. E. (2004). A beginner's guide to structural equation modeling. psychology press.

Raj, T., Shankar, R., & Suhaib, M. (2008). An ISM approach for modelling the enablers of flexible manufacturing system: The case for India. *International Journal of Production Research, 46*(24), 6883–6912. doi:10.1080/00207540701429926

Sandbhor, S. S., & Botre, R. P. (2014). Applying total interpretive structural modeling to study factors affecting construction labour productivity. *Construction Economics and Building, 14*(1), 20–31. doi:10.5130/AJCEB.v14i1.3753

Sushil, S. (2012). Interpreting the interpretive structural model. *Global Journal of Flexible Systems Management, 13*(2), 87–106. doi:10.100740171-012-0008-3

Yu, C. S. (2002). A GP-AHP method for solving group decision-making fuzzy AHP problems. *Computers & Operations Research, 29*(14), 1969–2001. doi:10.1016/S0305-0548(01)00068-5

KEY TERMS AND DEFINITIONS

AMOS: It is a visual program for Structural equation modelling (SEM), where models can be graphically drawn using simple drawing tools. It also performs the computations for SEM and displays the results.

Delphi Technique: It is a forecasting process framework based on the results of multiple rounds of questionnaires sent to a panel of experts. Several rounds of questionnaires are sent out to the group of experts, and the anonymous responses are aggregated and shared with the group after each round.

Driving and Dependence Power: The driving power of a particular enabler is the total number of enablers (including itself), which it may help to achieve and the dependence is the total number enablers which may help to achieve it.

Exploratory Factor Analysis and Confirmatory Factor Analysis (CFA): Confirmatory factor analysis (CFA) is a multivariate statistical procedure that is used to test how well the measured variables represent the number of constructs. Confirmatory factor analysis (CFA) and exploratory factor analysis (EFA) are similar techniques, but in exploratory factor analysis (EFA), data is simply explored and provides information about the numbers of factors required to represent the data. In exploratory factor analysis, all measured variables are related to every latent variable.

Multi Criteria Decision Analysis (MCDA): It is a general framework for supporting complex decision-making situations with multiple and often conflicting objectives that stakeholders groups and/ or decision-makers value differently.

Structural Equation Modelling: It is a multivariate statistical analysis technique that is used to analyze structural relationships. This technique is the combination of factor analysis and multiple regression analysis, and it is used to analyze the structural relationship between measured variables and latent constructs.

Chapter 2
Application of ISM in the Manufacturing Sector

Abhinav Pal
Symbiosis International University, India

Jisha Rajendran
Amity School of Economics, Amity University, India

Aastha Behl
Pranveer Singh Institute of Technology, India

ABSTRACT

This chapter discusses the application of Interpretive Structural Modelling (ISM) in the manufacturing sector. Authors provide a brief about ISM and its usage in the current scenario, and a comprehensive literature review that sheds light on the methodology used over the years in the application of ISM. The chapter assesses the method's advantages and disadvantages. It introduces the technique of ISM in the manufacturing sector, and discusses the applications of ISM in the manufacturing sector along the review of literature.

INTRODUCTION

The modern-day industry is evolving at a staggering space to a time where unparallel efforts are being put by various organisations by focusing on the manufacturing process alone in order to provide manufactured products and associated services of the highest quality and degree. Demands of the consumer are evolving along with competitiveness of the manufacturing industry, therefore its becoming extremely important for firms to implement advanced manufacturing technologies and techniques to keep pace with the increasing consumer demands and competition. Against this backdrop it is vital that the manufacturing process should be seen in an integrative manner. ISM as a method, can be very useful in this regard as it is very extensively employed as a qualitative tool in supply chain and quality management researches pertaining to the manufacturing sector (Goyal, Samalia, & Verma, 2017; Talib, Rahman, &

DOI: 10.4018/978-1-7998-2216-5.ch002

Qureshi, 2011; Kureshi, Qureshi, & Sajid 2010; Dewangan, Agrawal, & Sharma, 2015; Bouzon, Govindan, & Rodriguez, 2015).

It has been generally observed and identified that individuals or a group tend to face many difficulties and bottlenecks while facing complex systems or issues. These issues or complexity majorly arise due to large number of elements and interactions of these elements with each other. The existence of various relations, direct or indirect, among various elements of a system complicates the structure of the same. Since the structure is not clearly defined, it becomes difficult to work with the system. ISM (Interpretive Structural Modelling) is a methodology which helps in identification of a structure within a system (Singh and Kant, 2008; Malone, 1975; Singh, Shankar, Narain, & Agarwal 2003; Thakkar, Deshmukh, Gupta, & Shankar, 2007;Yeravdekar and Behl, 2017).

BACKGROUND

In the approach of ISM, there is a systematic application of various elements of graph theory in such a manner that conceptual, computational and theoretical aspects are fused together so as to explain certain complex pattern of an intricate system of various interlinked variables(Ravi, Shankar, & Tiwari, 2005; Janes, 1988; Singh, Garg, & Deshmukh, 2007; Singh, Shankar, Narain, & Agarwal, 2003). The idea behind the use of ISM stems from the desire to make use of structured and logical thinking in order to tackle a complex problem under consideration. The methodology is deemed as interpretive in the sense because the collective judgement of a group decides the various linkages that exist among the different variables of the system, it is structured on the various mutual relationships that exist among elements which leads to the determination of the holistic and the overall structure on the basis of all the elements that exists in the system(Bolaños, Fontela, Nenclares, & Pastor, 2005; Faisal, 2010; Warfield and Staley, 1996; Dubey and Ali, 2014). ISM as a modelling technique intends to determine and impose an order and direction on the relationships of various elements of the system. ISM is majorly a group exercise but can be used individually as well (Mangle, Phillips, Pitts, & Laver-Bradbury, 2014); Azevedo, Carvalho, & Cruz-Machado, 2013).

MAIN FOCUS OF THE CHAPTER

The chapter details the journey of ISM in the manufacturing sector and its applications in the same. The first and the current section introduces ISM in the manufacturing sector and its approach. The second and the subsequent section elaborates the review of literature and applications of ISM in the manufacturing sector. Lastly, the fourth section concludes the chapter with emphasis on the limitations. ISM is an interactive tool for learning process and active management. It is a well-established methodology for determining, identifying and summarising relationships that exists among various elements, which constitute a complex system and define a particular problem or an issue.ISM helps in ensuring that an order or a structure in formed in a complex system which has various elements that are directly or indirectly related, hence ISM helps in dealing with the complexities involved in a particular system (Yeravdekar and Behl, 2018; Behl et al., 2018). Literature in the past highlighted that ISM has been used to determine competitiveness in the manufacturing sector and also in the implementation of various of manufacturing technology (Bag, 2016; Cherrafi, Elfezazi, Garza-Reyes, Benhida, & Mokhlis 2017; Muruganantham, Vinodh, Arun, & Ramesh, 2018; Gardas, Raut, & Narkhede, 2017).

REVIEW OF LITERATURE AND ITS APPLICATION

The ISM methodology was first proposed by Warfield in 1973. Its Central idea was to use experts' practical experience and knowledge to form a deconstruct a complex structure of variables into a simpler multi-level structure of related variables and portrays the complex set of elements in a simpler form graphically, this process of ISM is a computer aided process (Jhankaria and Shankar, 2004); (Attri, Dev, & Sharma, 2013). The methodology and process of applying ISM is very well documented and has been established by various researchers in the past (Warfield, 1973; Sahney, 2008; Diabat, Khreishah, Kannan, Panikar, & Gunasekaran, 2013). In ISM researchers ensure that they establish the contextual relationship among various elements by incorporating expert opinions from various industry and academic experts with different number of respondents in a group. It helps in dealing with the complexities of the variables by imposing an order on the variables of a complex system(Luthra, Kumar, Kumar, & Haleem, 2011).The steps involved in the ISM methodology are as follows (Charan, Shankar, & Baisya, 2008):

1. Finalisation of the group of people that has the pertinent experience, knowledge and background towards the research topic.
2. Identification and selection of the relevant variables that are important to the system that is been studied.
3. Formation of the structural self-interaction matrix (SSIM). By incorporating the inputs of the experts based on their experience, the relationships among various elements of the system is hypothesized. The matrix would contain the pair wise relationships that exists among the variables of the system in consideration.
4. Determination of the reachability matrix. On the basis of the SSIM, the reachability matrix is formed. One of the assumptions in this matrix is that there is transitivity of relationships among variables of the system. If variable A is related to variable B, and Variable B is related variable C, then Variable A is necessarily related to variable C.
5. Decomposition of the reachability matrix into various structural levels in order to make a directed graph along with the removal of transitive links.

Literature in the past has established that ISM is very widely used as a qualitative tool in order to implement and gauge the effectiveness of various manufacturing technologies in various types of industry settings (Raj, Shankar, & Suhaib, 2008). Previous studies have highlighted that ISM can be employed in determining vendor-selection criteria (Mandal and Deshmukh, 1994; Kannan, Pokharel, & Sasi Kumar, 2009; Yang, Chiu, Tzeng, & Yeh, 2009), determination of choices of third-party logistics (Thakkar, Deshmukh, Gupta, & Shankar, 2005), The presence of supply chain risks are inevitable to the manufacturing process and ISM has been employed by researchers in order to gauge and mitigate supply chain risks that exists in the manufacturing processes (Ahuja, Sawhney, & Arif, 2017). ISM has also witnessed a number of uses in the development of a balance score card (Thakkar, Deshmukh, Gupta, & Shankar, 2007). In recent times Total Quality Management(TQM) has become the buzz word in the manufacturing processes and a lot of industrial companies are implementing the same in order to ensure better business optimization practices, ISM has been used by researchers in execution and implementation of TQM barriers (Talib, Rahman, & Qureshi, 2011). Sustainable manufacturing as a field has witnessed rapid growth in the manufacturing sector, which is validated by the growing body of literature pertinent to the topic. Sustainable manufacturing has immense benefits in the manufacturing process like product designing, supply chain, logistics, waste avoidance and various production processes (Seow and Rahimford, 2011; Despeisse, Mbaye, Ball, & Levers, 2012; Kara, Ibbotson, & Kayis (Dubey, Gunasekaran, Sushil, & Singh, 2015); (Jovane, Yoshikawa, Alting, Boer, Westkamper, Williams, & Paci, 2008). ISM as a modelling technique has been used in building a theory of sustainable manufacturing (Dubey, Gunasekaran, Sushil, & Singh, 2015); (Despeisse, Mbaye, Ball, & Levers, 2012).The role of information technology in effectively managing supply chains has been studied by a number of researchers in the past and substantial research has proven the significant improvement in competitive advantage due to investments in IT supported supply chain management(Lai, Zhao, & Wang, 2006; Goh, Prakash, & Yeo, 2007; Mueller and Seuring, 2008). ISM has proved useful in determining information technology enablers for Indian Manufacturing (Thakkar, Kanda, & Deshmukh, 2008); (Jharkaria and Shankar, 2004) ; (Jharkaria and Shankar, 2005;). ISM has also been used in assessment of lean performance in radial tyre manufacturing (Gupta, Acharya, & Patwardhan, 2013).The volatility that is present in the current market scenario has forced manufacturing managers to adopt flexible manufacturing systems in lieu of the traditional manufacturing systems in order to meet challenges caused due to everchanging demands of customers, market competition from both domestic and international players, technological changes and faster deliveries to market (Kulatilaka,1988; Koren and Shpitalni, 2010). ISM has been proved useful to gauge the mutual interactions of enablers of flexible manufacturing systems (Raj, Shankar, & Suhaib, 2008).The manufacturing sector has also witnessed the prominence of lean manufacturing since the 1990s, it has become a significant conceptual framework in many industrial companies in the recent times (Womack and Jones, 1994; Lewis, 2000; Yang, Hong, & Modi, 2011). Since lean manufacturing is a process that intends to produce a product in such a manner that it is exactly what a customer wants at the right time, lean manufacturing minimizes all non-value-added activities in the production process. Kumar, Kumar, Haleem, & Gahlot (2013) employ ISM to gauge the implementation of lean manufacturing in the manufacturing process. Even the automobile industry has witnessed the benefits of sustainable manufacturing practices, these practices are essential for automotive component manufacturing industry in order to obtain competitive advantage in the market. Thirupati and Vinodh (2016) have used the ISM technique for analysing and understanding the sustainable manufacturing factors in the Indian automotive component sector. Improvements in the manufacturing practices is essential for betterment of majority of the Industrial companies and various manufacturing hubs of the world, therefore an understanding of various world class practices is beneficial and essential to both academicians and practitioners. (Khan & Haleem, 2012) have used ISM to study and analyse the various critical success factors of world-class manufacturing practices. Research in the past has proven that supply chain of a company can be a major barrier to competition if there is a lasting and meaningful relationship between suppliers and consumers due to various direct and indirect consequences of supplier selection by the company(Jafarneid and Shahaei, 2007; De Boer, Labro & Morlacchi, 2001).The application of ISM has also been used to determine supplier selection criteria and ranking of suppliers (Beikkhakhian, Javanmardi, Karbasian, & Khayambashi, 2015). Also, in the recent times the manufacturing world has witnessed increasing environmental consciousness, as customers are becoming more sensitized to damages to the environment, industries need to reduce the adverse impact of supply chain on the environment (Chien & Shih, 2007; McWilliams & Siegel, 2000; Strandberg, 2009; Walker, Di

Sisto, & McBain, 2008). Against this backdrop, ISM has been used for barrier analysis in implementing green supply chain management (Mathiyazhagan, Govindan, NoorulHaq, & Geng, 2013; Saxena and Vrat, 1990; Kannan, Pokharel, & Sasi Kumar,2009). Lastly, ISM has also witnessed its application in the area of lean manufacturing (Jadhav, Mantha, & Rane, 2014; Kumar, Luthra, Govindan, Kumar, & Haleem, 2016; Sharma, Dixit, & Qadri, 2016; Sharma, Dixit, Qadri, & Kumar, 2015; Ravikumar, Marimuthu, & Parthiban, 2015).Success of any organisation would majorly depend on its competitive edge and implementation of lean manufacturing can significantly increase the competitive edge of the organisation which implements the same (see table 1).

Table 1. Applications of ISM

S. No	Application	References
1	ISM can be employed in determining vendor-selection criteria	Mandal and Deshmukh, 1994; Kannan, Pokharel, & Sasi Kumar, 2009; Yang, Chiu, Tzeng, & Yeh,2009
2	In determination of choices of third-party logistics	Thakkar, Deshmukh, Gupta, & Shankar, 2005
3	ISM has been employed by researchers in order to gauge and mitigate supply chain risks that exists in the manufacturing processes	(Ahuja, Sawhney, & Arif, 2017)
4	ISM has also witnessed a number of uses in the development of a balance score card	Thakkar, Deshmukh, Gupta, & Shankar, 2007
5	ISM has been used by researchers in execution and implementation of TQM barriers	Talib, Rahman, & Qureshi, 2011
6	ISM as a modelling technique has been used in building a theory of sustainable manufacturing	(Dubey, Gunasekaran, Sushil, & Singh, 2015); Despeisse, Mbaye, Ball, & Levers, 2012
7	ISM has proved useful in determining information technology enablers for Indian Manufacturing	(Thakkar, Kanda, & Deshmukh, 2008)
8	ISM has also been used in assessment of lean performance in radial tyre manufacturing	Gupta, Acharya, & Patwardhan, 2013
9	ISM has been proved useful to gauge the mutual interactions of enablers of flexible manufacturing systems	Raj, Shankar, & Suhaib, 2008
10	ISM to gauge the implementation of lean manufacturing in the manufacturing process.	Kumar, Kumar, Haleem, & Gahlot,2013
11	ISM technique for analysing and understanding the sustainable manufacturing factors in the Indian automotive component sector	Thirupati and Vinodh,2016
12	ISM to study and analyse the various critical success factors of world-class manufacturing practices.	(Khan & Haleem, 2012)
13	The application of ISM has also been used to determine supplier selection criteria and ranking of suppliers	Beikkhakhian, Javanmardi, Karbasian, & Khayambashi, 2015
14	ISM has been used for barrier analysis in implementing green supply chain management	Mathiyazhagan, Govindan, NoorulHaq, & Geng, 2013; Saxena and Vrat, 1990; Kannan, Pokharel, & Sasi Kumar, 2009
15	ISM has also witnessed its application in the area of lean manufacturing	Jadhav, Mantha, & Rane,2014; Kumar, Luthra, Govindan, Kumar, & Haleem, 2016; Sharma, Dixit, & Qadri, 2016; Sharma, Dixit, Qadri, & Kumar, 2015; Ravikumar, Marimuthu, & Parthiban, 2015

RESULTS AND ANALYSIS

It has been understood from the discussion so far that ISM is an advanced methodology that could be used for the identification of the relationships that tend to exist among particular items, which have the capacity to define the issue or problem at hand (Alawamleh & Popplewell, 2011). It is due to this reason that ISM method is garnering global acceptance across different fields, owing to the numerous advantages associated with its usage. As argued by Verma, Seth, & Singhal (2011), the method is being widely accepted by researchers for the purpose of representing the relationships that tend to exist between numerous elements associated to an issue. It commences with the recognition of the parameters that are contextually important for the issue or problem. This is followed by choosing a contextually important subordinate relation. After the contextual relationship is established, a structural self-interaction matrix (SSIM) is advanced that is dependent on the pairwise comparison of the parameters. This is followed by the conversion of the SSIM to a Reachability Matrix (RM), wherein the transitivity of the matrix is assessed. After the completion of the transitivity embedding, one can obtain the matrix model. Lastly, the process is followed by the derivation of the ISM through the process of segregating the elements and by extracting the structural model. It is useful for the derivation of hierarchical structures and obtaining relationship between factors and sub-factors. However, despite these advantages, the usage of ISM is still restricted and hasn't reached its full potential.

Firstly, several studies like that by Yudatama, Hidayanto, & Nazief (2018) have shown that ISM is an effective method for obtaining a hierarchical structure. Moreover, Attri, Dev, & Sharma (2013) argue that it is also effective for deriving a relationship between each factor and its subsequent sub-factor. By utilising a sequence of analytical procedures, ISM makes it possible to find and examine the important sub-factors and their relation with the factors. This is necessary because as argued by Thirupati & Vinodh (2016), several policymakers tend to divert their attention towards just one sub-factor. However, with ISM in the picture, policymakers can have a better understanding of the important sub-factors during the implementation of different policies based on the opinion of experts. According to Thakkar, Kanda, & Deshmukh (2008), this method is considered to be a better alternative than models like Technique for Order of Preference by Similarity to Ideal Solution (TOPSIS) and Analytic Hierarchy Process (AHP), owing to the fact that it not only identifies the priorities but also facilitates the provision of information regarding the relationship that tends to exist between the factors and the sub-factors, which is not applicable in the case of TOPSIS or AHP. In this regard, it is highly advantageous and is therefore preferred over its counterparts. Moreover, it has been proposed by Singh, Shankar, Narain, & Agarwal (2003) that one of the main traits of the ISM method is the validation or the accuracy of its data. It is mandatory for the data to be reliable and also be from a reliable source.

Secondly, it is often argued by several scholars like Govindan, Kannan, Mathiyazhagan, Jabbour, & Jabbour (2013), Singh, Sharma, & Garg (2010) and Tripathy, Sahu, & Ray (2013) that ISM would be highly useful during a high degree of abstraction like the ones required for long-range planning. Furthermore, Dubey, Gunasekaran, Sushil, & Singh (2015) suggests that it can also be utilised at a relatively more concrete degree of structure and process details that are associated to the activity or the issue like the electronic commerce, competitive analysis, human resources, financial decision making, difficult technical problems, re-engineering procedure, product design, engineering problems, strategic planning, career planning and process designing (Behl et al., 2016; Behl and Pal, 2016). This has been further reinstated by Attri, Dev, & Sharma (2013) who believe that ISM is advantageous in the current scenario, especially in the manufacturing sector, as it offers an extremely systematic process, wherein the computer is programmed in a manner to take into account the likely pairwise relations of all the elements of a system, either directly from the answers of the respondents or by making a transitive inference. Moreover, Ansari, Kharb, Luthra, Shimmi, & Chatterji (2013) its efficiency is further boosted, based on the context, the usage of transitive interpretations might end up reducing the quantity of the necessary queries by approximately 50%-80%.

Thirdly, the applicability and understandability of ISM to numerous fields has often been appreciated in different studies (Behl et al., 2016). According to Raj, Shankar, & Suhaib (2007), this method is considered to be easily comprehensible to a wide range of users across interdisciplinary groups, as it provides means to integrate the varied perceptions of the different participating groups. In other words, it helps in improving the quality of interpersonal as well as interdisciplinary communication within the realms of the research problem by diverting the attention of the respondents to just one particular question at a time (Faisal, 2010). The same has been stressed by Ahuja, Sawhney, & Arif (2017), who believe that no prior knowledge regarding the entire procedure is needed from the respondents. They should in fact, just possess sufficient understanding regarding the object system, in order to be able to respond to the wide array of relational queries that is being created by the computer. Moreover, Farris & Sage (1975) argue that the ISM method is also capable of conducting a wide range of components as well as relationships that is a typical part of a complex system. It is also considered to be heuristic with regard to the assessment of the suitability of the formulation of models, thus leading to insights regarding the system behaviour. Furthermore, as put forth by Watson (1978), it also possesses the advantage of its easy utilisation and the fact that it can be communicated easily to a larger set of audience. Such features of ISM approach have led to its widespread usage across the globe in numerous fields. As shown by Hughes, Dwivedi, Rana, & Simintiras (2016), ISM motivates issue analysis by facilitating participants to engage in exploration of the adequacy of the proposed systems elements list, along with the issue statements for illumination of the particular situation. In this light, it has been concluded by Shahabadkar (2012) that ISM serves the purpose of being a learning tool and forces participants for the development of a deeper understanding of the meaning as well as the significance of a particular list of elements and association.

Lastly, as argued by Qureshi, Kumar, & Kumar (2007), ISM also facilitates the provision of a directional and ordered framework for the difficult issues and helps in providing the decision makers an accurate picture of their situation, as well as the variables that are involved. Since, ISM process comprises of identifying factors and defining their interrelationships, along with the imposition of rank order and direction for illuminating difficult issues from the perspective of different systems. It facilitates the guiding and recording of the group results regarding to deliberations about complex subjects in a systematic and effective manner. As per Mangla, Madaan, Sarma, & Gupta (2014), ISM is known for creation of a structured graphical representation or model of the actual issue, which can be spread across to a wide range of people in an efficient manner. According to Mandal & Deshmukh (1994), the process of ISM helps in the transformation of blurred, poorly voiced mental models of the systems into well-defined as well as visible models. Such models help in finding the crucial issues or problems that are associated to each factor. This would help in the development of appropriate strategies to deal with the issue. ISM plays an important role of permitting policy or action analysis through the process of providing assistance to participants for the identification of specific areas for policy action, thereby offering advantages and other leverages to purse particular objectives (Dalvi-Esfahani, Ramayah, & Nilashi, 2017).

The discussion so far shed light on the numerous advantages of application of ISM. However, as argued by Jolhe & Subhash Babu (2014), like any other method that relies significantly on human judgment and their subsequent involvement in the process, ISM is also not devoid of any loopholes. Such

Table 2. Advantages and disadvantages of ISM

Advantages of ISM	• Effective in obtaining hierarchical structures. • ISM would be highly useful during a high degree of abstraction • Easily comprehensible to a wide range of users across interdisciplinary groups. • Facilitates the provision of a directional and ordered framework for the difficult issues and helps in providing the decision makers an accurate picture of their situation
Disadvantages of ISM	• Biased because based on human judgement • Difficulty while being use by a group of analysts.

limitations are seen to come into action to a large extent when ISM is utilised using a group of analysts who are known to be familiar with the issue. In this light, the aim of the underlying section is to highlight these limitations along with their toxic effects and also suggest ways to enhance and overcome these limitations. The major limitations to ISM have been highlighted by Attri, Dev, & Sharma (2013) who believe that there could be several variables to an issue or a problem. Increasing the number of variables to an issue or a problem, tends to raise the complexity of the methodology of ISM. Hence, one of the major limitations in ISM model is that only limited number of variables could be taken into account, while developing ISM model. Furthermore, help from experts have to be taken to analyse the power of dependence and driving force of the variable of an issue or a problem. However, as put forth by Lim, Tseng, Tan, & Bui (2017), this inclusion of experts will not provide models that can be statistically validated. SEM or also known as linear structural relationship approach possesses the ability to test the validity of all hypothetical models. Moreover, Jena, Sidharth, Thakur, Kumar Pathak, & Pandey (2017) have also identified a few limitations in the application of ISM. For instance, ISM model could only be utilised by people who are familiar with the methodology of ISM and hence are capable of deducing the information derived from it. Secondly, the benefit of implementing the methodology of ISM can be utilised an optimum manner, only when the adequate computer facilities are available. Thirdly, another major obstacle to the application of ISM is that the process of interpreting links would be weak and because of this reason, ISM methodology fails to give the same kind of clarifications of the given model for diverse people. This might end up misrepresenting the complete process of making decisions. As argued by Biswas (2017), usually relationships in a graphical model are interpreted through the utilisation of the edges of the link that helps in joining the two elements, thus facilitating the explanation of both the links as well as the nodes, which is clearly absent in the ISM model. Fourthly, as per Aoki, Saga, Ichinotsubo, Niu, & Tsuji (2013), ISM is restricted in its efforts to provide solutions as it only tends to solve the "how" and "what" aspect in building theories. However, it does not shed light on the on the causality of associations and is therefore not suitable for research questions that tend to deal with the "why" aspect of a problem. Lastly, it fails to take into consideration the transitive connections that tend to exist in a digraph. Due to these limitations, researchers developed models like TISM to curb the loopholes identified in the traditional ISM, without having to compromise its otherwise superior modelling methods in the current scenario (see table 2).

CONCLUSION

The aim of the underlying chapter was to discuss the application of Interpretive Structural Modelling (ISM) in the manufacturing sector. For this purpose, the chapter first gave a brief background to ISM and its application in different fields. This was followed by a comprehensive literature review that highlighted the methodology used over the years in the application of ISM. Lastly, the chapter discussed the application of ISM in the manufacturing sector specifically and assessed the advantages and disadvantages of relying on ISM method. From the discussion, it was evident that the primary aim of ISM is the identification of the relationship that tends to exist between the different elements taken into consideration, which in turn results in the perception regarding the system's structure in a much-improved manner (Salimifard, Abbaszadeh, & Ghorbangpur, 2010). According to Sushil (2012), ISM is a methodology that is utilised for the transformation of weak and vaguely expressed rational models of systems from a different zone into unambiguous and simple models.

Despite the numerous advantages in the application of ISM, several studies like that by Lee, Wang, & Lin (2010), the interpretation of the associations in ISM model is usually limited to just the contextual relationship that tends to exist between the elements as well as the direction of the association that tends to occur in a pair-wise comparison. This is because interpreting the directional graph in the ISM methodology is usually accomplished at two degrees, namely, the nodes and the links. The interpretation of the nodes on ISM is usually attained through the description of the particular element reflecting it. Due to this restriction, it has been indicated in the discussion above that the interpretation of the associations through the ISM methodology is relatively weaker, as it fails to answer the ways in which the links tend to attain a particular contextual relationship. To curb this issue, it has been suggested by Jayalakshmi & Pramod (2015) that the process of taking decisions could be increased by effectually interpreting the diagraph constructed from the depiction of the associations existing between the elements that have been identified. As shown by Pfohl, Gallus, & Thomas (2011), the issues arising from the limitation of ISM can be resolved through the development of "interpretive matrix" that is usually used as a managerial tool. This helps in the provision of a complete interpretation of the relationships that tend to exist in a structural model. In this regard, it can be concluded that the interpretive matrix's tools is extremely important for structural modelling, owing to the fact that it illustrates the interpretation of the associations in the form of a matrix for each of the pair-wise element in the particular cell, which can be termed as fuzzy or binary. Hence, with the addition of ISM to the interpretive matrix, it helps in directing the development of the framework and methodology of the total interpretive structural modelling (TISM). This is regarded as an advanced technique for qualitative modelling and is considered to be the current expansion of the traditional ISM.

REFERENCES

Ahuja, R., Sawhney, A., & Arif, M. (2017). Prioritising BIM Capabilities of an Organisation: An Interpretive Structural Modeling Analysis. *Procedia Engineering*, *86*, 2–10. doi:10.1016/j.proeng.2017.07.166

Alawamleh, M., & Popplewell, K. (2011). Interpretive Structural Modelling of Risk Sources in a Virtual Organisation. *International Journal of Production Research*, *49*(20), 6041–6063. doi:10.1080/00207543.2010.519735

Ansari, M. F., Kharb, R. K., Luthra, S., Shimmi, S. L., & Chatterji, S. (2013). Analysis of Barriers to Implement Solar Power Installations in India Using Interpretive Structural Modeling Technique. *Renewable & Sustainable Energy Reviews*, *27*, 163–174. doi:10.1016/j.rser.2013.07.002

Aoki, S., Saga, R., Ichinotsubo, T., Niu, W., & Tsuji, H. (2013). Dependency Extraction from Growth Trajectory using Sequential Pattern. *13th International Conference on Knowledge Management and Knowledge Technologies*, (pp. 1-6). 10.1145/2494188.2494197

Attri, R., Dev, N., & Sharma, V. (2013). Interpretive Structural Modelling (ISM) Approach: An Overview. *Research Journal of Management Sciences*, 3-8.

Azevedo, S., Carvalho, H., & Cruz-Machado, V. (2013). Using interpretive structural modelling to identify and rank performance measures: An application in the automotive supply chain. *Baltic Journal of Management*, *8*(2), 208–230. doi:10.1108/17465261311310027

Bag, S. (2016). Green strategy, supplier relationship building and supply chain performance: Total interpretive structural modelling approach. *International Journal of Procurement Management*, *9*(4), 398–426. doi:10.1504/IJPM.2016.077702

Behl, A., & Pal, A. (2016). Analysing the barriers towards sustainable financial inclusion using mobile banking in rural India. *Indian Journal of Science and Technology*, *9*(15), 1–7. doi:10.17485/ijst/2016/v9i15/92100

Behl, A., Pal, A., & Roy, K. K. (2016). Integrated framework for governance of cooperative: An Interpretive Structural Modeling approach. *Indian Journal of Economics and Development*, *4*, 2.

Behl, A., Rathi, P., & Kumar, V. A. (2018). Sustainability of the Indian auto rickshaw sector: Identification of enablers and their interrelationship using TISM. *International Journal of Services and Operations Management*, *31*(2), 137–168. doi:10.1504/IJSOM.2018.094750

Behl, A., Singh, M., & Venkatesh, V. G. (2016). Enablers and barriers of mobile banking opportunities in rural India: A strategic analysis. *International Journal of Business Excellence*, *10*(2), 209–239. doi:10.1504/IJBEX.2016.077999

Beikkhakhian, Y., Javanmardi, M., Karbasian, M., & Khayambashi, B. (2015). The application of ISM model in evaluating agile suppliers selection criteria and ranking suppliers using fuzzy TOPSIS-AHP methods. *Expert Systems with Applications*, *42*(15-16), 6224–6236. doi:10.1016/j.eswa.2015.02.035

Biswas, P. (2017). Modeling Reconfigurability in Supply Chains Using Total Interpretive Structural Modeling. *Journal of Advanced in Management Research*, *14*(2), 194–221. doi:10.1108/JAMR-09-2016-0071

Bolaños, R., Fontela, E., Nenclares, A., & Pastor, P. (2005). Using interpretive structural modelling in strategic decision-making groups. *Management Decision*, *43*(6), 877–895. doi:10.1108/00251740510603619

Bouzon, M., Govindan, K., & Rodriguez, C. M. T. (2015). Reducing the extraction of minerals: Reverse logistics in the machinery manufacturing industry sector in Brazil using ISM approach. *Resources Policy*, *46*, 27–36. doi:10.1016/j.resourpol.2015.02.001

Charan, P., Shankar, R., & Baisya, R. K. (2008). Analysis of interactions among the variables of supply chain performance measurement system implementation. *Business Process Management Journal*, *14*(4), 512–529. doi:10.1108/14637150810888055

Cherrafi, A., Elfezazi, S., Garza-Reyes, J. A., Benhida, K., & Mokhlis, A. (2017). Barriers in Green Lean implementation: A combined systematic literature review and interpretive structural modelling approach. *Production Planning and Control, 28*(10), 829–842. doi:10.1080/09537287.2017.1324184

Chien, M. K., & Shih, L. H. (2007). An empirical study of the implementation of green supply chain management practices in the electrical and electronic industry and their relation to organizational performances. *International Journal of Environmental Science and Technology, 4*(3), 383–394.

Dalvi-Esfahani, M., Ramayah, T., & Nilashi, M. (2017). Modelling Upper Echelons' Behavioural Drivers of Green IT/IS Adoption Using an Integrated Interpretive Structural Modelling–Analytic Network Process Approach. *Telematics and Informatics, 34*(2), 583–603. doi:10.1016/j.tele.2016.10.002

De Boer, L., Labro, E., & Morlacchi, P. (2001). A review of methods supporting supplier selection. *European Journal of Purchasing & Supply Management, 7*(2), 75-89.

Despeisse, M., Mbaye, F., Ball, P. D., & Levers, A. (2012). The emergence of sustainable manufacturing practices. *Production Planning and Control, 23*(5), 354–376. doi:10.1080/09537287.2011.555425

Dewangan, D. K., Agrawal, R., & Sharma, V. (2015). Enablers for competitiveness of Indian manufacturing sector: An ISM-fuzzy MICMAC analysis. *Procedia: Social and Behavioral Sciences, 189*, 416–432. doi:10.1016/j.sbspro.2015.03.200

Diabat, A., Khreishah, A., Kannan, G., Panikar, V., & Gunasekaran, A. (2013). Benchmarking the interactions among barriers in third-party logistics implementation: An ISM approach. *Benchmarking: An International Journal, 20*(6), 805–824. doi:10.1108/BIJ-04-2013-0039

Dubey, E., Gunasekaran, A., Sushil, A., & Singh, T. (2015). Building Theory of Sustainable Manufacturing Using Total Interpretive Structural Modelling. *International Journal of Systems Science: Operations & Logistics, 2*(4), 231–247.

Dubey, R., & Ali, S. S. (2014). Identification of flexible manufacturing system dimensions and their interrelationship using total interpretive structural modelling and fuzzy MICMAC analysis. *Global Journal of Flexible Systems Management, 15*(2), 131–143. doi:10.100740171-014-0058-9

Faisal, M. N. (2010). Analysing the Barriers to Corporate Social Responsibility in Supply Chains: An Interpretive Structural Modelling Approach. *International Journal of Logistics: Research and Applications, 13*(3), 179–195. doi:10.1080/13675560903264968

Farris, D. R., & Sage, A. P. (1975). On the Use of Interpretive Structural Modelling for Worth Assessment. *Computers & Electrical Engineering, 2*(2-3), 149–174. doi:10.1016/0045-7906(75)90004-X

Gardas, B. B., Raut, R. D., & Narkhede, B. E. (2017). A state-of the-art survey of interpretive structural modelling methodologies and applications. *International Journal of Business Excellence, 11*(4), 505–560. doi:10.1504/IJBEX.2017.082576

Goh, M., Prakash, S., & Yeo, R. (2007). Resource-based approach to IT shared services in a manufacturing firm. *Industrial Management & Data Systems, 107*(2), 251–270. doi:10.1108/02635570710723831

Govindan, K., Kannan, D., Mathiyazhagan, K., Jabbour, A. B., & Jabbour, C. J. (2013). Analysing Green Supply Chain Management Practices in Brazil's Electrical/Electornics Industry Using Interpretive Structural Modelling. *The International Journal of Environmental Studies*, *70*(4), 477–493. doi:10.1080/00207233.2013.798494

Goyal, G., Samalia, H. V., & Verma, P. (2017). Interpretive structural modeling for integrating quality management in manufacturing and service counterparts. *International Journal of Quality & Reliability Management*, *34*(9), 1568–1591. doi:10.1108/IJQRM-11-2015-0169

Gupta, V., Acharya, P., & Patwardhan, M. (2013). A strategic and operational approach to assess the lean performance in radial tyre manufacturing in India: A case-based study. *International Journal of Productivity and Performance Management*, *62*(6), 634–651. doi:10.1108/IJPPM-Jun-2012-0057

Haleem, A., Sushil, Qadri, M. A., & Kumar, S. (2012). Analysis of critical success factors of world-class manufacturing practices: An application of interpretative structural modelling and interpretative ranking process. *Production Planning and Control*, *23*(10-11), 722–734. doi:10.1080/09537287.2011.642134

Hughes, D. L., Dwivedi, Y. K., Rana, N. P., & Simintiras, A. (2016). Information Systems Project Failure-Analysis of Causal Links Using Interpretive Structural Modelling. *Production Planning and Control*, *27*(16), 1313–1333. doi:10.1080/09537287.2016.1217571

Jadhav, J. R., Mantha, S. S., & Rane, S. B. (2014). Development of framework for sustainable Lean implementation: An ISM approach. *Journal of Industrial Engineering International*, *10*(3), 72. doi:10.100740092-014-0072-8

Jafarnejad, A., & Shahaei, B. (2007). *Introduction to organizational agility and agile manufacturing* (pp. 25–79). Iran: Nashre Mehraban.

Janes, F. R. (1988). Interpretive structural modelling: A methodology for structuring complex issues. *Transactions of the Institute of Measurement and Control*, *10*(3), 145–154. doi:10.1177/014233128801000306

Jayalakshmi, B., & Pramod, V. R. (2015). Total Interpretive Structural Modeling (TISM) of the Enablers of a Flexible Control System for Industry. *Global Journal of Flexible Systems Management*, *16*(1), 63–85. doi:10.100740171-014-0080-y

Jena, J., Sidharth, S., Thakur, L. S., Kumar Pathak, D., & Pandey, V. C. (2017). Total Interpretive Structural Modeling (TISM): Approach and Application. *Journal of Advances in Management Research*, *14*(2), 162–181. doi:10.1108/JAMR-10-2016-0087

Jharkharia, S., & Shankar, R. (2004). Supply chain management: Some insights from Indian manufacturing companies. *Asian Academy of Management Journal*, *9*(1), 79–98.

Jharkharia, S., & Shankar, R. (2005). IT-enablement of supply chains: Understanding the barriers. *Journal of Enterprise Information Management*, *18*(1), 11–27. doi:10.1108/17410390510571466

Jolhe, D. A., & Subhash Babu, A. (2014). Modifications in Interpretive Structural Modelling Methodology to Enhance its Applicability in Group Decision Process and Power of Discrimination. *International Journal of Business Excellence*, *7*(3), 281–348. doi:10.1504/IJBEX.2014.060779

Jovane, F., Yoshikawa, H., Alting, L., Boer, C. R., Westkamper, E., Williams, D., ... Paci, A. M. (2008). The incoming global technological and industrial revolution towards competitive sustainable manufacturing. *CIRP Annals*, *57*(2), 641–659. doi:10.1016/j.cirp.2008.09.010

Kaluarachchi, K. A. S. P. (2010). Organizational culture and total quality management practices: A Sri Lankan case. *The TQM Journal*, *22*(1), 41–55. doi:10.1108/17542731011009612

Kannan, G., Pokharel, S., Sasi Kumar, P. (2009). A hybrid approach using ISM and fuzzy TOPSIS for the selection of reverse logistics provider. Resources, Conservation, and Recycling 54, pp. 28-36.

Kara, S., Ibbotson, S., & Kayis, B. (2014). Sustainable product development in practice: An international survey. *Journal of Manufacturing Technology Management*, *25*(6), 848–872. doi:10.1108/JMTM-09-2012-0082

Khan, U., & Haleem, A. (2012). Smart Organisations: Modelling of Enablers Using an Integrated ISM and Fuzzy-MICMAC Approach. *International Journal of Intelligent Enterprise*, *1*(3-4), 248–269. doi:10.1504/IJIE.2012.052556

Kulatilaka, N. (1988). Valuing the flexibility of flexible manufacturing systems. *IEEE Transactions on Engineering Management*, *35*(4), 250–257. doi:10.1109/17.7447

Kumar, N., Kumar, S., Haleem, A., & Gahlot, P. (2013). Implementing lean manufacturing system: ISM approach. [JIEM]. *Journal of Industrial Engineering and Management*, *6*(4), 996–1012. doi:10.3926/jiem.508

Kumar, S., Luthra, S., Govindan, K., Kumar, N., & Haleem, A. (2016). Barriers in green lean six sigma product development process: An ISM approach. *Production Planning and Control*, *27*(7-8), 604–620.

Kureshi, N., Qureshi, F., & Sajid, A. (2010). Current health of quality management practices in service sector SME: A case study of Pakistan. *The TQM Journal*, *22*(3), 317–329. doi:10.1108/17542731011035541

Lai, F., Zhao, X., & Wang, Q. (2006). The impact of information technology on the competitive advantage of logistics firms in China. *Industrial Management & Data Systems*, *106*(9), 1249–1271. doi:10.1108/02635570610712564

Lee, A. H., Wang, W., & Lin, T. (2010). An Evaluation Framework for Technology Transfer of New Equipment in High Technology Industry. *Technological Forecasting and Social Change*, *77*(1), 135–150. doi:10.1016/j.techfore.2009.06.002

Lewis, M. A. (2000). Lean production and sustainable competitive advantage. *International Journal of Operations & Production Management*, *20*(8), 959–978. doi:10.1108/01443570010332971

Lim, M. K., Tseng, M. L., Tan, K. H., & Bui, T. D. (2017). Knowledge Management in Sustainable Supply Chain Management: Improving Performance through an Interpretive Structural Modelling Approach. *Journal of Cleaner Production*, *62*, 806–816. doi:10.1016/j.jclepro.2017.06.056

Lin, Y. T., Lin, C. L., Yu, H. C., & Tzeng, G. H. (2011). Utilisation of interpretive structural modelling method in the analysis of interrelationship of vendor performance factors. *International Journal of Business Performance Management*, *12*(3), 260–275. doi:10.1504/IJBPM.2011.039890

Luthra, S., Kumar, V., Kumar, S., & Haleem, A. (2011). Barriers to implement green supply chain management in automobile industry using interpretive structural modeling technique: An Indian perspective. [JIEM]. *Journal of Industrial Engineering and Management*, *4*(2), 231–257. doi:10.3926/jiem.2011.v4n2.p231-257

Malone, D. W. (1975). An introduction to the application of interpretive structural modeling. *Proceedings of the IEEE*, *63*(3), 397–404. doi:10.1109/PROC.1975.9765

Mandal, A., & Deshmukh, S. G. (1994). Vendor Selection Using Interpretive Structural Modelling (ISM). *International Journal of Operations & Production Management*, *14*(6), 52–59. doi:10.1108/01443579410062086

Mangla, S., Madaan, J., Sarma, P. R., & Gupta, M. P. (2014). Multi-Objective Decision Modelling Using Interpretive Structural Modelling for Green Supply Chains. *International Journal of Logistics Systems and Management*, *17*(2), 125–142. doi:10.1504/IJLSM.2014.059113

Mangle, L., Phillips, P., Pitts, M., & Laver-Bradbury, C. (2014). Implementation of Independent Nurse Prescribing in UK Mental Health Settings: Focus on Attention-Deficit/Hyperactivity Disorder. *ADHD Attention Deficit and Hyperactivity Disorders*, *6*(4), 269–279. doi:10.100712402-014-0138-x PMID:24744052

Mathiyazhagan, K., Govindan, K., NoorulHaq, A., & Geng, Y. (2013). An ISM approach for the barrier analysis in implementing green supply chain management. *Journal of Cleaner Production*, *47*, 283–297. doi:10.1016/j.jclepro.2012.10.042

Müller, M., & Seuring, S. (2007). Reducing information technology-based transaction costs in supply chains. *Industrial Management & Data Systems*, *107*(4), 484–500. doi:10.1108/02635570710740652

Muruganantham, G., Vinodh, S., Arun, C. S., & Ramesh, K. (2018). Application of interpretive structural modelling for analysing barriers to total quality management practices implementation in the automotive sector. *Total Quality Management & Business Excellence*, *29*(5-6), 524–545. doi:10.1080/14783363.2016.1213627

Nishat Faisal, M., Banwet, D. K., & Shankar, R. (2006). Supply chain risk mitigation: Modeling the enablers. *Business Process Management Journal*, *12*(4), 535–552. doi:10.1108/14637150610678113

Pfohl, H. C., Gallus, P., & Thomas, D. (2011). Interpretive Structural Modeling of Supply Chain Risks. *International Journal of Physical Distribution & Logistics Management*, *41*(9), 839–859. doi:10.1108/09600031111175816

Qureshi, M. N., Kumar, D., & Kumar, P. (2007). Modelling the Logistics Outsourcing Relationships Variables to Enhance Shippers Productivity and Competitiveness in Logistics Supply Chain. *International Journal of Productivity and Performance Management*, *12*(4), 689–714. doi:10.1108/17410400710833001

Raj, T., Shankar, R., & Suhaib, M. (2007). An ISM Approach for Modelling the Enablers of Flexible Manufacturing System: The Case for India. *International Journal of Production Research*, *46*(24), 1–30.

Raj, T., Shankar, R., & Suhaib, M. (2008). An ISM approach for modelling the enablers of flexible manufacturing system: The case for India. *International Journal of Production Research, 46*(24), 6883–6912. doi:10.1080/00207540701429926

Ravi, V., Shankar, R., & Tiwari, M. K. (2005). Productivity improvement of a computer hardware supply chain. *International Journal of Productivity and Performance Management, 54*(4), 239–255. doi:10.1108/17410400510593802

Ravikumar, M. M., Marimuthu, K., & Parthiban, P. (2015). Evaluating lean implementation performance in Indian MSMEs using ISM and AHP models. *International Journal of Services and Operations Management, 22*(1), 21–39. doi:10.1504/IJSOM.2015.070881

Sahney, S. (2008). Critical success factors in online retail–an application of quality function deployment and interpretive structural modeling. *International Journal of Business and Information, 3*(1).

Salimifard, K., Abbaszadeh, M. A., & Ghorbangpur, A. (2010). Interpretive Structural Modeling of Critical Success Factors in Banking Process Re-Engineering. *International Journal of Business Research Papers, 6*(2), 95–103.

Saxena, J. P., & Vrat, P. (1990). Impact of indirect relationships in classification of variables—A micmac analysis for energy conservation. *Systems Research, 7*(4), 245–253. doi:10.1002res.3850070404

Seow, Y., & Rahimifard, S. (2011). A framework for modelling energy consumption within manufacturing systems. *CIRP Journal of Manufacturing Science and Technology, 4*(3), 258–264. doi:10.1016/j.cirpj.2011.03.007

Shahabadkar, P. (2012). Deployment of Interpretive Stuctural Modelling Methodology in Supply Chain Management- An Overview. *International Journal of Industrial Engineering & Production Research, 23*(3), 195–205.

Sharma, R., & Garg, S. (2010). Interpretive structural modelling of enablers for improving the performance of automobile service centre. *International Journal of Services Operations and Informatics, 5*(4), 351–372. doi:10.1504/IJSOI.2010.037003

Sharma, V., Dixit, A. R., & Qadri, M. A. (2016). Modeling lean implementation for manufacturing sector. *Journal of Modelling in Management, 11*(2), 405–426. doi:10.1108/JM2-05-2014-0040

Sharma, V., Dixit, A. R., Qadri, M. A., & Kumar, S. (2015). An interpretive hierarchical model for lean implementation in machine tool sector. *International Journal of Productivity and Quality Management, 15*(3), 381–406. doi:10.1504/IJPQM.2015.068475

Singh, M. D., & Kant, R. (2008). Knowledge management barriers: An interpretive structural modeling approach. *International Journal of Management Science and Engineering Management, 3*(2), 141–150. doi:10.1080/17509653.2008.10671042

Singh, M. D., Shankar, R., Narain, R., & Agarwal, A. (2003). An Interpretive Structural Modelling of Knowledge Management in Engineering Industries. *Journal of Advances in Management Research, 1*(1), 28–40. doi:10.1108/97279810380000356

Singh, R. K., Garg, S. K., & Deshmukh, S. G. (2007). Interpretive structural modelling of factors for improving competitiveness of SMEs. *International Journal of Productivity and Quality Management*, *2*(4), 423–440. doi:10.1504/IJPQM.2007.013336

Singh, R. K., Sharma, H. O., & Garg, S. K. (2010). Interpretive Structural Modelling for Selection of Best Supply Chain Practices. *International Journal of Business Performance and Supply Chain Modelling*, *2*(3-4), 237–257. doi:10.1504/IJBPSCM.2010.036201

Strandberg, C. (2009). *The role of human resource management in corporate social responsibility issue brief and roadmap. Report for Industry Canada*. Burnaby, BC: Strandberg Consulting.

Sushil, A. (2012). Interpreting the Interpretive Structural Model. *Global Journal of Flexible Systems Management*, *13*(2), 87–106. doi:10.100740171-012-0008-3

Talib, F., Rahman, Z., & Qureshi, M. N. (2011). Analysis of interaction among the barriers to total quality management implementation using interpretive structural modeling approach. *Benchmarking: An International Journal*, *18*(4), 563–587. doi:10.1108/14635771111147641

Thakkar, J., Deshmukh, S. G., Gupta, A. D., & Shankar, R. (2005, January). Selection of third-party logistics (3PL): A hybrid approach using interpretive structural modeling (ISM) and analytic network process (ANP). In *Supply Chain Forum*. Taylor & Francis. *International Journal (Toronto, Ont.)*, *6*(1), 32–46.

Thakkar, J., Deshmukh, S. G., Gupta, A. D., & Shankar, R. (2007). Development of a balanced scorecard. *International Journal of Productivity and Performance Management.*

Thakkar, J., Kanda, A., & Deshmukh, S. G. (2008). Interpretuve Structural Modelling (ISM) of IT-Enablers for Indian Manufacturing SMEs. *Information Management & Computer Security*, *16*(2), 113–136. doi:10.1108/09685220810879609

Thirupati, R. M., & Vinodh, S. (2016). Application of Interpretive Structural Modelling and Structural Equation Modelling for Analysis of Sustainable Manufacturing Factors in Indian Automotive Component Sector. *Journal of Production Research*, *54*(22), 6661–6682. doi:10.1080/00207543.2015.1126372

Tripathy, S., Sahu, S., & Ray, P. K. (2013). Interpretive Structural Modelling for Critical Success Factors of R&D Performance in Indian Manufacturing Firms. *Journal of Modelling in Management*, *8*(2), 212–240. doi:10.1108/JM2-11-2011-0061

Verma, A., Seth, N., & Singhal, N. (2011). Enablers of Supply Chain Competitiveness: An Interpretve Structural Modelling Approach. *International Journal of Value Chain Management*, *5*(3-4), 212–231. doi:10.1504/IJVCM.2011.043227

Walker, H., Di Sisto, L., & McBain, D. (2008). Drivers and barriers to environmental supply chain management practices: Lessons from the public and private sectors. *Journal of Purchasing and Supply Management*, *14*(1), 69–85. doi:10.1016/j.pursup.2008.01.007

Warfield, J. N. (1974). Developing interconnection matrices in structural modeling. *IEEE Transactions on Systems, Man, and Cybernetics*, *SMC-4*(1), 81–87. doi:10.1109/TSMC.1974.5408524

Warfield, J. N., & Staley, S. M. (1996). Structural thinking: Organizing complexity through disciplined activity. *Systems Research*, *13*(1), 47–67. doi:10.1002/(SICI)1099-1735(199603)13:1<47::AID-SRES27>3.0.CO;2-A

Watson, R. (1978). Interpretive Structural Modelling-A Useful Tool for Worth Assessment? *Technological Forecasting and Social Change*, *11*(2), 165–185. doi:10.1016/0040-1625(78)90028-8

Womack, J. P., & Jones, D. T. (1994). From lean production to the lean enterprise. *Harvard Business Review*, *72*(2), 93–103.

Yang, J. L., Chiu, H. N., Tzeng, G. H., & Yeh, R. H. (2009). Vendor selection by integrated fuzzy MCDM techniques with independent and interdependent relationships. *Information Sciences*, *178*(21), 4166–4183. doi:10.1016/j.ins.2008.06.003

Yang, M. G. M., Hong, P., & Modi, S. B. (2011). Impact of lean manufacturing and environmental management on business performance: An empirical study of manufacturing firms. *International Journal of Production Economics*, *129*(2), 251–261. doi:10.1016/j.ijpe.2010.10.017

Yeravdekar, A., & Behl, A. (2018). The unprecedented commercialisation of Indian cricket: A study using total interpretive structural modelling. *International Journal of Services and Operations Management*, *31*(3), 277–302. doi:10.1504/IJSOM.2018.095558

Yeravdekar, S., & Behl, A. (2017). Benchmarking model for management education in India: A total interpretive structural modeling approach. *Benchmarking: An International Journal*, *24*(3), 666–693. doi:10.1108/BIJ-06-2016-0082

Yudatama, U., Hidayanto, A. N., & Nazief, B. A. (2018). Approach Using Interpretive Structural Model (ISM) to Determine Key Sub-Factors at Factors: Benefits, Risk Reductions, Opportunities and Obstacles in Awareness IT Governance. *Journal of Theoretical and Applied Information Technology*, *96*(16), 5536–5549.

ADDITIONAL READING

Andejany, M., Elshennawy, A., Darwish, M., & Bahaitham, H. (2019). Developing an Industrial Engineering Study Plan Using ISM Approach. *International Journal of Engineering Pedagogy*, *9*(3).

Kumar, S. S., & Bhat, A. (2014). Modelling Supply Chain Agility Enablers Using ISM. *Journal of Modelling in Management*, *9*(2), 200–214. doi:10.1108/JM2-07-2012-0022

Li, Y., Sankarnarayanan, B., Kumar, D., & Diabat, A. (2019). Risks Assessment in Thermal Power Plants Using ISM Methodology. *Annals of Operations Research*, *279*(1-2), 89–113. doi:10.100710479-018-3121-7

Sahoo, T., Banwet, D. K., & Momaya, K. (2011). Developing a Conceptual Framework for Strategic Technology Management Using ISM and MICMAC Methodology: A Case of Automotive Industry in India. *Global Business Review*, *12*(1), 117–143. doi:10.1177/097215091001200108

Sushil, S. (2012). Interpreting the interpretive structural model. *Global Journal of Flexible Systems Management, 13*(2), 87–106. doi:10.100740171-012-0008-3

Zhou, F., Lim, M. K., He, Y., Lin, Y., & Chen, S. (2019). End-of-life vehicle (ELV) recycling management: Improving performance using an ISM approach. *Journal of Cleaner Production, 228*, 231–243. doi:10.1016/j.jclepro.2019.04.182

KEY TERMS AND DEFINITIONS

Analytic Hierarchy Process (AHP): AHP is a structured technique that is used for the organisation and analysis of multifaceted decisions, depending on the psychology and mathematics. It helps in the representation of the most precise approach for the quantification of weights of each criteria. Here, the experiences of each expert is used for the estimation of the relative scale of the parameters by using the method of pair-wise correlation. Each respondent is expected to strike a comparison between the relative importance of the two items in a questionnaire designed specially for this purpose.

Structural Equation Modelling (SEM): SEM is a multivariate statistical analysis technique that is usually utilised for the analysis of structural relationships. It is usually regarded as an amalgamation of multiple regression and factor analysis and is used to assess the structural relationships that tend to exist between the latent constructs and the variables used to measure these latent constructs.

Technique for Order of Preference by Similarity to Ideal Solution (TOPSIS): TOPSIS is an analysis method used for deriving multi-criteria decisions and was developed in 1981 by Yoon and Ching-Lai Hwang. It is dependent on the fact that the alternative that is chosen is should ideally have the least possible geometric distance from the PIS, otherwise known as the positive ideal solution and should be the farthest from negative ideal solution (NIS).

Chapter 3
Exploring Key Success Factors of Indian Pharmaceutical Supply Chain Using Interpretive Structural Modelling

Anurag Mishra
Indian Institute of Technology, Bombay, India

Pankaj Dutta
Indian Institute of Technology, Bombay, India

Suruj Kakoti
Indian Institute of Technology, Bombay, India

ABSTRACT

Indian pharmaceutical industry is witnessing enormous challenges due to varying patent laws, increasing demand, and continuous pressure from the government to provide medicines at a lower price. To overcome these challenges, there is a need for a more robust supply chain (SC) which will help in information sharing and reduce overall cost. The chapter determines the key drivers of Indian pharmaceutical SC, and draws the attention of industry, stakeholders, and top management to emphasise on these drivers to enhance the performance and profitability of SC. An interpretive structural modelling-based approach has been employed to model the pharmaceutical SC key drivers. The 16 key parameters have been identified across all major dimensions such as SC, HR, & organizational, market, technology, and reverse logistics. Further fuzzy MICMAC analysis is done to categorize based on their driving and dependence power. The factors like collaborative relationship among SC partners, quality regulations, third party logistics, and end-to-end responsive SC are found to be more important enablers.

DOI: 10.4018/978-1-7998-2216-5.ch003

INTRODUCTION

Indian pharmaceutical industry is experiencing major local and global challenges that are creating a pressure to tighten the Supply Chain (SC), which is an important link between the laboratory or manufacturing unit and marketplace. Now, the differentiating factor for a business is shifting from reverse engineering experts to one having improved operational performance measures such as service level and cost to deliver. The Indian Pharmaceutical Industry is expected to grow to $55 billion by 2020, thereby emerging as the sixth largest pharmaceutical market globally by absolute size. (India Brand Equity Foundation, 2018)

SC management is one of the vital components for industries to gain strategic success, by providing well balanced information flow which helps the organizations to stand against the challenges coming their way. (Rajeev et al, 2017). Understanding and practicing SCM in a proper way has become an essential requirement to stay in this competitive market.

In this paper, we have used interpretive structural modelling (ISM) for identifying and summarizing relationships among SC drivers specifically in the Indian Pharmaceutical Industry. It helps to divide the factors into different levels and then can act accordingly. In this paper, 16 primary key success factors of Indian pharmaceutical SCs have been identified by reviewing scientific journals and analysed by taking into account the opinions of experts and academia which was later used as an input in the ISM methodology from which interrelationships among the drivers and their hierarchical levels were developed. Then we have used fuzzy MICMAC analysis to categorize the drivers based on their driving and dependence power.

LITERATURE REVIEW

A well synchronized SC focuses on customer satisfaction, sustaining competency and continuous improvement in performance. These coordinating actions are tough to finalize due to different working cultures of organizations (Narayanan and Raman, 2004).

Cooper et al. (1997) said that support from the top management, business objectives that are being set are the major drivers influencing SC practices. Shah (2012) had done a thorough literature review addressing the key challenges, the drivers and major components working in a pharmaceutical supply chain. They also addressed the challenges with the solution strategy and future directions. Papageorgiou et al., (2001) used an optimization-based approach for the selection of strategy for product development, capacity and investment in case of pharmaceutical industries. The problem is formulated a s Mixed integer linear programming (MILP) and further an example is used to validate the model. Kumar et al., (2009) studies the control measures needed in the Supply chain of pharmaceutical industry, analysed the whole system using DMAIC process. The target of the study was to improve the reverse logistics process which in turn will help to reduce the harm to a consumer.

Kelle et al., (2012) studies the supply chain in pharmacy and explored the current managerial practices. The authors dealt with the inventory management at a local storage unit and then further suggested solutions for improvement. Surala and Karimi (2012) studied the integrated supply chain for multinational pharmaceutical companies. The authors have proposed a model which integrates the constraints of procurement, production and distribution. A MILP was formulated and two example problems were run to validate the model. Singh and Misra (2018) in their paper illustrate that awareness about SC performance measurement system (SCPMS) is a very significant enabler. Gupta and Ramesh (2015), in their research paper has used ISM in Healthcare SC in India and have identified 12 variables for Healthcare SC management. Their research mostly focuses on hospitals and the problems faced by the management in managing their hospital with respect to medicines, food, laundry, suppliers, etc. Singha and Mishra (2018) illustrates that risk can be prevented if a firm focuses on collaborative relationships, building trust and sharing of information.

From the above literature review, it can be seen that SC Management is one aspect of business that can lead to competitive advantage for an organization. There is a dearth of research in this field specifically that the SC mangers can utilize in order to bolster the growth of their firms through proper strategy planning that focuses on building collaborative relationships and using IT systems. The objective of this paper is to identify & categorize the main drivers of the pharmaceutical SC into broader categories such as SC, HR & organization, external factors, technology and reverse logistics based on their nature and then establish a relationship among them which will help in concurrent planning in addition to integrated planning.

Identification of Key Success Factors (CSF's) of SC

From the Literature Review (Enyinda, 2009) we found more than 80 drivers responsible for the smooth functioning of a Pharmaceutical SC. Then we removed the parameters that were part of a larger parameter and reduced the parameters to 28. After this, we validated the parameters with the panel of experts to remove a few more drivers and the brainstorming sessions resulted in a final list of 16 primary drivers that are most important in the efficient functioning of the Pharmaceutical SC.

Product Perishability

Product perishability is a major concern for the pharmaceutical SCs. Factors like Vulnerability to humidity, water, heat and other factors affect the performance of drug in the human body (Mahajan et al., 2015; Luthra et al., 2014). The critical issue is that expired or over date products may be overlooked and distributed to patients, which could be a potential disaster for them and in general to public relations.

Demand Management

In a pharmaceutical industry the manufacturer generally possesses a production capacity which is larger than the actual demand in the market (Gorane and Knat, 2013; Jyoti and Deshmukh, 2010). The industry is unique since the end consumer is usually not making the purchasing decision and payment decision; the industry has a network of various stakeholders that involves patients (consumers), doctors, pharmacies, regulatory bodies and other players like speciality stores and pharmacies, making the system more complex, therefore while demand forecasting everyone in the network should be considered (Mani et al., 2016).

Inventory Management

An effective inventory management along with higher service level of medical supplies is an essential objective of all entire healthcare industry. Pharmaceutical players find it difficult to manage proper inventory control management because they do not address how inventory management is being affected by other drivers of the SC. Inventory management for perishable products is different and difficult as compared to non-perishable (Mani et al., 2016; Devi et al., 2017).

Transportation Planning and Scheduling

Any global pharmaceutical company operates grown SC network with many warehouses in different countries and different contracting terms and diverse transportation companies. Pharmaceutical logistics account for about 2% of sales and 7-8% of the cost of goods sold (Reddy et al., 2017). Selection of suitable vehicles and its maintenance, adherence to the standards of operating procedures and to ensure that the vehicle is used for the intended purpose. Transportation planning is no longer a supportive system and no longer mere limited to the scheduling of the transportation and is a vital element in the strategic functioning of the companies (Gunasekaran et al., 2008; Zhang et al., 2013).

Warehouse Management

Warehouse is a control mechanism for the management of the most important link between the upstream (production) and downstream (distribution) entities but quite often, inconsistent pest control in warehouses may introduce contamination into the production line. Such an event will cause disruption of the production process and expensive manual inspections. This is easily fixed with education and periodic audits of the warehouse (Lee and Ng, 1997; Punniyamoorthy et al. 2013). In India, warehouse automation systems are not advance probably due to the involvement of large capital outlay and long pay back periods.

Top Management Commitment

Healthcare quality management is linked to human factors such as employee commitment. Top management of the firms, the leaders must comprehend and effectively communicate the vision and mission of the business with the ultimate goal to serve the end consumers to become more customers centric. (Mishra et al., 2012; Ahmad et al., 2009)

Collaborative and Strategic Planning

The failure or the success of the performance of a SC has been successfully linked to lack of collaborative and strategic planning within an organization (Bhaumik et al., 2010; Vishwakarma et al., 2016). The two most important things for managers to develop in a supply-chain risk management strategy are: firstly, creating an organization wide knowledge and understanding of the risks involved in a SC and secondly, determining ways to adapt to risk reducing approaches that are tailored to their own company.

Quality Regulations

The pharmaceutical industry has a significant importance and a potential for adverse health effects, thus the industry is subjected to very stringent regulation (Narayan et al., 2012). Especially in Indian Pharmaceutical SC the topic of quality is very important as it is coming from the global regulatory agencies.

Counterfeit Products

World health organization had defined Counterfeit as a medicine that is deliberately and fraudulently mislabelled or adulterant with respect to a drug. It can be applied to both generic and branded products. Counterfeit products in pharmaceutical industry can include products with wrong or correct ingredients without active ingredient or insufficient quantity of active ingredient (Chand et al., 2014).

Goods and Service Tax (GST)

The GST, introduced recently in the Indian context is a value added tax (VAT) and is a comprehensive indirect tax. Therefore, it will affect the entire SC from sourcing, manufacturing and distribution footprints with a specific impact on transportation and warehousing (Mohammad et al., 2008). GST is the major regulatory change companies gas been looking forward to, it brings along lot of consolidation of warehousing space. Today the warehouses are set up of tax rather than business purposes. This will also lead to setting up of modern warehouses like that in US or Europe (Ganguly et al., 2019).

Adoption of Analytics

Big data analytics are being used now in every sphere of science and technology. Through this public policy are modernized, and helps to make informed decision choices. (Prakash and Barau, 2016). Through use of analytics, the science that can transform data into meaningful and actionable insights, it offers a capability to increase and enable automation efficiencies, business intelligence for proactive and efficient decisions (Freeman et al. 2006).

Utilization of Information Technology

With the advancement of technology, getting fast and reliable information is a necessity for all the players involved in a SC (Dubey et al., 2014). The development of an IT infrastructure has made it possible to share information in real-time leading to an effective and efficient performance of the SC (Haq et al., 2016). But merely building the infrastructure cannot induce sharing of information as the managers who view information as a power are reluctant to share information also forms a major barrier for the proper utilization of information technology.

Collaborative Relationship Among SC Partners

Collaborative relationships are trust, which also helps in developing mutually advantageous associations bringing about a competitive advantage for all parties involved (Kumar et al., 2018). Such partnerships also help in the development of responsive and flexible SCs, with skill development in manufacturing at low-cost/low volume (Mehralian et al., 2015).Apart from trust, there also needs to be long-term cooperation in addition to the willingness for risk sharing (Chitoor et al., 2009). A SC functions well when the member organizations have their incentives aligned.

End-to-End Responsive SC

The most important element existing in the present business scenario is the awareness that it is the competition of SC and not the companies (Chitoor et al., 2009; Kanda and Deshmukh, 2008), this is very true in context to pharmaceutical SC. More advantages of end to end responsive SC can be significant inventory reduction, improved quality, greater product and volume flexibility specific to market needs.

Waste Management

Pharmaceutical SC is very complex nature and comprises of organization, operation and processes involved discovery, development and manufacture of medications and drugs (Jambulingam et al. 2008; Govindan et al., 2015). The main characteristics of pharma industry is its high R&D investments, long production times, shortening product cycles, quality constraints & regulation and high waste to product ratios. High waste to product ratio implies that there is a need to focus on research pertaining to environmental concerns and waste reduction in all the stages of value chain.

Dependency on Third Party Logistics

A 3PL is a service provider to perform the activities that are specifically asked by the purchasing enterprise pertaining to the firm need. 3PL helps to save the operating cost, improve the service level, capital cost reduction, etc (Kale et al., 2007; Aghalaya et al., 2012).

RESEARCH METHODS

We have 16 parameters, which were validated by the panel, to understand the primary drivers in the Indian Pharmaceutical SC. The primary drivers were then analysed through ISM and fuzzy MICMAC to provide insights into the industry and help the SC managers working in pharmaceutical industry in better decision making.

ISM is interpretive taking into account the group's decision, where they decide if the system elements are linked and how they are linked. The flowchart explains the various steps involved in the process from literature review to development of SSIM Matrix, Reachability matrix and then finally classifying the primary drivers.

The various steps involved in the ISM methodology are adapted from Kannan et al., (2009).

Self Structured Interaction Matrix (SSIM)

The Interrelationship for each driver, between the drivers is to be established by the expert opinions given by the industry experts. Four Alphabets V, A, X, O have been used in order to show the relationship of variables.

V: driver i will help to achieve driver j;
A: driver j will help to achieve driver i;
X: drivers i and j will help to achieve each other; and

Table 1. Initial SSIM matrix

D[i/j]	RL2	RL1	C2	C1	T2	T1	E3	E2	E1	HRO2	HRO1	SC5	SC4	SC3	SC2
SC1	O	O	V	A	A	A	O	O	A	A	A	A	A	A	O
SC2	V	O	V	A	A	A	O	O	O	A	A	V	V	V	
SC3	V	O	V	A	A	A	A	V	A	A	A	X	X		
SC4	V	O	V	A	A	A	A	V	A	A	A	X			
SC5	V	O	V	A	A	A	A	V	A	A	A				
HRO1	V	V	V	V	V	V	O	V	V	V					
HRO2	V	V	V	V	V	V	O	V	V						
E1	V	V	V	A	A	O	O	V							
E2	O	O	A	A	A	A	O								
E3	V	O	O	O	O	O									
T1	V	V	V	A	A										
T2	V	V	V	X											
C1	V	V	V												
C2	A	A													
RL1	V														

Legend: [SC1] Product perishability, [SC2] Demand Management, [SC3] Inventory management , [SC4] Transportation planning and scheduling, [SC5] Warehouse management, [HRO1] Top management commitment, [HRO2] Collaborative and strategic planning, [E1] Quality regulations , [E2] Counterfeit products, [E3] GST, [T1] Adoption of Analytics, [T2] Utilization of information technology, [C1] Collaborative relationships among supply chain partners, [C2] End to End responsive supply chain, [RL1] Waste Management, and [RL2] Dependency on third party logistics. D[*i*/*j*] = [Driver *i*/Driver *j*].

O: drivers i and j are not related.

Reachability Matrix

Once the SSIM is developed then further it is converted into binary matrix of 1, 0 as per the case (by substituting it for V, A, X, O). The substitution is done as stated below: -

- When the (i, j) entry in the SSIM is V, then (i, j) reachability matrix entry is set to 1 and then (j, i) entry is set to 0.

- When the (i, j) entry in the SSIM is A, then (i, j) reachability matrix entry is set to 0 and then (j, i) entry is set to 1.
- When the (i, j) entry in the SSIM is X, then (i, j) reachability matrix entry is set to 1 and then (j, i) entry is set to 1.
- When the (i, j) entry in the SSIM is O, then (i, j) reachability matrix entry is set to 0 and then (j, i) entry is set to 0.

After considering the transitivity rule in the initial reachability matrix of 15×15, and calculating the driving and dependence power we get the final reachability matrix.

Table 2. Reachability matrix

D[i/j]	SC1	SC2	SC3	SC4	SC5	HRO1	HRO2	E1	E2	E3	T1	T2	C1	C2	RL1	RL2
SC1	1	0	0	0	0	0	0	0	0	0	0	0	0	1	0	0
SC2	0	1	1	1	1	0	0	0	0	0	0	0	0	1	0	1
SC3	1	0	1	1	1	0	0	0	1	0	0	0	0	1	0	1
SC4	1	0	1	1	1	0	0	0	1	0	0	0	0	1	0	1
SC5	1	0	1	1	1	0	0	0	1	0	0	0	0	1	0	1
HRO1	1	1	1	1	1	1	1	1	1	0	1	1	1	1	1	1
HRO2	1	1	1	1	1	0	1	1	1	0	1	1	1	1	1	1
E1	1	0	1	1	1	0	0	1	1	0	0	0	0	1	1	1
E2	0	0	0	0	0	0	0	0	1	0	0	0	0	0	0	0
E3	0	0	1	1	1	0	0	0	0	1	0	0	0	0	0	1
T1	1	1	1	1	1	0	0	0	1	0	1	0	0	1	1	1
T2	1	1	1	1	1	0	0	1	1	0	1	1	1	1	1	1
C1	1	1	1	1	1	0	0	1	1	0	1	1	1	1	1	1
C2	0	0	0	0	0	0	0	0	1	0	0	0	0	1	0	0
RL1	0	0	0	0	0	0	0	0	0	0	0	0	0	1	1	1
RL2	0	0	0	0	0	0	0	0	0	0	0	0	0	1	0	1

Legend: [SC1] Product perishability, [SC2] Demand Management, [SC3] Inventory management , [SC4] Transportation planning and scheduling, [SC5] Warehouse management, [HRO1] Top management commitment, [HRO2] Collaborative and strategic planning, [E1] Quality regulations , [E2] Counterfeit products, [E3] GST, [T1] Adoption of Analytics, [T2] Utilization of information technology, [C1] Collaborative relationships among supply chain partners, [C2] End to End responsive supply chain, [RL1] Waste Management, and [RL2] Dependency on third party

Table 3. Final reachability matrix

D[i/j]	SC1	SC2	SC3	SC4	SC5	HRO1	HRO2	E1	E2	E3	T1	T2	C1	C2	RL1	RL2	DRP
SC1	1	0	0	0	0	0	0	0	0	0	0	0	0	1	0	0	2
SC2	1*	1	1	1	1	0	0	0	1*	0	0	0	0	1	0	1	8
SC3	1	0	1	1	1	0	0	0	1	0	0	0	0	1	0	1	7
SC4	1	0	1	1	1	0	0	0	1	0	0	0	0	1	0	1	7
SC5	1	0	1	1	1	0	0	0	1	0	0	0	0	1	0	1	7
HRO1	1	1	1	1	1	1	1	1	1	0	1	1	1	1	1	1	15
HRO2	1	1	1	1	1	0	1	1	1	0	1	1	1	1	1	1	14
E1	1	0	1	1	1	0	0	1	1	0	0	0	0	1	1	1	9
E2	0	0	0	0	0	0	0	0	1	0	0	0	0	0	0	0	1
E3	1*	0	1	1	1	0	0	0	1*	1	0	0	0	1*	0	1	8
T1	1	1	1	1	1	0	0	0	1	0	1	0	0	1	1	1	10
T2	1	1	1	1	1	0	0	1	1	0	1	1	1	1	1	1	13
C1	1	1	1	1	1	0	0	1	1	0	1	1	1	1	1	1	13
C2	0	0	0	0	0	0	0	0	1	0	0	0	0	1	0	0	2
RL1	0	0	0	0	0	0	0	0	0	0	0	0	0	1	1	1	3
RL2	0	0	0	0	0	0	0	0	0	0	0	0	0	1	0	1	2
DNP	12	6	11	11	11	1	2	5	13	1	5	4	4	15	7	13	

[Legend: 1*: shows transitivity, DNP: Dependence Power, DRP: Driving Power, D: Driver].

Building the ISM Model

Through the analysis of final reachability matrix, we have developed the final graphical model and portioned it into 10 levels. Then the digraph converted in the ISM model as shown in the fig 3.

ISM FUZZY MICMAC ANALYSIS

ISM Model has one limitation that it assigns either 0 or 1 to any relationship among the pair. It fails to show different aspects of relationship which may vary from very weak, weak, strong, and very strong or no relationship at all. Fuzzy Ism used for MICMAC analysis overcomes this drawback (Kumar et al., 2018).

Binary Direct Relationship Matrix

From the Initial Reachability Matrix i.e. Table 2, zero is assigned to the diagonal entries, this matrix so derived is called the Binary Direct Relationship Matrix. It is essentially the calculation of direct relationships among the primary drivers in the Pharmaceutical SC in India.

Table 4. Binary direct relationship matrix

D[i/j]	SC1	SC2	SC3	SC4	SC5	HRO1	HRO2	E1	E2	E3	T1	T2	C1	C2	RL1	RL2
SC1	0	0	0	0	0	0	0	0	0	0	0	0	0	1	0	0
SC2	0	0	1	1	1	0	0	0	0	0	0	0	0	1	0	1
SC3	1	0	0	1	1	0	0	0	1	0	0	0	0	1	0	1
SC4	1	0	1	0	1	0	0	0	1	0	0	0	0	1	0	1
SC5	1	0	1	1	0	0	0	0	1	0	0	0	0	1	0	1
HRO1	1	1	1	1	1	0	1	1	1	0	1	1	1	1	1	1
HRO2	1	1	1	1	1	0	0	1	1	0	1	1	1	1	1	1
E1	1	0	1	1	1	0	0	0	1	0	0	0	0	1	1	1
E2	0	0	0	0	0	0	0	0	0	0	0	0	0	0	0	0
E3	0	0	1	1	1	0	0	0	0	0	0	0	0	0	0	1
T1	1	1	1	1	1	0	0	0	1	0	0	0	0	1	1	1
T2	1	1	1	1	1	0	0	1	1	0	1	0	1	1	1	1
C1	1	1	1	1	1	0	0	1	1	0	1	1	0	1	1	1
C2	0	0	0	0	0	0	0	0	1	0	0	0	0	0	0	0
RL1	0	0	0	0	0	0	0	0	0	0	0	0	0	1	0	1
RL2	0	0	0	0	0	0	0	0	0	0	0	0	0	1	0	0

Fuzzy Direct Relationship Matrix

To increase the sensitivity by not only considering the binary values, fuzzy set theory (FST) is used. The chance of achievement can be described by a 0-1 scale through qualitative consideration mentioned in Table 5.

We have used our initial panel of experts, as mentioned in Section 3, again for this exercise and rate them based on the above table values. This value has then been used to create the below table.

Fuzzy MICMAC Stabilized Matrix

Once the Final direct reachability matrix is reached then the concept of fuzzy multiplication is used which is the generalization of the Boolean matrix multiplication (Kandasamy, 2007). The following rule is followed during multiplication:

AB = max k [min (aik, bkj)], where A = [aik] and B = [bkj]

The stabilized matrix so formed is illustrated in Table 7.

The above shows that there are no autonomous variables. Counterfeit products (E2), End to End responsive SC (C2), Dependency on third party logistics (RL2) and Waste Management (RL1), in Reverse Logistics, are the Dependent drivers. Collaborative relationships among SC partners (C1), Adoption of Analytics (T1), Utilization of information technology (T2), Quality regulations (E1), Product perish-

Table 5. Possibility of numerical value of achievability

Possibility of achievability	None	Very Weak	Weak	Medium	Strong	Very Strong	Perfect
Value	0	0.1	0.3	0.5	0.7	0.9	1

Table 6. Fuzzy direct relationship matrix

D[i/j]	SC1	SC2	SC3	SC4	SC5	HRO1	HRO2	E1	E2	E3	T1	T2	C1	C2	RL1	RL2
SC1	0.0	0.0	0.3	0.3	0.5	0.0	0.0	0.1	0.0	0.0	0.1	0.1	0.0	0.3	0.3	0.3
SC2	0.1	0.0	0.9	0.7	0.7	0.0	0.1	0.0	0.0	0.0	0.3	0.3	0.0	0.7	0.1	0.5
SC3	0.7	0.1	0.0	0.7	0.5	0.0	0.1	0.0	0.3	0.0	0.1	0.1	0.0	0.7	0.0	0.5
SC4	0.7	0.0	0.5	0.0	0.5	0.0	0.1	0.0	0.5	0.0	0.1	0.1	0.0	0.7	0.0	0.3
SC5	0.7	0.0	0.7	0.5	0.0	0.0	0.1	0.0	0.7	0.0	0.3	0.3	0.0	0.9	0.0	0.5
HRO1	0.5	0.9	0.7	0.7	0.7	0.0	1.0	0.7	0.7	0.0	0.5	0.9	0.9	1.0	0.7	0.7
HRO2	0.5	0.9	0.7	0.7	0.7	0.0	0.0	0.7	0.7	0.0	0.7	0.9	0.9	0.9	0.7	0.7
E1	0.7	0.0	0.3	0.5	0.5	0.0	0.0	0.0	0.3	0.0	0.0	0.0	0.0	0.1	0.7	0.3
E2	0.0	0.0	0.0	0.3	0.3	0.0	0.0	0.3	0.0	0.0	0.1	0.3	0.0	0.0	0.0	0.0
E3	0.0	0.0	0.3	0.7	0.9	0.0	0.0	0.0	0.0	0.0	0.0	0.0	0.0	0.0	0.0	0.9
T1	0.3	0.7	0.5	0.7	0.5	0.0	0.1	0.0	0.3	0.0	0.0	0.1	0.5	0.7	0.5	0.7
T2	0.3	0.7	0.5	0.7	0.7	0.0	0.1	0.1	0.3	0.0	0.7	0.0	0.7	0.9	0.7	0.7
C1	0.7	0.9	0.5	0.9	0.5	0.0	0.0	0.5	0.7	0.0	0.5	0.9	0.0	0.9	0.7	0.9
C2	0.0	0.0	0.0	0.0	0.0	0.0	0.0	0.0	0.7	0.0	0.0	0.0	0.0	0.0	0.0	0.0
RL1	0.0	0.0	0.0	0.0	0.0	0.0	0.0	0.0	0.0	0.0	0.0	0.0	0.0	0.7	0.0	0.5
RL2	0.0	0.0	0.0	0.0	0.0	0.0	0.0	0.0	0.0	0.0	0.0	0.0	0.0	0.7	0.3	0.0

Legend: [SC1] Product perishability, [SC2] Demand Management, [SC3] Inventory management , [SC4] Transportation planning and scheduling, [SC5] Warehouse management, [HRO1] Top management commitment, [HRO2] Collaborative and strategic planning, [E1] Quality regulations, [E2] Counterfeit products, [E3] GST, [T1] Adoption of Analytics, [T2] Utilization of information technology, [C1] Collaborative relationships among supply chain partners, [C2] End to End responsive supply chain, [RL1] Waste Management, and [RL2] Dependency on third party logistics. D[*i/j*] = [Driver *i*/Driver *j*].

ability (SC1), Demand Management (SC2), Inventory management (SC3), Transportation planning and scheduling (SC4) and Warehouse management (SC5) are present in the linkage category. The independent drivers are Top management commitment (HRO1), Collaborative and strategic planning (HRO2) and GST (E3).

The independent variables can be treated as the root cause of all other parameters and hence the top management should look over them more prudently.

MANAGERIAL IMPLICATIONS

As the Pharmaceutical Industry in India is very fragmented with no clear market leader, it is very important to build a responsive and efficient SC so that the company can have a competitive advantage over the others in the industry. In order to achieve this, the management should be aware of all the primary drivers of the SC and understand the interrelationship among them. With this objective in mind, this paper has identified 16 key parameters across all the major dimensions such as SC parameters, HR & Organiza-

Table 7. Fuzzy MICMAC stabilized matrix

D[I/J]	SC1	SC2	SC3	SC4	SC5	HRO1	HRO2	E1	E2	E3	T1	T2	C1	C2	RL1
SC1	0.3	0.3	0.5	0.5	0.5	0	0.1	0.3	0.5	0	0.3	0.3	0.3	0.5	0.3
SC2	0.5	0.3	0.5	0.5	0.5	0	0.1	0.3	0.5	0	0.3	0.3	0.3	0.5	0.3
SC3	0.5	0.3	0.5	0.5	0.5	0	0.1	0.3	0.5	0	0.3	0.3	0.3	0.5	0.3
SC4	0.5	0.3	0.5	0.5	0.5	0	0.1	0.3	0.5	0	0.3	0.3	0.3	0.5	0.3
SC5	0.5	0.3	0.5	0.5	0.5	0	0.1	0.3	0.5	0	0.3	0.3	0.3	0.5	0.3
HRO1	0.7	0.7	0.7	0.7	0.7	0	0.1	0.5	0.7	0	0.7	0.7	0.7	0.7	0.7
HRO2	0.7	0.7	0.7	0.7	0.7	0	0.1	0.5	0.7	0	0.7	0.7	0.7	0.7	0.7
E1	0.5	0.3	0.5	0.5	0.5	0	0.1	0.3	0.5	0	0.3	0.3	0.3	0.5	0.3
E2	0.3	0.3	0.3	0.3	0.3	0	0.1	0.3	0.3	0	0.3	0.3	0.3	0.3	0.3
E3	0.5	0.3	0.5	0.5	0.5	0	0.1	0.3	0.5	0	0.3	0.3	0.3	0.5	0.3
T1	0.5	0.5	0.5	0.5	0.5	0	0.1	0.5	0.5	0	0.5	0.5	0.5	0.5	0.5
T2	0.7	0.7	0.7	0.7	0.7	0	0.1	0.5	0.7	0	0.5	0.7	0.5	0.7	0.7
C1	0.7	0.7	0.7	0.7	0.7	0	0.1	0.5	0.7	0	0.7	0.5	0.7	0.7	0.7
C2	0.3	0.3	0.3	0.3	0.3	0	0.1	0.3	0.3	0	0.3	0.3	0.3	0.3	0.3
RL1	0.3	0.3	0.3	0.3	0.3	0	0.1	0.3	0.3	0	0.3	0.3	0.3	0.3	0.3
RL2	0.3	0.3	0.3	0.3	0.3	0	0.1	0.3	0.3	0	0.3	0.3	0.3	0.3	0.3
DNP	**7.8**	**6.6**	**8**	**8**	**8**	**0**	**1.6**	**5.8**	**8**	**0**	**6.4**	**6.4**	**6.4**	**8**	**6.6**

Legend: [SC1] Product perishability, [SC2] Demand Management, [SC3] Inventory manageme
Transportation planning and scheduling, [SC5] Warehouse management, [HRO1] Top ma
commitment, [HRO2] Collaborative and strategic planning, [E1] Quality regulations, [E2] C
products, [E3] GST, [T1] Adoption of Analytics, [T2] Utilization of information technol
Collaborative relationships among supply chain partners, [C2] End to End responsive supp
[RL1] Waste Management, and [RL2] Dependency on third party logistics. D[*i/j*] = [Driver *i/*
DNP: Dependence Power, DRP: Driving Power.

Figure 1. Driving power and dependence diagram

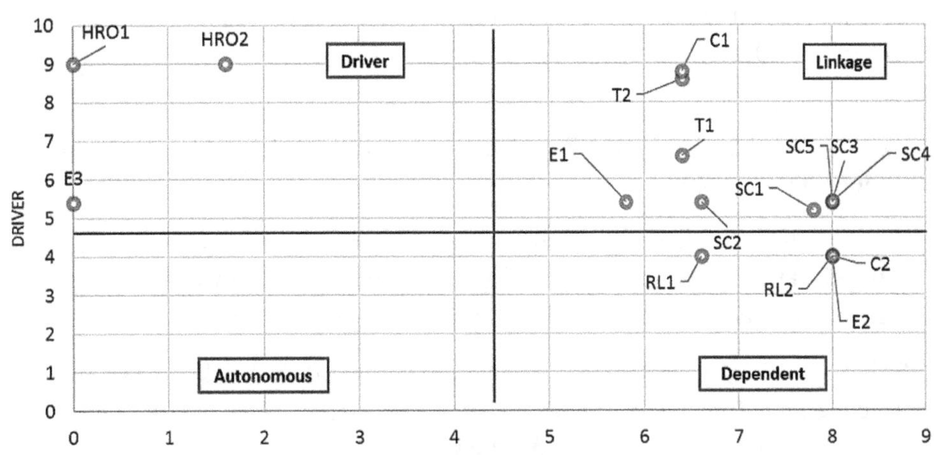

tion, External pressures, Collaboration and Reverse Logistics by reviewing several research articles and consulting several experts from the industry (Narayana et al., 2014; Thakkar et al., 2013). Managers were contacted and the key collecting and analysing their responses was one of the major milestone of this project, which helped us in identifying the primary drivers that significantly affect the operation of PSC so that management may efficiently strategize their SC initiatives keeping in mind such factors. As no single parameter can be self-determining driver in the PSC of India, it is very important to understand the relationship among the drivers. The SC managers can understand the relative importance of these factors and their interdependencies and can gain valuable insights about the how one factor influences another. The managers also need to keep a close eye on the drivers which have high driving power, as these are the parameters, which directly or indirectly influence the highly dependent parameters. The ISM methodology is used to develop the model which illustrates the relationships among the drivers. Further, in the second part of the paper, a fuzzy MICMAC analysis is done which helps in finding the driving and dependence power of the parameters. This segregation of parameters will help the SC managers to figure out which driver to target first in order to obtain an efficient SC.

CONCLUSION

The findings of this research provide valuable insights to both academicians and managers working in the industry. The major objective of this research was to identify the primary drivers that significantly affect the operation of PSC so that management may efficiently strategize their SC initiatives keeping in mind such factors. The study can be extended to include the small players in the pharmaceutical industry as a few parameters included in this research might not be relevant to the small companies. This will result in finalization of different set of parameters and will add a different dimension to the analysis. One other scope of future work would be to redesign the model using TISM and validate the relationship among latent variables using structural equation modelling.

REFERENCES

Aghalaya, S. N., Elias, A. A., & Pati, R. K. (2012). Analysing reverse logistics in the Indian pharmaceuticals industry: A systems approach. In 26th Australian and New Zealand Academy of Management (ANZAM) Conference 2012.

Ahmad, N., Usman Awan, M., Raouf, A., & Sparks, L. (2009). Development of a service quality scale for pharmaceutical SCs. *International Journal of Pharmaceutical and Healthcare Marketing*, *3*(1), 26–45. doi:10.1108/17506120910948494

Bhaumik, S. K., Driffield, N., & Pal, S. (2010). Does ownership structure of emerging-market firms affect their outward FDI? The case of the Indian automotive and pharmaceutical sectors. *Journal of International Business Studies*, *41*(3), 437–450. doi:10.1057/jibs.2009.52

Chand, M., Raj, T., & Shankar, R. (2014). Analysing the operational risks in SC by using weighted interpretive structure modelling technique. *International Journal of Services and Operations Management*, *18*(4), 378–403. doi:10.1504/IJSOM.2014.063242

Chittoor, R., Sarkar, M. B., Ray, S., & Aulakh, P. S. (2009). Third-world copycats to emerging multinationals: Institutional changes and organizational transformation in the Indian pharmaceutical industry. *Organization Science*, *20*(1), 187–205. doi:10.1287/orsc.1080.0377

Cooper, M. C., Lambert, D. M., & Pagh, J. D. (1997). SC management: More than a new name for logistics. *International Journal of Logistics Management*, *8*(1), 1–14. doi:10.1108/09574099710805556

Devi, P. U. M., Rao, B. S., & Shekhar, B. R. (2017). Service quality in the pharmaceutical SC: A case study with reference to a major Indian pharmaceutical company. *International Journal of Services Sciences*, *6*(2), 147–161. doi:10.1504/IJSSCI.2017.088753

Dubey, R., & Ali, S. S. (2014). Identification of flexible manufacturing system dimensions and their interrelationship using total interpretive structural modelling and fuzzy MICMAC analysis. *Global Journal of Flexible Systems Management*, *15*(2), 131–143. doi:10.100740171-014-0058-9

Enyinda, C. I. (2009). *Modeling risk management in the pharmaceutical industry global SC logistics using analytic hierarchy process model*. North Dakota State University.

Freeman, S., Edwards, R., & Schroder, B. (2006). How smaller born-global firms use networks and alliances to overcome constraints to rapid internationalization. *Journal of International Marketing*, *14*(3), 33–63. doi:10.1509/jimk.14.3.33

Ganguly, A., Chatterjee, D., & Talukdar, A. (2019). Knowledge Sharing Barriers Affecting Pharmaceutical SC Performance. In Global SCs in the Pharmaceutical Industry (pp. 269–291). Hershey, PA: IGI Global.

Gorane, S. J., & Kant, R. (2013). Modelling the SCM enablers: An integrated ISM-fuzzy MICMAC approach. *Asia Pacific Journal of Marketing and Logistics*, *25*(2), 263–286. doi:10.1108/13555851311314059

Govindan, K., Soleimani, H., & Kannan, D. (2015). Reverse logistics and closed-loop SC: A comprehensive review to explore the future. *European Journal of Operational Research*, *240*(3), 603–626. doi:10.1016/j.ejor.2014.07.012

Gunasekaran, A., Lai, K. H., & Cheng, T. E. (2008). Responsive SC: A competitive strategy in a networked economy. *Omega*, *36*(4), 549–564. doi:10.1016/j.omega.2006.12.002

Huq, F., Pawar, K. S., & Rogers, H. (2016). SC configuration conundrum: How does the pharmaceutical industry mitigate disturbance factors? *Production Planning and Control*, *27*(14), 1206–1220.

Jambulingam, T., Kathuria, R., & Nevin, J. R. (2009). How fairness garners loyalty in the pharmaceutical SC: Role of trust in the wholesaler-pharmacy relationship. *International Journal of Pharmaceutical and Healthcare Marketing*, *3*(4), 305–322. doi:10.1108/17506120911006029

Jyoti, B., Banwet, D. K., & Deshmukh, S. G. (2010). Modelling the success factors for national R&D organizations: A case of India. *Journal of Modelling in Management*, *5*(2), 158–175. doi:10.1108/17465661011061005

Kale, D., & Little, S. (2007). From imitation to innovation: The evolution of R&D capabilities and learning processes in the Indian pharmaceutical industry. *Technology Analysis and Strategic Management*, *19*(5), 589–609. doi:10.1080/09537320701521317

Kanda, A., & Deshmukh, S. G. (2008). SC coordination: Perspectives, empirical studies and research directions. *International Journal of Production Economics*, *115*(2), 316–335. doi:10.1016/j.ijpe.2008.05.011

Kelle, P., Woosley, J., & Schneider, H. (2012). Pharmaceutical supply chain specifics and inventory solutions for a hospital case. *Operations Research for Health Care*, *1*(2-3), 54–63. doi:10.1016/j.orhc.2012.07.001

Kumar, A., Zavadskas, E. K., Mangla, S. K., Agrawal, V., Sharma, K., & Gupta, D. (2018). When risks need attention: Adoption of green SC initiatives in the pharmaceutical industry. *International Journal of Production Research*, 1–23.

Kumar, S., Dieveney, E., & Dieveney, A. (2009). Reverse logistic process control measures for the pharmaceutical industry supply chain. *International Journal of Productivity and Performance Management*, *58*(2), 188–204. doi:10.1108/17410400910928761

Lee, H. L., & Ng, S. M. (1997). Introduction to the special issue on global SC management. *Production and Operations Management*, *6*(3), 191–192. doi:10.1111/j.1937-5956.1997.tb00425.x

Luthra, S., Garg, D., & Haleem, A. (2014). Greening the SC using SAP-LAP analysis: A case study of an auto ancillary company in India. *International Journal of Business Excellence*, *7*(6), 724–746. doi:10.1504/IJBEX.2014.065505

Mahajan, V., Nauriyal, D. K., & Singh, S. P. (2015). Trade performance and revealed comparative advantage of Indian pharmaceutical industry in new IPR regime. *International Journal of Pharmaceutical and Healthcare Marketing*, *9*(1), 56–73. doi:10.1108/IJPHM-05-2013-0030

Mani, V., Agarwal, R., Gunasekaran, A., Papadopoulos, T., Dubey, R., & Childe, S. J. (2016). Social sustainability in the SC: Construct development and measurement validation. *Ecological Indicators*, *71*, 270–279. doi:10.1016/j.ecolind.2016.07.007

Mehralian, G., Zarenezhad, F., & Rajabzadeh Ghatari, A. (2015). Developing a model for an agile SC in pharmaceutical industry. *International Journal of Pharmaceutical and Healthcare Marketing*, *9*(1), 74–91. doi:10.1108/IJPHM-09-2013-0050

Mishra, R. K. (2012). Measuring SC efficiency: A DEA approach. *Journal of Operations and SC Management*, *5*(1), 45–69.

Mohammed, I. R., Shankar, R., & Banwet, D. K. (2008). Creating flex-lean-agile value chain by outsourcing: An ISM-based interventional roadmap. *Business Process Management Journal*, *14*(3), 338–389. doi:10.1108/14637150810876670

Narayana, A., S., A. Elias, A., & K. Pati, R. (2014). Reverse logistics in the pharmaceuticals industry: A systemic analysis. *International Journal of Logistics Management*, *25*(2), 379–398. doi:10.1108/IJLM-08-2012-0073

Narayana, S. A., Pati, R. K., & Vrat, P. (2012). Research on management issues in the pharmaceutical industry: A literature review. *International Journal of Pharmaceutical and Healthcare Marketing*, *6*(4), 351–375. doi:10.1108/17506121211283235

Papageorgiou, L. G., Rotstein, G. E., & Shah, N. (2001). Strategic supply chain optimization for the pharmaceutical industries. *Industrial & Engineering Chemistry Research, 40*(1), 275–286. doi:10.1021/ie990870t

Prakash, C., & Barua, M. K. (2016). A combined MCDM approach for evaluation and selection of third-party reverse logistics partner for Indian electronics industry. *Sustainable Production and Consumption, 7*, 66–78. doi:10.1016/j.spc.2016.04.001

Punniyamoorthy, M., Thamaraiselvan, N., & Manikandan, L. (2013). Assessment of SC risk: Scale development and validation. Benchmarking. *International Journal (Toronto, Ont.), 20*(1), 79–105.

Reddy, M. R. S., Jigeesh, N., & Kumar, P. (2017). The Integration of Project Management with SC Management in Indian Pharmaceutical Projects. *IUP Journal of SC Management, 14*(4), 61–71.

Shah, N. (2004). Pharmaceutical supply chains: Key issues and strategies for optimisation. *Computers & Chemical Engineering, 28*(6-7), 929–941. doi:10.1016/j.compchemeng.2003.09.022

Singh, K., & Misra, S. (2018). Theory of Constraints for Managing Downstream SC in Indian FMCG Sector: A Literature Review. *Journal of SC Management Systems, 7*(1).

Susarla, N., & Karimi, I. A. (2012). Integrated supply chain planning for multinational pharmaceutical enterprises. *Computers & Chemical Engineering, 42*, 168–177. doi:10.1016/j.compchemeng.2012.03.002

Thakkar, J., Kanda, A., & Deshmukh, S. G. (2013). SC issues in SMEs: Select insights from cases of Indian origin. *Production Planning and Control, 24*(1), 47–71. doi:10.1080/09537287.2011.599119

Vishwakarma, V., Prakash, C., & Barua, M. K. (2016). Modeling the barriers of Indian Pharmaceutical SC using fuzzy AHP. *International Journal of Operational Research.*

Zhang, M. S., Pawar, K., Shah, J., & Mehta, P. (2013). Evaluating outsourcing partners' capability: A case study from the pharmaceutical SC. *Journal of Manufacturing Technology Management, 24*(8), 1080–1101. doi:10.1108/JMTM-02-2012-0023

Chapter 4 Hybrid Multi-Criteria Models: Joint Health and Safety Unit Selection on Hybrid Multi-Criteria Decision Making

Ömer Faruk Efe
https://orcid.org/0000-0001-8170-5114
Afyon Kocatepe University, Turkey

ABSTRACT

JHSUs should have occupational safety specialists, workplace physicians, and other health personnel to establish and provide services. To provide occupational safety services in the most effective operating environment, it is necessary to select the most appropriate JHSU. This chapter provides a hybrid model to assist the JHSU selection process. Using fuzzy logic linguistic variables makes an important contribution to decision making in uncertain environment. The hybrid model using Fuzzy AHP (Analytical Hierarchy Process) and Fuzzy TOPSIS (Technique for Similarity Sorting Preference for Ideal Solution) approaches were used in JHSU selection. The most important criterion was found to be the references of JHSU. Candidate JHSUs were evaluated on the basis of criteria with fuzzy TOPSIS. Five alternative JHSU were evaluated. Alternative 2 was found to be the most appropriate choice. A numerical example is presented to demonstrate the effectiveness of the proposed hybrid model.

INTRODUCTION

The need for OHS services is increasing daily. There are some deficiencies in performing these services. In order to eliminate the deficiencies, there is a need for the institutions where businesses can receive OHS services. The fact that the state alone is not sufficient in providing these services has paved the way for the provision of services through professional organizations from outsourcing. In particular, "The Sloguh Plan has been put into practice in order to provide OHS services for businesses in the UK. In the plan, group model implementation for OHS services has an important place (Rantanen ve Fedotov, 1995). This model, which is applied in the UK, is the first example of units providing external OHS

DOI: 10.4018/978-1-7998-2216-5.ch004

services. A similar unit of this model in Turkey, Joint Health Safety Unit (JHSU) it was implemented (Orhan and Özkan, 2017). JHSU creates to healthy and safe workplaces in order a working environment.

Today, for businesses, increasing competition conditions and customer-oriented quality services to increase and market share between companies to become more and more important is becoming. That's why; It is of great importance that companies restructure their relationships and trusts in coordination with the persons or organizations they have received external services in order to further increase their operational performance. It is seen that the harmony, trust and mutual cooperation developed with the service providers will have positive effects on issues such as lowering the cost of the product, increasing the quality, ensuring customer satisfaction, and being open to management developments and innovation. Therefore, the problem of how to provide the service, which is one of the most basic requirements for the businesses, is one of the important activities.

As a result of the literature surveys, the selection of JHSU using fuzzy AHP and fuzzy TOPSIS approaches was not found. Therefore, this study is a unique study. Experts cannot express certain evaluations clearly when using exact values during decision-making. However, using fuzzy logic linguistic variables makes a great success in decision making in uncertain environment. Fuzzy logic was used to determine the importance of criteria and to evaluate alternatives on the basis of criteria so that experts could express their views as linguistic variables. In the application, the importance of the criteria examined in the selection of JHSU with Fuzzy AHP was determined. With fuzzy TOPSIS, alternative JHSUs were assessed on the basis of criteria.

There are dozens of different JHSU that provide OHS services. In selection of JHSU, the criteria that will be the basis for measurement and evaluation and the weight of these criteria should be determined. Because the importance weight of each criterion varies in measuring and evaluating JHSU selection for that job. Therefore, these methods, which are not based on spesific criteria and weights, lead to objectivity in the measurement and evaluation process and therefore to make wrong decisions. These decisions are mostly complex and made in an uncertain environment. Many contradictory quantitative and qualitative criteria should be considered simultaneously. Fuzzy multi-criteria decision-making methods (MCDM) have been developed in order to solve these problems.

In this study, fuzzy TOPSIS method was used to evaluate alternative JHSUs. Fuzzy logic approach is proposed to make decision in uncertain environment. In recent years, fuzzy TOPSIS has been applied in different areas such as plant location selection, machine equipment selection and personnel selection (Efe, 2016). Fuzzy TOPSIS method is used to obtain the result of the positive and negative distance from the ideal solution is calculated.

Hybrid fuzzy AHP-fuzzy TOPSIS methods have been proposed for JHSU selection. The hierarchical structure of the problem is determined. Firstly, the fuzzy AHP approach was examined when determining criterion weights. As stated in the "Methodology" section, the opinions of the decision-makers have been translated into a single opinion and presented. "References" were the most important criteria in the selection of JHSU and "Compliance with OHS plan" was the least important criteria. According to this result, it is determined that the education level of OHS experts who will provide service in outsourcing OHS services is more important. In particular, it is necessary to select a expert who is suitable for the hazard type of the enterprise. According to the results obtained from this study, the most suitable JHSU was alternative 2. The worst selection was alternative 3 Although the proposed method helps decision-makers in an uncertain environment, it can be applied in many different areas. Different integrated MCDM methods can be used in future studies In addition, the proposed method can be applied in different decision making methods such as personnel selection, material selection, supplier selection, plant

Table 1. Linguistic values for criteria of JHSU selection

Definition	Numerical Rate
Absolutely strong (AS)	(7/2,4,9/2)
Very strong (VS)	(5/2,3,7/2)
Few strong (FS)	(3/2,2,5/2)
Poor (P)	(2/3,1,3/2)
Equal (E)	(1,1,1)

location selection, software selection (Efe et al., 2017; Kumlu & Tüdeş, 2018; Shaverdi et al., 2016; Kusumawardani & Agintiara, 2015).

MAIN FOCUS OF THE CHAPTER

In this study, solutions were investigated for the existing problems in selection of JHSU to OHS services by using fuzzy MCDM methods. There is limited information about this subject in the literature. The following methods have been utilized at this stage: Fuzzy AHP to determine the relative weights of criteria, and the fuzzy TOPSIS to select the JHSU.

HYBRID METHODOLOGY

In the literature, many methods based on classical or fuzzy set are used by researchers for solve the problems known as MCDM. AHP, analytical network process, MAUT, MACBETH, PROMETHEE, ELECTRE I, TOPSIS, data envelopment analysis; AHP, UTA, MACBETH, PROMETHEE, TOPSIS; FlowSort, classification; Methods such as GAIA and FS-Gaia are the recommended methods for identification (Ishizaka & Nemery, 2013). Among these MCDM techniques, AHP is the most preferred method. It can be used alone in MCDM problems or it can be used in combination with different methods (TOPSIS, VIKOR and others). In such cases, weights usually obtained by AHP are used as input in different methods. These methods are applied in a combination of studies called hybrid. In this study, hybrid fuzzy AHP-fuzzy TOPSIS methodology is utilized to order the JHSU options. Firstly, the main criteria are appropriately defined.

Fuzzy Set

Pairwise comparison matrixes of experts' opinions are established to obtain criteria by employing the linguistic scale. Linguistic variables are presented in Table 1.

Two triangular fuzzy numbers; $M_1(m_1^-, m_1, m_1^+)$ and $M_2(m_2^-, m_2, m_2^+)$ are demonstrated Figure 1 (Lee, 2009). $m_1^- \geq m_2^-, m_1 \geq m_2, m_1^+ \geq m_2^+$ while the degree of likelihood is determined as 1.

$V(M_1 \geq M_2) = 1$

Figure 1. Two triangular fuzzy sets

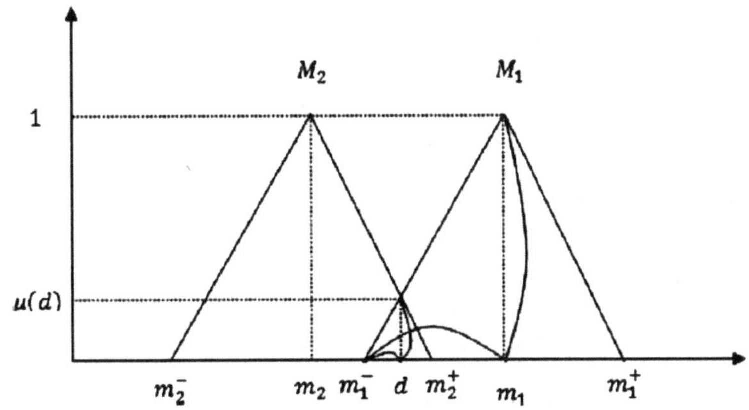

The TOPSIS method proposed by Hwang and Yoon (1981) examines the negative and positive ideal solutions when listing alternatives. In this study, fuzzy TOPSIS method was used to evaluate alternative JHSUs. Both distance-based calculations will be made. The articles of Junior et al. (2014) were used for fuzzy TOPSIS. Fuzzy set approach is proposed to make decision in uncertain environment. In recent years, fuzzy TOPSIS has been applied in different disciplines such as plant location selection, machine equipment selection and personnel selection (Efe, 2016; Dursun & Karsak, 2010).

When evaluating alternatives on the basis of criteria, decision makers used the linguistic variables in Table 2. The above-mentioned method has been utilized in converting the opinions of the decision makers into a single opinion.

Analytic Hierarchy Process (AHP)

AHP was developed by Thomas L. Saaty. It requires the judgment of the decision-maker (expert) in determining the relative significance of all criteria. Experts compare criteria by completing questionnaires prepared. After all criteria have been evaluated, the priority order of decision alternatives is determined (Anderson et al., 2008; Onder & Onder, 2015). There are various MCDM techniques in the literature. Among them AHP's, ease of use and objective judgments makes it superior to other techniques. AHP, has the ability to combine the views of multiple decision makers in a single view. AHP is a technique that combines many concepts under one roof.

Table 2. Linguistic expressions for ordering alternatives

Definition	Numerical Rate
Very poor (VP)	(1,1,3)
Poor (P)	(1,3,5)
Medium (M)	(3,5,7)
Good (G)	(5,7,9)
Very good (VG)	(7,9,11)

Table 3. AHP applications in literature

Author (s)	Problem
Dagdeviren & Yüksel (2008)	Safety management
Gungor et al. (2009)	Personnel selection
Chen & Wang (2009)	Risk assessment in construction projects
Podvezko et al. (2009)	Evaluation of contracts
Sivilevicius (2011)	Quality of technology
Ozkok & Pappalardo (2013)	E-marketplace selection
Thanki et al. (2016)	Impact of select lean and green practices
Macuzic et al. (2016)	Ranking of organizational flexibility factors in process industry
Dozic et al. (2018)	Passenger aircraft type selection
Krmac & Djordjevic (2018)	An evaluation of railway intelligent transportation systems
Promentilla et al. (2018)	Clean technologies selection
Darko et al. (2019)	Construction management

The hierarchical structure of the problem, pairwise comparison, multiple criteria, eigenvector with consistency ratio in obtaining weight coefficients are mentioned concepts. Saaty developed AHP method by making use of these concepts (Saaty, 1986; Onder & Onder, 2015; Forman & Selly, 2002). With the use of the expert selection package program, AHP applications have become widespread. AHP, which can make pairwise comparisons between criteria using eigenvalue approach; is a MCDM technique used in quantitative and qualitative performance measurement (Vaidya & Kumar, 2006). AHP is used effectively in the evaluation of decision alternatives and in the solution of decision-making problems. AHP is generally used for estimation, resource allocation, selection and ranking among criteria with varying degrees of importance (Forman & Selly, 2002). Although AHP method is used alone, it is more successful when used together with fuzzy logic and other MCDM techniques (Efe & Efe, 2018).

AHP is one of the broadly used MCDM techniques. The important advantage of this method is the relative ease with which it handles multiple criteria. Additionally, AHP is easier to understand and it can effectively handle both qualitative and quantitative data. Though the purpose of AHP is to capture the expert's knowledge, the conventional AHP still cannot reflect the human thinking style. Therefore, fuzzy AHP, a fuzzy extension of AHP, was developed to solve the hierarchical fuzzy problems (Mahmoodzadeh et al., 2007; Şengül & Eren, 2016). AHP method is applied in many different disciplines. The recent applications of AHP method in shortly are listed below Table 3. Generally, these are; expert choise and super decision. But an AHP application, it can be easily modeled in excel program.

The Steps of Implementation of AHP Method

The next steps are followed in the problem solved by using AHP technique.

Step 1: Define the decision-making problem, determining the purpose.
Step 2: Formation of hierarchical structure of decision problem.
Step 3: Creating of pairwise comparison matrix.

Step 4: Determination of relative importance weights.
Step 5: Calculation of consistency ratio.
Step 6: Ordering the alternatives.

In literature, pairwise comparisons generally use Saaty's scale. The comparison values are positive. If we want to compare n criteria according to their relative importance weights such that a1, a2, ..., an and weights are w1, w2, ..., wn, the general structure of the binary comparison matrix is shown below.

$$A = \begin{bmatrix} a_{11} & a_{12} & \cdots & a_{1n} \\ a_{21} & a_{22} & \cdots & a_{2n} \\ \vdots & \vdots & \vdots & \vdots \\ a_{n1} & a_{n2} & \cdots & a_{nn} \end{bmatrix} \tag{1}$$

The following equation is used to calculate the eigenvector value (Wi) of the criteria between the criteria and in the binary comparison matrix of alternatives for each criterion.

$$Wi = \frac{1}{n}\sum_{j=1}^{n} \frac{a_{ij}}{\sum_{j=1}^{n} a_{ij}} \tag{2}$$

After finding the eigenvector value of the criteria; consistency ratio, consistency indicator and eigenvalue are calculated. The consistency ratio indicates whether the values in the pairwise comparison matrix are related to each other. Consistency rate should be less than 0.10. If this value is greater than 0.10, it is assumed that there is inconsistency in AHP calculation or decision-makers' evaluations. Equalition for calculating the consistency ratio is below.

$$CR = \frac{CI}{RI} \tag{3}$$

The following equation is used to calculate the consistency indicator.

$$CI = \frac{\lambda_{\max - n}}{n-1} \tag{4}$$

The following equation is used to calculate the λ_{max} value.

$$\lambda \max = \frac{1}{n}\sum_{i=1}^{n} \frac{(aw)_i}{w} \tag{5}$$

The Random Index (RI) value shown in Equation 3 is shown in Table 4 (Podvezko, 2009).

Table 4. Random index

n	1	2	3	4	5	6	7	8	9	10
RI	0	0	0,58	0,90	1,12	1,24	1,32	1,41	1,45	1,49

After the consistency ratio calculation is made, the weight percentages are examined with the sum of 1. The obtained alternative scores are listed and the alternative with the highest value is determined as the best alternative.

TOPSIS

TOPSIS is a technique that makes the best selection among alternatives. TOPSIS suggested by Hwang and Yoon (1981) is a method, which ranks suitable solutions are the farthest distance from negative ideal solution (NIS) and the shortest distance from positive ideal solution (PIS) simultaneously (Lai et al., 1994). Recently, fuzzy TOPSIS method has been applied in different disciplines such as supplier, plant location, machinery equipment, software and personnel selection (Efe, 2016; Behzadian et al., 2012).

The recent applications of TOPSIS method in shortly are listed below Table 5.

Application steps of TOPSIS are as follows [Patil&Kant, 2014; Efe, 2016];

Step 1: Formation of decision matrix

$\tilde{A}_{ij}$ is the beginning matrix created by decision-makers. In the decision matrix, rows show alternatives and columns show criteria.

Table 5. TOPSIS applications in literature

Author (s)	Problem
Boran et al. (2009)	Supplier selection
Kelemenis & Askounis (2010)	Personnel selection
Dursun & Karsak (2010)	Industrial engineer selection
Başkaya & Öztürk (2011)	Salesperson selection
Rostampour (2012)	Ranking internet web browsers
Junior (2014)	Supplier selection
Temucin et al. (2014)	Machining process
Efe (2016)	ERP selection
Samantra et al. (2017)	Appropriate safety measure system for coal mines
Efe (2018)	Personnel selection

$$\tilde{A}_{ij} = \begin{bmatrix} \tilde{a}_{11} & \tilde{a}_{12} & \cdots & \tilde{a}_{1n} \\ \tilde{a}_{21} & \tilde{a}_{22} & \cdots & \tilde{a}_{2n} \\ \vdots & \vdots & \vdots & \vdots \\ \tilde{a}_{m1} & \tilde{a}_{m2} & \cdots & \tilde{a}_{mn} \end{bmatrix} \quad (6)$$

Step 2: Determining the normalized decision matrix

A normalized fuzzy decision matrix (R̃) is obtained from matrix $\tilde{A}_{ij}$:

$$\tilde{r}_{ij} = \frac{\tilde{a}_{ij}}{\sqrt{\sum_{k=1}^{m} a_{kj}^{2}}} \quad (7)$$

The matrix R is obtained as follows:

$$\tilde{R}_{ij} = \begin{bmatrix} \tilde{r}_{11} & \tilde{r}_{12} & \cdots & \tilde{r}_{1n} \\ \tilde{r}_{21} & \tilde{r}_{22} & \cdots & \tilde{r}_{2n} \\ \vdots & \ddots & \cdots & \vdots \\ \tilde{r}_{m1} & \tilde{r}_{m2} & \cdots & \tilde{r}_{mn} \end{bmatrix} \quad (8)$$

$$\tilde{r}_{ij} = \left(\frac{a_{ij}}{c_j^{+}}, \frac{b_{ij}}{c_j^{+}}, \frac{c_{ij}}{c_j^{+}} \right) vec_j^{+} = \max_{i^{cij}} \left(benefit\ criterion \right)$$

$$\tilde{r}_{ij} = \left(\frac{a_j^{-}}{c_{ij}}, \frac{a_j^{-}}{b_{ij}}, \frac{a_j^{-}}{a_{ij}} \right) vea_j^{-} = \min_{i^{aij}} \left(cost\ criterion \right)$$

Step 3: Determining of weighted normalized decision matrix

First, the weight values (*Wi*) of the evaluation factors are determined ($\sum_{i=1}^{n} Wi = 1$).

Then the elements in each column of the matrix R are multiplied by the corresponding value to form the V matrix. Matrix V is shown in below:

$$\tilde{v}_{ij} = \begin{bmatrix} w_1\tilde{r}_{11} & w_2\tilde{r}_{12} & \cdots & w_n\tilde{r}_{1n} \\ w_1\tilde{r}_{21} & w_2\tilde{r}_{22} & \cdots & w_n\tilde{r}_{2n} \\ . & . & . & . \\ . & . & . & . \\ . & . & . & . \\ w_1\tilde{r}_{m1} & w_2\tilde{r}_{m2} & \cdots & w_n\tilde{r}_{mn} \end{bmatrix}$$

$$i = 1,2,\ldots,m;\ j = 1,2,\ldots,n iken \tilde{v}_{ij} = \tilde{r}_{ij(\cdot)} w_j \tag{9}$$

Step 4: Calculating the positive ideal (A^+) and negative ideal (A^-) solutions

$$A^+ = \left\{\tilde{v}_1^+, \tilde{v}_2^+, \ldots, \tilde{v}_n^+\right\} iken \tilde{v}_j^+ = (1,1,1) \tag{10}$$

$$A^- = \left\{\tilde{v}_1^-, \tilde{v}_2^-, \ldots, \tilde{v}_n^-\right\} iken \tilde{v}_j^- = (0,0,0) \tag{11}$$

Step 5: Determining the discrimination scales

The determination of the separation measurements is as follows:

$$d_i^+ = \sum_{j=1}^{n} dv\left(\tilde{v}_{ij}, \tilde{v}_j^+\right), i = 1,2,\ldots,m \tag{12}$$

$$d_i^- = \sum_{j=1}^{n} dv\left(\tilde{v}_{ij}, \tilde{v}_j^-\right), i = 1,2,\ldots,m \tag{13}$$

$$\tilde{v}_{ij} = \left(\tilde{a}_{ij}, \tilde{b}_{ij}, \tilde{c}_{ij}\right) ve \tilde{v}_j^+ = (1,1,1)\ ve \tilde{v}_j^- = (0,0,0):$$

$$dv\left(\tilde{v}_{ij}, \tilde{v}_j^+\right) = \sqrt{\frac{1}{3}\left[\left(\tilde{a}_{ij} - 1\right)^2 + \left(\tilde{b}_{ij} - 1\right)^2 + \left(\tilde{c}_{ij} - 1\right)^2\right]},$$

$$dv\left(\tilde{v}_{ij}, \tilde{v}_j^-\right) = \sqrt{\frac{1}{3}\left[\left(\tilde{a}_{ij} - 0\right)^2 + \left(\tilde{b}_{ij} - 0\right)^2 + \left(\tilde{c}_{ij} - 0\right)^2\right]}.$$

Step 6: Determining the closeness coefficient (CC_i)

The relative score of each alternative is calculated by determining the closeness coefficients.

$$CC_i = \frac{d_i^-}{d_i^- + d_i^+} \tag{14}$$

Alternatives are listed according to the values of the coefficients obtained (C_i+). The closeness coefficient is between 0 and 1. Among the alternatives evaluated, the closest coefficient is considered to be the best.

Fuzzy AHP and Fuzzy TOPSIS methods are used as hybrid studies give successful results in the literature. The recent applications of hybrid fuzzy AHP- fuzzy TOPSIS method in shortly are listed below Table 6.

APPLICATION

Fuzzy AHP and Fuzzy TOPSIS hybrid method were used for JHSU selection. JHSU, in the absence of qualified personnel, the employer is an expert person or organization with an external qualification certificate in the provision of protective and preventive services related to health and safety in the workplace. Fuzzy extended AHP proposed by Chang (1996) was applied to determine criteria weights for JHSU selection. References (C1), OHS expert graduating (C2), periodic controls and inspection (C3), compliance with OHS plan/program (C4) and customer satisfaction (C5), evaluation criteria were determined by taking the opinions of the people working as OHS experts. Firstly, criteria were determined by taking opinions from 10 different experts. Then the criteria were interpreted with the data obtained from the evaluation of 3 decision makers. There is no study in the literature regarding the selection of JHSU. 5 alternatives that pass the pre-selection among JHSUs, providing OHS services are identified. In the study, the service prices of the JHSU's providing services are not taken into consideration because they are close to each other. The experts used the linguistic variables when creating pairwise comparison matrices. Fuzzy AHP-fuzzy TOPSIS methods have been proposed for JHSU selection. The weights of the criteria were determined by AHP method and the ordering was done by TOPSIS method. As a result of the study, the most appropriate JHSU was determined.

Table 6. Fuzzy AHP- fuzzy TOPSIS applications in literature

Author (s)	Problem
Yurdakul & İç (2005)	A performance measurement development
Ertuğrul & Karakaşoğlu (2008)	Facility location selection in textile firm
Dağdeviren et al. (2009)	Weapon selection
Wang et al. (2009)	Supplier selection
Taylan (2014)	Construction projects selection
Şengül & Eren (2016)	Digital marketing tools selection
Singh et al. (2018)	3PL selection
Roy & Dutta (2019)	Discharge machining process

Step 1: Define the decision-making problem, determining the purpose.

Weights of the criteria affecting OHS services were determined for JHSU selection of a textile firm. These criterias are: References (C1), graduation of OHS experts (C2), periodic control and inspection (C3), compliance with OHS plan/program (C4), customer satisfaction (C5).

References (C1): Information about that JHSU's has already provided services to business.

Graduation of OHS experts (C2): Information on the license / specialty training of OHS experts working under JHSU. Certificates of the enterprise according to the type of risk.

Periodic control and inspection (C3): Follow-up of the business periodically regarding the execution of OHS services.

Compliance with OHS plan/program (C4): Fulfill the operations / trainings related to annual OHS practices in a timely manner.

Customer satisfaction: The degree to which the business meets expectations of OHS services.

Step 2: Formation of hierarchical structure of problem

Firstly, a hierarchical structure is created which shows the criteria that are important in JHSU selection. The hierarchical structure of the problem is shown in Fig. 2. First, the fuzzy AHP approach was examined when determining criterion weights.

Step 3: Creating of pairwise comparison matrix.

In order to determine the order of decision elements in a decision problem, firstly, comparisons of decision elements should be made in an appropriate way (Onder & Onder, 2015; Ishizaka & Nemery, 2013). Determining the weights of a comparison matrix in AHP problems; with the help of matrix calculations, Ms. Excel operations can be done through or with the help of a package program (Super decision, expert choice et al.). Applications in this study is made with the help of excel.

Pairwise comparison matrixes containing fuzzy numbers of decision makers are shown in Table 7.

Figure 2. The hierarchical structure of JHSU selection

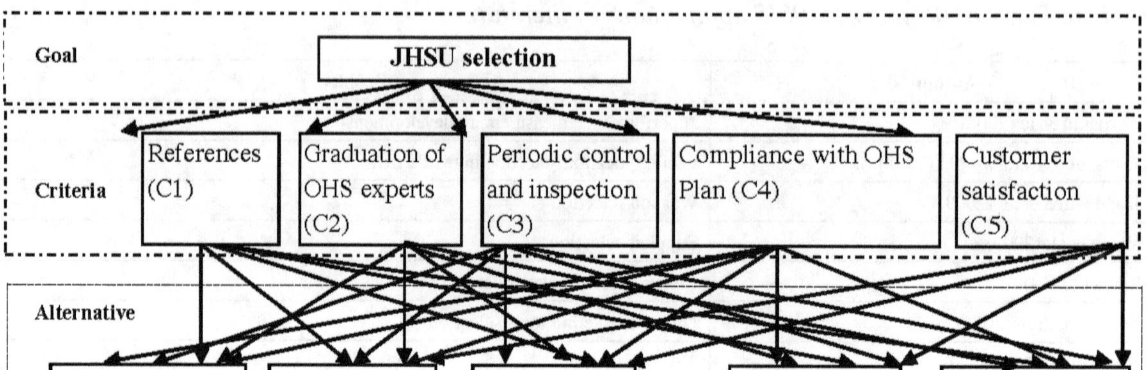

Table 7. Pairwise comparison matrixes containing fuzzy numbers of three decision makers

		C1	C2	C3	C4	C5
E1	C1	E	E	P	P	P
	C2		E	FS	P	E
	C3			E	FS	VS
	C4				E	P
	C5					E
		C1	C2	C3	C4	C5
E2	C1	E	FS	VS	VS	P
	C2		E	FS	FS	FS
	C3			E	VS	FS
	C4				E	E
	C5					E
		C1	C2	C3	C4	C5
E3	C1	E	E	FS	FS	1/VS
	C2		E	P	E	1/VS
	C3			E	FS	P
	C4				E	P
	C5					E

Pairwise comparison evaluations of three decision makers, the geometric average is converted to a single pairwise comparison matrix. All comparisons are positive. The comparisons on the main diagonal are 1 because a criterion is compared with itself.

Integrated pairwise comparison matrixes containing fuzzy numbers of decision makers are shown in Table 8.

Step 4-5: Determination of relative importance weights and calculation of consistency ratio

The consistency of pairwise comparisons by decision-makers is one of the important elements of AHP. Let's give a simple example of the concept of consistency. For example; When the reference criterion is compared with the customer satisfaction, the value of "2" is given so that the reference criterion

Table 8. Integrated pairwise comparison matrices of decision makers

	C1	C2	C3	C4	C5
C1	(1.00,1.00,1.00)	(1.14,1.26,1.36)	(1.36,1.82,2.36)	(1.36,1.82,2.36)	(0.56,0.79,1.14)
C2	(0.74,0.79, 0.87)	(1.00,1.00,1.00)	(1.14,1.59,2.11)	(1.00,1.26,1.55)	(0.84,1.00,1.19)
C3	(0.42,0.55,0.74)	(0.47,0.63, 0.87)	(1.00,1.00,1.00)	(1.78,2.29,2.80)	(1.36,1.82,2.36)
C4	(0.42,0.55,0.74)	(0.64,0.79,1.00)	(0.36,0.44,0.56)	(1.00,1.00,1.00)	(0.76, 1.00,1.31)
C5	(0.87,1.26, 1.78)	(0.84,1.00,1.19)	(0.42,0.55,0.74)	(0.76,1.00,1.31)	(1.00,1.00,1.00)

Table 9. Column sum account for normalization

	C1	C2	C3	C4	C5
C1	1	1,256935	1,830756	1,830756	0,813634
C2	0,797531	1	1,600483	1,26555	1,004844
C3	0,560338	0,644613	1	2,288814	1,830756
C4	0,560338	0,803077	0,444502	1	1,012252
C5	1,281952	1,004844	0,560338	1,012252	1
Sum	**4,200159**	**4,709468**	**5,436079**	**7,397373**	**5,661487**

For C1 column; (1+0,797531+0,560338+0,560338+1,281952) = 4,200159.

Table 10. Normalized matrix

	C1	C2	C3	C4	C5	Average
C1	0,238086	0,266895	0,336779	0,247487	0,143714	**0,246592**
C2	0,189881	0,212338	0,294419	0,171081	0,177488	**0,209041**
C3	0,133409	0,136876	0,183956	0,309409	0,32337	**0,217404**
C4	0,133409	0,170524	0,081769	0,135183	0,178796	**0,139936**
C5	0,305215	0,213367	0,103078	0,136839	0,176632	**0,187026**
Sum	1	1	1	1	1	

For C1 row; (0,238086+0,266895+0,336779+0,247487+0,143714)/5=0,246592.

is dominant. When customer satisfaction is compared with experts' graduating, "4" values should be given in such a way that customer satisfaction is dominant. Accordingly, when the reference criterion is compared with the training of experts, the reference criterion should be 8, predominantly. If the value "8" is given, the inconsistency will be "0". When another value is given instead of 8, such as "3" value is given. Inconsistency will be "0,1037". 0,1037> 0,10; because it is inconsistent. That is, when we give a value of 3, the weights (w) found will be invalid (Onder & Onder, 2015). Consistency ratio belong to integrated pairwise comparison matrices of decision makers and pairwise comparison matrixes containing fuzzy numbers of three decision makers were calculated separately.

Consistency ratio, as a result of calculations; integrated matrices (0,6443), expert1 (0,0839), expert2 (0,0224), expert3 (0,0774) is calculated.

e. g. the consistency ratio of the integrated pairwise comparison matrices of the decision makers was calculated as follows. The normalization process is performed and presented in Table 9.

Later, the same operation is done for each column. The normalized matrix is shown in Table 10.
Later, the same operation is done for each row. All priorities matrix is shown Table 11.
Later, the same operation is done for each row.
The resulting matrix elements are divided into elements of the priority vector.

0,246592/1,316= 5,3356

Table 11. All priorities matrix

	C1	C2	C3	C4	C5	Sum
C1	0,247	0,263	0,398	0,256	0,152	1,316
C2	0,197	0,209	0,348	0,177	0,188	1,119
C3	0,138	0,135	0,217	0,320	0,342	1,153
C4	0,138	0,168	0,097	0,140	0,189	0,732
C5	0,316	0,210	0,122	0,142	0,187	0,977

For C1 row; 0,247+0,263+0,398+0,256+0,152= 1,316.

0,209041/1,119= 5,3515

0,217404/1,153= 5,3035

0,139936/0,732= 5, 2305

0,187026/0,977= 5,2221

To calculate λ_{max}, 5 values are averaged.

λ_{max} = (5,3356; 5,3515; 5,3035; 5,2305; 5,2221)/5= 5,2886

Index of fit; $CI = \frac{\lambda_{\max - n}}{n-1}$, n=5.

CI= (5,2886- 5)/4= 0,07217.

Random index corresponding to "5" the number of decision alternatives: 1,12 in Table 5.

$$CR = \frac{CI}{RI}, CR = \frac{0,07217}{1,12} = 0,06443.$$

As a result, 0,06443<0,1. The result is within the limits of compliance. Inconsistency in comparisons is considered to be within acceptable limits.

Step 6: Determination of relative importance weights.

After consistency calculations, weights of criteria are presented as in Table 12. References (0.2769) were the most important criteria in the selection of JHSU and compliance with OHS plan/program (0.0811) was the least important criteria. Criterion ranking is C1>C3>C2>C5>C4. Secure references increase the preference of JHSU. After criterion weights were determined, alternatives were listed based on criteria using fuzzy TOPSIS.

Table 12. The weights of criteria

	Weights
C1	0,2769
C2	0,2169
C3	0,2566
C4	0,0811
C5	0,1685

Table 13. Integrated pairwise comparison matrices of decision makers

	C1	C2	C3	C4	C5
A 1	P	G	G	M	P
A 2	M	VG	G	G	G
A 3	VP	M	M	M	M
A4	P	G	VG	G	G
A5	P	M	G	G	G

The opinions of the decision makers were combined as described above and the results in Table 13 were obtained. If the problem is unfixed according to the method steps;

Step 1: Formation of decision matrix

Evaluations of the decision makers in the problem are shown in the Excel program as in the Table 10. After the decision matrix is created, step 2 is obtained to obtain the normalized matrix.

Step 2: Determining the normalized decision matrix

The decision criteria values corresponding to each alternative are squared, and then the values of each column are summed and square root is obtained and the following Table 14 is obtained.

Step 3: Determining of weighted normalized decision matrix

Table 14. Integrated pairwise comparison matrices of decision makers

	C1	C2	C3	C4	C5
A 1	(0.142, 0.428, 0.714)	(0.454, 0.636, 0.818)	(0.454, 0.636, 0.818)	(0.333, 0.555, 0.778)	(0.111, 0.333, 0.555)
A 2	(0.428, 0.714,1)	(0.636, 0.818, 1)	(0.454, 0.636, 0.818)	(0.555, 0.777, 1)	(0.555, 0.777, 1)
A 3	(0.142, 0.142, 0.428)	(0.272, 0.454, 0.636)	(0.272, 0.454, 0.636)	(0.333, 0.555, 0.778)	(0.333, 0.555,0.777)
A4	(0.142, 0.428, 0.714)	(0.454, 0.636, 0.818)	(0.636, 0.818, 1)	(0.555, 0.777, 1)	(0.555, 0.777, 1)
A5	(0.142, 0.428, 0.714)	(0.272, 0.454, 0.636)	(0.454, 0.636, 0.818)	(0.555, 0.777, 1)	(0.555, 0.777, 1)

Table 15. Weighted normalized decision matrix

	C1	C2	C3	C4	C5
Weights	**0.2769**	**0.2169**	**0.2567**	**0.081**	**0.1671**
A 1	(0.036, 0.108, 0.180)	(0.121, 0.169, 0.218)	(0.110, 0.155, 0.199)	(0.060, 0.099, 0.139)	(0.006, 0.019, 0.031)
A 2	(0.108, 0.180, 0.252)	(0.169, 0.218, 0.266)	(0.110, 0.155, 0.199)	(0.099, 0.139, 0.179)	(0.031, 0.044, 0.057)
A 3	(0.036, 0.036, 0.108)	(0.072, 0.121, 0.169)	(0.066, 0.110,0.151)	(0.060, 0.099, 0.139)	(0.019, 0.031, 0.044)
A4	(0.036, 0.108, 0.180)	(0.121, 0.169, 0.218)	(0.155, 0.199,0.243)	(0.099, 0.139, 0.179)	(0.031, 0.044, 0.057)
A5	(0.036, 0.108, 0.180)	(0.072, 0.121, 0.169)	(0.110,0.155,0.199)	(0.099, 0.139, 0.179)	(0.031, 0.044, 0.057)

Table 16. Calculating the positive ideal (A+)

	A1	A2	A3	A4	A5
C1	0,8569	0,8921	0,8957	0,8880	0,8782
C2	0,9375	0,9305	0,9066	0,9272	0,9415
C3	0,8781	0,8479	0,8765	0,9060	0,8678
C4	0,8966	0,8766	0,8523	0,9143	0,9091
C5	0,9405	0,9306	0,8912	0,9003	0,9163

Note: 4 digits after the comma.

Weighted normalized decision matrix is shown in Table 15.

Step 4: Calculating the positive ideal (A^+) and negative ideal (A^-) solutions

The maximum values for each column are considered for ideal solution values, while the minimum values for each column are considered for negative ideal solution values. Calculating the positive ideal (A^+) is shown Table 16.

Negative values for each decision criterion are shown in Table 17.

Step 5: Determining the discrimination scales

Calculated status of ideal discrimination criteria is shown in Table 18.

Table 17. Calculating the negative ideal (A-)

	A1	A2	A3	A4	A5
C1	0,1490	0,1180	0,1269	0,1218	0,1343
C2	0,0819	0,0983	0,1163	0,0859	0,0790
C3	0,1626	0,1876	0,1721	0,1248	0,1634
C4	0,1266	0,1352	0,1524	0,1015	0,1223
C5	0,0780	0,0818	0,1204	0,1090	0,1021

Table 18. Ideal discrimination criteria

	d_i^+	d_i^-
A1	4,4832	0,5559
A2	4,2721	0,7555
A3	4,5829	0,4480
A4	4,3438	0,6896
A5	4,4298	0,6058

Step 6: Determining the closeness coefficient (CC_i)

The formula $CC_i = \dfrac{d_i^-}{d_i^- + d_i^+}$ is used to calculating the closeness according to the ideal solution. Ranking is shown in Table 19.

Among the alternatives, the most suitable JHSU is alternative 2 with the highest value. The data in Table 16 was used in the fuzzy TOPSIS method. As seen in Table 19, alternative 2 (0.2476) was selected as the most suitable JHSU for distance-based measurements. The order of all alternatives in distance-based measurements was found as A2> A4> A5> A1> A3. The best JHSU was found to be A2 and the worst JHSU was A3.

FUTURE RESEARCH DIRECTIONS

Occupational health and safety services will continue to gain even more importance in the coming years. For this reason, it will be important to identify the persons / institutions that will carry out this service. As it is apparent, all mentioned subjects involve considering multiple criteria to determine and solve these problems. For this, many different methods can be proposed but MCDM techniques might be applied as one of the best. Integrated fuzzy set theory and MCDM techniques such as AHP, TOPSIS, ANP, PROMETHEE, VIKOR and etc, help researchers to find a more effectively results. Moreover, hybrid fuzzy MCDM methods and other techniques such as data envelopment analysis or goal programming will severely be recommended in term of applications and precedent studies.

Table 19. Closeness coefficient (CC_i)

	d_i^+	d_i^-	CC_i	Ranking
A1	4,4832	0,5559	0,1818	4
A2	4,2721	0,7555	0,2476*	1*
A3	4,5829	0,4480	0,1467	5
A4	4,3438	0,6896	0,2257	2
A5	4,4298	0,6058	0,1982	3

CONCLUSION

Businesses are responsible to ensure safe work environment for all employees due to legal requirements. Employees can work more efficiently when businesses build a safe work environment. Thus, productivity can be increased. The occupational accidents and occupational diseases can result in injury, disability or death. This situation may cause to loss of labor force, decrease in market share, decrease in productivity. For these causes, businesses must take all essential measures. OHS services is needed to build a safe work environment. All employees must participate to these activities. The considerable result of this study is the clear ranking of the organizations where the business can get the OHS services it needs. If these JHSUs are considered correctly, the work environment could be improved in terms of occupational safety. The managers can select the most suitable JHSU by using hybrid MCDM methods. This study handles the capacity of the business to make an effective OHS policy so that the managers can use this policy for long term. In real life applications, it provides more useful and effective information to managers such as determining the priorities of the OHS services, allocating the essential resources to the business appropriately, and creating an OHS policy to increase the system security. Awareness of the implementation of decision-making techniques between employees and managers is significant.

In this chapter, a MCDM hybrid model using fuzzy AHP-fuzzy TOPSIS integrated approach was developed by considering an JHSU selection problem. Distance and similarity based solutions are presented in the fuzzy TOPSIS approach. References (0.2769) were the foremost criteria in the selection of JHSU and "Compliance with OHS Plan" (0.0811) was the least important criteria. According to this result, it is determined that the references of JHSU who will provide service in outsourcing OHS services is more important. In particular, it is essential to select a expert who is appropriate for the hazard type of the business. Other companies working in that field are more easily able to prefer references in the business areas where JHSU has previously provided intensive services. The "Compliance with OHS Plan" criteria is considered to be the lowest since the companies receiving service from JHSU for OHS services leave the follow-up of these jobs directly to JHSU.

It is thought that enterprises consider OHS services as cost rather than as a culture. Looking at each OHS practices as a cost undermines the effectiveness of the studies. According to the results obtained from the study, the most appropriate JHSU was alternative 2 and the worst choice was alternative 3. Although the proposed method helps decision-makers in an uncertain environment, it can be implemented in many various areas. Another hybrid MCDM methods can be used in another studies. In addition, the proposed method can be applied in MCDM methods such as personnel selection, material selection, plant location selection, software selection.

REFERENCES

Anderson, D. R., Sweeney, D. J., & Williams, T. A. (2004). *Quantitative methods for business. Mason/ Ohio*. Thomson South-Western.

Başkaya, Z., & Öztürk, B. (2011). Evaluation of salesperson candidate's with fuzzy TOPSIS. *Business and Economics Research Journal*, *2*(2), 77–100.

Behzadian, M., Otaghsara, K., Yazdani, M., & Ignatius, J. (2012). A state of the art survey of TOPSIS applications. *Expert Systems with Applications*, *39*(17), 13051–13069. doi:10.1016/j.eswa.2012.05.056

Boran, F. E., Genc, S., Kurt, M., & Akay, D. (2009). A multi-criteria intuitionistic fuzzy group decision making for supplier selection with TOPSIS method. *Expert Systems with Applications*, *36*(8), 11363–11368. doi:10.1016/j.eswa.2009.03.039

Chang, D. Y. (1996). Applications of the extent analysis method on fuzzy AHP. *European Journal of Operational Research*, *95*(3), 649–655. doi:10.1016/0377-2217(95)00300-2

Chen, P., & Wang, J. (2009). Application of a fuzzy AHP method to risk assessment of international construction projects, In 2009 International Conference on Electronic Commerce and Business Intelligence, (pp. 459-462). IEEE.

Dagdeviren, M., Yavuz, S., & Kılınç, N. (2009). Weapon selection using the AHP and TOPSIS methods under fuzzy environment. *Expert Systems with Applications*, *36*(4), 8143–8151. doi:10.1016/j.eswa.2008.10.016

Dagdeviren, M., & Yüksel, İ. (2008). Developing a fuzzy analytic hierarchy process (AHP) model for behavior-based safety management. *Information Sciences*, *178*(6), 1717–1733. doi:10.1016/j.ins.2007.10.016

Darko, A., Chan, A. P. C., Ameyaw, E. E., Owusu, E. K., Parn, E., & Edwards, D. J. (2019). Review of application of analytic hierarchy process (AHP) in construction. *International Journal Construction Management*, *19*(5), 436–452. doi:10.1080/15623599.2018.1452098

Dozic, S., Lutovac, T., & Kalic, M. (2018). Fuzzy AHP approach to passenger aircraft type selection. *Journal of Air Transport Management*, *68*, 165–175. doi:10.1016/j.jairtraman.2017.08.003

Dursun, M., & Karsak, E. (2010). A fuzzy MDCM approach for personnel selection. *Expert Systems with Applications*, *37*(6), 4324–4330. doi:10.1016/j.eswa.2009.11.067

Efe, B. (2016). An integrated fuzzy multi criteria group decision making approach for ERP system selection. *Applied Soft Computing*, *38*, 106–117. doi:10.1016/j.asoc.2015.09.037

Efe, B., & Efe, Ö. F. (2018). Intuitionistic fuzzy number-based group decision making approach for personnel selection. *Uludağ University Journal of The Faculty of Engineering*, *23*(3), 11–26. doi:10.17482/uumfd.338406

Efe, B., Kurt, M., & Efe, Ö. F. (2017). An integrated intuitionistic fuzzy set and mathematical programming approach for an occupational health and safety policy. *Gazi University Journal of Science*, *30*(2), 73–95.

Ertuğrul, I., & Karakasoğlu, N. (2008). Comparison of fuzzy AHP and fuzzy TOPSIS methods for facility location selection. *International Journal of Advanced Manufacturing Technology*, *39*(7-8), 783–795. doi:10.100700170-007-1249-8

Forman, E. H., & Selly, M. A. (2002). *Decision by objectives: How to convince others that you are right.* Pittsburgh, PA: Scientific Pub Co.

Güngör, Z., Gürkan, K., & Saadettin, E. (2009). A fuzzy AHP approach to personnel selection problem. *Applied Soft Computing*, *9*(2), 641–646. doi:10.1016/j.asoc.2008.09.003

Hwang, C. L., & Yoon, K. (1981). *Multiple attributes decision making methods and applications*. Berlin, Germany: Springer-Verlag. doi:10.1007/978-3-642-48318-9

Ishizaka, A., & Nemery, P. (2013). Multi-criteria decision analysis methods and software, Wiley & Sons, Atrium, Southern Gate, Chichester, UK.

Junior, F. R. L., Osiro, L., & Carpinetti, L. C. R. (2014). A comparison between Fuzzy AHP and Fuzzy TOPSIS methods to supplier selection. *Applied Soft Computing*, *21*, 194–209. doi:10.1016/j.asoc.2014.03.014

Kelemenis, A., & Askounis, D. (2010). A new TOPSIS-based multi-criteria approach to personnel selection. *Expert Systems with Applications*, *37*(7), 4999–5008. doi:10.1016/j.eswa.2009.12.013

Krmac, E., & Djordjević, B. (2018). An evaluation of indicators of railway intelligent transportation systems using the group analytic hierarchy process. *Electronics Science Technology and Application*, *4*(2), 15–22. doi:10.18686/esta.v4i2.57

Kumlu, K. B., & Tüdeş, Ş. (2018). Multi criteria decision making techniques in urban planning and geology. In N. Ceryan (Ed.), *Handbook of Research on Trends and Digital Advances in Engineering Geology* (pp. 530–568). Hershey, PA: IGI Global; doi:10.4018/978-1-5225-2709-1.ch015

Kusumawardani, R. P., & Agintiara, M. (2015). Application of fuzzy AHP-TOPSIS method for decision making in human resource manager selection process. *Procedia Computer Science*, *72*, 638–646. doi:10.1016/j.procs.2015.12.173

Lai, Y. J., Liu, T. Y., & Hwang, C. L. (1994). TOPSIS for MODM. *European Journal of Operational Research*, *76*(3), 486–500. doi:10.1016/0377-2217(94)90282-8

Lee, A. H. I. (2009). A fuzzy supplier selection model with the consideration of benefits opportunities, costs and risks. *Expert Systems with Applications*, *36*(2), 2879–2893. doi:10.1016/j.eswa.2008.01.045

Macuzic, I., Tadic, D., Aleksic, A., & Stefanovic, M. (2016). A two-step fuzzy model for the assessment and ranking of organizational resilience factors in the process industry. *Journal of Loss Prevention in the Process Industries*, *40*, 122–130. doi:10.1016/j.jlp.2015.12.013

Mahmoodzadeh, S., Shahrabi, J., Pariazar, M., & Zaeri, M. S. (2007). Project selection by using fuzzy AHP and TOPSIS technique. *International Journal of Humanities and Social Science*, *1*(3), 135–140.

Onder, G., & Onder, E. (2015). *Çok kriterli karar verme yöntemleri, Analitik hiyerarşi süreci* (pp. 21–74). Bursa, Turkey: Dora Press.

Orhan, S., Ozkan, E., & Uysal, S. (2017). Outsourcing of health and safety service case from Turkey a case study joint health and safety units's efficiency. *Journal of Business Science*, *5*(3), 207–234. doi:10.22139/jobs.358810

Ozkok, B. A., & Pappalardo, E. (2013). Fuzzy analytic hierarchy process and its application to e-marketplace selection. In P. Papajorgji, A. Guimarães, & M. Guarracino (Eds.), *Enterprise Business Modeling, Optimization Techniques, and Flexible Information Systems* (pp. 26–44). Hershey, PA: IGI Global; doi:10.4018/978-1-4666-3946-1.ch003

Patil, S. K., & Kant, R. (2014). A fuzzy AHP-TOPSIS framework for ranking the solutions of knowledge management adoption in supply chain to overcome its barriers. *Expert Systems with Applications*, *41*(2), 679–693. doi:10.1016/j.eswa.2013.07.093

Podvezko, V. (2009). Application of AHP technique. *Journal of Business Economics and Management, 10*(2), 181–189. doi:10.3846/1611-1699.2009.10.181-189

Promentilla, M. A. B., Janairo, J. I. B., Yu, D. E. C., Pausta, C. M. J., Beltran, A. B., Huelgas-Orbecido, A. P., ... Tan, R. R. (2018). A stochastic fuzzy multicriteria decision-making model for optimal selection of clean technologies. *Journal of Cleaner Production, 183*, 1289–1299. doi:10.1016/j.jclepro.2018.02.183

Rantanen, J., & Fedotov, I. A. (1995). *ILO Standards, principles and approaches in occupational health services.* Retrieved from https://www.ilo.org/safework/info/publications/WCMS_110439/lang--en/index.htm

Rostampour, S. (2012). An application of TOPSIS for ranking internet web browsers. *Decision Science Letters, 1*(2), 53–58. doi:10.5267/j.dsl.2012.09.001

Roy, T., & Dutta, R. K. (2019). Integrated fuzzy AHP and fuzzy TOPSIS methods for multi-objective optimization of electro discharge machining process. *Soft Computing, 23*(13), 5053–5063. doi:10.100700500-018-3173-2

Saaty, T. L. (1986). Axiomatic foundation of the analytic hierarchy process. *Management Science, 32*(7), 841–855. doi:10.1287/mnsc.32.7.841

Samantra, C., Datta, S., & Mahapatra, S. S. (2017). A Risk-based decision support framework for selection of appropriate safety measure system for underground coal mines. *International Journal of Injury Control and Safety Promotion, 24*(1), 54–68. doi:10.1080/17457300.2015.1061561 PMID:26176824

Şengül, Ü., & Eren, M. (2016). Selection of digital marketing tools using fuzzy AHP-fuzzy TOPSIS. In A. Kumar, & M. Dash (Eds.), *Fuzzy optimization and multi-criteria decision making in digital marketing* (pp. 97–126). Hershey, PA: IGI Global; doi:10.4018/978-1-4666-8808-7.ch005

Shaverdi, M., Ramezani, I., & Rostamy, A. A. (2016). Multi-criteria decision-making models for sustainable and green supply chain management based on fuzzy approach. In A. Kumar, & M. Dash (Eds.), *Fuzzy optimization and multi-criteria decision making in digital marketing* (pp. 291–307). Hershey, PA: IGI Global; doi:10.4018/978-1-4666-8808-7.ch013

Singh, R. K., Gunasekaran, A., & Kumar, P. (2018). Third party logistics (3PL) selection for cold chain management: A fuzzy AHP and fuzzy TOPSIS approach. *Annals of Operations Research, 267*(1-2), 531–553. doi:10.100710479-017-2591-3

Sivilevicius, H. (2011). Application of expert evaluation method to determine the importance of operating asphalt mixing plant quality criteria rank correlation. *The Baltic Journal of Road and Bridge Engineering, 6*(1), 48–58. doi:10.3846/bjrbe.2011.07

Taylan, O., Bafail, A. O., Abdulaal, R. M. S., & Kabli, M. R. (2014). Construction projects selection and risk assessment by fuzzy AHP and fuzzy TOPSIS methodologies. *Applied Soft Computing, 17*, 105–116. doi:10.1016/j.asoc.2014.01.003

Temucin, T., Tozan, H., Vayvay, O., Valiček, J., & Harničarova, M. (2014). A fuzzy-based decision model for nontraditional machining process selection. *International Journal of Advanced Manufacturing Technology, 70*(9-12), 2275–2282. doi:10.100700170-013-5474-z

Thanki, S., Govindan, K., & Thakkar, J. (2016). An investigation on lean-green implementation practices in indian SMEs using analytical hierarchy process (AHP) Approach. *Journal of Cleaner Production, 135*, 284–295. doi:10.1016/j.jclepro.2016.06.105

Vaidya, O. S., & Kumar, S. (2006). Analytic hierarchy process: An overview of applications. *European Journal of Operational Research, 169*(1), 1–29. doi:10.1016/j.ejor.2004.04.028

Wang, J. W., Cheng, C. H., & Huang, K. C. (2009). Fuzzy hierarchical TOPSIS for supplier selection. *Applied Soft Computing, 9*(1), 377–386. doi:10.1016/j.asoc.2008.04.014

Yurdakul, M., & İç, Y. T. (2005). Development of a performance measurement model for manufacturing companies using the AHP and TOPSIS approaches. *International Journal of Production Research, 43*(21), 4609–4641. doi:10.1080/00207540500161746

ADDITIONAL READING

Buyukozkan, G., & Cifci, G. (2011). A novel fuzzy multi-criteria decision framework for sustainable supplier selection with incomplete information. *Computers in Industry,* 62(2), 164–174. doi:. compind.2010.10.009. doi:10.1016/j

Dagdeviren, M., Yavuz, S., & Kılınç, N. (2009). Weapon selection using the AHP and TOPSIS methods under fuzzy environment. *Expert Systems with Applications, 36*(4), 8143–8151. doi:10.1016/j.eswa.2008.10.016

Dereli, T., Durmuşoğlu, A., Seçkiner, S. U., & Avlanmaz, N. (2010). A fuzzy approach for personnel selection process. *Turkish Journal of Fuzzy Systems, 1*(2), 126–140.

Efe, B. (2019). Website evaluation using interval type-2 fuzzy-number-based TOPSIS approach. In K. Vatansever & Y. Akgül (Eds.), *Multi-criteria decision-making models for website evaluation* (pp. 166–185). Hershey, PA: IGI Global; doi:10.4018/978-1-5225-8238-0.ch009

Efe, B., & Efe, Ö. F. (2018). Intuitionistic fuzzy number based group decision making approach for personnel selection. *Uludağ University Journal of The Faculty of Engineering, 23*(3), 11–26. doi:10.17482/uumfd.338406

Kahraman, C., Cebeci, U., & Ulukan, Z. (2003). Multi-criteria supplier selection using fuzzy AHP. *Logistics Information Management, 16*(6), 382–394. doi:10.1108/09576050310503367

Kubler, S., Robert, J., Derigent, W., Voisin, A., & Traon, Y. L. (2016). A state-of the-art survey & testbed of fuzzy AHP (FAHP) applications. *Expert Systems with Applications, 65*, 398–422. doi:10.1016/j.eswa.2016.08.064

Massam, B. H. (1988). Multi-Criteria Decision Making (MCDM) techniques in planning. *Progress in Planning, 30*, 1–84. doi:10.1016/0305-9006(88)90012-8

Saaty, T. L. (2008). Decision making with analytic hierarchy process. *International Journal of Services Sciences, 1*(1), 83–98. doi:10.1504/IJSSCI.2008.017590

Zadeh, L. (1965). Fuzzy sets. *Information and Control*, *8*(3), 338–353. doi:10.1016/S0019-9958(65)90241-X

KEY TERMS AND DEFINITIONS

Alternative (A): Different options in the context of certain actions, which are present for decision makers.

Analytic Hierarchy Process (AHP): It is a multi-criteria decision making technique developed by Thomas Saaty.

Criteria (C): Properties used to evaluate alternatives.

Fuzzy Set: A set of ordered pairs composed of the elements and corresponding degrees of membership to this set.

Joint Health Safety Unit (JHSU): Organizations providing external occupational health and safety services.

Multi Criteria Decision Making (MCDM): MCDM is a research discipline that explicitly considers multiple criteria in decision-making process.

Occupational Health and Safety (OHS): All kinds of health and safety risks in the workplace preventive, preventive and corrective activities.

Technique for Order Preference by Similarity to Ideal Solution (TOPSIS): It is a multi-criteria decision-making technique developed by Hwang and Yoon.

Chapter 5
Multi-Criteria Decision-Making Process for Decentralized Healthcare Services Assessment

William Alberto Cruz Castañeda
https://orcid.org/0000-0002-9803-1387
Universidade do Estado de Santa Catarina, Brazil

ABSTRACT

Home health service, as decentralization form in many health systems, has an objective to deliver high-quality, long-term care inside the patient's home. However, management of those services is about handling a complex decision problem related with the care delivery process composed by technologies, patients, structures, and professionals. Consequently, the decision problem requires finding effective ways to involve assessment and management of several criterias to achieve continuous quality improvement. For this purpose, its useful implements structured approaches with multiple criteria decision analysis (MCDA) techniques. Nevertheless, there are many MCDA methods available and these differ not just in how they are put into practice but also in terms of fundamental theories underpinning them. Therefore, this chapter contributes with a methodological approach to establish a decision analysis for assessing home health services through MACBETH and ULOWA techniques. To demonstrate the feasibility of the methodology, a study case was applied into a homecare service.

INTRODUCTION

Decentralization in healthcare can adopt many different forms. One of them are home health services, which has the objective to deliver high-quality long-term care achieving better health outside of traditional facilities and inside of patient's home. Additionally, their management is about handling the complexity of the care delivery process composed by users, technologies, patients, structures, and professionals.

In order to maintain the interaction and stability of these elements, management strategies are required to plan and assess the process quality. Consequently, a decision problem is generated coming from the results of these strategies, which involves find effective ways to encompass both assessments and man-

DOI: 10.4018/978-1-7998-2216-5.ch005

agement of several criteria's as a way to achieve continuous quality improvement. Thus, patient safety, technology reliability and service effectiveness could be provided to produce quality of suitability for use.

Summarizing existing literature on decentralization and health systems performance (Panda & Thakur, 2016) literature review inspect 76 publications with the objective to clarify key concepts, essential variables, and develop a framework. (Panda & Thakur, 2016) results explain that the flexibility of decentralization has tremendous impact on health service functions; consequently, they must be adopted as a reform measure to increase efficiency and quality of service delivery.

Regarding to health outcomes, (Panda & Thakur, 2016) propose four categories:

1. Health status, which improve patient's health into hospital or a community health program;
2. Health-related knowledge, which concerns with the level of knowledge of the patient about preventive health procedures;
3. Health-seeking behavior, which include patient activities for improve or maintain health;
4. Satisfaction with care, which concerns with quality of care received.

Last but not least (Panda & Thakur, 2016) presents four challenges in assessment health service decentralization:

1. Measure decision making requires combine process and products;
2. Measure efficiency and quality in high and low levels;
3. Quality is a multidimensional element affected by process input/outputs that can be achieved through quantitative expressions;
4. Incomplete assessment from lack of fundamental references.

For this purpose, structured approaches as multiple criteria decision analysis (MCDA) into management strategies are useful due to the decisions involves multiple criteria that improve the quality of decision making. In addition, one things that should be consider by the MCDA users is that there are many methods available, which differs not just in how MCDA is put into practice but also in terms of the fundamental theories that underpinning them.

Therefore, the aim of this book chapter is to contribute with a methodological approach able to establish the implementation of a decision analysis process for assess and manage decentralized home health service through MACBETH and ULOWA multi-criteria decision-making techniques. A study case it was applied into a homecare service for chronic pulmonary diseases in order to demonstrate the feasibility of the methodological approach with several levels of management structures: rehabilitation center, regional development departments, municipalities and outsourced company.

The remainder of the chapter is organized as follows. Section II, Background, presents fundamentals of how measurements and decision making are put together to interact with decentralized health services . Section III, Main Focus of the Chapter, describes the three steps research methodological approach implementing MACBETH and ULOWA methods to establish a decision-making process for decentralized healthcare services assessment. Section IV, Results, presents a study case in a homecare service where it was applied the decision-making methodological approach as well as a standard representation of the decision analysis. Finally, discussions and conclusion are presented in Section V.

BACKGROUND

Decentralization in Health Services: How Measurement and Decision Making Is Involved

According to (World Health Organization, 2007) different classifications define decentralization in healthcare. Transfer of responsibility to a lower organization level its seen as delegation, the separation into a lower administrative level refers to de-concentration, transfers of authority to a lower political level is devolution, and the act to transfer from public into private ownership is privatization.

Home health services, a way of decentralization of health services, have been increasing their adoption for the reason that, in the last decade, increasing of ageing population as well as the prevalence of chronic diseases demands delivery and long-term care inside of patient's home. Nonetheless, to achieve quality of these services, the health system need to measure and control them given that involves a complex multilevel process among resources, outcomes, technologies, deliveries, information and environment.

Towards, to manage them, health systems need to be implement more highly responsive models, where locally available can help empower patients to personalized care. Examples of collaborative management approaches to long-term care are chronic models, which provide a multifactorial approach in the management of chronic illnesses identifying dependent and independent variables as well as his association among them.

The Chronic Care Model (CCM), developed by Wagner and the MacColl Institute for Healthcare Innovation, it was the result from a review of the quality improvement literature and from quality improvement program activities at the Group Health Cooperative of Puget Sound. This model take into consideration innovation in the prevention, control and care support to chronic noncommunicable diseases (Wagner E., 2019) (Coleman, Austin, Brach, & Wagner, 2009) (Nuño, 2009).

The CCM focuses on informed association among patients and professional team. Recognizes that chronic care takes place outside formal health facilities and proposes six elements to improve it (Bowen, et al., 2010) (Wagner, 2011)

1. Community Resources (CR);
2. The Health System (HS);
3. Self-Management Support (SMS);
4. Delivery System Design (DSD);
5. Decision Support (DS);
6. Clinical Information Systems (CIS).

DS component embed evidence-based guidelines into daily clinical practice, which is shared with the patients, use them to provide education models and integrate them with specialist expertise and primary care. On the other hand, CIS component covers telemonitoring, database, patient records and reminder systems.

CCM has been implemented in over 300 health care systems to improve quality of care for chronic illnesses. (Elissen, et al., 2013) meta-analysis expose the management of chronic care in diabetes programs for adult patients with the intervention of at least two CCM components. Charts (a) and (b) on Figure 1 depicts how 61 studies included in the analysis were classified.

Figure 1. Classification of 61 studies including number of CCM components (a) and classification by most frequent CMM components in the studies (b)
Source: Author

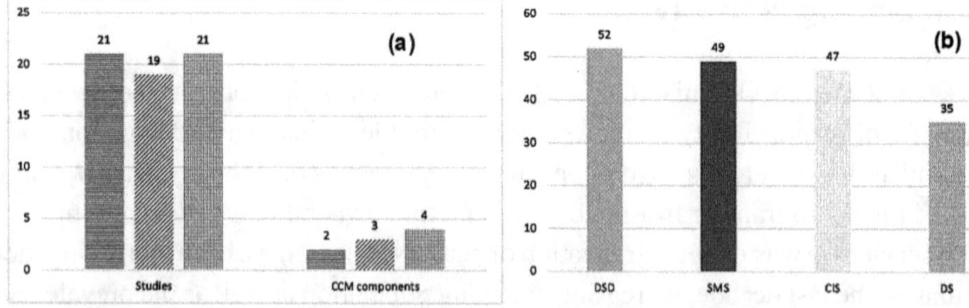

Furthermore, (Lemmens, et al., 2013) meta-analysis explore chronic care management in chronic obstructive pulmonary disease (COPD) programs using CCM. Figure 2 depicts how 29 studies included were classified. The DS component integrate evidence-based clinical guidelines into practice by reminder and feedback system as well as the CIS component mainly implements telephone follow-up of the patient.

(Bruin, et al., 2012) systematic review selects 42 publications describing 33 studies, which assess 28 programs for patients with multiple chronic conditions with CCM component intervention. Figure 3 depicts how these programs include the components. DS include evidence-based guidelines, training teams to implement new protocols, and supervising newly appointed case managers. CIS make use of technologies such as telemonitoring, messaging devices and video-call.

On the other hand, three other models discussed in the literature for the provision of decentralized health services are the approaches developed by Kaiser, EverCare, and Pfzier. These models are not mutually exclusive, but share patient care management. CCM-based Kaiser model integrates prevention and self-management services to identify and classify risk levels according to their complexity (Wallace P., 2005) (Wallace, 2005a) (Selevan, Kindermann, Pines, & Fields, 2015). EverCare (advanced nursing

Figure 2. Classification of 29 studies with number of CCM components in chronic obstructive pulmonary disease programs
Source: Author

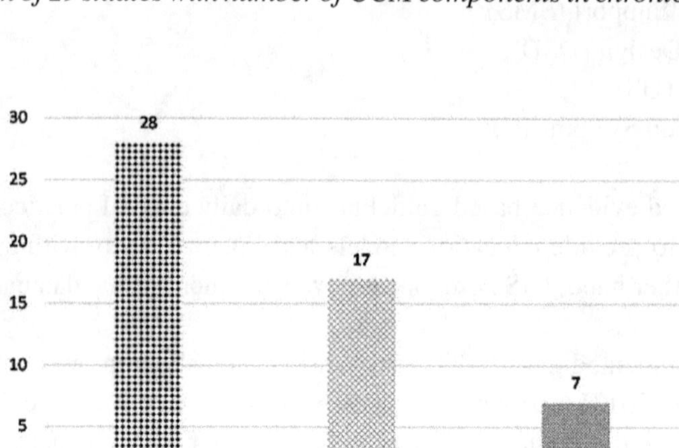

Figure 3. CCM component classification in 28 programs for patients with multiple chronic conditions
Source: Author

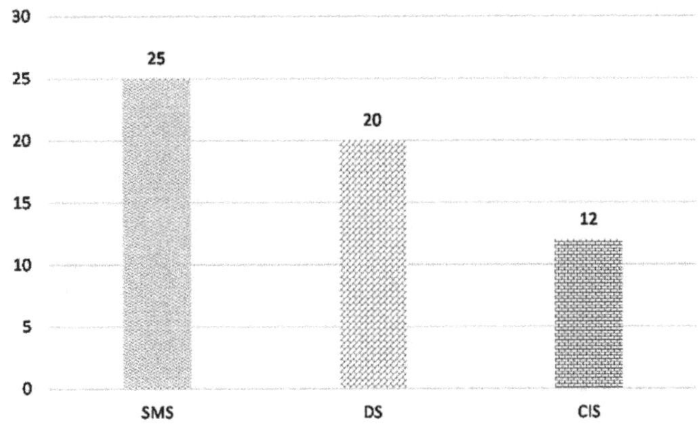

services) and Pfzier (telephone patient management) models focus on managing people at higher risk of hospitalization (Fraser, et al., 2005) (Abdallah, 2005) (Snoddon, 2010).

Guided Care is another service delivery model designed for older people with multiple chronic conditions. It integrates satisfactory experience techniques through specialized training of nursing teams. In addition, provides the following services: care planning and assessment, self-management, care coordination, access to community resources, teaching and family support (Boult, Karm, & Groves, 2008).

Regarding the implementation of ICT in this model, the studies of (Bruin, et al., 2012), (Boyd, et al., 2010) and (Boult, Karm, & Groves, 2008) present the development of systems with electronic patient records to monitor the performance of the nursing staff in relation to procedures and services offered.

The Program of All-Inclusive Care for the Elderly it´s an integrated care model for the elderly that aims to reduce the hospitalization and increase nursing care at home. The main feature of this model is the integration of acute care services. This allows older people with multiple problems to receive a single attention (Rich, 1999) (Hirth, Baskins, & Dever-Bumba, 2009) (Bouwmeester, 2012). Tele-health is used for palliative care or to make easier the management of chronic diseases (Felder, Alwan, & Zhang, 2008).

MAIN FOCUS OF THE CHAPTER

On the way to becoming useful and widely adopted the MACBETH and ULOWA multi-criteria decision-making techniques for assessment and management of decentralized healthcare services, a three steps methodological approach is proposed in order to establish a suitable solution. Figure 4, depicts, graphically the research methodology organized in conception, construction and implementation steps.

Figure 4. Research methodological approach organized in conception, construction, and implementation
Source: Author

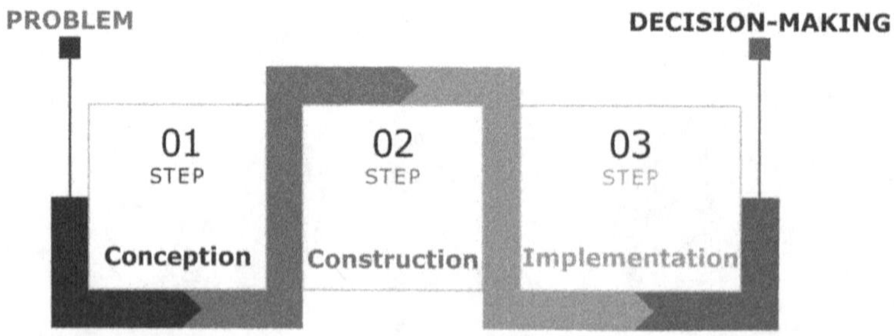

RESEARCH METHODOLOGY

Conception

Step focused on understand the problem. Involved actors must be identified for participation in interviews to allow the continuousness of the MCDA process. Descriptions are obtained about the context of the decentralized health service to identify, characterize, and organize a hierarchic structure with relevant factors in the decision-making process. A tree of viewpoints is this hierarchic structure with the purpose of: identify primary criteria's or areas of concern, and set out assessment dimensions that are the sub-criteria's or Fundamental Points of View (FPV) (Figueira, Greco, & Ehrogott, 2005) (Marafon, Ensslin, Oliveira, & Ensslin, 2015).

To determine a FPV, the area of concern must have the following properties: essential; controllable; complete; measurable; operational; isolable; non-redundant; concise, and comprehensible (Figueira, Greco, & Ehrogott, 2005). When all these properties are attended, a FPV set is reached.

Construction

From the tree hierarchical structure, a global quantitative assessment model is created using the MCDA MACBETH (Measuring Attractiveness by a Categorical Based Evaluation Technique) and ULOWA (Unbalanced Linguistic Ordered Weighted Average) methods. At this step, from each FPV of the tree hierarchical structure is defined and associate an ordinal scale. An ordinal scale is a set of impact levels that serve as a basis for describe the performances in each FPV. These should be ranked in terms of preference according to the perspective of the decision-makers. The most attractive level corresponds to an action whose performance would be the best possible. The least attractive level corresponds to an action with the worst performance.

The descriptor must be feasible, clear in its measure, unambiguous and contain the full range of possible situations that can measure the performance of the corresponding concept. The descriptor is the basis for describing performances of potential actions in each aspect considered in the model.

For each descriptor, anchor levels should be established and afterward transformed into cardinal scales. Anchor levels consist in the identification of three levels (excellence, competitive and compromising) within the ordinal scale constructed for each descriptor.

Excellence region defines levels that exceed service expectations, that is, has superior performance that is still achievable. Competitive region defines levels that perform within service expectations. Moreover, compromising region defines levels of underperforming but still acceptable performance (Figueira, Greco, & Ehrogott, 2005) (Bana e Costa A., Vansnick, Ensslin, & Corrêa, 1999).

In order to transform ordinal scales into cardinal scales (value function), it is necessary to verify, at the time of the construction of the descriptors, whether the difference in attractiveness among the descriptors levels is similar. In other words, if the change from one lower impact level to another higher impact level, immediately close, are similar, the cardinal scale can be considered linear. Otherwise, if exist some attractiveness difference between two levels, thereupon is used a semantic judgment where the value function is obtained through pair-to-pair comparisons of the difference in terms of attractiveness between the impact levels of the ordinal scale. In this sense, the aforementioned decision aiding process is implemented using MACBETH and ULOWA methods.

MACBETH Method

MCDA methods in which assignment of preference levels is involved for different criteria's by comparison, using pairs of alternatives. Attractiveness and degree are indicate by decision makers between two alternatives, on a semantic ordinal scale as follows (Bana e Costa & Vansnick, 1995):

Let A be a finite set of actions for which a decision maker D wants aid to quantify judgments of attractiveness of the elements of A. In such a decision context, the MACBETH approach facilitates the construction of a numerical scale $\nu : A \rightarrow \Re : a \rightarrow \nu\left(a\right)$ such that:

- $\forall\, a,b \in A$, $\upsilon(a) > \upsilon(b)$ if and only if D judges a more attractive than b ($a\, Pb$)
- $\forall\, a,b,c,d \in A$ with $a\, Pb$ and $c\, Pd$, $[\upsilon(a) - \upsilon(b)]/[\upsilon(c) - \upsilon(d)]$ reflects the ratio of the differences of attractiveness between a and b on the one hand and c and d on the other hand.

In fact, $\forall\, a,b \in A$ with $a\, Pb$, MACBETH questioning mode consists of asking D to express an absolute judgment of difference of attractiveness by assigning the pair (a, b) to one of three semantic categories:

$C_2 \rightarrow$ weak difference of attractiveness
$C_4 \rightarrow$ strong difference of attractiveness
$C_6 \rightarrow$ extreme difference of attractiveness

or, in the case of hesitation, to one of three intermediate categories:

$C_1 \rightarrow$ very weak difference of attractiveness (from nil to weak)
$C_3 \rightarrow$ moderate difference of attractiveness (from weak to strong)
$C_5 \rightarrow$ very strong difference of attractiveness (from strong to extreme)

From a mathematical point of view, the categories C_1, C_2, C_3, C_4, C_5, C_6 are asymmetric binary relations that constitute a partition of

$P = \{(a,b) \in A \times A \mid D$ judges a more attractive than $b\}$.

Figure 5. Representation of MACBETH's categories
Source: Adapted from (Bana e Costa & Vansnick, 1995)

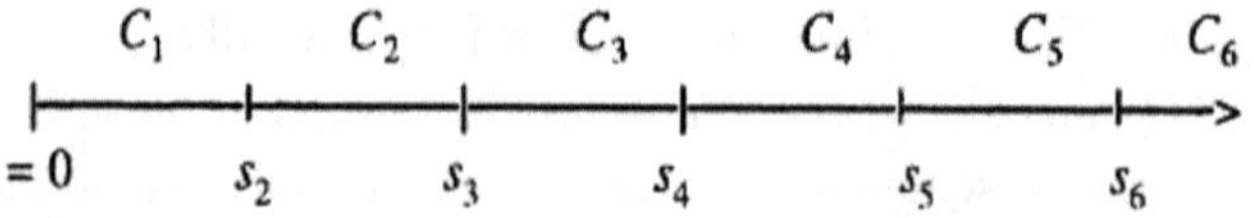

Whereas in MACBETH:

- Is associate to each of our six categories C_1 to C_6 an interval of the real line.
- The thresholds S_i=(1,2,3,4,5,6) defining the intervals associated with categories are not a priori fixed; on the other hand, they are determined simultaneously with the numerical scale *v* depicted on Figure 5.

Once *D* has assigned each pair *(a,b)*∈*P* to one of the six semantic categories of difference of attractiveness, MACBETH attempts to determine simultaneously:

- An application $\nu : A \rightarrow \Re$ associating each element *a* of A with a real number *v(a)*.
- Six real numbers S_1, S_2, S_3, S_4, S_5, S_6 such that

$$0 = S_1 < S_2 < S_3 < S_4 < S_5 < S_6$$

$$\forall a, b \in A : \left\{ \begin{matrix} \forall k \in \{1,2,3,4,5\} : S_k < v(a) - v(b) < S_{k+1} \text{ if and only if } (a,b) \in C_k \\ S_6 < v(a) - v(b) \text{ if and only if } (a,b) \in C_6 \end{matrix} \right\}$$

Let us see how MACBETH interacts with *D* to reach this purpose, assuming:

$$A = \{a_1, a_2, \ldots, a_{n-1}, a_n\}$$

such that:

$$\forall\, i \neq j \in \{1,2,\ldots,n\},\ a_i P a_j \text{ if and only if } i > j$$

that is, the complete ranking of the elements of *A* by order of decreasing attractiveness is $a_n P a_{n-1} P \ldots\ P a_2 P a_1$. In these conditions, to collect *D* absolute judgments of difference of attractiveness between the elements of *A* it is sufficient to fill in, row by row, the upper part of the *n*×*n* matrix depicted in Figure 6. Where,

$$\forall i > j \in \{1,2,\ldots,n\} \text{ and } \forall k \in \{1,2,3,4,5,6\} : a_{i,j} = k \text{ if and only if } (a_i, a_j) \in C_k$$

Figure 6. Representation of MACBETH's categories.
Source: Adapted from (Bana e Costa & Vansnick, 1995)

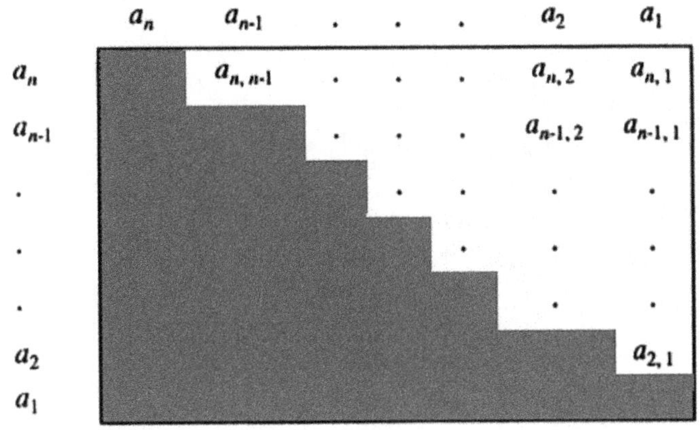

ULOWA Method

Operator defined by (Isern, Marin, Valls, & Moreno, 2010) as an extension of the LOWA operator with the purpose to deal with unbalanced linguistic terms. Define a value functions that measure the effort associated with ordinal descriptor scales as well as takes the same form as the LOWA, which is as follows:

If $A=\{a_1,\ldots,a_m\}$ is a set of labels to aggregate, ULOWA is defined as:

$$ULOWA\left(a_1,\ldots,a_m\right) = W \cdot B^T$$

$$= C^m \left\{w_k, b_k, k = 1,\ldots,m\right\}$$

$$= w_1 \otimes b_1 \oplus \left(1 - w_1\right) \otimes C^{m-1} \left\{\beta_h, b_h, h = 2,\ldots,m\right\}$$

Distinctiveness with LOWA is in the combination of two linguistic terms. Whereas LOWA implements a symbol-based approach, ULOWA works with fuzzy sets, taking into consideration the membership functions of the terms. In this way, it is able to take into account the information given by the fuzzy sets during the aggregation process, obtaining a more precise result. Consequently, when m=2, the combination of two terms, $b_1=s_j$ and $b_2=s_i$, with $s_j, s_i \in S$ ($j \geq i$), is calculated taking into account the membership functions of the labels s_j and s_i:

$$= C^2 \left\{w_i, b_i, i = 1,2\right\} = w_i \otimes s_i \oplus \left(1 - w_1\right) \otimes s_i = s_k,$$

where $s_k \in S$ with $k = \arg_{i \leq p \leq j} \max \left\{Sim\left(S_p, \delta\right)\right\}$

In this expression, δ is a crisp number defined as δ= (x_k, x_k, x_k, x_k) with $x_k = x^*_{si} + w_1\left(x^*_{sj} - x^*_{si}\right)$, where x^*_{si}, is the *x*-component of the center of gravity (COG) of the fuzzy set associated with the label $s_i = (p_1, p_2, p_3, p_4)$:

$$COG\left(S_A\right) = \left\{ \begin{bmatrix} y^*_A = \begin{cases} \frac{1}{6}\left(\frac{p_3 - p_2}{p_4 - p_1} + 2\right), if\ p_1 \neq p_4 \\ \frac{1}{2}, if\ p_1 \neq p_4 \end{cases} \\ x^*_A = \frac{y^*_A\left(p_3 + p_2\right) + \left(p_4 + p_1\right)\left(1 - y^*_A\right)}{2} \end{bmatrix} \right.$$

As a result, the aggregation s_k is the linguistic term consisting of s_j and s_i with the greatest similarity to the intermediate point δ. Standing out that the result is one of the terms available in the scale of reference *S*. The similarity is calculated between two fuzzy sets as follows:

$$Sim\left(P,Q\right) = \sqrt[4]{\prod_{i=1}^{4}\left(2 - \left|p_i - q_i\right|\right) - 1}$$

Afterwards, is calculated the aggregation procedure according to the importance of each linguistic term. Thus, are created a value function and a semantic judgments matrix to represents the transition from a normal to an excellence situation. When the comparison is carried out in the last level, then, the global assessment model can be determined and the profile of FPV can be established. The profile, as a result, is the performance of the current situation of the decentralized healthcare service with each constructed criterion under one FPV.

Implementation

Step that build the additive aggregation function, which represents the performance of the current situation of the global assessment model given by the criteria's, available alternatives, and by the association of a set of parameters to the criteria known as compensation weights.

The compensation weights within a multi-criteria assessment model represents the loss of performance in an affected action of one criterion to balance out the increase of performance in another criterion. Consequently, is implemented the additive aggregation function in the form of a weighted sum, in which the weighting of each criterion and the assessment dimensions are given by their compensation weights. Moreover, determines controllable feedback variables where actions should be developed to improve the quality of the decentralized healthcare services regarding to management (Figueira, Greco, & Ehrogott, 2005) (Marafon, Ensslin, Oliveira, & Ensslin, 2015).

Table 1. Homecare Services with management type and number of served patients descriptions

Decentralized Homecare Service – DHS	Management Type	Served Patients
DHS1 and DHS2	Full / Basic	45 / 251
DHS3, DHS4 and DHS5	Full / Basic / Full	165 / 203 / 285
DHS6	Full	288
DHS7	Basic	482

Source: (Author)

RESULTS

As part of state health departments, the oxygen-therapy homecare program (OHP) in Brazil, attends through outsourcing company, the population with respiratory chronic diseases indicated for oxygen treatment at home based on medical assessment. The OHP of Santa Catarina State it was used as a sample of this study case to apply the multi-criteria decision-making research methodology.

That program has been implementing a three-level spatial organization. Rehabilitation Center as a State level, which establish the attendance model as well as hold patient in their town. Thirty-six development departments as Regional level, which planning and execute health actions to keeps the citizen care of 295 municipalities avoiding their displacement to other centers.

Municipal level, which implements the service and perform health actions into the patient home with health professional team in order to maintain constant attendance. Although, at municipal level, the service can be classified in two management types according the source of financial resources: basic and full. Basic management receives financial resources only from state health department. Nonetheless, full management receives federal resources. Both types use financial resources in order to deploy and maintain the service. In this manner, health actions are decentralized, enabling the reduction of costs and number of hospital admissions to keep the patient at his home with their families and improves quality of life.

Into this context, the study case includes seven homecare services. Ethnography, interviews, questionnaires and brainstorming techniques were applied in loco to obtain service requirements from 11 health decision-makers at each organizational level of this sample. Table 1, describes the management type and the number of served patients of that services.

In addition, outsourcing company provide medical equipment (electronic oxygen concentrator with oxygen cylinder as a backup, BiPAP and CPAP) for patient treatment used in the OHP and therefore it is of great concern of management at State level. As depicted in Figure 7, among 2010 to 2015, medical devices has been rising incrementally and reveals the concern of extensive management actions and strategies.

Figure 7. Rises of medical devices among 2010 to 2015 in the oxygen-therapy homecare program
Source: Author

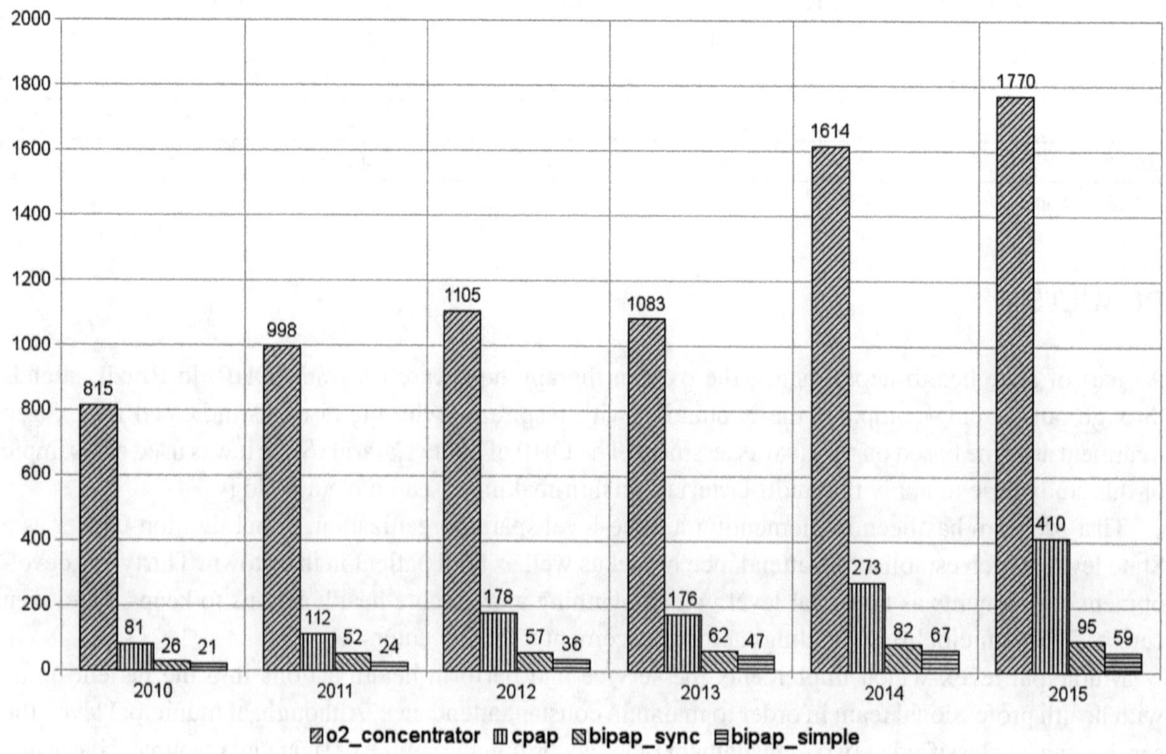

MCDA Assessment Model

According with the research methodology, the development of a tree of viewpoints its related to define a problem label, criteria's, sub-criteria's and descriptors. Thus, the problem label was defined as Assessment of decentralized healthcare services in the oxygen-therapy homecare program.

Conception Step

Afterward problem scope definition, eleven healthcare professionals at each organizational level contribute to identify criteria's (or areas of concern) and determined FPV about the healthcare service context. There were identified three criteria's of concern: Infrastructure, Human Resources, and Technology.

To establish the sub-criteria's of these three criteria, it was considered the study of (Boult, Karm, & Groves, 2008), which considers in home services of chronic diseases, family members and the efficiency of technological resources as desirable factors to improve the patient's quality of life. In addition, the systematic review by (Bruin, et al., 2012) reinforces these factors and includes indicators to identify technological use in home services, the implementation of electronic patient records and disease control.

Figure 8. Tree of viewpoints structure with problem label, criteria´s of concern and sub-criterias
Source: Author

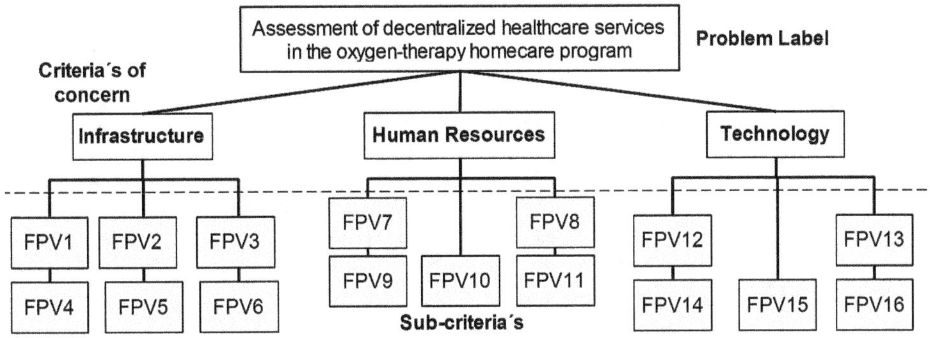

Finally, it was found that (Dorr, et al., 2006) highlight quality indicators for service implementation in the way to promote resources availability.

Therefore, taking into account both indicators from aforementioned studies and service requirements, 16 sub-criteria's were established. FPV´s for the criterion – Infrastructure are: FPV1 – Patient medical record; FPV2 – Health condition report and patient disease; FPV3 – Assessment report and service evolution; FPV4 – Communication system to logistic support; FPV5 – Domicile requirements for the patient attendance; and FPV6 – Personal protection for the attendance.

For the criterion – Human Resources are: FPV7 –Professional team for home care; FPV8 – Technical standards for procedures; FPV9 – Caregivers; FPV10 – Training; and FPV11 – Infection control program and adverse events. For the criterion – Technology are: FPV12 – Medical equipment related on the service; FPV13 – Medical equipment control system; FPV14 – Medical equipment maintenance program; FPV15 – Medical equipment calibration program; and FPV16 – Residue management plan.

Thereafter was generated the tree of viewpoints. Figure 8 depicts a three-level structure, illustrating at the highest level, the problem label or scope. Second level describes the three criteria's of concern. Subsequent level illustrates the 16 FPV or sub-criterias of the model.

Construction Step

MACBETH and ULOWA methods were implemented with M-MACBETH® software tool to build the global quantitative assessment model. To calculate the attractiveness, it was required that each decision maker identify the relevance that each criterion has regarding to the service management.

Consequently, using M-MACBETH®, were assigned semantic judgments to each criterion using the semantic categories: null, very weak, weak, moderate, strong, very strong and extreme. The same procedure was performed to calculate the attractiveness of sub-criteria.

Afterward, for each subcriterion, descriptors with an ordinal scale of (1–7) were established. This represents a set of impact levels that describe subcriterion performance. Each descriptor was organized in terms of preference where the most attractive level (7) corresponds actions that maximizes performance, and the fewer attractive level (1) corresponds actions whose performance that obstructs management of the healthcare service.

Figure 9. Anchored values for descriptor in three levels, compromising, competitive and excellence
Source: Author

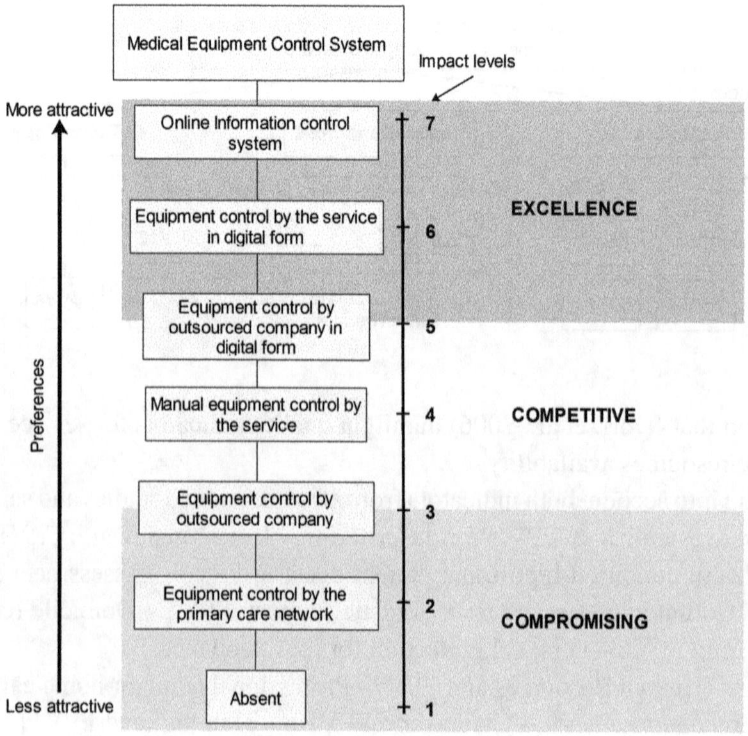

Additionally, it was anchored three levels in a scale for each descriptor: compromising, competitive and excellence. As an exemplification, Figure 9 depicts the structure of values for the descriptor constructed for medical equipment control system, which is part of the Technology criterion.

Afterward, the next step is to develop a semantic judgment to transform ordinal scales into interval cardinal scales and construct a value function. For this propose, it was used the ULOWA method. It was implemented the previously described operations in the M-MACBETH® software, which facilitates the retrieval of value functions implementing seven impact levels of the descriptor (Bana e Costa A., Vansnick, Ensslin, & Corrêa, 1999) (Bana e Costa & Vansnick, 1999).

Impact levels were established by Saaty's numerical scale 1-9 (Xu, 2013). The semantic judgment is described by Equation (1), which establishes the value function of linguistic terms that represents the transition from a normal situation to a situation of excellence.

$$S^t = \left\{ S^t_\alpha \mid \alpha = \frac{1}{\tau}, \frac{1}{\tau - 1}, \ldots, \frac{1}{2}, 1, 2, \ldots, \tau - 1, \tau \right\} \quad (1)$$

where τ is a positive integer, S^t_α it´s a linguistic term, $S_{1/\tau}$ and S_τ are lower and upper limits of the linguistic terms used in the value function. Figure 10, depicts the matrix of semantic transformation, and the anchored value function for the medical equipment control system descriptor.

Figure 10. Semantic transformation of descriptors into a value function using M-MACBETH®
Source: Author

M-MACBETH matrix semantic transformation

	7	6	5	4	3	2	1	Value function (anchored)
7	Null	very strong	very strong	extreme	extreme	extreme	extreme	100.00
6		Null	strong	very strong	very strong	extreme	extreme	69.57
5			Null	strong	very strong	very strong	very strong	47.83
4				Null	moderate	strong	strong	26.09
3					Null	very weak	very weak	8.70
2						Null	very weak	4.35
1							Null	0.00

7 - Online Information control system
6 - Equipment control by the service in digital form
5 - Equipment control by outsourced company in digital form
4 - Manual equipment control by the service
3 - Equipment control by outsourced company
2 - Equipment control by the primary care network
1 - Absent

Implementation Step

With the information of the previous step, it is feasible to build the additive aggregation function used by the global assessment model. That function transforms the local attractiveness unit (performances of criteria, sub-criteria and value functions) into a global attractiveness unit. In other words, transforms a model that has multiple criteria into a synthesis aggregation model.

In this manner, compensation weights are determined. The compensation weights reflect the loss of performance in an affected action of one criterion to balance out the increase of performance in another criterion. It was used the pairwise comparison method of the M-MACBETH® software to calculate the compensation weights. Figure 11 depicts the tree of viewpoints structure including compensation weights for all the 16 FPV´s and the criteria's of concern.

Thereafter, it is proceeded to perform the additive aggregation function, which helps to determine controllable feedback variables and transforms the multicriteria decision model into a model based on a single criterion as follows:

Figure 11. Tree of viewpoints structure including compensation weights of sub-criteria's and criteria´s of concern
Source: Author

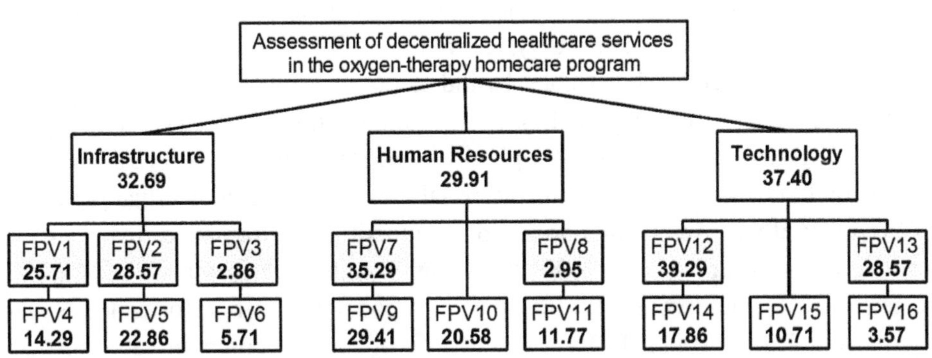

$$V(x) = \sum_{j=1}^{n} w_j \cdot \left(V_{FPV_j} \cdot (x)\right) \tag{2}$$

where, $V(x)$ is the global attractiveness of $x \in X$; X is the set of all controllable feedback variables; w_j is the compensation weights for criterion $j(j=1,\ldots,n)$; $\left(V_{FPV_j}(x)\right)$ is the impact indicator which includes the local attractiveness of controllable feedback variables of X, regarding to FPV_j; n is the number of FPV.

Considering $n=16$, Equation (2) afford the weighted sum of partial values acquire by a particular controllable feedback variable (x) at the several FPV. The weighting is conducted using the compensation weights of each FPV´s, which makes it possible transform units of local attractiveness into units of global attractiveness. Equations (3), (4) and (5) measure the impact of a controllable feedback variable x in each area of concern.

$$\begin{aligned} V_{Infrastructure}(x) = {} & 0.2571V_{FPV1}(x) + 0.2857V_{FPV2}(x) + 0.0286V_{FPV3}(x) \\ & +0.1429V_{FPV4}(x) + 0.2286V_{FPV5}(x) + 0.0571V_{FPV6}(x) \end{aligned} \tag{3}$$

$$\begin{aligned} V_{Human\ Resources}(x) = {} & 0.3529V_{FPV7}(x) + 0.0295V_{FPV8}(x) \\ & +0.2941V_{FPV9}(x) + 0.2058V_{FPV10}(x) + 0.1177V_{FPV11}(x) \end{aligned} \tag{4}$$

$$\begin{aligned} V_{Technology}(x) = {} & 0.3929V_{FPV12}(x) + 0.2857V_{FPV13}(x) \\ & +0.1786V_{FPV14}(x) + 0.1071V_{FPV15}(x) + 0.0357V_{FPV16}(x) \end{aligned} \tag{5}$$

The performance of a set of controllable feedback variable, by area of concern, can be determined by equation (6)

$$V(x) = 0.3269V_{Infrastructure}(x) + 0.2991V_{Human\ Resources}(x) + 0.3740V_{Technology}(x) \tag{6}$$

In order to improve the healthcare service quality, the controllable feedback variables of each FPV´s are organized in three indicators: patient safety, technology reliability, and service effectiveness. Table 2 classifies the controllable feedback variables by indicators and criterion of concern.

To illustrate the application of the global assessment model, it was scored current impact profiles of two DHS. Figure 12 (DHS7) and 13 (DHS6) depicts the performance values of the status quo in the three criterias of concern. In the performed assessment for DHS7, can be considered that in the Infrastructure criterion (7.43), FPV6 it was the one that obtained a competitive performance.

In Human Resources criterion (7.53), FPV9 had an excellent performance and FPV7 obtained a competitive performance. Otherwise, FPV10 and FPV11 had the lowest performance. Regarding to the technology criterion (7.97), FPV12, FPV13, and FPV14 obtained a competitive performance. FPV15

Table 2. Controllable feedback variables of the global assessment model classified by indicator and criterion of concern to improve the decentralized healthcare service quality regarding to management

Indicator	Criterion	Controllable Feedback Variables
Patient Safety	Infrastructure	FPV1, FPV2, FPV6.
	Human Resources	FPV9, FPV10, FPV11.
	Technology	FPV15, FPV16.
Technology Reliability	Infrastructure	FPV5.
	Human Resources	FPV8, FPV10.
	Technology	FPV12, FPV13, FPV14, FPV15.
Services Effectiveness	Infrastructure	FPV3, FPV4, FPV5.
	Human Resources	FPV7, FPV8, FPV10.
	Technology	FPV12, FPV14.

Source: (Author)

had the lowest performance. Nevertheless, were identified that FPV8 and FPV16 had a compromising performance as well as the lowest performance in the assessment. The score obtained was 22.93 points, which classifies it as a compromising to allow a suitable homecare service management. Figure 12 additionally depicts the radar chart illustrating the partial scores comparison of the technology criterion obtained with the equation (5).

Figure 12. Impact profile of criterions with performance values of each controllable feedback variables
Source: Author

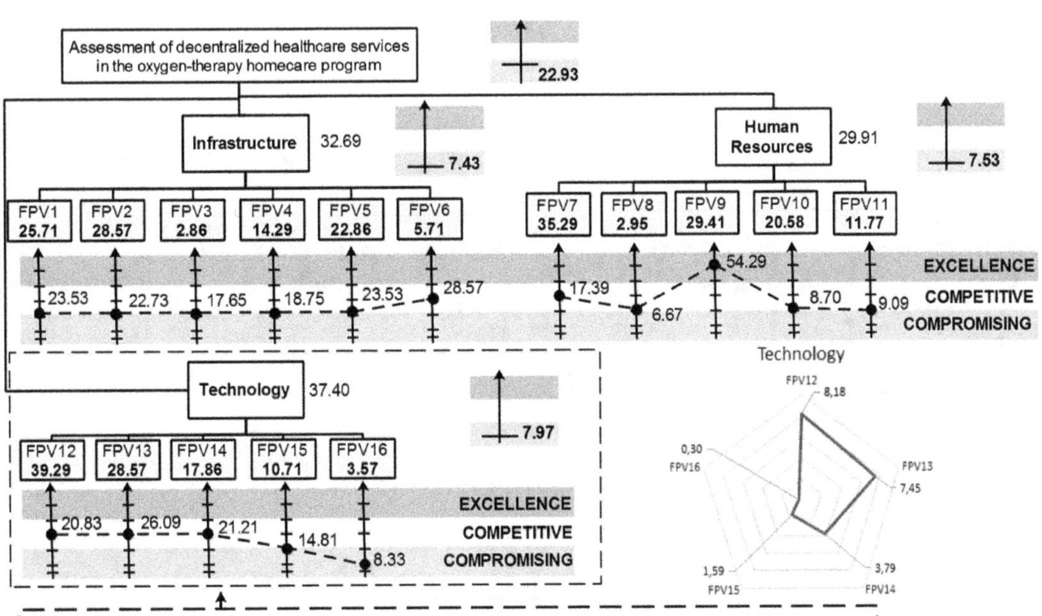

$$V_{Technology} = 0.3929V_{FPV12} + 0.2857V_{FPV13} + 0.1786V_{FPV14} + 0.1071V_{FPV15} + 0.0357V_{FPV16}$$

$$V_{Technology} = 0.3929*20.83 + 0.2857*26.09 + 0.1786*21.21 + 0.1071*14.81 + 0.0357*8.33 = 21.31$$

$$V_{(Technology)} = 0.3740*21.31 = 7.97$$

For the case of DHS6, (Figure 13) the performed assessment consider that in the Infrastructure criterion (14.23), FPV5 had an excellent performance, FPV1, FPV2, FPV4, and FPV6 obtained a competitive performance. FPV3 had the lowest performance.

Regarding to Human Resources criterion (11.79), FPV7 and FPV9 obtained an excellent performance. FPV11 had a competitive performance. FPV8 and FPV10 had the lowest performance. Finally, in the Technology criterion (9.37), FPV14 at the border of competitive - excellent performance, due to the accomplishment of maintenance log in physical document. FPV12, FPV13 and FPV16 obtained a competitive performance, due to satisfy the current requirements with an equipment control log in physical document and implementation of management residues; besides to provide oximeters, portable oxygen, and humidifiers jointly with the oxygen concentrator, BiPAP, and CPAP to the patient. Lastly, FPV15 had the lowest performance, due to do not exists calibration logs, activity performed by the outsourced company. However, FPV3, FPV8, and FPV10 had lowest performance due to lack of indicators related to the services evolution, incomplete technical documents for procedures, and verbal orientation for patients as training method. The score obtained was 35.39 points, which classifies it as a competitive to allow suitable management. Figure 13 additionally depicts the radar chart illustrating the partial scores comparison of the technology criterion obtained with the equation (5).

The same assessment procedure was performed in the others DHS (1 to 5). Table 3 summarize the current impact profile scores of the seven decentralized healthcare services.

Figure 13. Impact profile of criterions with performance values of each controllable feedback variables
Source: Author

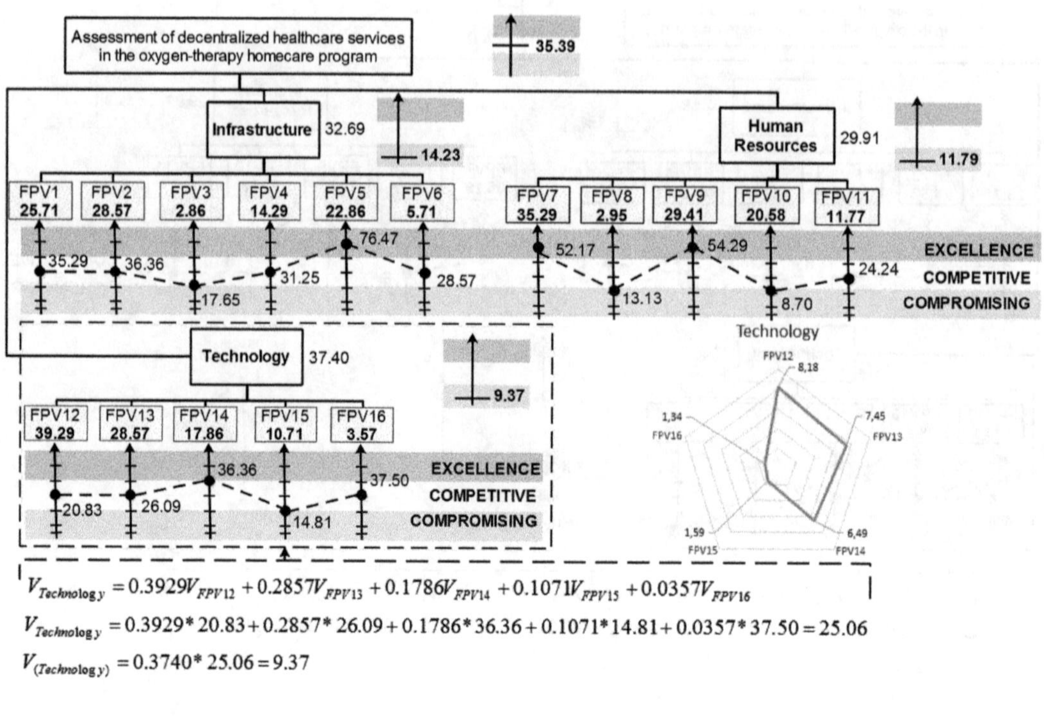

$$V_{Technology} = 0.3929V_{FPV12} + 0.2857V_{FPV13} + 0.1786V_{FPV14} + 0.1071V_{FPV15} + 0.0357V_{FPV16}$$

$$V_{Technology} = 0.3929*20.83+0.2857*26.09+0.1786*36.36+0.1071*14.81+0.0357*37.50=25.06$$

$$V_{(Technology)} = 0.3740*25.06=9.37$$

Table 3. Current impact profile scores of the seven decentralized healthcare services including partial scores in infrastructure, human resources, and technology criterions.

Decentralized Homecare Service – DHS	Performance Values			Impact Profile	Semantic Indicator
	Infrastructure	Human Resources	Technology		
DHS1	17.38	10.30	6.50	34.17	Competitive
DHS2	13.92	6.60	12.62	33.17	Competitive
DHS3	14.14	9.49	13.01	36.94	Competitive
DHS4	3.81	8.54	8.08	20.43	Compromised
DHS5	17.47	9.49	8.36	35.32	Competitive
DHS6	14.23	11.79	9.37	35.39	Competitive
DHS7	7.43	7.53	7.97	22.93	Compromised

Source: (Author)

Figure 14. Standard MCDA modeling language notation of the decision-making process flow
Source: Author

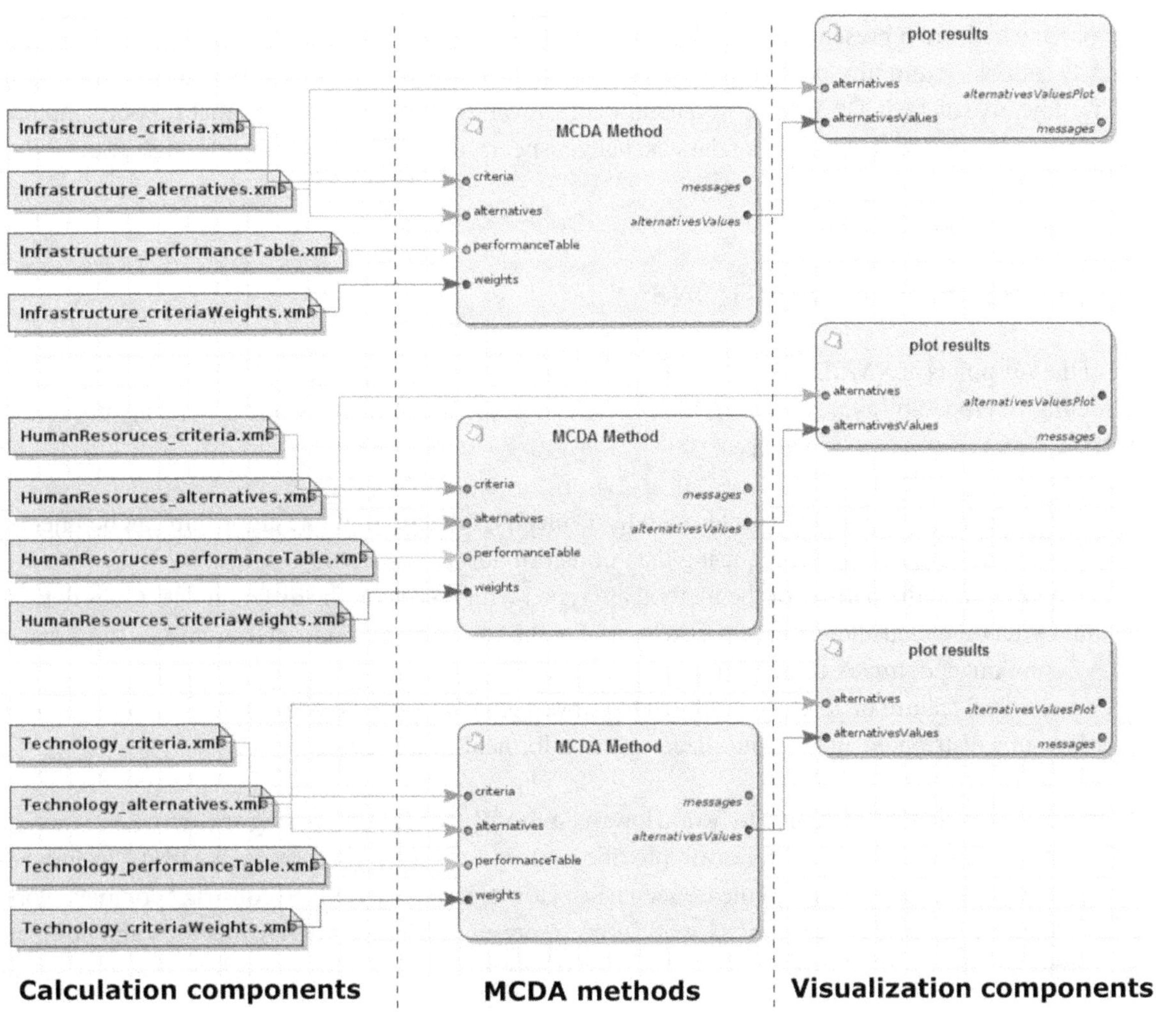

Standardizing the Decision – Making Problem

Towards to standardize the decision-making process, the Universal MCDA Modeling Language (UMCDA-ML) describes and express in a generic way inputs and outputs of a decision analysis workflow. To achieve this, MultiCriteria Decision Analysis data elements in XML (XMCDA) as an instance of UMCDA-ML, represents data and decision-making objects to allow a distributed and interoperable decision-making process. Figure 14 depicts the standardized UMCDA-ML notation for decentralized healthcare services assessment.

UMCDA-ML notation has three fundamental components:

1. Calculation, which consist of aggregation operators and analysis elements (alternative sets, relevant criteria sets, performance matrix sets and criterion weight sets);
2. Methods, which include full MCDA methods;
3. Visualization, which consist of modules for graphical representation of specific input and output data elements.

Abstract description of UMCDA-ML notation in Figure 14 is produced via a detailed XMCDA schema, in which are represented calculation components to allow several MCDA methods interact and be easily callable. Exemplifying, Figure 15 depicts the XMCDA overview of the calculation components.

The objective of XMCDA is to allow a meta-data knowledge base construction that supports interoperable decisions and decision-making data exchange, specifying MCDA concepts through general data structures coded in XML.

FUTURE RESEARCH DIRECTIONS

One of the key points of XMCDA data standard is the possibility of combining various MCDA algorithms, facilitating interoperability, and storing the inputs and outputs of MCDA workflows. This possibility has three direct research consequences:

1. The components available can interoperate. Typically, the output of one algorithm can be injected into other methods without requiring data transformations;
2. The inputs and the outputs of the method are typed with respect to the different data types defined in XMCDA, which allows very precise control of the various algorithms and simplifies the creation of component complex combinations;
3. A powerful feature of XML is exploited to convert XMCDA for the convenient content visualizations in a distributed and decentralized solution for healthcare scenarios.

Design and execution of XMCDA workflows is a useful tool for comparing the outputs of several methods on the same input data. Moreover, provide a unified software platform for XMCDA techniques in distributed and decentralized healthcare scenarios. However, it is possible to construct complex workflows, connect a set of data for various workflows, represent different MCDA methods and compare their outputs.

Figure 15. XMCDA meta-data representation of the decision-making process
Source: Author

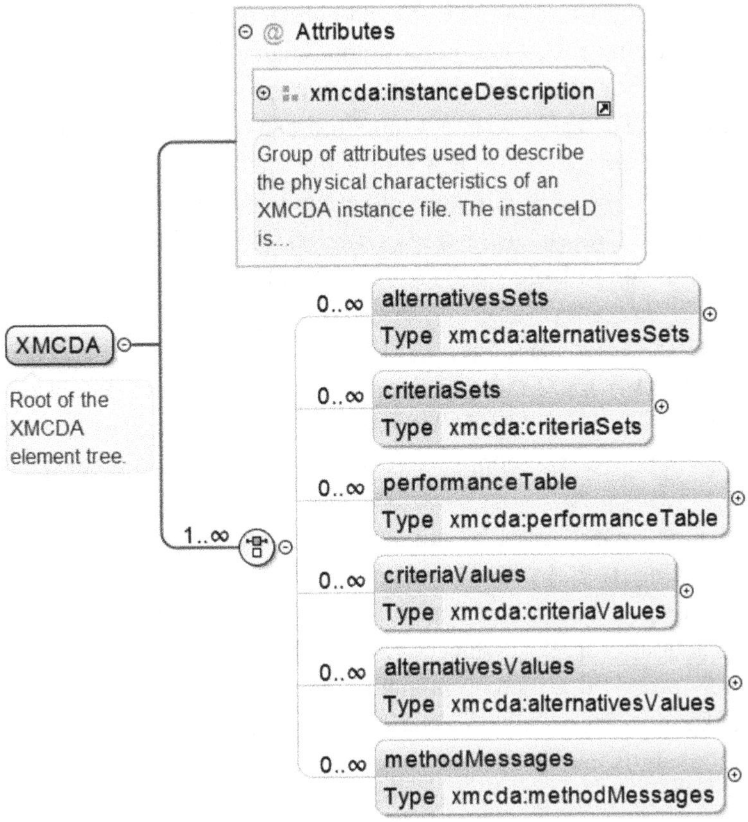

CONCLUSION

This chapter brings the multi-criteria decision-making process as an intervention instrument for a suitable management in homecare service. The results of the MCDA model exposes that two of three basic management DHS (7 and 4) has a global impact profile classified as compromising. In the case of DHS 4, it was the lowest score of the sample (20.43). This score evidence that the infrastructure criterion (3.81) and all its controllable feedback variables are in a compromising condition and require improvement actions. Human resources (8.54) and technology (8.08) criterions, even with a compromising condition, evidence that controllable feedback variables of highest weight (FPV7, FPV10, FPV11, FPV12, FPV13, FPV14 and FPV15), are performed minimal improvement actions.

Regarding to the remaining five DHS, the MCDA model presents current impact profiles classified as competitive. The DHS2 (basic management) has a global impact profile score of 33.14. This score evidence that the human resources criterion (6.60) focus the improvement actions in only one controllable feedback variables of highest weight (FPV7). Infrastructure criterion (13.92) and technology (12.62) evidences similarly, improvement actions in controllable feedback variables of highest weight (FPV5, FPV13).

Concerning to DHS1, has a global impact profile score of 34.17. The score evidence that in technology criterion (6.50) only one controllable feedback variables of highest weight (FPV12) is attended with improvement actions. Infrastructure (17.38) and human resources (10.30) criterions evidences an equivalent contribution, seeing that, three controllable feedback variables of highest weight (FPV1, FPV2, FPV5, FPV7, FPV9, FPV10) are performed with improvement actions.

About DHS6 (35.39) and DHS5 (35.32), they has almost an equivalent global impact profile, however different in some partial assessments. In DHS5 infrastructure criterion (17.47), the difference was in improvement actions in FPV1 and FPV6. On the other hand, human resources criterion (9.49) evidence falling performance only in FPV7 and technology criterion (8.36) evidence falling performance only in FPV14 related to the same controllable feedback variables of highest weight in DHS6 for improvement actions.

Last but not least, DHS3 evidence the highest score of the sample (36.94). The score evidence that infrastructure criterion (14.14) applies improvement actions in three of the controllable feedback variables of highest weight (FPV1, FPV2, FPV5). Human resources (9.49) and technology (13.01) criterions evidences improvement actions in two controllable feedback variables of highest weight (FPV7, FPV9, FPV12, FPV13).

In this manner, changes in delivering health services results in the need for a proper management adjustment of those services. Thus, in this chapter it was proposed multi-criteria decision-making techniques for assess and manage decentralized healthcare services, as an effort of continuous evolution that guides a new focus of action where the distance is not an obstacle to perform the efficient management.

Additionally, it was proposed a methodological approach for management and decision-making, addressing, in particular, the support and integration with decentralized health services. Consequently, multicriteria decision analysis enable everywhere management activities and becomes the backbone where decentralized healthcare services will operate and enhance patient safety, technology reliability and services effectiveness.

Regarding to the homecare program used in the study case is possible to emphasize by the MCDA assessment of the whole sample that the improvement actions are focused on a continuous enhancement of the infrastructure. Although, deficiency in the dimensioning of technological resources, requirements in the patient´s residence for the attendance, and relationship of health professionals with patients and caregivers are highlighted. The fact, that partial assessments of human resources evidence had a lower number of improvement actions, may be due to the support of the primary health teams, and rare training methods for patients and families. In the case of technology, it may be due to the maintenance and calibration of equipment's depends by the outsourced company, as well as, the lack of information concerning with medical devices.

REFERENCES

Abdallah, L. (2005). EverCare Nurse Practitioner Practice Activities: Similarities and Differences across Five Sites. *Journal of the American Academy of Nurse Practitioners*, *17*(9), 355–362. doi:10.1111/j.1745-7599.2005.00063.x PMID:16115114

Boult, C., Karm, L., & Groves, C. (2008). Improving Chronic Care: The "Guided Care" Model. *The Permanente Journal*, 50–54. Retrieved from https://www.ncbi.nlm.nih.gov/pmc/articles/PMC3042340 PMID:21369513

Bouwmeester, C. (2012). The PACE Program: Home-Based Long-Term Care. *The Consultant Pharmacist*, *27*(1), 24–30. doi:10.4140/TCP.n.2012.24 PMID:22231995

Bowen, J., Stevens, D., Sixta, C., Provost, L., Johnson, J., Woods, D., & Wagner, E. (2010). Developing measures of educational change for academic health care teams implementing the chronic care model in teaching practices. *Journal of General Internal Medicine*, *25*(S4), 586–592. doi:10.100711606-010-1358-1 PMID:20737234

Boyd, C., Reider, L., Frey, K., Scharfstein, D., Leff, B., Wolff, J., ... Boult, C. (2010). The Effects of Guided Care on the Perceived Quality of Health Care for Multi-morbid Older Persons: 18-Month Outcomes from a Cluster-Randomized Controlled Trial. *Journal of General Internal Medicine*, *25*(3), 235–242. doi:10.100711606-009-1192-5 PMID:20033622

Bruin, S., Versnel, N., Lemmens, L., Molema, C., Schellevis, F., Nijpels, G., & Baan, C. (2012). Comprehensive care programs for patients with multiple chronic conditions: A systematic literature review. *Health Policy (Amsterdam)*, *107*(2-3), 108–145. doi:10.1016/j.healthpol.2012.06.006 PMID:22884086

Coleman, K., Austin, B., Brach, C., & Wagner, E. (2009). Evidence On The Chronic Care Model In The New Millennium. *Health Affairs*, *28*(1), 75–85. doi:10.1377/hlthaff.28.1.75 PMID:19124857

Dorr, D., Wilcox, A., Burns, L., Brunker, C., Narus, S., & Clayton, P. (2006). Implementing a Multidisease Chronic Care Model in Primary Care Using People and Technology. *Disease Management*, *9*(1), 1–15. doi:10.1089/dis.2006.9.1 PMID:16466338

e Costa, C. A. B., & Vansnick, J. C. (1999). The MACBETH Approach: Basic Ideas, Software, and an Application. In N. Meskens, & M. Roubens (Eds.), Advances in Decision Analysis. Mathematical Modelling: Theory and Applications (pp. 131-157). The Netherlands: Springer. doi:10.1007/978-94-017-0647-6_9

e Costa, C. A. B., & Vansnick, JEnsslin, C., & Corrêa, L., C. (1999). Decision support systems in action: Integrated application in a multicriteria decision aid process. *European Journal of Operational Research*, *113*(2), 315–335. doi:10.1016/S0377-2217(98)00219-7

e Costa, C. A. B., & Vansnick, J. C. (1995). General Overview of the Macbeth Approach. In P. Pardalos, Y. Siskos, & C. Zopounidis (Eds.), *Advances in Multicriteria Analysis. Nonconvex Optimization and Its Applications* (pp. 93–100). Boston, MA: Springer; doi:10.1007/978-1-4757-2383-0_6

Elissen, A., Steuten, L., Lemmens, L., Drewes, H., Lemmens, K., Meeuwissen, J., ... Vrijhoef, H. (2013). Meta-analysis of the effectiveness of chronic care management for diabetes: Investigating heterogeneity in outcomes. *Journal of Evaluation in Clinical Practice*, 753–762. doi:10.1111/j.1365-2753.2012.01817.x PMID:22372830

Felder, R., Alwan, M., & Zhang, M. (2008). *Systems Engineering Approach to Medical Automation*. Norwood, MA: Artech House.

Figueira, J., Greco, S., & Ehrogott, M. (2005). *Multiple Criteria Decision Analysis: State of the Art Surveys*. New York: Springer; doi:10.1007/b100605

Fraser, A., Howard, M., Alder, J., Boobier, S., Burke, V., & Chambers, J. (2005). Across cultures implementing the Evercare model. 16-19. doi:10.7748/nop2005.10.17.7.16.c2388

Hirth, V., Baskins, J., & Dever-Bumba, M. (2009). Program of all-inclusive care (PACE): Past, present, and future. *Journal of the American Medical Directors Association*, *10*(3), 155–160. doi:10.1016/j.jamda.2008.12.002 PMID:19233054

Isern, D., Marin, L., Valls, A., & Moreno, A. (2010). The Unbalanced Linguistic Ordered Weighted Averaging operator. *International Conference on Fuzzy Systems* (pp. 1-8). Barcelona, Spain: IEEE. 10.1109/FUZZY.2010.5584199

Lemmens, K., Lemmens, L., Boom, J., Drewes, H., Meeuwissen, J., Steuten, L., ... Baan, C. (2013). Chronic care management for patients with COPD: A critical review of available evidence. *Journal of Evaluation in Clinical Practice*, 734–752. doi:10.1111/j.1365-2753.2011.01805.x PMID:22133473

Marafon, A., Ensslin, L., Oliveira, R., & Ensslin, S. (2015). The effectiveness of multi-criteria decision aid methodology. *European Journal of Innovation Management*, *18*(1), 86–109. doi:10.1108/EJIM-10-2013-0106

Nuño, R. (2009). Atención innovadora a las condiciones crónicas: más necesaria que nunca. Revista de Innovación Sanitaria y Atención Integrada, 1-8. Retrieved from https://www.researchgate.net/publication/33544067_Atencion_innovadora_a_las_condiciones_cronicas_mas_necesaria_que_nunca

Panda, B., & Thakur, H. P. (2016). Decentralization and health system performance - a focused review of dimensions, difficulties, and derivatives in India. *BMC Health Services Research*, 1–14. doi:10.118612913-016-1784-9 PMID:28185593

Rich, M. (1999). The PACE model: Description and impressions of a capitated model of long-term care for the elderly. *Care Management Journals*, *1*(1), 62–70. doi:10.1891/1521-0987.1.1.62 PMID:10835798

Selevan, J., Kindermann, D., Pines, J., & Fields, W. (2015). What Accountable Care Organizations Can Learn from Kaiser Permanente California's Acute Care Strategy. *Population Health Management, 233-236*. doi:10.1089/pop.2014.0157 PMID:25856631

Snoddon, J. (2010). *Case management of long-term conditions. Principles and practice for nurses*. Oxford, UK: Wiley-Blackwell. doi:10.1002/9781444319866

Wagner, E. H. (2019). Organizing Care for Patients With Chronic Illness Revisited. Milbank Quarterly Classics, 659-664. doi:10.1111/1468-0009.12416

Wagner, E. H. (2011). Counterpoint: chronic illness and primary care. Medical care, 49(11), 973-975.

Wallace, P. (2005). Physician involvement in disease management as part of the CCM. *Health Care Financing Review*, 19–31. Retrieved from https://www.ncbi.nlm.nih.gov/pmc/articles/PMC4194903/ PMID:17288075

Wallace, P. (2005a). The Care Management Institute: Making the Right Thing Easier to Do. *The Permanente Journal,* 56-57. doi:10.7812/TPP/05-026

World Health Organization - WHO. (2007). Decentralization in health care. Strategies and outcomes. New York: McGraw-Hill. Retrieved from http://www.euro.who.int/en/publications/abstracts/decentralization-in-health-care.-strategies-and-outcomes-2007

Xu, Z. (2013). *Linguistic Decision Making: Theory and Methods.* Beijing, China: Science Press Beijing; doi:10.1007/978-3-642-29440-2

ADDITIONAL READING

Belton, V., & Stewart, T. (2002). *Multiple criteria decision analysis: an integrated approach.* Boston: Kluwer; doi:10.1007/978-1-4615-1495-4

Dolan, J. (2010). Multi-Criteria Clinical Decision Support: A Primer on the Use of Multiple-Criteria Decision-Making Methods to Promote Evidence-Based, Patient-Centered Healthcare. *The Patient: Patient-Centered Outcomes Research,* 229-248. doi:10.2165/11539470-000000000-00000

Dong, Y., & Xu, J. (2019). *Linguistic Decision Making: Numerical Scale Model and Consistency-Driven Methodology.* Singapore: Springer; doi:10.1007/978-981-13-2916-6

Hansen, P., & Devlin, N. (2019). *Multi-Criteria Decision Analysis (MCDA) in Healthcare Decision-Making.* Oxford: Oxford Research Enciclopedias; doi:10.1093/acrefore/9780190625979.013.98

Lasorsa, I., Padoano, E., Marceglia, S., & Accardo, A. (2018). Multi-criteria decision analysis for the assessment of non-clinical hospital services: Methodology and case study. *Operations Research for Health Care,* 1–8. doi:10.1016/j.orhc.2018.08.002

Marsh, K., Lanitis, T., Neasham, D., Orfanos, P., & Caro, J. (2014). Assessing the Value of Healthcare Interventions Using Multi-Criteria Decision Analysis: A Review of the Literature. *PharmacoEconomics, 32*(4), 345–36. doi:10.100740273-014-0135-0 PMID:24504851

Mühlbacher, A., & Kaczynski, A. (2016). Making Good Decisions in Healthcare with Multi-Criteria Decision Analysis: The Use, Current Research and Future Development of MCDA. *Applied Health Economics and Health Policy, 14*(1), 29–40. doi:10.100740258-015-0203-4 PMID:26519081

Weernink, M., Janus, S., van Til, J., Raisch, D., van Manen, J., & IJzerman, M. (2014). A Systematic Review to Identify the Use of Preference Elicitation Methods in Healthcare Decision Making. *Pharmaceutical Medicine, 28*(4), 175–185. doi:10.100740290-014-0059-1

KEY TERMS AND DEFINITIONS

Decentralized Healthcare Service: Authority delegation for planning, decision-making and management, from higher to lower health organizational levels that explores a variety of applications of patient-centered delivery models in the way of delivery care that is effective, inclusive, flexible, and in tune with the current era of preventive and evidence-based healthcare.

Healthcare Service Assessment: Process for determining and addressing the gaps between the current situation, and the desired one. Identifies and defines requirements with regard to existing facilities and infrastructures, long-term plan of use, performance of medical equipment users, delivery of services within the context of health system capabilities and service delivery priorities.

Healthcare Service Management: Quantitative and qualitative aspects to improve quality and efficiency, implement new technology, and ensure compliance with changing regulations.

Home Care: short and long-term supportive care provided at home, including medical equipment for monitoring, by healthcare professionals or by other caregivers to ensure the activities related to hospice care or rehabilitative therapies.

Medical Device: Apparatus or machine that is used in the prevention, diagnosis or treatment of disease to measure, restore, correct or modify the structure or function of the body for some health purpose.

Medical Equipment: Medical device that require calibration, maintenance, repair, user training, and decommissioning. Used for purposes of diagnosis and treatment of disease or rehabilitation following disease or injury. It can be used either alone or in combination with any accessory, consumable.

XMCDA: Data standard that represents multicriteria decision analysis elements in an interoperable and reusable structure to develop and test a given problem instance on various algorithms of a decision aid process.

Chapter 6
Multicriteria Decision Support Model for Selection of Tinplate Suppliers:
A Case Study in CAN Company

Rafaela Ribeiro Pinho
Polytechnic of Porto, Portugal

Ana Paula Lopes
https://orcid.org/0000-0003-1603-6959
Polytechnic of Porto, Portugal

ABSTRACT

The evaluation and selection of suppliers has been an issue of great strategic importance over time. In this way, a structured evaluation is crucial, considering several criteria. This work reviews several multi-criteria decision support methodologies explored in the literature to solve the supplier evaluation process based on CAN company specifications, strategies, and requirements. Considering the characteristics of each supplier and a set of criteria with different weights, the AHP method and the PROMETHEE method are applied to establish a ranking according to the performance in the selected criteria. In addition, to help the company make the best decision, an analysis of ranking stability is performed by varying the weights assigned to the criteria. The study and models developed were easy to apply and understand, meeting the specified objectives.

INTRODUCTION

With the constant changes and demands of the market, the competition between supply chains has assumed global importance and an increasingly aggressive stance, requiring companies to make greater efforts to develop new management tools. Regardless of the sector in which companies are inserted,

DOI: 10.4018/978-1-7998-2216-5.ch006

the activities related to the process of selection and evaluation of suppliers, are of extreme importance (Alencar, Almeida, & Mota, 2007).

The CAN company is a leading global company in the production of consumer goods packaging, where its main raw material is tinplate, which is acquired from several suppliers around the world. In this way, not being responsible for the production of this raw material, the evaluation and selection of suppliers is one of the critical activities so that the company obtains a competitive advantage.

The delivery of materials with quality problems, long lead times, high acquisition costs, among other things, can cause losses to the company. It is therefore extremely important to have a portfolio of reliable suppliers with positive characteristics.

Usually, suppliers tend to have similar characteristics to their competitors, which does not allow their evaluation and selection to be a simple process. In this way, a thorough evaluation of the criteria in supplier selection becomes crucial. However, this task frequently involves multiple criteria (quantitative and qualitative), which present different forms of measurement, thus being a multicriteria decision problem (Wang, 2010).

According to (de Boer, Labro, & Morlacchi, 2001), in industrial companies, as in the case of the company under study, the weight of purchases represents between 50% and 90% of its total turnover, which makes purchasing operations a determining factor for profit maximization.

In order to assist analysts and decision-makers in situations where there is a conflict of interests, considering a set of criteria, the Multicriteria Decision Analysis (MCDA) arise, which aim to help in choosing the best alternative (Gomes, Pereira, & Lins, 2002).

Applying two methods to support multi-criteria decision making, the **AHP** (Analytic Hierarchy Process) and **PROMETHEE** (Preference Ranking Organization Method for Enrichment Evaluation), the main intention is to obtain a ranking of the best suppliers. The application of both methods will allow to enrich the conclusions obtained, since, according to (Bruno, Esposito, Genovese, & Passaro, 2009), while the AHP approach structures the problem hierarchically, comparing judgments made by the decision makers (between alternatives and criteria) on a par and synthesizes in a simple way the priorities, the PROMETHEE method seeks to order potential alternatives by comparing them by pair, establishing a degree of preference, where the importance of each criterion is determined by the decision maker, by assigning a weight to it (Almeida, 2011).

The chapter is organized in 3 sections. Initially it addresses concepts, problems in supplier selection and multicriteria decision analysis. Subsequently, the methodologies of the criteria and the AHP and PROMETHEE methods will be deepened. Finally, both methods are applied in the evaluation of the suppliers of the CAN company in order to establish a ranking and to conclude which suppliers best fit the company's requirements.

BACKGROUND

1. Selection of Suppliers

The selection of suppliers should consider customer needs and the ability of the company has to meet those needs. Thus, it is considered that the initial point to start the process of production and distribution of a product, begins with the supplier (Sonmez, 2006). As stated by (Azadfallah, 2016; de Santis, Golliat, & de Aguiar, 2017; Rodrigues Lima-Junior & Ribeiro Carpinetti, 2016), supplier selection can be defined as a decision making process by which possible suppliers are review, evaluated and selected to become part of the company's supply chain.

According to (Mendes, 2013), supplier selection encompasses a range of variables that serve to filter the requirements to be met in accordance with the supply chain management process. It is increasingly intended to create a lasting relationship with the supplier, promoting trust and greater control over the production process, with the aim of creating barriers for new competitors (Mendes, 2013).

The problem in the selection of suppliers arises when a process of purchase of raw material is initiated, resorting to the current suppliers or the search of new suppliers (Cunha, 2008). According to (Dias, 2015), it is noted that there are high costs in the purchase of goods and, therefore, the company should consider the selection decision of suppliers based on several criteria. The supplier to be chosen must meet the necessary requirements to obey, in the agreed place, the desired quality and quantity.

The significance of the supplier selection comes from both external and internal aspects. Concerning the former, over the past few decades, supplier selection has gained even more importance due to the global markets and the increasing of competitive pressure. The growth in the number of competitors have force the companies to focus on core competences and to outsource less lucrative activities to suppliers (Ortiz-Barrios, Kucukaltan, Carvajal-Tinoco, Neira-Rodado, & Jiménez, 2017).

Therefore, competition has become a problem of supply chains rather than companies (Azadfallah, 2016). Suppliers have turn out to be key elements to acquire the products of higher quality in the required amount and time, at a cheap cost, and with the satisfaction of customer (Sarkar, Pratihar, & Sarkar, 2018; Valipour Parkouhi & Safaei Ghadikolaei, 2017). In this situation, supplier selection have emerged as a critical decision and buyer-supplier relationship have become more strategic and based on close collaboration and sustainability (Wetzstein, Hartmann, Benton jr., & Hohenstein, 2016).

The better the relationship between the company and the supplier, the more effective the entire production and distribution process of the products will be in the competitive environment that companies face. It is also a competitive advantage that becomes increasingly valued.

In this way, the company can operate more effectively and use the Lean and JIT philosophy (Ohno, 1997). Based on (Ho, Xu, & Dey, 2010), it is confirmed that the best choice of the supplier generates impact on the costs, performance and competitiveness of the company. This selection is considered reliable when considering quantitative and qualitative criteria.

According to (de Boer et al., 2001), the selection of suppliers is divided into two types: pre-qualification and decision. The supplier prequalification method encompasses qualitative methods, cluster analysis, Data Envelopment Analysis (DEA), linear weighting, and cost of ownership. The author also argues that the definition of the problem, the formulation and qualification of the criteria strongly influence the results in the choice of supplier.

The definition of the problem consists of selecting new suppliers, turning to usual suppliers, or producing in-house. After this filter, it is formulated the criteria that will satisfy the needs of the company. Subsequently, it will be the qualification phase that requires several steps for a method of elimination if the alternatives do not satisfy the selection rule. Once the qualification phase is identified, the final choice is based on ordering the suppliers and selecting them (de Boer et al., 2001).

The selection process, according to (Sonmez, 2006), is divided into two components:

- Evaluation and assessment process: identification of the criteria for scale creation and determination of the best and worst results. An attribute of the criterion can be subdivided into sub-attributes;

- Aggregation of evaluation in decision making: it uses scales based on the attributes previously indicated.

2. Multicriteria Decision Analysis (MCDA)

According to (Anderson, Sweeney, Williams, Camm, & Martin, 2011), problem solving integrates steps that are associated with the decision-making process. As shown in Figure 1, once the problem is identified and the alternatives and the criteria to be considered are identified, an evaluation is required that will aim at choosing an alternative. These phases are not only part of the problem-solving steps but are also associated with decision-making.

In everyday life, in fact they are considered not only an objective, criterion or point of view in decision making. In this sense, the multicriteria analysis serves as support in developing appropriate methodologies for, in the various situations, with multiple conflicting factors to be considered simultaneously, the option for an alternative in specific or classification/evaluation is simpler (Figueira, Greco, & Ehrogott, 2005).

As a tool to support decision-making, the multicriteria analysis emerged in the 1960s. In order to support organizations to make decisions that best suit their needs, even considering a number of criteria, the Multi-criteria Decision Making or Multi-criteria Decision Analysis presents a set of methods (Carmo, Neto, & Dutra, 2011; L. Ensslin, Giffhorn, R. Ensslin, Petri, & Vianna, 2010).

What differs from the multicriteria approach of traditional approaches to operational research is the concept of subjectivity that the multicriteria approach introduces (Costa, Brazil, & Oliveira, 2003). The same criterion can be analysed in different ways, depending on the decision maker that is evaluating, thus involving the subjectivity of the agents that are part of it.

Thus, the purpose of this analysis is to provide the decision maker with the best solution or recommendation among a finite set of alternatives, while being evaluated under different points of view, or in other words, different criteria. Nevertheless, and as (A. T. Almeida, 2011) alert, there is no solution that is simultaneously optimal for all criteria. Unlike the conventional techniques of Operational Research that are oriented towards the optimization of an objective function, the intention of the methods of multicriteria analysis is to find a solution that is more appropriate to the preferences of the decision maker.

There are several solutions to this problem that include methods such as Weighted Sum Model (WSM), Analytical Hierarchy Processes (AHP), Analytic Network Process (ANP), Data Envelopment Analysis (DEA), approaches such as PROMETHEE which consists in organization of preference ranking for

Figure 1. Relationship between problem-solving and decision-making
(Adapted from (Anderson et al., 2011))

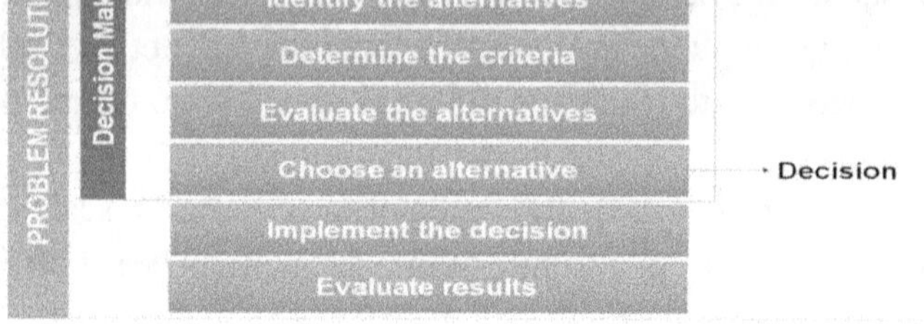

enrichment evaluation, approaches based on Artificial Neural Networks (ANN), simple techniques for assigning multiple attributes (SMART), among others (Agarwal, Sahai, Mishra, Bag, & Singh, 2011).

According to (Mendes, 2013), multicriteria techniques can be subdivided into four categories:

- **Multi-attribute utility methods:** ANP e AHP (try to assign a value to each alternative)
- ***Outranking*:** ELECTRE e PROMETHEE (construct a binary preference relation for the whole potential of alternatives)
- **Compromise Methods**: TOPSIS e VIKOR (compromise solution is the closest solution to the ideal and evidences an agreement based on mutual concessions)
- **Other methods:** SMART e DEMATEL (sum of exact weights to generate rating indices)
- Based on (Kumar et al., 2017), multicriteria can be classified into three types:
    - Miscellaneous models: NAIADE
    - Utility-based model: SAW, AHP, MAUT
    - Model via prevalence: ELECTRE e PROMETHEE

According to these authors, this classification is complex since it covers several factors, such as social, economic or the selection of stakeholders. This procedure can be considered ambiguous since the objectives can create different solutions at different moments, according to the priority defined by the agents in the decision making.

The Hierarchical Analysis method, also known as AHP, allows a hierarchical structure to be defined, through several criteria and multiple decision making (Hatcher, 2008). According to (Forsberg, Mooz, & Cotterman, 2005), the decision-making process is easily structured, since to each criterion and alternative is applied a process to calculate its relative importance, allowing to obtain the best general alternative.

Based on (Roy & Vincke, 1981), the outranking methods are composed of two phases: the design of one or several prevalence relations over the alternatives, and later, in the analysis of the consequent relations in function of the formalization of the problem. The construction of a prevalence relationship implies a dominance relationship, in order to facilitate the resolution of the decision problem.

Based on (Terrientes, 2015), a prevalence relation is a binary relation of "*S*" defined in the set of alternatives A, such that, *aSb* translates into "*a* is at least as good as *b*", that is, *a* is not worse than *b*, where *a* and *b* are decision criteria. This method is successful because it is based on natural realistic assumptions inspired by the theory of social choice and intends to find the set of the best alternatives in comparison to the others. Therefore, the outranking methods do not consider strong assumptions about preference between alternatives, however, are rare cases in which a hierarchy of criteria is considered.

The PROMETHEE method consists in the construction of a value classification relationship, in which the decision maker establishes a weight for each criterion that increases according to its importance (Almeida & Costa, 2002).

METHODOLOGY

1. Definition of Decision Criteria

Over the years, the criteria cover aspects that go beyond the financial aspect, with an increase in the number of qualitative and intangible criteria, such as quality, delivery, performance, among others. With this addition of variables, complexity increases in the selection (Mendes, 2013). According to (Sonmez, 2006), the decision criteria can be the demographic characteristics of the purchasing managers, the size of the company, the acquisition strategy, the existence of a supply chain strategy and the type of products purchased. Other authors, as identified by (Mendes, 2013), Other authors, as identified by Mendes, determine new criteria such as cost of raw material, quality, service, experience, risk factors, knowledge of information technology, availability, environment, etc.

Based on (Dias, 2015), the criteria must meet the following requirements: easy to interpret, simple, clear, comparable, precise, universal and easily organized by hierarchy. After validation of the criteria, it is important to pre-evaluate them, to confirm the need to redefine and reduce the list of criteria to improve the decision-making process. It is also recommended that the number of criteria be identified in a range of three to seven, not exceeding nine to maintain consistency, simplicity and avoid abandonment, since too many criteria do not allow an individual assessment of the behavior of each (Dias, 2015).

The selected criteria were distributed as shown in Table 1.

The criteria referred to above will now be detailed in terms of definition.

- **Quality of Material** – the material delivered by the supplier must meet the minimum quality requirements set by the company. With more and more demanding customers, it is crucial to ensure the quality of products. In this way, a company that favours high quality parameters will achieve a strategic advantage over its competitors. In the company under study, in order to define the tinplate in terms of quality, the following criteria are generally considered: the quality, hardness and appearance of the tin. Being a qualitative criterion, it was necessary to transform qualitative data into quantifiable data, to be analysed and interpreted later.
- **Cost Acquisition** – this quantitative criterion refers to the cost that the company has to bear to acquire the raw material, which is considered in net terms and by Coil. Coil is the term assigned to a tin sheet coil. Being a cost to the company, it is intended to minimize it. It is necessary to find a balance between cost and benefit. Once there is a lot of suppliers in the market, the price of this becomes crucial in the negotiation and choice of suppliers.

Table 1. Definition of criteria

Supplier	Quality of Material	Cost Acquisition (€)	Logistic Lead Time (days)	Attendance Capacity	Certification	Flexibility	Financial Stability
1	4	909	56	3	2	3	4
2	4	954	56	4	2	3	4
3	2	630	110	1	1	1	2
4	3	801	70	2	2	3	3
5	3	783	110	1	1	1	3
6	2	774	110	1	1	1	4
7	2	765	110	1	1	1	4
8	3	918	70	2	2	2	3
9	2	792	110	1	1	1	4
10	3	936	110	1	1	1	3

(Source: Own)

- **Logistic Lead time–** lead time is the period of time it takes from the time the customer places an order to the delivery of the final product. In this way, the time it takes each supplier to complete the production of tinplate is crucial to ensure that the company can guarantee deliveries to customers on time in full (OTIF).
- **Attendance Capacity –** this criterion refers to the supplier's production capacity. In other words, the supplier's ability to respond to volumes ordered by the company. In a win-win logic, it is in the interest of both parties that, when the company orders a certain amount of material, the supplier can deliver it in full and not only partially.
- **Certification –** currently, certifications are part of the company's strategy as being indispensable. For this criterion there are two possible results: the supplier can be certified by the European standard *EN-10202-2001*, assuming the value 2; or Japanese standard *JIS G 3303_2008,* assuming the value 1. The European standard *EN-10202-2001* (CEN national Members, 2001) was drawn up by the Technical Committee ECISS/TC and specifies the requirements that must be met for products such as tinplate, specifying the quality standards, size, tolerances and specific tests to be performed. According to the experience of those responsible for purchasing department of this company, the European standard is more stringent and meets the requirements of conformity defined by the company, being preferred.
- **Flexibility –** the concept of flexibility is considered, in this context, such as the degree of ease with which the supplier, in the face of an unexpected or unforeseeable need on the part of the customers to whom it supplies, can anticipate the delivery of the raw material.
- **Financial Stability –** according to (Schinasi, 2004), the concept of financial stability is broad, including the role of financial infrastructure, institutions themselves and markets. In order to measure this criterion, aspects such as the number of factories it owns, the volume of invoicing and the number of responsible employees are considered.

2. Multicriteria Decision Methods

AHP Method: Analytic Hierarchy Process

The Analytic Hierarchy Process, better known as the AHP method, was developed by Thomas L. Saaty in the 1970s with the purpose of giving aid in making complex decisions, based on mathematics and psychology (Saaty, 1980).

As a methodology to measure, structure and synthesize a problem, the AHP method is widely used in multicriteria environments (Forman & Gass, 2001). According to these authors, the method comprises three functions:

1. The **measurement** through a scale defined by (T. L. Saaty, 1980) of positive and real numbers, ranging from 1 to 9, making possible the association to each element of a certain degree of importance, obtained through the binary comparison between the factors at various levels;
2. The **hierarchical structuring** of complexity, in an environment where there are several factors that are equally relevant in the decision making, allowing to order the problem in hierarchical levels, according to the characteristics of each element;

3. **Synthesize**, that is, combine the multiplicity of factors in a hierarchy. Based on the weight of the factors and in the preferences of the decision makers, to obtain a final ranking with the classification of the alternatives.

In this way, the AHP method allows to structure a complex problem in a hierarchy, comprising at least three levels: objectives, criteria and alternatives (Saaty, 2008).

According to (Saaty, 1991, 2008), the application of the AHP method is summarized in four steps:

- Define the problem, establish the objectives and the type of knowledge that is needed;
- Hierarchical decomposition of the decision problem: it comprises a higher level, the general objective, following the criteria to be taken into account in the decision problem, and finally, a last level that is represented by the possible alternatives. The criteria may also be subdivided into sub-criteria, depending on the decision problem to be addressed.
- Once the logical hierarchy is constructed, a set of square matrices is constructed, where comparisons are made alongside the criteria and the alternatives, whose objective is to establish a relative importance among the elements. In a first step, for each criterion a comparison is made in pairs. Subsequently, in a second stage, the alternatives for each criterion are compared. To convert human perception into numbers, the Fundamental scale of Saaty is used (Table 2).

As shown in Table 2, the fundamental scale of (TL Saaty, 1980), ranges from 1 to 9, where the value 1 expresses indifference in the selection of one element in relation to another, that is, one is equally preferable in relation to, and, on the other hand, the value 9 indicates that one element is absolutely preferable in relation to another. It should also be noted that one of the assumptions made is reciprocity in the comparisons made, that is, if, for example, it is considered by the decision-maker that the comparison of pairs from criterion A to criterion B assumes the value 3, then the comparison of criterion B pairs in relation to criterion A assumes the ratio of 1 to 3 (T. L. Saaty, 1980).

Table 2. Fundamental scale of Saaty

Intensity of Importance	Definition	Explanation
1	Equal importance	Two activities contribute equally to the objective.
3	Moderate importance of one over the other	Experience and judgment slightly favor one activity over another.
5	Strong or essential importance	Experience and judgment strongly favor one activity over another.
7	Very strong or demonstrated importance	An activity is strongly favored and Its dominance demonstrated in practice.
9	Extreme importance	The evidence favoring one activity over another is of the highest possible order of affirmation.
2, 4, 6, 8	Intermediate values between the two adjacent judgments	When you are looking for a compromise condition between two settings.
Reciprocals	If activity *i* has one of the above numbers assigned to it when compared with activity *j*, then *j* has the reciprocal value when compared with *i*.	

(adapted from (T. L. Saaty, 1980))

According to (T. L. Saaty, 1980) in the elaboration of the square matrices or decision matrices, where i represents the line number of the matrix, j the columns and a_{ij} represents the comparison between criteria and alternatives A_i and A_j, the following rules must be respected:

$$A = \begin{bmatrix} a_{11} & \cdots & a_{1n} \\ \vdots & \ddots & \vdots \\ a_{n1} & \cdots & a_{nn} \end{bmatrix} \quad (1)$$

where,

1. $a_{ij} = \frac{1}{a_{ji}}$, so, if $a_{ij} = k$ then $a_{ji} = \frac{1}{k}$ for all $k>0$;
2. $a_{ii}=1$ for all i. That is, any criterion compared to itself assumes equal importance in the fundamental scale.

Based on (T. L. Saaty, 1991), subsequently the decision matrices are normalized in order to obtain the relative weights (w), this normalized matrix being defined by:

$$A' = \left[a'_{ij}\right] \quad (2)$$

where, $a'_{ij} = \frac{a_{ij}}{\sum_{k=1}^{n} a_{ik}}$ for $1 \leq i \leq n$, and $1 \leq j \leq n$.

Normalized to the matrix, in order to determine the relative weight of each alternative, the average value in each line is calculated, being determined by (T. L. Saaty, 1991):

$$W = \left[w_k\right] \quad (3)$$

where, $w_k = \frac{\sum_{k=1}^{n} a'_{ij}}{n}$ for $1 \leq i \leq n$, e $1 \leq j \leq n$.

Since a_{ij} are values that are based on subjective judgments, it means that the values they assume may have a deviation from the ideal ratio, and it is crucial that, in order to ascertain if the propositions made are minimally plausible, be measured the consistency of the matrices (T. L. Saaty, 1991).

If $A=[a_{ij}]$ is a matrix of $n \times n$ positive elements, then $a_{ij} = a_{ji}^{-1}$, such that, A is consistent, if and only if, the eigenvectors $\lambda_{max} \geq n$.

Thus, to measure consistency, we will base two axioms (T. L. Saaty, 1991):

- There exist eigenvectors λ_i, $i=1,2,\ldots,n$, such that $AX=\lambda X$ (where X is a vector of weights).

If the matrix A is consistent, then all the eigenvectors assume a value equal to 0, with the exception of one that will assume a value n, the maximum value of λ_i;

- If the diagonal of matrix A assumes values with a_{ij}=1 and considering that A is consistent, then the largest eigenvectors λ_{max} with small variations of a_{ij} will remain close to n and the remaining eigenvectors close to 0.

Thus, it is necessary to determine the proper vector w of weights that obeys the following equation:

$$Aw = \lambda_{max} w \tag{4}$$

The eigenvectors of weights w will determine the disposition by level of relevance of the elements corresponding to matrix A, since it considers the actual weights given to the elements that were being compared.

Finally, in order to evaluate the proximity between λ_{max} and n, that is, to verify whether the evaluations were consistent or not, it is necessary to calculate the Consistency Ratio (CR) which correlates the Consistency Index (CI) with the Random Consistency Index (RI), and is given by the following expression:

$$CR = \frac{CI}{RI} \tag{5}$$

The Consistency Index (CI) s obtained by the following formula (T. L. Saaty, 1991):

$$CI = \frac{\lambda_{max} - n}{n - 1} \tag{6}$$

where, n is the number of elements (criteria or alternatives).

The values for the Random Consistency Index are obtained from Table 3.

According to (Saaty, 1990), the value of CR, to indicate consistency, can take as maximum value 0.10. However, if the result is greater than this value, the evaluation process must be repeated to establish consistency for acceptable values.

- Finally, in order to establish priorities (that is, to define a global ranking), use the precedencies previously obtained in the comparisons.

Table 3. The RI values

Matrix Size	1	2	3	4	5	6	7	8	9	10
RI	0	0	0,58	0,9	1,12	1,24	1,32	1,41	1,45	1,49

(adapted from (Saaty, 1987))

Method PROMETHEE: Preference Ranking Organization Method for Enrichment Evaluation

The PROMETHEE method is based on the ordering of a finite set of actions, where a given weight is assigned to each criterion, taking into account its importance. Thus, preference is calculated by combining pairs of alternatives, considering the deviation between two alternatives in a single criterion. This means that the higher the deviation, the higher the preference (Morte, 2013). (Rezaei-kelidbari, Homayounfar, & Foumani, 2016) argue that this is a method for a finite set of actions that will be classified and selected among the criteria, which may generate conflict. It is quite simple to apply comparatively with the other methods for analysis of multiple criteria.

PROMETHEE I and II, were the first of this family of methods to be developed by Jean-Pierre Brans, having been presented for the first time in 1982 (Brans & Mareschal, 2005).

Since then, other methods of the family have been continuously developed, as illustrated in Table 4.

According to (A. T. Almeida, 2011), in the first stage a weight *w* is established for each criterion, which reflects its relative importance. From this point it is possible to obtain a degree of preference that the criterion *a* has on *b*, for each pair of alternatives through the following expression:

$$\pi\left(a,b\right)=\sum_{i=1}^{n}w_iP_i\left(a,b\right) \tag{7}$$

where,

$$\sum_{i=1}^{n}w_i=1 \tag{8}$$

Table 4. PROMETHEE family of methods

Method	Problematic	Characteristic
PROMETHEE I	Choice	Partial pre-order
PROMETHEE II	Ordering	Complete pre-order
PROMETHEE III	Ordering	Stochastic treatment of flows (interval preference)
PROMETHEE IV	Choice and sorting	Continuous set of actions
PROMETHEE V	Ordering	Full pre-order including targeting restrictions
PROMETHEE VI	Choice and sorting	Pre-order complete or partial
PROMETHEE-GAIA	Extension of PROMETHEE results	Visual and interactive procedure

(Adapted from (Brans & Mareschal, 2005))

and $P_i(a,b)$ – Preference function that depends on the difference between the performance of the alternatives for each criterion i, d_i, where $d_i=g_i(a) - g_i(b)$.

Presented by (Brans & Mareschal, 2005), there are six preference functions used in PROMETHEE that allow the decision maker to express their preferences in a more timely manner to each criterion, which are illustrated in Figure 2, where:

p corresponds to a threshold of preference, that is, the lowest value for d_i above which there is a strict preference among alternatives;
q corresponds to the indifference threshold, that is, the highest value for d_i above which there is an indifference between the alternatives;
s is an intermediate value between p and q, which follows a normal distribution;
Valor 1 – strict preference;
Valor 0 – indifference.

After the first phase, two indicators are used to evaluate the preference relationship between alternatives (Brans & Mareschal, 2005), the positive preference flow, $\phi^+(a)$, and the negative preference flow, $\phi^-(a)$, which admit values between -1 and 1.

The positive preference flow reflects the intensity with which an alternative surpasses all others, that is, the greater the value of $\phi^+(a)$, the better the alternative. On the other hand, the negative preference flow shows the intensity with which an alternative is exceeded by the others, that is, the lower the value of $\phi^-(a)$, the better the alternative (Brans & De Smet, 2016).

Finally, in order to extrapolate a complete pre-order, the global flow of the alternative ($\phi(a)$) resulting from the difference between $\phi^+(a)$ and $\phi^-(a)$ is used, comprising values on a scale which goes from -1 to 1. Thus, the higher this value, the better sorted will be the alternative (Brans & De Smet, 2016).

In a multicriteria problem, it is not always easy to compare two alternatives, since one can be much better in one set of criteria and the other better in another set of criteria, that is, decision-making often involves evaluating criteria that are conflicting. In this way, different forms of evaluation (considering, respectively, the values of ϕ^- and ϕ^+) can culminate in different rankings (Mareschal, 2013).

Figure 2. Preference functions used in PROMETHEE - graphical representation
(Adapted from (Brans & De Smet, 2016))

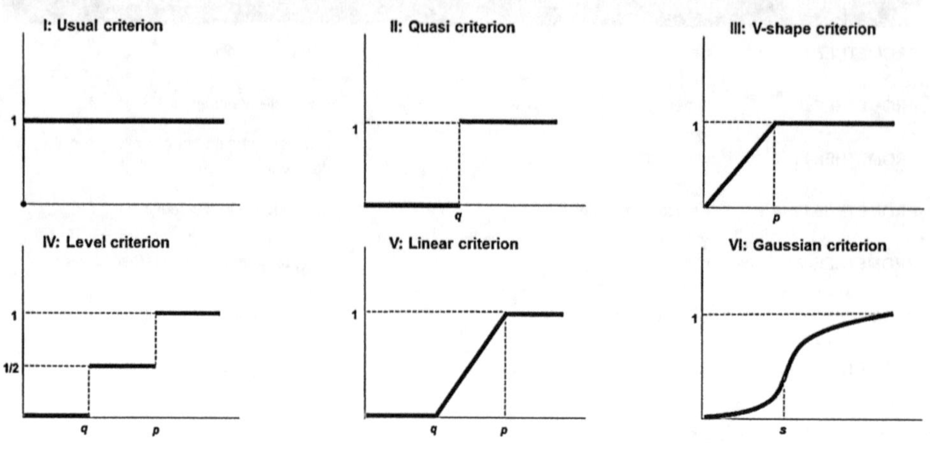

The PROMETHEE I, is a cautious indicator, as it confronts the two rankings obtained for both ϕ^+ and ϕ^-, including only the preferences that are confirmed in both rankings. For this reason, it is denominated as partial ranking, in the sense that, when two rankings are not consensual for a given alternative, no comparison is made, introducing the concept of incomparability between actions (Mareschal, 2013).

However, PROMETHEE II presents a complete ranking, considering, like the flow table, the global flow ϕ which, as previously mentioned, results from the difference between ϕ^+ and ϕ^- of each supplier, being all the better, the greater the value obtained (Mareschal, 2013).

The PROMETHEE GAIA is used to minimize the loss of information, starting from a multidimensional representation of the decision problem. The objective is to graphically describe the main characteristics of the decision problems, determining if the alternatives are different or similar from each other, which criteria conflict, what is the impact of the weighting assigned to the criteria in the ranking obtained, among other aspects (Mareschal, 2013).

(Brans & Mareschal, 2005) state that the analysis of the GAIA plan helps the decision maker to perceive the structure of the problem, being the best two-dimensional representation of the multicriteria problem, since it provides information on three crucial points, namely:

- Actions, which are represented by points;
- Criteria, which are represented by axes;
- Weights of the criteria, which are represented by the decision axis.

In practice, the 2D representation is considered reliable when the quality level is higher than 70%.

APPLICATION OF METHODOLOGY OF MULTICRITERIA ANALYSIS: RESULTS / DISCUSSION

1. Problem Identification and Structuring

For the process of collecting and obtaining data for subsequent employment in the selected models, it was necessary to access the database of the company's computer system for the collection of quantitative data and, on the other hand, to collect qualitative data, hold informal meetings with those responsible for the company's purchasing department. In this way, the criteria and the possible alternatives were indicated by the professionals responsible for the purchasing department of the CAN company, who work daily with the suppliers and know closely the relevant aspects of the raw material in question, tinplate, for the productive process. The main objective will be to establish a ranking of the best suppliers, so that the company can make decisions in this scope.

As for the PROMETHEE method, the weight assigned to each criterion was also indicated by the buyers of this company. The same happens when it comes to the AHP method, where the trade-offs determined in the pairwise comparison of the alternatives and criteria are carried out jointly with the decision makers of the purchasing sector.

Figure 3. Problem hierarchical structure
(Source: Own)

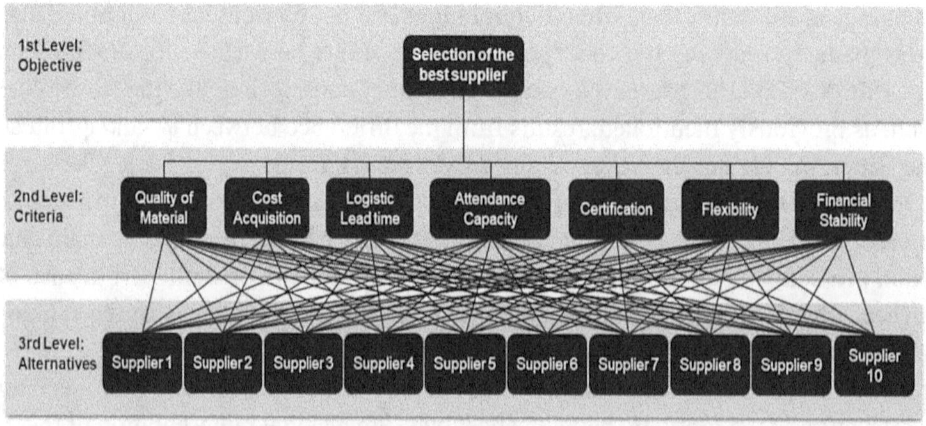

2. Application of the AHP Method

In order to apply the AHP method in this study, it was considered a hierarchical structure that Figure 3 illustrates.

At the top of the hierarchical structure is the main objective, the selection of the best supplier. Below is the second level that includes the seven criteria considered for the evaluation process, and finally, in the third level, there are the ten possible alternatives of suppliers.

Once the hierarchies have been defined, it is necessary to compare in pairs a total of 7 criteria of the second level in relation to the first hierarchical level. For this comparison the fundamental scale of (T. L. Saaty, 1980), as referred in Table 1. At this stage the objective is to establish the relative importance of each criterion in the objective to be fulfilled.

If there is only one element in the first hierarchical level, only one matrix is constructed with the intention of measuring the degree of intensity in pairs according to the seven criteria.

Then, this matrix is normalized, matching all the criteria to the same unit, dividing each value of the matrix by the total of its column. Thus, by calculating the mean value is obtained the weight assigned to each criterion, that is, the relative importance that each criterion has in selecting the best supplier (Table 5).

As shown in Figure 4, the criterion "Cost Acquisition" is one that, according to the evaluation of the decision makers, represents a greater portion in the final choice, followed by the criterion "Quality of Material" weighing about 27% . In this way, the cost criterion will be the one that will impact the objective more, following the criterion "Quality of Material". With a lower portion, "Lead time Logistic" appears, with a weighting of about 14% in the final decision. Regarding the criteria "Attendance Capacity", "Certification" and "Flexibility", these have the same impact on the selection of the best supplier, having a weight of about 6%. Finally, and with a relative lower importance, the "Financial Stability" criterion appears, which although important for the evaluator is less important than the other criteria.

The next step is to carry out the consistency test of the comparisons made, trying to verify if the evaluations are logically related. For this, the element that corresponds to the greatest importance (λ_{max}) that is obtained through the sum of the products of the column vector w_n, obtained in Table 5, is calculated with the sum vector of the matrix.

Table 5. Standard matrix and its weight for each criterion

Matrix A Normalized	Quality of Material	Cost Acquisition	Logistic Lead Time	Attendance Capacity	Certification	Flexibility	Financial Stability	Weight (w_n)
Quality of Material	0,2439	0,2095	0,3636	0,2703	0,2703	0,2703	0,2400	26,7%
Cost Acquisition	0,4878	0,4190	0,3636	0,3784	0,3784	0,3784	0,3200	38,9%
Logistic Lead Time	0,0813	0,1397	0,1212	0,1622	0,1622	0,1622	0,1600	14,1%
Attendance Capacity	0,0488	0,0599	0,0404	0,0541	0,0541	0,0541	0,0800	5,6%
Certification	0,0488	0,0599	0,0404	0,0541	0,0541	0,0541	0,0800	5,6%
Flexibility	0,0488	0,0599	0,0404	0,0541	0,0541	0,0541	0,0800	5,6%
Financial Stability	0,0407	0,0524	0,0303	0,0270	0,0270	0,0270	0,0400	3,5%
Sum	1	1	1	1	1	1	1	100%

(Source: Own)

Figure 4. Relative weight of each criterion
(Source: Own)

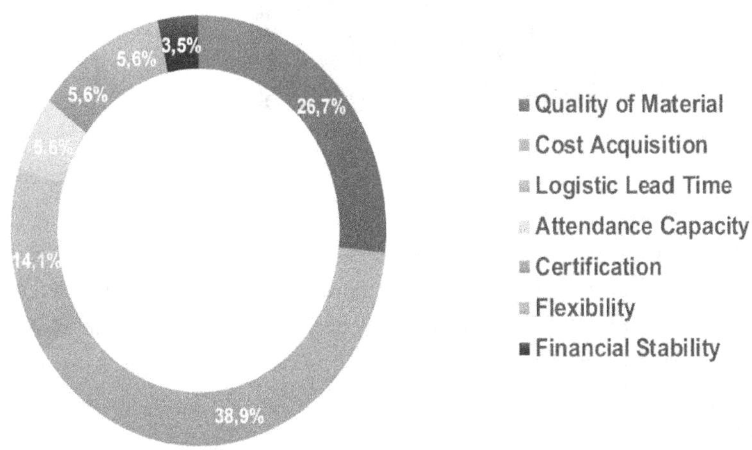

Then, the Consistency Index (*CI*) and the Consistency Ratio (*CR*) are calculated. As the value of *CR*<0,10, then it can be concluded that the comparisons made are consistent.

The next step is to perform the pairwise comparison of each element of the third level with each element of the second hierarchical level, that is, the comparison of suppliers with each other, regarding the performance in each of the criteria.

The final step of applying the AHP method to the problem under study is to use the weights (w_k) obtained by supplier in each criterion, weighted by weight (w_n), both values obtained in the previous steps. In order to obtain a ranking of the best suppliers, we calculate the weighted average of these parcels, which will allow to find the final value of importance of each supplier and establish priorities. Table 6 presents a summary table with the global ranking obtained.

With the application of the AHP method, it is concluded that the best performance was from supplier 1 with 16,16%, followed by supplier 2 with about 15,56%. Although these suppliers perform very

Table 6. Ranking of suppliers

RANKING		
1º	Supplier 1	16,16%
2º	Supplier 2	15,56%
3º	Supplier 3	13,56%
4º	Supplier 4	11,70%
5º	Supplier 8	8,94%
6º	Supplier 5	8,33%
7º	Supplier 7	7,81%
8º	Supplier 6	7,15%
9º	Supplier 9	5,76%
10º	Supplier 10	5,04%

(Source: Own)

closely, with a difference of only about 0,6%, which distinguishes favourably the first supplier of the second, it is the lowest price it presents. On the other hand, Supplier 2 stands out positively from Supplier 1, when the criterion of Attendance Capacity is analysed. However, since the cost of acquisition is the criterion with greater weight in the final decision, it is the one that has the most impact in the decision vector, since, while the cost of acquisition has a weight of about 39% in the final choice, the Attendance Capacity only weighs in 6%.

Observing in detail the criteria "Cost Acquisition", since it is one that has more impact on the final selection, it is possible to conclude that the supplier that performs more favourably (about 30%) is the supplier 3. However, this supplier only ranks 3rd in the ranking. Although it has the lowest cost, it performs negatively on the other evaluation fields, since the quality of the material, the second criterion that weighs most in the decision, is only reasonable, as is the financial stability. On the other hand, this supplier is governed by the least beneficial standard, the Japanese standard, has a flexibility and a weak service capacity and, finally, a very long lead time (of about 110 days), double the lead time that the suppliers 1 and 2 have.

Below the supplier 3, the supplier 4 appears, although having good material quality and financial stability and, on the other hand, following the standards defined by the European standard, has a cost acquisition of € 801/coil, a lead time of 70 days and an attendance capacity that is not of the best.

Finally, in the last places of the ranking, the suppliers 9 and 10 appear. The supplier 9 demonstrates a more favourable performance in relation to the supplier 10, occupying the penultimate position of the ranking, since, despite having a low performance in all the criteria, it has a lower acquisition cost than the supplier 10, achieving position ninth. The supplier 10, when presenting a cost of acquisition of the highest, although having a good material quality, does not compensate it in the other criteria, obtaining a low performance, being classified in the last position.

In order to determine the weight variation of each criterion that will result in the fact that the chosen alternative is not selected, a sensitivity analysis was performed.

This analysis makes it possible to gauge the robustness of the choice of supplier 1, and the choice could only change with a relatively different opinion on the part of the decision makers, the heads of the purchasing department of CAN. The cost acquisition is the criterion that presents the most sensitivity in the variation of its weighting and this is perceptible given the nature of the criterion in question. Considering the current weight of the criterion "Cost Acquisition" (39%), the selected option is the supplier 1. However, lowering this criterion from 39% to 20%, the preferred option becomes supplier 2. On the other hand, increasing the weighting of this criterion by 6%, the option selected becomes the supplier 3, being this the supplier with the most competitive price. For the criterion "Quality of Material", which currently has a weight of 27%, the selected alternative is the supplier 1. Only with a reduction of more than 10 percentage points in the weight of this criterion, is the supplier 1 no longer the best positioned in the ranking.

Regarding the criteria "Certification", "Flexibility" and "Financial Stability", in all three cases the selected option is the supplier 1, regardless of the weighting assigned.

The criteria "Lead time Logistic" and " Attendance Capacity ", with only a reduction of more than 10% in the first criterion and an increase in the weight assigned to the second criterion to more than double, is that supplier 1 ceases to be the chosen one, wherein in the first case the supplier 1 gives place to the supplier 3 and in the second case, the supplier 2.

3. Application of the PROMETHEE Method

In the PROMETHEE method pairwise comparisons are made for the alternatives, indicating the performance of each alternative in relation to each criterion (Brans & Mareschal, 2005). However, unlike the AHP method, where the decision makers make a set of judgments to express the relative importance that each criterion taking into account the fundamental scale of (T. L. Saaty, 1980), in the PROMETHEE method is assigned a weight for each criterion, which reflects its relative importance, that is, it assumes that the decision maker can weigh the criteria adequately (A. T. Almeida, 2011).

In the problem under study, the weights assigned to each criterion consider the importance that each takes in decision-making by purchasers of tinplate CAN company, which have a high technical knowledge about this stuff, interacting daily with suppliers. This is the weight that the decision-makers responsible of the purchasing department consider in the selection of suppliers, which will be, in turn, reflected in the PROMETHEE method.

The PROMETHEE & GAIA software was used to support the PROMETHEE Method, which resulted in the interface below. In column, the criteria are listed and, in line, the available alternatives. In this way, a set of 7 criteria and 10 suppliers is presented, as shown in Figure 5.

a. Network

For this indicator each action is represented as a node and preferences are represented by arrows. The nodes are located in relative positions corresponding to the PROMETHEE Diamond, so that the proximity

Figure 5. PROMETHEE software interface
(Source: Visual PROMETHEE)

Empresa CAN	Quality	Cost	Leadtime	Capacity	Certification	Flexibility	Financial
Unit	Scale 1-4	€	Days	Scale 1-4	Scale 1-2	Scale 1-3	Scale 1-4
Cluster/Group							
Preferences							
Min/Max	max	min	min	max	max	max	max
Weight	2,00	3,00	1,50	1,00	1,00	1,00	0,50
Preference Fn.	Usual	V-shape	V-shape	Usual	Usual	Level	Level
Thresholds	absolute	absolute	absolute	absolute	absolute	absolute	absolute
-Q: Indifference	n/a	n/a	n/a	n/a	n/a	0,89	0,64
-P: Preference	n/a	200,00	49,32	n/a	n/a	1,89	1,39
-S: Gaussian	n/a	n/a	n/a	n/a	n/a	n/a	n/a
Statistics							
Minimum	2,00	630,00	56,00	1,00	1,00	1,00	2,00
Maximum	4,00	954,00	110,00	4,00	2,00	3,00	4,00
Average	2,80	826,20	91,20	1,70	1,40	1,70	3,40
Standard Dev.	0,75	96,08	23,45	1,00	0,49	0,90	0,66
Evaluations							
Supplier 1	Very good	909,00	56,00	Good	European	High	Very good
Supplier 2	Very good	954,00	56,00	Very good	European	High	Very good
Supplier 3	Reasonable	630,00	110,00	Weak	Japanese	Low	Reasonable
Supplier 4	Good	801,00	70,00	Reasonable	European	High	Good
Supplier 5	Good	783,00	110,00	Weak	Japanese	Low	Good
Supplier 6	Reasonable	774,00	110,00	Weak	Japanese	Low	Very good
Supplier 7	Reasonable	765,00	110,00	Weak	Japanese	Low	Very good
Supplier 8	Good	918,00	70,00	Reasonable	European	Average	Good
Supplier 9	Reasonable	792,00	110,00	Weak	Japanese	Low	Very good
Supplier 10	Good	936,00	110,00	Weak	Japanese	Low	Good

between the flow values appears clearly. That is, it relates suppliers that have dominance over others and isolates suppliers that are incomparable. It resorts to ϕ^- and ϕ^+ to determine dominance, that is, if ϕ^+ is superior relative to another, then there is one vendor that dominates. In the case of ϕ^- it treats inversely, the lower the value, the more dominant the supplier.

The supplier 10 reveals the lowest ϕ^+ and the highest ϕ^- compared to the others, with 0.09 and 0.41 respectively. The best suppliers are suppliers 1 and 2, with ϕ^+ of 0.55 and 0.54 and with ϕ^- of 0.15 and 0.19, respectively. This means that the best suppliers show a higher ϕ^+, with a difference of 0.46 (supplier 1) and 0.45 (supplier 2) values above the last one, in addition to having a lower ϕ^- of about 0.22 when compared to the supplier 2, and about 0.26 when compared to supplier 1. This represents a significant difference in the determination of the preference of the selection and a more evident disparity between the remaining suppliers.

Interpreting the hierarchy of the diagram of Figure 6, it is verified that:

- The supplier 10 is easily surpassed by the suppliers 9, 6 and 7, as they positively vary the cost and stability, unlike the supplier 10 which only demonstrates a quality of the raw material above these suppliers;

- The supplier 3 also overlays the supplier 10 since it carries a substantially lower cost, promoting ϕ^+, notwithstanding the financial stability and the quality of the good that are unsuitable for the requirements of the decision maker, which promotes that ϕ^- is less than the supplier 10;
- Suppliers 9, 6 and 7 are below supplier 5 (with ϕ^+ of 0.19 and $\phi^-$of 0.28). This does not establish a comparison with the supplier 3, since the ϕ^+ is inferior, notwithstanding the ϕ^- being smaller, that is, it establishes a relationship of incomparability. All of these suppliers are homogeneous as a result of extended lead time, attendance capacity and flexibility of anticipation of orders are weak, as well as being governed by Japanese certification;
- Vendor 8 dominates suppliers 3 and 5, because ϕ^+ is higher and ϕ^- is lower with 0.35 and 0.25 respectively. It holds the criteria more favourably, except in the cost of acquisition that assumes a higher value. It should be noted that when compared to the supplier 5, the supplier 8 exhibits the same quality of the material and is classified as having the same level of financial stability;
- The provider 4 (with $\phi^+$of 0.46 and ϕ^- of 0.13) is superior compared to the supplier 8, and establishes a relation of incomparability for suppliers 1 and 2, since it has, on the one hand, a lower ϕ^+ and, for other side, a lower ϕ^-;
- The supplier 1 shows the best results, since it assumes a higher ϕ^+ and a lower ϕ^- with respect to the supplier 2. The latter, has all the positive criteria but a higher raw material cost.

b. PROMETHEE GAIA

As previously mentioned, PROMETHEE GAIA is the best two-dimensional representation of the multicriteria problem, providing information regarding the alternatives, criteria and weights of the criteria (Brans & Mareschal, 2005).

Figure 6. Network
(Source: PROMETHEE-GAIA software)

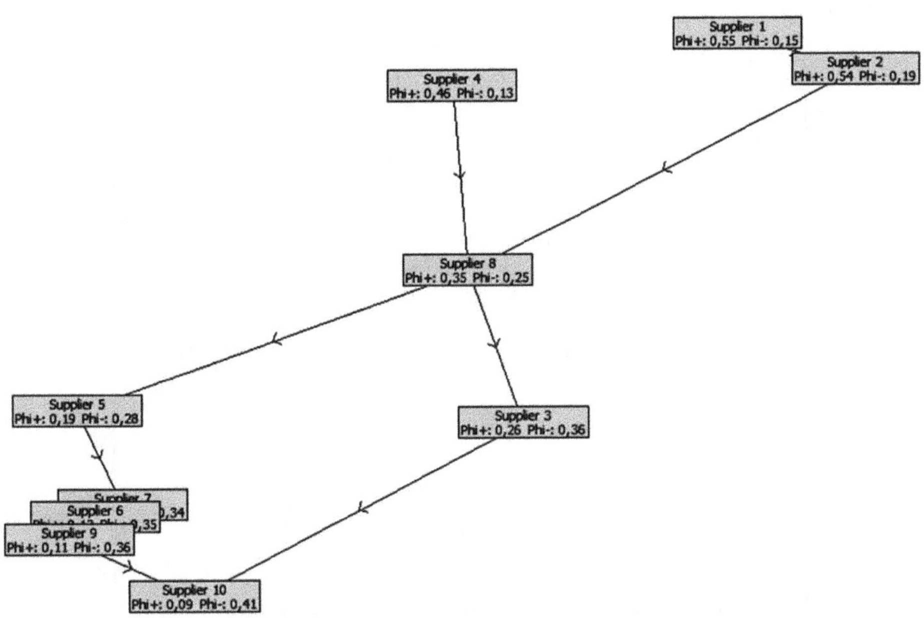

A first aspect to consider is the fact that the 2D representation obtained has a quality level of 89,7%, which means that it is extremely reliable.

For actions or alternatives, these will be similar the closer they are, and vice versa. Analysing the obtained graph, the suppliers 1 and 2 are very close to each other, being considered actions with similar characteristics. On the other hand, suppliers 4 and 8 also appear close to each other, thus concluding that they are analogous alternatives.

However, the supplier 3, being isolated from the other suppliers, is considered disparate from the others. In fact, considering the values of the criteria, the supplier 3 is the one that exhibits the lowest cost, however, in the other criteria the same values as the suppliers 6, 7 and 9, except for the financial stability that, while these have excellent stability the supplier has only a reasonable financial stability. Finally, in the same quadrant, but further away, the supplier 10 appears, which, although similar in all respects to suppliers 5, 6, 7 and 9, the major difference lies in the price which is substantially higher. This aspect means that, although the supplier 10 is in the same quadrant distances himself from the other suppliers.

As for the criteria, these are portrayed by axes drawn from the center of the plane, where criteria with an analogous preference will be represented by axes oriented in similar directions. On the other hand, criteria with divergent or conflicting preferences are portrayed by axes with opposing directions.

In this case, the axis that represents logistic lead time, attendance capacity, flexibility and certification exhibit the same orientation, these criteria being very close, indicating that they assume a similar behaviour.

The cost, appearing isolated, indicates that it conflicts with the other criteria. Looking at the detail, it is noteworthy that, for example, observing suppliers 1 and 2, in spite of practicing a high price, are suppliers with a more favourable performance in the other criteria. It is possible, therefore, that when the price is analysed in parallel with the quality, it turns out that the company will have to make a trade-off between quality/price, in the sense that the best quality suppliers will be those who practice higher prices.

Figure 7. PROMETHEE GAIA
(Source: PROMETHEE-GAIA software)

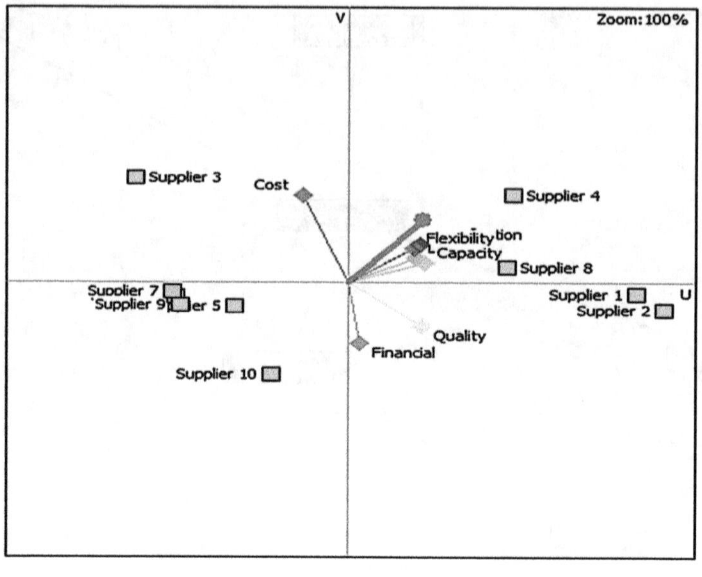

The same analysis can be carried out with the other criteria. When comparing the certification with the price, it is concluded that the suppliers who practice the highest price are governed by the European standard, with the exception of the supplier 10 who, practicing the second highest price in the table, follows the Japanese standard and not the standard considered most beneficial to the CAN company, the European standard. In this way, there is a conflict of interest since, when the decision maker seeks the raw material at the lowest cost, it will have to make several trade-offs, since it will find a favourable price performance, but the same may not occur in the other criteria.

Finally, the criterion of "Quality of Material" appearing below the logistic lead time criterion, attendance capacity, flexibility and certification, with a relatively identical direction, indicates that these criteria, not being completely consensual, also do not reveal a completely different behavior. Conversely, by displaying an axis with an entirely opposite orientation, the criterion of the acquisition cost indicates a total divergent preference. When analysing the values of these two criteria, it is found that, in order to obtain a high quality of the raw material, a higher price is requested and there is, therefore, a conflict of interests and a trade-off that the decision makers will have to consider and in decision-making, as mentioned in the previous paragraph.

As for the criterion of financial stability, there are suppliers who, despite having a high performance, are charged with higher prices. On the other hand, the supplier 3, being the one who practices the lowest price, is also the supplier with less financial stability, existing conflict. Looking at the quality of the material in parallel with this criterion, since both axes are relatively close (albeit with a slightly different orientation), it is perceptible that suppliers with excellent financial standing reveal a very good quality for suppliers 1 and 2, or only reasonable, as is the case with suppliers 6, 7 and 9.

In addition to the orientation of the axis, its size is also relevant, since it indicates how the variation observed in a criterion is more or less important.

Figure 8. PROMETHEE GAIA with the axis of the criterion "acquisition cost" evidenced
(Source: PROMETHEE-GAIA software)

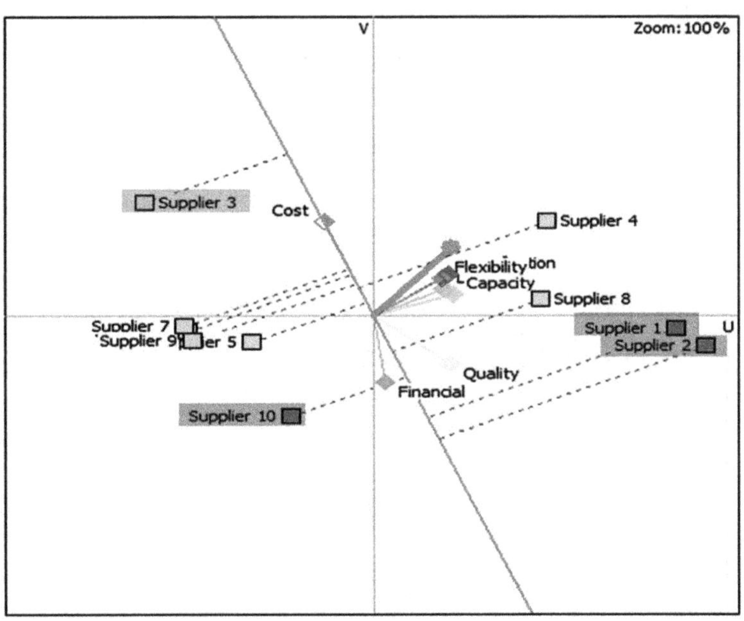

Contemplating simultaneously the relative positions of alternatives and criteria, the information to be extrapolated is quite interesting.

Analysing the cost criterion (Figure 8), since this is the one that weighs the most in the choice of the best supplier, it is verified that the supplier 3 is the one that is more aligned with the orientation of the axis of this criterion, positioning to the left, demonstrating that this supplier is the best ranked in this criterion. However, suppliers 1, 2, 8 and 10, practicing the highest prices, are in the opposite orientation to this criterion and at the same time more distant.

As for the criterion "quality of the material" (Figure 9), suppliers 1 and 2 assume the preference, being positioned more to the right of the axis to yellow stroke, having a quality considered very good. Next to these suppliers and, moving in the axis to the left, the suppliers 8, 4, 10 and 5 appear, being the suppliers that have a good quality of the material. Finally, the remaining suppliers, who are still further left on this axis, are the worst suppliers classified in this criterion, with a raw material quality considered only reasonable (suppliers 3, 7, 6 and 9).

In order to assess the robustness of the obtained ranking, a sensitivity analysis is performed through the Visual Stability Intervals output. This output determines in detail the impact of a change in the weights of the criteria. It shows how the value of the global flow ϕ modifies according to the weight of each criterion and is complementary to the previous model, which allows manual weight variation. This graph allows us to visualize an approximation of how suppliers behave by changing the weights of each criterion. It also reveals the same conclusions obtained in Walking Weight, but in a more comprehensive way. Thus, it is concluded that the cost is a very sensitive criterion to the weight variation, being the supplier 3 the most benefited with the increment of the weight attributed to this criterion. On the other hand, an increase in the weight attributed to quality benefits the supplier 10 since it is the criterion that, by contributing about 30% to the final decision, is the one in which this supplier qualifies best.

Figure 9. PROMETHEE GAIA with the criterion axis "quality of material" evidenced
(Source: PROMETHEE-GAIA software)

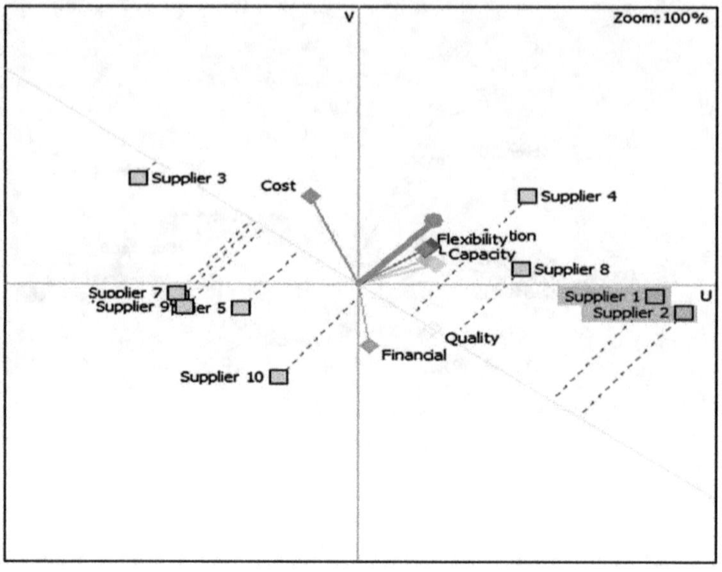

Figure 10. Visual stability intervals for the acquisition cost criterion
(Source: PROMETHEE-GAIA software)

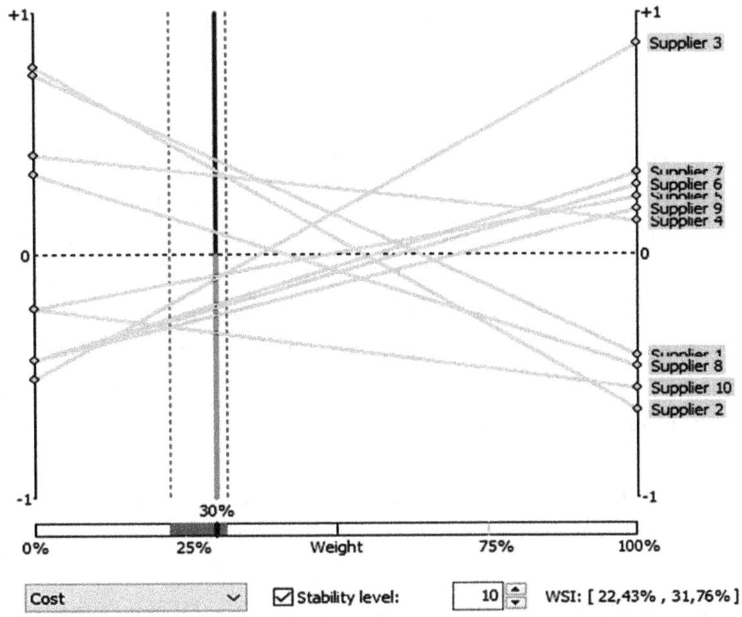

Figure 11. Visual stability intervals for the quality of material criterion
(Source: PROMETHEE-GAIA software)

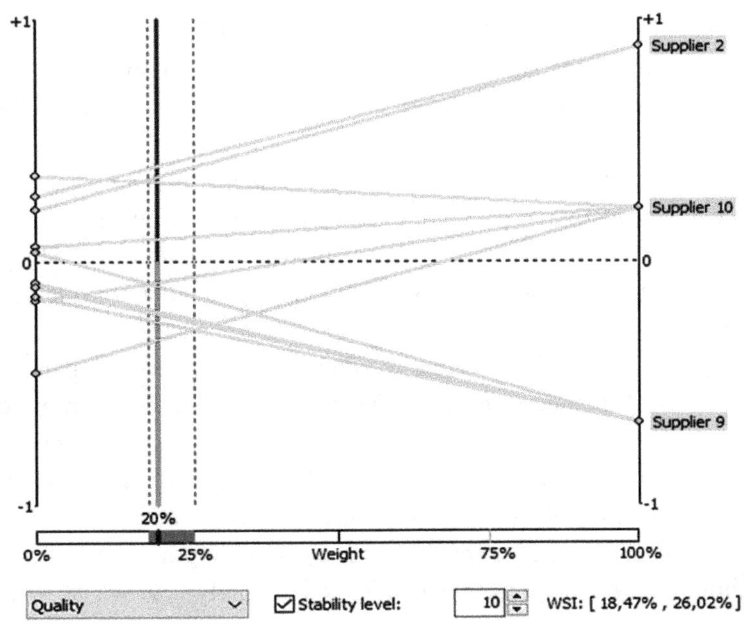

Finally, flexibility in anticipation of deliveries, certification by suppliers, and logistic lead time are the three criteria that most contribute to the stability of the ranking, while cost and quality are the criteria that provide some instability when re-weighting the assigned weights.

CONCLUSION

The need to establish a good relationship and build trust between a company and its suppliers is becoming increasingly important to make it more competitive in the market, differentiating itself from its competitors. Given the diversity of quantitative and qualitative criteria, as well as the number of suppliers to consider, the evaluation and selection of suppliers becomes more complex. Unlike the traditional approach, where cost alone would determine suppliers' ranking, methodologies that address different aspects show that, although a supplier may have a highly competitive acquisition cost, when compared to others, it does not establish your preference.

With the application of both methods, AHP and PROMETHEE, the intention is to help the CAN company, not to find an optimal solution, but to find the alternatives that best suit the requirements and needs of the company.

Analysing both methods applied to the problem of selection of suppliers for the raw material tinplate in the CAN company, it is possible to obtain a clear conclusion that the supplier 1 is the one that meets the best conditions of supply, taking into account the criteria defined for the process. Still for both methods, as second option is the supplier 2.

Considering the AHP method, supplier 3 appears in third place, in the PROMETHEE method, occupying the sixth place, descending three positions in the ranking. Consequently, suppliers 4, 8 and 5, which, being soon in the positions below the supplier 3 in the AHP method, when in the PROMETHEE method the supplier 3 occupies the sixth place in the ranking, the suppliers 4, 8 and 5 move up one position each. These small differences can be explained by the fact that the weights used are distinct and interpreted differently.

The AHP method, by allowing formal structure of the problem, taking into account experiences and perceptions in a logical way, making it possible to perform priority or weight scales, proves to be very advantageous in the analysis (T. L. Saaty, 1990). On the other hand, this method is based on the selection and preferences of decision makers who, being subjective, have a considerable influence on the results (Ayağ, 2005).

On the other hand, as for the PROMETHEE method, the obtained ranking can be manipulated according to the preferences of the decision maker. That is, depending on the preferences of the agents responsible for decision making, how the weights are assigned will have a great impact and will determine the ranking obtained, not being anything linear. The way the weights are assigned creates a major impact and reshapes the entire ranking, subject to oscillations in results and ranking of suppliers. However, PROMETHEE-GAIA software that uses this method, by providing a variety of outputs, is extremely advantageous and allows the decision maker, depending on the analysis he wants, to have different results to re-evaluate and compare different scenarios.

Through the results presented, it is verified that the suppliers 1 and 2 are more appealing, according to the proposed criteria. Both suppliers have a high quality in the product, a reduced lead time, a greater capacity to meet the company's volume requirements, are governed by the European standard (considered the most appropriate by the CAN company), have flexibility in the face of unforeseen, as well as excellent financial stability. The only criterion that these suppliers distance themselves from the requirements of the company is the cost, having a weight for decision making of 30%. This means that although the heavier criterion is less favourable to the supplier, it stands out from the rest when evaluating all criteria and all suppliers. In short, the cost that a priori would classify the ranking of suppliers, does not guarantee the best selection, reinforcing the need to consider other aspects.

In terms of future work, it would be interesting to extend these methodologies to other raw materials that the company consumes from other suppliers. The proposed method can also be extended to constitute a tool that allows the professionals of the purchasing department of the CAN company to evaluate and select the suppliers in a fast and objective way.

REFERENCES

Agarwal, P., Sahai, M., Mishra, V., Bag, M., & Singh, V. (2011). A review of multi-criteria decision-making techniques for supplier evaluation and selection. *International Journal of Industrial Engineering Computations*, *2*(4), 801–810. doi:10.5267/j.ijiec.2011.06.004

Alencar, L. H., de Almeida, A. T., & Mota, C. M. de M. (2007). Sistemática proposta para seleção de fornecedores em gestão de projetos. *Gestão & Produção*, *14*(3), 477–487. doi:10.1590/S0104-530X2007000300005

Almeida, A. T. (2011). O conhecimento e o uso de métodos multicritério de apoio a decisão. Recife: Editora Universitária Da UFPE., 232.

Almeida, A. T. de, & Costa, A. P. C. S. (2002). Modelo de decisão multicritério para priorização de sistemas de informação com base no método PROMETHEE. *Gestão & Produção*, *9*(2), 201–214. doi:10.1590/S0104-530X2002000200007

Anderson, D. R., Sweeney, D. J., Williams, T. A., Camm, J. D., & Martin, R. K. (2011). *An Introduction to Management Science: Quantitative Approaches to Decision Making* (13th ed.). Cengage Learning.

Ayağ, Z. (2005). A fuzzy AHP-based simulation approach to concept evaluation in an NPD environment. *IIE Transactions*, *37*(9), 827–842. doi:10.1080/07408170590969852

Azadfallah, M. (2016). Supplier Selection using MADM Method Under Uncertainty. *Journal of Supply Chain Management Systems*, *5*(3), 1–8. doi:10.21863/jscms/2016.5.3.034

Brans, J.-P., & De Smet, Y. (2016). PROMETHEE Methods (pp. 187–219). doi:10.1007/978-1-4939-3094-4_6

Brans, J.-P., & Mareschal, B. (2005). Promethee Methods. In *Multiple Criteria Decision Analysis: State of the Art Surveys* (pp. 163–186). New York: Springer-Verlag; doi:10.1007/0-387-23081-5_5

Bruno, G., Esposito, E., Genovese, A., & Passaro, R. (2009). *The Analytic Hierarchy Process in the Supplier Selection Problem.*

Carmo, B. B. T. do, Neto, J. F. B., & Dutra, N. G. da S. (2011). Análise do impacto nos custos de transporte de um modelo de seleção de fornecedores baseado em variáveis socioambientais e de competitividade, *21*(3), 466–483. doi:10.1590/S0103-65132011005000013

CEN national Members. (2001). [*COMITÉ EUROPÉEN DE NORMALISATION.*]. *EUROPEAN STANDARD EN, 10202*, 2001.

Costa, J. F. da S., Brazil, C. H. A., & De Oliveira, M. B. (2003). Metodologia multicritério e ECR: Utilização no mercado varejista. *Revista Produção, 13*(2), 114–122. doi:10.1590/S0103-65132003000200011

Cunha, S. M. A. (2008). *Selecção de Fornecedores – Estudo de Caso*. Universidade de Aveiro.

de Boer, L., Labro, E., & Morlacchi, P. (2001). A review of methods supporting supplier selection. *European Journal of Purchasing and Supply Management, 7*(2), 75–89. doi:10.1016/S0969-7012(00)00028-9

de Santis, R. B., Golliat, L., & de Aguiar, E. P. (2017). Multi-Criteria Supplier Selection Using Fuzzy Analytic Hierarchy Process: Case Study from a Brazilian Railway Operator. *Brazilian Journal of Operations & Production Management, 14*(3), 428–437. doi:10.14488/BJOPM.2017.v14.n3.a15

Dias, E. M. P. da S. (2015). *Modelo de apoio à decisão multicritério para selecção de fornecedores de azeite*. Faculdade de Economia do Porto.

Ensslin, L., Giffhorn, E., Ensslin, S. R., Petri, S. M., & Vianna, W. B. (2010). Avaliação do desempenho de empresas terceirizadas com o uso da metodologia multicritério de apoio à decisão - construtivista. *Pesquisa Operacional, 30*(1), 125–152. doi:10.1590/S0101-74382010000100007

Figueira, J., Greco, S., & Ehrogott, M. (2005). *Multiple Criteria Decision Analysis: State of the Art Surveys* (Vol. 78). Boston, MA: Springer New York; doi:10.1007/b100605

Forman, E. H., & Gass, S. I. (2001). The Analytic Hierarchy Process—An Exposition. *Operations Research, 49*(4), 469–486. doi:10.1287/opre.49.4.469.11231

Forsberg, K., Mooz, H., & Cotterman, H. (2005). *Visualizing project management: models and frameworks for mastering complex systems.* Wiley.

Gomes, E. G., Pereira, M., & Lins, E. (2002). Integrating Geographical Information Systems and Multi-Criteria Methods: A Case Study. *Annals of Operations Research, 116*(1/4), 243–269. doi:10.1023/A:1021344700828

Hatcher, M. (2008). Asset Evaluation and Selection Using The Analytic Hierarchy Process. *International Journal of Business Research, 8*(3), 118–124.

Ho, W., Xu, X., & Dey, P. K. (2010). Multi-criteria decision-making approaches for supplier evaluation and selection: A literature review. *European Journal of Operational Research, 202*(1), 16–24. doi:10.1016/j.ejor.2009.05.009

Kumar, A., Sah, B., Singh, A. R., Deng, Y., He, X., Kumar, P., & Bansal, R. C. (2017). A review of multi criteria decision making (MCDM) towards sustainable renewable energy development. *Renewable & Sustainable Energy Reviews, 69*, 596–609. doi:10.1016/j.rser.2016.11.191

MareschalB. (2013). *Visual PROMETHEE.*

Mendes, L. P. L. (2013). *Análise dos métodos de seleção de fornecedores*. Instituto Superior de Engenharia do Porto.

Morte, R. C. G. (2013). *Modelo De Apoio À Decisão Multicritério Para a Avaliação De Desempenho De Motoristas Numa Empresa Portuguesa De Transporte Rodoviário*. Faculdade de Economia do Porto.

Ohno, T. (1997). O sistema Toyota de produção: além da produção em larga escala. (Bookman, Ed.). Bookman.

Ortiz-Barrios, M. A., Kucukaltan, B., Carvajal-Tinoco, D., Neira-Rodado, D., & Jiménez, G. (2017). Strategic hybrid approach for selecting suppliers of high-density polyethylene. *Journal of Multi-Criteria Decision Analysis*, *24*(5/6), 296–316. doi:10.1002/mcda.1617

Rezaei-kelidbari, H. R., Homayounfar, M., & Foumani, S. F. A. (2016). A Combined Group EA-PROMETHEE Method for a Supplier Selection Problem. *Iranian Journal of Optimization*, *8*(2), 87–100.

Rodrigues Lima-Junior, F., & Ribeiro Carpinetti, L. C. (2016). A multicriteria approach based on fuzzy QFD for choosing criteria for supplier selection. *Computers & Industrial Engineering*, *101*, 269–285. doi:10.1016/j.cie.2016.09.014

Roy, B., & Vincke, P. (1981). Multicriteria analysis: Survey and new directions. *European Journal of Operational Research*, *8*(3), 207–218. doi:10.1016/0377-2217(81)90168-5

Saaty, R. W. (1987). The analytic hierarchy process—What it is and how it is used. *Mathematical Modelling*, *9*(3–5), 161–176. doi:10.1016/0270-0255(87)90473-8

Saaty, T. L. (1980). *The Analytic Hierarchy Process*. New York: McGraw-Hill.

Saaty, T. L. (1990). How to make a decision: The analytic hierarchy process. *European Journal of Operational Research*, *48*(1), 9–26. doi:10.1016/0377-2217(90)90057-I

Saaty, T. L. (1991). *Método de Análise Hierárquica. Tradução e Revisão por Wainer da Silveira e Silva*. São Paulo, Brazil: McGraw-Hill.

Saaty, T. L. (2008). Decision making with the analytic hierarchy process. *International Journal of Services Sciences*, *1*(1), 83. doi:10.1504/IJSSCI.2008.017590

Sarkar, S., Pratihar, D. K., & Sarkar, B. (2018). An integrated fuzzy multiple criteria supplier selection approach and its application in a welding company. *Journal of Manufacturing Systems*, *46*, 163–178. doi:10.1016/j.jmsy.2017.12.004

Schinasi, G. J. (2004). Defining Financial Stability.

Sonmez, M. (2006). *A review and critique of supplier selection process and practices*. Loughborough University.

Terrientes, L. M. D. V. (2015). *Hierarchical outranking methods for multi-criteria decision aiding*. Universitat Rovira i Virgili.

Valipour Parkouhi, S., & Safaei Ghadikolaei, A. (2017). A resilience approach for supplier selection: Using Fuzzy Analytic Network Process and grey VIKOR techniques. *Journal of Cleaner Production*, *161*, 431–451. doi:10.1016/j.jclepro.2017.04.175

Wang, W. P. (2010). A fuzzy linguistic computing approach to supplier evaluation. *Applied Mathematical Modelling*, *34*(10), 3130–3141. doi:10.1016/j.apm.2010.02.002

Wetzstein, A., Hartmann, E., Benton, W. C. Jr, & Hohenstein, N.-O. (2016). A systematic assessment of supplier selection literature – State-of-the-art and future scope. *International Journal of Production Economics*, *182*, 304–323. doi:10.1016/j.ijpe.2016.06.022

Chapter 7
The Technique for Order of Preference by Similarity to Ideal Solution Method in Fuzzy Environment:
Fuzzy TOPSIS Method

Merve Cengiz Toklu
Sakarya University, Turkey

ABSTRACT

Decision-making process is the selection of the most appropriate one among the alternatives. Different selection criteria are considered in the decision-making process. Simultaneous assessment of different evaluation criteria may not always be possible. Multi-criteria decision-making techniques provide an easily applicable mathematical solution in this respect. Technique for Order Preference by Similarity to Ideal Solution (TOPSIS) method is one of the multi-criteria decision-making techniques. This method is used in many problems in literature and allows multiple decision makers to choose the most suitable alternative by evaluating them together with different criteria. Assessments of decision makers may include linguistic statements. In this case, the Fuzzy Logic approach can be used. In this chapter, Fuzzy TOPSIS method is explained with a detailed numerical example.

INTRODUCTION

The decision-making process is carried out at every stage of life. Even in daily life, people constantly decide on specific issues. Basically, the decision-making mechanism works to select the most appropriate one from among a set of feasible alternatives. However, it is not always easy to decide on real-world problems. It may be necessary to evaluate the conflicting objectives together, such as high quality and low cost. Similarly, companies may need to choose between alternatives when seeking solutions to their problems such as supplier selection, personnel selection, product range selection, raw material selec-

DOI: 10.4018/978-1-7998-2216-5.ch007

tion, workbench selection. For instance, in the personnel selection problem, several criteria such as age, experience, and demanded salary are evaluated together. These problems are defined as multi-criteria decision-making (MCDM) problems. MCDM methods provide solutions to researchers in various MCDM problems. These methods develop an analytical solution for the simultaneous evaluation of multiple criteria. In addition to this, MCDM methods provide the flexibility to evaluate multiple decision makers' views at the same time.

Technique for Order Preference by Similarity to Ideal Solution (TOPSIS) method is one of the MCDM techniques that commonly used in literature. It was developed by Hwang & Yoon (1981). In this chapter, the TOPSIS method in the fuzzy environment was investigated. The application steps of the method are described step by step on a numerical example.

When the literature is examined, it is seen that the TOPSIS method is used in many problems such as supplier selection, material selection, personnel selection, and handling equipment selection. Some studies have applied the Fuzzy TOPSIS method with different MCDM methods. For instance, there are studies that use the Fuzzy Analytic Hierarchy Process (AHP) method and Fuzzy TOPSIS method together. In these studies, criterion weights are obtained from Fuzzy AHP method. Afterward, the ranking order of the alternatives can be calculated by the Fuzzy TOPSIS method. Jee & Kang (2000) used Entropy and TOPSIS method in the procedure of the material selection process for a flywheel product. Shanian & Savadogo (2006) used the TOPSIS method to material selection for metallic bipolar plates for polymer electrolyte fuel cell. Boran et al. (2009) proposed Intuitionistic Fuzzy TOPSIS method and applied this method to supplier selection problem. Kelemenis & Askounis (2010) proposed a Fuzzy TOPSIS method and applied on the problem of the top management team selection. Aikhuele & Turan (2017) and Aikhuele & Turan (2018) proposed Intuitionistic Fuzzy TOPSIS method and they introduced modified exponential score function-based separation method to calculate each alternative from the positive ideal solution (PIS) and the negative ideal solution (NIS). Gupta & Barua (2017) proposed a framework for green supplier selection. They ranked the suppliers according to selection criteria by using fuzzy TOPSIS method. Tian et al. (2017) proposed a model for automotive components remanufacturing industry by using fuzzy AHP and combined gray relation analysis with TOPSIS methods. Daneshvar Rouyendegh, Yildizbasi, & Arikan (2018) used Intuitionistic Fuzzy TOPSIS method to select the in wind power plants site in Turkey. Abdel-Basset, Manogaran, Gamal, & Smarandache (2019) analyzed smart medical devices for diabetics' patients by using Neutrosophic TOPSIS method. Nabeeh, Smarandache, Abdel-Basset, El-Ghareeb, & Aboelfetouh (2019) proposed a model by combining Neutrosophic AHP with the TOPSIS method and applied on a personnel selection problem. In summary, TOPSIS method can be used in many problems, including multiple evaluation criteria, multiple decision makers and multiple alternatives.

The aim of this study is to introduce the TOPSIS method which is one of the multi-criteria decision-making techniques to the readers and to explain how to use it in fuzzy environment. The remainder of the study is organized as follows: In the Background section, the fuzzy logic approach is addressed and fundamental definitions and notations of the Fuzzy TOPSIS method are introduced. The Fuzzy TOPSIS method was applied to a problem in the Numerical Example section. The solution of the problem is explained step by step in the Solutions and Recommendations section. Future studies and researches on the Fuzzy TOPSIS method are given in the Future Research Directions section. Finally, in the Conclusions section, an overview of the topic is given and method and problem results are discussed.

BACKGROUND

In this section, the fuzzy set theory and the Fuzzy TOPSIS method are described briefly.

Fuzzy Set Theory

The fuzzy set theory was developed by Zadeh in 1965. In the fuzzy set theory, Zadeh has extended the sense of conventional mathematics with membership function (MF). In real-world problems, classical mathematical methods may not be sufficient due to incomplete information or difficulties in determining the numerical value of linguistic expressions. In this case, the MF is used when processing data. Fuzzy numbers can properly indicate imprecise parameters. In the fuzzy logic approach, since indefinite parameters are treated as indefinite values rather than certain ones, it will be more useful in real-world problems and its results will be more credible. The fuzzy set theory is applied to various problems in engineering, business, medical and related health sciences, and the natural sciences (Kahraman, 2006). In the fuzzy set theory, a positive triangular fuzzy number $\tilde{n} = \left(n_1, n_2, n_3\right)$ and a positive trapezoidal fuzzy number $\tilde{m} = \left(m_1, m_2, m_3, m_4\right)$ can be shown in Figure 1.

In this chapter, trapezoidal fuzzy numbers (TFNs) are used to express the linguistic variables. The membership function $\mu_{\tilde{m}}\left(x\right)$ can be defined as Eq.(1) (Castillo & Melin, 2008).

Figure 1(a). Triangular fuzzy number $\tilde{n}$, 1(b). Trapezoidal fuzzy number $\tilde{m}$

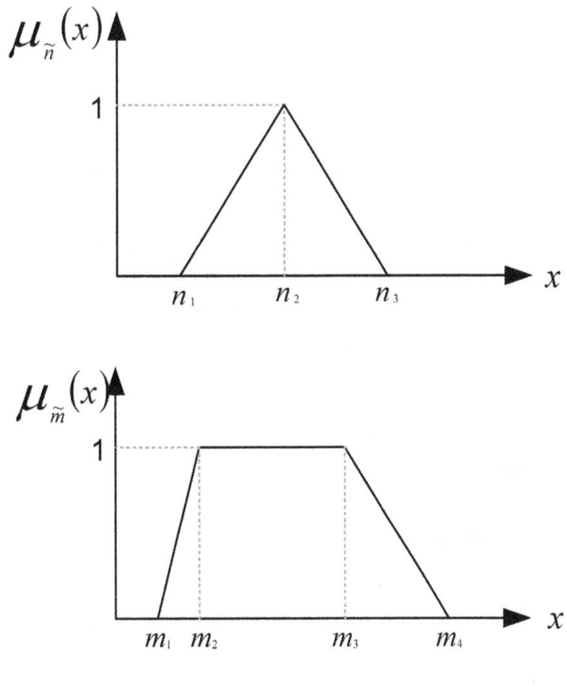

$$\mu_{\tilde{m}}\left(x\right)=\begin{cases} 0, x < m_1, \\ \dfrac{x-m_1}{m_2-m_1}, m_1 \le x \le m_2, \\ 1, m_2 \le x \le m_3, \\ \dfrac{m_4-x}{m_4-m_3}, m_3 \le x \le m_4, \\ 0, x > m_4. \end{cases} \quad (1)$$

TOPSIS Method

The TOPSIS method is one of the commonly used MCDM methods in the literature. This method takes into consideration the distances to both the PIS and the NIS. When the method is applied, the selected alternative should have the shortest distance from PIS and the farthest distance from the NIS (Hwang & Yoon, 1981). In 2000, the TOPSIS method was extended to use in the fuzzy environment based on Type1 Fuzzy sets by C.-T. Chen. In 2006 TOPSIS method was further extended to the concept of TOPSIS by C.-T. Chen et al. by using linguistic ratings in trapezoidal or triangular fuzzy numbers. Another development of the TOPSIS method is that the method is combined with the Interval Type 2 Fuzzy sets approach. Interval Type 2 Fuzzy TOPSIS method is proposed (Lee & Chen, 2008b, 2008a; S.-M. Chen & Lee, 2010). On the other hand, the TOPSIS method combined with the intuitionistic fuzzy set (Boran et al., 2009). In the other study, the TOPSIS method is extended to use in the single-valued neutrosophic environment (Biswas, Pramanik, & Giri, 2016). In this section, the Fuzzy TOPSIS method introduced by C.-T. Chen et al. (2006) is discussed.

Fuzzy TOPSIS Method

Decision makers evaluate both criteria and alternatives according to their importance by using the TOPSIS method. Decision makers can use linguistic expressions as medium poor, fair, medium good in these evaluations. The fuzzy logic approach can be used when decision makers use linguistic expressions rather than numerical expressions. In addition to this, in real-world problems, preferred ratings can be usually referred to the subjective uncertainty. For this reason, the TOPSIS method can be extended to the fuzzy numbers (Tzeng & Huang, 2011). As stated previously, TOPSIS method was extended to use in the fuzzy environment based on Type 1 Fuzzy sets (C.-T. Chen, 2000). TOPSIS method was further extended by C.-T. Chen et al. in 2006 by using linguistic ratings in trapezoidal or triangular fuzzy numbers. In their study, C.-T. Chen et al. (2006) suggested that the decision makers can use the linguistic variables shown in Figure 2 and Figure 3 to evaluate the criteria and alternatives.

Steps of Fuzzy TOPSIS Method

The Fuzzy TOPSIS method (C.-T. Chen et al., 2006) is described below.

Decision makers = $D_k = D_1, D_2, D_3, \ldots, D_k$

Figure 2. Linguistic variables for importance weight of each criterion

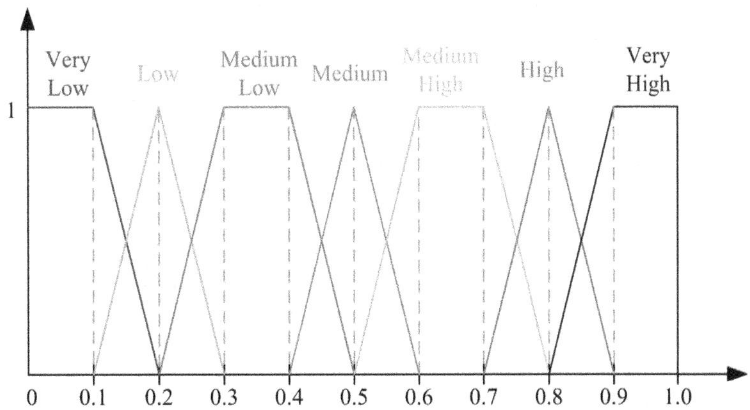

Alternatives = $A_m = A_1, A_2, A_3,\ldots,A_m$

Criteria = $C_n = C_1, C_2, C_3,\ldots,C_n$

Step 1. Assume that a decision group has K decision makers. The decision makers' evaluations are collected. Decision makers use linguistic expressions in the evaluation process.

Step 2. The linguistic expressions of the decision makers are converted to trapezoidal fuzzy numbers (TFNs) by using Table 1 and Table 2.

Table 1 and Table 2 are generated by using Figure 2 and Figure 3. For instance, if a decision maker determines the importance of a criterion as High (H), the TFNs equivalent of the "High" statement can be read from Figure 2 as (0.7;0.8;0.8;0.9). Likewise, if a decision maker evaluates an alternative as Fair (F) according to a criterion, the TFNs equivalent of the "Fair" statement can be read from Figure 3 as (4;5;5;6).

Figure 3. Linguistic variables for ratings

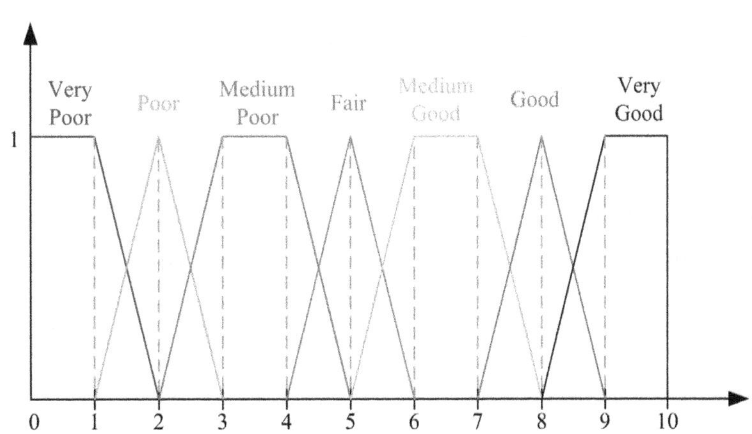

Table 1. Linguistic variables for importance weight of each criterion

	a	b	c	d
Very Low (VL)	0	0	0.1	0.2
Low (L)	0.1	0.2	0.2	0.3
Medium Low (ML)	0.2	0.3	0.4	0.5
Medium (M)	0.4	0.5	0.5	0.6
Medium High (MH)	0.5	0.6	0.7	0.8
High (H)	0.7	0.8	0.8	0.9
Very High (VH)	0.8	0.9	1	1

Table 2. Linguistic variables for ratings

	a	b	c	d
Very Poor (VP)	0	0	1	2
Poor (P)	1	2	2	3
Medium Poor (MP)	2	3	4	5
Fair (F)	4	5	5	6
Medium Good (MG)	5	6	7	8
Good (G)	7	8	8	9
Very Good (VG)	8	9	10	10

Step 3. Aggregated fuzzy rating (R_k) are calculated by applying an aggregation method to all decision-makers' fuzzy ratings. Fuzzy rating of each decision maker ($\tilde{R}_k$) can be represented as a positive trapezoidal fuzzy number $\tilde{R}_k = (a_k, b_k, c_k, d_k)$. Aggregated fuzzy rating (R_k) can be defined as

$$R_k = (a,b,c,d);\ k=1,2,3,\ldots,k \tag{2}$$

where

$$a = \min_k \{a_k\} \quad b = \frac{1}{K}\sum_{k=1}^{K} b_k \quad c = \frac{1}{K}\sum_{k=1}^{K} c_k \quad d = \max_k \{d_k\}$$

Step 4. Assume that $\tilde{x}_{ijk} = \left(a_{ijk}, b_{ijk}, c_{ijk}, d_{ijk}\right)$ is the fuzzy rating and $\tilde{w}_{ijk} = \left(w_{jk1}, w_{jk2}, w_{jk3}, w_{jk4}\right)$ is the fuzzy importance weight the kth decision maker respectively (i=1,2,…,m and j=1,2,…,n). The aggregated fuzzy ratings $(\tilde{x}_{ij})$ of alternatives with respect to each criterion can be calculated as

$$\tilde{x}_{ij} = \left(a_{ij}, b_{ij}, c_{ij}, d_{ij}\right) \tag{3}$$

where

$$a_{ij} = \min_k \left\{a_{ijk}\right\} \quad b_{ij} = \frac{1}{K}\sum_{k=1}^{K} b_{ijk} \quad c_{ij} = \frac{1}{K}\sum_{k=1}^{K} c_k \quad d_{ij} = \max_k \left\{d_{ijk}\right\}$$

The aggregated fuzzy weights $(\tilde{w}_j)$ of each criterion can be calculated as

$$\tilde{w}_j = \left(w_{j1}, w_{j2}, w_{j3}, w_{j4}\right) \tag{4}$$

where

$$w_{j1} = \min_k \left\{w_{jk1}\right\} \quad w_{j2} = \frac{1}{K}\sum_{k=1}^{K} w_{jk2} \quad w_{j3} = \frac{1}{K}\sum_{k=1}^{K} w_{jk3} \quad w_{j4} = \max_k \left\{w_{jk4}\right\}$$

The problem can be expressed in matrix form as follows:

$$\tilde{D} = \begin{pmatrix} \tilde{x}_{11} & \tilde{x}_{12} & \cdots & \tilde{x}_{1n} \\ \tilde{x}_{21} & \tilde{x}_{22} & \cdots & \tilde{x}_{2n} \\ \vdots & \vdots & \ddots & \vdots \\ \tilde{x}_{m1} & \tilde{x}_{m2} & \cdots & \tilde{x}_{mn} \end{pmatrix}$$

$$\tilde{W} = \left[\tilde{w}_1, \tilde{w}_2, \ldots, \tilde{w}_n\right]$$

where

$\tilde{x}_{ij}$ and $\tilde{w}_j$ can be approximated by positive TFNs.

Step 5. A normalized fuzzy decision matrix is determined. C.-T. Chen et al. (2006) suggested the linear scale transformation to transform the various criteria scales into comparable scales to avoid the complexity of mathematical operations. Each criterion can be grouped as a benefit or cost. The normalized fuzzy decision matrix can be represented as

$$\tilde{R} = \left[\tilde{r}_{ij}\right]_{m \times n} \tag{5}$$

where

$$\tilde{r}_{ij} = \left(\frac{a_{ij}}{d_j^*}, \frac{b_{ij}}{d_j^*}, \frac{c_{ij}}{d_j^*}, \frac{d_{ij}}{d_j^*} \right), j \in \text{Benefit}$$

$$\tilde{r}_{ij} = \left(\frac{a_j^-}{d_{ij}}, \frac{a_j^-}{c_{ij}}, \frac{a_j^-}{b_{ij}}, \frac{a_j^-}{a_{ij}} \right), j \in \text{Cost}$$

$$d_j^* = \max_i d_{ij}$$

$$a_j^- = \min_i a_{ij}$$

Step 6. The weighted normalized decision matrix is generated by multiplying the aggregated fuzzy weights $(\tilde{w}_j)$ of each criterion in the normalized fuzzy decision matrix. The weighted normalized fuzzy decision matrix $(\tilde{V})$ is constructed as

$$\tilde{V} = \left[\tilde{v}_{ij} \right]_{m \times n} \left(i = 1,2,\ldots,m \; and \; j = 1,2,\ldots,n \right) \tag{6}$$

where

$$\tilde{v}_{ij} = \tilde{r}_{ij} (\cdot) \tilde{w}_j$$

Step 7. The fuzzy PIS (A^*) and fuzzy NIS (A^-) are defined as

$$A^* = \left(\tilde{v}_1^*, \tilde{v}_2^*, \ldots, \tilde{v}_n^* \right) \tag{7}$$

$$A^- = \left(\tilde{v}_1^-, \tilde{v}_2^-, \ldots, \tilde{v}_n^- \right) \tag{8}$$

where

$\tilde{v}_j^* = \max_i \left\{ v_{ij4} \right\}$ and $\tilde{v}_j^- = \min_i \left\{ v_{ij1} \right\}$ (i=1,2,…,m and j=1,2,…,n)

Step 8. The distance of each alternative from A^* and A^- can be calculated as

$$d_i^* = \sum_{j=1}^{n} d_v \left(\tilde{v}_{ij}, \tilde{v}_j^* \right), \; i=1,2,\ldots,m \tag{9}$$

$$d_i^- = \sum_{j=1}^{n} d_v\left(\tilde{v}_{ij}, \tilde{v}_j^-\right),\ i=1,2,\ldots,m \tag{10}$$

where $d_v(\bullet,\bullet)$ is the distance measurement between two fuzzy numbers.

C.-T. Chen (2000) and C.-T. Chen et al. (2006) defined the distance between two fuzzy numbers as follows:

Assume that there are two triangular fuzzy numbers which are $\tilde{m} = \left(m_1, m_2, m_3, m_4\right)$ and $\tilde{n} = \left(n_1, n_2, n_3, n_4\right)$. Distance between these two numbers can be calculated using the vertex method as following.

$$d\left(\tilde{m}, \tilde{n}\right) = \sqrt{\left(1/4\right)\left[\left(m_1 - n_1\right)^2 + \left(m_2 - n_2\right)^2 + \left(m_3 - n_3\right)^2 + \left(m_4 - n_4\right)^2\right]} \tag{11}$$

Step 9. Finally, Closeness Coefficient (CC_i) is calculated. The ranking order of feasible alternatives can be concluded according to the descending order of CC_i.

$$CC_i = \frac{d_i^-}{d_i^* + d_i^-},\ i = 1, 2, 3, \ldots, m \tag{12}$$

MAIN FOCUS OF THE CHAPTER

The TOPSIS method is a multi-criteria decision-making technique and can be applied to a variety of problems to choose between alternatives or to sort alternatives according to suitability. The method is preferred by many researchers because of the easy applicability of mathematical calculations and flexibility. In addition to this, the Fuzzy TOPSIS method is preferred when decision makers use linguistic expressions to evaluate alternatives and criteria. The chapter focuses on the Fuzzy TOPSIS method and its applications. The aim of this chapter is to introduce the TOPSIS method to the readers who want to work with multi-criteria decision-making techniques and to explain how to use it in fuzzy environment. The solution to the problem in the numerical example is explained step by step in detail so that the readers who want to study the fuzzy TOPSIS method can understand this technique without difficulty. In the numerical example, a real problem in the manufacturing sector is discussed. In this way, it is aimed to contribute to the field with the use of Fuzzy TOPSIS method in a selection problem in the manufacturing sector.

RESEARCH METHODOLOGY

In this section, a numerical example is performed to clarify the Fuzzy TOPSIS method. In the numerical example, it is aimed to select the material handling equipment for a manufacturing company by using the Fuzzy TOPSIS method. The main purpose of material handling systems is the safe delivery of the correct quantity of material to the desired location at the appropriate time with minimum cost. There is a large variety of material handling equipment in the manufacturing industry. Conveyors, crane and hoist systems, industrial trucks, automated guided vehicles (AGVs), and robots are among the equipment. AGVs are battery-powered and unmanned vehicles. Due to the fact that AGVs are an unmanned vehicle, they can be programmed for path selection and positioning. AGV is one of the fastest growing material handling equipment thanks to its ability to be integrated with fully automatic intelligent control systems and to respond to different transport methods (Sawant, Mohite, & Patil, 2011).

Although many different evaluation criteria for material handling systems were used in the literature, (Chan, Ip, & Lau, 2001; Chan, 2002; Kulak, 2005; Maniya & Bhatt, 2011; Sawant et al., 2011; Eko Saputro & Daneshvar Rouyendegh, 2016; Nguyen, Md Dawal, Nukman, P. Rifai, & Aoyama, 2016) 9 evaluation criteria were determined for the numerical example. The main structure of the problem is based on 3 decision makers (D_1, D_2, D_3), 5 alternative equipment (A_1, A_2, A_3, A_4, A_5) and 9 evaluation criteria.

The evaluation criteria are determined as; Accuracy (C_1), Battery Capacity (C_2), Controllability (C_3), Cost (C_4), Dimensional Compliance (C_5), Flexibility (C_6), Load Capacity (C_7), Reliability (C_8), and Speed (C_9). In this criteria list; C_1, C_2, C_3, C_5, C_6, C_7, C_8, and C_9 are classified as benefit criteria. C_2 is classified as cost criteria. The hierarchical representation of this problem is shown in Figure 4.

SOLUTIONS AND RECOMMENDATIONS

The main goal of the problem is the selection of the most suitable AGV for a manufacturing company according to 9 evaluation criteria. In this study, the Fuzzy TOPSIS method is used to solve the problem. The solution steps of the problem are explained in detail below.

Step 1: Initially decision makers evaluated the criteria set by using Figure 2 and Table 1. For instance, D_1 and D_2 determined the importance of the "Accuracy" criterion (C_1) as "Very High" while D_3 determined as "High". Likewise, D_1 and D_2 determined the importance of the "Battery Capacity" criterion (C_2) as "Medium" while D_3 determined as "Medium High". The decision makers evaluated all criteria and Table 3 was obtained.

Figure 4. The hierarchical representation of the problem

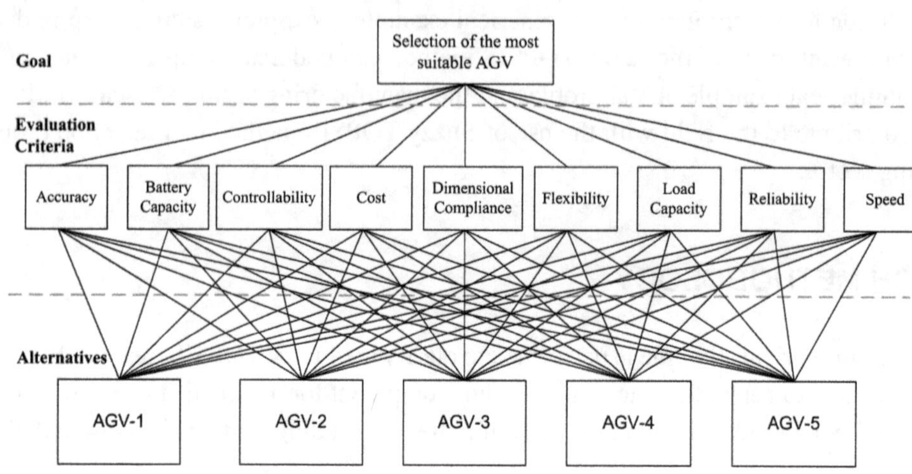

Table 3. Linguistic evaluations of criteria from D_1, D_2, and D_3

Evaluation Criteria	Decision Makers		
	D_1	D_2	D_3
C_1:Accuracy	VH	VH	H
C_2:Battery Capacity	M	M	MH
C_3:Controllability	ML	ML	M
C_4:Cost	VH	VH	VH
C_5:Dimensional Compliance	L	L	M
C_6:Flexibility	M	M	ML
C_7:Load Capacity	M	M	M
C_8:Reliability	H	H	VH
C_9:Speed	L	ML	M

*VL:Very Low, L:Low, ML:Medium Low, M:Medium, MH:Medium High, H:High, VH:Very High

In Table 3, evaluations of decision-makers about the criteria set consist of linguistic expressions. For this reason, these expressions have been converted into TFNs by using Table 1. For instance, D_1 determined the importance of the "Accuracy" criterion (C_1) as "Very High" as seen in Table 3. The TFNs equivalent of the "Very High" which is a linguistic expression can be read from Table 1 as (0.8;0.9;1;1). Likewise, D_1 determined the importance of the "Battery Capacity" criterion (C_2) as "Medium" as seen in Table 3. The TFNs equivalent of the "Medium" which is a linguistic expression can be read from Table 1 as (0.4;0.5;0.5;0.6). Similarly, all linguistic expressions are read from Table 1. Table 4 was obtained as a result of this process.

Aggregated fuzzy weights in Table 4 are calculated as follows by using Eq. (4).

Table 4. Importance weight of criteria from all decision makers (D_1, D_2, and D_3)

Criteria	Decision Makers			Aggregated Fuzzy Weights
	D_1	D_2	D_3	
C_1	(0.8;0.9;1;1)	(0.8;0.9;1;1)	(0.7;0.8;0.8;0.9)	(0.7;0.87;0.93;1)
C_2	(0.4;0.5;0.5;0.6)	(0.4;0.5;0.5;0.6)	(0.5;0.6;0.7;0.8)	(0.4;0.53;0.57;0.8)
C_3	(0.2;0.3;0.4;0.5)	(0.2;0.3;0.4;0.5)	(0.4;0.5;0.5;0.6)	(0.2;0.37;0.43;0.6)
C_4	(0.8;0.9;1;1)	(0.8;0.9;1;1)	(0.8;0.9;1;1)	(0.8;0.9;1;1)
C_5	(0.1;0.2;0.2;0.3)	(0.1;0.2;0.2;0.3)	(0.4;0.5;0.5;0.6)	(0.1;0.3;0.3;0.6)
C_6	(0.4;0.5;0.5;0.6)	(0.4;0.5;0.5;0.6)	(0.2;0.3;0.4;0.5)	(0.2;0.43;0.47;0.6)
C_7	(0.4;0.5;0.5;0.6)	(0.4;0.5;0.5;0.6)	(0.4;0.5;0.5;0.6)	(0.4;0.5;0.5;0.6)
C_8	(0.7;0.8;0.8;0.9)	(0.7;0.8;0.8;0.9)	(0.8;0.9;1;1)	(0.7;0.83;0.87;1)
C_9	(0.1;0.2;0.2;0.3)	(0.2;0.3;0.4;0.5)	(0.4;0.5;0.5;0.6)	(0.1;0.33;0.37;0.6)

For Accuracy (C_1);

"a" value in aggregated fuzzy weights is calculated as min(0.8;0.8;0.7) = 0.70
"b" value in aggregated fuzzy weights is calculated as arithmetic mean(0.9;0.9;0.8) = 0.87
"c" value in aggregated fuzzy weights is calculated as arithmetic mean(1;1;0.8) = 0.93
"d" value in aggregated fuzzy weights is calculated as max(1;1;0.9) = 1

For Battery Capacity (C_2);

"a" value in aggregated fuzzy weights is calculated as min(0.4;0.4;0.5) = 0.40
"b" value in aggregated fuzzy weights is calculated as arithmetic mean(0.5;0.5;0.6) = 0.53
"c" value in aggregated fuzzy weights is calculated as arithmetic mean(0.5;0.5;0.7) = 0.57
"d" value in aggregated fuzzy weights is calculated as max(0.6;0.6;0.8) = 0.80

For Controllability (C_3);

"a" value in aggregated fuzzy weights is calculated as min(0.2;0.2;0.4) = 0.20
"b" value in aggregated fuzzy weights is calculated as arithmetic mean(0.3;0.3;0.5)= 0.37
"c" value in aggregated fuzzy weights is calculated as arithmetic mean(0.4;0.4;0.5)= 0.43
"d" value in aggregated fuzzy weights is calculated as max(0.5;0.5;0.6) = 0.60

For Cost (C_4);

"a" value in aggregated fuzzy weights is calculated as min(0.8;0.8;0.8) = 0.8
"b" value in aggregated fuzzy weights is calculated as arithmetic mean(0.9;0.9;0.9) = 0.9
"c" value in aggregated fuzzy weights is calculated as arithmetic mean(1;1;1) = 1
"d" value in aggregated fuzzy weights is calculated as max(1;1;1) = 1

For Dimensional Compliance (C_5);

"a" value in aggregated fuzzy weights is calculated as min(0.1;0.1;0.4) = 0.10
"b" value in aggregated fuzzy weights is calculated as arithmetic mean(0.2;0.2;0.5) = 0.30
"c" value in aggregated fuzzy weights is calculated as arithmetic mean(0.2;0.2;0.5) = 0.30
"d" value in aggregated fuzzy weights is calculated as max(0.3;0.3;0.6) = 0.60

For Flexibility (C_6);

"a" value in aggregated fuzzy weights is calculated as min(0.4;0.4;0.2) = 0.20
"b" value in aggregated fuzzy weights is calculated as arithmetic mean(0.5;0.5;0.3) = 0,43
"c" value in aggregated fuzzy weights is calculated as arithmetic mean(0.5;0.5;0.4) = 0.47
"d" value in aggregated fuzzy weights is calculated as max(0.6;0.6;0.5) = 0.60

For Load Capacity (C_7);

"a" value in aggregated fuzzy weights is calculated as min(0.4;0.4;0.4) = 0.40
"b" value in aggregated fuzzy weights is calculated as arithmetic mean(0.5;0.5;0.5) = 0.50
"c" value in aggregated fuzzy weights is calculated as arithmetic mean(0.5;0.5;0.5) = 0.50
"d" value in aggregated fuzzy weights is calculated as max(0.6;0.6;0.6) = 0.60

For Reliability (C_8);

"a" value in aggregated fuzzy weights is calculated as min(0.7;0.7;0.8) = 0.70
"b" value in aggregated fuzzy weights is calculated as arithmetic mean(0.8;0.8;0.9)= 0.83
"c" value in aggregated fuzzy weights is calculated as arithmetic mean(0.8;0.8;1)= 0.87
"d" value in aggregated fuzzy weights is calculated as max(0.9;0.9;1) = 1

For Speed (C_9);

"a" value in aggregated fuzzy weights is calculated as min(0.1;0.2;0.4) = 0.10
"b" value in aggregated fuzzy weights is calculated as arithmetic mean(0.2;0.3;0.5) = 0.33
"c" value in aggregated fuzzy weights is calculated as arithmetic mean(0.2;0.4;0.5) = 0.37
"d" value in aggregated fuzzy weights is calculated as max(0.3;0.5;0.6) = 0.60

Step 2: In Table 5, decision makers determined the ratings of alternatives with respect to each criterion by using linguistic variables for ratings shown in Figure 3 and Table 2.

The decision makers evaluated all alternatives respect to 9 criteria and Table 5 was obtained. For instance, D_1, D_2, D_3 evaluated Alternative-1 as "Medium Good" according to "Accuracy" criterion (C_1). Likewise, D_1 evaluated Alternative-2 as "Medium Poor" while D_2 and D_3 evaluated Alternative-2 as "Very Poor" according to "Accuracy" criterion (C_1). D_1, D_2, D_3 evaluated Alternative-1 as "Fair" according to "Battery Capacity" criterion (C_2). D_1 evaluated Alternative-2 as "Medium Poor" while D_2 and

Table 5. Linguistic ratings of the alternatives with respect to each criterion from D_1, D_2, and D_3

Criteria	Alternatives	D_1	D_2	D_3	Criteria	Alternatives	D_1	D_2	D_3	Criteria	Alternatives	D_1	D_2	D_3
	A_1	MG	MG	MG		A_1	VG	VG	VG		A_1	F	MG	F
	A_2	MP	VP	VP		A_2	F	F	F		A_2	MP	MP	MP
C_1	A_3	G	G	MG	C_4	A_3	MG	MG	F	C_7	A_3	G	G	MG
	A_4	P	VP	VP		A_4	F	F	F		A_4	P	VP	P
	A_5	VG	VG	G		A_5	F	F	MP		A_5	MG	F	MG
	A_1	F	F	F		A_1	F	F	F		A_1	MP	MP	F
	A_2	MP	P	P		A_2	F	MP	MP		A_2	MP	F	MP
C_2	A_3	G	G	G	C_5	A_3	MG	MG	F	C_8	A_3	G	G	VG
	A_4	P	P	MP		A_4	MP	MP	MP		A_4	MP	MP	MP
	A_5	G	G	VG		A_5	MG	MG	F		A_5	G	G	VG
	A_1	P	P	P		A_1	P	MP	F		A_1	VG	VG	VG
	A_2	P	P	VP		A_2	P	P	P		A_2	G	G	MG
C_3	A_3	G	G	MG	C_6	A_3	MG	F	MG	C_9	A_3	VG	VG	VG
	A_4	MG	MG	G		A_4	VP	P	P		A_4	MP	F	F
	A_5	G	G	MG		A_5	VG	G	G		A_5	G	G	VG

D_3 evaluated Alternative-2 as "Poor" according to "Battery Capacity" criterion (C_2). Table 5 consists of linguistic expressions. The linguistic expressions have been converted into TFNs by using Table 2.

For instance, D_1, D_2, D_3 evaluated Alternative-1 as "Medium Good" according to "Accuracy" criterion (C_1) as seen in Table 5. The TFNs equivalent of the "Medium Good" linguistic expression can be read from Table 2 as (5;6;7;8). Likewise, D_1 evaluated Alternative-2 as "Medium Poor" while D_2 and D_3 evaluated Alternative-2 as "Very Poor" according to "Accuracy" criterion (C_1) as seen in Table 5. The TFNs equivalent of the "Medium Poor" linguistic expression can be read from Table 2 as (2;3;4;5) and The TFNs equivalent of the "Very Poor" linguistic expression can be read from Table 2 as (0;0;1;2). Similarly, all linguistic expressions are read from Table 2. As a result of this process Table 6 was obtained. Aggregated fuzzy weights in Table 6 are calculated as follows by using Eq. (3).

For Alternative-1 (A_1) according to C_1

"a" value in aggregated fuzzy weights is calculated as min(5;5;5)=5
"b" value in aggregated fuzzy weights is calculated as arithmetic mean(6;6;6)=6
"c" value in aggregated fuzzy weights is calculated as arithmetic mean(7;7;7)=7
"d" value in aggregated fuzzy weights is calculated as max(8;8;8)=8

For Alternative-2 (A_2) according to C_1

"a" value in aggregated fuzzy weights is calculated as min(2;0;0)=0
"b" value in aggregated fuzzy weights is calculated as arithmetic mean(3;0;0)=1
"c" value in aggregated fuzzy weights is calculated as arithmetic mean(4;1;1)=2
"d" value in aggregated fuzzy weights is calculated as max(5;2;2)=5

For Alternative-3 (A_3) according to C_1

"a" value in aggregated fuzzy weights is calculated as min(7;7;5)=5
"b" value in aggregated fuzzy weights is calculated as arithmetic mean(8;8;6)=7.33
"c" value in aggregated fuzzy weights is calculated as arithmetic mean(8;8;7)=7.67
"d" value in aggregated fuzzy weights is calculated as max(9;9;8)=9

For Alternative-4 (A_4) according to C_1

"a" value in aggregated fuzzy weights is calculated as min(1;0;0)=0
"b" value in aggregated fuzzy weights is calculated as arithmetic mean(2;0;0)=0.67
"c" value in aggregated fuzzy weights is calculated as arithmetic mean(2;1;1)=1.33
"d" value in aggregated fuzzy weights is calculated as max(3;2;2)=3

For Alternative-5 (A_5) according to C_1

"a" value in aggregated fuzzy weights is calculated as min(8;8;7)=7
"b" value in aggregated fuzzy weights is calculated as arithmetic mean(9;9;8)=8.67
"c" value in aggregated fuzzy weights is calculated as arithmetic mean(10;10;8)=9.33
"d" value in aggregated fuzzy weights is calculated as max(10;10;9)=10

Table 6. Numerical ratings of the alternatives with respect to each criterion from D_1, D_2, and D_3

Criteria	Alternatives	D_1	D_2	D_3	Aggregated Fuzzy Weights
C_1	A_1	(5;6;7;8)	(5;6;7;8)	(5;6;7;8)	(5;6;7;8)
	A_2	(2;3;4;5)	(0;0;1;2)	(0;0;1;2)	(0;1;2;5)
	A_3	(7;8;8;9)	(7;8;8;9)	(5;6;7;8)	(5;7.33;7.67;9)
	A_4	(1;2;2;3)	(0;0;1;2)	(0;0;1;2)	(0;0.67;1.33;3)
	A_5	(8;9;10;10)	(8;9;10;10)	(7;8;8;9)	(7;8.67;9.33;10)
C_2	A_1	(4;5;5;6)	(4;5;5;6)	(4;5;5;6)	(4;5;5;6)
	A_2	(2;3;4;5)	(1;2;2;3)	(1;2;2;3)	(1;2.33;2.67;5)
	A_3	(7;8;8;9)	(7;8;8;9)	(7;8;8;9)	(7;8;8;9)
	A_4	(1;2;2;3)	(1;2;2;3)	(2;3;4;5)	(1;2.33;2.67;5)
	A_5	(7;8;8;9)	(7;8;8;9)	(8;9;10;10)	(7;8.33;8.67;10)
C_3	A_1	(1;2;2;3)	(1;2;2;3)	(1;2;2;3)	(1;2;2;3)
	A_2	(1;2;2;3)	(1;2;2;3)	(0;0;1;2)	(0;1.33;1.67;3)
	A_3	(7;8;8;9)	(7;8;8;9)	(5;6;7;8)	(5;7.33;7.67;9)
	A_4	(5;6;7;8)	(5;6;7;8)	(7;8;8;9)	(5;6.67;7.33;9)
	A_5	(7;8;8;9)	(7;8;8;9)	(5;6;7;8)	(5;7.33;7.67;9)
C_4	A_1	(8;9;10;10)	(8;9;10;10)	(8;9;10;10)	(8;9;10;10)
	A_2	(4;5;5;6)	(4;5;5;6)	(4;5;5;6)	(4;5;5;6)
	A_3	(5;6;7;8)	(5;6;7;8)	(4;5;5;6)	(4;5.67;6.33;8)
	A_4	(4;5;5;6)	(4;5;5;6)	(4;5;5;6)	(4;5;5;6)
	A_5	(4;5;5;6)	(4;5;5;6)	(2;3;4;5)	(2;4.33;4.67;6)
C_5	A_1	(4;5;5;6)	(4;5;5;6)	(4;5;5;6)	(4;5;5;6)
	A_2	(4;5;5;6)	(2;3;4;5)	(2;3;4;5)	(2;3.67;4.33;6)
	A_3	(5;6;7;8)	(5;6;7;8)	(4;5;5;6)	(4;5.67;6.33;8)
	A_4	(2;3;4;5)	(2;3;4;5)	(2;3;4;5)	(2;3;4;5)
	A_5	(5;6;7;8)	(5;6;7;8)	(4;5;5;6)	(4;5.67;6.33;8)
C_6	A_1	(1;2;2;3)	(2;3;4;5)	(4;5;5;6)	(1;3.33;3.67;6)
	A_2	(1;2;2;3)	(1;2;2;3)	(1;2;2;3)	(1;2;2;3)
	A_3	(5;6;7;8)	(4;5;5;6)	(5;6;7;8)	(4;5.67;6.33;8)
	A_4	(0;0;1;2)	(1;2;2;3)	(1;2;2;3)	(0;1.33;1.67;3)
	A_5	(8;9;10;10)	(7;8;8;9)	(7;8;8;9)	(7;8.33;8.67;10)
C_7	A_1	(4;5;5;6)	(5;6;7;8)	(4;5;5;6)	(4;5.33;5.67;8)
	A_2	(2;3;4;5)	(2;3;4;5)	(2;3;4;5)	(2;3;4;5)
	A_3	(7;8;8;9)	(7;8;8;9)	(5;6;7;8)	(5;7.33;7.67;9)
	A_4	(1;2;2;3)	(0;0;1;2)	(1;2;2;3)	(0;1.33;1.67;3)
	A_5	(5;6;7;8)	(4;5;5;6)	(5;6;7;8)	(4;5.67;6.33;8)
C_8	A_1	(2;3;4;5)	(2;3;4;5)	(4;5;5;6)	(2;3.67;4.33;6)
	A_2	(2;3;4;5)	(4;5;5;6)	(2;3;4;5)	(2;3.67;4.33;6)
	A_3	(7;8;8;9)	(7;8;8;9)	(8;9;10;10)	(7;8.33;8.67;10)
	A_4	(2;3;4;5)	(2;3;4;5)	(2;3;4;5)	(2;3;4;5)
	A_5	(7;8;8;9)	(7;8;8;9)	(8;9;10;10)	(7;8.33;8.67;10)
C_9	A_1	(8;9;10;10)	(8;9;10;10)	(8;9;10;10)	(8;9;10;10)
	A_2	(7;8;8;9)	(7;8;8;9)	(5;6;7;8)	(5;7.33;7.67;9)
	A_3	(8;9;10;10)	(8;9;10;10)	(8;9;10;10)	(8;9;10;10)
	A_4	(2;3;4;5)	(4;5;5;6)	(4;5;5;6)	(2;4.33;4.67;6)
	A_5	(7;8;8;9)	(7;8;8;9)	(8;9;10;10)	(7;8.33;8.67;10)

For Alternative-1 (A_1) according to C_2

"a" value in aggregated fuzzy weights is calculated as min(4;4;4)=4
"b" value in aggregated fuzzy weights is calculated as arithmetic mean(5;5;5)=5
"c" value in aggregated fuzzy weights is calculated as arithmetic mean(5;5;5)=5
"d" value in aggregated fuzzy weights is calculated as max(6;6;6)=6

For Alternative-2 (A_2) according to C_2

"a" value in aggregated fuzzy weights is calculated as min(2;1;1)=1
"b" value in aggregated fuzzy weights is calculated as arithmetic mean(3;2;2)=2.33
"c" value in aggregated fuzzy weights is calculated as arithmetic mean(4;2;2)=2.67
"d" value in aggregated fuzzy weights is calculated as max(5;3;3)=5

For Alternative-3 (A_3) according to C_2

"a" value in aggregated fuzzy weights is calculated as min(7;7;7)=7
"b" value in aggregated fuzzy weights is calculated as arithmetic mean(8;8;8)=8
"c" value in aggregated fuzzy weights is calculated as arithmetic mean(8;8;8)=8
"d" value in aggregated fuzzy weights is calculated as max(9;9;9)=9

For Alternative-4 (A_4) according to C_2

"a" value in aggregated fuzzy weights is calculated as min(1;1;2)=1
"b" value in aggregated fuzzy weights is calculated as arithmetic mean(2;2;3)=2.33
"c" value in aggregated fuzzy weights is calculated as arithmetic mean(2;2;4)=2.67
"d" value in aggregated fuzzy weights is calculated as max(3;3;5)=5

For Alternative-5 (A_5) according to C_2

"a" value in aggregated fuzzy weights is calculated as min(7;7;8)=7
"b" value in aggregated fuzzy weights is calculated as arithmetic mean(8;8;9)=8.33
"c" value in aggregated fuzzy weights is calculated as arithmetic mean(8;8;10)=8.67
"d" value in aggregated fuzzy weights is calculated as max(9;9;10)=10

For Alternative-1 (A_1) according to C_3

"a" value in aggregated fuzzy weights is calculated as min(1;1;1)=1
"b" value in aggregated fuzzy weights is calculated as arithmetic mean(2;2;2)=2
"c" value in aggregated fuzzy weights is calculated as arithmetic mean(2;2;2)=2
"d" value in aggregated fuzzy weights is calculated as max(3;3;3)=3

For Alternative-2 (A_2) according to C_3

"a" value in aggregated fuzzy weights is calculated as min(1;1;0)=0
"b" value in aggregated fuzzy weights is calculated as arithmetic mean(2;2;0)=1.33
"c" value in aggregated fuzzy weights is calculated as arithmetic mean(2;2;1)=1.67
"d" value in aggregated fuzzy weights is calculated as max(3;3;2)=3

For Alternative-3 (A_3) according to C_3

"a" value in aggregated fuzzy weights is calculated as min(7;7;5)=5
"b" value in aggregated fuzzy weights is calculated as arithmetic mean(8;8;6)=7.33
"c" value in aggregated fuzzy weights is calculated as arithmetic mean(8;8;7)=7.67
"d" value in aggregated fuzzy weights is calculated as max(9;9;8)=9

For Alternative-4 (A_4) according to C_3

"a" value in aggregated fuzzy weights is calculated as min(5;5;7)=5
"b" value in aggregated fuzzy weights is calculated as arithmetic mean(6;6;8)=6.67
"c" value in aggregated fuzzy weights is calculated as arithmetic mean(7;7;8)=7.33
"d" value in aggregated fuzzy weights is calculated as max(8;8;9)=9

For Alternative-5 (A_5) according to C_3

"a" value in aggregated fuzzy weights is calculated as min(7;7;5)=5
"b" value in aggregated fuzzy weights is calculated as arithmetic mean(8;8;6)=7.33
"c" value in aggregated fuzzy weights is calculated as arithmetic mean(8;8;7)=7.67
"d" value in aggregated fuzzy weights is calculated as max(9;9;8)=9

For Alternative-1 (A_1) according to C_4

"a" value in aggregated fuzzy weights is calculated as min(8;8;8)=8
"b" value in aggregated fuzzy weights is calculated as arithmetic mean(9;9;9)=9
"c" value in aggregated fuzzy weights is calculated as arithmetic mean(10;10;10)=10
"d" value in aggregated fuzzy weights is calculated as max(10;10;10)=10

For Alternative-2 (A_2) according to C_4

"a" value in aggregated fuzzy weights is calculated as min(4;4;4)=4
"b" value in aggregated fuzzy weights is calculated as arithmetic mean(5;5;5)=5
"c" value in aggregated fuzzy weights is calculated as arithmetic mean(5;5;5)=5
"d" value in aggregated fuzzy weights is calculated as max(6;6;6)=6

For Alternative-3 (A_3) according to C_4

"a" value in aggregated fuzzy weights is calculated as min(5;5;4)=4
"b" value in aggregated fuzzy weights is calculated as arithmetic mean(6;6;5)=5.67

"c" value in aggregated fuzzy weights is calculated as arithmetic mean(7;7;5)=6.33
"d" value in aggregated fuzzy weights is calculated as max(8;8;6)=8

For Alternative-4 (A_4) according to C_4

"a" value in aggregated fuzzy weights is calculated as min(4;4;4)=4
"b" value in aggregated fuzzy weights is calculated as arithmetic mean(5;5;5)=5
"c" value in aggregated fuzzy weights is calculated as arithmetic mean(5;5;5)=5
"d" value in aggregated fuzzy weights is calculated as max(6;6;6)=6

For Alternative-5 (A_5) according to C_4

"a" value in aggregated fuzzy weights is calculated as min(4;4;2)=2
"b" value in aggregated fuzzy weights is calculated as arithmetic mean(5;5;3)=4.33
"c" value in aggregated fuzzy weights is calculated as arithmetic mean(5;5;4)=4.67
"d" value in aggregated fuzzy weights is calculated as max(6;6;5)=6

For Alternative-1 (A_1) according to C_5

"a" value in aggregated fuzzy weights is calculated as min(4;4;4)=4
"b" value in aggregated fuzzy weights is calculated as arithmetic mean(5;5;5)=5
"c" value in aggregated fuzzy weights is calculated as arithmetic mean(5;5;5)=5
"d" value in aggregated fuzzy weights is calculated as max(6;6;6)=6

For Alternative-2 (A_2) according to C_5

"a" value in aggregated fuzzy weights is calculated as min(4;2;2)=2
"b" value in aggregated fuzzy weights is calculated as arithmetic mean(5;3;3)=3.67
"c" value in aggregated fuzzy weights is calculated as arithmetic mean(5;4;4)=4.33
"d" value in aggregated fuzzy weights is calculated as max(6;5;5)=6

For Alternative-3 (A_3) according to C_5

"a" value in aggregated fuzzy weights is calculated as min(5;5;4)=4
"b" value in aggregated fuzzy weights is calculated as arithmetic mean(6;6;5)=5.67
"c" value in aggregated fuzzy weights is calculated as arithmetic mean(7;7;5)=6.33
"d" value in aggregated fuzzy weights is calculated as max(8;8;6)=8

For Alternative-4 (A_4) according to C_5

"a" value in aggregated fuzzy weights is calculated as min(2;2;2)=2
"b" value in aggregated fuzzy weights is calculated as arithmetic mean(3;3;3)=3
"c" value in aggregated fuzzy weights is calculated as arithmetic mean(4;4;4)=4
"d" value in aggregated fuzzy weights is calculated as max(5;5;5)=5

For Alternative-5 (A_5) according to C_5

"a" value in aggregated fuzzy weights is calculated as min(5;5;4)=4
"b" value in aggregated fuzzy weights is calculated as arithmetic mean(6;6;5)=5.67
"c" value in aggregated fuzzy weights is calculated as arithmetic mean(7;7;5)=6.33
"d" value in aggregated fuzzy weights is calculated as max(8;8;6)=8

For Alternative-1 (A_1) according to C_6

"a" value in aggregated fuzzy weights is calculated as min(1;2;4)=1
"b" value in aggregated fuzzy weights is calculated as arithmetic mean(2;3;5)=3.33
"c" value in aggregated fuzzy weights is calculated as arithmetic mean(2;4;5)=3.67
"d" value in aggregated fuzzy weights is calculated as max(3;5;6)=6

For Alternative-2 (A_2) according to C_6

"a" value in aggregated fuzzy weights is calculated as min(1;1;1)=1
"b" value in aggregated fuzzy weights is calculated as arithmetic mean(2;2;2)=2
"c" value in aggregated fuzzy weights is calculated as arithmetic mean(2;2;2)=2
"d" value in aggregated fuzzy weights is calculated as max(3;3;3)=3

For Alternative-3 (A_3) according to C_6

"a" value in aggregated fuzzy weights is calculated as min(5;4;5)=4
"b" value in aggregated fuzzy weights is calculated as arithmetic mean(6;5;6)=5.67
"c" value in aggregated fuzzy weights is calculated as arithmetic mean(7;5;7)=6.33
"d" value in aggregated fuzzy weights is calculated as max(8;6;8)=8

For Alternative-4 (A_4) according to C_6

"a" value in aggregated fuzzy weights is calculated as min(0;1;1)=0
"b" value in aggregated fuzzy weights is calculated as arithmetic mean(0;2;2)=1.33
"c" value in aggregated fuzzy weights is calculated as arithmetic mean(1;2;2)=1.67
"d" value in aggregated fuzzy weights is calculated as max(2;3;3)=3

For Alternative-5 (A_5) according to C_6

"a" value in aggregated fuzzy weights is calculated as min(8;7;7)=7
"b" value in aggregated fuzzy weights is calculated as arithmetic mean(9;8;8)=8.33
"c" value in aggregated fuzzy weights is calculated as arithmetic mean(10;8;8)=8.67
"d" value in aggregated fuzzy weights is calculated as max(10;9;9)=10

For Alternative-1 (A_1) according to C_7

"a" value in aggregated fuzzy weights is calculated as min(4;5;4)=4
"b" value in aggregated fuzzy weights is calculated as arithmetic mean(5;6;5)=5.33
"c" value in aggregated fuzzy weights is calculated as arithmetic mean(5;7;5)=5.67
"d" value in aggregated fuzzy weights is calculated as max(6;8;6)=8

For Alternative-2 (A_2) according to C_7

"a" value in aggregated fuzzy weights is calculated as min(2;2;2)=2
"b" value in aggregated fuzzy weights is calculated as arithmetic mean(3;3;3)=3
"c" value in aggregated fuzzy weights is calculated as arithmetic mean(4;4;4)=4
"d" value in aggregated fuzzy weights is calculated as max(5;5;5)=5

For Alternative-3 (A_3) according to C_7

"a" value in aggregated fuzzy weights is calculated as min(7;7;5)=5
"b" value in aggregated fuzzy weights is calculated as arithmetic mean(8;8;6)=7.33
"c" value in aggregated fuzzy weights is calculated as arithmetic mean(8;8;7)=7.67
"d" value in aggregated fuzzy weights is calculated as max(9;9;8)=9

For Alternative-4 (A_4) according to C_7

"a" value in aggregated fuzzy weights is calculated as min(1;0;1)=0
"b" value in aggregated fuzzy weights is calculated as arithmetic mean(2;0;2)=1.33
"c" value in aggregated fuzzy weights is calculated as arithmetic mean(2;1;2)=1.67
"d" value in aggregated fuzzy weights is calculated as max(3;2;3)=3

For Alternative-5 (A_5) according to C_7

"a" value in aggregated fuzzy weights is calculated as min(5;4;5)=4
"b" value in aggregated fuzzy weights is calculated as arithmetic mean(6;5;6)=5.67
"c" value in aggregated fuzzy weights is calculated as arithmetic mean(7;5;7)=6.33
"d" value in aggregated fuzzy weights is calculated as max(8;6;8)=8

For Alternative-1 (A_1) according to C_8

"a" value in aggregated fuzzy weights is calculated as min(2;2;4)=2
"b" value in aggregated fuzzy weights is calculated as arithmetic mean(3;3;5)=3.67
"c" value in aggregated fuzzy weights is calculated as arithmetic mean(4;4;5)=4.33
"d" value in aggregated fuzzy weights is calculated as max(5;5;6)=6

For Alternative-2 (A_2) according to C_8

"a" value in aggregated fuzzy weights is calculated as min(2;4;2)=2
"b" value in aggregated fuzzy weights is calculated as arithmetic mean(3;5;3)=3.67

"c" value in aggregated fuzzy weights is calculated as arithmetic mean(4;5;4)=4.33
"d" value in aggregated fuzzy weights is calculated as max(5;6;5)=6

For Alternative-3 (A_3) according to C_8

"a" value in aggregated fuzzy weights is calculated as min(7;7;8)=7
"b" value in aggregated fuzzy weights is calculated as arithmetic mean(8;8;9)=8.33
"c" value in aggregated fuzzy weights is calculated as arithmetic mean(8;8;10)=8.67
"d" value in aggregated fuzzy weights is calculated as max(9;9;10)=10

For Alternative-4 (A_4) according to C_8

"a" value in aggregated fuzzy weights is calculated as min(2;2;2)=2
"b" value in aggregated fuzzy weights is calculated as arithmetic mean(3;3;3)=3
"c" value in aggregated fuzzy weights is calculated as arithmetic mean(4;4;4)=4
"d" value in aggregated fuzzy weights is calculated as max(5;5;5)=5

For Alternative-5 (A_5) according to C_8

"a" value in aggregated fuzzy weights is calculated as min(7;7;8)=7
"b" value in aggregated fuzzy weights is calculated as arithmetic mean(8;8;9)=8.33
"c" value in aggregated fuzzy weights is calculated as arithmetic mean(8;8;10)=8.67
"d" value in aggregated fuzzy weights is calculated as max(9;9;10)=10

For Alternative-1 (A_1) according to C_9

"a" value in aggregated fuzzy weights is calculated as min(8;8;8)=8
"b" value in aggregated fuzzy weights is calculated as arithmetic mean(9;9;9)=9
"c" value in aggregated fuzzy weights is calculated as arithmetic mean(10;10;10)=10
"d" value in aggregated fuzzy weights is calculated as max(10;10;10)=10

For Alternative-2 (A_2) according to C_9

"a" value in aggregated fuzzy weights is calculated as min(7;7;5)=5
"b" value in aggregated fuzzy weights is calculated as arithmetic mean(8;8;6)=7.33
"c" value in aggregated fuzzy weights is calculated as arithmetic mean(8;8;7)=7.67
"d" value in aggregated fuzzy weights is calculated as max(9;9;8)=9

For Alternative-3 (A_3) according to C_9

"a" value in aggregated fuzzy weights is calculated as min(8;8;8)=8
"b" value in aggregated fuzzy weights is calculated as arithmetic mean(9;9;9)=9
"c" value in aggregated fuzzy weights is calculated as arithmetic mean(10;10;10)=10
"d" value in aggregated fuzzy weights is calculated as max(10;10;10)=10

For Alternative-4 (A_4) according to C_9

"a" value in aggregated fuzzy weights is calculated as min(2;4;4)=2
"b" value in aggregated fuzzy weights is calculated as arithmetic mean(3;5;5)=4.33
"c" value in aggregated fuzzy weights is calculated as arithmetic mean(4;5;5)=4.67
"d" value in aggregated fuzzy weights is calculated as max(5;6;6)=6

For Alternative-5 (A_5) according to C_9

"a" value in aggregated fuzzy weights is calculated as min(7;7;8)=7
"b" value in aggregated fuzzy weights is calculated as arithmetic mean(8;8;9)=8.33
"c" value in aggregated fuzzy weights is calculated as arithmetic mean(8;8;10)=8.67
"d" value in aggregated fuzzy weights is calculated as max(9;9;10)=10

Fuzzy-decision matrix and fuzzy weights of alternatives are shown in Table 7.

Step 3: The normalized fuzzy-decision matrix is constructed by using Eq.(5) shown in Table 8.

For instance, for Criteria 1 initially, $d_j^* = \max_i d_{ij}$ value is determined due to C_1 is a benefit criterion. When the 1st column of Table 7 is examined, the maximum value is determined as 10. All values of this column are divided into 10 as shown in Eq.(5). In Table 7, fuzzy weights of Alternative 1 (A_1) according to Criteria 1 (C_1) are (5;6;7;8). So normalized fuzzy weights are calculated as (0.5;0.6;0.7;0.8). Likewise, in Table 7 fuzzy weights of Alternative 2 (A_2) according to Criteria 1 (C_1) are (0;1;2;5). So normalized fuzzy weights are calculated as (0;0.1;0.2;0.5).

Note that, C_4 (cost) is a cost criterion, so $a_j^- = \min_i a_{ij}$ value is determined. When the column of cost criterion in Table 7 is examined, the minimum value is determined as 2. All values of this column are divided into 2 as shown in Eq.(5). It is important to observe the rules in the formula when dividing. For instance, in Table 7, fuzzy weights of Alternative 1 (A_1) according to Criteria 4 (C_4) are (8;9;10;10). As mentioned above, the minimum value of the related column was determined as 2. So normalized fuzzy weights are calculated as (2/10;2/10;2/9;2/8) = (0.2;0.2;0.22;0.25). Likewise, in Table 7, fuzzy weights of Alternative 2 (A_2) according to Criteria 4 (C_4) are (4;5;5;6). As mentioned above, the minimum value of the related column was determined as 2. So normalized fuzzy weights are calculated as (2/6;2/5;2/5;2/4) = (0.33;0.4;0.4;0.5).

Step 4: Weighted normalized fuzzy-decision matrix is calculated by using Eq.(6) as in Table 9. For instance, in the normalized fuzzy-decision matrix (Table 8), ratings of Alternative 1 according to C_1 is (0.5;0.6;0.7;0.8). Weight of the C_1 (from Table 7) is (0.7;0.87;0.93;1). So ratings of Alternative 1 according to C_1 in Weighted normalized fuzzy-decision matrix can be calculated as (0.5x0.7;0.6x0.87;0.7x0.93;0.8x1) = (0.35;0.52;0.65;0.8).

Step 5: Fuzzy PIS and Fuzzy NIS are determined by using Eq.(7) and Eq.(8) as shown in Table 10.

Step 6: The distance of each alternative from Fuzzy PIS and Fuzzy NIS with respect to each criterion are calculated by using Eq.(11) and shown in Table 11 and Table 12 respectively. d_i^* and d_i^- values for five possible alternatives are calculated by using Eq.(9) and Eq.(10). For instance, distance between Alternative 1 and A* according to C_1 is calculated as follows:

$$d\left(A_1,A^*\right)=\sqrt{\left(1/4\right)\left[\left(1-0.35\right)^2+\left(1-0.52\right)^2+\left(1-0.65\right)^2+\left(1-0.80\right)^2\right]}=0.45$$

Likewise, distance between Alternative 1 and A^- according to C_1 is calculated as follows;

$$d\left(A_1,A^-\right)=\sqrt{\left(1/4\right)\left[\left(0-0.35\right)^2+\left(0-0.52\right)^2+\left(0-0.65\right)^2+\left(0-0.80\right)^2\right]}=0.60$$

d_i^* value of Alternative 1 is calculated as:

$$d_i^*=0.45+0.52+0.50+0.80+0.41+0.44+0.30+0.67+0.32=4.41$$

Likewise, d_i^* value of Alternative 1 is calculated as:

$$d_i^-=0.60+0.28+0.12+0.06+0.24+0.21+0.35+0.27+0.37=2.51$$

Step 7: The CC_i values are calculated by using Eq.(12) and shown in Table 13.

For instance, for Alternative 1 CC_i value is calculated as:

$$CC_1=\frac{2.51}{2.51+4.41}=0.36$$

Likewise, CC_i values of the other alternatives are calculated as:

$$CC_2=\frac{1.96}{4.99+1.96}=0.28$$

$$CC_3=\frac{3.78}{3.36+3.78}=0.53$$

$$CC_4=\frac{1.79}{5.10+1.79}=0.26$$

$$CC_5=\frac{4.22}{3.11+4.22}=0.58$$

Table 7. Fuzzy-decision matrix and fuzzy weights of alternatives

Alternatives	C_1	C_2	C_3	C_4	C_5	C_6	C_7	C_8	C_9
A_1	(5;6;7;8)	(4;5;5;6)	(1;2;2;3)	(8;9;10;10)	(4;5;5;6)	(1;3.33;3.67;6)	(4;5.33;5.67;8)	(2;3.67;4.33;6)	(8;9;10;10)
A_2	(0;1;2;5)	(1;2.33;2.67;5)	(0;1.33;1.67;3)	(4;5;5;6)	(2;3.67;4.33;6)	(1;2;2;3)	(2;3;4;5)	(2;3.67;4.33;6)	(5;7.33;7.67;9)
A_3	(5;7.33;7.67;9)	(7;8;8;9)	(5;7.33;7.67;9)	(4;5.67;6.33;8)	(4;5.67;6.33;8)	(4;5.67;6.33;8)	(5;7.33;7.67;9)	(7;8.33;8.67;10)	(8;9;10;10)
A_4	(0;0.67;1.33;3)	(1;2.33;2.67;5)	(5;6.67;7.33;9)	(4;5;5;6)	(2;3;4;5)	(0;1.33;1.67;3)	(0;1.33;1.67;3)	(2;3;4;5)	(2;4.33;4.67;6)
A_5	(7;8.67;9.33;10)	(7;8.33;8.67;10)	(5;7.33;7.67;9)	(2;4.33;4.67;6)	(4;5.67;6.33;8)	(7;8.33;8.67;10)	(4;5.67;6.33;8)	(7;8.33;8.67;10)	(7;8.33;8.67;10)
Weight	(0.7;0.87;0.93;1)	(0.4;0.53;0.57;0.8)	(0.2;0.37;0.43;0.6)	(0.8;0.9;1;1)	(0.1;0.3;0.3;0.6)	(0.2;0.43;0.47;0.6)	(0.4;0.5;0.5;0.6)	(0.7;0.83;0.87;1)	(0.1;0.33;0.37;0.6)

Table 8. Normalized fuzzy-decision matrix

Alternatives	C_1	C_2	C_3	C_4	C_5	C_6	C_7	C_8	C_9
A_1	(0.5;0.6;0.7;0.8)	(0.4;0.5;0.5;0.6)	(0.11;0.22;0.22;0.33)	(0.2;0.2;0.22;0.25)	(0.5;0.63;0.63;0.75)	(0.1;0.33;0.37;0.6)	(0.44;0.59;0.63;0.89)	(0.2;0.37;0.43;0.6)	(0.8;0.9;1;1)
A_2	(0;0.1;0.2;0.5)	(0.1;0.23;0.27;0.5)	(0;0.15;0.19;0.33)	(0.33;0.4;0.4;0.5)	(0.25;0.46;0.54;0.75)	(0.1;0.2;0.2;0.3)	(0.22;0.33;0.44;0.56)	(0.2;0.37;0.43;0.6)	(0.5;0.73;0.77;0.9)
A_3	(0.5;0.73;0.77;0.9)	(0.7;0.8;0.8;0.9)	(0.56;0.81;0.85;1)	(0.25;0.32;0.35;0.5)	(0.5;0.71;0.79;1)	(0.4;0.57;0.63;0.8)	(0.56;0.81;0.85;1)	(0.7;0.83;0.87;1)	(0.8;0.9;1;1)
A_4	(0;0.07;0.13;0.3)	(0.1;0.23;0.27;0.5)	(0.56;0.74;0.81;1)	(0.33;0.4;0.4;0.5)	(0.25;0.38;0.5;0.63)	(0;0.13;0.17;0.3)	(0;0.15;0.19;0.33)	(0.2;0.3;0.4;0.5)	(0.2;0.43;0.47;0.6)
A_5	(0.7;0.87;0.93;1)	(0.7;0.83;0.87;1)	(0.56;0.81;0.85;1)	(0.33;0.43;0.46;1)	(0.5;0.71;0.79;1)	(0.7;0.83;0.87;1)	(0.44;0.63;0.7;0.89)	(0.7;0.83;0.87;1)	(0.7;0.83;0.87;1)

Table 9. Weighted normalized fuzzy-decision matrix

Alternatives	C_1	C_2	C_3	C_4	C_5	C_6	C_7	C_8	C_9
A_1	(0.35;0.52;0.65;0.8)	(0.16;0.27;0.28;0.48)	(0.02;0.08;0.1;0.2)	(0.16;0.18;0.22;0.25)	(0.05;0.19;0.19;0.45)	(0.02;0.14;0.17;0.36)	(0.18;0.3;0.31;0.53)	(0.14;0.31;0.38;0.6)	(0.08;0.3;0.37;0.6)
A_2	(0;0.09;0.19;0.5)	(0.04;0.12;0.15;0.4)	(0;0.05;0.08;0.2)	(0.27;0.36;0.4;0.5)	(0.03;0.14;0.16;0.45)	(0.02;0.09;0.09;0.18)	(0.09;0.17;0.22;0.33)	(0.14;0.31;0.38;0.6)	(0.05;0.24;0.28;0.54)
A_3	(0.35;0.64;0.72;0.9)	(0.28;0.43;0.45;0.72)	(0.11;0.3;0.37;0.6)	(0.2;0.28;0.35;0.5)	(0.05;0.21;0.24;0.6)	(0.08;0.25;0.3;0.48)	(0.22;0.41;0.43;0.6)	(0.49;0.69;0.75;1)	(0.08;0.3;0.37;0.6)
A_4	(0;0.06;0.12;0.3)	(0.04;0.12;0.15;0.4)	(0.11;0.27;0.35;0.6)	(0.27;0.36;0.4;0.5)	(0.03;0.11;0.15;0.38)	(0;0.06;0.08;0.18)	(0;0.07;0.09;0.2)	(0.14;0.25;0.35;0.5)	(0.02;0.14;0.17;0.36)
A_5	(0.49;0.75;0.87;1)	(0.28;0.44;0.49;0.8)	(0.11;0.3;0.37;0.6)	(0.27;0.39;0.46;1)	(0.05;0.21;0.24;0.6)	(0.14;0.36;0.4;0.6)	(0.18;0.31;0.35;0.53)	(0.49;0.69;0.75;1)	(0.07;0.28;0.32;0.6)

Table 10. Fuzzy PIS and Fuzzy NIS

	C_1	C_2	C_3	C_4	C_5	C_6	C_7	C_8	C_9
$A*$	(1;1;1;1)	(0.8;0.8;0.8;0.8)	(0.6;0.6;0.6;0.6)	(1;1;1;1)	(0.6;0.6;0.6;0.6)	(0.6;0.6;0.6;0.6)	(0.6;0.6;0.6;0.6)	(1;1;1;1)	(0.6;0.6;0.6;0.6)
$A-$	(0;0;0;0)	(0.04;0.04;0.04;0.04)	(0;0;0;0)	(0.16;0.16;0.16;0.16)	(0.03;0.03;0.03;0.03)	(0;0;0;0)	(0;0;0;0)	(0.14;0.14;0.14;0.14)	(0.02;0.02;0.02;0.02)

Table 11. Distances between alternatives and A with respect to each criterion*

	C_1	C_2	C_3	C_4	C_5	C_6	C_7	C_8	C_9	d_i^*
d (A_1, $A*$)	0.45	0.52	0.50	0.80	0.41	0.44	0.30	0.67	0.32	4.41
d (A_2, $A*$)	0.83	0.64	0.52	0.62	0.44	0.51	0.41	0.67	0.37	4.99
d (A_3, $A*$)	0.40	0.37	0.31	0.67	0.38	0.35	0.23	0.32	0.32	3.36
d (A_4, $A*$)	0.89	0.64	0.32	0.62	0.45	0.53	0.51	0.70	0.44	5.10
d (A_5, $A*$)	0.29	0.35	0.31	0.55	0.38	0.28	0.29	0.32	0.34	3.11

Table 12. Distances between alternatives and A⁻ with respect to each criterion

	C_1	C_2	C_3	C_4	C_5	C_6	C_7	C_8	C_9	d_i^-
d (A_1, $A-$)	0.60	0.28	0.12	0.06	0.24	0.21	0.35	0.27	0.37	2.51
d (A_2, $A-$)	0.27	0.19	0.11	0.24	0.23	0.11	0.22	0.27	0.31	1.96
d (A_3, $A-$)	0.68	0.46	0.39	0.21	0.32	0.31	0.43	0.62	0.37	3.78
d (A_4, $A-$)	0.16	0.19	0.38	0.24	0.19	0.10	0.12	0.21	0.20	1.79
d (A_5, $A-$)	0.80	0.50	0.39	0.46	0.32	0.41	0.37	0.62	0.35	4.22

Table 13.

Alternatives	d_i^*	d_i^-	CC_i
A_1	4.41	2.51	0.36
A_2	4.99	1.96	0.28
A_3	3.36	3.78	0.53
A_4	5.10	1.79	0.26
A_5	3.11	4.22	0.58

Table 13 is obtained as a result of mathematical calculations of Fuzzy TOPSIS method. As a result of the calculations, alternatives are ranked according to Closeness Coefficient. According to the closeness coefficients of five AGV alternatives, the ranking order determined as $A_5 > A_3 > A_1 > A_2 > A_4$. In the numerical example, A_5 is determined as the most suitable alternative.

FUTURE RESEARCH DIRECTIONS

The TOPSIS method has been used in many problems since the first day it was developed. At the same time, this method is also being developed. In this study, a multiple criteria decision making problem is solved by using the Fuzzy TOPSIS method. There are 9 evaluation criteria for the problem. In future research, more different evaluation criteria can be determined to the numerical example.

The problem produces a result in the light of the linguistic expressions of the decision-makers. How are the results affected when decision-makers change the linguistic expressions they use to evaluate criteria and alternatives? In the next step of the study, sensitivity analysis can be added to answer this question.

However, in practice, there is a limitation of the method. As the number of criteria and / or alternatives increases, it is time-consuming to collect evaluations of decision-makers. In these and similar problems, decision-makers are usually composed of managers who are experts in their fields. Due to the workload and time constraints of the managers, the method may become difficult to implement. The main reason for this is that decision makers evaluate each alternative individually according to all criteria. A more efficient collection of evaluations from decision-makers can be considered as a topic for future research.

CONCLUSION

A fuzzy logic approach can be used in cases where decision makers' interpretations are unclear or use linguistic expressions. The fuzzy logic approach does not require an element to belong to a set precisely. One criterion may be less important than the other criterion. The expression "less important" needs to be digitized. By this means, a result can be reached with mathematical calculations. With the fuzzy TOPSIS method, these operations can be performed easily. The Fuzzy TOPSIS method is flexible due to the closeness coefficient. In addition to determining the ranking order, the status of all possible alternatives can be assessed by using this method (C.-T. Chen et al., 2006).

In this section, the TOPSIS method which is one of the multi-criteria decision-making methods is investigated and the calculations are detailed with a numerical example. In the numerical example, it is aimed to select the most appropriate material handling equipment from five alternatives for a manufacturing company. In order to solve this problem, 3 decision makers evaluated the alternatives. Decision-makers made their evaluations within the scope of 9 criteria. Decision makers first evaluated the criteria and then evaluated the alternatives according to these criteria. In the evaluations, linguistic expressions were used. The problem was solved by Fuzzy TOPSIS method as a suitable solution technique for the structure of the problem. As a result of the calculations, Alternative-5 (A5) was determined as the most suitable alternative. All alternatives are listed by using Closeness Coefficient. This ranking will be a guide to the manager when making a decision.

There are 3 main inputs in the decision-making process. These are evaluation criteria, alternatives, and decision-makers. As the number of these main inputs increases, the problem becomes more complex. This complex problem can be solved easily by the TOPSIS method. With the TOPSIS method, alternatives can be examined in the light of multiple criteria. The evaluation criteria may be contradictory criteria such as cost and quality. In the TOPSIS method, all criteria can be evaluated by labeling the criteria as benefit or cost. In addition to this, the fuzzy TOPSIS method can deal with the ratings of both quantitative as well as qualitative criteria (C.-T. Chen et al., 2006). The contribution of this study is to explain how to use fuzzy TOPSIS method in an industrial problem. Similarly, the same method can be easily applied by changing the existing alternatives and criteria for problems such as personnel selection, operator selection, and machine selection.

REFERENCES

Abdel-Basset, M., Manogaran, G., Gamal, A., & Smarandache, F. (2019). A Group Decision Making Framework Based on Neutrosophic TOPSIS Approach for Smart Medical Device Selection. *Journal of Medical Systems*, *43*(2), 38. doi:10.100710916-019-1156-1 PMID:30627801

Aikhuele, D. O., & Turan, F. M. (2017). An Intuitionistic Fuzzy Multi-Criteria Decision-Making Method Based on an Exponential-Related Function. *International Journal of Fuzzy System Applications*, *6*(4), 33–46. doi:10.4018/IJFSA.2017100103

Aikhuele, D. O., & Turan, F. M. (2018). A modified exponential score function for troubleshooting an improved locally made Offshore Patrol Boat engine. *Journal of Marine Engineering & Technology*, *17*(1), 52–58. doi:10.1080/20464177.2017.1286841

Biswas, P., Pramanik, S., & Giri, B. C. (2016). TOPSIS method for multi-attribute group decision-making under single-valued neutrosophic environment. *Neural Computing & Applications*, *27*(3), 727–737. doi:10.100700521-015-1891-2

Boran, F. E., Genç, S., Kurt, M., & Akay, D. (2009). A multi-criteria intuitionistic fuzzy group decision making for supplier selection with TOPSIS method. *Expert Systems with Applications*, *36*(8), 11363–11368. doi:10.1016/j.eswa.2009.03.039

Castillo, O., & Melin, P. (2008). Type-2 Fuzzy Logic: Theory and Applications. Berlin, Germany: Springer-Verlag. doi:10.1007/978-3-540-76284-3

Chan, F. T. S. (2002). Design of material handling equipment selection system: An integration of expert system with analytic hierarchy process approach. *Integrated Manufacturing Systems*, *13*(1), 58–68. doi:10.1108/09576060210411512

Chan, F. T. S., Ip, R. W. L., & Lau, H. (2001). Integration of expert system with analytic hierarchy process for the design of material handling equipment selection system. *Journal of Materials Processing Technology*, *116*(2–3), 137–145. doi:10.1016/S0924-0136(01)01038-X

Chen, C.-T. (2000). Extensions of the TOPSIS for group decision-making under fuzzy environment. *Fuzzy Sets and Systems*, *114*(1), 1–9. doi:10.1016/S0165-0114(97)00377-1

Chen, C.-T., Lin, C.-T., & Huang, S.-F. (2006). A fuzzy approach for supplier evaluation and selection in supply chain management. *International Journal of Production Economics*, *102*(2), 289–301. doi:10.1016/j.ijpe.2005.03.009

Chen, S.-M., & Lee, L.-W. (2010). Fuzzy multiple attributes group decision-making based on the interval type-2 TOPSIS method. *Expert Systems with Applications*, *37*(4), 2790–2798. doi:10.1016/j.eswa.2009.09.012

Daneshvar Rouyendegh, B., Yildizbasi, A., & Arikan, Ü. Z. B. (2018). Using Intuitionistic Fuzzy TOPSIS in Site Selection of Wind Power Plants in Turkey. *Advances in Fuzzy Systems*, *2018*, 1–14. doi:10.1155/2018/6703798

Eko Saputro, T., & Daneshvar Rouyendegh, B. (2016). A hybrid approach for selecting material handling equipment in a warehouse. *International Journal of Management Science and Engineering Management, 11*(1), 34–48. doi:10.1080/17509653.2015.1042535

Gupta, H., & Barua, M. K. (2017). Supplier selection among SMEs on the basis of their green innovation ability using BWM and fuzzy TOPSIS. *Journal of Cleaner Production, 152*, 242–258. doi:10.1016/j.jclepro.2017.03.125

Hwang, C.-L., & Yoon, K. (1981). *Multiple attribute decision making, methods and applications. Lecture Notes in Economics and Mathematical Systems* (Vol. 186). New York: Springer-Verlag.

Jee, D.-H., & Kang, K.-J. (2000). A method for optimal material selection aided with decision making theory. *Materials & Design, 21*(3), 199–206. doi:10.1016/S0261-3069(99)00066-7

Kahraman, C. (Ed.). (2006). *Fuzzy applications in industrial engineering* (Vol. 201). Berlin, Germany: Springer. doi:10.1007/3-540-33517-X

Kelemenis, A., & Askounis, D. (2010). A new TOPSIS-based multi-criteria approach to personnel selection. *Expert Systems with Applications, 37*(7), 4999–5008. doi:10.1016/j.eswa.2009.12.013

Kulak, O. (2005). A decision support system for fuzzy multi-attribute selection of material handling equipments. *Expert Systems with Applications, 29*(2), 310–319. doi:10.1016/j.eswa.2005.04.004

Lee, L.-W., & Chen, S.-M. (2008a). Fuzzy interpolative reasoning using interval Type-2 fuzzy sets. In *Proceedings of the International Conference on Industrial, Engineering, and Other Applications of Applied Intelligent Systems* (pp. 92-101). Berlin, Germany: Springer. 10.1007/978-3-540-69052-8_10

Lee, L.-W., & Chen, S.-M. (2008b). Fuzzy multiple attributes group decision-making based on the extension of TOPSIS method and interval type-2 fuzzy sets. In *Proceedings of the 2008 International Conference on Machine Learning and Cybernetics* 6, pp. 3260-3265. IEEE 10.1109/ICMLC.2008.4620968

Maniya, K. D., & Bhatt, M. G. (2011). A multi-attribute selection of automated guided vehicle using the AHP/M-GRA technique. *International Journal of Production Research, 49*(20), 6107–6124. doi:10.1080/00207543.2010.518988

Nabeeh, N. A., Smarandache, F., Abdel-Basset, M., El-Ghareeb, H. A., & Aboelfetouh, A. (2019). An Integrated Neutrosophic-TOPSIS Approach and Its Application to Personnel Selection: A New Trend in Brain Processing and Analysis. *IEEE Access: Practical Innovations, Open Solutions, 7*, 29734–29744. doi:10.1109/ACCESS.2019.2899841

Nguyen, H.-T., Md Dawal, S. Z., Nukman, Y., Rifai, A., & Aoyama, H. (2016). An Integrated MCDM Model for Conveyor Equipment Evaluation and Selection in an FMC Based on a Fuzzy AHP and Fuzzy ARAS in the Presence of Vagueness. *PLOS ONE, 11*(4). . pone.0153222 doi:10.1371/journal

Sawant, V. B., Mohite, S. S., & Patil, R. (2011). *A Decision-Making Methodology for Automated Guided Vehicle Selection Problem Using a Preference Selection Index Method.* 176–181. Berlin, Germany: Springer-Verlag.

Shanian, A., & Savadogo, O. (2006). TOPSIS multiple-criteria decision support analysis for material selection of metallic bipolar plates for polymer electrolyte fuel cell. *Journal of Power Sources*, *159*(2), 1095–1104. doi:10.1016/j.jpowsour.2005.12.092

Tian, G., Zhang, H., Feng, Y., Jia, H., Zhang, C., Jiang, Z., ... Li, P. (2017). Operation patterns analysis of automotive components remanufacturing industry development in China. *Journal of Cleaner Production*, *164*, 1363–1375. doi:10.1016/j.jclepro.2017.07.028

Tzeng, G.-H., & Huang, J.-J. (2011). *Multiple Attribute Decision Making: Methods and Applications*. Chapman and Hall/CRC. doi:10.1201/b11032

Zadeh, L. A. (1965). Fuzzy sets. *Information and Control*, *8*(3), 338–353. doi:10.1016/S0019-9958(65)90241-X

ADDITIONAL READING

Behzadian, M., Khanmohammadi Otaghsara, S., Yazdani, M., & Ignatius, J. (2012). A state-of the-art survey of TOPSIS applications. *Expert Systems with Applications*, *39*(17), 13051–13069. doi:10.1016/j.eswa.2012.05.056

Boran, F. E., Genç, S., Kurt, M., & Akay, D. (2009). A multi-criteria intuitionistic fuzzy group decision making for supplier selection with TOPSIS method. *Expert Systems with Applications*, *36*(8), 11363–11368. doi:10.1016/j.eswa.2009.03.039

Büyüközkan, G., & Güleryüz, S. (2016)... *Fuzzy Multi Criteria Decision Making Approach for Evaluating Sustainable Energy Technology Alternatives.*, *1*, 6.

Chen, C.-T. (2000). Extensions of the TOPSIS for group decision-making under fuzzy environment. *Fuzzy Sets and Systems*, *114*(1), 1–9. doi:10.1016/S0165-0114(97)00377-1

Chen, C.-T., Lin, C.-T., & Huang, S.-F. (2006). A fuzzy approach for supplier evaluation and selection in supply chain management. *International Journal of Production Economics*, *102*(2), 289–301. doi:10.1016/j.ijpe.2005.03.009

Shukla, R. K., Garg, D., & Agarwal, A. (2014). An integrated approach of Fuzzy AHP and Fuzzy TOPSIS in modeling supply chain coordination. *Production & Manufacturing Research*, *2*(1), 415–437. do i:10.1080/21693277.2014.919886

Wang, J.-W., Cheng, C.-H., & Huang, K.-C. (2009). Fuzzy hierarchical TOPSIS for supplier selection. *Applied Soft Computing*, *9*(1), 377–386. doi:10.1016/j.asoc.2008.04.014

Wang, T.-C., & Chang, T.-H. (2007). Application of TOPSIS in evaluating initial training aircraft under a fuzzy environment. *Expert Systems with Applications*, *33*(4), 870–880. doi:10.1016/j.eswa.2006.07.003

KEY TERMS AND DEFINITIONS

Alternative: A set of options to be decided upon as a result of an assessment.

Criteria: A level of quality that can be used when making a decision.

Decision: Choosing alternatives under certain constraints.

Decision Maker: Senior official with expertise in the relevant field.

Fuzzy: Incomplete and/or unclear.

Fuzzy Logic: Fuzzy logic is an approach that defines the belonging of an element to the related set with membership functions rather than 1-0 Boolean logic.

Importance Weight: The degree of priority.

Chapter 8
Intuitionistic Fuzzy TOPSIS Model Based on Reliability Criteria and a Dynamic Mathematical Operator for Solving MCGDM Problems

Daniel Osezua Aikhuele
https://orcid.org/0000-0001-9274-4530
Bells University of Technology, Nigeria

ABSTRACT

This chapter proposes a model based on the IF-TOPSIS method and the DIFWGϵ operator for the evaluation of renewable power plants. The model uses five reliability-based criteria and addresses the dynamic factors associated with renewable power plant operations. The factors include: the changing energy demand and consumption, the changing environmental conditions, rapidly increasing population, social activities, and awareness. The result from the evaluation shows that the Solar power plant (S3) is the most preferred power source considering the dynamic factors associated with the plant operation, the plant location, and the reliability-based criteria used for the assessment.

INTRODUCTION

Intuitionistic fuzzy set (IFS) was introduced by Atanassov, (1986), who extend the traditional Fuzzy Set (FS) theory to include a non-membership function ($\upsilon_A(x)$) to the ready existing membership function ($\mu_A(x)$) in the FS theory. The IFS which was developed mainly to address and solve problems that cannot be fully expressed with the FS theory, due to complexity and fuzziness in most decision-making information, has remained a very active research theme in industrial engineering and among decision-making researchers (Aikhuele & Turan, 2017b).

DOI: 10.4018/978-1-7998-2216-5.ch008

Example of complex decision-making information; "during voting, if there are ten persons voting for an issue, and three of them give the "agree'', four of them give the "disagree", and the others abstain, obviously, FS cannot fully express the polling information"(Liu & Zhang, 2014).

IFS which is used for solving complex decision-making problems recently has been integrated to solve Multi-criteria Group Decision-making (MCGDM) problems, which requires the simultaneous consideration of several attributes/criteria before decision alternatives are ranked. In integrating the IFS for MCGDM problems, an intuitionistic fuzzy number(s) (IFNs), which is/are relatively independent and bounded with the conditions that, the summation of the membership and non-membership function must not exceed one (Deschrijver & Kerre, 2007), are used for the mathematical computations in the integrated IFS theory.

An extensive review of the IFS for solving MCGDM problems, however, has shown an increase in their application over the last decade. Some of their applications when integrated with MCGDM techniques include; the use of IFS in the fuzzy analytic network process method (Saeedi & Malek, 2008). IFS in Analytical network process and in intuitionistic fuzzy preference relations (Zhou, et al, 2018). Others include the IFS in the Technique for Order of Preference by Similarity to Ideal Solution (FTOPSIS) (Daneshvar, et al, 2018), IFS in fuzzy data envelopment analysis (Puri & Prasad Yadav, 2015). IFS in the Evaluation based on Distance from Average Solution (EDAS) (Kahraman et al., 2017), IFS in Decision Making Experiment and Evaluation Laboratories (DEMATEL) method (Gan & Luo, 2017) and IFS in the elimination et choice translating reality (ELECTRE) method (Rouyendegh, 2018). IFS in multi-objective optimization on the basis of ratio analysis (MOORA) method (Yazdani, 2015), IFS in Gray relational analysis method (Wei, 2011), IFS in Linear programming method (Parvathi & Malathi, 2012) and the use of IFS in VlseKriterijumska Optimizacija I Kompromisno Resenje (Serbian term) (Wan, et al, 2013) and IFS in C-means clustering method (Chaira, 2001).

Furthermore, IFS has also been applied in several integrated MCGDM methods, some which include, IFS in Grey-Intuitionistic Fuzzy-ELECTRE and VIKOR used for the assessment of contractors in a construction project (Hashemi, et al., 2018). IFS in an integrated GRA Technique and Fuzzy Entropy-Based TOPSIS Method for the selection of sustainable building materials supplier (Chen, 2019). IFS in an integrated model that is based on integrated weighting approach and fuzzy VIKOR (Suh, et al., 2019). IFS in a model based on the integration of fuzzy entropy and distance measure that uses TOPSIS method for decision-making (Joshi & Kumar, 2014).

From the foregoing, it is obvious that IFS has been applied in several MCGDM methods and for solving decision-making problems in literature. The literature review has provided a critical assessment of previous and related work within the research area and scope, by highlighting the research gaps not currently addressed or accounted for by the reviewed methods and approaches. However, in this study, the application of IFS in the MCGDM method is further extended to solve problems that are inherently dynamic, which are problems that required the dynamics of the decisions to be accounted for in the final decision-making process. Hence in this study, an integrated MCGDM model which is based on the Intuitionistic Fuzzy Technique for Order of Preference by Similarity to Ideal Solution (IF-TOPSIS) method and the Dynamic intuitionistic fuzzy Einstein geometric averaging (DIFWGϵ) operator is proposed to address an account for dynamic issues in the decision-making process.

The main advantages and contributions of the integrated MCGDM model are; (1) the model addresses the dynamic issues in the decision-making process and (2) its accounts for the uncertainty in the decision-making process. To the best of my knowledge, this is the first study to present an IFTOPSIS model that addresses dynamic issues in the decision-making process. The rest of the paper is organized as follows. In Section 2, the concept of intuitionistic fuzzy set, the dynamic intuitionistic fuzzy Einstein geometric averaging (DIFWGϵ) operator and the IFTOPSIS model are introduced. This is followed by the algorithm of the proposed integrated model in Section 3. In Section 4, a real-life numerical case study for the selection of a renewable energy source is presented to demonstrate the feasibility of the model. Finally, a concluding remark is presented in Section 5.

PRELIMINARIES

In this section, the basic definitions for the *IFS* concepts as described in Pérez-Domínguez et al. (Pérez-Domínguez, Alvarado-Iniesta, Rodríguez-Borbón, & Vergara-Villegas, 2015) and Despic and Simonovic (Despic & Simonovic, 2000) is presented. Furthermore, the dynamic intuitionistic fuzzy Einstein geometric averaging (DIFWGϵ) operator (Gümüş & Bali, 2017) and the IFTOPSIS model (Aikhuele & Turan, 2017b) is introduced.

Intuitionistic Fuzzy Set (IFS)

Fuzzy set theory was introduced by Zadeh in 1965. Its concept is based on the fact that the range of true value of membership function (relations) is the closed interval [0,1] of real numbers (Zadeh, 1965). The Fuzzy set theory is designed in such a way that it can deal with problems in which source of vagueness and uncertainties are involved. The concept has been successfully utilized in modeling and incorporating imprecise and vague information into the decision framework and judgments of decision-makers.

Mathematically fuzzy set (e.g. fuzzy set $\tilde{A}$) are defined by means of membership function $\mu_A(x)$, which associates with each element x in the universe of discourse X a real number in the interval [0, 1]. A triangular fuzzy number $\widetilde{A}$ which can be defined by the triplet (l_1,m_1,u_1), their membership function are express as;

$$\mu_A\left(x\right)=\begin{cases}\dfrac{x-1}{m-1} & for\, l\leq x\leq m,\\ \dfrac{u-x}{x-m} & for\, m\leq x\leq u,\\ 0 & for\, x>u,\end{cases} \tag{1}$$

Where l, m and u are real numbers and $l < m < u$. Outside the interval [l, u], the pertinence degree is null, and m represents the point in which the pertinence degree is maximum. Basic arithmetic operations on the triangular fuzzy numbers are shown below;

The fuzzy membership function which is designated by μ can be said to be the whole essence of the fuzzy sets theory, and it is defined as a curve that shows how each point in an input space is mapped to a degree of membership usually taken as a real number in the interval [0, 1]. The construction of the fuzzy membership functions depends on the identification of a suitable universe of discourse and the specification of an appropriate membership function (Jang & Sun, 1995). The construction helps in defining the functional overlap between the inputs and then determines the responses of the outputs, where the input membership values are used as weighting factors in determining the influence of the fuzzy output sets for the final output conclusion (Cai, 2011). The commonly used membership functions include the triangular, trapezoidal, Gaussian, sigmoid and bell membership functions.

In this study, the Intuitionistic fuzzy set (IFS) originally introduced by Atanassov, (1986), which is an extension of the traditional Fuzzy Set (FS) theory described above is applied using the intuitionistic non-membership function ($\upsilon_A(x)$) and the existing membership function ($\mu_A(x)$) in the FS theory.

Definition 1

Let A in $X=\{x\}$ be the nonempty fuzzy set with a closed unit interval $I=[0,1]$. Then the *IFS* is therefore given as;

$$A=\left\{x,\mu_A\left(x\right),v_A\left(x\right)\middle|x\in X\right\}. \quad (2)$$

where the mapping μ_A: $X\to[0,1]$ is the membership function of the fuzzy set A; and υ_A: $X\to[0,1]$ is the non-membership function of the fuzzy set, such that $0\leq\mu_A(x)+\upsilon_A(x)\leq1, \forall x\in X$ for each element $x\in X$ in A.

From the above, it is clear that every fuzzy set A, on the nonempty set $X=\{x\}$ is *IFS* that can be defined as;

$$A=\left\{x,\mu_A\left(x\right),1-v_A\left(x\right)\middle|x\in X\right\} \quad (3)$$

The intuitionistic fuzzy hesitation (or the non-determinacy or uncertainty) degree of whether x belong to A or not is given as;

$$\pi_A\left(x\right)=1-\mu_A\left(x\right)-v_A\left(x\right) \quad (4)$$

This degree will arise when there is a relative lack of knowledge, personal error or uncertainty of any form, particularly when; $1-\mu_A(x)-\upsilon_A(x)=0$. For every element $x\in X$ in A, the *IFS A* belongs to the fuzzy set, where $0\leq\pi_A\leq1$, hence, the intuitionistic fuzzy number(s) (IFN(s)) is given as $\alpha=(\mu_A,\upsilon_A,\pi_A)$ or as $\alpha=(\mu_A,\upsilon_A)$.

Definition 2 (Atanassov, 1994)

If the *IFN* is given as $\alpha=(\mu_A,\upsilon_A,\pi_A)$ or as $\alpha=(\mu_A,\upsilon_A)$, then their operational laws are given as (5) to (8) when $\lambda>0$;

$$A.B=\left\{x,\mu_A\left(x\right).\mu_B\left(x\right),v_A\left(x\right)+v_B\left(x\right)-v_A\left(x\right).v_B\left(x\right)\middle|x\in X\right\} \quad (5)$$

$$A+B=\left\{x,\mu_A\left(x\right)+\mu_B\left(x\right)-\mu_A\left(x\right).\mu_B\left(x\right),v_A\left(x\right).v_B\left(x\right)\middle|x\in X\right\} \quad (6)$$

$$\lambda A = \{x, 1-(1-\mu_A(x))^{\lambda}, (v_A(x))^{\lambda} | x \in X\}, \ \ \lambda > 0. \tag{7}$$

$$A^{\lambda} = \{x, (\mu_A(x))^{\lambda}, 1-(1-v_A(x))^{\lambda} | x \in X\}, \ \ \lambda > 0 \tag{8}$$

Intuitionistic Fuzzy Aggregation Operators

Aggregation operators are the mathematical model used for joining and summarizing information gathered from a variety of sources and then use for making real-time decisions. Some of the most common and popular aggregation operators that have found application in engineering management include; the ordered weighted averaging (OWA) operator (Yager, 1988), the weighted OWA (WOWA) operator and its interpolation function (Torra, 2000), continuous ordered weighted geometric (C-OWG) operator (Yager & Xu, 2006), the ordered weighted geometric averaging (OWGA) operator (Xu & Da, 2002), the generalized ordered weighted proportional averaging (GOWPA) operator (Zhou & Chen, 2014), the generalized ordered weighted averaging (GOWA) operator and the weighted generalized mean (WGM) operator (Jose-M & Montserrat, 2010), the uncertain dynamic linguistic weighted harmonic mean (UDLWHM) operator (Park et al., 2011), linguistic harmonic mean (LHM) operator, linguistic weighted harmonic mean (LWHM) operator, linguistic ordered weighted harmonic mean operator, and linguistic hybrid harmonic mean (LHHM) operator by (Park, Gwak, & Kwun, 2011). The generalized triangular intuitionistic fuzzy geometric averaging operator (Aikhuele & Odofin, 2017). Uncertain dynamic linguistic weighted harmonic mean (UDLWHM) operator (Park, Kwun, et al., 2011) and the dynamic intuitionistic fuzzy Einstein geometric averaging (DIFWG϶) operator (Gümüş & Bali, 2017). In this study, however, we will be concerned only with the dynamic intuitionistic fuzzy Einstein geometric averaging (DIFWG϶) operator for aggregating decision-making information. Detail definition of the operation is given below.

Definition 3 (Gümüş & Bali, 2017)

Let $\alpha(t_i) = \left(\mu_{\alpha(t_i)}, v_{\alpha(t_i)}\right)$ for all (i=1,2,3,…,p) is a set of Intuitionistic Fuzzy Numbers (IFN) for P different periods (i=1,2,3,…,p), where $\delta = \left(\left(\delta(t_1), \delta(t_2), \delta(t_3), \ldots, \delta(t_p)\right)^T\right.$ is the weight vector of periods such that $\sum_{i=1}^{n} \delta_{(t_i)} = 1$ and DIFWG϶: $\Omega^n \rightarrow \Omega$, if

$$\begin{aligned} & DIFWG \in_{\delta(t)} \left(\left(\delta(t_1), \delta(t_2), \delta(t_3), \ldots, \delta(t_p)\right)\right) = \otimes_{i=1}^{p} \in . \left(\delta_{ij}(t_i)\right)^{\delta(t_i)} \\ & = \left(\delta_{ij}(t_1)\right)^{\delta(t_1)} \otimes \in \left(\delta_{ij}(t_2)\right)^{\delta(t_2)} \otimes \in \ldots.. \otimes \in \left(\delta_{ij}(t_p)\right)^{\delta(t_p)} \\ & = \left(\frac{2\prod_i^p \left(\mu_{ij}(t_i)\right)^{\delta(t_i)}}{\prod_i^p \left(2-\mu_{ij}(t_i)\right)^{\delta(t_i)} + \prod_i^p \left(\mu_{ij}(t_i)\right)^{\delta(t_i)}}, \frac{\prod_i^p \left(1+v_{ij}(t_i)\right)^{\delta(t_i)} - \prod_i^p \left(1-v_{ij}(t_i)\right)^{\delta(t_i)}}{\prod_i^p \left(1+v_{ij}(t_i)\right)^{\delta(t_i)} + \prod_i^p \left(1-v_{ij}(t_i)\right)^{\delta(t_i)}} \right) \end{aligned} \tag{9}$$

IF-TOPSIS Model

TOPSIS which is an abbreviation of Technique for Order Preference by Similarity to the Ideal Solution which was originally proposed by Hwang & Yoon, (1981) has remained one of the most widely used MCDM methods. The choice of using intuitionistic fuzzy set in a TOPSIS model in this study is based on the fact that it is more capable than the traditional fuzzy sets at handling vagueness and uncertain information in practice (Aikhuele & Turan, 2017a). Also, introducing the TOPSIS model in an intuitionistic fuzzy environment by using the dynamic operator for aggregating experts' opinions and in the separation, measures provide a whole new approach to solving multi-criteria decision-making problems.

It is based on the concept that the chosen or most appropriate alternative should have the shortest distance from the positive ideal solution and the farthest distance from the negative ideal solution, where the positive ideal solution tends to maximize the benefit criteria and minimizes the cost criteria, whereas the negative ideal solution maximizes the cost criteria and minimizes the benefit criteria (Behzadian, et al., 2012).

The method is said to have a compensatory aggregation that compares sets of alternatives (A_i, i=1,2,3,…,n) by identifying the weights for each criterion, normalizing the scores for the criterion and then calculating the geometric distance from the alternatives to the positive ideal (A^+) and negative ideal (A^-) solutions. In calculating the separation measure from A_i to A^+ and A^- solutions, in the traditional TOPSIS model, the Euclidean distance method is used, which implicitly assumes that the attributes contemplated for ordering alternatives are independent (Aguarón-Joven et al., 2015; Behzadian et al., 2012). But, the independence of criteria rarely exists in real-life cases.

The IF-TOPSIS is one of the most popular multi-criteria decision-making model, used for decision-making in industrial engineering management. The model which measures distances in the Euclidean norm, assume all contemplated attributes/criteria are independent. Several authors have contributed to the study of IF-TOPSIS models, some of which include, Chen & Tsao, (2008) who proposed an extension to the IF-TOPSIS model by using an interval-valued fuzzy set in decision analysis, the result of the study was achieved by using a comprehensive experimental analysis to observe the interval-valued fuzzy TOPSIS results yielded by different distance measures. Yüce & Temiz, (2017), applied the TOPSIS, MOORA and VIKOR methods for the selection of asynchronous motors. In another study, Lozano-Minguez, et al., (2011), proposed an MCDM approach for wind turbine structural analysis. Their model, which is a TOPSIS-based model, was designed to select a suitable support structure for OFW turbines. With this model, they were able to justify the selection of a suitable foundation on the basis of techno-economic and environmental criteria. Chu, (2002) applied the fuzzy TOPSIS model for the selection of plant location, such that the ratings and weights assigned by decision-makers were computed and then normalized into a comparable scale. Tan, et al., (2010) applies the Fuzzy TOPSIS approach in assisting contractors in selecting appropriate projects, the model which considered multiple attributes, integrates the opinions of a group of experts. Linguistic terms were used in gathering the expert's opinion and was later converted to the triangular fuzzy numbers for onward ratings of alternatives.

Tsaura, et al., (2002) applies the fuzzy set theory for the evaluation of service quality of an airline company. Ding, (2011) uses the fuzzy TOPSIS model for improving the quality of decision making and for ranking alternatives, the fuzzy TOPSIS model also accounts for the classification of criteria by integrating the weight of criteria and that of the sub-criteria.

The integrated fuzzy 'technique for order preference by similarity to ideal solution' (TOPSIS) and fuzzy 'analytical hierarchy process' (AHP) was presented by Kutlu & Ekmekçioğlu, (2012). The intuitionistic fuzzy hybrid TOPSIS method was for failure detection was proposed by Liu et al. (2015). Due to the characteristics and capabilities of the TOPSIS method, it has continued to receive increasing attention and application for the evaluation of power system. In this paper, the Technique for Order of Preference by Similarity to Ideal Solution (TOPSIS) originally proposed in (Hung & Chen, 2009) is adopted and applied in the intuitionistic fuzzy environment where it is integrated with the DIFWG϶ operator for group decision-making in power system evaluation.

Group Decision-Making

Decision making which is a critical area of artificial intelligence can be referred to as an essential component in many intelligent systems. Where the decisions made in/for such systems are often in the form of group decision-making. Group decision-making (GDM) is a situation where individuals are tasked to collectively make a choice from a list of alternatives with respect to some criteria. Let consider a group of n DMs tasked to evaluate one or more alternatives. If each of the DMs expresses their preference evaluation of the alternatives on a numerical scale (which is the strength of DMs preference), the goal, therefore, is to aggregate all the group of DMs preference judgments into a single score (Dubois & Prade, 2004). By using the numerical scale say [0, 1], to represent the DMs preference judgment, we can obtain a vector of inputs$X=(x_1,\dots,x_n)$, where x_1 is the degree of preference of the i-th Decision-maker (DM) and the overall aggregated scores is represented in the form $y=f(x)$.

In the case where the DMs are of different standing, then their preference scores are assigned different weights, which is termed 'the weight of the DMs'. In correlating the DMs preference (opinions), one has to model their interactions and groupings. However, 'from the mathematical point of view, the function f needs to be monotone non-decreasing (i.e. the increase in one DM's score cannot lead to the decrease of the overall score) and satisfy the boundary conditions. Thus f is an aggregation function' used in MCDM (Beliakov et al., 2007).

Multi-Criteria Group Decision-Making Method (MCGDM)

Multi-criteria group decision making which is a sub-discipline of operation research and engineering management, is concerns with problems of prioritizing, screening, ranking or selecting alternative(s) from among a finite set of candidates with multiple criteria, usually conflicting, by considering them simultaneously to select the best candidate (Braglial et al., 2003).

Many of our everyday decision-making problems involve the consideration of multiple criteria or attributes. Also, even corporate decision-making, which often involves a complex decision process in which fuzzy conditions and requirements have to be considered rarely involves a single criterion (Leonardi, 2016; Roszkowska, 2013).

THE ALGORITHM OF THE PROPOSED INTEGRATED MODEL

In presenting the algorithm of the integrated model, let's consider a multi-attribute decision-making (MADM) problem where a set of alternatives said ($S=S_1,S_2,S_3,\dots,S_n$) are to be evaluated with respect to a set of attributes ($T=T_1,T_2,T_3,..,T_n$). If the level of importance (weight) of the different attributes are known by the evaluator and the evaluation needs to be carried out in a dynamic process due to changes in the attributes. Then the algorithm of the proposed integrated model can be implemented by following the steps:

Step 1: Select a group of experts with relevant experience and expertise in the subject matter. To ensure accuracy in the evaluation, experts from the academic and from the industry should be chosen.

Step 2: Construct an intuitionistic fuzzy decision matrix $(S_{m\times n}(x_{ij}))$, using the preferences information by the group of experts. The information should be collected using a scale of linguistic variables, which will then be converted to the intuitionistic fuzzy number (IFN) used in the model. The sample of the intuitionistic fuzzy decision matrix is given below, while the scale of linguistic variables is given in Table 1.

The concept of linguistic variable is very important and plays a key role in the application of the fuzzy system. A fuzzy linguistic variable can be referred to as variable whose values are expressed qualitatively by linguistic terms and quantitatively by a pertinence function (Ganga & Carpinetti, 2011). The Linguistic variables are very useful tools when dealing with complex or ill-defined situations. For example, "attending classes before an exam" the example can be valued by expressing them in linguistic terms that are it is; moderately important (MI), important (I), very important (VI) and absolutely important (AI)).

$$S_{mxn}(x_{ij}) = \begin{bmatrix} (\mu_{11}, v_{11}, \pi_{11}) & (\mu_{12}, v_{12}, \pi_{12}) & \cdots & (\mu_{1n}, v_{1n}, \pi_{1n}) \\ (\mu_{21}, v_{21}, \pi_{21}) & (\mu_{22}, v_{22}, \pi_{22}) & \cdots & (\mu_{2n}, v_{2n}, \pi_{2n}) \\ \vdots & \vdots & \ddots & \vdots \\ \vdots & \vdots & \ddots & \vdots \\ (\mu_{m1}, v_{m1}, \pi_{m1}) & (\mu_{m2}, v_{m2}, \pi_{m2}) & \cdots & (\mu_{mn}, v_{mn}, \pi_{mn}) \end{bmatrix} \tag{10}$$

Step 3: The preference information given by the individual experts are aggregated to construct the collective decision matrix ($R_{pk}(x_{ij})$), using the DIFWGε operator - equation (8).

Step 4: Using the pre-determined weights vectors of the attributes, construct the weighted normalization from the collective decision matrix ($R_{pk}(x_{ij})$).

Step 5: Determine the Intuitionistic Positive Ideal Solution (IPIS) and the Negative Ideal Solutions (INIS), that is:

Table 1. Linguistic values for evaluating the power plans

Linguistic Terms	Intuitionistic Fuzzy Number (IFN)
Very low (VL)	(0.65, 0.10)
Low (L)	(0.70, 0.20)
High (HG)	(0.80, 0.10)
Very High (VH)	(0.85, 0.15)
Really Very High (RH)	(0.95, 0.20)

$$S^{+} = \left\{ \begin{matrix} T_j, \left(\left(\max \mu_{ij}\left(T_j\right) \mid j \in Z \right), \left(\min \mu_{ij}\left(T_j\right) \mid j \in G \right) \right), \\ \left(\left(\min v_{ij}\left(T_j\right) \mid j \in Z \right), \left(\max v_{ij}\left(T_j\right) \mid j \in G \right) \right) \end{matrix} \mid i \in m \right\} \tag{11}$$

$$S^{-} = \left\{ \begin{matrix} T_j, \left(\left(\min \mu_{ij}\left(T_j\right) \mid j \in Z \right), \left(\max \mu_{ij}\left(T_j\right) \mid j \in G \right) \right), \\ \left(\left(\max v_{ij}\left(T_j\right) \mid j \in Z \right), \left(\min v_{ij}\left(T_j\right) \mid j \in G \right) \right) \end{matrix} \mid i \in m \right\} \tag{12}$$

where Z be a collection of benefit attributes and G the collection of cost attributes when the attributes are categorized into benefit and cost.

Step 6: Calculate the distances of each of the alternatives to the positive and negative ideal solutions using the intuitionistic Euclidean distance.

$$d_{IFS}\left(S^{+}\right) = \sqrt{\sum_{j=1}^{n} \left[\left(\mu_{ij}\left(T_j\right) - \mu_{(PT^{+})}\left(T_j\right) \right)^2 + \left(v_{ij}\left(T_j\right) - v_{(PT^{+})}\left(T_j\right) \right)^2 \right]} \tag{13}$$

$$d_{IFS}\left(PT^{-}\right) = \sqrt{\sum_{j=1}^{n} \left[\left(\mu_{ij}\left(T_j\right) - \mu_{(PT^{-})}\left(T_j\right) \right)^2 + \left(v_{ij}\left(T_j\right) - v_{(PT^{-})}\left(T_j\right) \right)^2 \right]} \tag{14}$$

Step 7: Calculation of the Closeness Coefficient (CC) of all the alternatives;

$$CC_i = \frac{d_{IFS}\left(S^{-}\right)}{d_{IFS}\left(S^{-}\right) + d_{IFS}\left(S^{+}\right)} \tag{15}$$

Step 8: Rank the alternatives

A NUMERICAL ILLUSTRATION OF THE MODEL

Power experts are of the opinion that the use of sub-stations is capable of improving energy distribution in a community. Such sub-stations are to be used to manage the loads on a distributed network, visa-vice the installation of step down transformers in these stations (Siemens, 2012). Apart from technical issues that have caused changes in power system management, this system structure and operation are affected by ideological and finance factors (Saxena et al., 2010). For example, the innovation in renewable energy technologies has changed the orientation of how energy generated, transmitted and distributed across the world. And this has increased the interest in distributed systems. It is now a common experience to see a facility is run on a national grid and a stand-alone renewable energy source; in most cases, this is required to enhance the safety, reliability and efficiency of a facility. Thus, a detailed evaluation of the characteristics of facilities that are connected to a national grid and renewable energy sources must be carried in order to select a suitable renewable power technology. While the short-run benefits of this evaluation will be improved facility efficiency - technical benefit, the long-term benefits will be both economic and environmental, and social to a facility owner(s) and host community (Matsuo et al., 2013; Husain et al., 2018). Thus, energy experts now approach renewable energy analysis from a multi-criteria perspective (Zhang and Tao, 2014; Ighravwe and Babatunde, 2018).

A new power company intends to build a 20MW power generating plant in the west of Lagos. According to the feasibility report of the project, five preliminary power source plants are presented to the management of the power company to select. The power sources which include the establishment of a wind power (S_1), hydroelectricity (S_2), solar power (S_3), geothermal power (S_4) and biomass (S_5) plants, are to be evaluated with respect to the following reliability-based attributes, the risk factor (T_1), payback reliability (T_2), social benefit (T_3), change in demand (T_4) and cost (T_5).

In selecting a power source plant for a company, the management intends to consider the dynamic factor associated with power plant operations, some of which include; the changing energy demand and consumption, the changing environmental conditions, rapidly increasing population, social activities, and awareness. These information's are accounted for in the selection of the power source plants by evaluating their impact around the west of Lagos for a period of two (2) years within the last ten (10) years using expert-based opinion. If the following weight vector is assumed to be the impact of the dynamic factors $\delta(t)$= {0.167, 0.333, 0.500, 0.630, 0.652} respectively. Then these factors can be accounted for in the decision-making process.

Following the algorithm of the proposed model, five (5) experts with equal weight vector, are contracted by the company to give their preference judgment for the selection of the power plant. the preference rating of the power plants by the different experts (E_i) (intuitionistic fuzzy decision matrix) are given in Table 2. This is in line with previous literature like Liu et al., (2014) who used five (5) experts' opinions for the reliability assessment of thin-film transistor liquid crystal display (TFT-LCD) products. Song et al., (2013) used four (4) experts opinions for reliability assessment of reheat valve system in nuclear steam turbine, Liu et al., (2014), used five (5) experts opinions for the reliability assessment of horizontal directional drilling (HDD) machine. Liu et al., (2015) used four (4) experts' opinions for the reliability assessment thin film transistor liquid crystal display (TFT-LCD) product. Kutlu & Ekmekçioğlu, (2012) uses three (3) experts' opinions for the reliability assessment of manufacturing facility and. Alarcin et al., (2014) uses three (3) experts' opinions for troubleshooting auxiliary systems of ship main engines.

Table 2. Rating by the experts for the establishment of power plants

	E1	E2	E3	E4	E5	E1	E2	E3	E4	E5	E1	E2	E3	E4	E5	E1	E2	E3	E4	E5	E1	E2	E3	E4	E5
	T_1					T_2					T_3					T_4					T_5				
S_1	VH	L	L	HG	L	VH	L	RH	HG	L	RH	HG	VH	VH	HG	VH	HG	HG	VH	HG	RH	HG	VH	L	RH
S_2	L	HG	HG	VH	HG	RH	HG	RL	VH	HG	RL	VH	L	RH	VH	L	VH	VH	RH	VH	RL	VH	RH	HG	RL
S_3	HG	VH	VH	RH	VH	RL	VH	L	RH	VH	L	RH	HG	RL	RH	HG	RH	RH	RL	RH	L	RH	RL	VH	L
S_4	VH	HG	HG	VH	HG	RH	GH	VG	VH	HG	HG	VH	VH	L	VH	HG	VH	VH	L	VH	L	VH	RH	L	RH
S_5	HG	VH	VH	L	VH	HG	HG	L	RH	VH	VH	VH	HG	VH	HG	VH	L	HG	VH	RH	VH	HG	HG	VH	HG

Using the DIFWGϵ operator, the individual preference rating given by the experts is aggregated, where this is achieved by converting the linguistic opinion/variables in Table 2 to the IFN using the information in Table 1. The aggregated result which constructs the collective decision matrix ($R_{pk}(x_{ij})$) is shown in Table 3. The result addresses and account for the dynamic factors within the stated periods in the power plant evaluation. Furthermore, the weighted normalization is constructed using the weighted vectors of the reliability-based criteria in Table 3 from the collective decision matrix ($R_{pk}(x_{ij})$). The results of the normalization are given in Table 4.

With the result of the weighted normalization matrix, the intuitionistic positive ideal solution (IPIS) and the intuitionistic negative ideal solutions (INIS) is determined and used for calculating the distances of each of the alternative to the positive and negative ideal solutions using Equation 13 and 14 and finally, the closeness coefficient of the alternatives is calculated using Equation 15. The results from the calculation and their rankings are presented in Table 5.

From the result presented in Table 5, it is not hard to see that the power plant (Solar power plant) is the most preferred power plant source considering the dynamic factors associated with the plants, within and around the west of Lagos Nigeria. The study has not only revealed the suitability of the proposed integrated model for ranking and selecting a suitable power source for power companies but has also revealed the capability of the model to evaluate and select sets of alternatives under dynamic environment, while addressing uncertainty in the decision-making process.

Table 3. Aggregation of the expert's opinions using the dynamic operator

	T_1	T_2	T_3	T_4	T_5
S_1	(0.454, 0.360, 0.186)	(0.551, 0.360, 0.088)	(0.638, 0.289, 0.073)	(0.602, 0.257, 0.141)	(0.638, 0.372, -0.010)
S_2	(0.580, 0.265, 0.155)	(0.549, 0.265, 0.186)	(0.623, 0.368, 0.009)	(0.702, 0.360, -0.062)	(0.536, 0.283, 0.181)
S_3	(0.718, 0.345, -0.063)	(0.623, 0.368, 0.009)	(0.593, 0.322, 0.085)	(0.674, 0.353, -0.027)	(0.501, 0.351, 0.148)
S_4	(0.602, 0.257, 0.141)	(0.638, 0.289, 0.073)	(0.575, 0.345, 0.080)	(0.575, 0.345, 0.080)	(0.659, 0.408, -0.068)
S_5	(0.575, 0.345, 0.080)	(0.632, 0.353, 0.015)	(0.616, 0.273, 0.111)	(0.657, 0.343, 0.000)	(0.602, 0.257, 0.141)
	0.487814	0.428525	0.010064	0.036799	0.036799

Table 4. The weighted normalization of the power plants evaluation

	T_1	T_2	T_3	T_4	T_5
S_1	(0.221, 0.176, 0.091)	(0.236, 0.154, 0.038)	(0.006, 0.003, 0.001)	(0.022, 0.009, 0.005)	(0.023, 0.014, 0.000)
S_2	(0.283, 0.129, 0.076)	(0.235, 0.114, 0.080)	(0.006, 0.004, 0.000)	(0.026, 0.013, -0.002)	(0.020, 0.010, 0.007)
S_3	(0.350, 0.168, -0.031)	(0.267, 0.158, 0.004)	(0.006, 0.003, 0.001)	(0.025, 0.013, -0.001)	(0.018, 0.013, 0.005)
S_4	(0.294, 0.125, 0.069)	(0.274, 0.124, 0.031)	(0.006, 0.003, 0.001)	(0.021, 0.013, 0.003)	(0.024, 0.015, -0.002)
S_5	(0.281, 0.168, 0.039)	(0.271, 0.151, 0.007)	(0.006, 0.003, 0.001)	(0.024, 0.013, 0.000)	(0.022, 0.009, 0.005)

Table 5. The closeness coefficient of the alternatives

	$d_{IFS}(S^{+})$	$d_{IFS}(S^{-})$	CC_i	Ranking
S_1	0.381205	0.231368	0.377699	5
S_2	0.354545	0.232109	0.395649	4
S_3	0.46239	0.355725	0.434811	1
S_4	0.378765	0.280948	0.425863	2
S_5	0.409781	0.296402	0.419724	3

To prove the rationality and feasibility of the integrated model, the result from the evaluation above is compared with a similar computational model in the literature. The model reviewed at this instead includes; the extended VIKOR method under fuzzy environment by Liu, et al., (2012) and the value-index ranking method (Biswas, et al, 2016). The comparison which focuses on the ranking result shows total agreement with the proposed integrated model; the results are presented in Table 6.

CONCLUSION

An integrated MCGDM model which is based on an IF-TOPSIS method and the DIFWGε operator has been proposed in this study, for the evaluation and selection of a renewable power plant by a new power company located in the west of Lagos city in Nigeria. The model uses some reliability-based criteria for the evaluation of the power source plants presented to the management of the company after a preliminary study by a team of consultants. The study addresses, the dynamic factors associated with the power plant operations and the factors due to the location (Lagos west). The dynamic factors include; the changing energy demand and consumption, the changing environmental conditions, rapidly increasing population, social activities, and awareness issues.

The result from the evaluation shows that the power plant S_3 (Solar power plant) is the most preferred power plant source considering the dynamic factors associated with the plant and operation of a new power plant, as well as the reliability-based criteria used for the assessment. The main advantage and contribution of the proposed model for the selection and evaluation study of power plants include; (1) the ability of the model to address and account for uncertainty and dynamic issues in the decision-making process, which is a major drawback in currently existing models used for the selection and evaluation

Table 6. The closeness coefficient of the alternatives

	Proposed Integrated Model		(Liu et al., 2012)		(Biswas et al., 2016b)	
	CC_i	Ranking	Q_i	Ranking	$S(r_i)$	Ranking
S_1	0.377699	5	0.1227	5	0.246352	5
S_2	0.395649	4	0.0954	4	0.244353	4
S_3	0.434811	1	0.0641	1	0.366392	1
S_4	0.425863	2	0.0892	3	0.290729	3
S_5	0.419724	3	0.0650	2	0.30774	2

of power plans. (2) The use of a dynamic intuitionistic fuzzy Einstein geometric averaging (DIFWG∊) operator for aggregating expert's opinions for power technology plans and finally. (3) The user of the IF-TOPSIS and the dynamic operator for evaluating and ranking the alternatives, which to the best knowledge is novel in the selection of power technology plans.

To prove the rationality and feasibility of the integrated model, the result from the study is compared with a similar computational model in the literature which includes the extended VIKOR method under fuzzy environment by Liu et al., (2012) and the value-index ranking method (Biswas et al., 2016b). The comparison which focuses on the ranking result shows a total agreement with the proposed integrated model.

Key Observation on Its Future Application

Although the integrated model proposed in this study have been able to solve the research problem and fill the identified gaps. However, there are still some aspects that the method can be applied in. Also, some of the identified limitations of the method can be improved in future research. Here are some observations that will allow for future research and application of the proposed model in the future.

1. Due to the mathematical computation involved with the integrated model, consultants, academics or experts of some sort are identified as the most probable eventual end-users of the developed model where they may get involved with companies to aid its usage, this can be a disadvantage of some sort.
2. The model may be ideal for a company that has made up its mind to address dynamic issues, flexibility, and agility in their decision-making process, especially for power/energy selection.
3. The ideal usage of the proposed integrated model may lie on the possibilities of gathering the power/energy data and concepts assessment information from the different stakeholders and knowing their different levels of experience and expertise as it relates to the system/technology.

REFERENCES

Aguarón-Joven, J., Escobar-Urmeneta, M. T., García-Alcaraz, J. L., Moreno-Jiménez, J. M., & Vega-Bonilla, A. (2015). A new synthesis procedure for TOPSIS based on AHP. *Dyna (Bilbao), 82*(191), 11–19. doi:10.15446/dyna.v82n191.51140

Aikhuele, D. O., & Odofin, S. (2017). A Generalized Triangular Intuitionistic Fuzzy Geometric Averaging Operator for Decision-Making in Engineering and Management. *Information, 8*(3), 1–17. doi:10.3390/info8030078

Aikhuele, D. O., Sorooshian, S., Ansah, R. H., & Turan, F. M. (2017). Application of intuitionistic fuzzy topsis model for troubleshooting an offshore patrol boat engine. *Polish Maritime Research, 24*(94), 68–76. doi:10.1515/pomr-2017-0051

Aikhuele, D. O., & Turan, F. M. (2017a). A modified exponential score function for troubleshooting an improved locally-made Offshore Patrol Boat engine. *Journal of Marine Engineering & Technology*, (February). doi:10.1080/20464177.2017.1286841

Aikhuele, D. O., & Turan, F. M. (2017b). Extended TOPSIS model for solving multi-attribute decision making problems in engineering. *Decision Science Letters*, *6*, 365–376. doi:10.5267/j.dsl.2017.2.002

Alarcin, F., Balin, A., & Demirel, H. (2014). Fuzzy AHP and Fuzzy TOPSIS integrated hybrid method for auxiliary systems of ship main engines. *Journal of Marine Engineering & Technology*, *13*(1), 3–11. doi:10.1080/20464177.2014.11020288

Atanassov, K. T. (1986). Intuitionistic fuzzy sets. *Fuzzy Sets and Systems*, *20*(1), 87–96. doi:10.1016/S0165-0114(86)80034-3

Atanassov, K. T. (1994). New operations defined over the intuitionistic fuzzy sets. *Fuzzy Sets and Systems*, *61*(2), 137–142. doi:10.1016/0165-0114(94)90229-1

Behzadian, M., Khanmohammadi Otaghsara, S., Yazdani, M., & Ignatius, J. (2012). A state-of the-art survey of TOPSIS applications. *Expert Systems with Applications*, *39*(17), 13051–13069. doi:10.1016/j.eswa.2012.05.056

Beliakov, G., Pradera, A., & Calvo, T. (2007). *Aggregation Functions: A Guide for Practitioners. Soft Computing* (Vol. 18). doi:10.1007/3-540-32367-8_3

Biswas, P., Pramanik, S., & Giri, B. C. (2016a). TOPSIS method for multi-attribute group decision-making under single-valued neutrosophic environment. *Neural Computing & Applications*, *27*(3), 727–737. doi:10.100700521-015-1891-2

Biswas, P., Pramanik, S., & Giri, B. C. (2016b). Value and ambiguity index based ranking method of single-valued trapezoidal neutrosophic numbers and its application to multi-attribute decision making. *Neutrosophic Sets and Systems*, *12*(July), 127–138.

Braglia, M., Frosolini, M., & Montanari, R. (2003). Fuzzy TOPSIS approach for failure mode, effects and criticality analysis. *Quality and Reliability Engineering International*, *19*(5), 425–443.

Cai, T. (2011). *A conceptual framework for value creation management in the lean product development process (Unpublished master's thesis)*. University of Calgary, Calgary, AB. doi:10.11575/PRISM/4026.

Chaira, T. (2001). A novel intuitionistic fuzzy C means clustering algorithm and its application to medical images. *Applied Soft Computing*, *11*(2), 1711–1717. doi:10.1016/j.asoc.2010.05.005

Chen, T. Y., & Tsao, C. Y. (2008). The interval-valued fuzzy TOPSIS method and experimental analysis. *Fuzzy Sets and Systems*, *159*(11), 1410–1428. doi:10.1016/j.fss.2007.11.004

Chu, T. C. (2002). Selecting plant location via a fuzzy TOPSIS approach. *International Journal of Advanced Manufacturing Technology*, *20*(11), 859–864. doi:10.1007001700200227

Chun-ho, C. (2019). A New Multi-Criteria Assessment Model Combining GRA Techniques with Intuitionistic Fuzzy Entropy-Based TOPSIS Method for Sustainable Building Materials Supplier Selection. *Sustainability*, *11*(2265).

Daneshvar, B., Erdebilli, R. B., Yildizbasi, A., & Arikan, Ü. Z. B. (2018). Using Intuitionistic Fuzzy TOPSIS in Site Selection of Wind Power Plants in Turkey. *Advances in Fuzzy Systems, 2018*(Mcdm), 1–14.

Deschrijver, G., & Kerre, E. E. (2007). On the position of intuitionistic fuzzy set theory in the framework of theories modelling imprecision. *Information Sciences*, *177*(8), 1860–1866. doi:10.1016/j.ins.2006.11.005

Despic, O., & Simonovic, S. P. (2000). Aggregation operators for soft decision making in water resources. *Fuzzy Sets and Systems*, *115*(1), 11–33. doi:10.1016/S0165-0114(99)00030-5

Ding, J. F. (2011). An integrated fuzzy topsis method for ranking alternatives and its application. *Journal of Marine Science and Technology*, *19*(4), 341–352.

Dubois, D., & Prade, H. (2004). On the use of aggregation operations in information fusion processes. *Fuzzy Sets and Systems*, *142*(1), 143–161. doi:10.1016/j.fss.2003.10.038

Gan, J., & Luo, L. (2017). Using DEMATEL and Intuitionistic Fuzzy Sets to Identify Critical Factors Influencing the Recycling Rate of End-Of-Life Vehicles in China. *Sustainability, 9*(1873), 1–22. doi:10.3390u9101873

Ganga, G. M. D., & Carpinetti, L. C. R. (2011). A fuzzy logic approach to supply chain performance management. *International Journal of Production Economics*, *134*(1), 177–187. doi:10.1016/j.ijpe.2011.06.011

Ghazanfari, M., Rouhani, S., & Jafari, M. (2014). A fuzzy TOPSIS model to evaluate the Business Intelligence competencies of Port Community Systems. *Polish Maritime Research*, *21*(2), 86–96. doi:10.2478/pomr-2014-0023

Gümüş, S., & Bali, O. (2017). Dynamic Aggregation Operators Based on Intuitionistic Fuzzy Tools and Einstein Operations. *Fuzzy Information and Engineering*, *9*(1), 45–65. doi:10.1016/j.fiae.2017.03.003

Hashemi, H., Mousavi, S. M., & Zavadskas, E. K. (2018). A New Group Decision Model Based on Grey-Intuitionistic Fuzzy-ELECTRE and VIKOR for Contractor Assessment Problem. *Sustainability*, *10*(1635), 1–19. doi:10.3390u10051635 PMID:30607262

Hung, C.-C., & Chen, L.-H. (2009). A Fuzzy TOPSIS Decision Making Model with Entropy Weight under Intuitionistic Fuzzy Environment. *Proceedings of the International MultiConference of Engineers and Computer Scientists IMECS 2009, Hong Kong, I*, 18–21.

Husain, A. A. F., Hasan, W. Z. W., Shafie, S., Hamidon, M. N., & Pandey, S. S. (2018). A review of transparent solar photovoltaic technologies. *Renewable & Sustainable Energy Reviews*, *94*(3), 779–791. doi:10.1016/j.rser.2018.06.031

Hwang, C. L., & Yoon, K. (1981). *Multiple Attribute Decision Making Methods and Applications*. Berlin, Germany: Springer. doi:10.1007/978-3-642-48318-9

Jang, J. S. R., & Sun, C. T. (1995). Neuro-fuzzy modeling and control. *Proceedings of the IEEE*, *83*(3), 378–406. doi:10.1109/5.364486

Jose-M, M. L., & Montserrat, C. R. (2010). The Generalized Hybrid Averaging Operator and its Application in Decision Making. *REVISTA DE METODOS CUANTITATIVOS PARA LA ECONOMIA Y LA EMPRESA*, (9), 69–84.

Joshi, D., & Kumar, S. (2014). Intuitionistic fuzzy entropy and distance measure based TOPSIS method for multi-criteria decision making. *Egyptian Informatics Journal, 15*(2), 97–104. doi:10.1016/j.eij.2014.03.002

Kahraman, C., Keshavarz Ghorabaee, M., Zavadskas, E. K., Cevik Onar, S., Yazdani, M., & Oztaysi, B. (2017). Intuitionistic fuzzy EDAS method: an application to solid waste disposal site selection. *Journal of Environmental Engineering and Landscape Management, 25*(1).

Kutlu, A. C., & Ekmekçioğlu, M. (2012). Fuzzy failure modes and effects analysis by using fuzzy TOPSIS-based fuzzy AHP. *Expert Systems with Applications, 39*(1), 61–67. doi:10.1016/j.eswa.2011.06.044

Leonardi, G. (2016). A Fuzzy Model for a Railway-Planning Problem. *Applied Mathematical Sciences, 10*(27), 1333–1342. doi:10.12988/ams.2016.63106

Liu, H.-C., Liu, L., & Li, P. (2014). Failure mode and effects analysis using intuitionistic fuzzy hybrid weighted Euclidean distance operator. *International Journal of Systems Science, 45*(10), 2012–2030. doi:10.1080/00207721.2012.760669

Liu, H.-C., Liu, L., & Li, P. (2015). Failure mode and effects analysis using intuitionistic fuzzy hybrid TOPSIS approach. *Soft Computing, 19*(4), 1085–1098. doi:10.100700500-014-1321-x

Liu, H.-C., Liu, L., Liu, N., & Mao, L.-X. (2012). Risk evaluation in failure mode and effects analysis with extended VIKOR method under fuzzy environment. *Expert Systems with Applications, 39*(17), 12926–12934. doi:10.1016/j.eswa.2012.05.031

Liu, H.-C., You, J.-X., Lin, Q.-L., & Li, H. (2014). Risk assessment in system FMEA combining fuzzy weighted average with fuzzy decision-making trial and evaluation laboratory. *International Journal of Computer Integrated Manufacturing, 28*(7), 701–714. doi:10.1080/0951192X.2014.900865

Liu, P., & Zhang, L. (2014). *The Extended VIKOR Method for Multiple Criteria Decision Making Problem Based on Neutrosophic Hesitant Fuzzy Set.*

Lozano-Minguez, E., Kolios, A. J., & Brennan, F. (2011). Multi-criteria assessment of offshore wind turbine support structures. *Renewable Energy, 36*(11), 2831–2837. doi:10.1016/j.renene.2011.04.020

Madlener, R., & Sunak, Y. (2011). Impacts of urbanization on urban structures and energy demand: What can we learn for urban energy planning and urbanization management? *Sustainable Cities and Society, 1*(1), 45–53. doi:10.1016/j.scs.2010.08.006

Matsuo, Y., Yanagisawa, A., & Yamashita, Y. (2013). A global energy outlook to 2035 with strategic considerations for Asia and Middle East energy supply and demand interdependencies. *Energy Strategy Reviews, 2*(1), 79–91. doi:10.1016/j.esr.2013.04.002

Park, J. H., Gwak, M. G., & Kwun, Y. C. (2011). Linguistic harmonic mean operators and their applications to group decision making. *International Journal of Advanced Manufacturing Technology, 57*(1–4), 411–419. doi:10.100700170-011-3295-5

Park, J. H., Kwun, Y. C., & Koo, J. H. (2011). Dynamic uncertain linguistic weighted harmonic mean operators applied to decision making. In *Proceedings 2011 International Conference on System Science and Engineering, ICSSE 2011* (pp. 101–106). 10.1109/ICSSE.2011.5961882

Parvathi, R., & Malathi, C. (2012). Intuitionistic fuzzy linear optimization. *Notes on Intuitionistic Fuzzy Sets*, *18*(1), 48–56.

Pérez-Domínguez, L., Alvarado-Iniesta, A., Rodríguez-Borbón, I., & Vergara-Villegas, O. (2015). Intuitionistic Fuzzy MOORA for Supplier Selection. *Dyna (Bilbao)*, *82*(191), 34–41. doi:10.15446/dyna.v82n191.51143

Puri, J., & Prasad Yadav, S. (2015). Intuitionistic fuzzy data envelopment analysis: An application to the banking sector in India. *Expert Systems with Applications*, *42*(11), 4982–4998. doi:10.1016/j.eswa.2015.02.014

Roszkowska, E. (2013). Rank ordering criteria weighting methods – a comparative overview. *Optimum Studia Ekonomiczne Nr*, *5*(65), 14–33. doi:10.15290/ose.2013.05.65.02

Rouyendegh, B. D. (2018). The Intuitionistic Fuzzy ELECTRE model The Intuitionistic Fuzzy ELECTRE model. *International Journal of Management Science and Engineering Management*, (September 2017), 1–7. doi:10.1080/17509653.2017.1349625

Saeedi, S., & Malek, M. R. (2008). An intuitionistic fuzzy analytic network process for parking site selection Intuitionistic Fuzzy Analytical Network Process (IF-ANP) for Spatial Multi Criteria Decision Making under Uncertainty, (August 2015). doi:10.1142/9789812799470

Saxena, D., Singh, S., & Verma, K. (2010). Application of computational intelligence in emerging power systems. *International Journal of Engineering Science and Technology*, *2*(3), 1–7. doi:10.4314/ijest.v2i3.59166

Siemens, A. G. (2012). *Power Engineering Guide*. Siemens; doi:10.100710342-012-0675-9

Song, W., Ming, X., Wu, Z., & Zhu, B. (2013). Failure modes and effects analysis using integrated weight-based fuzzy TOPSIS. *International Journal of Computer Integrated Manufacturing*, *26*(12), 1172–1186. doi:10.1080/0951192X.2013.785027

Suh, Y., Park, Y., & Kang, D. (2019). Evaluating mobile services using integrated weighting approach and fuzzy VIKOR. *PLoS One*, *14*(9). doi:10.1371/journal.pone.0222312 PMID:31487317

Tan, Y., Shen, L., Langston, C., & Liu, Y. (2010). Construction project selection using fuzzy TOPSIS approach. *Journal of Modelling in Management*, *5*(3), 302–315. doi:10.1108/17465661011092669

Torra, V. (2000). The WOWA operator and the interpolation function W*: Chen and Otto's interpolation method revisited. *Fuzzy Sets and Systems*, *113*(3), 389–396. doi:10.1016/S0165-0114(98)00040-2

Tsaura, S. H., Chang, T. Y., & Yen, C. H. (2002). The evaluation of airline service quality by fuzzy MCDM. *Tourism Management*, *23*(2), 107–115. doi:10.1016/S0261-5177(01)00050-4

Wan, S. P., Wang, Q. Y., & Dong, J. Y. (2013). The extended VIKOR method for multi-attribute group decision making with triangular intuitionistic fuzzy numbers. *Knowledge-Based Systems*, *52*, 65–77. doi:10.1016/j.knosys.2013.06.019

Wei, G.-W. (2011). Gray relational analysis method for intuitionistic fuzzy multiple attribute decision making. *Expert Systems with Applications*, *38*(9), 11671–11677. doi:10.1016/j.eswa.2011.03.048

Xu, Z. S., & Da, Q. L. (2002). The ordered weighted geometric averaging operators. *International Journal of Intelligent Systems, 17*(7), 709–716. doi:10.1002/int.10045

Yager, R. R. (1988). On ordered weighted averaging aggregation operators in multi criteria decision making. *IEEE Transactions on Systems, Man, and Cybernetics, 18*(1), 183–190. doi:10.1109/21.87068

Yager, R. R., & Xu, Z. (2006). The continuous ordered weighted geometric operator and its application to decision making. *Fuzzy Sets and Systems, 157*(10), 1393–1402. doi:10.1016/j.fss.2005.12.001

Yazdani, M. (2015). New intuitionistic fuzzy approach with multi-objective optimisation on the basis of ratio analysis method. *International Journal of Business and Systems Research, 9*(4), 355–374. doi:10.1504/IJBSR.2015.072584

Yüce, G., & Temiz, İ. (2017). Multi Criteria Decision Making Methods Approach to Asynchronous Electric. *The Journal of Operations Research, Statistics, Econometrics, and Management Information Systems, 5*(2), 171–190. doi:10.17093/alphanumeric.313270

Zadeh, L. A. (1965). Fuzzy sets. *Information and Control, 8*(3), 338–353. doi:10.1016/S0019-9958(65)90241-X

Zhou, L., & Chen, H. (2014). Generalized Ordered Weighted Proportional Averaging Operator and Its Application to Group Decision Making. *Informatica, 25*(2), 327–360. doi:10.15388/Informatica.2014.17

Zhou, X., Ding, Y., & Lu, M. (2018). Study on bond selection under intuitionistic fuzzy conditions. *Journal of Algorithms & Computational Technology, 12*(4), 376–386. doi:10.1177/1748301818791505

ADDITIONAL READING

Ahmad, S., & Tahar, R. M. (2014). Selection of renewable energy sources for sustainable development of electricity generation system using analytic hierarchy process: A case of Malaysia. *Renewable Energy, 63*, 458–466. doi:10.1016/j.renene.2013.10.001

Aikhuele, D. O. (2017). Systematic model for lean product development implementation in an automotive related company. *Management Science Letters, 7*(7). doi:10.5267/j.msl.2017.4.003

Aikhuele, D. O. (2018). Reliability evaluation using MAGDM based on triangular intuitionistic attitudinal ranking and aggregating model. *Journal of Modern Technology & Engineering, 3*(2), 165–178.

Aikhuele, D. O., Sorooshian, S., Ansah, R. H., & Turan, F. M. (2017). Application of intuitionistic fuzzy topsis model for troubleshooting an offshore patrol boat engine. *Polish Maritime Research, 24*(94), 68–76. doi:10.1515/pomr-2017-0051

Arif-uz-zaman, K. (2012). *A Fuzzy TOPSIS Based Multi Criteria Performance Measurement Model for Lean Supply Chain.*

Biswas, P., Pramanik, S., & Giri, B. C. (2016). TOPSIS method for multi-attribute group decision-making under single-valued neutrosophic environment. *Neural Computing & Applications, 27*(3), 727–737. doi:10.100700521-015-1891-2

Braglial, M., Frosolini, M., & Montanari, R. (2003). Fuzzy TOPSIS approach for failure mode, effects and criticality analysis. *Quality and Reliability Engineering International, 19*(5), 425–443.

Chang, K. H., & Cheng, C. H. (2011). Evaluating the risk of failure using the fuzzy OWA and DEMATEL method. *Journal of Intelligent Manufacturing*, *22*(2), 113–129. doi:10.100710845-009-0266-x

Chang, S. H., & Tseng, H. E. (2008). Fuzzy TOPSIS decision method for configuration management. *International Journal of Industrial Engineering : Theory Applications and Practice*, *15*(3), 304–313.

Chen, S. M., & Chiou, C. H. (2015). A new method for multiattribute decision making based on interval-valued intuitionistic fuzzy sets, PSO techniques and evidential reasoning methodology. *Proceedings - International Conference on Machine Learning and Cybernetics*, *1*(6), 403–409. doi:10.1109/ICMLC.2014.7009149

Chen, S.-M., & Tan, J.-M. (1994). Handling multicriteria fuzzy decision-making problems based on vague set theory. *Fuzzy Sets and Systems*, *67*(2), 163–172. doi:10.1016/0165-0114(94)90084-1

Ghazanfari, M., Rouhani, S., & Jafari, M. (2014). A fuzzy TOPSIS model to evaluate the Business Intelligence competencies of Port Community Systems. *Polish Maritime Research*, *21*(2), 86–96. doi:10.2478/pomr-2014-0023

Jadidi, O., Hong, T., & Firouzi, F. (2008). TOPSIS and fuzzy multi-objective model integration for supplier selection problem. *Journal of Achievements in Materials and Manufactuing Engineering*, *31*(2), 762–769. Retrieved from http://157.158.19.167/papers_vol31_2/31288.pdf

Mohammad, S., Hojjati, H., & Anvary, A. (2013). An Integrated SAW. *TOPSIS Method for Ranking the Major Lean Practices Based on Four Attributes*, *28*(11), 1862–1871. doi:10.5829/idosi.wasj.2013.28.11.2079

Şengül, Ü., Eren, M., Eslamian Shiraz, S., Gezder, V., & Şengül, A. B. (2015). Fuzzy TOPSIS method for ranking renewable energy supply systems in Turkey. *Renewable Energy*, *75*, 617–625. doi:10.1016/j.renene.2014.10.045

Tyagi, S. K. (2014). Reliability Analysis of a Powerloom Plant Using Interval Valued Intuitionistic Fuzzy Sets. *Applied Mathematics*, *5*(13), 2008–2015. doi:10.4236/am.2014.513193

Xu, Z. (2011). Approaches to multiple attribute group decision making based on intuitionistic fuzzy power aggregation operators. *Knowledge-Based Systems*, *24*(6), 749–760. doi:10.1016/j.knosys.2011.01.011

Yue, Z. (2011). An extended TOPSIS for determining weights of decision makers with interval numbers. *Knowledge-Based Systems*, *24*(1), 146–153. doi:10.1016/j.knosys.2010.07.014

Zhang, H., & Yu, L. (2012). MADM method based on cross-entropy and extended TOPSIS with interval-valued intuitionistic fuzzy sets. *Knowledge-Based Systems*, *30*(l), 115–120. doi:10.1016/j.knosys.2012.01.003

KEY TERMS AND DEFINITIONS

μ_A: Membership function of the fuzzy set *A*.

υ_A: Non-membership function of the fuzzy set *A*.
CC: Closeness Coefficient.
(A^+): Positive ideal solutions.
(A^-): Negative ideal solutions.

Chapter 9
Modified TOPSIS Method With Banking Case Study

Semra Erpolat Taşabat
https://orcid.org/0000-0001-6845-8278
Mimar Sinan Fine Art University, Turkey & Bahçeşehir University, Turkey

Tuğba Kıral Özkan
https://orcid.org/0000-0002-7050-3805
Bahçeşehir University, Turkey

ABSTRACT

In this chapter, an alternative measure to Euclidean distance measurement is proposed which is used to calculate positive and negative ideal solutions in the traditional TOPSIS method. Lp Minkowski family and L1 family distance measures were used for this purpose. By taking the averages of the distance measurements in the Lq and L1 families, more general and accurate level units were tried to be obtained. Thus, it was shown that TOPSIS method can give different results according to the distance measure used. The importance of the distance measurement unit was emphasized to rank the alternatives correctly. The implementation and evaluation of the proposed method was carried out through the financial performance of the deposit bank operating in the Turkish Banking Sector. It was seen that the rankings of the alternatives changed according to the distance measurements used. By referring to the distance measurements that can be used in the TOPSIS method, it was shown that the rank of the alternatives can vary according to the preferred distance measure.

INTRODUCTION

We have to make a choice among alternatives for actions we think we are doing or are considering to do in many of our lives. The selection process starts with the formation of at least two alternatives, the process works and one of the alternatives is selected. This selection process is one of the simplest definitions of decision making. Decision making is called Multi Criteria Decision Making (MCDM), which has a lot of criteria in particular. The development of MCDM dates back to the 1960s. The objective of

DOI: 10.4018/978-1-7998-2216-5.ch009

the MCDM is to make the decision-making process as easy and quick as possible, in cases where the alternative and criterion numbers are far too many.

MCDM is actually a part of real life, in which we face many problems and have to make decisions. When things get complicated, people have a hard time in making a decision and they may need help. In that case, applying some simple rules and procedures to the problem rather than adding too much information and trying to make a decision will lead to a more rational decision and the final decision will be more appropriate in a given condition (Taha, 1997).

There are various MCDM methods in the literature and they do not have superiority over the other. Evaluating quantitative and qualitative criteria together is the most significant advantage of these methods..

There are many methods developed in the literature to solve MCDM problems. Although none of these methods is superior to the other, they can provide advantage or disadvantage according to the problem structure discussed. Often the results of several methods are evaluated before the final decision is made. ELECTRE, TOPSIS, PROMITHEE, VIKOR MCDM methods are the most basic methods known. Numerous MCDM methods have been introduced into the literature since the beginning. There are also studies in the literature on the modification of these and other methods, or the development of hybrid methods consisting of a combination of several MCDM methods.

In this study, TOPSIS, one of the MCDM methods, was tried to be modified. For this purpose, the Euclidean distance used to rank alternatives in the traditional TOPSIS method is focused. An alternative measure for Euclidean distance has been developed. This unit of measure is composed of distances in L_p Minkowski family (Sorensen, Gower, Soergel, Kulczyynski, Canberra, Lorentzian) and L_l family (Euclidean, City block, Chebyshev). Thus, a more powerful unit of measurement was tried to be obtained.

In the following sections, firstly the steps of TOPSIS method will be elaborated. Then, the distances in L_p Minkowski family and L_l family which are mentioned with emphasis on distance concept will be discussed in detail.

BACKGROUND

The first known application in the field of MCDM was performed Churchman et al. (1957). In this application for solving a decision-making problem the Simple Additive Weighting (SAW) method was used. Then, various studies for MCDM were performed. It is possible to list the most used ones as follows: TOPSIS (Technique for Order Preference ny Similarity to an IdealSolution) (Hwang and Yoon, 1981; Deng et al., 2000), AHP (Analitic Hierarchy Process) (Saaty 1980, 2000; Belton and Gear 1983; Lootsma 1999), ELECTRE (Elimination Et Choix Traduisant La Realite´-Elimination and Choice Expressing The Reality) (Roy 1989, 1991; Roy and Vincke 1981), VIKOR (Visekriterijumska Optimizacija I Kompromisno Resenje - Multicriteria Optimization and Compromise Solution) (Yu, 1973; Zeleny, 1982; Opricovic 1998; Tzeng and Huang, 2011), PROMITHEE (Preference Ranking Organization Methods for Enrichment Evaluation(Brans et al., 1984), etc.

In order to solve the problems of uncertainty, blurred states of MCDM methods have been discussed (Bass and Kwakernaak, 1977; Chen et al., 1992; Figueira et al., 2004, etc.). Additionally, different versions and modifications of these MCDM methods have been studied for solving various decision problems (Deng et al.,2000; Olson,2004; Vommi,2017, etc.).

The TOPSIS method is a MCDM method aiming at getting closer to the most ideal alternative while getting away from the least ideal solution. Some of these are as follows:

Taşabat (2019) proposed a novel method based on TOPSIS, which was named as DSC TOPSIS. She proposed a new distance measure by using distance, similarity and correlation concept.

Soto et al. (2018) introduced a ranking method for instructional videos on Youtube based on three decision criteria type: precise and imprecise and an ideal solution. taking into account decision criteria of different nature: precise and imprecise and a reference solution (ideal solution). According to them, classical normalization procedures sometimes fail to account for the different nature of the data, which makes it almost unstable to rank the alternatives. Therefore, they came up with a new normalization technique so that this problem can be resolved.

Anandan V. and Uthra G. (2017) proposed a modified TOPSIS approach using the various distance measures of L_1 family. The comparisons indicated that the proposed distance measures were suitable to solve similar multi criteria decision problems.

In order to reach the best alternatives, procedures were developed making use of the statistical and weighted statistical distances in combination. The results indicated that while getting at the most ideal solutions, the above-mentioned methods could be used as alternatives (Vommi, 2017).

Ting (2017) attempted to draw attention to the design flaw in the original TOPSIS and suggest a more appropriate way to deal with it. His study proposed a new ranking index which was intelligible and intrinsically superior to the original TOPSIS in terms of compromised solutions. This ranking index could be applied to other versions of modified TOPSIS such as the fuzzy TOPSIS as well.

Hu et al. (2016) proposed a new method, called weighted technique (or weighted TOPSIS). In their method, they took into account various centrality measures as the multi-attribute to the network and moreover, their new algorithm can compute each attribute's weight.

Another evaluation method built on the TOPSIS was proposed by Cables et al. (2012). It is thought that when there is a linguistic input in a decision process, the output should be the same. Their modified TOPSIS algorithm can be used as a linguistic classifier. In this new approach, modifications to the classic algorithm had been considered, which enable linguistic outputs and could be checked through the inclusion of an applied example to demonstrate the goodness of the new proposed model.

Shih et al. (2007) attempted to apply the extension of TOPSIS to a group decision environment. To get a broad view of the techniques used, they provided a few options for the operations, such as normalization, distance measures and mean operators, at each of the corresponding steps of TOPSIS. In addition, the TOPSIS procedure involved having more than one decision maker and identifying their preferences. Unlike in previous developments, their group preferences were aggregated within the procedure.

Olson (2004) reviewed several applications of TOPSIS where different weighting procedures and different distance metrics were used. The results of different sets of weights attributed to a previously-used set of data were compared as well. Another comparison was against SMART and centroid weighting schemes.

Deng et al. (2000) formulated the inter-company comparison process as a MCDM and modified the TOPSIS effectively. With this modified method, the relevance of the financial ratios to the evaluation result can be identified and thus, the performance difference between companies on each financial ratio can be compared. This type of modified TOPSIS is favourable over the other methods in selecting the favourable by using the entropy measure.

Pinter U. and Pšunder I. (2013) presented a systematic analysis of a general construction project success evaluation. The MCDM method M-TOPSIS orders the results starting with the ideal solution and finishes with the negative ideal solution, generating an exact, non-dimensional ordering of project success based on the given project execution criteria.

Aikhuele and Turan (2017) attempted to propose a reliable, simple and a more objective approach for the ranking and determination of the preferences in a MCDM problem through extending the MTOPSIS into the intuitionistic fuzzy environment. The improved score function matrix was applied in order to represent the accumulated effect of positive and negative evaluations in the performance ratings of the alternatives depending on interval-valued intuitionistic fuzzy set (IVIFS) data and in conjunction with the weighted normalized Euclidean distance method to calculate the separation measures of alternative(s) for the intuitionistic positive and negative ideal solutions while using the fuzzy Delphi (FD) method was determined by the weighted criteria.

Aikhuele and Turan (2016) introduced a new approach to be used during the selection and decision design concept as well as the ranking and determining choice in a MCDM problem. Their new approach included a combination of M-TOPSIS model and fuzzy Delphi model which uses interval fuzzy values on a score function along with a weighted Normalized Hamming distance method. The aim was to calculate the how much each alternative is separated from the most ideal and least ideal solutions.

MAIN FOCUS OF THE CHAPTER

In this chapter, firstly the traditional TOPSIS method will be discussed and the process steps of the method will be explained in detail. Then, attention is paid to the Euclidean distance measure used in the TOPSIS method and the distance measurements in the literature will be examined on the basis of the families they are included. The usability of distance measurements in Lp (that include Euclidean distance) and L_1 families in TOPSIS method will be emphasized. Thus, the traditional TOPSIS method will be modified in terms of the distance used. The effects of the proposed modified TOPSIS method will be applied to the data compiled by the Turkish Banking Unity (TBU) to measure the performances of the deposit banks operating in Turkey at the end of the chapter.

In the following sub-sections, the traditional TOPSIS method will be discussed first and then the proposed TOPSIS method will be elaborated.

RESEARCH METHODOLOGY

TOPSIS Method

The implementation steps of the TOPSIS method are given below.

Step 1. Determining the decision matrix:

$$X = \begin{bmatrix} x_{11} & x_{12} & \cdots & x_{1m} \\ x_{21} & x_{22} & \cdots & x_{2m} \\ \cdots & \cdots & x_{ij} & \cdots \\ x_{n1} & x_{n2} & \cdots & x_{nm} \end{bmatrix} \tag{1}$$

In a decision matrix alternatives and criterias are shown as A_i $(i=1,2,...,n)$ and C_j $(j=1,2, ...,m)$, respectively.

Step 2. Determining the weighting vector as below:

$$W = \left(w_1, \cdots, w_j, \cdots, w_m\right) \tag{2}$$

w_j is represented as the relative importance of criterion C_j.

Step 3. Normalizing the decision matrix by using Euclidean normalization:

$$x'_{ij} = \frac{x_{ij}}{\left(\sum_{k=1}^{n} x_{ik}^2\right)^{1/2}} \tag{3}$$

The normalized decision matrix is shown in (4).

$$X' = \begin{bmatrix} x'_{11} & x'_{12} & \cdots & x'_{1m} \\ x'_{21} & x'_{22} & \cdots & x'_{2m} \\ \cdots & \cdots & x'_{ij} & \cdots \\ x'_{n1} & x'_{n2} & \cdots & x'_{nm} \end{bmatrix} \tag{4}$$

Step 4. Calculating the performance matrix:

By multiplying the normalized decision matrix (11) by the weight vector (9) the weighted performance matrix is determined.

$$Y = \begin{bmatrix} w_1 x'_{11} & w_2 x'_{12} & \cdots & w_m x'_{1m} \\ w_1 x'_{21} & w_2 x'_{22} & \cdots & w_m x'_{2m} \\ \cdots & \cdots & w_i x'_{ij} & \cdots \\ w_1 x'_{n1} & w_2 x'_{n2} & \cdots & w_m x'_{nm} \end{bmatrix} = \begin{bmatrix} y_{11} & y_{12} & \cdots & y_{1m} \\ y_{21} & y_{22} & \cdots & y_{2m} \\ \cdots & \cdots & y_{ij} & \cdots \\ y_{n1} & y_{n2} & \cdots & y_{nm} \end{bmatrix} \tag{5}$$

Step 5. Calculation of the PIS and the NIS:

The positive or negative ideal solution corresponds to the best or worst criterion values, considering all criteria respectively. According to Deng (2007), "these two concepts are simple and comprehensible, have a computational efficiency as they can measure the relative performance of the alternatives with a simple mathematical formula".

$$I^{+} = \left\{ (\max_{i} y_{ij} \left| j \in J), (\min_{i} y_{ij} \right| j \in J^{'} \right\} \tag{6}$$

$$I^{+} = \left\{ y_{1}^{+}, y_{2}^{+}, \ldots, y_{n}^{+} \right\}$$

and,

$$I^{-} = \left\{ (\min_{i} y_{ij} \left| j \in J), (\max_{i} y_{ij} \right| j \in J^{'} \right\} \tag{7}$$

$$I^{-} = \left\{ y_{1}^{-}, y_{2}^{-}, \ldots, y_{n}^{-} \right\}$$

Both formulas benefit or maximization is shown as J and loss or minimization is shown as $J^{'}$ value.

Step 6. Calculating the degree of distance of the alternatives between each alternative and the PIS and the NIS:

By using Euclid Distance.

$$d_{i}^{+} = \sqrt{\sum_{j=1}^{n} (y_{ij} - y_{j}^{+})^{2}} \tag{8}$$

$$d_{i}^{-} = \sqrt{\sum_{j=1}^{n} (y_{ij} - y_{j}^{-})^{2}} \tag{9}$$

Step 7. Calculating the overall performance index for each alternative across all criteria:

This index can be calculated as in (10):

$$P_{i} = \frac{d_{i}^{-}}{d_{i}^{-} + d_{i}^{+}} \tag{10}$$

$0 \leq P_i \leq 1$. The P_i value indicates the absolute closeness of the ideal solution. If $P_i = 1$ then A_i is the ideal solution, if $P_i = 0$ then A_i is the negative ideal solution.

Step 8. Ranking the alternatives.

The ranking should be made from large to small in the case of earnings, and from small to large in the case of costs.

Distance Measure

From a scientific and mathematical perspective, distance can be defined as a quantitative degree of how far two objects are from each other. Dissimilarity can be considered as a synonym for distance. Synonyms for distance include dissimilarity. Metric distance measures are the ones that satisfy the metric features while divergence is seldom the name for other non-metric distance measures. Proximity is another word for similarity and similarity measures are usually named similarity coefficients (Jornocode, 2019).

The choice of distance/similarity measures depends on the measurement type (nominal, ordinal, interval, or proportional scale) or representation (continuous or discrete) of the data. Properties of Distance Function;

$$d\left(x,y\right)\geq 0 \tag{11}$$

$$d\left(x,y\right)=0\Leftrightarrow x=y \tag{12}$$

$$d\left(x,z\right)=d\left(y,x\right) \tag{13}$$

$$d\left(x,z\right)\leq d\left(x,y\right)+d\left(x,z\right) \tag{14}$$

In the appendix section, the formulas of distances/similarities, including: L_p Minkowski family, L_1 family, Intersection family, Inner Product family, Fidelity family or Squared-chord family, Squared L_2 family or χ^2 family, Shannon's entropy family and family derived from combinations of different methods are shown (Cha, 2007).

Proposed Method

In this study, TOPSIS method has been modified by considering distances in the L_p Minkowski family and L_1 family from the distance/similarity families mentioned appendix briefly. In the proposed method, Steps 6 and 7 of the traditional TOPSIS method are modified as follows.

Proposed Step 6. Calculating the degree of similarity of the alternatives between each alternative and the PIS and the NIS:

While the separation measures for L_p Minkowski family are given below formulas, for L_1 family these values are given in Equations 17-28 (Anandan V. and Uthra G., 2017) collectively.

For L_p Minkowski family:

$$d_i^+ = \left(\sum_{j=1}^{n}\left|a_{ij} - b_{ij}^+\right|^p\right)^{\frac{1}{r}} \quad (15)$$

$$d_i^- = \left(\sum_{j=1}^{n}\left|a_{ij} - b_{ij}^-\right|^p\right)^{\frac{1}{r}} \quad (16)$$

For $p = r \geq 1$, it is the l_p**-metric** ($p = 2$ **Euclidean**, $p = 1$ **Manhattan** (or magnitude, or city block), $p = \infty$ **Chebyshev** and for $(p, r) = (2, 1)$ **squared Euclidean distance**).

For L_1 family (Source: Anandan V. and Uthra G. (2017)):

Sorensen (or) Bray-Curtis:

$$d_i^+ = \frac{\sum_{j=1}^{n}\left|a_{ij} - b_{ij}^+\right|}{\sum_{j=1}^{n}\left(a_{ij} + b_{ij}^+\right)} \quad (17)$$

$$d_i^- = \frac{\sum_{j=1}^{n}\left|a_{ij} - b_{ij}^-\right|}{\sum_{j=1}^{n}\left(a_{ij} + b_{ij}^-\right)} \quad (18)$$

Gower:

$$d_{ij}^+ = \frac{1}{n}\sum_{j=1}^{n}\left|a_{ij} - b_{ij}^+\right| \quad (19)$$

$$d_i^- = \frac{1}{n}\sum_{j=1}^{n}\left|a_{ij} - b_{ij}^-\right| \quad (20)$$

Soergel:

$$d_i^+ = \frac{\sum_{j=1}^{n} \left| a_{ij} - b_{ij}^+ \right|}{\sum_{j=1}^{n} \max\left(a_{ij}, b_{ij}^+\right)} \tag{21}$$

$$d_i^- = \frac{\sum_{j=1}^{n} \left| a_{ij} - b_{ij}^- \right|}{\sum_{j=1}^{n} \max\left(a_{ij}, b_{ij}^-\right)} \tag{22}$$

Kulczynski:

$$d_i^+ = \frac{\sum_{j=1}^{n} \left| a_{ij} - b_{ij}^+ \right|}{\sum_{j=1}^{n} \min\left(a_{ij}, b_{ij}^+\right)} \tag{23}$$

$$d_i^- = \frac{\sum_{j=1}^{n} \left| a_{ij} - b_{ij}^- \right|}{\sum_{j=1}^{n} \min\left(a_{ij}, b_{ij}^-\right)} \tag{24}$$

Canberra:

$$d_i^+ = \sum_{j=1}^{n} \frac{\left| a_{ij} - b_{ij}^+ \right|}{\left(a_{ij} + b_{ij}^+\right)} \tag{25}$$

$$d_i^- = \sum_{j=1}^{n} \frac{\left| a_{ij} - b_{ij}^- \right|}{\left(a_{ij} + b_{ij}^-\right)} \tag{26}$$

Lorentzian:

$$d_i^+ = \sum_{j=1}^{n} \ln(1 + \left| a_{ij} - b_{ij}^+ \right|) \tag{27}$$

$$d_i^- = \sum_{j=1}^{n} \ln(1 + |a_{ij} - b_{ij}^-|) \tag{28}$$

The proposed d^+ and d^- values for the L_p and L_1 families were calculated by taking the average of the d^+ and d^- values obtained from the distances of L_p and L_1 families.

$$Proposed\_D_i^+ = \frac{\sum_i^k d_i^+}{k} \tag{29}$$

$$Proposed\_D_i^- = \frac{\sum_i^k d_i^-}{k} \tag{30}$$

Where k is represent the number of methods.

Proposed Step 7. Calculating the overall performance index:

The P_i value is obtained from the D^+ and D^- value.

$$Proposed\_P_i = \frac{D_i^-}{D_i^- + D_i^+} \tag{31}$$

SOLUTIONS AND RECOMMENDATIONS

In this study, L_p Minkowski family and $L1$ Family distance measures were used instead of Euclidean distance. The financial performance of the deposit bank that operates in the Turkish Banking Union (TBU) was analyzed through the use of the modified TOPSIS methods. The results obtained indicated the significance of the distance measures used in the TOPSIS method. For this purpose, data on deposit banks for the period of 2017 published by the TBU were used. A total of 28 banks were considered as alternatives in the study. The list of these banks is as in Table 1.

There are various ratios that measure the financial performance of the banks. As a result of literature review made from these ratios; a set of criteria was established by considering the 15 financial ratios observed most frequently under six main headings as capital adequacy, exchange rate risk, asset quality, liquidity status, profitability status and income-expenditure structure. These criteria are listed in Table 2 (Taşabat et al. 2015).

The performance of the criterion analyzed at the analysis stage has been made positive by applying the conversion to the ones that are negative. In the literature there are two different methods used for the transformation process. The first is the $x_{ij}^* = 1 / x_{ij}$ transformation and the second is the

Table 1. List of the deposit banks in Turkey

The Name of the Bank	Code
Adabank A.Ş.	A1
Akbank T.A.Ş.	A2
Alternatifbank A.Ş.	A3
Anadolubank A.Ş.	A4
Arap Türk Bankası A.Ş.	A5
Bank of Tokyo-Mitsubishi UFJ Turkey A.Ş.	A6
Birleşik Fon Bankası A.Ş.	A7
Burgan Bank A.Ş.	A8
Citibank A.Ş.	A9
Denizbank A.Ş.	A10
Deutsche Bank A.Ş.	A11
Fibabanka A.Ş.	A12
Finans Bank A.Ş.	A13
HSBC Bank A.Ş.	A14
ICBC Turkey Bank A.Ş.	A15
ING Bank A.Ş.	A16
Odea Bank A.Ş.	A17
Rabobank A.Ş.	A18
Şekerbank T.A.Ş.	A19
Turkish Bank A.Ş.	A20
Turkland Bank A.Ş.	A21
Türk Ekonomi Bankası A.Ş.	A22
Türkiye Cumhuriyeti Ziraat Bankası A.Ş.	A23
Türkiye Garanti Bankası A.Ş.	A24
Türkiye Halk Bankası A.Ş.	A25
Türkiye İş Bankası A.Ş.	A26
Türkiye Vakıflar Bankası T.A.O.	A27
Yapı ve Kredi Bankası A.Ş.	A28

Source: TBU (2017).

$x_{ij}^{*} = \underset{i}{maks}\, x_{ij} - x_{ij}$ transformation. In this study, by applying the second approach, the criterions with negative effect on performance and the criterions with negative value were transformed into TOPSIS method.

Weighting Criteria

Determining the weight of performance criteria in multi-criteria decision making is another important step. This is due to the fact that the decision makers of performance evaluation give different weights

Table 2. Financial ratios used as criteria

Rate Group	Criteria Code	Ratios	Performance Effect
Capital Adequacy	C1	Equity / (Credit + Market + Operational Ratio)	Positive
	C2	Equity / Total Assets	Positive
	C3	(Equity - Fixed Assets) / Total Assets	Positive
	C4	Equity / (Deposits + Non-Deposit Sources)	Positive
Exchange Rate	C5	Net Balance Sheet Position / Equity (*)	Negative
	C6	(Net Balance Sheet Position + Net Off-Balance Sheet Position) / Equity*	Negative
Active Quality	C7	Total Loans / Equity	Negative
	C8	Credits in the Sector (Gross) / Total Loans	Negative
	C9	Consumer Loans / Total Loans	Positive
Liquidity	C10	Liquid Assets / Short Term Liabilities	Positive
	C11	Liquid Assets / (Deposits + Non-Deposit Sources)	Positive
Profitability	C12	Net Period Profit (Loss) / Total Assets	Positive
	C13	Net Period Profit / Equity	Positive
Income/Expense Structure	C14	Net Interest Income After Specific Provisions / Total Operating Income	Positive
	C15	Non-interest Income / Other Operating Expenses	Positive

* Calculated by taking absolute values.
Source: Taşabat et al. (2015).

(importance) to each criterion. Different weights give different performance orders. Different techniques are used in the literature to weight the criteria. In this study, "Equal Weighted Method" is considered. Equal Weighted Method is a method based on equal weighting of the criteria considered in evaluating alternatives.

$$w_{ij} = \frac{1}{n} \tag{32}$$

At this formula *n* is the number of criteria. The formula is used when the weight for the criteria is determined since the weights must be "1". The application of the modified TOPSIS methods is explained step by step below.

Step 1. Determining the decision matrix

The decision matrix was established with 28 banks as alternatives and 15 ratios as criteria. The decision matrix is shown at Table 3.

Step 2. Determining the weighting vector

Table 3. The decision matrix with original data

	C1	C2	C3	C4	C5	C6	C7	C8	C9	C10	C11	C12	C13	C14	C15
A1	211.3	84.6	79.9	711.3	0.0	0.0	0.0	-	-	775.6	791.1	3.1	3.6	94.7	7.6
A2	14.6	11.4	10.2	13.6	-32.7	-0.8	60.4	2.4	27.9	61.3	39.4	1.3	11.2	53.8	71.8
A3	15.5	7.6	4.2	9.2	-57.8	5.8	71.1	5.1	2.8	64.9	30.8	0.5	6.0	49.5	46.8
A4	14.5	12.4	8.6	14.9	-26.5	-5.6	62.1	3.7	4.5	62.4	40.1	1.3	10.6	61.4	44.9
A5	18.6	15.0	12.6	17.9	-5.1	2.1	33.8	1.0	0.1	116.5	67.8	1.7	11.6	62.0	81.7
A6	14.1	9.7	9.0	11.0	-218.7	-0.4	53.5	0.0	0.0	92.3	51.7	0.3	2.8	143.7	-69.5
A7	61.0	19.6	17.9	70.3	3.3	3.3	44.6	3.9	0.2	89.9	90.0	0.7	3.5	84.7	30.6
A8	16.0	9.5	5.5	11.5	-53.8	3.1	76.7	2.6	1.7	42.0	22.9	0.5	5.2	67.0	25.4
A9	17.6	14.9	14.7	18.3	-74.0	-2.8	44.1	2.2	0.0	64.4	62.2	2.0	13.7	85.7	25.1
A10	16.1	9.8	3.6	12.6	-102.4	6.3	61.0	5.2	31.9	51.3	36.2	0.9	9.2	55.9	32.8
A11	20.7	17.0	16.4	21.0	5.1	7.7	57.9	0.0	0.0	122.6	50.1	2.4	14.2	65.1	66.8
A12	13.6	9.3	6.8	10.9	-15.4	-10.9	77.0	1.7	5.6	44.8	23.9	0.7	7.9	72.7	23.4
A13	15.4	10.5	7.0	14.3	-141.8	-2.6	66.8	6.6	37.8	40.1	28.4	0.8	7.8	63.5	31.5
A14	15.7	8.4	6.4	10.6	-105.1	2.9	64.7	6.1	36.1	56.9	40.0	-1.0	-12.5	29.7	50.7
A15	12.8	8.9	7.4	9.9	-112.0	-2.1	61.9	4.4	11.8	99.7	40.6	-0.3	-2.9	78.1	5.8
A16	15.8	9.1	7.3	11.1	-159.0	1.4	71.5	3.0	32.1	46.6	28.4	0.2	2.6	70.4	15.3
A17	12.2	4.2	2.4	4.7	-232.0	8.8	68.0	2.2	10.1	57.6	32.6	0.2	3.7	87.8	-20.9
A18	227.9	82.8	82.0	536.6	-0.6	-0.6	13.9	0.0	0.0	43,449.7	550.5	3.2	3.8	95.1	10.1
A19	13.7	10.3	3.6	12.5	-98.5	-0.5	68.5	6.0	9.8	35.0	23.4	0.4	4.1	51.8	36.7
A20	19.9	15.6	10.3	19.1	8.2	7.8	67.0	1.5	0.9	67.2	31.1	0.3	2.0	81.3	14.2
A21	15.6	12.8	8.9	15.1	4.0	0.0	68.1	6.1	0.2	59.5	35.1	0.2	2.0	61.0	30.5
A22	13.9	9.7	7.8	11.9	-90.2	8.0	73.9	2.3	28.2	37.7	27.4	1.2	12.7	60.0	36.4
A23	15.1	10.4	7.5	12.1	-2.6	2.3	61.7	1.7	26.9	51.2	36.8	1.7	16.4	73.0	51.6
A24	15.0	12.2	8.7	15.2	-25.1	5.5	62.6	2.8	33.0	46.0	29.2	1.3	11.0	64.0	47.1
A25	13.8	10.3	7.1	12.0	-7.3	1.5	67.5	3.1	21.1	37.6	23.1	1.2	11.9	63.0	56.9
A26	15.6	11.6	6.2	14.4	-51.4	-7.3	64.5	2.0	26.1	53.1	34.1	1.1	9.6	62.2	50.3
A27	14.5	9.2	6.3	11.0	2.2	10.7	67.7	3.9	29.6	44.4	29.2	1.1	11.5	58.5	59.0
A28	13.8	10.5	6.0	13.4	-35.2	3.3	67.5	4.1	29.4	46.5	30.8	0.8	8.1	55.4	52.2

Source: TBU (2017).

Since 15 criteria were used in this study, the criteria weights were determined as 1/15 = 0.06667. Table 4 was formed to show how the weights of the criteria are.

Step 3. Normalizing the decision matrix through Euclidean normalization:

Before normalizing data the criterions with negative effect on performance and the criterions with negative value were transformed. And then data are normalized. For this purpose the formula (18) is applied. The result is shown in Table 5.

Table 4. Weight of the criteria

	C1	C2	C3	C4	C5	C6	C7	C8	C9	C10	C11	C12	C13	C14	C15
w_i	0.067	0.067	0.067	0.067	0.067	0.067	0.067	0.067	0.067	0.067	0.067	0.067	0.067	0.067	0.067

Source: Authors

Table 5. Normalized data

	C1	C2	C3	C4	C5	C6	C7	C8	C9	C10	C11	C12	C13	C14	C15
A1	0.648	0.640	0.648	0.794	0.238	0.272	0.585	0.000	0.000	0.018	0.802	0.348	0.151	0.247	0.137
A2	0.045	0.086	0.083	0.015	0.205	0.254	0.126	0.204	0.261	0.001	0.040	0.196	0.222	0.140	0.251
A3	0.048	0.057	0.034	0.010	0.179	0.128	0.045	0.074	0.026	0.001	0.031	0.126	0.173	0.129	0.207
A4	0.045	0.094	0.070	0.017	0.211	0.133	0.113	0.140	0.042	0.001	0.041	0.199	0.216	0.160	0.203
A5	0.057	0.113	0.102	0.020	0.233	0.219	0.328	0.272	0.001	0.003	0.069	0.235	0.226	0.162	0.269
A6	0.043	0.073	0.073	0.012	0.014	0.263	0.178	0.319	0.000	0.002	0.052	0.111	0.143	0.374	0.000
A7	0.187	0.148	0.145	0.078	0.235	0.190	0.246	0.132	0.002	0.002	0.091	0.147	0.150	0.221	0.178
A8	0.049	0.072	0.044	0.013	0.183	0.194	0.002	0.195	0.016	0.001	0.023	0.130	0.165	0.174	0.169
A9	0.054	0.113	0.119	0.020	0.162	0.204	0.250	0.213	0.000	0.001	0.063	0.261	0.245	0.223	0.168
A10	0.049	0.074	0.029	0.014	0.133	0.114	0.122	0.068	0.298	0.001	0.037	0.165	0.203	0.146	0.182
A11	0.064	0.128	0.133	0.023	0.233	0.079	0.145	0.319	0.000	0.003	0.051	0.291	0.250	0.170	0.242
A12	0.042	0.070	0.055	0.012	0.222	0.000	0.000	0.237	0.052	0.001	0.024	0.150	0.191	0.189	0.165
A13	0.047	0.080	0.057	0.016	0.093	0.208	0.078	0.000	0.353	0.001	0.029	0.158	0.190	0.165	0.180
A14	0.048	0.064	0.052	0.012	0.130	0.200	0.093	0.027	0.338	0.001	0.041	0.000	0.000	0.077	0.214
A15	0.039	0.067	0.060	0.011	0.123	0.221	0.114	0.108	0.110	0.002	0.041	0.067	0.090	0.203	0.134
A16	0.048	0.069	0.059	0.012	0.075	0.239	0.042	0.175	0.300	0.001	0.029	0.108	0.141	0.183	0.151
A17	0.037	0.032	0.020	0.005	0.000	0.051	0.068	0.211	0.094	0.001	0.033	0.102	0.152	0.229	0.086
A18	0.699	0.626	0.665	0.599	0.237	0.258	0.479	0.319	0.000	1.000	0.558	0.356	0.153	0.248	0.141
A19	0.042	0.078	0.029	0.014	0.137	0.261	0.064	0.029	0.091	0.001	0.024	0.124	0.155	0.135	0.189
A20	0.061	0.118	0.084	0.021	0.230	0.077	0.076	0.246	0.008	0.002	0.032	0.115	0.136	0.212	0.149
A21	0.048	0.097	0.072	0.017	0.234	0.272	0.067	0.026	0.002	0.001	0.036	0.109	0.135	0.159	0.178
A22	0.043	0.073	0.063	0.013	0.146	0.072	0.023	0.207	0.264	0.001	0.028	0.192	0.236	0.156	0.188
A23	0.046	0.079	0.061	0.014	0.235	0.216	0.116	0.238	0.252	0.001	0.037	0.232	0.270	0.190	0.215
A24	0.046	0.092	0.070	0.017	0.212	0.136	0.109	0.186	0.309	0.001	0.030	0.201	0.220	0.167	0.207
A25	0.042	0.078	0.058	0.013	0.231	0.234	0.072	0.168	0.198	0.001	0.023	0.192	0.228	0.164	0.225
A26	0.048	0.088	0.050	0.016	0.185	0.090	0.095	0.221	0.244	0.001	0.035	0.183	0.207	0.162	0.213
A27	0.045	0.069	0.051	0.012	0.236	0.003	0.071	0.131	0.277	0.001	0.030	0.177	0.225	0.152	0.228
A28	0.042	0.079	0.049	0.015	0.202	0.190	0.072	0.121	0.275	0.001	0.031	0.159	0.192	0.144	0.216

Source: Authors

Step 4. Calculating the performance matrix:

The weighted performance matrix (Table 6) is determined by multiplying the normalized decision matrix (Table 5) with the weight vector (Table 4).

Step 5. Determining the PIS and the NIS

By using formula (8)-(9) the PIS and NIS values are obtained. These values are shown in Table 7 for all criteria.

Step 6. Calculating the degree of distance of the alternatives between each alternative and the PIS and the NIS:

Tables for the L_p and L_1 families with PIS and NIS distance values are given respectively below (Table 8 and Table 9). The abbreviations used in the following tables are as follows; D_1: Euclidean, D_2: City blok, D_3: Chebyshev, D_4: Sorensen, D_5: Gower, D_6: Soergel, D_7: Kulczyynski, D_8: Canberra, D_9: Lorentzian.

Step 7. Calculating the overall performance index for each alternative across all criteria:

The overall performance index for L_p and L_1 families are given in Table 10.

The order of alternatives for the L_p and L_1 families according to the overall performance index are given in Table 11.

The proposed D^+ and D^- values and also P_i value are calculated according to formulas (29)-(30). The solutions are summarized in Table 12 and shown in Figure 1.

In Figure 1 the following definitions apply. 1: Euclidean, 2: City blok, 3: Chebyshev, 4: Sorensen, 5: Gower, 6: Soergel, 7: Kulczyynski, 8: Canberra, 9: Lorentzian, 10: Proposed Method for L_p family, 11: Proposed Method for L_1 family. The first ten banks which are ranked through modified methods are reported in Table 13.

FUTURE RESEARCH DIRECTIONS

Whether in our personal or business life, we often face events with multiple criteria and multiple alternatives. In particular, the importance of MCDM methods in the banking sector where financial transactions are performed is indisputable. In this context, the contribution of the book to the literature will be quite valuable. The case study, which is covered in the chapter, is adaptable to each country. The solution of the proposed model was carried out with the excel program.

Table 6. Performance matrix

	C1	C2	C3	C4	C5	C6	C7	C8	C9	C10	C11	C12	C13	C14	C15
A1	0.043	0.043	0.043	0.053	0.016	0.018	0.039	0.000	0.000	0.001	0.053	0.023	0.010	0.016	0.009
A2	0.003	0.006	0.006	0.001	0.014	0.017	0.008	0.014	0.017	0.000	0.003	0.013	0.015	0.009	0.017
A3	0.003	0.004	0.002	0.001	0.012	0.009	0.003	0.005	0.002	0.000	0.002	0.008	0.012	0.009	0.014
A4	0.003	0.006	0.005	0.001	0.014	0.009	0.008	0.009	0.003	0.000	0.003	0.013	0.014	0.011	0.014
A5	0.004	0.008	0.007	0.001	0.016	0.015	0.022	0.018	0.000	0.000	0.005	0.016	0.015	0.011	0.018
A6	0.003	0.005	0.005	0.001	0.001	0.018	0.012	0.021	0.000	0.000	0.003	0.007	0.010	0.025	0.000
A7	0.012	0.010	0.010	0.005	0.016	0.013	0.016	0.009	0.000	0.000	0.006	0.010	0.010	0.015	0.012
A8	0.003	0.005	0.003	0.001	0.012	0.013	0.000	0.013	0.001	0.000	0.002	0.009	0.011	0.012	0.011
A9	0.004	0.008	0.008	0.001	0.011	0.014	0.017	0.014	0.000	0.000	0.004	0.017	0.016	0.015	0.011
A10	0.003	0.005	0.002	0.001	0.009	0.008	0.008	0.005	0.020	0.000	0.002	0.011	0.014	0.010	0.012
A11	0.004	0.009	0.009	0.002	0.016	0.005	0.010	0.021	0.000	0.000	0.003	0.019	0.017	0.011	0.016
A12	0.003	0.005	0.004	0.001	0.015	0.000	0.000	0.016	0.003	0.000	0.002	0.010	0.013	0.013	0.011
A13	0.003	0.005	0.004	0.001	0.006	0.014	0.005	0.000	0.024	0.000	0.002	0.011	0.013	0.011	0.012
A14	0.003	0.004	0.003	0.001	0.009	0.013	0.006	0.002	0.023	0.000	0.003	0.000	0.000	0.005	0.014
A15	0.003	0.004	0.004	0.001	0.008	0.015	0.008	0.007	0.007	0.000	0.003	0.004	0.006	0.014	0.009
A16	0.003	0.005	0.004	0.001	0.005	0.016	0.003	0.012	0.020	0.000	0.002	0.007	0.009	0.012	0.010
A17	0.002	0.002	0.001	0.000	0.000	0.003	0.005	0.014	0.006	0.000	0.002	0.007	0.010	0.015	0.006
A18	0.047	0.042	0.044	0.040	0.016	0.017	0.032	0.021	0.000	0.067	0.037	0.024	0.010	0.017	0.009
A19	0.003	0.005	0.002	0.001	0.009	0.017	0.004	0.002	0.006	0.000	0.002	0.008	0.010	0.009	0.013
A20	0.004	0.008	0.006	0.001	0.015	0.005	0.005	0.016	0.001	0.000	0.002	0.008	0.009	0.014	0.010
A21	0.003	0.006	0.005	0.001	0.016	0.018	0.004	0.002	0.000	0.000	0.002	0.007	0.009	0.011	0.012
A22	0.003	0.005	0.004	0.001	0.010	0.005	0.002	0.014	0.018	0.000	0.002	0.013	0.016	0.010	0.013
A23	0.003	0.005	0.004	0.001	0.016	0.014	0.008	0.016	0.017	0.000	0.002	0.015	0.018	0.013	0.014
A24	0.003	0.006	0.005	0.001	0.014	0.009	0.007	0.012	0.021	0.000	0.002	0.013	0.015	0.011	0.014
A25	0.003	0.005	0.004	0.001	0.015	0.016	0.005	0.011	0.013	0.000	0.002	0.013	0.015	0.011	0.015
A26	0.003	0.006	0.003	0.001	0.012	0.006	0.006	0.015	0.016	0.000	0.002	0.012	0.014	0.011	0.014
A27	0.003	0.005	0.003	0.001	0.016	0.000	0.005	0.009	0.018	0.000	0.002	0.012	0.015	0.010	0.015
A28	0.003	0.005	0.003	0.001	0.013	0.013	0.005	0.008	0.018	0.000	0.002	0.011	0.013	0.010	0.014

Source: Authors

Table 7. PIS and NIS value

	C1	C2	C3	C4	C5	C6	C7	C8	C9	C10	C11	C12	C13	C14	C15
I^+	0.699	0.640	0.665	0.794	0.238	0.272	0.585	0.319	0.353	1.000	0.802	0.356	0.270	0.374	0.269
I^-	0.037	0.032	0.020	0.005	0.000	0.000	0.000	0.000	0.000	0.001	0.023	0.000	0.000	0.077	0.000

Source: Authors

Table 8. D^+ and D^- value L_p family

	Positive Distances (D^+)			Negative Distances (D^-)		
	D_I	D_2	D_3	D_I	D_2	D_3
A1	0.07428	0.14053	0.06546	0.11605	0.35546	0.05256
A2	0.12603	0.36709	0.06656	0.04184	0.12890	0.01740
A3	0.13292	0.42445	0.06655	0.02571	0.07154	0.01377
A4	0.12842	0.39680	0.06656	0.03248	0.09919	0.01439
A5	0.12281	0.35512	0.06648	0.04647	0.14087	0.02190
A6	0.12926	0.39852	0.06651	0.03824	0.09747	0.02124
A7	0.11844	0.36555	0.06652	0.03812	0.13044	0.01641
A8	0.13223	0.41364	0.06659	0.02935	0.08235	0.01302
A9	0.12353	0.36919	0.06656	0.04066	0.12680	0.01738
A10	0.12918	0.40004	0.06658	0.03316	0.09595	0.01988
A11	0.12476	0.36695	0.06647	0.04328	0.12904	0.02124
A12	0.13249	0.41502	0.06659	0.03051	0.08097	0.01577
A13	0.12979	0.39877	0.06659	0.03576	0.09723	0.02356
A14	0.13257	0.42258	0.06657	0.03187	0.07341	0.02250
A15	0.13030	0.41626	0.06650	0.02587	0.07973	0.01475
A16	0.12991	0.40021	0.06658	0.03359	0.09578	0.02003
A17	0.13363	0.43423	0.06657	0.02353	0.06176	0.01408
A18	0.03528	0.08649	0.02356	0.12467	0.40950	0.06660
A19	0.13213	0.41753	0.06660	0.02834	0.07846	0.01738
A20	0.12897	0.40468	0.06655	0.03050	0.09131	0.01642
A21	0.13113	0.41216	0.06656	0.03053	0.08383	0.01812
A22	0.12974	0.39540	0.06660	0.03509	0.10059	0.01757
A23	0.12629	0.36214	0.06658	0.04351	0.13385	0.01801
A24	0.12676	0.37545	0.06658	0.03954	0.12054	0.02060
A25	0.12848	0.38047	0.06660	0.03838	0.11552	0.01562
A26	0.12785	0.38652	0.06657	0.03610	0.10947	0.01629
A27	0.12993	0.39521	0.06659	0.03629	0.10078	0.01843
A28	0.12893	0.38972	0.06658	0.03585	0.10627	0.01832

Source: Authors

Table 9. D^+ and D^- value for L_1 family

	Positive Distances (D^+)						Negative Distances (D^-)					
	D_4	D_5	D_6	D_7	D_8	D_9	D_4	D_5	D_6	D_7	D_8	D_9
A1	0.160	0.009	0.276	0.381	3.840	0.138	0.932	0.024	0.965	27.289	12.104	0.349
A2	0.564	0.024	0.721	2.587	7.287	0.359	0.832	0.009	0.908	9.896	10.480	0.128
A3	0.715	0.028	0.834	5.019	9.666	0.416	0.733	0.005	0.846	5.492	9.695	0.071
A4	0.639	0.026	0.780	3.536	8.487	0.389	0.792	0.007	0.884	7.615	10.569	0.099
A5	0.536	0.024	0.698	2.307	7.234	0.348	0.844	0.009	0.915	10.815	11.419	0.140
A6	0.643	0.027	0.783	3.607	9.598	0.390	0.789	0.007	0.882	7.483	8.935	0.097
A7	0.560	0.024	0.718	2.548	7.615	0.359	0.834	0.009	0.909	10.014	12.465	0.130
A8	0.684	0.028	0.813	4.337	9.195	0.405	0.760	0.005	0.863	6.322	9.805	0.082
A9	0.569	0.025	0.725	2.640	7.672	0.362	0.830	0.008	0.907	9.735	10.294	0.126
A10	0.647	0.027	0.786	3.671	8.675	0.392	0.786	0.006	0.880	7.366	9.910	0.095
A11	0.564	0.024	0.721	2.583	7.712	0.359	0.832	0.009	0.908	9.906	10.542	0.128
A12	0.688	0.028	0.815	4.415	9.519	0.407	0.757	0.005	0.861	6.216	0.000	0.081
A13	0.644	0.027	0.783	3.617	8.868	0.391	0.789	0.006	0.882	7.464	9.074	0.097
A14	0.710	0.028	0.830	4.889	10.226	0.414	0.738	0.005	0.849	5.636	7.809	0.073
A15	0.692	0.028	0.818	4.487	9.337	0.408	0.754	0.005	0.860	6.121	10.454	0.079
A16	0.648	0.027	0.786	3.678	8.710	0.392	0.786	0.006	0.880	7.353	10.060	0.095
A17	0.744	0.029	0.853	5.806	10.499	0.426	0.703	0.004	0.826	4.741	0.000	0.061
A18	0.093	0.006	0.170	0.205	2.249	0.086	0.940	0.027	0.969	31.437	13.170	0.402
A19	0.695	0.028	0.820	4.564	9.407	0.409	0.751	0.005	0.858	6.024	9.406	0.078
A20	0.660	0.027	0.795	3.878	9.011	0.397	0.778	0.006	0.875	7.010	9.973	0.091
A21	0.680	0.027	0.810	4.255	9.395	0.404	0.763	0.006	0.866	6.436	10.543	0.083
A22	0.635	0.026	0.777	3.480	8.464	0.387	0.794	0.007	0.885	7.722	9.887	0.100
A23	0.552	0.024	0.711	2.466	7.112	0.354	0.837	0.009	0.911	10.276	10.327	0.133
A24	0.584	0.025	0.738	2.811	7.617	0.368	0.822	0.008	0.902	9.254	10.307	0.120
A25	0.597	0.025	0.747	2.960	7.741	0.372	0.816	0.008	0.899	8.869	9.816	0.115
A26	0.612	0.026	0.759	3.155	8.044	0.379	0.808	0.007	0.894	8.404	10.294	0.109
A27	0.635	0.026	0.776	3.473	8.677	0.387	0.795	0.007	0.886	7.737	8.875	0.100
A28	0.620	0.026	0.766	3.267	8.131	0.382	0.803	0.007	0.891	8.159	9.988	0.106

Source: Authors

Table 10. P_i value for L_p and L_1 families

	P_i Value For L_p Family Distances			P_i Value For L_1 Family Distances					
	D_I	**D_2**	**D_3**	**D_4**	**D_5**	**D_6**	**D_7**	**D_8**	**D_9**
A1	0.61	0.72	0.45	0.85	0.72	0.78	0.99	0.76	0.72
A2	0.25	0.26	0.21	0.60	0.26	0.56	0.79	0.59	0.26
A3	0.16	0.14	0.17	0.51	0.14	0.50	0.52	0.50	0.15
A4	0.20	0.20	0.18	0.55	0.20	0.53	0.68	0.55	0.20
A5	0.27	0.28	0.25	0.61	0.28	0.57	0.82	0.61	0.29
A6	0.23	0.20	0.24	0.55	0.20	0.53	0.67	0.48	0.20
A7	0.24	0.26	0.20	0.60	0.26	0.56	0.80	0.62	0.27
A8	0.18	0.17	0.16	0.53	0.17	0.52	0.59	0.52	0.17
A9	0.25	0.26	0.21	0.59	0.26	0.56	0.79	0.57	0.26
A10	0.20	0.19	0.23	0.55	0.19	0.53	0.67	0.53	0.20
A11	0.26	0.26	0.24	0.60	0.26	0.56	0.79	0.58	0.26
A12	0.19	0.16	0.19	0.52	0.16	0.51	0.58	0.00	0.17
A13	0.22	0.20	0.26	0.55	0.20	0.53	0.67	0.51	0.20
A14	0.19	0.15	0.25	0.51	0.15	0.51	0.54	0.43	0.15
A15	0.17	0.16	0.18	0.52	0.16	0.51	0.58	0.53	0.16
A16	0.21	0.19	0.23	0.55	0.19	0.53	0.67	0.54	0.20
A17	0.15	0.12	0.17	0.49	0.12	0.49	0.45	0.00	0.13
A18	0.78	0.83	0.74	0.91	0.83	0.85	0.99	0.85	0.82
A19	0.18	0.16	0.21	0.52	0.16	0.51	0.57	0.50	0.16
A20	0.19	0.18	0.20	0.54	0.18	0.52	0.64	0.53	0.19
A21	0.19	0.17	0.21	0.53	0.17	0.52	0.60	0.53	0.17
A22	0.21	0.20	0.21	0.56	0.20	0.53	0.69	0.54	0.21
A23	0.26	0.27	0.21	0.60	0.27	0.56	0.81	0.59	0.27
A24	0.24	0.24	0.24	0.58	0.24	0.55	0.77	0.58	0.25
A25	0.23	0.23	0.19	0.58	0.23	0.55	0.75	0.56	0.24
A26	0.22	0.22	0.20	0.57	0.22	0.54	0.73	0.56	0.22
A27	0.22	0.20	0.22	0.56	0.20	0.53	0.69	0.51	0.21
A28	0.22	0.21	0.22	0.56	0.21	0.54	0.71	0.55	0.22

Source: Authors

Table 11. Ranking alternatives

	Ranking For L_p Family Distance			*Ranking* For L_l Family Distance					
	D_1	D_2	D_3	D_4	D_5	D_6	D_7	D_8	D_9
A1	2	2	2	2	2	2	2	2	2
A2	6	7	16	7	7	7	7	6	7
A3	27	27	27	27	27	27	27	23	27
A4	19	15	25	15	15	15	15	12	15
A5	3	3	5	3	3	3	3	4	3
A6	11	16	7	16	16	16	16	25	16
A7	8	5	20	5	5	5	5	3	5
A8	24	22	28	22	22	22	22	20	22
A9	7	8	17	8	8	8	8	9	8
A10	18	18	10	18	18	18	18	16	18
A11	4	6	6	6	6	6	6	7	6
A12	23	23	22	23	23	23	23	27	23
A13	15	17	3	17	17	17	17	21	17
A14	20	26	4	26	26	26	26	26	26
A15	26	24	24	24	24	24	24	18	24
A16	17	19	9	19	19	19	19	15	19
A17	28	28	26	28	28	28	28	28	28
A18	1	1	1	1	1	1	1	1	1
A19	25	25	18	25	25	25	25	24	25
A20	21	20	19	20	20	20	20	19	20
A21	22	21	13	21	21	21	21	17	21
A22	16	14	15	14	14	14	14	14	14
A23	5	4	14	4	4	4	4	5	4
A24	9	9	8	9	9	9	9	8	9
A25	10	10	23	10	10	10	10	11	10
A26	12	11	21	11	11	11	11	10	11
A27	13	13	11	13	13	13	13	22	13
A28	14	12	12	12	12	12	12	13	12

Source: Authors

Table 12. Proposed method solutions

	L_p Family			Rank	L_l Family			Rank
	D^+	D^-	P_i		D^+	D^-	P_i	
A1	0.093	0.175	0.652	1	0.265	9.534	0.973	1
A2	0.187	0.063	0.252	18	1.222	3.644	0.749	18
A3	0.208	0.037	0.151	5	2.090	2.136	0.506	5
A4	0.197	0.049	0.198	23	1.568	2.866	0.646	23
A5	0.181	0.070	0.278	11	1.118	3.957	0.780	7
A6	0.198	0.052	0.209	2	1.593	2.820	0.639	11
A7	0.184	0.062	0.251	7	1.208	3.684	0.753	2
A8	0.204	0.042	0.169	9	1.852	2.422	0.567	9
A9	0.186	0.062	0.248	24	1.242	3.589	0.743	24
A10	0.199	0.050	0.200	25	1.616	2.781	0.632	25
A11	0.186	0.065	0.257	26	1.221	3.648	0.749	26
A12	0.205	0.042	0.172	28	1.879	2.386	0.559	28
A13	0.198	0.052	0.208	6	1.597	2.814	0.638	27
A14	0.207	0.043	0.170	13	2.044	2.186	0.517	22
A15	0.204	0.040	0.164	27	1.904	2.353	0.553	4
A16	0.199	0.050	0.200	22	1.619	2.776	0.632	6
A17	0.211	0.033	0.135	16	2.362	1.876	0.443	13
A18	0.048	0.200	0.805	10	0.153	10.936	0.986	10
A19	0.205	0.041	0.168	4	1.931	2.320	0.546	16
A20	0.200	0.046	0.187	20	1.690	2.659	0.611	20
A21	0.203	0.044	0.178	21	1.823	2.461	0.575	21
A22	0.197	0.051	0.206	12	1.548	2.903	0.652	8
A23	0.185	0.065	0.260	14	1.177	3.773	0.762	12
A24	0.190	0.060	0.241	8	1.305	3.425	0.724	15
A25	0.192	0.057	0.228	19	1.360	3.294	0.708	19
A26	0.194	0.054	0.218	15	1.431	3.135	0.687	14
A27	0.197	0.052	0.208	3	1.545	2.908	0.653	3
A28	0.195	0.053	0.215	17	1.471	3.052	0.675	17

Source: Authors

Figure 1. L_p family distance, L_1 family distance and proposed method
Source: Authors

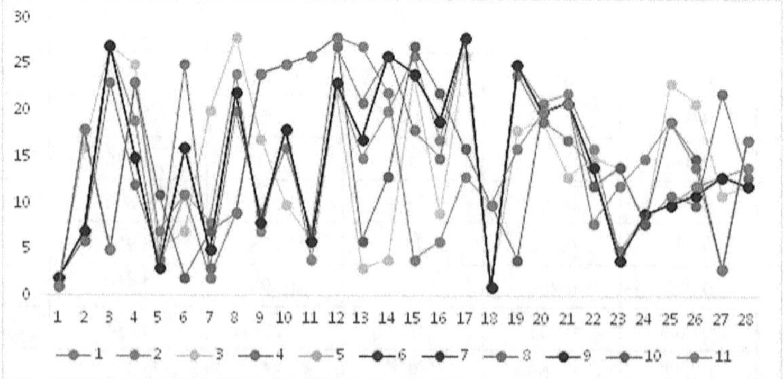

Table 13. Top five banks with high performance value

L_p Family Distances				L_1 Family Distances						
D_1	D_2	D_3	Proposed_D	D_4	D_5	D_6	D_7	D_8	D_9	Proposed_D
A18	A18	A18	A1	A18	A18	A18	A18	A18	A18	A1
A1	A1	A1	A18	A1	A1	A1	A1	A1	A1	A18
A5	A5	A13	A5	A5	A5	A5	A5	A7	A5	A5
A11	A23	A14	A23	A23	A23	A23	A23	A5	A23	A23
A23	A7	A5	A11	A7	A7	A7	A7	A23	A7	A7

Source: Authors

CONCLUSION

With this study, it has been tried to present a different approach to evaluate alternatives in cases where there are many criteria for decision makers, by modifying the TOPSIS method, one of the well-known MCDM methods.

Performance evaluation, which has a very important role in the banking sector, was dealt with and a model was proposed to evaluate different alternatives within the framework of the various criteria considered to affect the financial performance of the banks. The proposed model was evaluated on a real sample and the results obtained were interpreted. For this purpose, the financial performance of 28 deposit banks, which account for more than 90% of assets size in the Turkish banking sector and operate in Turkey as of 2017, has been evaluated.

In order for the banks to be ranked according to their financial performances in the study, 15 financial ratios (criteria) used in many applications in the literature, calculated from year-end financial tables related to capital adequacy, exchange rate risk, asset quality, profitability and income-expenditure status were used. The evaluation of the performance of the banks is not based on the individual criteria; all the criteria were taken together with the modified versions of the TOPSIS method, which were taken into account together. The criteria discussed in the methods are weighted by Equal weighting technique.

In the study, distances of Manhattan and Chebyshev in the L_p family and distances of Sorensen, Gower, Soergel, Kulczyynski, Canberra and Lorentzian in the L_1 family were used as an alternative to the distance of Euclid included in the L_p family used in the traditional TOPSIS method. Also in the study, the average d^+ and d^- values for the L_p and L_1 families are proposed, taking the averages of the distance measures considered.

From the results obtained, it is seen that the alternative rankings may vary according to the distance used. This was expected. Because both L_q and L_1 families have different mathematical formulations and structures. Thus, it was seen that TOPSIS method may show differences according to the distance measure used (Table 14). On the other hand, the recommended distance measurements showed similar ranking. According to the proposed method, it is seen that the banks receiving the first four orders from the results obtained for the families L_p and L_1 are the same. The banks in question are respectively: Adabank A.Ş. (A1), Rabobank A.Ş. (A18), Arab Türk Bankası A.Ş. (A5), Türkiye Cumhuriyeti Ziraat Bankası A.Ş (A23).

ACKNOWLEDGMENT

This research received no specific grant from any funding agency in the public, commercial, or not-for-profit sectors.

REFERENCES

Aikhuele, D. O., & Turan, F. B. M. (2016). An Interval Fuzzy-Valued M-TOPSIS Model for Design Concept Selection. *The National Conference for Postgraduate Research 2016*, Universiti Malaysia Pahang, 374–384.

Aikhuele, D. O., & Turan, F. B. M. (2017). An integrated fuzzy dephi and interval-valued intuitionistic fuzzy M-Topsis model for design concept selection. *Pakistan Journal of Statistics and Operation Research, 13*(2), 425. doi:10.18187/pjsor.v13i2.1413

Anandan, V., & Uthra, G. (2017). Extension of TOPSIS using L1 Family of Distance Measures. Advances in Fuzzy Mathematics, 12, 4 (pp. 897–908). Research India Publications; Retrieved from http://www.ripublication.com

Bankacılık Düzenleme ve Denetleme Kurumu. (2017). Retrieved from http://www.bddk.org.tr/WebSitesi/default.aspx

Bass, S. J., & Kwakernaak, H. (1977). Rating and ranking of multi-aspects alternatives using fuzzy sets. *Automatica, 13*(1), 47–58. doi:10.1016/0005-1098(77)90008-5

Belton, V., & Gear, T. (1983). On a short-coming of Saaty's method of analytic hierarchies. *Omega, 11*(3), 228–230. doi:10.1016/0305-0483(83)90047-6

Brans, J. P., Mareschal, B., & Vincke, Ph. (1984). PROMITHEE: A new family of outranking methods in MCDM. *Operations Research, 84*, 477–490.

Cables, E., García-Cascales, M. S., & Lamata, M. T. (2012). The LTOPSIS: An alternative to TOPSIS decision-making approach for linguistic variables. *Expert Systems with Applications*, *39*(2), 2119–2126. doi:10.1016/j.eswa.2011.07.119

Cha, S. H. (2007). Comprehensive Survey on Distance/Similarity Measures between Probability Density Functions. *International Journal of Mathematical Models and Methods in Applied Sciences*, *1*(4), 300–307.

Chen, S. J., Hwang, C. L., & Hwang, F. P. (1992). *Fuzzy multiple attribute decision making (methods and applications)*. Lecture Notes in Economics and Mathematical Systems. doi:10.1007/978-3-642-46768-4

Churchman, C. W., Ackoff, R. L., & Arnoff, E. L. (1957). *Introduction to operations research*. New York: John Wiley & Sons.

Deng, H. (2007). A Similarity-Based Approach to Ranking Multicriteria Alternatives. *International Conference on Intelligent Computing ICIC 2007: Advanced Intelligent Computing Theories and Applications with Aspects of Artificial Intelligence*, pp. 253-262. 10.1007/978-3-540-74205-0_28

Deng, H., Yeh, C. H., & Willis, R. J. (2000). Inter-company comparison using modified TOPSIS with objective weights. *Computers & Operations Research*, *27*(10), 963–973. doi:10.1016/S0305-0548(99)00069-6

Figueira, J., Greco, S., & Ehrgott, M. (2004). *Multiple criteria decision analysis; state of the art surveys*. New York: Springer.

Hu, J., Du, Y., Mo, H., Wei, D., & Deng, Y. (2016). A modified weighted TOPSIS to identify influential nodes in complex networks. *Physica A*, *444*, 73–85. doi:10.1016/j.physa.2015.09.028

Hwang, C. L., & Yoon, K. P. (1981). *Multiple attribute decision making: methods and applications. Lecture notes in Economics and Mathematical Systems, 186*. New York: Springer-Verlag. doi:10.1007/978-3-642-48318-9

Jornocode. (2019). *Similarity and distance in data: Part 1*. Retrieved from http://journocode.com/2016/03/10/ similarity-and-distance-part-1/

Lootsma, F. A. (2007). *Multi-criteria decision analysis via ratio and difference judgement. Science and Business Media* (Vol. 29). Springer.

Olson, D. L. (2004). Comparison of weights in TOPSIS models. *Mathematical and Computer Modelling*, *40*(7), 721–727. doi:10.1016/j.mcm.2004.10.003

Opricovic, S. (1998). Multicriteria optimization of civil engineering systems. Faculty of Civil Engineering, Belgrade, 2(1), 5-21.

Pinter, U., & Pšunder, I. (2013). Evaluating construction project success with use of the M-TOPSIS method. *Journal of Civil Engineering and Management*, *19*(1), 16–23. doi:10.3846/13923730.2012.734849

Roy, B. (1989). *The outranking approach and the foundations of ELECTRE methods*. University of Paris-Dauphine, Document Du Lamsade.

Roy, B. (1991). The outranking approach and the foundations of ELECTRE methods. *Theory and Decision*, *31*(1), 49–73. doi:10.1007/BF00134132

Roy, B., & Vincke, P. (1981). Multicriteria analysis: Survey and new directions. *European Journal of Operational Research*, *8*(3), 207–218. doi:10.1016/0377-2217(81)90168-5

Saaty, T. L. (1980). *The analytic hierarchy process*. New York: McGraw Hill.

Saaty, T. L. (2000). *Fundamentals of decision making and priority theory with the analytic hierarchy process* (Vol. 6). RWS Publications.

Shih, H. S., Shyur, H. J., & Lee, E. S. (2007). An extension of TOPSIS for group decision making. *Mathematical and Computer Modelling*, *45*(7), 801–813. doi:10.1016/j.mcm.2006.03.023

Soto, C. M. A., Liern, V., & Pérez-Gladish, B. (2018). Normalization in TOPSIS-based approaches with data of different nature: Application to the ranking of mathematical videos. *Annals of Operations Research. Springer, 2018*. doi:10.100710479-018-2945-5

Taha, H. A. (1997). *Operations Research*. Fayetteville: Pearson Education.

Taşabat, E. S. (2019). A novel Multi Criteri Decision Making Method: DSC TOPSIS. *Mathematical Problems in Engineering*.

Taşabat, S. E., Cinemre, N., & Şen, S. (2005). Farklı Ağırlıklandırma Tekniklerinin Denendiği Çok Kriterli Karar Verme Yöntemleri İle Türkiye'deki Mevduat Bankalarının Mali Performanslarının Değerlendirilmesi. *Social Sciences Research Journal*, *4*(2), 96-110.

Ting, K. (2017, July 1). A modified TOPSIS with a different ranking index. *European Journal of Operational Research*, *260*(1), 152–160. doi:10.1016/j.ejor.2016.11.052

Türkiye Bankalar Birliği Seçilmiş Rasyolar 2016 Raporu. (2017, December 1). Retrieved from http://www.tbb.org.tr/Content/Upload/istatistiki raporlar/tumu/903/Secilmis_Rasyolar-2016.zip

Tzeng, G. H., & Huang, J. J. (2011). Multiple attribute decision making: methods and applications. Boca Raton, FL: CRC Press. doi:10.1201/b11032

Vommi, V. B. (2017). TOPSIS with statistical distances: A new approach to MADM. *Decision Science Letters*, *6*, 49–66. doi:10.5267/j.dsl.2016.8.001

Yu, P. L. (1973). A class of solutions for group decision problems. *Management Science*, *19*(8), 936–946. doi:10.1287/mnsc.19.8.936

Zeleny, M. (1982). *Multiple criteria decision making*. New York: McGraw-Hill.

ADDITIONAL READING

Anandan, V., & Uthra, G. (2017). Extension of TOPSIS using L1 Family of Distance Measures. Advances in Fuzzy Mathematics. ISSN 0973-533X: Vol. 12. *Number 4* (pp. 897–908). Research India Publications; http://www.ripublication.com

Churchman, C. W., Ackoff, R. L., & Arnoff, E. L. (1957). *Introduction to operations research*. New York: John Wiley and Sons, Inc.

Taşabat, E. S. (in press). A novel Multi Criteri Decision Making Method: DSC TOPSIS. *Mathematical Problems in Engineering*.

Taşabat, S. E., Cinemre, N., & Şen, S. (2005). Farklı Ağırlıklandırma Tekniklerinin Denendiği Çok Kriterli Karar Verme Yöntemleri İle Türkiye'deki Mevduat Bankalarının Mali Performanslarının Değerlendirilmesi. *Social Sciences Research Journal*, Volume 4, Issue 2, 96-110, ISSN: 2147

Ting, K. (2017, July 1). A modified TOPSIS with a different ranking index. *European Journal of Operational Research*, *260*(1), 152–160. doi:10.1016/j.ejor.2016.11.052

Tzeng, G. H., & Huang, J. J. (2011). *Multiple attribute decision making: methods and applications*. CRC press. doi:10.1201/b11032

Zeleny, M. (1982). *Multiple criteria decision making*. New York: McGraw-Hill.

KEY TERMS AND DEFINITIONS

Decision Making: Selection of the best among the various alternatives.

Distance: A quantitative degree of how far apart two objects are.

Euclidean Distance: The "ordinary" straight-line distance between two points in Euclidean space.

Financial Performance: Calculation of a general financial score using various financial criteria.

L_q Distance Family: The family that hosts the distances of Euclidean, Manhattan, Minkowski and Chebyshev.

L_1 Distance Family: The family that hosts the distances Sørensen, Gower, Soergel, Kulczynski, Canberra and Lorentzian.

MCDM: Decision making when there are multiple criteria decision making.

TOPSIS: A MCDM method.

APPENDIX

L_p Minkowski Family

The distance formulas of the L_p Minkowski family are given in Equations 33-36 (Source: Anandan V. and Uthra G., 2017).

Euclidean L_2:

$$d_i = \sqrt{\sum_{j=1}^{n} \left| a_{ij} - b_{ij} \right|^2} \tag{33}$$

City block L_1:

$$d_i = \sum_{j=1}^{n} \left| a_{ij} - b_{ij} \right| \tag{34}$$

Minkowski L_p:

$$d_i = \sqrt[p]{\sum_{j=1}^{n} \left| a_{ij} - b_{ij} \right|^p} \tag{35}$$

Chebyshev L_∞:

$$d_i = \left| a_{ij} - b_{ij} \right| \tag{36}$$

L_1 Family

The distance formulas of the L_1 family are given in Equations 37-43 (Source: Anandan V. and Uthra G., 2017).

Sørensen:

$$d_i = \frac{\sum_{j=1}^{n} \left| a_{ij} - b_{ij} \right|}{\sum_{j=1}^{n} \left(a_{ij} + b_{ij} \right)} \tag{37}$$

Gower:

$$d_{ij} = \frac{1}{n}\sum_{j=1}^{n}\frac{\left|a_{ij} - b_{ij}\right|}{c_{ij}} \tag{38}$$

$$d_{ij} = \frac{1}{n}\sum_{j=1}^{n}\left|a_{ij} - b_{ij}\right| \tag{39}$$

Soergel:

$$d_{i} = \frac{\sum_{j=1}^{n}\left|a_{ij} - b_{ij}\right|}{\sum_{j=1}^{n}\max\left(a_{ij}, b_{ij}\right)} \tag{40}$$

Kulczynski *d*:

$$d_{i} = \frac{\sum_{j=1}^{n}\left|a_{ij} - b_{ij}\right|}{\sum_{j=1}^{n}\min\left(a_{ij}, b_{ij}\right)} \tag{41}$$

Canberra:

$$d_{i} = \sum_{j=1}^{n}\frac{\left|a_{ij} - b_{ij}\right|}{\left(a_{ij} + b_{ij}\right)} \tag{42}$$

Lorentzian:

$$d_{i} = \sum_{j=1}^{n}\ln(1 + \left|a_{ij} - b_{ij}\right|) \tag{43}$$

* L_1 family ⊃ {Intersectoin (45), Wave Hedges (47), Czekanowski (48), Ruzicka (53), Tanimoto (55), etc}.

Intersection Family

The distance formulas of the Intersection family are given in Equations 44-54 (Source: Anandan V. and Uthra G., 2017).

Intersection:

$$s_i = \sum_{j=1}^{n} \min\left(a_{ij}, b_{ij}\right) \tag{44}$$

$$d_i = 1 - s_i \frac{1}{2}\sum_{j=1}^{n}\left|a_{ij} - b_{ij}\right| \tag{45}$$

Wave Hedges:

$$d_i = \sum_{j=1}^{n}\left(1 - \frac{\min\left(a_{ij}, b_{ij}\right)}{\max\left(a_{ij}, b_{ij}\right)}\right) \tag{46}$$

$$= \sum_{j=1}^{n}\frac{\left|a_{ij} - b_{ij}\right|}{\max\left(a_{ij}, b_{ij}\right)} \tag{47}$$

Czekanowski:

$$s_i = \frac{2\sum_{j=1}^{n}\min\left(a_{ij}, b_{ij}\right)}{\sum_{j=1}^{n}\left(a_{ij} + b_{ij}\right)} \tag{48}$$

$$d_i = 1 - s_i = \frac{\sum_{j=1}^{n}\left|a_{ij} - b_{ij}\right|}{\sum_{j=1}^{n}\left(a_{ij} + b_{ij}\right)} \tag{49}$$

Motyka:

$$s_i = \frac{\sum_{j=1}^{n} \min\left(a_{ij}, b_{ij}\right)}{\sum_{j=1}^{n}\left(a_{ij} + b_{ij}\right)} \tag{50}$$

$$d_i = 1 - s_i = \frac{\sum_{j=1}^{n} \max\left(a_{ij}, b_{ij}\right)}{\sum_{j=1}^{n}\left(a_{ij} + b_{ij}\right)} \tag{51}$$

Kulczynski s:

$$s_i = \frac{1}{d_i} = \frac{\sum_{j=1}^{n} \min\left(a_{ij}, b_{ij}\right)}{\sum_{j=1}^{n}\left|a_{ij} - b_{ij}\right|} \tag{52}$$

Ruzicka:

$$s_i = \frac{\sum_{j=1}^{n} \min\left(a_{ij}, b_{ij}\right)}{\sum_{j=1}^{n} \max\left(a_{ij}, b_{ij}\right)} \tag{53}$$

Tani-moto:

$$d_i = \frac{\sum_{j=1}^{n} a_{ij} + \sum_{j=1}^{n} b_{ij} - 2\sum_{j=1}^{n} \min\left(a_{ij}, b_{ij}\right)}{\sum_{j=1}^{n} a_{ij} + \sum_{j=1}^{n} b_{ij} - \sum_{j=1}^{n} \min\left(a_{ij}, b_{ij}\right)} \tag{54}$$

$$= \frac{\sum_{j=1}^{n}\left(\max\left(a_{ij}, b_{ij}\right) - \min\left(a_{ij}, b_{ij}\right)\right)}{\sum_{j=1}^{n} \max\left(a_{ij}, b_{ij}\right)} \tag{55}$$

Inner Product Family

The distance formulas of the Inner Product family are given in Equations 56-63 (Source: Anandan V. and Uthra G., 2017).

Inner Product:

$$s_i = a_{ij} \bullet b_{ij} = \sum_{j=1}^{n} a_{ij} b_{ij} \tag{56}$$

Harmonic mean:

$$s_i = 2\sum_{j=1}^{n} \frac{a_{ij} b_{ij}}{a_{ij} + b_{ij}} \tag{57}$$

Cosine:

$$s_i = \frac{\sum_{j=1}^{n} a_{ij} b_{ij}}{\sqrt{\sum_{j=1}^{n} a_{ij}^2} \sqrt{\sum_{j=1}^{n} b_{ij}^2}} \tag{58}$$

KumarHassebrook:
(PCE):

$$s_i = \frac{\sum_{j=1}^{n} a_{ij} b_{ij}}{\sum_{j=1}^{n} a_{ij}^2 + \sum_{j=1}^{n} b_{ij}^2 - 2\sum_{j=1}^{n} a_{ij} b_{ij}} \tag{59}$$

Jaccard:

$$s_i = \frac{\sum_{j=1}^{n} a_{ij} b_{ij}}{\sum_{j=1}^{n} a_{ij}^2 + \sum_{j=1}^{n} b_{ij}^2 - \sum_{j=1}^{n} a_{ij} b_{ij}} \tag{60}$$

$$d_i = 1 - s_i = \frac{\sum_{j=1}^{n} \left(a_{ij} - b_{ij}\right)^2}{\sum_{j=1}^{n} a_{ij}^2 + \sum_{j=1}^{n} b_{ij}^2 - \sum_{j=1}^{n} a_{ij} b_{ij}} \tag{61}$$

Dice:

$$s_i = \frac{2\sum_{j=1}^{n} a_{ij} b_{ij}}{\sum_{j=1}^{n} a_{ij}^2 + \sum_{j=1}^{n} b_{ij}^2} \tag{62}$$

$$d_i = 1 - s_i = \frac{\sum_{j=1}^{n} \left(a_{ij} - b_{ij}\right)^2}{\sum_{j=1}^{n} a_{ij}^2 + \sum_{j=1}^{n} b_{ij}^2} \tag{63}$$

Fidelity Family or Squared-Chord Family

The distance formulas of the Fidelity family or Squared-chord family are given in Equations 64-71 (Source: Anandan V. and Uthra G., 2017).

Fidelity:

$$s_i = \sum_{j=1}^{n} \sqrt{a_{ij} b_{ij}} \tag{64}$$

Bhattacharyya:

$$d_i = -\ln \sum_{j=1}^{n} \sqrt{a_{ij} b_{ij}} \tag{65}$$

Hellinger:

$$d_i = \sqrt{2\sum_{j=1}^{n} \left(\sqrt{a_{ij}} - \sqrt{b_{ij}}\right)^2} \tag{66}$$

$$= 2\sqrt{1 - \sum_{j=1}^{n} \sqrt{a_{ij} b_{ij}}} \tag{67}$$

Matusita:

$$d_i = \sqrt{\sum_{j=1}^{n} \left(\sqrt{a_{ij}} - \sqrt{b_{ij}}\right)^2} \tag{68}$$

$$= \sqrt{2 - 2\sum_{j=1}^{n} \sqrt{a_{ij} b_{ij}}} \tag{69}$$

Squared-chord:

$$d_i = \sum_{j=1}^{n} \left(\sqrt{a_{ij}} - \sqrt{b_{ij}}\right)^2 \tag{70}$$

$s_{sqc} = 1\text{-}d_{sqc}$:

$$s_i = 2\sum_{j=1}^{n} \sqrt{a_{ij} b_{ij}} - 1 \tag{71}$$

Squared L_2 Family or χ2 Family

The distance formulas of the Squared L_2 family or $\chi 2$ family or Squared-chord family are given in Equations 72-79 (Source: Anandan V. and Uthra G., 2017).

Squared Euclidean:

$$d_i = \sum_{j=1}^{n} \left(a_{ij} - b_{ij}\right)^2 \tag{72}$$

Pearson $\chi 2$:

$$d_i = \sum_{j=1}^{n} \frac{\left(a_{ij} - b_{ij}\right)^2}{a_{ij}} \tag{73}$$

Neyman $\chi 2$:

$$d_i = \sum_{j=1}^{n} \frac{\left(a_{ij} - b_{ij}\right)^2}{b_{ij}} \tag{74}$$

Squared χ2:

$$d_i = \sum_{j=1}^{n} \frac{\left(a_{ij} - b_{ij}\right)^2}{a_{ij} + b_{ij}} \tag{75}$$

Probabilistic Symmetric χ2:

$$d_i = 2\sum_{j=1}^{n} \frac{\left(a_{ij} - b_{ij}\right)^2}{a_{ij} + b_{ij}} \tag{76}$$

Divergence:

$$d_i = 2\sum_{j=1}^{n} \frac{\left(a_{ij} - b_{ij}\right)^2}{\left(a_{ij} + b_{ij}\right)^2} \tag{77}$$

Clark:

$$d_i = \sqrt{\sum_{j=1}^{n} \left(\frac{\left|a_{ij} - b_{ij}\right|}{a_{ij} + b_{ij}} \right)^2} \tag{78}$$

Additive Symmetric χ2:

$$d_i = \sum_{j=1}^{n} \frac{\left(a_{ij} - b_{ij}\right)^2 \left(a_{ij} + b_{ij}\right)}{a_{ij} b_{ij}} \tag{79}$$

* Squared L_2 family ⊃ {Jaccard (61), Dice (63)}

Shannon's Entropy Family

The distance formulas of the Squared L_2 family or χ2 family or Squared-chord family are given in Equations 80-85 (Source: Anandan V. and Uthra G., 2017).

Kullback– Leibler:

$$d_i = \sum_{j=1}^{n} a_{ij} \ln \frac{a_{ij}}{b_{ij}} \tag{80}$$

Jeffreys:

$$d_i = \sum_{j=1}^{n} \left(a_{ij} - b_{ij}\right) \ln \frac{a_{ij}}{b_{ij}} \tag{81}$$

K divergence:

$$d_i = \sum_{j=1}^{n} a_{ij} \ln \frac{2a_{ij}}{a_{ij} + b_{ij}} \tag{82}$$

Topsøe:

$$d_i = \sum_{j=1}^{n} \left(a_{ij} \ln \left(\frac{2a_{ij}}{a_{ij} + b_{ij}} \right) + b_{ij} \ln \left(\frac{2b_{ij}}{a_{ij} + b_{ij}} \right) \right) \tag{83}$$

Jensen-Shannon:

$$d_i = \tfrac{1}{2} \left[\sum_{j=1}^{n} \left(a_{ij} \ln \left(\frac{2a_{ij}}{a_{ij} + b_{ij}} \right) + \sum_{j=1}^{n} b_{ij} \ln \left(\frac{2b_{ij}}{a_{ij} + b_{ij}} \right) \right) \right] \tag{84}$$

Jensen difference:

$$d_i = \sum_{j=1}^{n} \left(\frac{a_{ij} \ln a_{ij} + b_{ij} \ln b_{ij}}{2} - \left(\frac{a_{ij} + b_{ij}}{2} \right) \ln \left(\frac{a_{ij} + b_{ij}}{2} \right) \right) \tag{85}$$

Combinations

The distance formulas of combinations of families are given in Equations 86-88 (Source: Anandan V. and Uthra G., 2017).

Taneja:

$$d_i = \sum_{j=1}^{n} \left(\frac{a_{ij} + b_{ij}}{2} \right) \ln \left(\frac{a_{ij} + b_{ij}}{2\sqrt{a_{ij} b_{ij}}} \right) \tag{86}$$

Kumar Johnson:

$$d_i = \sum_{j=1}^{n} \left(\frac{\left(a_{ij}^2 - b_{ij}^2\right)^2}{2\left(a_{ij} b_{ij}\right)^{3/2}} \right) \tag{87}$$

Avg (L_1, L_∞):

$$d_i = \sum_{j=1}^{n} \frac{\left|a_{ij} - b_{ij}\right| + \max\left|a_{ij} - b_{ij}\right|}{2} \tag{88}$$

It is briefly summarized in Table 14 that the cases mentioned in the methods can be confronted (Cha, 2007). Here 0/0 and 0 log0 are treated as 0. The zero is replaced by a very small value for the division by zero and log of zero.

Table 14. Grouping of distance/similarity measures by caveats to implementation

Vector Ops	Equations (33~41), (43~45), (48~51), (53~55), (58~72), and (87~88)
0 / 0	Canberra (42), Wave Hedges (46), Harmonic mean (57), Squared χ2 (75), Probabilistic Symmetric χ2 (76), Divergence (77), Clark (78), and Additive Symmetric χ2 (79)
division by zero	Kulczynski (41) (52), Pearson χ2 (73), Neyman χ2 (74), KL (80), Jeffreys (81), Taneja (86), and Kumar-Johnson (87)
0 log0	KL (80), K divergence (82), Topsøe (83), Jensen-Shannon (84), Jensen difference (85), and Taneja (86)
Log of 0	Jeffreys (81)

Source: Anandan V. and Uthra G., 2017.

Chapter 10
TOPSIS vs. VIKOR:
A Case Study for Determining Development Level of Countries

Semra Erpolat Taşabat
https://orcid.org/0000-0001-6845-8278
Mimar Sinan Fine Art University, Turkey & Bahçeşehir University, Turkey

Tuğba Kıral Özkan
https://orcid.org/0000-0002-7050-3805
Bahçeşehir University, Turkey

ABSTRACT

Evaluating multiple criteria and selecting and/or ranking alternatives is called Multi Criteria Decision Making (MCDM). These methods which are considered important decision-making tools for decision makers due to their multidisciplinary nature have been developed over the years. As a result, there are many MCDM methods in the literature. In this chapter, TOPSIS and VIKOR, widely used in the literature, will be discussed. The major reason for examining these two methods is that the aggregating function used by both methods is similar because VIKOR method uses linear normalization and TOPSIS method uses vector normalization. The process of the methods is shown on a data set that includes the Human Development Index (HDI) indicators, which have been developed to measure the development levels of countries as well as the unemployment indicator. It was observed that the methods yielded similar results.

INTRODUCTION

It is possible to define decision making as the process of choosing the best among various alternatives, which is an indispensable behavior that we exhibit in almost every moment of our lives. This process can become quite complex when evaluating the many alternatives we have to choose among many criteria. Various methods have been developed to minimize the complexities to be encountered as much as possible, and to help decision makers make the right and effective decision.

DOI: 10.4018/978-1-7998-2216-5.ch010

In the literature, decision making process can be defined by different methods and procedures since it is used by various disciplines such as operational research, computer science, cognitive science, sociology, decision theory, economics, psychology, management, political science, statistics (Berger (1990), Edwards and Fasolo (2001), Hastie (2001), Matlin (1998), Wilson and Keil (2001)).

Decision-making processes with multiple criteria are called MCDM. MCDM has been developing since the beginning of 1960s. Then, researchers have developed various methods to solve such decision problems and they still continue to develop. Because in real life, whether in our daily lives or business, we are constantly faced with many criteria and alternatives. MCDM is a very important area whose main objective is to keep the decision-making mechanism under control and make the decision-making process as easy and fast as possible when the number of alternatives and criteria is too high. Although there are many MCDM methods in the literature, none of them has any superiority over the other. The validity and reliability of the methods can vary according to the decision problem. At this point, it can be the right approach to evaluate the results of MCDM methods which can be applied to the same decision problem altogether and to suggest the most appropriate one (or ones) according to the results obtained. Churchman et al. (1957) performed the first known method in the field of MCDM which is called SAW (Simple Additive Weighting). Then, various studies for MCDM were performed. It is possible to list the most used ones as follows: TOPSIS (Technique for Order Preference by Similarity to an Ideal Solution) (Hwang and Yoon, 1981; Deng et al., 2000), AHP (Analitic Hierarchy Process) (Saaty 1980, 2000; Belton and Gear 1983; Lootsma 1999), ELECTRE (Elimination Et Choix Traduisant La Realite´-Elimination and Choice Expressing The Reality) (Roy 1989, 1991; Roy and Vincke 1981), VIKOR (Vlse Kriterijumska Optimizacija Kompromisno Resenje - Multicriteria Optimization and Compromise Solution) (Yu, 1973; Zeleny, 1982; Opricovic 1998; Tzeng and Huang, 2011), PROMITHEE (Preference Ranking Organization Methods for Enrichment Evaluation (Brans et al., 1984), etc. Apart from these methods, there is also a large number of methods in the literature where fuzzy structures are tested, hybrid methods are created by combining different methods together and methods have been modified.

In this chapter, TOPSIS and VIKOR methods will be discussed. The most important reason for the comparison of various MCDM methods, especially TOPSIS and VIKOR, is that the two methods are similar. Namely: Both methods are based on an aggregating function that represents closeness to the ideal solution. However, for eliminating decision-making units, VIKOR method uses linear normalization while TOPSIS method uses vector normalization. TOPSIS method is based on the principle of choosing the alternative that has the shortest distance to the positive ideal solution and the longest to the negative ideal solution. VIKOR method is based on the principle of determining a possible solution closest to the ideal solution. This method lists alternatives by considering the maximum group benefit and minimum regret. VIKOR is also known as the Compromise Ranking Method.

In the following sections, first, TOPSIS and VIKOR methods will be discussed in detail. Their similar and different aspects will be emphasized. Then, the process steps of the methods will be carried out on the data that is used to compare countries' level of development. And finally, the results obtained will be compared.

BACKGROUND

In the literature, TOPSIS and VIKOR are used to solve a wide range of decision problems. However, among these studies, there are no studies that measure the development levels of countries with TOPSIS and VIKOR, taking into account unemployment indicators in addition to the indicators used in HDI.

The most similar study is Shiraz and et all's (2013). In this study they sorted the countries according to their level of development by using TOPSIS and VIKOR with Shannon entropy weighting method.

Some other similar studies are: Mateusz and et all. (2018) were applied TOPSIS and VIKOR methods to study sustainable development, by using selected indices out from objectives defined by Sustainable Development Goals (SDGs).

Soltanpanah and et al. (2010) used Entropy and AHP methods to obtain the weights of indexes constituting HDI. They also used SAW and TOPSIS techniques and Numerical Taxonomy analysis rather than arithmetic average method to rank countries with reference to human development range.

MAIN FOCUS OF THE CHAPTER

The main focus of this chapter is to compare TOPSIS and VIKOR methods. Another aim is to examine the computability of HDI by different methods. For this purpose, firstly the steps of TOPSIS and VIKOR methods will be explained in detail and then the application of the two methods will be shown on HDI data. Finally, the results will be evaluated with the results of HDI rankings.

RESEARCH METHODOLOGY

Technique for Order Preference by Similarity to an Ideal Solution (TOPSIS) Method

TOPSIS method was first put forward by Hwang and Yoon in 1981 and later in 1992 was developed by Chen and Hwang. The method is based on the principle that the chosen alternative should have the farthest Euclidean distance from the negative ideal solution (NIS), and the shortest from the positive ideal solution (PIS) (Chen and Chen, 2010).

The TOPSIS method is one of the most commonly used methods for solving MCDM problems. Basic features of the method are being simple and understandable, being based on a simple mathematical equation to calculate the relative performance of each alternative, having a good calculation efficiency, and a limited number of subjective input (only criteria weights) needs to be listed (Yeh, 2002). The stages of the method are given below (Taşabat E. S., 2019).

Step1. Determining the decision matrix:

$$X = \begin{bmatrix} x_{11} & x_{12} & \cdots & x_{1m} \\ x_{21} & x_{22} & \cdots & x_{2m} \\ \cdots & \cdots & x_{ij} & \cdots \\ x_{n1} & x_{n2} & \cdots & x_{nm} \end{bmatrix} \tag{1}$$

A general multiple criteria analysis problem is represented as a decision matrix which consists of a set of alternatives A_i *(i=1,2,...,n)* to be evaluated against a set of criteria C_j *(j=1,2, ...,m)*.

Step2. Determining the weighting vector as below:

$$W = \left(w_1, \cdots, w_j, \cdots, w_m\right) \tag{2}$$

In which the relative importance of criterion C_j with respect to the overall objective of the problem is represented as w_j.

Step 3. Normalizing the decision matrix through Euclidean normalization:

$$x'_{ij} = \frac{x_{ij}}{\left(\sum_{k=1}^{n} x_{ik}^2\right)^{1/2}} \tag{3}$$

As a result, a normalized decision matrix can be determined as:

$$X' = \begin{bmatrix} x'_{11} & x'_{12} & \cdots & x'_{1m} \\ x'_{21} & x'_{22} & \cdots & x'_{2m} \\ \cdots & \cdots & x'_{ij} & \cdots \\ x'_{n1} & x'_{n2} & \cdots & x'_{nm} \end{bmatrix} \tag{4}$$

Step 4. Calculating the performance matrix:

The weighted performance matrix which reflects the performance of each alternative with respect to each criterion is determined by multiplying the normalized decision matrix (4) by the weight vector (2).

$$Y = \begin{bmatrix} w_1 x'_{11} & w_2 x'_{12} & \cdots & w_m x'_{1m} \\ w_1 x'_{21} & w_2 x'_{22} & \cdots & w_m x'_{2m} \\ \cdots & \cdots & w_i x'_{ij} & \cdots \\ w_1 x'_{n1} & w_2 x'_{n2} & \cdots & w_m x'_{nm} \end{bmatrix} = \begin{bmatrix} y_{11} & y_{12} & \cdots & y_{1m} \\ y_{21} & y_{22} & \cdots & y_{2m} \\ \cdots & \cdots & y_{ij} & \cdots \\ y_{n1} & y_{n2} & \cdots & y_{nm} \end{bmatrix} \tag{5}$$

Step 5. Determining the PIS and the NIS:

The Positive Ideal Solution (PIS) and The Negative Ideal Solution (NIS) embodies the best or the worst criteria values from the alternatives. According to Deng (2007), these two concepts are simple and comprehensible, have a computational efficiency as they can measure the relative performance of the alternatives with a simple mathematical formula. For PIS (I^+):

$$I^+ = \left\{(\max_i y_{ij} \middle| j \in J), (\min_i y_{ij} \middle| j \in J'\right\} \quad (6)$$

$$I^+ = \left\{y_1^+, y_2^+, \ldots, y_n^+\right\} \quad (7)$$

And for NIS (I^-):

$$I^- = \left\{(\min_i y_{ij} \middle| j \in J), (\max_i y_{ij} \middle| j \in J'\right\} \quad (8)$$

$$I^- = \left\{y_1^-, y_2^-, \ldots, y_n^-\right\} \quad (9)$$

At both formulas J shows benefit (maximization) and J' show loss (minimization) value.

Step 6. Calculating the degree of distance of the alternatives between each alternative and the PIS and the NIS:

The D^+ and the D^- formulas are as the follow, by using Euclidean distance.

$$D_i^+ = \sqrt{\sum_{j=1}^{n} (y_{ij} - y_j^+)^2} \quad (10)$$

$$D_i^- = \sqrt{\sum_{j=1}^{n} (y_{ij} - y_j^-)^2} \quad (11)$$

Step 7. Calculating the overall performance index for each alternative across all criteria:

This index can be calculated based on the concept of the degree of similarity of alternative A_i relative to the ideal solutions.

$$P_i = \frac{D_i^-}{D_i^- + D_i^+} \tag{12}$$

$0 \leq P_i \leq 1$. The P_i value indicates the absolute closeness of the ideal solution. If $P_i = 1$ then A_i is the ideal solution, if $P_i = 0$ then A_i is the negative ideal solution.

Step 8. Ranking the alternatives in the descending order of the performance index value.

Multicriteria Optimization and Compromise Solution (Visekriterijumska Optimizacija I Kompromisno Resenje-VIKOR) Method

VIKOR stands for "VIsekriterijumska optimizacija i Kompromisno Resenje" in Serbian language (Opricovic, 1998) also known as the compromise ranking method. VIKOR is a multiple criteria ranking method providing a compromise solution to a problem that involves conflicting or non-commensurable criteria (Tae and et al. 2018).

It is used when decision makers cannot specify their preferences at the beginning (Opricovic and Tzeng, 2007). The comparison structure is simple, easy and understandable. Obtaining a compromise sorting among the alternatives can be listed as the most prominent feature of the method (Bernroider and Stix, 2003).

The procedure of traditional VIKOR for compromise-ranking can be described as the stages below (Taşabat and et al. 2018):

Stage 1: Determine the best x_j^* and the worst x_i^- values of all criterion functions, where j = 1,2, ..., n;

$$x_j^* = \max_j x_{ij} \tag{13}$$

and

$$x_j^- = \min_j x_{ij} \tag{14}$$

After these values are found, the following formula is used for normalization.

$$r_{ij} = \frac{(x_j^* - x_{ij})}{(x_j^* - x_j^-)} \tag{15}$$

Stage 2: Compute the values of S_i and R_i, where i= 1,2, ..., m;

$$S_i = \sum_{j=1}^{n} w_j \frac{x_j^* - x_{ij}}{x_j^* - x_j^-} \tag{16}$$

$$R_i = \max \left[w_j \frac{x_j^* - x_{ij}}{x_j^* - x_j^-} \right] \tag{17}$$

S_j and R_j denote the utility measure and the regret measure, respectively, for the alternative Ai. w_j is the weight of the j-th criterion.

Stage 3: Compute the value Q_i, where, i=1,2, ..., m.

$$Q_i = v\left(\frac{S_i - S^*}{S^- - S^*}\right) + (1-v)\left(\frac{R_i - R^*}{R^- - R^*}\right) \tag{18}$$

$S^* = \min_i S_i$, $S^- = \max_i S_i$ and $R^* = \min_i R_i$, $R^- = \max_i R_i$

where, v is the weight for the strategy of maximum group utility and *(1-v)* is the weight of the individual regret. v is usually set to "0.5" (Opricovic 1998).

Stage 4: Sort the values S, R and Q in decreasing order and rank the alternatives accordingly, which results in three ranking lists.

If the value of Q_i is less, A_i is the better decision of the alternatives.

Stage 5: Suggest a compromise solution, the alternative (A') ranked the best by the minimum value of Q, if the two conditions below are met:

C1. "Acceptable advantage": $Q(A'') - Q(A') \geq D$, in which A'' is the alternative with second position in the ranking list by Q; $DQ = 1/(j-1)$ and m is the number of alternatives.

C2. "Acceptable stability in decision making": The alternative A' should also be the best with respect to S and/or R value (The lower the value of S/R is, the better).

If one of these conditions is not met, it is impossible to pick out directly the best solution of the set but a subset of preferable options can be defined, which consists of (Opricovic and Tzeng 2007):

1. Alternatives A' and A'' if only the condition C2 is not satisfied, or
2. Alternatives $A', A'', \cdots, A^{(M)}$ if the condition C1 is not satisfied, where $A^{(M)}$ is determined by the relation $Q\left(A^{(M)}\right) - Q\left(A'\right) < DQ$ for maximum *M*.

SOLUTIONS AND RECOMMENDATIONS

Case Study: Development Level of Countries

The Human Development Report in 1990 was the first to propose a new perspective into human flourishing. Human development became a topic of discussion in the 20th century as there were ongoing discussions about the relationship between economic growth and development. In the early 1960s, GDP was considered to be the leading objective and indicator of national progress in many countries although it never intended to be used that way. Therefore, alternative forces were proposed to measure the wellbeing of the countries in the 70s and 80s. These alternatives included a greater emphasis on employment, growth redistribution and whether people can meet their basic needs. (HDR, 2019).

According to the glossary definition, Development Indicators is defined as "a numerical measure of quality of life in a country". Indicators showing the progress of countries in achieving economic, social and potential goals may be inconsistent, as they are calculated differently by various organizations ("GreenFacts", n.d.).

The World Development Indicators (WDI) is a compilation of relevant, high-quality, and internationally comparable statistics about global development and the fight against poverty. The online database includes 1,600 indicators for almost 220 economies, with some data series extending back more than 50 years. Some of the indicators in WDI are formed by the World Bank Group, while the majority are based on data generated by other sources, including UN expert institutions, national statistical bureaus, and other international organizations such as organizations (World Bank, 2019).

While GDP and population indicators are the focus of much attention, other topics such as including inflation, military expenditure, CO2 emissions, or health expenditure, are also of great interest for data seekers. The most popular top ten WDI indicators can be listed as: GDP (current US$); population, total; GDP growth (annual %); GDP per capita (current US$); GINI index (World Bank estimate); Population, female (% of total); fertility rate, total (births per woman); GDP per capita, PPP (current international $); Life expectancy at birth, total (years); Military expenditure (% of GDP) (World Bank, 2019).

Various indices are developed by using different combinations of the above-mentioned world development indicators. One of them is undoubtedly Human Development Index (HDI). Human development aims to develop the richness of human life rather than the economy (Taşabat, 2019). HDI consists of three dimensions blended into each other. The first one is having a decent life standard which is about GNI per capita and thus creates the "GNI Index". The second dimension is life expectancy creating the "Life Expectancy Index". And the final dimension is about longevity of schooling which generates the "Education Index". In calculation of HDI, these dimensions are placed in a (0,1) scale. The next step is calculating the geometric mean of the dimensions and thus generating the HDI. (UNDP, 2011). And ultimately, the order of the countries of the world from the most developed to the least, with the help of this formula the calculated HDI values can be obtained by ordering from big to small (Taşabat, 2019).

In this study, the indicators used by the HDI will be taken into consideration in determining the development levels of the countries around the world: Life expectancy at birth (years) (Life), Gross national income (GNI) per capita (2011 PPP$) (Income), Expected years of schooling (years) (Education). In addition, Unemployment, total (% of labour force) indicator is included in the data since it is an important factor for many countries. Data for these indicators were obtained from the 2017 HDR (Human Development Reports) (HDR, 2017). Countries where the unemployment rate is not calculated are excluded from the analysis. These are: Andorra, Antigua and Barbuda, Dominican Republic, Grenada, Kiribati,

Liechtenstein, Marshall Islands, Micronesia (Federated), Palau, Saint Kitts and Nevis, Seychelles. Even though there are unemployment values for Korea (Democratic) and Somalia, school indicator for Korea (Democratic) and life indicator for Somalia are not calculated. For this reason, these countries are also discarded from the analysis. Thus, out of 188 countries in the HDI index, 178 are included in the data.

Development Level with TOPSIS Method

Step1. Determining the decision matrix

In this matrix, 178 countries which were investigated in the 2017 HDR, are considered to be alternatives and the four development indicators mentioned above form the criteria. The decision matrix shown at Table 1 is for the first and last five countries.

As the unemployment criterion had a negative effect on the level of development, its impact was made positive by applying the transformation to this criterion. From Table 2, the new value of the "unemployment" criterion is shown as "unemployment *".

In the literature, different methods have been developed to change the effect state of variables from negative to positive. One of these methods is to subtract all the values of the criterion from its maximum value (Taşabat and et al, 2015). In this study, this method was applied. Table 2 shows the decision matrix after the transformation.

Step 2. Determining the weighting vector:

In this study "**equally weighted**" method is used. "Equal weighting" can be defined as attributing equal importance to the criteria in hand. As this study uses three criteria, the weight of each criterion is "**1/4 = 0.25**", which is shown in the bottom row of Table 2.

Table 1. The original data for the first and last five countries: decision matrix

Country	Life	Income	Education	Unemployment
Afghanistan	64	1824	10.4	8.8
Albania	78.5	11886	14.8	13.9
Algeria	76.3	13802	14.4	10
Angola	61.8	5790	11.8	8.2
Argentina	76.7	18461	17.4	8.7
. . .	. . .	. . .	. . .	. . .
Venezuela (Bolivarian Republic of)	74.7	10672	14.3	8.1
Viet Nam	76.5	5859	12.7	2.1
Yemen	65.2	1239	9	13.8
Zambia	62.3	3557	12.5	7.8
Zimbabwe	61.7	1683	10.3	5.2

Source: HDR, 2017.

Table 2. Initial decision matrix

Country	Life	Income	Education	Unemployment*
Afghanistan	64	1824	10.4	19.1
Albania	78.5	11886	14.8	14.0
Algeria	76.3	13802	14.4	17.9
Angola	61.8	5790	11.8	19.7
Argentina	76.7	18461	17.4	19.2
. . .	. . .	. . .	. . .	. . .
Venezuela (Bolivarian Republic of)	74.7	10672	14.3	19.8
Viet Nam	76.5	5859	12.7	25.8
Yemen	65.2	1239	9	14.1
Zambia	62.3	3557	12.5	20.1
Zimbabwe	61.7	1683	10.3	22.7
Weights	**0.25**	**0.25**	**0.25**	**0.25**

Source: Authors

Step 3. Normalizing the decision matrix:

Before ranking the countries, to put data on a common scale normalization method are used. It was performed with formula (3). The result is shown in Table 3.

Step 4. Calculating the performance matrix:

The performance matrix is obtained by multiplying the weight vector by the matrix of the normalized values (Table 4).

Step 5. Determining the PIS and the NIS

The PIS and the NIS are attainable from all the alternatives (178 countries) across all three criteria according to formula (15)-(16), respectively. These values are shown in Table 5.

Step 6. Calculating the degree of distance of the alternatives between each alternative and the PIS and the NIS:

Step 7. Calculating the overall performance index for each alternative across all criteria:

The calculated P_i values are given in Table 6. Then, according to P_i values alternatives are ranked in the descending order. Thus, according to TOPSIS, it is concluded that which countries are the most developed and which ones are the least developed. The results for first ten and last ten countries are given in Table 7. The results of TOPSIS is given in appendix for all countries (Table 15).

Table 3. Normalized data (or performance matrix) for the first and last five countries

Country	Life	Income	Education	Unemployment*
Afghanistan	0.06622	0.00527	0.05756	0.06822
Albania	0.08122	0.03432	0.08191	0.05000
Algeria	0.07894	0.03985	0.07970	0.06393
Angola	0.06394	0.01672	0.06531	0.07036
Argentina	0.07936	0.05330	0.09630	0.06858
. . .	. . .	. . .	. . .	. . .
Venezuela (Bolivarian Republic of)	0.07729	0.03081	0.07914	0.06225
Viet Nam	0.07915	0.01692	0.07029	0.01614
Yemen	0.06746	0.00358	0.04981	0.10605
Zambia	0.06446	0.01027	0.06918	0.05994
Zimbabwe	0.06384	0.00486	0.05701	0.03996
Weights	**0.25**	**0.25**	**0.25**	**0.25**

Source: Authors

Table 4. Performance matrix for the first and last five countries

Country	Life	Income	Education	Unemployment*
Afghanistan	0.01655	0.00132	0.01439	0.01705
Albania	0.02030	0.00858	0.02048	0.01250
Algeria	0.01974	0.00996	0.01992	0.01598
Angola	0.01599	0.00418	0.01633	0.01759
Argentina	0.01984	0.01332	0.02408	0.01714
. . .	. . .	. . .	. . .	. . .
Venezuela (Bolivarian Republic of)	0.01932	0.00770	0.01979	0.01556
Viet Nam	0.01979	0.00423	0.01757	0.00403
Yemen	0.01686	0.00089	0.01245	0.02651
Zambia	0.01611	0.00257	0.01730	0.01499
Zimbabwe	0.01596	0.00121	0.01425	0.00999

Source: Authors

Table 5. PIS (I^+) and NIS (I^-) value

PIS and NIS	Life	Income	Education	Unemployment*
I^+	0.02175	0.08432	0.03169	0.02473
I^-	0.01350	0.00048	0.00678	0.00000

Source: Authors

Table 6. D^+ and D^- values for the first and last five countries

Country	D^+	D^-	P_i
Afghanistan	0.08529	0.01894	0.18173
Albania	0.07755	0.02135	0.21588
Algeria	0.07581	0.02360	0.23741
Angola	0.08211	0.02050	0.19982
Argentina	0.07183	0.02825	0.28231
. . .	. . .	. . .	. . .
Venezuela (Bolivarian Republic of)	0.08640	0.02204	0.20322
Viet Nam	0.09526	0.01354	0.12446
Yemen	0.08993	0.02695	0.23059
Zambia	0.09172	0.01830	0.16635
Zimbabwe	0.09563	0.01244	0.11509

Source: Authors

Development Level with VIKOR Method

Step 1: Determining the decision matrix

The decision matrix shown in Table 1 was also used in the VIKOR method.

Step 2: Determine the best x_j^* and the worst x_i^- values of all criterion functions acoording to formula (13) and (14). Life, Education, Income criteria were evaluated as benefit-oriented and Unemployment criteria were evaluated as cost-oriented. These values are shown in Table 8.

Table 7. Top ten and last ten countries with high performance value

Most Developed Countries	Least Developed Countries
Qatar	Sudan
Singapore	South Sudan
Brunei Darussalam	Yemen
Kuwait	Haiti
Norway	Namibia
United Arab Emirates	Syrian Arab Republic
Luxembourg	Palestine, State of
Hong Kong, China (SAR)	Eswatini (Kingdom of)
Switzerland	Lesotho
United States	Mozambique

Source: Authors

Step 3: Normalizing the decision matrix:

The normalized decision matrix and weighted decision matrix are shown in Table 9 and Table 10 respectively.

Step 4: Compute the values of S_i, R_i and Q_i (Q_i calculated acoording to v=0,5) formula (16), (17) and (18). These values are shown in Table 11.

$S^* = \min_i S_i,\ S^- = \max_i S_i$ and $R^* = \min_i R_i,\ R^- = \max_i R_i$

where, v is the weight for the strategy of maximum group utility and $(1-v)$ is the weight of the individual regret. The v value of 0.5 was used.

Step 5: Rank the alternatives, sorting by the S, R and Q values in a decreasing order. These values are shown in Table 12.

Table 8. The best x_j^* and the worst x_i^- values

	Life	Income	Education	Unemployment
x_j^*	84.1	116818	22.9	0.2
x_i^-	52.2	663	4.9	27.9

Source: Authors

Table 9. Normalized decision matrix

Country	Life	Income	Education	Unemployment
Afghanistan	0.630	0.990	0.694	0.310
Albania	0.176	0.903	0.450	0.495
Algeria	0.245	0.887	0.472	0.354
Angola	0.699	0.956	0.617	0.289
Argentina	0.232	0.847	0.306	0.307
. . .	. . .	. . .	. . .	. . .
Venezuela (Bolivarian Republic of)	0.295	0.914	0.478	0.285
Viet Nam	0.238	0.955	0.567	0.069
Yemen	0.592	0.995	0.772	0.491
Zambia	0.683	0.975	0.578	0.274
Zimbabwe	0.702	0.991	0.700	0.181
Weights	**0.25**	**0.25**	**0.25**	**0.25**

Source: Authors

Table 10. Weighted decision matrix

Country	Life	Income	Education	Unemployment
Afghanistan	0.158	0.248	0.174	0.078
Albania	0.044	0.226	0.113	0.124
Algeria	0.061	0.222	0.118	0.088
Angola	0.175	0.239	0.154	0.072
Argentina	0.058	0.212	0.076	0.077
⋮	⋮	⋮	⋮	⋮
Venezuela (Bolivarian Republic of)	0.074	0.228	0.119	0.071
Viet Nam	0.060	0.239	0.142	0.017
Yemen	0.148	0.249	0.193	0.123
Zambia	0.171	0.244	0.144	0.069
Zimbabwe	0.176	0.248	0.175	0.045

Source: Authors

Table 11. The values of S_i, R_i and Q_i

Country	Si	R_i			Q_i
Afghanistan	0.656	0.248	S^*	0.177	0.644
Albania	0.506	0.226	S^-	0.891	0.496
Algeria	0.489	0.222	R^*	0.093	0.476
Angola	0.640	0.239	R^-	0.250	0.616
Argentina	0.423	0.212			0.409
⋮	⋮	⋮			⋮
Venezuela (Bolivarian Republic of)	0.493	0.228			0.492
Viet Nam	0.457	0.239			0.488
Yemen	0.713	0.249			0.686
Zambia	0.628	0.244			0.617
Zimbabwe	0.643	0.248			0.636

Source: Authors

Step 6: Propose a compromise solution,

The results of the VIKOR rankings obtained from the analysis are shown in Table 13. The accuracy of the given ranking is first tested with the condition "acceptable advantage".

Since $DQ = 1 / (m - 1) = 1 / (178 - 1) = 0.006$ (*m*: number of alternatives and $Q_2 - Q_1 = 0.048 \geq DQ$, C1 provides able "Acceptable advantage". When the data shown in Table 13 are sorted according to the Rj value, Singapore is also in the first place and C2 "Acceptable stability in decision making" condition

Table 12. Top ten and last ten countries with high performance value for S_i, R_i and Q_i

S_i	R_i	Qi
Most Developed Countries		
Qatar	Singapore	Singapore
Singapore	Norway	Norway
Australia	Brunei Darussalam	Qatar
Norway	Luxembourg	Hong Kong. China (SAR)
Iceland	Hong Kong. China (SAR)	Switzerland
Hong Kong. China (SAR)	Switzerland	Ireland
Ireland	Kuwait	Brunei Darussalam
Switzerland	United Arab Emirates	Luxembourg
Netherlands	Qatar	Australia
Denmark	United States	United Arab Emirates
Least Developed Countries		
Sudan	Mozambique	Sierra Leone
Mali	Malawi	Mali
Namibia	Niger	Chad
Chad	Congo (Democratic Republic of the)	South Africa
Central African Republic	Burundi	Central African Republic
South Africa	Liberia	Eswatini (Kingdom of)
South Sudan	Central African Republic	South Sudan
Eswatini (Kingdom of)	Palestine, State of	Mozambique
Mozambique	Sierra Leone	Lesotho
Lesotho	South Sudan	Sierra Leone

Source: Authors

is provided. Due to both conditions being fulfilled, VIKOR has maintained its position as the best-performing country in the Singapore ranking.

Table 13 shows the results of the ten most developed and ten least developed countries. Respectively, the most developed countries Singapore, Norway, Qatar, Hong Kong, Switzerland, Ireland, Brunei Darussalam, Luxembourg, Australia, United Arab Emirates. Respectively, the least developed countries Haiti, Sierra Leone, Mali, Chad, South Africa, Central African Republic, Eswatini, South Sudan, Mozambique, Lesotho. The results of VIKOR are given in appendix for all countries (Table 16).

Finally, a comparison was made between the HDI ranking of 178 countries and the scores obtained from TOPSIS and VIKOR methods, which were proposed to be used in this study. For this purpose, firstly the ranking of the countries is compared with the line graph. Then Spearman Rank Correlation was calculated to measure whether HDI, TOPSIS and VIKOR sequences were consistent with each other.

When Figure 1 is examined, it can be seen that Singapore is in the 1st place according to VIKOR method while it is in 9th position in HDI and in 2nd place according to the TOPSIS method. Norway, which is in the 1st place in HDI, takes the 2nd place in VIKOR method and 5th place in TOPSIS method. Qatar is ranked 3rd by VIKOR method and TOPSIS while it is ranked 1st in HDI. When differences in

Table 13. Top ten and last ten countries

Most Developed Countries	Least Developed Countries
Singapore	Haiti
Norway	Sierra Leone
Qatar	Mali
Hong Kong, China (SAR)	Chad
Switzerland	South Africa
Ireland	Central African Republic
Brunei Darussalam	Eswatini (Kingdom of)
Luxembourg	South Sudan
Australia	Mozambique
United Arab Emirates	Lesotho

Source: Authors

ranking are taken into account, Austria is ranked 20th in HDI and 10th in vikor and topsis methods. HDI-TOPSIS and HDI-VIKOR show 1 rank difference, but there is no difference between VIKOR and TOPSIS methods. No difference in the ranking of Malta was observed among the three calculation methods.

When Table 14 is examined, there is a strong significant relationship between HDI and TOPSIS rankings ($r = 0.819$), a very strong significant relationship between HDI and VIKOR rankings ($r = 0.937$), and a very strong significant relationship between TOPSIS rankings and VIKOR rankings ($r = 0.946$).

Figure 1. Country rankings line graph
Source: Authors

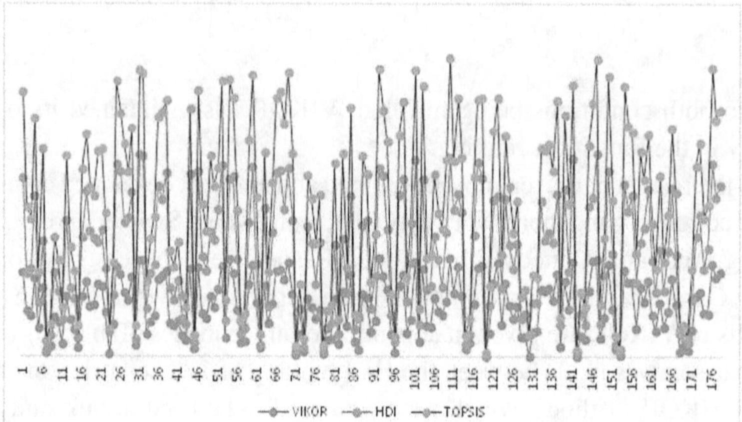

Table 14. Spearman rank correlation results

		HDI	TOPSIS	VIKOR
HDI	Correlation Coefficient	1.000		
	Sig. (2-tailed)			
	N	178		
TOPSIS	Correlation Coefficient	0.819**	1.000	
	Sig. (2-tailed)	0.000		
	N	178	178	
VIKOR	Correlation Coefficient	0.937**	0.946**	1.000
	Sig. (2-tailed)	0.000	0.000	
	N	178	178	178

Source: Authors

FUTURE RESEARCH DIRECTIONS

Some of the MCDM methods are important methods to rank alternatives. Indicators and calculation methods used in ranking countries according to development levels have been criticized in various studies. In this context, the contribution of this chapter to the literature will be very valuable. In this section, it is shown that VIKOR and TOPSIS methods can be used in HDI ranking and it can be an alternative to HDI calculation. The solution of the proposed model was realized with the MS excel program. In future research, researchers can combine all three calculation methods to achieve a single ranking.

CONCLUSION

In this chapter, the well-known MCDM methods, TOPSIS and VIKOR methods were examined as an alternative to HDI calculation.

For this purpose, firstly the data set used in HDI is discussed. The Unemployment variable was added to the data set along with life, income and education variables. Then, TOPSIS and VIKOR methods were used to determine the development levels of the countries. And by ranking the values obtained, countries are ranked according to their development level.

After the countries were sorted separately by VIKOR and TOPSIS method, spearman rho was calculated for the consistency of HDI, VIKOR and TOPSIS methods. When the consistency of rankings with Spearman Rank Correlation is examined, it can be interpreted that all three methods have high correlation among each other.

Thus, it has been tried to show that in addition to the variables of life, income and education, unemployment variable can also be used in the measurement of countries' development levels and different methods can be used instead of HDI's calculation method.

ACKNOWLEDGMENT

This research received no specific grant from any funding agency in the public, commercial, or not-for-profit sectors.

REFERENCES

Belton, V., & Gear, T. (1983). On a shortcoming of Saaty's method of analytic hierarchies. *Omega, 11*(3), 228–230. doi:10.1016/0305-0483(83)90047-6

Bernroider, E. W. N., & Stix, V. (2003). The Evaluation of ERP Systems Using Data Envelopment Analysis. *The Proceedings CD of IRMA 2003- Information Resources Management Association International Conference*, pp. 283-386.

Brans, J. P., Mareschal, B., & Vincke, Ph. (1984). PROMITHEE: A new family of outranking methods in MCDM. *Operations Research, 84*, 477–490.

Chen, J. K., & Chen, S. (2010). A Pro-Performance Appraisal System for The University. *Expert Systems with Applications, 37*(3), 2108–2116. doi:10.1016/j.eswa.2009.07.063

Chen, J. K., & Chen, S. (2010). Using A Novel Conjunctive MCDM Approach Based On DEMATEL, Fuzzy Anp, And TOPSIS As An Innovation Support System For Taiwanese Higher Education. *Expert Systems with Applications, 37*(3), 1981–1990. doi:10.1016/j.eswa.2009.06.079

Churchman, C. W., Ackoff, R. L., & Arnoff, E. L. (1957). *Introduction to operations research.* New York: John Wiley & Sons.

Deng, H., Yeh, C. H., & Willis, R. J. (2000). Inter-company comparison using modified TOPSIS with objective weights. *Computers & Operations Research, 27*(10), 963–973. doi:10.1016/S0305-0548(99)00069-6

greenfacts. (n.d.). Retrieved from https://www.greenfacts.org/glossary/index.htm

Human Development Reports. (n.d.). Retrieved from http://hdr.undp.org/en/humandev

Hwang, C. L., & Yoon, K. P. (1981). *Multiple attribute decision making: methods and applications. Lecture notes in Economics and Mathematical Systems, 186.* New York: Springer-Verlag. doi:10.1007/978-3-642-48318-9

Lootsma, F. A. (2007). *Multi-criteria decision analysis via ratio and difference judgement* (Vol. 29). Springer Science and Business Media.

Opricovic, S., & Tzeng, G. H. (2007). Extended VIKOR Method in Comparison With Other Outranking Methods. *European Journal of Operational Research, 178*(2), 514–529. doi:10.1016/j.ejor.2006.01.020

Paksoy, S. (2015). Assessment of Country Indicators with VIKOR Method. *The International Journal of Economic and Social Research, 11*(11), 2.

Roy, B. (1989). *The outranking approach and the foundations of ELECTRE methods.* University of Paris-Dauphine, Document Du Lamsade.

Roy, B. (1991). The outranking approach and the foundations of ELECTRE methods. *Theory and Decision, 31*(1), 49–73. doi:10.1007/BF00134132

Roy, B., & Vincke, P. (1981). Multicriteria analysis: Survey and new directions. *European Journal of Operational Research, 8*(3), 207–218. doi:10.1016/0377-2217(81)90168-5

Saaty, T. L. (1980). *The analytic hierarchy process*. New York: McGraw Hill.

Saaty, T. L. (2000). *Fundamentals of decision making and priority theory with the analytic hierarchy process* (Vol. 6). RWS Publications.

Shiraz, S. E., Şengül, Ü., & Eren, M. (2013). Ranking of Countries According to Their Level of Development with the Vikor and Topsis Using Entropy. *6th International Conference of Iranian Operations Research Society, Research Center of Operations Research.*

Tae, P., Lee, W., & Yang, Z. (2018). *Multi Criteria Decision Making in Maritime Studies and Logistics*. Springer.

Taşabat, E. S. (2019). A Novel Multi Criteria Decision Making Method: DSC TOPSIS. *Mathematical Problems in Engineering, 2019.*

Taşabat, E. S., Aydın, O., & Sayi, H. (2018). *Multi Criteria Decision Making Methods*. Gece Akademi Press.

Taşabat, E. S., Cinemre, N., & Şen, S. (2015). Financial Performance Evaluation of Turkish Deposit Banks By Application of Different Weighting Techniques in Multi-Criteria Decision Making Methods. *Social Sciences Research Journal*, 4(2), 96-110 (June 2015).

World Development Indicators. The Story. (n.d.). Retrieved from http://datatopics.worldbank.org/world-development-indicators/stories/world-development-indicators-the-story.html

Yeh, C. H. (2002). A Problem Based Selection of Multi-Attribute Decision-Making Methods. *International Transactions in Operational Research, 9*(2), 169–181. doi:10.1111/1475-3995.00348

ADDITIONAL READING

Anandan, V., & Uthra, G. (2017). Extension of TOPSIS using L1 Family of Distance Measures. Advances in Fuzzy Mathematics. ISSN 0973-533X: Vol. 12. *Number 4* (pp. 897–908). Research India Publications; http://www.ripublication.com

Berger, J. (1990). *Statistical decision theory. Foundations, concepts, and methods*. Springer-Verlag.

Churchman, C. W., Ackoff, R. L., & Arnoff, E. L. (1957). *Introduction to operations research*. New York: John Wiley and Sons, Inc.

Edwards, W., & Fasolo, B. (2001). Decision technology. *Annual Review of Psychology, 52*(1), 583. doi:10.1146/annurev.psych.52.1.581 PMID:11148318

Hastie, R. (2001). Problems for judgment and decision-making. *Annual Review of Psychology*, *52*(1), 654. doi:10.1146/annurev.psych.52.1.653 PMID:11148321

Mateusz, P., Danuta, M., Malgorzata, L., Mariusz, B., & Kesra, N. (2018). TOPSIS and VIKOR methods in study of sustainable development in the EU countries. *Procedia Computer Science*, *126*, 1683–1692. doi:10.1016/j.procs.2018.08.109

Matlin, M. W. (1998). *Cognition* (4th ed.). Orlando, FL: Harcourt Brace College Publishers.

Soltanpanah, H., Farughi, H., & Golabi, M. (2010). Utilization and Comparison of Multi Attribute Decision Techniques to Rank Countries upon Human Development Rate. *International Journal of Finance & Economics*, *60*(60), 175.

Taşabat, E. S. (2019). A novel Multi Criteri Decision Making Method: DSC TOPSIS. *Mathematical Problems in Engineering*, *2019*.

Taşabat, S. E., Cinemre, N., & Şen, S. (2005). Farklı Ağırlıklandırma Tekniklerinin Denendiği Çok Kriterli Karar Verme Yöntemleri İle Türkiye'deki Mevduat Bankalarının Mali Performanslarının Değerlendirilmesi. *Social Sciences Research Journal*, Volume 4, Issue 2, 96-110, ISSN: 2147.

Ting, K. (2017, July 1). A modified TOPSIS with a different ranking index. *European Journal of Operational Research*, *260*(1), 152–160. doi:10.1016/j.ejor.2016.11.052

Tzeng, G. H., & Huang, J. J. (2011). *Multiple attribute decision making: methods and applications*. CRC press. doi:10.1201/b11032

Wilson, R. A., & Keil, F. C. (2001). *The MIT Encyclopedia of the Cognitive Sciences*. MIT Press.

Zeleny, M. (1982). *Multiple criteria decision making*. New York: McGraw-Hill.

KEY TERMS AND DEFINITIONS

Correlation: The process of establishing a relationship or connection between two or more things.

Decision Making: Selection of the best among the various alternatives.

Development: The process of developing or being developed.

HDI: Human Development Index. Index for comparing development levels of countries.

MCDM: Decision making when there are multiple criteria decision making.

TOPSIS: Technique for Order Preference by Similarity to an Ideal Solution Method. One of the MCDM methods.

VIKOR: Multicriteria Optimization and Compromise Solution (Visekriterijumska Optimizacija I Kompromisno Resenje) MethodOne of the MCDM methods.

APPENDIX

Table 15. TOPSIS results

Country	D^+	D^-	P_i	Rank	Country	D^+	D^-	P_i	Rank
Afghanistan	0.085288	0.018942	0.181730	154	Latvia	0.067508	0.029184	0.301827	47
Albania	0.077547	0.021349	0.215878	120	Lebanon	0.076238	0.024855	0.245861	76
Algeria	0.075813	0.023602	0.237407	89	Lesotho	0.087476	0.008147	0.085199	177
Angola	0.082111	0.020504	0.199818	139	Liberia	0.085910	0.024001	0.218366	116
Argentina	0.071826	0.028253	0.282306	54	Libya	0.079051	0.017450	0.180831	157
Armenia	0.080570	0.016501	0.169985	165	Lithuania	0.064907	0.031899	0.329518	37
Australia	0.053104	0.045119	0.459354	17	Luxembourg	0.039674	0.052615	0.570111	7
Austria	0.052605	0.041739	0.442412	19	Madagascar	0.085193	0.024877	0.226012	107
Azerbaijan	0.074595	0.026025	0.258647	63	Malawi	0.085530	0.021400	0.200132	138
Bahamas	0.067492	0.026383	0.281041	56	Malaysia	0.066797	0.031629	0.321350	42
Bahrain	0.055177	0.041393	0.428629	21	Maldives	0.076014	0.025720	0.252817	71
Bangladesh	0.083334	0.023544	0.220287	113	Mali	0.086064	0.018370	0.175899	160
Barbados	0.074152	0.025088	0.252804	72	Malta	0.060390	0.036387	0.375988	29
Belarus	0.073310	0.031155	0.298238	50	Mauritania	0.084727	0.016996	0.167079	167
Belgium	0.054445	0.041396	0.431925	20	Mauritius	0.070891	0.027819	0.281828	55
Belize	0.080715	0.022197	0.215691	122	Mexico	0.073188	0.028582	0.280851	57
Benin	0.084279	0.025186	0.230080	101	Moldova (Republic of)	0.081968	0.023673	0.224088	109
Bhutan	0.079954	0.025970	0.245179	79	Mongolia	0.078030	0.025096	0.243354	83
Bolivia (Plurinational State of)	0.080549	0.026230	0.245645	77	Montenegro	0.074420	0.021950	0.227769	105
Bosnia and Herzegovina	0.080108	0.016581	0.171487	162	Morocco	0.080779	0.021094	0.207062	130
Botswana	0.076296	0.017921	0.190209	146	Mozambique	0.088562	0.007343	0.076562	178
Brazil	0.075991	0.022731	0.230253	100	Myanmar	0.082383	0.025728	0.237977	88
Brunei Darussalam	0.032031	0.059618	0.650505	3	Namibia	0.081720	0.013114	0.138285	173
Bulgaria	0.071918	0.027647	0.277675	58	Nepal	0.083953	0.025153	0.230540	98
Burkina Faso	0.085865	0.020056	0.189350	149	Netherlands	0.050381	0.044409	0.468497	14
Burundi	0.085509	0.025341	0.228608	103	New Zealand	0.060202	0.037873	0.386161	28
Cabo Verde	0.081807	0.020104	0.197270	142	Nicaragua	0.082082	0.024228	0.227902	104
Cambodia	0.083395	0.026903	0.243913	82	Niger	0.087312	0.024746	0.220831	112
Cameroon	0.083592	0.023505	0.219474	115	Nigeria	0.083086	0.020227	0.195782	143
Canada	0.054012	0.040449	0.428211	22	Norway	0.036080	0.056524	0.610385	5
Central African Republic	0.087136	0.019813	0.185255	150	Oman	0.061119	0.031167	0.337722	35
Chad	0.086097	0.020124	0.189453	148	Pakistan	0.083072	0.022511	0.213208	123

continues on following page

Table 15. Continued

Country	D^+	D^-	P_i	Rank	Country	D^+	D^-	P_i	Rank
Chile	0.069366	0.029786	0.300411	48	Palestine, State of	0.085567	0.012656	0.128849	175
China	0.074504	0.027039	0.266283	62	Panama	0.072051	0.027144	0.273639	60
Colombia	0.076340	0.023867	0.238179	87	Papua New Guinea	0.083948	0.023921	0.221758	111
Comoros	0.085104	0.023010	0.212834	124	Paraguay	0.079737	0.023799	0.229864	102
Congo	0.082483	0.018246	0.181140	156	Peru	0.076944	0.026804	0.258356	64
Congo (Democratic Republic of the)	0.085964	0.022737	0.209169	129	Philippines	0.079133	0.025937	0.246850	74
Costa Rica	0.074854	0.025779	0.256168	66	Poland	0.066216	0.032458	0.328945	39
Croatia	0.069853	0.026703	0.276558	59	Portugal	0.065719	0.030995	0.320484	44
Cuba	0.079877	0.027290	0.254647	69	Qatar	0.013230	0.088456	0.869894	1
Cyprus	0.063312	0.031068	0.329178	38	Romania	0.069184	0.029468	0.298709	49
Czechia	0.062858	0.035781	0.362747	31	Russian Federation	0.067835	0.030651	0.311226	45
C'e d'Ivoire	0.084419	0.023386	0.216927	117	Rwanda	0.084688	0.025622	0.232270	96
Denmark	0.050273	0.044613	0.470178	13	Saint Lucia	0.079198	0.016829	0.175254	161
Djibouti	0.085395	0.020094	0.190482	145	Saint Vincent and the Grenadines	0.079588	0.016993	0.175943	159
Dominica	0.079712	0.024327	0.233824	93	Samoa	0.081680	0.021673	0.209700	128
Ecuador	0.077819	0.026350	0.252955	70	Sao Tome and Principe	0.084391	0.017181	0.169148	166
Egypt	0.078815	0.020053	0.202829	136	Saudi Arabia	0.049469	0.044206	0.471909	12
El Salvador	0.080764	0.024522	0.232911	94	Senegal	0.084804	0.021979	0.205830	131
Equatorial Guinea	0.073269	0.023999	0.246729	75	Serbia	0.076838	0.021147	0.215821	121
Eritrea	0.086821	0.019531	0.183647	151	Sierra Leone	0.085852	0.021970	0.203766	133
Estonia	0.064376	0.032507	0.335531	36	Singapore	0.026496	0.065824	0.713003	2
Eswatini (Kingdom of)	0.084059	0.010271	0.108879	176	Slovakia	0.064383	0.031426	0.328006	40
Ethiopia	0.085678	0.021185	0.198242	140	Slovenia	0.063022	0.034115	0.351207	33
Fiji	0.079278	0.025135	0.240730	85	Solomon Islands	0.084890	0.024676	0.225213	108
Finland	0.055735	0.038831	0.410626	24	South Africa	0.080871	0.014476	0.151826	168
France	0.057334	0.036815	0.391032	26	South Sudan	0.088106	0.014705	0.143026	170
Gabon	0.075935	0.017822	0.190085	147	Spain	0.061925	0.032621	0.345027	34
Gambia	0.085958	0.017646	0.170320	164	Sri Lanka	0.077264	0.026500	0.255387	68
Georgia	0.079157	0.021795	0.215897	119	Sudan	0.085020	0.014506	0.145752	169
Germany	0.051765	0.043367	0.455861	18	Suriname	0.076430	0.023178	0.232696	95
Ghana	0.083052	0.024866	0.230417	99	Sweden	0.050722	0.043375	0.460964	16
Greece	0.069603	0.026169	0.273240	61	Switzerland	0.043911	0.049252	0.528666	9

continues on following page

Table 15. Continued

Country	D^+	D^-	P_i	Rank	Country	D^+	D^-	P_i	Rank
Guatemala	0.080892	0.025033	0.236331	90	Syrian Arab Republic	0.086018	0.013521	0.135837	174
Guinea	0.085301	0.021819	0.203690	134	Tajikistan	0.084058	0.018729	0.182211	153
Guinea-Bissau	0.085382	0.021011	0.197483	141	Tanzania (United Republic of)	0.084790	0.023929	0.220099	114
Guyana	0.081316	0.018050	0.181649	155	Thailand	0.074030	0.030129	0.289260	51
Haiti	0.086268	0.014154	0.140943	172	The former Yugoslav Republic of Macedonia	0.079146	0.016275	0.170557	163
Honduras	0.083283	0.022981	0.216263	118	Timor-Leste	0.080739	0.025245	0.238196	86
Hong Kong, China (SAR)	0.043211	0.050410	0.538446	8	Togo	0.084758	0.025607	0.232025	97
Hungary	0.066997	0.031624	0.320659	43	Tonga	0.081243	0.027919	0.255757	67
Iceland	0.051551	0.044947	0.465781	15	Trinidad and Tobago	0.065364	0.031279	0.323652	41
India	0.081219	0.024795	0.233888	92	Tunisia	0.078829	0.020334	0.205060	132
Indonesia	0.077933	0.025246	0.244680	80	Turkey	0.068021	0.027646	0.288983	52
Iran (Islamic Republic of)	0.072325	0.024131	0.250174	73	Turkmenistan	0.075125	0.026040	0.257398	65
Iraq	0.073786	0.023551	0.241954	84	Uganda	0.084820	0.024929	0.227144	106
Ireland	0.046085	0.048047	0.510421	11	Ukraine	0.079701	0.022820	0.222591	110
Israel	0.061584	0.035679	0.366831	30	United Arab Emirates	0.037708	0.055527	0.595560	6
Italy	0.060363	0.034026	0.360489	32	United Kingdom	0.056719	0.039645	0.411409	23
Jamaica	0.080592	0.019568	0.195367	144	United States	0.045700	0.047776	0.511104	10
Japan	0.057226	0.039214	0.406617	25	Uruguay	0.070970	0.027942	0.282495	53
Jordan	0.080614	0.018084	0.183226	152	Uzbekistan	0.081369	0.021917	0.212200	126
Kazakhstan	0.069061	0.029890	0.302072	46	Vanuatu	0.083990	0.022575	0.211840	127
Kenya	0.084246	0.018212	0.177754	158	Venezuela (Bolivarian Republic of)	0.077890	0.023828	0.234257	91
Korea (Republic of)	0.059129	0.037818	0.390089	27	Viet Nam	0.081363	0.026472	0.245485	78
Kuwait	0.035927	0.057029	0.613509	4	Yemen	0.086605	0.014219	0.141024	171
Kyrgyzstan	0.083324	0.022451	0.212254	125	Zambia	0.083473	0.021068	0.201531	137
Lao People's Democratic Republic	0.081679	0.026377	0.244103	81	Zimbabwe	0.085225	0.021754	0.203349	135

Source: Authors

Table 16. VIKOR results

Countries	Si	Rank	Ri	Rank	Qi	Rank	Countries	Si	Rank	Ri	Rank	Qi	Rank
Afghanistan	0.656253	151	0.247501	153	0.644396	152	Latvia	0.450219	56	0.197615	46	0.400268	46
Albania	0.505878	82	0.225845	81	0.495725	81	Lebanon	0.455831	62	0.222634	76	0.454237	65
Algeria	0.489353	72	0.221721	73	0.475899	73	Lesotho	0.891031	178	0.244585	141	0.803059	178
Angola	0.640099	145	0.238965	120	0.616006	141	Liberia	0.614374	135	0.249991	174	0.620035	144
Argentina	0.422791	47	0.211693	60	0.409207	51	Libya	0.611467	134	0.227536	85	0.573088	121
Armenia	0.604585	128	0.231746	97	0.576686	124	Lithuania	0.420090	44	0.190487	40	0.364902	40
Australia	0.215149	3	0.157673	19	0.155684	9	Luxembourg	0.301201	19	0.123611	4	0.147852	8
Austria	0.313984	21	0.153680	18	0.216947	19	Madagascar	0.573276	119	0.248504	167	0.588265	128
Azerbaijan	0.496883	77	0.217851	67	0.473435	72	Malawi	0.629414	140	0.249137	170	0.628863	148
Bahamas	0.511240	88	0.194002	42	0.435795	62	Malaysia	0.419294	43	0.195237	44	0.373844	43
Bahrain	0.323338	25	0.161934	22	0.240009	24	Maldives	0.459544	65	0.222227	75	0.456025	67
Bangladesh	0.529699	99	0.243513	131	0.547751	109	Mali	0.728456	170	0.247224	151	0.694430	171
Barbados	0.471320	69	0.217328	66	0.454478	66	Malta	0.335917	29	0.177397	30	0.279746	29
Belarus	0.407987	40	0.216295	65	0.408039	50	Mauritania	0.694785	161	0.243696	132	0.663783	158
Belgium	0.290676	12	0.160695	21	0.214645	18	Mauritius	0.451585	58	0.207974	54	0.421943	57
Belize	0.548868	111	0.236004	109	0.546163	107	Mexico	0.420256	45	0.214958	62	0.413961	53
Benin	0.590272	123	0.246991	150	0.597147	133	Moldova (Republic of)	0.532405	100	0.239473	123	0.541567	105
Bhutan	0.506946	84	0.234069	103	0.512921	90	Mongolia	0.508252	86	0.229682	93	0.505063	83
Bolivia (Plurinational State of)	0.501181	80	0.236976	113	0.514697	93	Montenegro	0.522316	93	0.215314	63	0.486179	75
Bosnia and Herzegovina	0.631145	142	0.229242	91	0.590286	129	Morocco	0.526288	97	0.235629	107	0.529594	100
Botswana	0.651911	149	0.217993	69	0.582338	126	Mozambique	0.853727	177	0.249075	169	0.785901	177
Brazil	0.506440	83	0.221822	74	0.488073	79	Myanmar	0.560391	116	0.239445	122	0.561119	115
Brunei Darussalam	0.318382	23	0.116667	3	0.146001	7	Namibia	0.738183	171	0.231223	94	0.669244	162
Bulgaria	0.450747	57	0.211093	59	0.427594	59	Nepal	0.523082	95	0.246109	146	0.548306	110
Burkina Faso	0.685532	158	0.247876	161	0.665659	161	Netherlands	0.275264	9	0.148332	14	0.179121	14
Burundi	0.623436	136	0.249916	173	0.626233	147	New Zealand	0.292745	13	0.178313	32	0.251332	26
Cabo Verde	0.559751	115	0.238550	117	0.558880	114	Nicaragua	0.494064	74	0.240328	127	0.516413	94
Cambodia	0.515624	90	0.244081	135	0.539026	102	Niger	0.679172	155	0.249477	171	0.664406	159
Cameroon	0.629750	141	0.244292	139	0.619409	143	Nigeria	0.717384	166	0.240168	126	0.672561	164
Canada	0.316720	22	0.157946	20	0.227395	21	Norway	0.224697	4	0.105045	2	0.057118	2
Central African Republic	0.764916	173	0.250000	177	0.725528	174	Oman	0.494211	75	0.173320	27	0.382501	44
Chad	0.748212	172	0.247660	156	0.709145	172	Pakistan	0.610051	132	0.239996	125	0.597015	132
Chile	0.390403	36	0.204270	53	0.371668	42	Palestine, State of	0.713113	165	0.250000	175	0.689233	168
China	0.445909	53	0.218561	71	0.439141	63	Panama	0.446792	54	0.210150	57	0.422937	58
Colombia	0.495510	76	0.223581	79	0.483932	74	Papua New Guinea	0.590033	122	0.244103	136	0.591203	131
Comoros	0.606227	129	0.248416	166	0.611175	139	Paraguay	0.511022	87	0.233391	98	0.514421	92
Congo	0.645270	148	0.239172	121	0.620042	145	Peru	0.453780	60	0.226054	82	0.459640	69

continues on following page

Table 16. Continued

Countries	Si	Rank	Ri	Rank	Qi	Rank	Countries	Si	Rank	Ri	Rank	Qi	Rank
Congo (Democratic Republic of the)	0.652118	150	0.249714	172	0.645924	153	Philippines	0.515017	89	0.231725	96	0.513888	91
Costa Rica	0.431134	50	0.219926	72	0.431518	61	Poland	0.378117	34	0.195144	43	0.344809	37
Croatia	0.458491	64	0.203728	52	0.418289	55	Portugal	0.384886	35	0.192637	41	0.344537	36
Cuba	0.413420	42	0.235233	105	0.449721	64	Qatar	0.177399	1	0.131944	9	0.077778	3
Cyprus	0.421075	46	0.183483	34	0.351585	38	Romania	0.433871	51	0.202686	50	0.398956	45
Czechia	0.335851	28	0.185593	36	0.296092	31	Russian Federation	0.448272	55	0.199270	49	0.402214	48
C'e d'Ivoire	0.693761	160	0.243935	134	0.663543	157	Rwanda	0.550051	113	0.247529	154	0.570043	120
Denmark	0.277593	10	0.148293	13	0.180676	15	Saint Lucia	0.608979	130	0.226256	83	0.568783	119
Djibouti	0.695108	162	0.244126	137	0.664870	160	Saint Vincent and the Grenadines	0.610160	133	0.228830	88	0.574759	123
Dominica	0.470774	68	0.233468	99	0.486376	77	Samoa	0.525105	96	0.238709	118	0.534924	101
Ecuador	0.444242	52	0.229157	90	0.459165	68	Sao Tome and Principe	0.644255	147	0.245097	144	0.631182	150
Egypt	0.569830	118	0.229140	89	0.547123	108	Saudi Arabia	0.351141	31	0.144501	12	0.224621	20
El Salvador	0.499230	78	0.236645	111	0.512667	89	Senegal	0.602142	127	0.246296	147	0.604073	137
Equatorial Guinea	0.664117	153	0.209429	56	0.573762	122	Serbia	0.533101	101	0.223406	78	0.509921	87
Eritrea	0.692441	159	0.247660	155	0.670069	163	Sierra Leone	0.719511	167	0.250000	176	0.693715	170
Estonia	0.393193	37	0.189025	38	0.343134	35	Singapore	0.190210	2	0.093056	1	0.008976	1
Eswatini (Kingdom of)	0.836183	176	0.236462	110	0.748384	175	Slovakia	0.422865	48	0.188005	37	0.361883	39
Ethiopia	0.635487	144	0.247727	157	0.630299	149	Slovenia	0.348727	30	0.185580	35	0.305087	33
Fiji	0.501488	81	0.233511	100	0.507981	84	Solomon Islands	0.543599	109	0.247398	152	0.565260	118
Finland	0.333881	27	0.163179	23	0.249883	25	South Africa	0.769519	174	0.248195	164	0.725143	173
France	0.353930	32	0.166941	24	0.271456	28	South Sudan	0.811371	175	0.250000	178	0.758076	176
Gabon	0.669362	154	0.216063	64	0.590704	130	Spain	0.408642	41	0.177694	31	0.331295	34
Gambia	0.700277	163	0.248164	163	0.676567	165	Sri Lanka	0.454647	61	0.227050	84	0.462240	71
Georgia	0.528122	98	0.231656	95	0.522932	97	Sudan	0.723595	169	0.242562	129	0.681700	166
Germany	0.288389	11	0.152129	16	0.195910	17	Suriname	0.534501	102	0.222789	77	0.509666	86
Ghana	0.584772	121	0.242611	130	0.584533	127	Sweden	0.293554	14	0.148620	15	0.192513	16
Greece	0.488651	71	0.198377	48	0.428719	60	Switzerland	0.266675	8	0.127401	6	0.131241	5
Guatemala	0.507886	85	0.235763	108	0.516967	95	Syrian Arab Republic	0.680274	157	0.246397	148	0.659018	155
Guinea	0.661623	152	0.246978	149	0.647113	154	Tajikistan	0.599040	126	0.244288	138	0.597884	134
Guinea-Bissau	0.679671	156	0.248087	162	0.661975	156	Tanzania (United Republic of)	0.597706	125	0.245713	145	0.599799	135
Guyana	0.635394	143	0.235399	106	0.605577	138	Thailand	0.407442	39	0.218032	70	0.411130	52
Haiti	0.721939	168	0.247843	159	0.691103	169	The former Yugoslav Republic of Macedonia	0.627885	138	0.224513	80	0.578543	125
Honduras	0.538274	105	0.242355	128	0.551443	112	Timor-Leste	0.522622	94	0.236692	112	0.529151	99

continues on following page

Table 16. Continued

Countries	Si	Rank	Ri	Rank	Qi	Rank	Countries	Si	Rank	Ri	Rank	Qi	Rank
Hong Kong, China (SAR)	0.244432	6	0.125690	5	0.112235	4	Togo	0.593526	124	0.248300	165	0.602044	136
Hungary	0.404807	38	0.196774	45	0.366768	41	Tonga	0.453381	59	0.239488	124	0.486230	76
Iceland	0.236603	5	0.152830	17	0.161030	11	Trinidad and Tobago	0.474461	70	0.189824	39	0.401671	47
India	0.534665	103	0.237753	115	0.539711	103	Tunisia	0.537288	104	0.229312	92	0.524666	98
Indonesia	0.520568	91	0.228083	86	0.510494	88	Turkey	0.468646	67	0.198041	47	0.414031	54
Iran (Islamic Republic of)	0.499703	79	0.210254	58	0.460215	70	Turkmenistan	0.540976	107	0.217864	68	0.504354	82
Iraq	0.561121	117	0.213140	61	0.509020	85	Uganda	0.609255	131	0.247858	160	0.612182	140
Ireland	0.257115	7	0.135732	11	0.141206	6	Ukraine	0.521630	92	0.233929	102	0.522929	96
Israel	0.326221	26	0.181023	33	0.280206	30	United Arab Emirates	0.300703	18	0.129167	7	0.158614	10
Italy	0.374354	33	0.175453	29	0.302790	32	United Kingdom	0.299439	16	0.167238	25	0.233871	22
Jamaica	0.544358	110	0.234540	104	0.540076	104	United States	0.296023	15	0.133178	10	0.163357	12
Japan	0.299495	17	0.167518	26	0.234470	23	Uruguay	0.427994	49	0.208532	55	0.406530	49
Jordan	0.577606	120	0.233589	101	0.561468	116	Uzbekistan	0.551597	114	0.237502	114	0.551071	111
Kazakhstan	0.463983	66	0.202729	51	0.420140	56	Vanuatu	0.549250	112	0.244981	142	0.564385	117
Kenya	0.628701	139	0.245054	143	0.620198	146	Venezuela (Bolivarian Republic of)	0.492869	73	0.228458	87	0.491836	80
Korea (Republic of)	0.308765	20	0.174063	28	0.254055	27	Viet Nam	0.457192	63	0.238817	119	0.487557	78
Kuwait	0.318837	24	0.129167	8	0.171320	13	Yemen	0.712679	164	0.248760	168	0.686449	167
Kyrgyzstan	0.542326	108	0.244421	140	0.558414	113	Zambia	0.627654	137	0.243771	133	0.616899	142
Lao People's Democratic Republic	0.539388	106	0.238363	116	0.544238	106	Zimbabwe	0.643480	146	0.247805	158	0.636054	151

Source: Authors

Chapter 11
Entropy-Based VIKOR Method and a Case Study:
An Evaluation of Websites' Technical and Popularity Performances

Burcu Avcı Öztürk
Bursa Uludag University, Turkey

ABSTRACT

Due to the rapid advances in Internet technology, the number of websites and the amount of information obtained from websites are increasing day by day. Internet users want to access the website and the information they need more easily and quickly. This is also the case getting news so effectiveness of newspapers' websites in terms of content and the speed at which pages are opened is also an important indicator for users. The purpose of this chapter is to investigate the technical and popularity performance of the newspapers' websites in Turkey. The study will show the applicability of an objective weight-determining method, Entropy technique, for finding the weights of criteria and VIKOR for evaluating websites' technical and popularity performance. As a result of the evaluation, the best websites were determined in terms of technique and popularity, and ranked in terms of overall performance.

INTRODUCTION

With the rapid increase in internet usage, the use of websites in activities of the obtainment of information has become inevitable. With the imporvement of World Wide Web (www) in the recent decade, the websites have played a central role not only in business communities but also in our daily lives. Web users look for more comfortable browsing experiences that require the www environment to be both effective and efficient. With effective browsing, the users can easily search the most interesting websites and reach the target website with just a few clicks in seconds (Yin & Guo, 2013). For this reason, the importance of the use of the websites of newspapers and their speed and performance is increasing day by day. Websites need to be constantly renewed and updated according to the wishes and needs of their users.

DOI: 10.4018/978-1-7998-2216-5.ch011

Many features such as the speed, content, design of newspaper websites, and the fact that the published news is interesting and reflects the truth increase the number of visitors. Therefore, the performance evaluation of websites from the technical and popularity point of view becomes a necessary issue.

There are numerous websites and web documents on the Internet prepared for various purposes such as commercial, corporate, official or personal purposes. Evaluating websites according to certain criteria, is especially important for web sites that serve corporate and social purposes. When looking at the publishing purposes of websites, they can be classified as follows: Information sharing, education, and training, commerce and advertising, entertainment, communication, news publishing, etc. The content and designs of the websites differ according to these basic publishing purposes, and the point of view of the internet users varies according to the content. Reading news online is among the most preferred types of Internet usage (Gürcan, 2003).

The websites of newspapers have developed rapidly on the internet and are continuously developing, and that communicate instant and daily developments to Internet users straightaway. Due to the news constantly changing and the contents getting old very quickly, the internet users look for websites where they can quickly follow instantaneous developments (Gürcan, 2003).

The measurement of website performance, which can be evaluated in various aspects, can be referred to as a multi-criteria decision making (MCDM) problem. When analyzing the content, design and technical competence of newspaper websites, using concrete criteria in the evaluation will increase the objectivity of the analysis. In this study, website performances are evaluated by using criteria that are objective and can be expressed in numbers. And the importance weights of these criteria are calculated with Entropy, an objective weighting method. Therefore, the subjective judgments of decision-makers or users are not included. It is more appropriate to use fuzzy numbers and fuzzy MCDM methods in studies where subjective judgments of decision-makers will be used.

The aim of the study is to investigate the technical and popularity performance of the newspapers' websites in Turkey by an integrated Entropy-based VIKOR method with its step by step analysis. In the first section, a general introduction to the subject is presented, and information about the course of the study is given. The second section includes a literature review of studies evaluating website performance using MCDM methods and those using Entropy-based VIKOR method. In the third section, the methodology to be used in the analysis is explained. In this section, the algorithms of Entropy and VIKOR methods and the equations to be used in the calculations are given. In the fourth section of the study, technical and popularity performances and total performance of newspaper websites are evaluated using the Entropy-based VIKOR method, and related calculations are included. And in the results section, results and comments regarding the technical and popularity performances and the total performance rankings are given.

BACKGROUND

When the literature on website performance measurement is reviewed, it is seen that the majority of the studies are composed of availability evaluation and content analysis. In terms of the implementation of multi-criteria decision making (MCDM) methods, it can be said that most of the studies focus on issues such as testing consumer perceptions, e-commerce, evaluating shopping sites in terms of consumer satisfaction, or measuring the effects of websites on consumers' buying behaviors. Most of the studies using MCDM methods have been carried out using data obtained from the preferences of the decision-makers (from their subjective evaluations) or the survey results applied to the decision-makers. In the literature review, there were no studies measuring the speed or popularity performance of newspaper websites or evaluating their effectiveness by using their users' (readers) opinions about the websites. In this study, objective real numbers are used in performance evaluation.

The literature review will be carried out in terms of two aspects. In this section, the studies that have made the website performance measurement or evaluation with MCDM methods and the studies which have used the Entropy-based VIKOR method in an integrated manner will be included.

Some of the studies using MCDM methods for website performance evaluation are summarized below.

Chou and Cheng (2012) built an integrated approach that combines fuzzy ANP (Analytic Network Process) and fuzzy VIKOR for evaluating website quality of four professional accounting firms. The results showed that the firms didn't utilize the internet to its full potential and needed to improve their websites.

Çebi (2013) evaluated the perceived design quality of websites while considering the interactions among design characteristics. A new approach, which includes the fuzzy set theory, DEMATEL, and generalized Choquet integral techniques are proposed, and the researchers used the proposed method to evaluate the quality of the most used shopping websites in Turkey.

Akıncılar and Dağdeviren (2014) proposed a robust and reliable model that evaluates the quality of hotel websites. A hybrid model including AHP and PROMETHEE was used to evaluate the performance of websites of five-star hotels in Ankara. The researchers used AHP to determine the weights of criteria and PROMETHEE to rank the alternatives.

Chung, Liu, Wang, and Pang (2015) applied fuzzy MCDM methods to the evaluation of portal website service quality. To overcome the obstacles of subjective respondents, the researchers adopted the fuzzy set theory as the measurement of performance and obtained the weights of criteria, and they used VIKOR to rank each performance of service quality.

Büyükozan and Güleryüz (2016) proposed a solution to the problem of quality performance evaluation for websites in the logistic industry. For this purpose, an integrated approach based on MCDM and fuzzy logic is used to assess the quality of logistic firms' websites. The weights of website evaluation criteria are calculated with fuzzy AHP, and the websites of 15 logistic companies in Turkey are ranked based on quality using fuzzy TOPSIS method. The researchers used decision-makers' subjective preferences to evaluate website performance.

Durmuş and Tayyar (2017) aimed to determine the methods which give the closest results to the decision-makers' opinions using AHP, TOPSIS, Max 100 and SWARA methods. Three Turkish best-known online shopping sites had been used as alternatives. Max 100 and SWARA methods provided closer results to decision-makers' opinions than AHP and TOPSIS methods.

Kabak, Özceylan, Dağdeviren, and Genç (2017) provided an evaluation model that prioritizes the relative weights of various distance education websites. The researchers weighted the criteria with stakeholders of distance education websites using ANP and used TOPSIS to rank the alternatives.

The studies using Entropy-based VIKOR, are summarized below.

Shemshadi, Shirazi, Toreihi, and Tarokh (2011) used the Shannon entropy concept to regulate subjective weights assigned by decision-makers. The researchers solved a group MCDM problem with objective weights based on the Shannon entropy concept.

Malekian and Azarnivand (2016) applied entropy and VIKOR methods in prioritization of flood risk in Shemshak watershed Iran. Shannon's entropy is used to determine the weights of criteria, and it successfully attached little importance to the factors which are in contrast with the non-permanent characteristics of flood analysis phenomena.

Rao, Sai, and Babu (2017) used entropy to determine the objective weights of the supplier selection problem and ranked the supplier alternatives with the VIKOR method.

Mohsen and Fereshteh (2017) proposed a new framework for evaluation of the equipment failure models by the FMEA (Failure models and effect analysis) method applying z-numbers, entropy, and an extended VIKOR method. The researchers used the z-numbers to handle the partial reliability in the experts' opinions about the FMEA risk factors.

Lee and Tseng (2018) selected qualified and stable employees with an integrated fuzzy membership function, entropy, and VIKOR method. The researchers integrated VIKOR with the entropy method to design a systematic model to deal with the personnel selection problem.

Gök-Kısa and Perçin (2018) performed the performance measurement of hardware companies in the information technology sector, which were included in the Global 2000 list, with integrated Entropy weight and VIKOR methods. During the performance measurement, the weights of financial evaluation criteria were calculated using Entropy, and the ranking was done using the VIKOR method, and the ranking was compared with the ranking published by FORBES magazine.

Çelebi-Demirarslan, Küçükönder, and Kıngır (2019) applied a survey to academic staff about burnout, job satisfaction, emotional labor and intention to leave. The researchers weighted the scales (criteria) by entropy method and then respectively TOPSIS, and VIKOR methods are used to evaluate academic staffs' performance. According to their observation, the first and the last person in the ranking were the same in both methods.

ENTROPY AND VIKOR METHODS

Entropy

Objective weighting methods are suitable for situations that decision-makers' preferences are not available and situations that the researchers want to use objective weights only based on the known data of the MCDM problem. The entropy method is the most representative objective weighting method to determine the relative importance weights of the criteria used in MCDM problems. This method also determines how the criteria are related to the evaluation or final result (Arce, Saavedra, Miguez, & Granada, 2015). The entropy shows that how much the decision criteria reflect the all MCDM problem and how great uncertainty of criteria is (Wang, Jing, Zhang, & Zhao, 2009).

Entropy is a measure of uncertainty, which is developed by Shannon (1948) in the paper 'A Mathematical Theory of Communication'. Entropy method has been widely used in many fields such as engineering, management, etc. 'According to the idea of information Entropy, the number or quality of information acquired from decision-making setting is one of the determinants of accuracy and reliability of decision-making problem'. Entropy value is a very good scale that can be used for different cases of evaluation in the different decision-making processes and used to measure the quantity of useful information provided by data itself (Wu, Sun, Liang, & Zha, 2011). The idea of Entropy is useful for examining the contrast between datasets. If a criterion has very similar values, then the Entropy method gives this criterion little importance. Even if all the alternatives have the same values, the criterion can be ignored (Apan, Öztel, & İslamoğlu, 2018).

A MCDM problem is expressed in a matrix in which columns indicate criteria and in which rows list the alternatives to the problem. The problem has m alternatives (A_1, A_2, ….., A_m) that are evaluated by n criteria (C_1, C_2, ….., C_n) can be viewed as a geometric system that has m points in dimensional space. X_{ij} indicates the performance score of the ith alternative A_i, with respect to the jth criterion C_j, (i = 1, 2,….., m; j = 1,2,….., n) and the decision matrix D is shown in (1) (El-Santawy, 2012).

$$D = \begin{bmatrix} X_{11} & X_{12} & \cdots & X_{1n} \\ X_{21} & X_{22} & \cdots & X_{2n} \\ . & . & \cdots & . \\ . & . & \cdots & . \\ X_{m1} & X_{m2} & \cdots & X_{mn} \end{bmatrix} \tag{1}$$

The calculation steps of determining the objective weights of each criterion based on the concept of Entropy are introduced below (Wang & Lee, 2009; Wu et al., 2011; Li et al., 2011; Ömürbek, Eren, & Dağ, 2017):

1. **Standardization of X_{ij} values:** In order to eliminate the influence of value dimension on incommensurability, it is necessary to standardize the values of the decision matrix using the equations of relative optimum membership degree. Equation (2) is used to transform the values for the benefit criteria and Equation (3) is used for the cost criteria.

$$r_{ij} = \frac{X_{ij}}{\max_j X_{ij}} \tag{2}$$

$$r_{ij} = \frac{\min_j X_{ij}}{X_{ij}}, \quad \min_j X_{ij} \neq 0 \tag{3}$$

After standardization, the standardized decision matrix $R' = \left[r_{ij}\right]_{mxn}$ is obtained.

2. **Normalization of r_{ij} values:** To determine the weights of criteria by the Entropy measure, the standardized decision matrix needs to be normalized for each criterion to obtain the projection value of each criterion P_{ij}.

$$P_{ij} = \frac{r_{ij}}{\sum_{i=1}^{m} r_{ij}} \tag{4}$$

3. **Calculation of Entropy values (E_j):** The Entropy values of each criterion are calculated by equation (5), k is a constant number, $k=(ln(m))^{-1}$.

$$E_j = -k\sum_{j=1}^{n} P_{ij} \,.\, \ln P_{ij} \tag{5}$$

4. **Determining the degree of divergence (d_j):** The degree of divergence is calculated by equation (6) for each criterion.

$$d_j = 1 - E_j \tag{6}$$

d_j value represents the inherent contrast intensity of the criterion C_j. The higher the d_j is, the more important the criterion C_j.

5. **Calculation of Entropy weights of criteria (w_j):** The objective weight for each criterion can be calculated with equation (7). w_j is a parameter that can describe how much importance the criterion is. The larger Entropy-based weight means that the specific criterion provides more information about the decision-making process.

$$w_j = \frac{d_j}{\sum_{j=1}^{n} d_j}, \sum_{j=1}^{n} w_j = 1 \tag{7}$$

VIKOR

VIKOR (VlseKriterijumsa Optimizacija I Kompromisno Resenje = Multi-criteria optimization and Compromise Solution) method was developed by Opricovic (1998) for multi-criteria optimization of complex systems. VIKOR determines a compromise ranking list, the compromise solution obtained with the weights of criteria. This method focuses on ranking and selecting from a set of alternatives with respect to conflicting criteria. VIKOR introduces the multi-criteria ranking index based on the particular measure of closeness to the ideal solution (Opricovic, 1998; Opricovic & Tzeng, 2004; Shemshadi, Shirazi, Toreihi, & Tarakh, 2011).

In some MCDM methods, each alternative is evaluated according to each criterion and, the ranking could be performed by comparing the measure of closeness to the ideal alternative. In compromise programming method, the multi-criteria measure for compromise ranking is developed from the L_p-metric used as an aggregating function. Development of VIKOR method started with the form of L_p-metric (Yu, 1973; Zeleny, 1982; Opricovic & Tzeng, 2004).

$$L_{pi} = \left\{ \sum_{j=1}^{n} \left[\frac{wj\left(f_j^* - f_{ij}\right)}{\left(f_j^* - f_j^-\right)} \right]^p \right\}^{\frac{1}{p}} \quad 1 \le p \le \infty \tag{8}$$

Figure 1. Ideal and compromise solutions
(Opricovic &Tzeng, 2004)

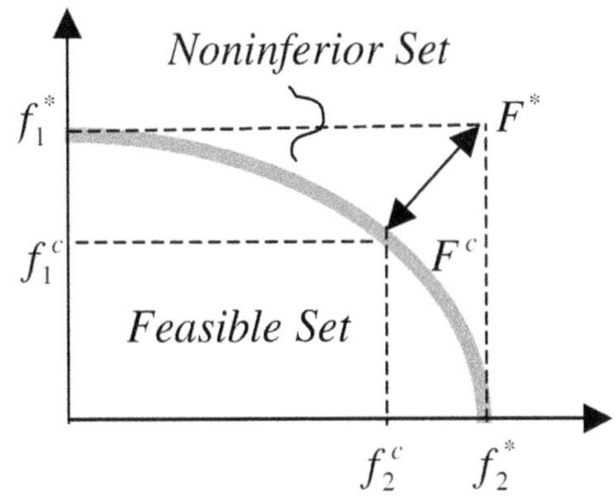

'The compromise solution F^c is a feasible solution that is the ideal F^*, and compromise means an agreement established by mutual concessions, as is shown in Figure 1 by $\Delta f_1 = f_1^* - f_1^c$ and $\Delta f_2 = f_2^* - f_2^c$' (Opricovic & Tzeng, 2004).

The compromise ranking algorithm VIKOR has the following steps (Opricovic & Tzeng, 2004; Opricovic & Tzeng, 2007; Chatterjee & Chakraborty, 2016; Yalçın & Ünlü, 2018):

1. Determine the best f_j* and the worst f_j^- values of all criteria, j=1,2,…..,n. If the function represents benefit criteria then:

$$f_j^* = \max_i f_{ij} \quad f_j^- = \min_i f_{ij} \tag{9}$$

If the function represents cost criteria then:

$$f_j^* = \min_i f_{ij} \quad f_j^- = \max_i f_{ij} \tag{10}$$

2. Calculate the normalized values of f_{ij} with equation (11):

$$r_{ij} = \frac{\left(f_j^* - f_{ij}\right)}{\left(f_j^* - f_j^-\right)} \tag{11}$$

3. Calculate weighted normalize values with equation (12):

$$r_{ij} \; x \; w_j = w_j \frac{\left(f_j^* - f_{ij}\right)}{\left(f_j^* - f_j^-\right)} \tag{12}$$

4. Compute the values S_i, and R_i, i = 1,2,….., m, by the following equations:

$$S_i = \sum_{j=1}^{n} \left[\frac{wj\left(f_j^* - f_{ij}\right)}{\left(f_j^* - f_j^-\right)} \right] \tag{13}$$

$$R_i = \max_j \left[\frac{wj\left(f_j^* - f_{ij}\right)}{\left(f_j^* - f_j^-\right)} \right] \tag{14}$$

w_j are the weights of criteria, expressing their relative importance.

5. Calculate the values Q_i by the equation (15)

$$Q_i = \frac{v\left(S_i - S^*\right)}{\left(S^- - S^*\right)} + \frac{(1-v)\left(R_i - R^*\right)}{\left(R^- - R^*\right)} \tag{15}$$

$$S^* = \min_i S_i \quad S^- = \max_i S_i,$$

$$R^* = \min_i R_i \quad R^- = \max_i R_i,$$

and v is introduced as the weight of strategy of 'the majority of criteria' (or maximum group utility), whereas (1 – v) is the weight of the individual regret, usually v = 0.50. When v is larger than 0.50, the index of Q_i follows majority rule. The value of v affects the ranking of alternatives and is usually determined externally by the decision experts.

6. Rank the alternatives, sorted by the values S_i, R_i, and Q_i, in decreasing order. The results are three ranking lists.
7. Propose as a compromise solution the alternative $A^{(1)}$ which is ranked the best ranked by the measure Q_i (minimum) if the two conditions below are satisfied:
   C1. The condition of acceptable advantage: $Q(A^{(2)}) - Q(A^{(1)}) \geq DQ$, $A^{(2)}$ is the second alternative in the ranking list by Q_i ; DQ = 1/(m – 1), m is the number of alternatives.
   C2. The condition of acceptable stability: 'Alternative $A^{(1)}$ must also be the best ranked by S_i or/and R_i. This compromise solution is stable within a decision-making process, which could be: voting by majority rule (when v > 0.5 is needed), or by consensus v = 0.5, or with veto (v < 0.5). Here, v is the weight of the decision-making strategy the majority of criteria (or the maximum group utility)'.

$A^{(1)}$ is the best alternative when $A^{(1)}$ and $A^{(2)}$ satisfy both C1 and C2 conditions.

If one of the conditions is not satisfied, then a set of compromise solutions is proposed, which includes the following two-judge rules:

1. If only condition C2 is not satisfied, alternatives $A^{(1)}$ and $A^{(2)}$ are the best alternatives as a compromise solution.
2. If condition C1 is not satisfied, alternatives $A^{(1)}, A^{(2)}, \ldots\ldots, A^{(m)}$ is determined by the relation $Q(A^{(m)}) - Q(A^{(1)}) < DQ$ for maximum m (the positions of these alternatives are ''in closeness'').

RESEARCH METHODOLOGY

In this study, an integrated MCDM method called Entropy-based VIKOR is used to evaluate the technical and popularity performances of Turkish newspapers. Entropy-based VIKOR method's steps can be summarized as follows:

1. Select the alternatives from Turkish newspapers' websites
2. Identify criteria for websites' technical performance
3. Identify criteria for websites' popularity performance
4. Collect the data for technical and popularity performance evaluation
5. Determine the Entropy weights of criteria
6. Evaluate the website alternatives by VIKOR
7. Determine the best and the worst values of criteria
8. Calculate S_i and R_i values by using Entropy weights
9. Calculate the Qi values
10. Rank the website alternatives by sorting $S_{i,}$ $R_{i,}$ and Q_i in decreasing order
11. Propose a solution according to the verification rules

Determining Criteria and Alternatives

In the first step, alternative newspapers to be evaluated and performance-determining criteria were determined, and the hierarchical structure of the problem is created. As alternatives, the 10 most widely read and known newspapers of Turkey are selected. For the evaluation, the speed and performance criteria of "Google PageSpeed Insights", which determine the technical performance of the websites, are used, and the performance criteria of "SimilarWeb - Traffic Rank & Website Analysis" are used for popularity performance. Criteria and the codes to be used for the criteria are given in Table 1.

The criteria used to measure the technical performance of Web sites are the performance criteria used by Google PageSpeed Insights (PSI). PSI shows the page speeds of websites, reports on the performance of a page on both mobile and desktop devices and provides suggestions on how that page may be improved. Criteria used for measuring popularity performance are the performance criteria determined and measured by SimilarWeb - Traffic Rank & Website Analysis. Website traffic and key metrics for any website, including engagement rate, traffic ranking, keyword ranking, and traffic source can be seen in SimilarWeb. The SimilarWeb allows researchers to gain insights into any website's statistics and strategy as they're browsing, with the click of a button. Traffic and engagement statistics for any website can be seen. SimilarWeb provides users with all this information about the popularity and main traffic sources.

Table 1. Criteria, codes, and speciality of criteria

Main Criteria	Criteria	Codes	Specialty of Criteria
Mobile Technical Performance (MTP)	Performance Score	PS	Max
	First Contentful Paint	FCP	Min
	First Meaningful Paint	FMP	Min
	Speed Index	SI	Min
	Time to Interactive	TTI	Min
	Estimated Input Latency	EIL	Min
Desktop Technical Performance (DTP)	Performance Score	PS	Max
	First Contentful Paint	FCP	Min
	First Meaningful Paint	FMP	Min
	Speed Index	SI	Min
	Time to Interactive	TTI	Min
	Estimated Input Latency	EIL	Min
Popularity Performance (PP) Traffic and Engagement	Monthly visits	MV	Max
	Global Traffic Rank	GTR	Min
	Country Traffic Rank	CTR	Min
	Category Traffic Rank	CGTR	Min
	Average Visit Duration	AVD	Max
	Page Views/Visit	PV	Max
	Bounce Rate	BR	Min

Forming Decision Matrices by Collecting Data

Since the data to be used to determine technical performance may vary according to content and pages, measurements were made every week during July 2019, and average values were used. The data that will be used to determine the popularity performance is the monthly data for July 2019. Technical performance data were measured separately for mobile and desktop computers, and they were evaluated using two different decision matrices. Therefore, 3 decision matrices were used to determine the weights of criteria with the Entropy method and to the application of the VIKOR method. A separate ranking will be done for each decision matrix, and a ranking will be done to show the overall performance by taking the average of the S_i and R_i values. Decision matrices are given in Tables 2, 3 and 4.

Determining the Entropy Weights of Criteria

In this study, the entropy that is an objective technique for determining the weights of criteria is used. After the decision matrices are created, the weights of criteria are determined using the relevant values. The first step is to determine the characteristics of the criteria. Criteria can be benefit-specific or cost-specific. The benefit criteria are the criteria that are desired to have high values and the cost criteria are those preferred to have low values. Criteria properties are coded using max. for benefit criteria and min. for cost criteria and are given in Table 5. Standardization and normalization processes are performed

Table 2. Decision matrix of MTP

Alternatives	PS	FCP	FMP	SI	TTI	EIL
NP_1	25.2	1.8	3.4	14.8	38.7	780
NP_2	19.3	3.6	4.4	21.1	35.7	710
NP_3	25.1	3.7	4.1	7.3	19.6	740
NP_4	31.4	3.3	3.5	6.3	17.7	420
NP_5	16.2	3.7	3.7	13.1	29.8	1700
NP_6	37.6	1.3	4.4	6.1	16.7	540
NP_7	7.8	5.6	8.2	16.7	28.6	6240
NP_8	45.6	2.3	2.4	5.2	13.7	310
NP_9	19.4	3.6	3.6	10.6	23.1	1820
NP_{10}	20.4	2.9	4.3	11.8	25.9	1430
Max-Min	45.6	1.3	2.4	5.2	13.7	310

Table 3. Decision matrix of DTP

Alternatives	PS	FCP	FMP	SI	TTI	EIL
NP_1	84.4	0.6	0.8	1.4	3.4	140
NP_2	27.1	0.9	1.1	4.1	16.2	640
NP_3	79.3	0.8	1.2	1.5	4	220
NP_4	63.4	0.9	0.9	2.1	4.9	160
NP_5	29.8	0.8	0.8	4.7	12.4	250
NP_6	85.1	0.4	1.1	1.5	3.2	93
NP_7	42.3	1.3	1.1	3.2	6.1	780
NP_8	82.1	0.6	0.6	1.6	3.4	120
NP_9	17.3	2.2	2.3	3.8	7.4	560
NP_{10}	35.2	0.9	1.2	3.2	7.6	230
Max-Min	85.1	0.4	0.6	1.4	3.2	93

for the values coded according to cost and benefit characteristics. In the standardization process, the problems that may arise from the different characteristics of the criteria (max, min) and in the normalization process, the problems that might arise from having different scales are eliminated. Equation (2) and (3) are used for the standardization process, and the values obtained are given in Tables 5, 6 and 7.

Example for benefit criteria standardization: Mobile Technical Performance/PS Criteria/A_1

$$X_{11} = \frac{25.2}{45.6} = 0.5526$$

Example for cost criteria standardization: Mobile Technical Performance/FCP Criteria/ A_1

Table 4. Decision matrix of PP

Alternatives	MV	GTR	CTR	CGTR	AVD	PV	BR
NP_1	50.78	2307	64	326	4.49	4.71	51.46
NP_2	114.3	1179	42	180	9.03	5.38	43.06
NP_3	238.8	382	19	63	7.25	6.89	46.34
NP_4	358.7	243	9	39	7.29	7.08	48.54
NP_5	198.1	348	17	57	12.39	11.95	36.93
NP_6	45.95	1986	59	285	6.21	9.03	43.64
NP_7	300.2	266	13	42	3.18	8.11	42.49
NP_8	394	248	11	41	10.12	7.47	43.19
NP_9	122	699	30	109	2.24	7.96	48.89
NP_{10}	50.05	2489	73	349	5.37	6.19	41.03
Max-Min	394	243	9	39	12.39	11.95	36.93

Table 5. Standardized matrix of MTP

Alternatives	PS	FCP	FMP	SI	TTI	EIL
NP_1	0.5526	0.7222	0.7059	0.3514	0.3540	0.3974
NP_2	0.4232	0.3611	0.5455	0.2464	0.3838	0.4366
NP_3	0.5504	0.3514	0.5854	0.7123	0.6990	0.4189
NP_4	0.6886	0.3939	0.6857	0.8254	0.7740	0.7381
NP_5	0.3553	0.3514	0.6486	0.3969	0.4597	0.1824
NP_6	0.8246	1.0000	0.5455	0.8525	0.8204	0.5741
NP_7	0.1711	0.2321	0.2927	0.3114	0.4790	0.0497
NP_8	1.0000	0.5652	1.0000	1.0000	1.0000	1.0000
NP_9	0.4254	0.3611	0.6667	0.4906	0.5931	0.1703
NP_{10}	0.4474	0.4483	0.5581	0.4407	0.5290	0.2168
TOTAL	5.4386	4.7867	6.2340	5.6275	6.0919	4.1843

$$X_{12} = \frac{1.3}{1.8} = 0.7222$$

Equation (4) is used for the normalization, and normalized decision matrices are given in Tables 8, 9 and 10.

Example for scale normalization: Mobile Technical Performance/PS Criteria/ A_1

$$P_{11} = \frac{0.5526}{5.4386} = 0.1016$$

Table 6. Standardized matrix of DTP

Alternatives	PS	FCP	FMP	SI	TTI	EIL
NP_1	0.9918	0.6667	0.7500	1.0000	0.9412	0.6643
NP_2	0.3184	0.4444	0.5455	0.3415	0.1975	0.1453
NP_3	0.9318	0.5000	0.5000	0.9333	0.8000	0.4227
NP_4	0.7450	0.4444	0.6667	0.6667	0.6531	0.5813
NP_5	0.3502	0.5000	0.7500	0.2979	0.2581	0.3720
NP_6	1.0000	1.0000	0.5455	0.9333	1.0000	1.0000
NP_7	0.4971	0.3077	0.5455	0.4375	0.5246	0.1192
NP_8	0.9647	0.6667	1.0000	0.8750	0.9412	0.7750
NP_9	0.2033	0.1818	0.2609	0.3684	0.4324	0.1661
NP_{10}	0.4136	0.4444	0.5000	0.4375	0.4211	0.4043
TOTAL	6.4160	5.1562	6.0639	6.2911	6.1691	4.6502

Table 7. Standardized matrix of PP

Alternatives	MV	GTR	CTR	CGTR	AVD	PV	BR
NP_1	0.1289	0.1053	0.1406	0.1196	0.3624	0.3941	0.7176
NP_2	0.2901	0.2061	0.2143	0.2167	0.7288	0.4502	0.8576
NP_3	0.6061	0.6361	0.4737	0.6190	0.5851	0.5766	0.7969
NP_4	0.9104	1.0000	1.0000	1.0000	0.5884	0.5925	0.7608
NP_5	0.5028	0.6983	0.5294	0.6842	1.0000	1.0000	1.0000
NP_6	0.1166	0.1224	0.1525	0.1368	0.5012	0.7556	0.8462
NP_7	0.7619	0.9135	0.6923	0.9286	0.2567	0.6787	0.8691
NP_8	1.0000	0.9798	0.8182	0.9512	0.8168	0.6251	0.8551
NP_9	0.3096	0.3476	0.3000	0.3578	0.1808	0.6661	0.7554
NP_{10}	0.1270	0.0976	0.1233	0.1117	0.4334	0.5180	0.9001
TOTAL	4.7535	5.1068	4.4443	5.1257	5.4536	6.2569	8.3589

By taking the natural logarithms (ln) of normalized values, entropy values are calculated by equation (5), and ln P_{ij} values are given in Tables 11, 12, and 13.

Example of the entropy value: Mobile Technical Performance/PS Criteria/A_1

$$\ln(P_{11}) = \ln(0.1016) = -2.2866$$

P_{ij} . Ln P_{ij} values are calculated and given in Tables 14, 15, and 16.

Example for P_{ij} . Ln P_{ij}: Mobile Technical Performance/PS Criteria/ A_1

$$P_{11}x\ln(P_{11}) = 0.1016x - 2.2866 = -0.2323$$

Table 8. Normalized decision matrix of MTP

Alternatives	PS	FCP	FMP	SI	TTI	EIL
NP_1	0.1016	0.1509	0.1132	0.0624	0.0581	0.0950
NP_2	0.0778	0.0754	0.0875	0.0438	0.0630	0.1043
NP_3	0.1012	0.0734	0.0939	0.1266	0.1147	0.1001
NP_4	0.1266	0.0823	0.1100	0.1467	0.1271	0.1764
NP_5	0.0653	0.0734	0.1040	0.0705	0.0755	0.0436
NP_6	0.1516	0.2089	0.0875	0.1515	0.1347	0.1372
NP_7	0.0315	0.0485	0.0469	0.0553	0.0786	0.0119
NP_8	0.1839	0.1181	0.1604	0.1777	0.1642	0.2390
NP_9	0.0782	0.0754	0.1069	0.0872	0.0974	0.0407
NP_{10}	0.0823	0.0936	0.0895	0.0783	0.0868	0.0518

Table 9. Normalized decision matrix of DTP

Alternatives	PS	FCP	FMP	SI	TTI	EIL
NP_1	0.1546	0.1293	0.1237	0.1590	0.1526	0.1429
NP_2	0.0496	0.0862	0.0900	0.0543	0.0320	0.0312
NP_3	0.1452	0.0970	0.0825	0.1484	0.1297	0.0909
NP_4	0.1161	0.0862	0.1099	0.1060	0.1059	0.1250
NP_5	0.0546	0.0970	0.1237	0.0473	0.0418	0.0800
NP_6	0.1559	0.1939	0.0900	0.1484	0.1621	0.2150
NP_7	0.0775	0.0597	0.0900	0.0695	0.0850	0.0256
NP_8	0.1504	0.1293	0.1649	0.1391	0.1526	0.1667
NP_9	0.0317	0.0353	0.0430	0.0586	0.0701	0.0357
NP_{10}	0.0645	0.0862	0.0825	0.0695	0.0683	0.0870

Table 10. Normalized decision matrix of PP

Alternatives	MV	GTR	CTR	CGTR	AVD	PV	BR
NP_1	0.0271	0.0206	0.0316	0.0233	0.0664	0.0630	0.0859
NP_2	0.0610	0.0404	0.0482	0.0423	0.1336	0.0720	0.1026
NP_3	0.1275	0.1246	0.1066	0.1208	0.1073	0.0921	0.0953
NP_4	0.1915	0.1958	0.2250	0.1951	0.1079	0.0947	0.0910
NP_5	0.1058	0.1367	0.1191	0.1335	0.1834	0.1598	0.1196
NP_6	0.0245	0.0240	0.0343	0.0267	0.0919	0.1208	0.1012
NP_7	0.1603	0.1789	0.1558	0.1812	0.0471	0.1085	0.1040
NP_8	0.2104	0.1919	0.1841	0.1856	0.1498	0.0999	0.1023
NP_9	0.0651	0.0681	0.0675	0.0698	0.0332	0.1065	0.0904
NP_{10}	0.0267	0.0191	0.0277	0.0218	0.0795	0.0828	0.1077

Table 11. Ln P_{ij} values of MTP

Alternatives	PS	FCP	FMP	SI	TTI	EIL
NP_1	-2.2866	-1.8913	-2.1783	-2.7736	-2.8454	-2.3541
NP_2	-2.5533	-2.5844	-2.4362	-3.1283	-2.7647	-2.2600
NP_3	-2.2906	-2.6118	-2.3655	-2.0669	-2.1651	-2.3014
NP_4	-2.0666	-2.4974	-2.2073	-1.9196	-2.0631	-1.7350
NP_5	-2.7284	-2.6118	-2.2629	-2.6516	-2.5841	-3.1331
NP_6	-1.8864	-1.5658	-2.4362	-1.8873	-2.0050	-1.9863
NP_7	-3.4593	-3.0262	-3.0587	-2.8944	-2.5430	-4.4335
NP_8	-1.6935	-2.1364	-1.8300	-1.7277	-1.8070	-1.4313
NP_9	-2.5482	-2.5844	-2.2355	-2.4399	-2.3294	-3.2014
NP_{10}	-2.4979	-2.3682	-2.4132	-2.5471	-2.4438	-2.9602

Table 12. Ln P_{ij} values of DTP

Alternatives	PS	FCP	FMP	SI	TTI	EIL
NP_1	-1.8671	-2.0457	-2.0900	-1.8391	-1.8802	-1.9460
NP_2	-3.0031	-2.4511	-2.4085	-2.9136	-3.4414	-3.4658
NP_3	-1.9294	-2.3333	-2.4955	-1.9081	-2.0427	-2.3979
NP_4	-2.1532	-2.4511	-2.2078	-2.2446	-2.2456	-2.0795
NP_5	-2.9081	-2.3333	-2.0900	-3.0502	-3.1741	-2.5258
NP_6	-1.8588	-1.6402	-2.4085	-1.9081	-1.8196	-1.5369
NP_7	-2.5578	-2.8189	-2.4085	-2.6658	-2.4647	-3.6636
NP_8	-1.8947	-2.0457	-1.8024	-1.9727	-1.8802	-1.7918
NP_9	-3.4519	-3.3449	-3.1461	-2.8377	-2.6579	-3.3323
NP_{10}	-2.7416	-2.4511	-2.4955	-2.6658	-2.6845	-2.4424

Table 13. Ln P_{ij} values of PP

Alternatives	MV	GTR	CTR	CGTR	AVD	PV	BR
NP_1	-3.6077	-3.8812	-3.4533	-3.7576	-2.7113	-2.7647	-2.4551
NP_2	-2.7964	-3.2099	-3.0321	-3.1637	-2.0126	-2.6317	-2.2769
NP_3	-2.0596	-2.0829	-2.2388	-2.1138	-2.2322	-2.3843	-2.3503
NP_4	-1.6527	-1.6306	-1.4916	-1.6343	-2.2267	-2.3571	-2.3967
NP_5	-2.2465	-1.9897	-2.1276	-2.0138	-1.6963	-1.8337	-2.1233
NP_6	-3.7077	-3.7314	-3.3719	-3.6232	-2.3870	-2.1139	-2.2903
NP_7	-1.8308	-1.7210	-1.8594	-1.7084	-3.0563	-2.2213	-2.2636
NP_8	-1.5589	-1.6509	-1.6923	-1.6843	-1.8987	-2.3035	-2.2799
NP_9	-2.7312	-2.6872	-2.6956	-2.6621	-3.4067	-2.2400	-2.4039
NP_{10}	-3.6222	-3.9572	-3.5849	-3.8258	-2.5323	-2.4915	-2.2286

Table 14. P_{ij} . Ln P_{ij} values of MTP

Alternatives	PS	FCP	FMP	SI	TTI	EIL
NP_1	-0.2323	-0.2854	-0.2467	-0.1732	-0.1653	-0.2236
NP_2	-0.1987	-0.1950	-0.2132	-0.1370	-0.1742	-0.2358
NP_3	-0.2318	-0.1917	-0.2221	-0.2616	-0.2484	-0.2304
NP_4	-0.2617	-0.2055	-0.2428	-0.2815	-0.2621	-0.3061
NP_5	-0.1782	-0.1917	-0.2355	-0.1870	-0.1950	-0.1365
NP_6	-0.2860	-0.3271	-0.2132	-0.2859	-0.2700	-0.2725
NP_7	-0.1088	-0.1468	-0.1436	-0.1602	-0.2000	-0.0526
NP_8	-0.3114	-0.2523	-0.2936	-0.3070	-0.2966	-0.3421
NP_9	-0.1993	-0.1950	-0.2391	-0.2127	-0.2268	-0.1303
NP_{10}	-0.2055	-0.2218	-0.2161	-0.1995	-0.2122	-0.1534
TOTAL	-2.2138	-2.2122	-2.2656	-2.2056	-2.2506	-2.0833

Table 15. P_{ij} . Ln P_{ij} values of DTP

Alternatives	PS	FCP	FMP	SI	TTI	EIL
NP_1	-0.2886	-0.2645	-0.2585	-0.2923	-0.2868	-0.2780
NP_2	-0.1491	-0.2113	-0.2166	-0.1581	-0.1102	-0.1083
NP_3	-0.2802	-0.2263	-0.2058	-0.2831	-0.2649	-0.2180
NP_4	-0.2500	-0.2113	-0.2427	-0.2379	-0.2377	-0.2599
NP_5	-0.1587	-0.2263	-0.2585	-0.1444	-0.1328	-0.2021
NP_6	-0.2897	-0.3181	-0.2166	-0.2831	-0.2949	-0.3305
NP_7	-0.1982	-0.1682	-0.2166	-0.1854	-0.2096	-0.0939
NP_8	-0.2849	-0.2645	-0.2972	-0.2744	-0.2868	-0.2986
NP_9	-0.1094	-0.1180	-0.1353	-0.1662	-0.1863	-0.1190
NP_{10}	-0.1767	-0.2113	-0.2058	-0.1854	-0.1832	-0.2124
TOTAL	-2.1855	-2.2196	-2.2538	-2.2103	-2.1933	-2.1207

Entropy values are obtained by equation (5). The degree of divergence using entropy values are calculated by equation (6) finally, the degree of divergence of each criterion is divided by the sum of the degree of divergence, the entropy weights are calculated using equation (7), and entropy values, divergence values, and importance weights for each criterion are summarized in Table 17.

Example for entropy weight: PS Criteria

$k = 1/\ln 10 = 1/2.302585 = 0.4343$

$E_1 = -0.4343 \text{ x } (-2.2138) = 0.9614$

$1 - E_1 = 1 - 0.9614 = 0.0386$

Table 16. P_{ij} . Ln P_{ij} values of PP

Alternatives	MV	GTR	CTR	CGTR	AVD	PV	BR
NP_1	-0.0978	-0.0801	-0.1093	-0.0877	-0.1802	-0.1742	-0.2108
NP_2	-0.1707	-0.1295	-0.1462	-0.1337	-0.2690	-0.1894	-0.2336
NP_3	-0.2626	-0.2595	-0.2386	-0.2553	-0.2395	-0.2197	-0.2241
NP_4	-0.3165	-0.3193	-0.3356	-0.3188	-0.2402	-0.2232	-0.2181
NP_5	-0.2376	-0.2721	-0.2534	-0.2688	-0.3110	-0.2931	-0.2540
NP_6	-0.0910	-0.0894	-0.1157	-0.0967	-0.2194	-0.2553	-0.2319
NP_7	-0.2935	-0.3079	-0.2896	-0.3095	-0.1438	-0.2409	-0.2354
NP_8	-0.3279	-0.3168	-0.3115	-0.3126	-0.2844	-0.2301	-0.2332
NP_9	-0.1779	-0.1829	-0.1820	-0.1858	-0.1129	-0.2385	-0.2172
NP_{10}	-0.0968	-0.0757	-0.0994	-0.0834	-0.2013	-0.2063	-0.2400
TOTAL	-2.0723	-2.0330	-2.0815	-2.0524	-2.2017	-2.2706	-2.2983

Table 17. Entropy weights of mobile, desktop and popularity performance criteria

Mobile Performance								
	PS	FCP	FMP	SI	TTI	EIL		
E_j	0.9614	0.9607	0.9839	0.9579	0.9774	0.9048		Total
$1-E_j$	0.0386	0.0393	0.0161	0.0421	0.0226	0.0952		0.2538
w_j	0.1520	0.1547	0.0633	0.1660	0.0889	0.3751		
Desktop Performance								
	PS	FCP	FMP	SI	TTI	EIL		
E_j	0.9492	0.9640	0.9788	0.9599	0.9526	0.9210		Total
$1-E_j$	0.0508	0.0360	0.0212	0.0401	0.0474	0.0790		0.2746
w_j	0.1852	0.1312	0.0772	0.1460	0.1728	0.2877		
Popularity Performance								
	MV	GTR	CTR	CGTR	AVD	PV	BR	
E_j	0.9000	0.8829	0.9040	0.8913	0.9562	0.9861	0.9981	Total
$1-E_j$	0.1000	0.1171	0.0960	0.1087	0.0438	0.0139	0.0019	0.4814
w_j	0.2078	0.2432	0.1995	0.2257	0.0911	0.0289	0.0039	

$$w_1 = \frac{0.0386}{0.2538} = 0.1520$$

Evaluation of The Website Alternatives By VIKOR Method

Step by step analysis and evaluation of the newspapers' website alternatives by VIKOR method are given below:

1. **Determining the best and the worst vales of criteria:** By using equation (9) and equation (10), the best and worst values for the criteria are determined. While the best value for the criteria with benefit characteristic is maximum, and the worst value is minimum, the opposite is the case for the criteria with cost characteristics. Decision matrices, the best and worst values are given in Tables 18, 19 and 20.
2. **Constructing the normalized decision matrix:** With the help of equation (11), the values in the decision matrix are normalized by normalization process in order to eliminate the problems that may arise from the unit differences and to make them comparable, and the decision matrices were constructed and given in Tables 21, 22, and 23.

Example calculation for normalization process: Mobile Technical Performance/PS Criteria/ A_1

$$r_{11} = \frac{45.6 - 25.2}{37.8} = 0.5397$$

3. **Constructing the weighted normalized decision matrix:** By using the weights of criteria obtained with Entropy, equation (12) is applied, and weighted normalized decision matrices are constructed, and they are given in Tables 24, 25, and 26.

Example for weighting process: Mobile Technical Performance/PS Criteria/ A_1

$$r_{11} \times w_1 = 0.5397 \times 0.1520 = 0.0820$$

Table 18. Decision matrix, the best and the worst values of mobile performance criteria

Alternatives	PS	FCP	FMP	SI	TTI	EIL
NP_1	25.2	1.8	3.4	14.8	38.7	780
NP_2	19.3	3.6	4.4	21.1	35.7	710
NP_3	25.1	3.7	4.1	7.3	19.6	740
NP_4	31.4	3.3	3.5	6.3	17.7	420
NP_5	16.2	3.7	3.7	13.1	29.8	1700
NP_6	37.6	1.3	4.4	6.1	16.7	540
NP_7	7.8	5.6	8.2	16.7	28.6	6240
NP_8	45.6	2.3	2.4	5.2	13.7	310
NP_9	19.4	3.6	3.6	10.6	23.1	1820
NP_{10}	20.4	2.9	4.3	11.8	25.9	1430
Best f_j^*	45.6	1.3	2.4	5.2	13.7	310
Worst f_j^-	7.8	5.6	8.2	21.1	35.7	6240
$f_j^* - f_j^-$	37.8	-4.3	-5.8	-15.9	-22	-5930

Table 19. Decision matrix, the best and the worst values of desktop performance criteria

Alternatives	PS	FCP	FMP	SI	TTI	EIL
NP_1	84.4	0.6	0.8	1.4	3.4	140
NP_2	27.1	0.9	1.1	4.1	16.2	640
NP_3	79.3	0.8	1.2	1.5	4	220
NP_4	63.4	0.9	0.9	2.1	4.9	160
NP_5	29.8	0.8	0.8	4.7	12.4	250
NP_6	85.1	0.4	1.1	1.5	3.2	93
NP_7	42.3	1.3	1.1	3.2	6.1	780
NP_8	82.1	0.6	0.6	1.6	3.4	120
NP_9	17.3	2.2	2.3	3.8	7.4	560
NP_{10}	35.2	0.9	1.2	3.2	7.6	230
Best f_j^*	85.1	0.4	0.6	1.4	3.2	93
Worst f_j^-	17.3	2.2	2.3	4.7	16.2	780
$f_j^* - f_j^-$	67.8	-1.8	-1.7	-3.3	-13	-687

Table 20. Decision matrix, the best and the worst values of popularity performance criteria

Alternatives	MV	GTR	CTR	CGTR	AVD	PV	BR
NP_1	50.78	2307	64	326	4.49	4.71	51.46
NP_2	114.3	1179	42	180	9.03	5.38	43.06
NP_3	238.8	382	19	63	7.25	6.89	46.34
NP_4	358.7	243	9	39	7.29	7.08	48.54
NP_5	198.1	348	17	57	12.39	11.95	36.93
NP_6	45.95	1986	59	285	6.21	9.03	43.64
NP_7	300.2	266	13	42	3.18	8.11	42.49
NP_8	394	248	11	41	10.12	7.47	43.19
NP_9	122	699	30	109	2.24	7.96	48.89
NP_{10}	50.05	2489	73	349	5.37	6.19	41.03
Best f_j^*	394	243	9	39	12.39	11.95	36.93
Worst f_j^-	45.95	2489	73	349	2.24	4.71	51.46
$f_j^* - f_j^-$	348.05	-2246	-64	-310	10.15	7.24	-14.53

4. **Calculation of S_i and R_i values:** For each alternative, S_i and R_i values are calculated using equation (13) and (14).

   Example for S_i and R_i values: A_1

$$S_1 = 0.0820 + 0.0180 + 0.0109 + 0.1002 + 0.1010 + 0.0297 = 0.3419$$

Table 21. Normalized decision MTP

Alternatives	PS	FCP	FMP	SI	TTI	EIL
NP_1	0.5397	0.1163	0.1724	0.6038	1.1364	0.0793
NP_2	0.6958	0.5349	0.3448	1.0000	1.0000	0.0675
NP_3	0.5423	0.5581	0.2931	0.1321	0.2682	0.0725
NP_4	0.3757	0.4651	0.1897	0.0692	0.1818	0.0185
NP_5	0.7778	0.5581	0.2241	0.4969	0.7318	0.2344
NP_6	0.2116	0.0000	0.3448	0.0566	0.1364	0.0388
NP_7	1.0000	1.0000	1.0000	0.7233	0.6773	1.0000
NP_8	0.0000	0.2326	0.0000	0.0000	0.0000	0.0000
NP_9	0.6931	0.5349	0.2069	0.3396	0.4273	0.2546
NP_{10}	0.6667	0.3721	0.3276	0.4151	0.5545	0.1889
w_j	0.1520	0.1547	0.0633	0.1660	0.0889	0.3751

Table 22. Normalized decision matrix for DTP

Alternatives	PS	FCP	FMP	SI	TTI	EIL
NP_1	0.0103	0.1111	0.1176	0.0000	0.0154	0.0684
NP_2	0.8555	0.2778	0.2941	0.8182	1.0000	0.7962
NP_3	0.0855	0.2222	0.3529	0.0303	0.0615	0.1849
NP_4	0.3201	0.2778	0.1765	0.2121	0.1308	0.0975
NP_5	0.8156	0.2222	0.1176	1.0000	0.7077	0.2285
NP_6	0.0000	0.0000	0.2941	0.0303	0.0000	0.0000
NP_7	0.6313	0.5000	0.2941	0.5455	0.2231	1.0000
NP_8	0.0442	0.1111	0.0000	0.0606	0.0154	0.0393
NP_9	1.0000	1.0000	1.0000	0.7273	0.3231	0.6798
NP_{10}	0.7360	0.2778	0.3529	0.5455	0.3385	0.1994
w_j	0.1852	0.1312	0.0772	0.1460	0.1728	0.2877

R_1 = Maximum (0.0820; 0.0180; 0.0109; 0.1002; 0.1010; 0.0297) = 0.1010

5. **Calculation of Q_i values:** By using equation (11), Q_i values are calculated for different q parameters (0; 0.25; 0.50; 0.75; 1). The calculated S_i, R_i and Q_i values for each alternative are given in Table 27, 28, 29 and 30.

Example for Q_i values: A_1/ v = 0.5

S^* = Minimum S_i = 0.0360 R^* = Minimum R_i = 0.0322

S^- = Maximum S_i = 0.8894 R^- = Maximum R_i = 0.3751

Table 23. Normalized decision matrix for PP

Alternatives	MV	GTR	CTR	CGTR	AVD	PV	BR
NP_1	0.9861	0.9190	0.8594	0.9258	0.7783	1.0000	1.0000
NP_2	0.8036	0.4167	0.5156	0.4548	0.3310	0.9075	0.4219
NP_3	0.4459	0.0619	0.1563	0.0774	0.5064	0.6989	0.6476
NP_4	0.1014	0.0000	0.0000	0.0000	0.5025	0.6727	0.7990
NP_5	0.5629	0.0467	0.1250	0.0581	0.0000	0.0000	0.0000
NP_6	1.0000	0.7760	0.7813	0.7935	0.6089	0.4033	0.4618
NP_7	0.2695	0.0102	0.0625	0.0097	0.9074	0.5304	0.3827
NP_8	0.0000	0.0022	0.0313	0.0065	0.2236	0.6188	0.4308
NP_9	0.7815	0.2030	0.3281	0.2258	1.0000	0.5511	0.8231
NP_{10}	0.9882	1.0000	1.0000	1.0000	0.6916	0.7956	0.2822
w_j	0.2078	0.2432	0.1995	0.2257	0.0911	0.0289	0.0039

Table 24. Weighted normalized decision MTP

Alternatives	PS	FCP	FMP	SI	TTI	EIL
NP_1	0.0820	0.0180	0.0109	0.1002	0.1010	0.0297
NP_2	0.1057	0.0827	0.0218	0.1660	0.0889	0.0253
NP_3	0.0824	0.0863	0.0185	0.0219	0.0238	0.0272
NP_4	0.0571	0.0719	0.0120	0.0115	0.0162	0.0070
NP_5	0.1182	0.0863	0.0142	0.0825	0.0651	0.0879
NP_6	0.0322	0.0000	0.0218	0.0094	0.0121	0.0145
NP_7	0.1520	0.1547	0.0633	0.1201	0.0602	0.3751
NP_8	0.0000	0.0360	0.0000	0.0000	0.0000	0.0000
NP_9	0.1053	0.0827	0.0131	0.0564	0.0380	0.0955
NP_{10}	0.1013	0.0576	0.0207	0.0689	0.0493	0.0709

Table 25. Weighted normalized DTP

Alternatives	PS	FCP	FMP	SI	TTI	EIL
NP_1	0.0019	0.0146	0.0091	0.0000	0.0027	0.0197
NP_2	0.1584	0.0364	0.0227	0.1195	0.1728	0.2291
NP_3	0.0158	0.0292	0.0272	0.0044	0.0106	0.0532
NP_4	0.0593	0.0364	0.0136	0.0310	0.0226	0.0281
NP_5	0.1510	0.0292	0.0091	0.1460	0.1223	0.0657
NP_6	0.0000	0.0000	0.0227	0.0044	0.0000	0.0000
NP_7	0.1169	0.0656	0.0227	0.0796	0.0385	0.2877
NP_8	0.0082	0.0146	0.0000	0.0088	0.0027	0.0113
NP_9	0.1852	0.1312	0.0772	0.1062	0.0558	0.1956
NP_{10}	0.1363	0.0364	0.0272	0.0796	0.0585	0.0574

Table 26. Weighted normalized decision matrix for popularity performance

Alternatives	MV	GTR	CTR	CGTR	AVD	PV	BR
NP_1	0.2049	0.2235	0.1714	0.2090	0.0709	0.0289	0.0039
NP_2	0.1670	0.1014	0.1029	0.1027	0.0301	0.0262	0.0016
NP_3	0.0926	0.0151	0.0312	0.0175	0.0461	0.0202	0.0025
NP_4	0.0211	0.0000	0.0000	0.0000	0.0458	0.0194	0.0031
NP_5	0.1169	0.0114	0.0249	0.0131	0.0000	0.0000	0.0000
NP_6	0.2078	0.1887	0.1559	0.1791	0.0554	0.0116	0.0018
NP_7	0.0560	0.0025	0.0125	0.0022	0.0826	0.0153	0.0015
NP_8	0.0000	0.0005	0.0062	0.0015	0.0204	0.0179	0.0017
NP_9	0.1624	0.0494	0.0655	0.0510	0.0911	0.0159	0.0032
NP_{10}	0.2053	0.2432	0.1995	0.2257	0.0630	0.0230	0.0011

Table 27. S_i, R_i and Q_i values for MTP

Alternatives	S_i	R_i	Q_i	Q_i	Q_i	Q_i	Q_i
			v = 0	v = 0.25	v = 0.5	v = 0.75	v = 1
NP_1	0.3419	0.1010	0.2008	0.2366	0.2724	0.3082	0.3440
NP_2	0.4905	0.1660	0.3903	0.4205	0.4507	0.4809	0.5111
NP_3	0.2603	0.0863	0.1580	0.1815	0.2051	0.2286	0.2522
NP_4	0.1756	0.0719	0.1160	0.1263	0.1365	0.1468	0.1570
NP_5	0.4542	0.1182	0.2509	0.3057	0.3606	0.4154	0.4702
NP_6	0.0901	0.0322	0.0000	0.0152	0.0304	0.0456	0.0608
NP_7	0.9254	0.3751	1.0000	1.0000	1.0000	1.0000	1.0000
NP_8	0.0360	0.0360	0.0111	0.0083	0.0056	0.0028	0.0000
NP_9	0.3911	0.1053	0.2133	0.2598	0.3063	0.3528	0.3993
NP_{10}	0.3687	0.1013	0.2016	0.2447	0.2878	0.3310	0.3741
S^*	0.0360	R^*	0.0322				
S^-	0.9254	R^-	0.3751				
$S^- - S^*$	0.8894	$R^- - R^*$	0.3430				

$$Q_{1(v=0.5)} = \frac{0.5(0.3419-0.0360)}{0.8894} + \frac{(1-0.5)(0.1010-0.0322)}{0.3430} = 0.2724$$

6. **Checking the acceptable advantage and acceptable stability conditions:** S_i, R_i, and Q_i (v = 0.5) values are ranked from smallest to largest. After ranking, whether the alternative with the minimum Q_i value provided acceptable advantage and acceptable stability conditions are checked the ranking in order to test the accuracy of the ranking. The rankings are shown in Table 31, and acceptable advantage and stability conditions are shown in Table 32.

Table 28. S_i, R_i and Q_i values for desktop performance

Alternatives	S_i	R_i	Q_i	Q_i	Q_i	Q_i	Q_i
			v = 0	v = 0.25	v = 0.5	v = 0.75	v = 1
NP_1	0.0479	0.0197	0.0187	0.0212	0.0237	0.0262	0.0287
NP_2	0.7388	0.2291	0.7853	0.8348	0.8842	0.9336	0.9830
NP_3	0.1405	0.0532	0.1414	0.1452	0.1490	0.1528	0.1566
NP_4	0.1909	0.0593	0.1636	0.1793	0.1949	0.2106	0.2263
NP_5	0.5233	0.1510	0.4996	0.5460	0.5924	0.6389	0.6853
NP_6	0.0271	0.0227	0.0298	0.0223	0.0149	0.0074	0.0000
NP_7	0.6111	0.2877	1.0000	0.9516	0.9033	0.8549	0.8065
NP_8	0.0456	0.0146	0.0000	0.0064	0.0127	0.0191	0.0255
NP_9	0.7511	0.1956	0.6627	0.7470	0.8313	0.9157	1.0000
NP_{10}	0.3954	0.1363	0.4456	0.4614	0.4772	0.4929	0.5087
S*	0.0271	R*	0.0146				
S^-	0.7511	R^-	0.2877				
$S^- - S^*$	0.7240	$R^- - R^*$	0.2731				

Table 29. S_i, R_i and Q_i values for popularity performance

Alternatives	S_i	R_i	Q_i	Q_i	Q_i	Q_i	Q_i
			v = 0	v = 0.25	v = 0.5	v = 0.75	v = 1
NP_1	0.9124	0.2235	0.9116	0.9204	0.9293	0.9381	0.9470
NP_2	0.5318	0.1670	0.6578	0.6259	0.5939	0.5619	0.5300
NP_3	0.2251	0.0926	0.3243	0.2917	0.2591	0.2265	0.1939
NP_4	0.0893	0.0458	0.1139	0.0967	0.0795	0.0623	0.0452
NP_5	0.1664	0.1169	0.4334	0.3574	0.2814	0.2055	0.1295
NP_6	0.8004	0.2078	0.8409	0.8367	0.8326	0.8284	0.8242
NP_7	0.1725	0.0826	0.2794	0.2436	0.2079	0.1721	0.1363
NP_8	0.0481	0.0204	0.0000	0.0000	0.0000	0.0000	0.0000
NP_9	0.4383	0.1624	0.6372	0.5848	0.5324	0.4800	0.4275
NP_{10}	0.9608	0.2432	1.0000	1.0000	1.0000	1.0000	1.0000
S*	0.0481	R*	0.0204				
S^-	0.9608	R^-	0.2432				
$S^- - S^*$	0.9127	$R^- - R^*$	0.2228				

Table 30. S_i, R_i and Q_i values for overall performance

Alternatives	S_i	R_i	Q_i	Q_i	Q_i	Q_i	Q_i
			v = 0	v = 0.25	v = 0.5	v = 0.75	v = 1
NP_1	0.4341	0.1147	0.4052	0.4836	0.5619	0.6403	0.7187
NP_2	0.5871	0.1873	0.7281	0.7961	0.8640	0.9320	1.0000
NP_3	0.2086	0.0774	0.2390	0.2553	0.2716	0.2879	0.3041
NP_4	0.1520	0.0590	0.1572	0.1679	0.1786	0.1893	0.2000
NP_5	0.3813	0.1287	0.4673	0.5059	0.5445	0.5830	0.6216
NP_6	0.3058	0.0875	0.2842	0.3339	0.3836	0.4332	0.4829
NP_7	0.5697	0.2485	1.0000	0.9920	0.9840	0.9760	0.9680
NP_8	0.0432	0.0236	0.0000	0.0000	0.0000	0.0000	0.0000
NP_9	0.5268	0.1544	0.5817	0.6586	0.7355	0.8124	0.8893
NP_{10}	0.5750	0.1603	0.6076	0.7002	0.7927	0.8852	0.9778
S*	0.0432	R*	0.0236				
S^-	0.5871	R^-	0.2485				
$S^- - S^*$	0.5438	$R^- - R^*$	0.2248				

Table 31. Rankings of each criterion and overall performance

Alternatives	Mobile Technical Performance			Desktop Technical Performance			Popularity Performance			Overall Performance		
	S_i	R_i	Q_i	S_i	R_i	Q_i	S_i	R_i	Q_i	S_i	R_i	Q_i
NP_1	5	5	5	3	2	3	9	9	9	6	5	6
NP_2	9	9	9	9	9	9	7	7	7	10	9	9
NP_3	4	4	4	4	4	4	5	4	4	3	3	3
NP_4	3	3	3	5	5	5	2	2	2	2	2	2
NP_5	8	8	8	7	7	7	3	5	5	5	6	5
NP_6	2	1	2	1	3	2	8	8	8	4	4	4
NP_7	10	10	10	8	10	10	4	3	3	8	10	10
NP_8	1	2	1	2	1	1	1	1	1	1	1	1
NP_9	7	7	7	10	8	8	6	6	6	7	7	7
NP_{10}	6	6	6	6	6	6	10	10	10	9	8	8

Acceptable advantage conditions are tested and shown below:

Mobile Technical Performance Scores:

$Q(A^{2th}) - Q(A^{1th}) = 0.0304 - 0.0056 = 0.0248 < 0.1111$ Not-satisfied.

Desktop Technical Performance Scores:

$Q(A^{2th}) - Q(A^{1th}) = 0.0149 - 0.0127 = 0.0021 < 0.1111$ Not-satisfied.

Table 32. Acceptable advantage and stability conditions

	Mobile Technical Performance	Desktop Technical Performance	Popularity Performance	Overall Performance
$Q(A^{2th})$	0.0304 (NP_6)	0.0149 (NP_6)	0.0795 (NP_4)	0.1786 (NP_4)
$Q(A^{1th})$	0.0056 (NP_8)	0.0127 (NP_8)	0.0000 (NP_8)	0.0000 (NP_8)
$Q(A^{2th})$-$Q(A^{1th})$	0.0248	0.0021	0.0795	0.1786
DQ(1/m-1)	0.1111	0.1111	0.1111	0.1111
1. Condition	Not-Satisfied	Not-Satisfied	Not-Satisfied	Satisfied
2. Condition	Satisfied	Not-Satisfied	Satisfied	Satisfied

Popularity Performance Scores:

$Q(A^{2th}) - Q(A^{1th}) = 0.0795 - 0 = 0.0795 < 0.1111$ Not-satisfied.

Overall Performance Scores:

$Q(A^{2th}) - Q(A^{1th}) = 0.1786 - 0 = 0.1786 > 0.1111$ Satisfied.

C1 and C2 conditions are only satisfied for overall performance evaluation, and A_8 has the best popularity performance.

C1 condition is not satisfied for the technical and popularity performances. Compromise solutions will be proposed, and they are determined by the relation $Q(A^{(m)}) - Q(A^{(1)})<DQ$

Mobile Technical Performance:

$Q(A^{2th}) - Q(A^{1th}) = 0.0304 - 0.0056 = 0.0248 < 0.1111$

$Q(A^{3th}) - Q(A^{1th}) = 0.1949 - 0.0056 = 0.1893 > 0.1111$

As the results of the calculation, the compromise solution set of mobile technical performance consists of A_8 and A_6.

Desktop Technical Performance:

$Q(A^{2th}) - Q(A^{1th}) = 0.0149 - 0.0127 = 0.0022 < 0.1111$

$Q(A^{3th}) - Q(A^{1th}) = 0.0237 - 0.0127 = 0.011 < 0.1111$

$Q(A^{4th}) - Q(A^{1th}) = 0.1490 - 0.0127 = 0.2079 > 0.1111$

The compromise solution set of desktop technical performance consists of A_8, A_6 and A_1.

$Q(A^{2th}) - Q(A^{1th}) = 0.0795 - 0 = 0.0795 < 0.1111$

$Q(A^{3th}) - Q(A^{1th}) = 0.2079 - 0 = 0.2079 > 0.1111$

The compromise solution set of popularity performance consists of A_8 and A_4.

RESEARCH DIFFICULTIES AND GAPS

When the subject of the study was decided, the speed and performance criteria used by Google PageSpeed Insight were presented in a different format. After collecting data for over 15 days, it was seen that the criteria had changed, and performance evaluation was performed with different measures. Therefore, the collected data have become unusable, and data collection was performed again. The biggest problem in the study was the instant changing in performance data. Therefore, this problem was tried to eliminate this problem by using average values. In the application stage of the VIKOR method, it was seen that the acceptable advantage condition was not satisfied due to the fact that the values of some criteria were very close to each other. But since the VIKOR method provides compromised solutions, a set of best solutions has been proposed.

Since an objective criteria weighting method was used in the study, the preferences of decision-makers were ignored, and the subjective judgments were not included. If the subjective judgments of decision-makers were used, different criteria could be added to the assessment.

FUTURE RESEARCH DIRECTIONS

For further studies, other MCDM methods which can perform objective or subjective measurements can be used to evaluate the performance of newspaper websites and to determine benchmark weights. The subjective judgments of decision-makers can be compared by being included in the decision process. The criteria which can be expressed in numbers both subjectively and objectively can be evaluated together. For subjective evaluations, criteria weights and performances can be calculated using fuzzy MCDM methods.

CONCLUSION

The main objective of this study is to analyze the technical and popularity performances of Turkish newspapers with an integrated MCDM method which includes Entropy and VIKOR methods. An objective weighting method is used to calculate the weights of criteria and the results of performances are determined by the VIKOR method. VIKOR is applied to determine the compromise solution of a MCDM problem with respect to conflicting criteria, rank, and select among possible alternatives.

When the decision matrices are examined, it can be said that the technical performances of all newspaper mobile websites are poor. Technically, the most important area that needs to be emphasized and improved is the performance of mobile websites. Although desktop technical performances are generally good, many of them need to be improved. Google PSI recommends several improvements that are generally required to enhance both mobile and desktop technical performances. Prominent improvements are uploading images of the right size, publishing the images in the right formats, using the images efficiently, enabling text compression, avoiding huge network loads, and editing fonts. Such measures will increase the speed and performance of the website. Popularity performances vary depending on the principles of journalism such as the fact that the news published is interesting, accurate and reliable. Therefore, it is possible to increase the number of users and the time spent on the website by improving the visual and content features.

Objective weights of criteria can be obtained from objective weighting methods like Entropy. Objective weights of criteria have no relationship with the subjective preferences of decision-makers'. When the objective importance weights found with Entropy are reviewed, it is determined that the criterion which has the highest importance weight is EIL and the criterion which has the lowest importance weight is FMP among the mobile technical performance criteria. This is the same for desktop technical performance criteria. Among the popularity performance criteria, while the highest importance weight is given to GTR, the lowest importance weight is given to BR.

According to the VIKOR method, among the rankings, only the overall performance ranking satisfied acceptable advantage and stability conditions together. Thus, in terms of overall performance, the NP_8 alternative has the best performance. In the evaluation made in terms of mobile technical performance, a compromise solution can be proposed since acceptable advantage condition isn't satisfied. NP_8 and NP_6 are the best alternatives in the compromise solution set. In the evaluation of desktop technical performance, it is seen that neither of the conditions is satisfied. Here, the compromise solution set consists of NP_8, NP_6 and NP_1. According to the evaluation with respect to popularity performance, whereas the acceptable advantage condition is not satisfied, the condition of stability is satisfied. The compromise solution set is composed of NP_8 and NP_4. Failure to meet acceptable advantage conditions is due to the fact that the differences between the best alternatives are not large enough. Although NP_8 alternative takes the first place in all rankings, since the acceptable alternative conditions are not satisfied, compromise solutions are proposed.

Entropy-based VIKOR method is a MCDM method that can be used in cases where subjective judgments of decision-makers are not available and the values of the criteria to be used are real numbers. The most important advantage of the VIKOR method is that it can provide compromised solutions when the ranking values are close to each other. With these features, it can provide researchers and practitioners a solution when they encounter these kinds of problems.

REFERENCES

Akıncılar, A., & Dağdeviren, M. (2014). A hybrid multi-criteria decision-making model to evaluate hotel websites. *International Journal of Hospitality Management*, *36*, 263–271. doi:10.1016/j.ijhm.2013.10.002

Apan, M., Öztel, A., & İslamoğlu, M. (2018). Comparative empirical analysis of financial failures of enterprises with Altman z-score and VIKOR methods: BIST food sector application. *AABFJ*, *12*(1), 77–101. doi:10.14453/aabfj.v12i1.6

Arce, M. E., Saavedra, A., Míguez, J. L., & Granada, E. (2015). The use of grey-based methods in multi-criteria decision analysis for the evaluation of sustainable energy systems: A review. *Renewable & Sustainable Energy Reviews*, *47*, 924–932. doi:10.1016/j.rser.2015.03.010

Büyüközkan, G., & Güleryüz, S. (2016). Lojistik firma web sitelerinin performanslarının çok kriterli değerlendirilmesi. *Journal of the Faculty of Engineering and Architecture of Gazi University*, *31*(4), 889–902.

Çebi, S. (2013). A quality evaluation model for the design quality of online shopping websites. *Electronic Commerce Research and Applications*, *12*(2), 124–135. doi:10.1016/j.elerap.2012.12.001

Çelebi Demirarslan, P., Küçükönder, H., & Kıngır, S. (2019). Entropi tabanlı TOPSIS ve VIKOR yaklaşımı ile akademisyenler üzerinde duygusal performans değerlendirme: Bartın örneği. *Elektronik Sosyal Bilimler Dergisi, 18*(69), 232–251.

Chou, W. C., & Cheng, Y. P. (2012). A hybrid fuzzy MCDM approach for evaluating website quality of Professional accounting firms. *Expert Systems with Applications, 39*(3), 2783–2793. doi:10.1016/j.eswa.2011.08.138

Chung, Y. F., Liu, S. H., Wang, C.H. & Pang, C. T. (2015). Applying fuzzy MCDM methods to the evaluation on portal website service quality. *The SIJ Transactions on Computer Science Engineering & its Applications (CSEA), 3*(1), 8-15.

Durmuş, M., & Tayyar, N. (2017). AHP ve TOPSIS ile farklı kriter ağırlıklandırma yöntemlerinin kullanılması ve karar verici görüşleriyle karşılaştırılması. *Eskişehir Osmangazi Üniversitesi İİBF Dergisi, 12*(3), 65–80.

El-Santawy, M. F. (2012). A VIKOR method for solving personnel training selection problem. *International Journal of Computational Science, 1*(2), 9–12.

Gök-kısa, A. C., & Perçin, S. (2018). Bütünleşik entropi ağırlık-VIKOR yöntemi ile bilişim teknolojisi sektöründe performans ölçümü. *Ekonomik ve Sosyal Araştırmalar Dergisi, 14*(1), 1–13.

Google PageSpeed Insights (PSI). (2019). *About PageSpeed Insights.* Retrieved from https://developers.google.com/speed/docs/insights/v5/about?hl=trTR&utm_source=PSI&utm_medium=incoming-link&utm_campaign=PSI

Gürcan, H. İ. (2003). Haber sitelerinde içerik ve tasarıma yönelik değerlendirme ölçütlerine bir yaklaşım. *Selçuk İletişim Dergisi, 2*(4), 90–99.

Kabak, M., Özceylan, E., Dağdeviren, M., & Genç, T. (2017). Evaluation of distance education websites: A hybrid multicriteria approach. *Turkish Journal of Electrical Engineering and Computer Sciences, 25*, 2809–2819. doi:10.3906/elk-1512-271

Lee, C. C., & Tseng, H. C. (2018). Integrating fuzzy membership function, entropy method and VIKOR to select qualified and stable employee. *2018 International Conference on Information Management and Processing* (vol. 1, pp. 26-31). Global: IEEE Press. 10.1109/ICIMP1.2018.8325836

Li, X., Wang, K., Liu, L., Xin, J., Yang, H., & Gao, C. (2011). Application of the entropy weight and TOPSIS method in safety evaluation of coal mines. *Procedia Engineering, 26*, 2085–2091. doi:10.1016/j.proeng.2011.11.2410

Malekian, A., & Azarnivand, A. (2016). Application of integrated Shannon's entropy and VIKOR techniques in prioritization of flood risk in the Shemshak Watershed, Iran. *Water Resources Management, 30*(1), 409–425. doi:10.100711269-015-1169-6

Mohsen, O., & Fereshteh, N. (2017). An extended VIKOR method based on entropy measure for the failure modes risk assessment – A case study of the geothermal power plant (GPP). *Safety Science, 92*, 160–172. doi:10.1016/j.ssci.2016.10.006

Ömürbek, N., Eren, H., & Dağ, O. (2017). Entropi-Aras ve Entropi-Moosra yöntemleri ile yaşam kalitesi açısından AB ülkelerinin değerlendirilmesi. *Ömer Halisdemir Üniversitesi İktisadi ve İdari Bilimler Fakültesi Dergisi, 10*(2), 29-48.

Opricovic, S. (1998). *Multi-criteria optimization of civil engineering systems*. Belgrade, Serbia: Faculty of Civil Engineering.

Opricovic, S., & Tzeng, G. H. (2004). Compromise solution by MCDM methods: A comparative analysis of VIKOR and TOPSIS. *European Journal of Operational Research, 156*(2), 445–455. doi:10.1016/S0377-2217(03)00020-1

Opricovic, S., & Tzeng, G. H. (2007). Extended VIKOR method in comparison with outranking methods. *European Journal of Operational Research, 178*(2), 514–529. doi:10.1016/j.ejor.2006.01.020

Rao, D. A., Sai, V. N., & Babu, K. P. (2017). An Integrated approach using VIKOR and Entropy methods for a Supplier selection problem. [IJIET]. *International Journal of Innovations in Engineering and Technology, 8*(3), 1–9.

Shannon, E. (1948). A mathematical theory of communication. *The Bell System Technical Journal, 27*(3), 379–423. doi:10.1002/j.1538-7305.1948.tb01338.x

Shemshadi, A., Shirazi, H., Toreihi, M., & Tarokh, M. J. (2011). A fuzzy VIKOR method for supplier selection based on entropy measure for objective weighting. *Expert Systems with Applications, 38*(10), 12160–12167. doi:10.1016/j.eswa.2011.03.027

SimilarWeb. (2019). Retrieved from https://www.similarweb.com/website/

Wang, J. J., Jing, Y. Y., Zhang, C. F., & Zhao, J. H. (2009). Review on multi-criteria decision analysis aid in sustainable energy decision-making. *Renewable & Sustainable Energy Reviews, 13*(9), 2263–2278. doi:10.1016/j.rser.2009.06.021

Wang, T. C., & Lee, H. D. (2009). Developing a fuzzy TOPSIS approach based on subjective weights and objective weights. *Expert Systems with Applications, 36*(5), 8980–8985. doi:10.1016/j.eswa.2008.11.035

Wu, J., Sun, J., Liang, L., & Zha, Y. (2011). Determination of weights for ultimate cross efficiency using Shannon Entropy. *Expert Systems with Applications, 38*(5), 5162–5165. doi:10.1016/j.eswa.2010.10.046

Yalçın, N., & Ünlü, U. (2018). A multi-criteria performance analysis of initial public offering (IPO) firms using CRITIC and VIKOR methods. *Technological and Economic Development of Economy, 24*(2), 534–560. doi:10.3846/20294913.2016.1213201

Yin, P. Y., & Guo, Y. M. (2013). Optimization of multi-criteria website structure based on enhanced tabu search and web usage mining. *Applied Mathematics and Computation, 219*(24), 11082–11095. doi:10.1016/j.amc.2013.05.033

Yu, P. L. (1973). A class of solutions for group decision problems. *Management Science, 19*(8), 936–946. doi:10.1287/mnsc.19.8.936

Zeleny, M. (1982). *Multiple criteria decision making*. New York: McGraw-Hill.

ADDITIONAL READING

Abdullah, R., & Wei, K. T. (2008). Usability Measurement of Malaysia Online News Websites. *International Journal of Computer Science and Network Security*, *8*(5), 159–166.

Alp, İ., Öztel, A., & Köse, M. S. (2015). Entropi tabanlı maut yöntemi ile kurumsal sürdürülebilirlik performansı ölçümü: Bir vaka çalışması. *Ekonomik ve Sosyal Araştırmalar Dergisi*, *11*(2), 65–81.

Bahry, F. D. S., Masroml, M., & Masrek, M. N. (2015). Website evaluation measures, website user engagement and website credibility for municipal website. *Journal of Engineering and Applied Sciences (Asian Research Publishing Network)*, *10*(23), 18228–18238.

Chiu, W. Y., Tzeng, G. H., & Li, H. L. (2013). A new hybrid MCDM model combining DANP with VIKOR to improve e-store business. *Knowledge-Based Systems*, *37*, 48–61. doi:10.1016/j.knosys.2012.06.017

Dickinger, A., & Stang, B. (2013). Optimization of multi-criteria website structure based on enhanced tabu search and web usage mining. *Journal of Business Research*, *66*(6), 771–777. doi:10.1016/j.jbusres.2011.09.017

Kang, D., & Park, Y. (2014). Review-based measurement of customer satisfaction in mobile service: Sentiment analysis and VIKOR approach. *Expert Systems with Applications*, *41*(4), 1041–1050. doi:10.1016/j.eswa.2013.07.101

Kaya, T. (2013). Multi-attribute evaluation of website quality in e-business using an integrated fuzzy AHP-TOPSIS methodology. *International Journal of Computational Intelligence Systems*, *3*(3), 301–314. doi:10.1080/18756891.2010.9727701

Larsson, A. O. (2012). Interactivity on Swedish newspaper websites: What kind, how much and why? *Convergence (London)*, *18*(2), 195–213. doi:10.1177/1354856511430184

KEY TERMS AND DEFINITIONS

AHP: Analytic Hierarchy Process

ANP: Analytic Network Process

Average Visit Duration: Average time spent by users on a website, per visit in seconds. Includes both desktop and mobile web.

Bounce Rate: Percentage of visitors to the site who navigate away after viewing only one page.

Category Traffic Rank: Traffic rank of website, as compared to all other sites in its main category.

Country Traffic Rank: Traffic rank of website, as compared to all other sites in its leading country.

DEMATEL: The Decision Making Trial and Evaluation Laboratory

Estimated Input Latency (EIL): Input responsiveness is a key factor in how users perceive the performance of websites' applications (apps).

First Contentful Paint (FCP): There are multiple moments during the load experience that can affect whether a user perceives it as "fast" or "slow". FCP measures the time from navigation to the time when the browser renders the first bit of content from the DOM.

First Meaningful Paint (FMP): FMP is the time when the page's primary content appeared on the mobile or desktop devices' screen.

Fuzzy number: A fuzzy number is a generalization of a real number in the sense that it does not refer to one single value but rather to a connected set of possible values, where each possible value has its own weight between 0 and 1.

Global Traffic Rank: Traffic rank of website, as compared to all other sites on the web.

Multi-criteria decision making (MCDM): MCDM is a general framework for supporting complex decision-making systems with multiple and conflicting criteria that decision-makers value differently.

NP: Newspaper

Page Views/Visit: Average number of pages viewed by users in each visit to a site in the last month. Includes both desktop and mobile web.

Performance score (PS): PS provides a score that shows the webpage's technical performance.

PROMETHEE: Preference Ranking Organization Method For Encrichment Evaluations

Speed Index (SI): SI is a page load performance metric that shows how quickly the contents of a page are visibly populated.

The Time to Interactive (TTI): TTI measures how long it takes a page to become interactive.

TOPSIS: Technique for Order Preference by Similarity to Ideal Solution

World Wide Web: An information system on the Internet which allows documents to be connected to other documents by hypertext links, enabling the user to search for information by moving from one document to another.

Chapter 12
Promethee:
A Tool for Multi-Criteria Decision Analysis

Priyam Verma
https://orcid.org/0000-0003-1860-3312
Symbiosis International University, India

ABSTRACT

This chapter decodes the techniques of PROMETHEE (Preference Ranking Organization Method for Enrichment Evaluation) in MCDA. Rigorous literature review will assist in deciphering and rationalising the progressions in the techniques since the inception of PROMETHEE. The chapter shall extensively review literature on PROMETHEE and shall concisely explore relevant cases. The literature shall include journal articles, research paper based on case studies and conference proceedings concentrating mainly in the discipline of management science. The chapter will untangle the essential steps that will simplify the mathematical component used in PROMETHEE I and PROMETHEE II with a hypothetical case and a practical case. In the final phase of the chapter the limitations of PROMETHEE I and II shall be accentuated.

INTRODUCTION

To tackle the complex problems in today's world, the Multi-criteria decision Analysis (MCDA) tools have been evolving constantly. The last three decades have not only witnessed significant revisions to the existing tools but also the addition of the new methods. The primary objective of these methods has been to help decision-makers solve complex problems having multiple criteria which are both, conflicting and qualitative in nature. The strategies of MCDA tools have been implemented in various fields. It solves a wide range of problems related to sorting, ranking and selection. The fundamental idea of MCDA is to rank multiple alternatives according to their efficacy, which in turn would enhance the decisions which would be befitting for an entity. According to Cho (2003) cited in Terrientes & Miguel (2015) the steps of MCDA are - identify the relevant attributes; assign quantifiable criteria to each of the attributes and specify their restrictions; construct a utility function for each criterion, all providing ratings in the same range; aggregate the individual ratings using operators like presented before; evaluate the alternatives

DOI: 10.4018/978-1-7998-2216-5.ch012

using the global utility function and choose, rank or sort them accordingly. All MCDA tools follow the same rubric. These tools are not only used in the realm of business and management but also in diversified fields such as medicine, agriculture, chemistry, engineering, education, sports etc.

In the present world, people deal with the issues related to urbanization and industrialization, increase of water and energy demands, environmental pollution, shortage of natural resources and food, and many other challenges. To deal with these in a manner which is both, less time consuming and efficient, various methods have emerged in the last couple of decades to evaluate and implement the most efficient option of tackling these issues. There have been numerous alterations in the MCDA methods and PROMETHEE (Preference Ranking Organization Method for Enrichment Evaluation) has emerged as one of the most feasible methods. This method was developed by J.P. Brans in the year 1982 which was extended by Vincke and Brans in 1985. PROMETHEE is a simple ranking method in conceptual terms and in application in comparison to the other methods of multi-criteria analysis. Since 1985, there have been over 200 scholarly articles published on PROMETHEE under the topic of MCDA. The flexibility offered by this method due to its mathematical properties increases its efficiency and usage in diverse fields.

This chapter would focus on the application of PROMETHEE in various fields. Rigorous literature review mentioned under the theoretical background of the chapter shall accentuate the applicability of PROMETHEE in diverse fields. The methodology will guide how to sail through the discussion and analysis section in order to decipher the steps involved in taking a rational decision using PROMETHEE as a tool. Moreover, the concepts of PROMETHEE I and PROMETHEE II shall be discussed at length taking a hypothetical case and a real-life case proving the consistency of the decision from both methods. The conclusion shall highlight the criticism of PROMETHEE on the grounds of existing literature and will entail the basic requirements to be fulfilled and kept in mind in order to undertake PROMETHEE as a decision-making tool.

THEORETICAL BACKGROUND

The PROMETHEE family initially included the PROMETHEE I method for partial ranking and PROMETHEE II for complete ranking of the alternatives. These methods were developed and presented by JP Brans in the year 1982 at a conference at the University of Laval, Quebec, Canada. Thus Behzadian, Kazemzadeh, Albadvi, & Aghdasi (2010) suggests that 1985 must be chosen as a starting date for search. In the same year, the first paper on PROMETHEE and its application was published by Management Science journal and it is adopted as the starting point for review.

The next decade was marked by further advancements in the methods of PROMETHEE. The new versions of PROMETHEE such as PROMETHEE III was derived for ranking alternatives in a range of intervals. PROMETHEE IV derived the partial and complete rankings of alternatives when the plausible solution set was continuous in nature. In the year 1992, Brans & Mareschal (1992) proposed PROMETHEE V for the problem with segmentation constraints. PROMETHEE VI was an attempt by JP Brans and Mareschal to evaluate the degree of hardness of a multicriteria decision problem with respect to the weights given to the criteria (Brans & Mareschal, 1995). To visualise the decisions of the PROMETHEE methods, Geometrical Analysis for Interactive Aid (GAIA) was introduced for graphical representation to assist in more complex decision-making scenarios. In the year 2004, Figueira, de Smeth & Brans (2004) proposed two approaches called PROMETHEE TRI for the purpose of sorting and the PROMETHEE CLUSTER to deal with the problem of assigning weights in clustering decisions.

PROMETHEE is used as tool of weighing best alternatives in various fields. These fields include Environment management, Business and Financial Management, Water Management, Transportation, Manufacturing and Assembly, energy management and other miscellaneous decision-making fields. The literature review shall focus on the applicability of PROMETHEE in these fields.

PROMETHEE has a wide scope of applicability in Environment Management and Waste Management. According to Behzadian, Kazemzadeh, Albadvi & Aghdasi (2010), Environment Management is considered as the most popular topic in PROMETHEE applications and a large amount of the papers are related to this topic, Environment Management has covered several specific areas such as waste management, Life Cycle Assessment (LCA), Environmental Impact Assessment (EIA) and land-use planning.

Al-Rashdan, Al-Kloub, Dean & Al-Shemmeri (1999) used PROMETHEE as one of the Multi-criteria Decision tools to develop a reliable methodology to prioritise environmental projects in Jordan and to evaluate their environmental impacts. This paper used PROMETHEE I and PROMETHEE II as decision making tool. In this case 15 criteria were shortlisted and weights were assigned to each of them. These included the factors such as water supply, urgency, effects on human life, number of people, effects on the water quality, certainty of outcome, cultural feasibility, flexibility, opportunity, etc. From these factors, some were to be minimised while some were to be maximised and thus each project was evaluated based on this rubric.

In the area of nuclear waste management, Briggs, Kunsch & Mareschal (1990) states that radioactive waste must be dealt with utmost caution as the time span between the electricity production itself and the final disposal in geological formations can represent decades. This time-lag in the process of disposal can prove to be fatal and thus a multicriteria analysis was applied, using the PROMETHEE methods and the geometrical representation GAIA. These methods are well adapted to this problem with many actions and few very conflicting criteria. Three scenarios were evaluated based on four normalised criteria. These scenarios had further sub-divisions wherein 27 actions were listed. These actions were then evaluated based on the technique of PROMETHEE I, PROMETHEE II and GAIA which helped in determining which scenario would be befitting for nuclear waste disposal in Belgium.

In the year 2004, European regulation of waste electrical and electronic equipment (WEEE) required installation of new recycling plants and alteration of the existing ones in Spain. In this context, Queiruga, Walther, González-Benito & Spengler (2008) suggested that PROMETHEE must be used as a tool for ranking the Spanish municipalities according to their efficacy for the installation of these plants in South and Central Spain. Fifteen autonomous communities were evaluated based on the broad criteria of economic objectives, infrastructural objectives and legal objectives. Each criterion was assigned a weight and each has different sub-parameters of evaluation. Based on this mechanism, the fifteen autonomous communities were ranked according to their appropriateness for installation of recycling plant.

With the increasing damage inflicted on Earth due to human activities, protecting Biodiversity has been of paramount importance in the last two decades. Moffett & Sarkar (2006) stresses on this issue and review majority of the MCDM tools to evaluate which methods is most feasible for the conservation of Biodiversity. The paper is basically a taxonomy of MCDM methods including PROMETHEE. Moreover, there has been a research on developing a mechanism to allocate equitable international greenhouse gases (GHGs) emission entitlements for different countries (Vaillancourt, 2004). The main criteria were egalitarianism, basic needs, polluter pays, historical responsibility, sovereignty, efficiency, geography and energy. These criteria were assigned weights and each of them had certain sub-parameters for evaluation. The countries were divided into North and South region and PROMETHEE II was applied for comparison of the current and targeted GHG emission level for countries. Thus, the allocations made were equitable in nature for developed and developing countries.

Motor vehicles have provided individuals with the flexibility of reaching out at a destination according to their feasibility, but the toll that it takes on the environment in terms of the chemical emission from these vehicles is far graver in nature. According to a research by Beynon & Wells (2008), PROMETHEE was used for ranking of a small set of motor vehicles based on constituents of their exhaust emissions. As a model of an interested party's preference ranking of the motor vehicles, the subsequent uncertainty (sensitivity) analysis considered minimal (lean) changes and identified what would be necessary to a vehicle's emissions so that their preference ranking is improved. For instance, it identified the necessary engineering performance modifications that can be made to improve the perceived consumer-based ranking of a manufacturer.

Environmental management is a domain where the problem coexists in the form of qualitative and quantitative nature which makes the environmental impact assessment (EIA) cumbersome. Often the MCDM tools for EIA makes a trade off in terms of assigning less or no weight to qualitative factors and more weight to quantitative factors for evaluation. This bias is overcome by the introduction of PROMETHEE. While ranking sites for the construction of bus stations, Martín, Fajardo, Blanco & Requena (2003) use modified PROMETHEE I and II for the purpose of comparison. Similarly, Kiker, Bridges, Varghese, Seager & Linkov (2005) presents a review paper on MCDM tools which includes PROMETHEE as one of the techniques. The paper aims to rationalise the decision-making strategies in environmental projects by considering cost, public acceptance, human health and ecological health as the broad criteria in the model. This increases the efficiency of EIA and makes it more reliable in nature. Further amendments were made by Klauer, Drechsler & Messner (2006) to the above research by factoring in the decisions under uncertainty for sustainable development. This study focuses on developing a method, Integrated assessment of decisions under uncertainty for sustainable development (IANUS), to assist decision-making efforts towards sustainable development and has a wide range of applications in the Torgau region of Germany. The efficacy of IANUS is increased using PROMETHEE as a tool of ranking projects.

The concepts of Multi Criteria Decision Making (MCDM) seem a suitable means in order to implement Life Cycle Assessment (LCA) into integrated decision processes. The outranking methods as a special subgroup of MCDM methods are particularly suitable for integral decision making through the notion of weak preference and incomparability, which better represent the real decision situation, as demonstrated in this paper. Especially the outranking method PROMETHEE brings together flexibility and simplicity for the user (Geldermann, Spengler, & Rentz, 2000). This claim is further justified by Geldermann & Rentz (2005), wherein the research considers a case-based study of the sector called surface coating. Environmentally relevant installation options are then compared and ranked by PROMETHEE II as a tool.

The domain of financial and business management focuses mainly on the aspects of performance management, portfolio management, general management and investment analysis. This makes the field of financial and business management one of the domains where PROMETHEE is readily applicable. Numerous papers in this domain have adopted PROMETHEE as a decision-making tool to select superior stocks, figure out more feasible investment options, evaluating a less risky venture and allocating budget.

Portfolio managers are individuals who are vested with the responsibility of making the investment decisions. These investments can result in procuring enough funds to break even, gaining a hefty amount and in worst case scenario, losing majority of your investments. Thus, the job of a portfolio manager is not all plain sailing as there is a potential risk of losing out on the investment that one makes. Hababou

& Martel (1998) accentuate this fact and implement PROMETHEE II as the MCDM tool for defining a rubric for selecting a portfolio manager. For this purpose, he narrows a broad list (*A*) of criteria to a small list (*N*). The refined list *N,* includes criteria of returns, investment philosophy, staff allocation and corporate criteria. Each criterion is assigned a weight. From the list *N,* the most efficient portfolio manager is selected using PROMETHEE II.

Since 1990s, the complexity of financial decisions has increased globally. This required highly sophisticated methods of evaluating options involved in financial decisions. Zopounidis & Doumpos (2002) evaluate majority of MCDM tools which assist in these financial decisions which vary from credit risk management, portfolio selection and management, corporate performance evaluation and investment appraisal. Apart from evaluating various MCDM tools, the paper claims that PROMETHEE is the most applicable method while ranking choices associated with the financial decisions.

Stock trading is often associated with selecting the right stock at the right time. In order to select the superior stock (alternatives) for investment, a finite number of alternatives have to be ranked considering several and sometimes conflicting criteria (Albadvi, Chaharsooghi & Esfahanipour, 2007). The proposed model was structured around two pillars: Industry evaluation and company evaluation. For this PROMETHEE was applied in the Tehran Stock Exchange (TSE) to select superior stocks. Moreover, a correlation matrix was formed for the 42 criteria of evaluation of the superior stocks. Mitkova, Mlynarovic & Tus (2007) and Mareschal (1986) use PROMETHEE II to classify the financial problems of a business along the factor of uncertainty and risk analysis.

Behzadian, Kazemzadeh, Albadvi, & Aghdasi (2010) claims that, "Manufacturing and Assembly is also an important application area in literature of the PROMETHEE methods that is mainly related to the aspects of manufacturing systems and planning, maintenance programming, and assembly line planning." Araz (2005) conducted a study to rank and select the most feasible dispatching rubric for a Dual Resource Constrained (DRC) by integrating a simulation model, Back-Propagation Neural Network (BPNN), and PROMETHEE II. Apart from these fields, numerous research papers have highlighted the importance of PROMETHEE in Hydrology and water management, chemistry, energy management and other significant issues.

METHODOLOGY

The chapter is an amalgamation of rigorous literature review and a strong discussion which decodes the steps involved in PROMETHEE I and PROMETHEE II. The significance of these two methods is that these act as a prerequisite for the understanding of PROMETHEE family and visualising tools for multi-criteria decision analysis. The literature briefly discusses all the major developments in the PROMETHEE family and the applicability of this strategy in real world cases. The discussion section shall illustrate the steps of PROMETHEE in the simple manner for enhanced understanding. These illustrations would be bifurcated into two parts. The first one being a hypothetical example while the second one shall be on a case study of choosing the most feasible supplier.

Figure 1. Preference functions in PROMETHEE
(Source: Brans & Smet (2016))

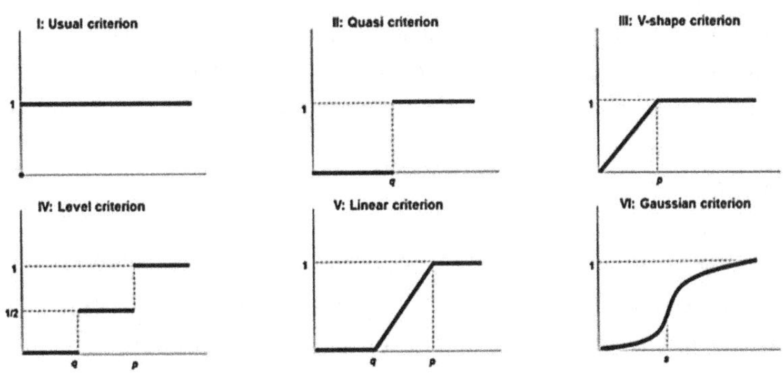

DISCUSSION

PROMETHEE is based on valued outranking relation based on a preference index which ranges between 0 and 1. Each variant of P(a,b) represents the preference of a over b for each criterion. The closer P(a,b) is to 0, the greater the indifference between a and b. Likewise, the closer to 1, the greater the preference of a over b is (Figueira, Mousseau & Roy, 2005).

In figure 1, 'p' is the lowest value for d_i above which there is a strict preference among alternatives. The highest value for d_i, 'q' is the value above which there is an indifference between the alternatives while 's' is a value that lies between p and q and which follows a normal distribution.

Decisions are accompanied by choices or alternatives. The primary aim behind every choice is to optimise each criterion affecting an individual's choice and the rationale behind this action is the fact that humans tend to maximise their satisfaction. The criteria and alternatives are denoted by

- A={a1,...,an} A={a1,...,an} - set of alternatives
- F={f1,...,fq} F={f1,...,fq} - set of criteria

The task of a decision-maker is to evaluate which is the best alternative that optimises all the criteria. Thus, the trait of almost all existing problems is multicriteria in nature. In purview of the above example, this chapter shall discuss the simplified steps of PROMETHEE I and PROMETHEE II with respect to two examples. The first one where each of the criterion is assigned equal weights while in the second example, each criterion shall be assigned different weights.

Example A- Hypothetical Scenario

For instance, X wants to buy a car. X is confused whether to buy car A, B, C or D. In order to make a rational choice, X uses the factor of cost, mileage, car safety rating and looks to judge a car. Among these, only the factor of cost is to be minimised and the rest are to be maximised. X then compares A, B, C and D based on these factors and figures out which car will be the most suitable.

Step 1: Determining and assigning the weights to the broad the criteria

The initial step of assigning weights to the broader criteria is one of the most important one. In the aforementioned case, weights shall be assigned to the criteria of cost (i), mileage (ii), car safety (iii) and looks (iv). It should be noted that the sum of these weights ideally should be equal to one to increase the feasibility of calculation. The rationale behind this is the fact that weights signify the importance of each criterion in the overall decision. Hence, the sum of these weights ideally must be equal to unity.

$$W_i + W_{ii} + W_{iii} + W_{iv} = 1 \quad (1)$$

However, even if the sum of these weights is greater than 1 the rubric of PROMETHEE is such that at the end, the evaluation matrix would be normalised by taking into consideration the weighted averages. For the purpose of simplicity in this example, the weights assigned to each of the criterion are equal. Thus,

$$W_i = W_{ii} = W_{iii} = W_{iv} = 0.25 \quad (2)$$

In the same step it is suggested that the linguistic terms should be converted to nominal scale. Basically, the qualitative criteria should be converted into numerical values (quantitative values) to facilitate evaluation. For instance, each of the car A, B, C and D should be rated on a scale of 1-5 for its looks as it is a qualitative parameter. Now, hypothetically scaling the criterion of looks for the alternatives A, B, C and D to be 4, 5, 3 and 4 respectively. Note that the value in the table are hypothetical and simplified for better understanding.

Step 2: Normalisation of the Evaluation Matrix

To normalise the evaluation matrix, the decision maker must identify the beneficiary and non-beneficiary criteria. Here, the aim is to identify which criterion should be maximized and which should be minimised. In the aforementioned case, the criterion of cost has to be minimised (hence non-beneficiary criterion) while the rest are to be maximised (beneficiary criterion) for driving the maximum utility out of the decision.

For this purpose, the decision maker must identify the maximum and minimum value of each criterion from the given alternatives.

The equation to normalise the criterion are-

1. Beneficiary Criteria (Maximisation)

Table 1. The evaluation matrix

Criteria (Weight)→ Alternatives↓	Cost (0.25)	Mileage (0.25)	Car Safety (0.25)	Looks (0.25)
A	600	20	4	4
B	800	20	5	5
C	700	24	3	3
D	650	22	4	4

Table 2. Determining maximising and minimising criteria

Criteria (Weight)→ Alternatives↓	Cost (0.25)	Mileage (0.25)	Car Safety (0.25)	Looks (0.25)
A	600	20	4	4
B	800	20	5	5
C	700	24	3	3
D	650	22	4	4
Maximum (f_{ij}) Minimum (f_{ij})	800 600	24 20	5 3	5 3

$$R_{ij} = [f_{ij} - \text{Min}\ (f_{ij})]/[\ \text{Max}\ f_{ij}) - \text{Min}\ f_{ij})] \quad (3)$$

Here, $i=\{a_1,...,a_n\}$ and $j=\{f_1,...,f_q\}$

In simpler terms, beneficial criteria is the difference of the current alternative value with the minimum value divided by difference of maximum value and minimum value of that criterion from all the alternatives.

2. Non-Beneficiary Criteria (Minimisation)

$$R_{ij} = [\text{Max}\ (f_{ij}) - f_{ij}\ ]/[\ \text{Max}\ f_{ij}) - \text{Min}\ f_{ij})] \quad (4)$$

Here, $i=\{a_1,...,a_n\}$ $j=\{f_1,...,f_q\}$

Thus, non-beneficial criteria is the difference of the maximum value and the current alternative value divided by the difference of maximum value and minimum value of that criterion from all alternatives.

Based on the above formula, the normalised evaluation table would thus be calculated as-

On solving, the ratios would be reflected as follows

Now, the task would be the compare each alternative with the rest of the alternatives. For instance,

- A must be compared with B, C and D individually,
- B must be compared with A, C and D individually,
- C must be compared with A, B and D individually and

Table 3. Calculations in the evaluation matrix

Criteria (Weight)→ Alternatives↓	Cost (0.25)	Mileage (0.25)	Car Safety (0.25)	Looks (0.25)
A	(800-600)/ (800-600)	(20-20)/ (24-20)	(4-3)/ (5-3)	(4-3)/ (5-3)
B	(800-800)/ (800-600)	(20-20)/ (24-20)	(5-3)/ (5-3)	(5-3)/ (5-3)
C	(800-700)/ (800-600)	(24-20)/ (24-20)	(3-3)/ (5-3)	(3-3)/ (5-3)
D	(800-650)/ (800-600)	(22-20)/ (24-20)	(4-3)/ (5-3)	(4-3)/ (5-3)

Table 4. Results of the calculation in the evaluation matrix

Criteria (Weight)→ Alternatives↓	Cost (0.25)	Mileage (0.25)	Car Safety (0.25)	Looks (0.25)
A	1	0	0.5	0.5
B	0	0	1	1
C	0.5	1	0	0
D	0.75	0.5	0.5	0.5

- D must be compared with A, B and C individually.

For this purpose, another table depicting the comparisons of the alternatives are depicted as follows-

Table A2.4 represents the normalised matrix. Following this step, the next shall be to calculate preference function from the evaluation matrix.

Step 3: Determining the Preference Function

The value of the Preference Function shall be determined by the following equations-

1. If the value of the difference of any two alternative is less than zero then the value of the preference function is equal to zero.

$$P(A,B) = 0 \text{ if } D(f_{ai} - f_{bi}) \leq 0 \tag{5}$$

Table 5. Calculating the difference of each alternative with respect to other

Criteria (Weight)→ Alternatives↓	Cost (0.25)	Mileage (0.25)	Car Safety (0.25)	Looks (0.25)
D(A-B)	1	0	-0.5	-0.5
D(A-C)	0.5	-1	0.5	0.5
D(A-D)	0.25	-0.5	0	0
D(B-A)	-1	0	0.5	0.5
D(B-C)	-0.5	-1	1	1
D(B-D)	-.075	-0.5	0.5	0.5
D(C-A)	-0.5	1	-0.5	-0.5
D(C-B)	0.5	1	-1	-1
D(C-D)	-0.25	0.5	-0.5	-0.5
D(D-A)	-0.25	0.5	0	0
D(D-B)	0.75	0.5	-0.5	-0.5
D(D-C)	0.25	-0.5	-0.5	0.5

2. If the value of the difference of any two alternative is greater than zero then the value of the preference function is same as that of the difference between the two alternatives

$$P(A,B) = D(A\text{-}B) \text{ if } D(f_{ai} - f_{bi}) \geq 0 \tag{6}$$

Now, the aim is to calculate the aggregate sum of preference function or, as many authors refer it to, the Global Preference Index (GPI). As the term suggests, GPI is the weighted sum of all criteria of a given alternative. In simpler term, in this step the preference functions are multiplied by the respective weights of its criterion and then for each alternative these values are aggregated. This aggregated value is then divided by the sum of weights. It is calculated by the following equation-

$$\pi(a_i,a_j)= \sum w_f \cdot \pi(a_i,a_j)/ \sum w_f \tag{7}$$

The steps of calculating the Global Preference Function can be bifurcated into three steps

- Calculating the value of Preference Function
- Calculating the value of Aggregate Preference Function
- Calculating the value of Global Preference Function.

Thus, the evaluation matrix would now be represented as

The average preference function is represented in the table below which is followed by the table depicting global preference function

There are certain properties of aggregate preference and these should hold. These properties can also be regarded as a proxy for the correctness and accuracy of the decision. The properties are-

Table 6. Calculating the value of preference function

Criteria (Weight)→ Alternatives↓	Cost (0.25)	Mileage (0.25)	Car Safety (0.25)	Looks (0.25)
P(A,B)	1	0	0	0
P(A,C)	0.5	0	0.5	0.5
P(A,D)	0.25	0	0	0
P(B,A)	0	0	0.5	0.5
P(B,C)	0	0	1	1
P(B,D)	0	0	0.5	0.5
P(C,A)	0	1	0	0
P(C,B)	0.5	1	0	0
P(C,D)	0	0.5	0	0
P(D,A)	0	0.5	0	0
P(D,B)	0.75	0.5	0	0
P(D,C)	0.25	0	0	0.5

Table 7. Calculating the value of aggregate preference function

Criteria (Weight)→ Alternatives↓	Cost (0.25)	Mileage (0.25)	Car Safety (0.25)	Looks (0.25)	$\pi(a_i,a_j)$
P(A,B)	1 x 0.25	0 x 0.25	0 x 0.25	0 x 0.25	0.25
P(A,C)	0.5 x 0.25	0 x 0.25	0.5 x 0.25	0.5 x 0.25	0.375
P(A,D)	0.25 x 0.25	0 x 0.25	0 x 0.25	0 x 0.25	0.0625
P(B,A)	0 x 0.25	0 x 0.25	0.5 x 0.25	0.5 x 0.25	0.25
P(B,C)	0 x 0.25	0 x 0.25	1 x 0.25	1 x 0.25	0.50
P(B,D)	0 x 0.25	0 x 0.25	0.5 x 0.25	0.5 x 0.25	0.25
P(C,A)	0 x 0.25	1 x 0.25	0 x 0.25	0 x 0.25	0.25
P(C,B)	0.5 x 0.25	1 x 0.25	0 x 0.25	0 x 0.25	0.375
P(C,D)	0 x 0.25	0.5 x 0.25	0 x 0.25	0 x 0.25	0.125
P(D,A)	0 x 0.25	0.5 x 0.25	0 x 0.25	0 x 0.25	0.125
P(D,B)	0.75 x 0.25	0.5 x 0.25	0 x 0.25	0 x 0.25	0.3125
P(D,C)	0.25 x 0.25	0 x 0.25	0 x 0.25	0.5 x 0.25	0.1875

Table 8. Calculating the value of global preference function

	$\pi(a_i,a_j)$
P(A,B)	0.25
P(A,C)	0.375
P(A,D)	0.0625
P(B,A)	0.25
P(B,C)	0.50
P(B,D)	0.25
P(C,A)	0.25
P(C,B)	0.375
P(C,D)	0.125
P(D,A)	0.125
P(D,B)	0.3125
P(D,C)	0.1875

- $\pi(a_i,a_i)$ is always equal to zero as the difference between any alternative with itself shall always be equal to zero.

$$\pi(a_i,a_i) = 0 \quad (8)$$

- The value $\pi(a_i,a_j)$ lies between 0 and 1.

$$0 \leq \pi(a_i,a_j) \leq 1 \quad (9)$$

- The value $\pi(a_j,a_i)$ lies between 0 and 1.

$$0 \leq \pi(a_j,a_i) \leq 1 \quad (10)$$

- The sum of two aggregate preference function of the same pair of alternatives lies between 0 and 1

$$0 \leq \pi(a_i,a_j)+\pi(a_j,a_i) \leq 1 \quad (11)$$

The implications of the aggregate preference function value are as follows-

- If $\pi(a_i,a_j) \sim 0$ then there is weak Global Preference Index
- If $\pi(a_i,a_j) \sim 1$ then there is weak Global Preference Index

Step 4: Determining the Leaving and Entering outranking flow

To determine the leaving and entering outranking flow, procedure is to formulate the aggregated preference function matrix which is represented as-

From this matrix the leaving and entering outranking flows are calculated as follows-

- Positive/Leaving outranking flow basically tells how an alternative outrank the others and the decision maker would desire to maximize this parameter. It is calculated using the following formula

$$\Phi^{+}_{(ai)=}1/n-1(\sum_{aj\in A} \pi(a_{i,}a_j))\ (a_{i\neq}a_j) \quad (12)$$

- Negative/entering outranking flow basically tells how an alternative is outranked by others and the decision maker must desire to minimize this parameter. It is calculated using the following formula

$$\Phi\text{-}(ai)=1/n-1(\sum aj\in A\ \pi(aj,ai))\ (ai \neq aj) \quad (13)$$

In both the above cases, n represents the number of alternatives offered while deciding (in this case, n is equal to 4). The higher the leaving outflow is, the better it is. Whereas, the lower the entering outflow

Table 9. The aggregate preference function matrix

Criteria→ Alternatives↓	A	B	C	D
A	-	0.25	0.25	0.125
B	0.25	-	0.375	0.3125
C	0.375	0.50	-	0.1875
D	0.0625	0.25	0.125	-

Table 10. Calculating the entering and leaving flow

Criteria→ Alternatives↓	A	B	C	D	Leaving Flow (Φ^+)
A	-	0.25	0.25	0.125	0.2083
B	0.25	-	0.375	0.3125	0.3125
C	0.375	0.50	-	0.1875	0.354
D	0.0625	0.25	0.125	-	0.1458
Entering Flow (Φ^-)	0.2292	0.3333	0.25	0.2083	

is better it is. In simpler terms, positive outflow can be regarded as a strength of the alternative while negative outflow can be regarded as the weakness of an alternative.

Step 5: Applying PROMETHEE I or Partial Ranking

PROMETHEE I evaluate alternatives based on three conditions. It compares the two alternatives and deem their relationship as

- P^I – Preference
- I^I – Indifference
- R^I – incompatibility

a is preferred over b (aP^Ib) iff

$$\Phi^+_a > \Phi^+_b \text{ and } \Phi^-_a < \Phi^-_b \text{ or} \tag{14}$$

$$\Phi^+_a = \Phi^+_b \text{ and } \Phi^-_a < \Phi^-_b \text{ or} \tag{15}$$

$$\Phi^+_a > \Phi^+_b \text{ and } \Phi^-_a = \Phi^-_b \tag{16}$$

If one these conditions is satisfied (simultaneously fulfilling both the clauses in a single condition), then alternative a is preferred over b.

a is indifferent to b (aI^Ib) iff

$$\Phi^+_a = \Phi^+_b \text{ and } \Phi^-_a = \Phi^-_b \tag{17}$$

If this condition is satisfied (simultaneously fulfilling both the clauses), alternative a is indifferent to b.

a is incompatible to b (aR^Ib) iff

$$\Phi^+_a > \Phi^+_b \text{ and } \Phi^-_a > \Phi^-_b \text{ or} \tag{18}$$

$$\Phi^+_a < \Phi^+_b \text{ and } \Phi^-_a < \Phi^-_b \quad (19)$$

If any of these conditions is satisfied (simultaneously fulfilling both the clauses in a single condition), then alternative a is incompatible to b.

While comparing A with other alternatives based on the aforementioned rubric, it is found that

- A R^I B
- A R^I C
- A R^I D

Similarly evaluating B, C and D

PROMETHEE I suggest that all the incompatible alternatives should be discarded and only the preferred ones should be evaluated. Table A5.2 proves that the only scenario exists where an alternative is preferred over the other, that is, C P^I B.

Figure 2 depicts the partial ranking of alternatives or the outcome of PROMETHEE I. To find the consistency of the results, PROMETHEE II must be applied and evaluated.

step 6: Applying PROMETHEE II or Complete Ranking

In order to evaluate the most feasible alternative, PROMETHEE II suggests that the decision maker must calculate the net outranking flow. The net outranking flow is the difference between the leaving (positive) flow and the entering (negative) flow. It is represented as

$$\Phi^n = (\Phi^+) - (\Phi^-) \quad (20)$$

Table 11. Representation of the entering and leaving flows of each alternative

Alternatives	Leaving Flow (Φ^+)	Entering Flow (Φ^-)
A	0.2083	0.2292
B	0.3125	0.3333
C	0.354	0.25
D	0.1458	0.2083

Table 12. PROMETHEE I result of partial comparison of alternatives

Alternatives	A	B	C	D
A	-	B R^I A	C R^I A	D R^I A
B	A R^I B	-	N/A (as C P^I B)	D R^I B
C	A R^I C	C P^I B	-	D R^I C
D	A R^I D	B R^I D	C R^I D	-

Figure 2. Partial ranking of alternatives
(source: own)

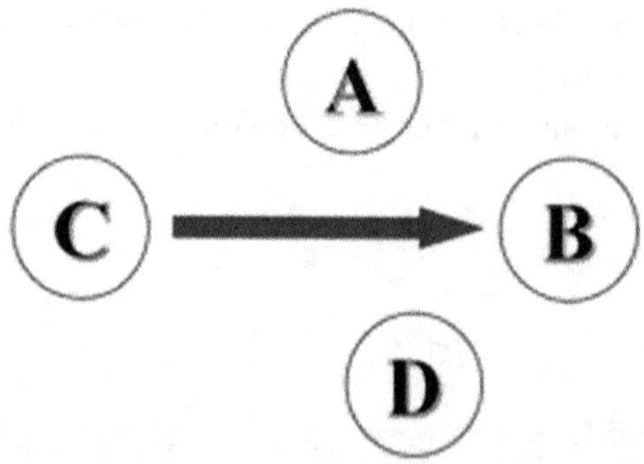

It must be noted that one of the properties of PROMETHEE II is that the value of net outranking flow is between -1 and 1.

$$-1 < \Phi^n < 1 \quad (21)$$

PROMETHEE II offers only two implications, that is, it does not consider the parameter of incompatibility, unlike PROMETHEE I. Hence, the conditions for PROMETHEE II are as follows-

- $aP^{II}b$ iff $\Phi_a > \Phi_b$ Here, P^{II} denotes Preference of a over b
- $aI^{II}b$ iff $\Phi_a = \Phi_b$ Here, I^{II} denotes indifference of a and b

Thus, the net outranking flow shall be represented as
Thus, according to PROMETHEE II the alternatives in order of their feasibility is

C > B > A > D

Table 13. Calculating the entering flow, leaving flow and ranking of the alternatives

Alternatives	Leaving Flow (Φ^+)	Entering Flow (Φ^-)	Net Flow (Φ^n)	Ranking
A	0.2083	0.2292	-0.0209	3
B	0.3125	0.3333	-0.0208	2
C	0.354	0.25	0.104	1
D	0.1458	0.2083	-0.0625	4

Figure 3. The complete ranking of alternatives
(source: own)

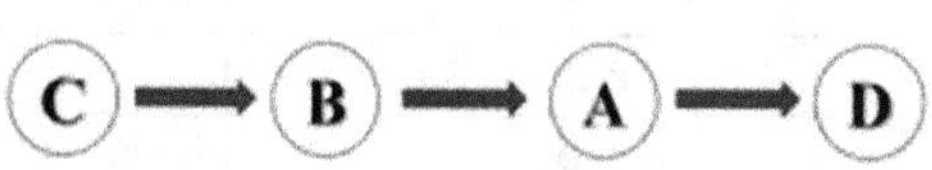

The results in Figure 3 are in conformity with the results in PROMETHEE I.

Example B: Supplier Selection Decision

The example that follows is an excerpt from the work of Rezaei-kelidbari, Homayounfar M & Foumani (2016). This would help to elaborate as to how PROMETHEE assists in real life problems such as selection of suppliers. The selection of a supplier is completed on the basis of suppliers Reliability (A), Average delay (B), Quality of transport place (B), Product price (D), Experience (E) and Reputation (F). The payoffs assigned to them are as follows

Step 1: Determining and assigning the weights to the broad the criteria

Assigning weights is an important step as it can be taken as a proxy for the trade-off that a decision maker is willing to take between the criteria. Weights are usually assigned by the Analytical hierarchy Process (AHP) though there more evolved techniques such as ANP to facilitate the process of assigning weights. Weights shall be assigned to the criteria of Reliability (A), Average delay (B), Quality of transport place (B), Product price (D), Experience (E) and Reputation (F). The weightage of each criterion playing a role in the decision is highly subjective in nature but AHP rationalise the weights that are assigned to them. The weights assigned to criteria are as follows

Here, it is to be noted that the sum of the weights of these criteria is approximately equal to unity or 1. In the same step it is suggested that the linguistic terms should be converted to nominal scale.

Step 2: Normalisation of the Evaluation Matrix

To normalise the evaluation matrix, the decision maker must identify the beneficiary and non-beneficiary criteria. Here, the aim is to identify which criterion should be maximized and which should be minimised. In the aforementioned case, the criterion of cost has to be minimised (hence non-beneficiary criterion) while the rest are to be maximised (beneficiary criterion) for driving the maximum utility out of the decision.

For this purpose, the decision maker must identify the maximum and minimum value of each criterion from the given alternatives.

The equation to normalise the criterion are-

1. Beneficiary Criteria (Maximisation)

Figure 4. Evaluation matrix
(Source: Rezaei-kelidbari, Homayounfar M & Foumani (2016))

	Reliability	Average Delay	Quality of transport place	Product price	Experience	Reputation
Supplier A	7.766	90	7.268	2000	6.446	7.766
Supplier B	8.32	90	7.268	1900	8.277	8.653
Supplier C	5.323	60	3.684	2100	2.757	4.866
Supplier D	6.9	75	6.997	2200	7.435	7.908

Figure 5. List of criteria and assigned weights
(Source: Rezaei-kelidbari, Homayounfar M & Foumani (2016))

Criterion name	Type	Weight
Reliability	Max	0.122
Average delay	Min	0.281
Quality of transport place	Max	0.143
Product price	Min	0.340
Experience	Max	0.082
Reputation	Max	0.031

Table 14. The evaluation matrix after step 1

Criteria (Weight)→ Alternatives↓	A (0.122)	B (0.281)	C (0.143)	D (0.340)	E (0.082)	F (0.031)
SA	7.766	90	7.268	2000	6.446	7.766
SB	8.320	90	7.268	1900	8.277	8.653
SC	5.323	60	3.684	2100	2.757	4.866
SD	6.900	75	6.997	2200	7.435	7.908

Table 15. Determining maximising and minimising criteria

Criteria (Weight)→ Alternatives↓	A (0.122)	B (0.281)	C (0.143)	D (0.340)	E (0.082)	F (0.031)
SA	7.766	90	7.268	2000	6.446	7.766
SB	8.320	90	7.268	1900	8.277	8.653
SC	5.323	60	3.684	2100	2.757	4.866
SD	6.900	75	6.997	2200	7.435	7.908
Maximum (f_{ij}) Minimum (f_{ij})	8.320 5.323	90 60	7.268 3.684	2200 1900	8.277 2.757	8.653 4.866

$$R_{ij} = [f_{ij} - \text{Min}(f_{ij})]/[\text{Max}\, f_{ij}) - \text{Min}\, f_{ij})] \tag{22}$$

Here, $i=\{a_1,...,a_n\}$ and $j=\{f_1,...,f_q\}$

2. Non-Beneficiary Criteria (Minimisation)

$$R_{ij} = [\text{Max}(f_{ij}) - f_{ij}]/[\text{Max}\, f_{ij}) - \text{Min}\, f_{ij})] \tag{23}$$

Here, $i=\{a_1,...,a_n\}$ $j=\{f_1,...,f_q\}$
Based on the above formula, the normalised evaluation table would thus be calculated as-
On solving, the ratios would be reflected as follows

Table 16. Calculations in the evaluation matrix

Criteria (Weight)→ Alternatives↓	A (0.122)	B (0.281)	C (0.143)	D (0.340)	E (0.082)	F (0.031)
SA	(7.766-5.323) / (8.320-5.323)	(90-90) / (90-60)	(7.268-3.684) / (7.268-3.684)	(2200-2000) / (2200-1900)	(6.446-2.757) / (8.277-2.757)	(7.766-4.866) / (8.653-4.866)
SB	(8.320-5.323) / (8.320-5.323)	(90-90) / (90-60)	(7.268-3.684) / (7.268-3.684)	(2200-1900) / (2200-1900)	(8.277-2.757) / (8.277-2.757)	(8.653-4.866) / (8.653-4.866)
SC	(5.323-5.323) / (8.320-5.323)	(90-60) / (90-60)	(3.684-3.684) / (7.268-3.684)	(2200-2100) / (2200-1900)	(2.757-2.757) / (8.277-2.757)	(4.866-4.866) / (8.653-4.866)
SD	(6.900-5.323) / (8.320-5.323)	(90-75) / (90-60)	(6.997-3.684) / (7.268-3.684)	(2200-2200) / (2200-1900)	(7.435-2.757) / (8.277-2.757)	(7.908-4.866) / (8.653-4.866)

Table 17. Results of the calculation in the evaluation matrix

Criteria (Weight)→ Alternatives↓	A (0.122)	B (0.281)	C (0.143)	D (0.340)	E (0.082)	F (0.031)
SA	0.815	0	1	0.667	0.668	0.765
SB	1	0	1	1	1	1
SC	0	1	0	0.333	0	0
SD	0.526	0.5	0.924	0	0.847	0.803

Now, the task would be the compare each alternative with the rest of the alternatives. For this purpose, another table depicting the comparisons of the alternatives are depicted as follows

Table B2.4 represents the normalised matrix. Following this step, the next shall be to calculate preference function from the evaluation matrix.

Step 3: Determining the Preference Function

The value of the Preference Function shall be determined by the following equations-

If the value of the difference of any two alternative is less than zero then the value of the preference function is equal to zero.

$$P(A,B) = 0 \text{ if } D(f_{ai} - f_{bi}) \leq 0 \quad (24)$$

If the value of the difference of any two alternative is greater than zero then the value of the preference function is same as that of the difference between the two alternatives

$$P(A,B) = D(A\text{-}B) \text{ if } D(f_{ai} - f_{bi}) \geq 0 \quad (25)$$

Table 18. Calculating the difference of each alternative with respect to other

Criteria (Weight)→ Alternatives↓	A (0.122)	B (0.281)	C (0.143)	D (0.340)	E (0.082)	F (0.031)
D(A-B)	-0.185	0	0	-0.333	-0.322	-0.235
D(A-C)	0.815	-1	1	0.334	0.668	0.765
D(A-D)	0.289	-0.5	0.076	0.667	-0.179	-0.038
D(B-A)	0.185	0	0	0.333	0.322	0.235
D(B-C)	1	-1	1	0.667	1	1
D(B-D)	0.474	-0.5	0.076	1	0.153	0.197
D(C-A)	-0.815	1	-1	-0.334	-0.668	-0.765
D(C-B)	-1	1	-1	-0.667	-1	-1
D(C-D)	-0.526	0	-0.924	-0.333	-0.847	-0.803
D(D-A)	-0.289	0.5	-0.076	-0.667	0.179	0.038
D(D-B)	-0.474	0.5	-0.076	-1	-0.153	-0.197
D(D-C)	0.526	-0.5	0.924	-0.333	0.847	0.803

Table 19. Calculating the value of preference function

Criteria (Weight)→ Alternatives↓	A (0.122)	B (0.281)	C (0.143)	D (0.340)	E (0.082)	F (0.031)
D(A-B)	0	0	0	0	0	0
D(A-C)	0.815	0	1	0.334	0.668	0.765
D(A-D)	0.289	0	0.076	0.667	0	0
D(B-A)	0.185	0	0	0.333	0.322	0.235
D(B-C)	1	0	1	0.667	1	1
D(B-D)	0.474	0	0.076	1	0.153	0.197
D(C-A)	0	1	0	0	0	0
D(C-B)	0	1	0	0	0	0
D(C-D)	0	0	0	0	0	0
D(D-A)	0	0.5	0	0	0.179	0.038
D(D-B)	0	0.5	0	0	0	0
D(D-C)	0	0	0	0	0.847	0.803

Thus, the evaluation matrix would now be represented as

Now, the aim is to calculate the aggregate sum of preference function or, as many authors refer it to, the Global Preference Index (GPI). As the term suggests, GPI is the weighted sum of all criteria of a given alternative.

$$\pi(a_i,a_j)= \sum w_f \cdot \pi(a_i,a_j) / \sum w_f \quad (26)$$

Table 20. Calculating the value of aggregate preference function

Criteria (Weight)→ Alternatives↓	A (0.122)	B (0.281)	C (0.143)	D (0.340)	E (0.082)	F (0.031)	$\pi(a_i,a_j)$
D(A-B)	0x0.122	0x0.281	0x0.143	0x0.340	0x0.082	0x0.031	0
D(A-C)	0.815 x0.122	0 x0.281	1 x0.143	0.334 x0.340	0.668 x0.082	0.765 x0.031	0.434
D(A-D)	0.289 x0.122	0 x0.281	0.076 x0.143	0.667 x0.340	0 x0.082	0 x0.031	0.273
D(B-A)	0.185 x0.122	0 x0.281	0 x0.143	0.333 x0.340	0.322 x0.082	0.235 x0.031	0.170
D(B-C)	1 x0.122	0 x0.281	1 x0.143	0.667 x0.340	1 x0.082	1 x0.031	0.605
D(B-D)	0.474 x0.122	0 x0.281	0.076 x0.143	1 x0.340	0.153 x0.082	0.197 x0.031	0.339
D(C-A)	0 x0.122	1 x0.281	0 x0.143	0 x0.340	0 x0.082	0 x0.031	0.281
D(C-B)	0 x0.122	1 x0.281	0 x0.143	0 x0.340	0 x0.082	0 x0.031	0.281
D(C-D)	0 x0.122	0 x0.281	0 x0.143	0 x0.340	0 x0.082	0 x0.031	0
D(D-A)	0 x0.122	0.5 x0.281	0 x0.143	0 x0.340	0.179 x0.082	0.038 x0.031	0.156
D(D-B)	0 x0.122	0.5 x0.281	0 x0.143	0 x0.340	0 x0.082	0 x0.031	0.281
D(D-C)	0 x0.122	0 x0.281	0 x0.143	0 x0.340	0.847 x0.082	0.803 x0.031	0.094

Table 21. Calculating the value of aggregate preference function

	$\pi(a_i,a_j)$
P(A,B)	0
P(A,C)	0.434
P(A,D)	0.273
P(B,A)	0.170
P(B,C)	0.605
P(B,D)	0.339
P(C,A)	0.281
P(C,B)	0.281
P(C,D)	0
P(D,A)	0.156
P(D,B)	0.281
P(D,C)	0.094

Step 4: Determining the Leaving and Entering Outranking flow

To determine the leaving and entering outranking flow, procedure is to formulate the aggregated preference function matrix which is represented as-

From this matrix the leaving and entering outranking flows are calculated as follows-

- Positive/Leaving outranking flow is calculated using the following formula

Table 22. The aggregate preference function matrix

Criteria→ Alternatives↓	A	B	C	D
A	-	0.170	0.281	0.156
B	0	-	0.281	0.281
C	0.434	0.605	-	0.094
D	0.273	0.339	0	-

$$\Phi^{+}_{(ai)=} 1/n-1(\textstyle\sum_{aj\in A} \pi(a_{i,} a_j))\ (a_{i\neq} a_j) \tag{27}$$

- Negative/entering outranking flow it is calculated using the following formula

$$\Phi^{-}_{(ai)=} 1/n-1(\textstyle\sum_{aj\in A} \pi(a_j, a_i))\ (a_{i\neq} a_j) \tag{28}$$

In both the above cases, n represents the number of alternatives offered (in this case, n is equal to 4) while taking a decision. The higher the leaving outflow is, the better it is. Whereas, the lower the entering outflow is better it is.

Step 5: Applying PROMETHEE I or Partial Ranking

PROMETHEE I evaluate alternatives based on three conditions. It compares the two alternatives and deem their relationship as-

- P^I – Preference
- I^I – Indifference
- R^I – incompatibility

a is preferred over b (aP^Ib) iff

$$\Phi^{+}_{a} > \Phi^{+}_{b} \text{ and } \Phi^{-}_{a} < \Phi^{-}_{b} \text{ or} \tag{29}$$

Table 23. Calculating the entering and leaving flow

Alternatives→ Alternatives↓	A	B	C	D	Leaving Flow (Φ^+)
A	-	0.170	0.281	0.156	0.2023
B	0	-	0.281	0.281	0.1873
C	0.434	0.605	-	0.094	0.3777
D	0.273	0.339	0	-	0.2040
Entering Flow (Φ^-)	0.2357	0.3713	0.1873	0.1770	

$$\Phi^+_a = \Phi^+_b \text{ and } \Phi^-_a < \Phi^-_b \text{ or} \tag{30}$$

$$\Phi^+_a > \Phi^+_b \text{ and } \Phi^-_a = \Phi^-_b \tag{31}$$

If one these conditions is satisfied (simultaneously fulfilling both the clauses in a single condition), then alternative a is preferred over b.

a is indifferent to b ($aI^{I}b$) iff

$$\Phi^+_a = \Phi^+_b \text{ and } \Phi^-_a = \Phi^-_b \tag{32}$$

If this condition is satisfied (simultaneously fulfilling both the clauses), alternative a is indifferent to b.

a is incompatible to b ($aR^{I}b$) iff

$$\Phi^+_a > \Phi^+_b \text{ and } \Phi^-_a > \Phi^-_b \text{ or} \tag{33}$$

$$\Phi^+_a < \Phi^+_b \text{ and } \Phi^-_a < \Phi^-_b \tag{34}$$

If any of these conditions is satisfied (simultaneously fulfilling both the clauses in a single condition), then alternative a is incompatible to b.

While comparing A with other alternatives based on the aforementioned rubric, it is found that

- A R^{I} B
- A R^{I} C
- A R^{I} D

Similarly evaluating B, C and D

The results of PROMETHEE I are represented in the table B5.2. PROMETHEE I suggest that all the incompatible alternatives should be discarded and only the preferred ones should be evaluated. Figure 6 illustrates that there exist five scenarios where an alternative is preferred over the other, that is, A P^{I} B, C P^{I} A, C P^{I} B, D P^{I} A and D P^{I} B. To find the consistency of the results, PROMETHEE II must be applied and evaluated.

Step 6: Applying PROMETHEE II or Complete Ranking

Table 24. Representation of the entering and leaving flows of each alternative

Alternatives	Leaving Flow (Φ^+)	Entering Flow (Φ^-)
A	0.2023	0.2357
B	0.1873	0.3713
C	0.3777	0.1873
D	0.2040	0.1770

Table 25. PROMETHEE I result of partial comparison of alternatives

Alternatives	A	B	C	D
A	-	N/A	C P^I A	D P^I A
B	A P^I B	-	C P^I B	D P^I B
C	N/A		-	D R^I C
D	N/A	N/A	C R^I D	-

Figure 6. Partial ranking of alternatives
(source: own)

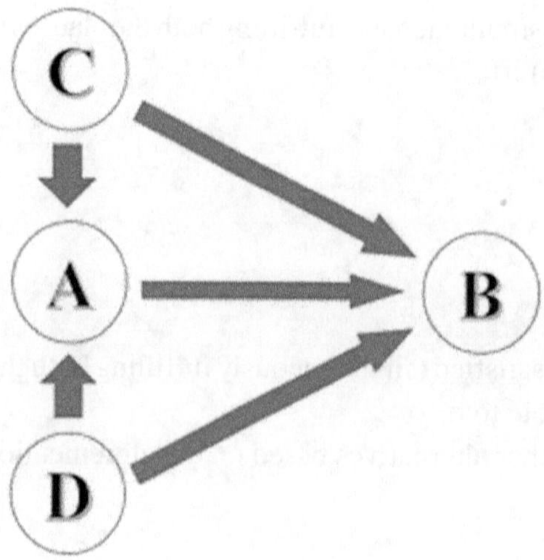

In order to evaluate the most feasible alternative, PROMETHEE II suggests that the decision maker must calculate the net outranking flow. The net outranking flow is the difference between the leaving (positive) flow and the entering (negative) flow. It is represented as

$$\Phi^n = (\Phi^+) - (\Phi^-) \quad (35)$$

It must be noted that one of the properties of PROMETHEE II is that the value of net outranking flow is between -1 and 1.

$$-1 < \Phi n < 1 \quad (36)$$

PROMETHEE II offers only two implications, that is, it does not consider the parameter of incompatibility, unlike PROMETHEE I. Hence, the conditions for PROMETHEE II are as follows-

- $aP^{II}b$ iff $\Phi_a > \Phi_b$ Here, P^{II} denotes Preference of a over b
- $aI^{II}b$ iff $\Phi_a = \Phi_b$ Here, I^{II} denotes indifference of a and b

Thus, the net outranking flow shall be represented as

Table 26. Calculating the entering flow, leaving flow and ranking of the alternatives

Alternatives	Leaving Flow (Φ^+)	Entering Flow (Φ^-)	Net Flow (Φ^n)	Ranking
A	0.2023	0.2357	-0.0334	3
B	0.1873	0.3713	-0.184	4
C	0.3777	0.1873	0.1904	1
D	0.2040	0.1770	0.027	2

Figure 7. Complete ranking of the alternatives
(source: own)

Thus, according to PROMETHEE II the alternatives in order of their feasibility is

C > D > A > B

Figure 7 illustrates that the ranking is consistent with the results of PROMETHEE I.

CONCLUSION

Albeit PROMETHEE is one of the most feasible strategy that any decision maker can adopt, there exists some implicit limitations that are present in the rubric of PROMETHEE. The primary drawback which can easily be overcome by existing software is that it is time consuming in nature. Terrientes & Miguel (2015) stresses on the fact that the decision maker can express their preferences between two actions on all the criteria on ratio scales or they can express the importance they have attached to the criteria on a ratio scale. The decision maker would want to take all criteria into account knowing that the weights are representing trade-offs between each criterion. Thus, for all criteria the difference between evaluations must be meaningful. None of the possible differences on any of the criteria can give fulfil the clauses of discordance. Moreover, while performing PROMETHEE the decision maker precisely knows what can be the effect on the final decision if there is an addition or removal of an action.

Though PROMETHEE tries to ascertain that along with the quantifiable parameters, the qualitative parameters should also be considered while making a rational and most appropriate decision in any given scenario (Araz, 2005). The first and the foremost limitation of PROMETHEE methods is that its applicability is subjected to the stipulation wherein the decision maker can express his preferences or choices between two actions on a ratio scale for any given criterion.

The second issue that a decision maker must take care of is that PROMETHEE methods is applicable only after the decision maker bifurcates the criteria based on their importance or simply the decision maker attaches weights to each criterion mentioned on the ratio scale. The weights of the criteria express trade-offs between the criteria (De Keyser, Wim & Peeters, Peter, 1996). PROMETHEE methods may only be used with criteria which are quantifiable in nature, thus the qualitative criteria are to be moulded in meaningful manner. Attaching weights in itself is a subjective task which, in a certain sense, is rationalised by techniques such as AHP which itself has some drawback (Martin, Fajard, Blanco, & Requena, 2003). The consistency condition is difficult to achieve via AHP as several consistency indices have been proposed, as well as methods to obtain a transitive matrix (Bana e Costa & Vansnick, 2008). The second drawback of AHP which is its additive nature of the aggregation forces another drawback in the framework of PROMETHEE as it generates rank reversals (Ishizaka & Labib, 2011).

An outranking relation is deemed credible if for any assertion, both the necessity condition (concordance test) and sufficient condition (discordance test) are satisfied. This factor of "credibility" is precisely what is one of the drawbacks of PROMETHEE. The PROMETHEE method does not account for is discordance. According to Terrientes & Miguel (2015), concordance is referred to as "the respect of the majority" that measures the strength of the coalition of criteria that supports the assertion while discordance is referred to as " the respect of minoritites" that accounts for criteria that disagrees with the assertion (Adalı, Işık, & Kundakcı, 2016). The issue with PROMETHEE is that it only fulfills or take into consideration the test of concordance but neglects the test of discordance which is an equally significant subset of decision making.

The next limitation arises in the form of addition or removal of an action. The relative position in the pre-order scenario is susceptible to change with an addition or removal of an action which is dominated by all other actions or which is equal to another action does not only change the PROMETHEE pre-orders but can also influence the final decision. This seems reasonable when 'the best action' is deleted or 'a better action' is added (Terrientes & Miguel, 2015).

The chapter proves that PROMETHEE offers a flexibility in MCDM with its quantitative approach. Apart from considering the qualitative criteria affecting a decision, consistency of results evaluated from PROMETHEE I and PROMETHEE II is another aspect of this approach that makes it one of the most applicable tools in the regime of decision making. The literature proves the applicability of PROMETHEE in diverse fields, varying from environmental management to nuclear management. The future scope of research can be in terms of explaining the evolution of PROMETHEE, its association with GAIA and visualising its decision plane.

REFERENCES

Adalı, E., Işık, A., & Kundakcı, K. (2016). An alternative approach based on Fuzzy PROMETHEE method for the supplier selection problem. *Uncertain Supply Chain Management, 4*(3), 183–194. doi:10.5267/j.uscm.2016.2.002

Al-Rashdan, D., Al-Kloub, B., Dean, A., & Al-Shemmeri, T. (1999). Environmental impact assessment and ranking the environmental projects in Jordan. *European Journal of Operational Research, 118*(1), 30–45. doi:10.1016/S0377-2217(97)00079-9

Albadvi, A., Chaharsooghi, S. K., & Esfahanipour, A. (2007). Decision making in stock trading: An application of PROMETHEE. *European Journal of Operational Research, 177*(2), 673–683. doi:10.1016/j.ejor.2005.11.022

Araz, O. U. (2005, December). A simulation based multi-criteria scheduling approach of dual-resource constrained manufacturing systems with neural networks. In *Australasian Joint Conference on Artificial Intelligence* (pp. 1047-1052). Berlin, Germany: Springer. 10.1007/11589990_138

Bana e Costa, C., & Vansnick, J. (2008). A critical analysis of the eigenvalue method used to derive priorities in AHP. *European Journal of Operational Research, 187*(3), 1422–1428. doi:10.1016/j.ejor.2006.09.022

Behzadian, M., Kazemzadeh, R. B., Albadvi, A., & Aghdasi, M. (2010). PROMETHEE: A comprehensive literature review on methodologies and applications. *European Journal of Operational Research, 200*(1), 198–215. doi:10.1016/j.ejor.2009.01.021

Beynon, M. J., & Wells, P. (2008). The lean improvement of the chemical emissions of motor vehicles based on preference ranking: A PROMETHEE uncertainty analysis. *Omega, 36*(3), 384–394. doi:10.1016/j.omega.2006.04.015

Brans, J.-P., & De Smet, Y. (2016). PROMETHEE Methods (pp. 187–219). doi:10.1007/978-1-4939-3094-4_6

Brans, J. P., & Mareschal, B. (1992). PROMETHEE V: MCDM problems with segmentation constraints. *INFOR, 30*(2), 85–96. doi:10.1080/03155986.1992.11732186

Brans, J. P., & Mareschal, B. (1995). The PROMETHEE VI procedure: How to differentiate hard from soft multicriteria problems. *Journal of Decision Systems, 4*(3), 213–223. doi:10.1080/12460125.1995.10511652

Briggs, T., Kunsch, P. L., & Mareschal, B. (1990). Nuclear waste management: An application of the multicriteria PROMETHEE methods. *European Journal of Operational Research, 44*(1), 1–10. doi:10.1016/0377-2217(90)90308-X

De Keyser, W., & Peeters, P. (1996). A note on the use of PROMETHEE multicriteria methods. *European Journal of Operational Research, 89*(3), 457–461. doi:10.1016/0377-2217(94)00307-6

Figueira, J., de Smet, I., & Brans, J. P. (2004). *MCDA methods for sorting and clustering problems: PROMETHEE TRI and PROMETHEE CLUSTER. Université Libre de Bruxelles*. Service de Mathématiques de la Gestion.

Figueira, J., Mousseau, V., & Roy, B. (2005). ELECTRE methods. In Multiple criteria decision analysis: State of the art surveys, 133-153, Springer New York. doi:10.1007/0-387-23081-5_4

Geldermann, J., & Rentz, O. (2005). Multi-criteria Analysis for Technique Assessment: Case Study from Industrial Coating. *Journal of Industrial Ecology, 9*(3), 127–142. doi:10.1162/1088198054821591

Geldermann, J., Spengler, T., & Rentz, O. (2000). Fuzzy outranking for environmental assessment. Case study: Iron and steel making industry. *Fuzzy Sets and Systems, 115*(1), 45–65. doi:10.1016/S0165-0114(99)00021-4

Hababou, M., & Martel, J. M. (1998). A multicriteria approach for selecting a portfolio manager. *INFOR, 36*(3), 161–176. doi:10.1080/03155986.1998.11732354

Ishizaka, A., & Labib, A. (2011). Review of the main developments in the analytic hierarchy process. *Expert Systems with Applications*. doi:10.1016/j.eswa.2011.04.143

Kiker, G. A., Bridges, T. S., Varghese, A., Seager, T. P., & Linkov, I. (2005). Application of multicriteria decision analysis in environmental decision making. *Integrated Environmental Assessment and Management: An International Journal, 1*(2), 95–108. doi:10.1897/IEAM_2004a-015.1 PMID:16639891

Klauer, B., Drechsler, M., & Messner, F. (2006). Multicriteria analysis under uncertainty with IANUS—Method and empirical results. *Environment and Planning. C, Government & Policy, 24*(2), 235–256. doi:10.1068/c03102s

Mareschal, B. (1986). Stochastic multicriteria decision making and uncertainty. *European Journal of Operational Research, 26*(1), 58–64. doi:10.1016/0377-2217(86)90159-1

Martin, J. M., Fajardo, W., Blanco, A., & Requena, I. (2003). Constructing linguistic versions for the multicriteria decision support systems preference ranking organization method for enrichment evaluation I and II. *International Journal of Intelligent Systems, 18*(7), 711–731. doi:10.1002/int.10112

Mitkova, V., Mlynarovic, V., & Tus, B. (2007). A performance and risk analysis on the Slovak private pension funds market. *Ekonomický časopis. Journal of Economics, 3*(55), 232–249.

Moffett, A., & Sarkar, S. (2006). Incorporating multiple criteria into the design of conservation area networks: A minireview with recommendations. *Diversity & Distributions, 12*(2), 125–137. doi:10.1111/j.1366-9516.2005.00202.x

Queiruga, D., Walther, G., Gonzalez-Benito, J., & Spengler, T. (2008). Evaluation of sites for the location of WEEE recycling plants in Spain. *Waste Management (New York, N.Y.), 28*(1), 181–190. doi:10.1016/j.wasman.2006.11.001 PMID:17198752

Rezaei-kelidbari, H. R., Homayounfar, M., & Foumani, S. F. A. (2016). A Combined Group EA-PROMETHEE Method for a Supplier Selection Problem. *Iranian Journal of Optimization, 8*(2), 87–100.

Senvar, O., Tuzkaya, G., & Kahraman, C. (2014). Multi criteria supplier selection using fuzzy PROMETHEE method. In *Supply chain management under fuzziness* (pp. 21–34). Berlin, Germany: Springer. doi:10.1007/978-3-642-53939-8_2

Terrientes, D. V., & Miguel, L. (2015). *Hierarchical outranking methods for multi-criteria decision aiding*. Universitat Rovira i Virgili.

Vaillancourt, K., & Waaub, J. P. (2004). Equity in international greenhouse gases abatement scenarios: A multicriteria approach. *European Journal of Operational Research, 153*(2), 489–505. doi:10.1016/S0377-2217(03)00170-X

Zopounidis, C., & Doumpos, M. (2002). Multi-criteria decision aid in financial decision making: Methodologies and literature review. *Journal of Multi-Criteria Decision Analysis, 11*(4-5), 167–186. doi:10.1002/mcda.333

ADDITIONAL READING

De Smet, Y. (2019). Beyond Multicriteria Ranking Problems: The Case of PROMETHEE. In *New Perspectives in Multiple Criteria Decision Making* (pp. 95–114). Cham: Springer. doi:10.1007/978-3-030-11482-4_3

Rezaei-kelidbari, H. R., Homayounfar, M., & Foumani, S. F. A. (2016). A Combined Group EA-PROMETHEE Method for a Supplier Selection Problem. *Iranian Journal of Optimization*, *8*(2), 87–100.

Saaty, T. L. (2008). Decision making with the analytic hierarchy process. *International Journal of Services Sciences*, *1*(1), 83. doi:10.1504/IJSSCI.2008.017590

Senvar, O., Tuzkaya, G., & Kahraman, C. (2014). Multi criteria supplier selection using fuzzy PROMETHEE method. In *Supply chain management under fuzziness* (pp. 21–34). Berlin, Heidelberg: Springer. doi:10.1007/978-3-642-53939-8_2

Zhang, K., Kluck, C., & Achari, G. (2009). A comparative approach for ranking contaminated sites based on the risk assessment paradigm using fuzzy PROMETHEE. *Environmental Management*, *44*(5), 952–967. doi:10.100700267-009-9368-7 PMID:19763684

KEY TERMS AND DEFINITIONS

Criteria: One of the options or the ideal way of judgment of an alternative.

Evaluation: The assessment of an alternative.

MCDM: Stands for Multicriteria-decision making which is the process of selecting the most feasible alternative in order to achieve an objective.

PROMETHEE: Stands for Preference Ranking Organization Method for Enrichment Evaluation which is a decision-making tool.

Chapter 13
Fuzzy Failure Mode and Effects Analysis in a Pharmaceutical Production Process With Fuzzy PROMETHEE Method

Sündüz Dağ
Istanbul University, Turkey

ABSTRACT

Failure mode and effects analysis (FMEA) is a quality improvement technique that defines potential errors and ranks them according to their degree of effectiveness in both service and production processes. While enterprises want to produce quality products or services, they also strive to reduce the cost of quality. At this point, the FMEA method provides a proactive approach to decision makers by ensuring that the types of errors in products sent to both internal and external customers and the probability of occurrence of these errors are predicted. In recent years, the FMEA method has begun to be evaluated in the frame of fuzzy logic to obtain more effective results. In this way, results have become realistic and objective. This chapter analyzes pharmaceutical production process to define potential error types and the effect of these errors. Risk priority order of error types is determined by Fuzzy PROMETHEE Method.

INTRODUCTION

In recent year, firms have entered into a challenging struggle for competition, due to the rapid development of technology and the change in customer understanding. Firms have to differentiate with the products or services they offer in order to be able to survive in intense competition conditions. In addition, it has become a necessity for them to develop themselves. One of the important points that firms can make a difference is the quality of the product or service. Observing errors which causes the fail of the production processes and taking corrective actions in every process ensures the quality of the final products that will go to the external customer while increasing the quality of the products used by internal customers. Also these errors can lead to defects and waste outcomes for the customers. Preserving and improving the

DOI: 10.4018/978-1-7998-2216-5.ch013

quality level is closely related to the design of the product, the production process, and the sales process. In order to create customer satisfaction, the operation of all these processes should be planned correctly.

The main objective of this chapter is to propose a practical and efficient model to determine the potential failure types in a pharmaceutical process and, rank them according to the RPN number using a multi-criteria decision-making (MCDM) method. In this study, firstly, a fuzzy approach, allowing decision makers to use linguistic variables for determining the weights of risk factors: severity (S), occurrence (O), and detectability (D) is considered for FMEA. Then, failure types in the pharmaceutical process are evaluated according to the RPN values using the Fuzzy PROMETHEE method. This proposed model permitting the use of different importance weights for the risk factors (S, O, D) in fuzzy PROMETHEE for scoring and sorting of the potential failure modes, can be taken as a contribution in the Fuzzy FMEA literature. Also, there is no research implements the Fuzzy PROMETHEE to improve the FMEA for a pharmaceutical process. Therefore, there is a necessity to present a risk sorting model for FMEA by including the advantages of the Fuzzy PROMETHEE method.

In this study, pharmaceutical production, which is one of the most important actors in the health sector, has been selected. Pharmaceutical production involves crucial processes related to human life. Therefore, Good Manufacturing Practice (GMP) which is a set of rules and practices that minimize production risks and failures, is implemented in pharmaceutical production. This rules system requires process-oriented operations from raw material procurement to final product packaging. Process –oriented operations are carried out with standard operations procedures (SOP) which is unchanged rule of GMP. The SOP is a guideline to apply every operation in the production process in the same way. All of the production processes are performed and followed in accordance with the quantity and quality written in the SOP's. In this way, risks and failures lead to variability and deviation in production can be prevented. Therefore, pharmaceutical companies have to comply with GMP standards to deliver the guaranteed full product to the customer.

Nowadays, the FMEA method has been widely used to determine potential errors which cause variability and deviation and its' impactsin the pharmaceutical processes. FMEA method has emerged as a quality improvement technique for prevention before errors occur. FMEA focuses on the risks that may cause poor quality in production processes. The traditional FMEA method prioritizes the types of failure by determining the risk priority number (RPN) of the failure types. In other words, it ensures the types of errors that may contain high risk or danger are considered as a priority (Şimşir, Demir, & Azdemir, 2018, p.24).

When the studies in the literature are examined, it has been determined that the traditional FMEA technique has some deficiencies which are described under the Fuzzy FMEA title of this study. for real-life problems. These deficiencies are mostly related to detection and evaluation o frisk factors which is showed S, O, and D. Several methods have been proposed in the literature to eliminate these deficiencies. One of these methods is to combine the FMEA with MCDM techniques.

Some Studies which combine AHP (Analytic Hierarchy Process) with the FMEA technique in the literature: Braglia (2000) developed a multi-feature error analysis method that works based on AHP technique. According to the study, risk factors is decision criterion, error causes are decision alternatives and priority order of error causes are accepted as objective function.Hu et al. (2009) determined the relative weight of risk factors by the Fuzzy AHP method and proposed the green component risk priority number for the analysis of hazardous substances in green components. Shahrabi and Shojaei (2014) attempted to identify the root causes of failures in one of the oldest refineries in the world by using FMEA and AHP techniques and to minimize these expenditures. Illangkumaran et al. (2014) proposed a method based on FMEA and AHP techniques to evaluate the risk priority values of critical components in the paper industry. They used Fuzzy AHP method to determine risk factor weights. Özfırat (2014) aimed to bring together the positive aspects of FMEA and fuzzy AHP methods in order to analyze the risks on occupational health and safety in the mining field. Bao et al. (2017) assessed an occupational disease in mining industry. An FMEA-based method and an improved AHP model have been established to prevent the risk of occupational health and to ensure the reliability of weight. Cheraghi et al.(2018) tried to evaluate the environmental risk of Iran's oil field using FMEA and AHP. At the end of the study, they obtained the most important criteria (manpower, vehicles, materials, and operations) to reduce the environmental pollution.

Some studies which combine VIKOR (VIše Kriterijumska Optimizacija I Kompromisno Resenje) or TOPSIS (Technique for Order Preference by Similarity to Ideal Solution) methods that provide compromise solutions with the FMEA: Braglia et al. (2003) were the first to implement the fuzzy TOPSIS method to prioritize error types in FMEA. The grading of the causes of error in the method is based on the measure of the Euclidean distance of an alternative to the ideal target. Sachdeva et al. (2009) proposed an FMEA method that takes into account risk factors such as failure occurrence, detection, maintenance, spare parts and cost in prioritizing error types. They used the Shannon entropy method to calculate the weights of these six risk factors. Liu et al. (2012) proposed the extended VIKOR method in a fuzzy environment to determine the risk priorities of error types. They used linguistic expressions in trapezoidal fuzzy numbers for the assessment of risk factors and determined the risk priorities of the identified error types with the extended VIKOR.

Helvacıoğlu & Özen (2014) used FMEA method for reliability analysis in yacht systems and proposed fuzzy TOPSIS method in order to overcome the deficiencies of FMEA method. Emovon et al. (2015) integrated an averaging technique with the Compromise Programming (CP)technique and VIKOR method in order to determine the error types in marine machinery systems and to determine the risk priorities of these error types. Chang (2015) proposed a risk assessment method in order to meet customer demands accurately in a high-tech design company. The method consists of computerized application of FMEA and fuzzy TOPSIS methods. Sisman (2017) proposed fuzzy set theory to increase the efficiency of risk assessment process and to sort error types according to their priorities effectively and precisely. In this study, Fuzzy AHP and Fuzzy VIKOR methods are used to evaluate risks in an automotive production firm. Firstly fuzzy AHP method was used to determine the significance weights of the risk factors, and then the risk priority of the error types was listed using fuzzy VIKOR method. Mangeli et. Al (2019) proposed a hybrid method based on support vector machine and fuzzy system to reduce the effects of subjective opinions in identifying FMEA factors. Then, authors ranked type of risks according to the fuzzy TOPSIS method. Some studies using ELECTRE (Elemination and Choice Translating Reality English) or PROMETHEE (The Preference Ranking Organization Method for Enrichment Evaluation) methods that provide a solution by sorting. Liu et al. (2016) performed ELECTRE based ranking approach for FMEA using the two tuple interval. Authors used a hybrid averaging operator by taking into account the evaluations of different team members to form a group assessment matrix. Emovon (2016) conducted a risk analysis of diesel marine engines by combining Dempster Shafer Theory and ELECTRE. Dempster Shafer Theory was used to collect the ratings of uncertain error types from experts, while ELECTRE method was used to rate error types. Silvia et al. (2018) advised an alternative approach to compute the RPN number. ELECTRE method was used to specify the most important failure types. In contrast to classical RPN, proposed method allow to consider the relative importance of the risk factors. Yerlikaya et al. (2016) applied the Fuzzy PROMETHE method to determine the risk priorities of error types in a construction company. Lolli et al. (2015) proposed a novel group decision support system which is named as Flow Sort-GDSS to rank the failure types in the plastic bottle manufacturing system. Then, authors used PROMETHEE method to compare failure types with the reference profiles set by the decision-makers. Mokrini et al. (2016) investigated for failure modes in pharmaceutical supply chain. Authors combined Fuzzy AHP and PROMETHEE methods to assess the risks of critical. Liu et al. (2017) used the cloud model and PROMETHEE method for the analysis of error types. The cloud model is used to identify risk assessment types recognized by FMEA experts and to model personal uncertainties; The PROMETHEE method has been proposed to determine the risk priorities of the error types and the most dangerous error types.

This chapter is organized as follow: Initially, a brief overview of the literature dealing with the FMEA and MCDM techniques is presented. Secondly, FMEA, and thirdly Fuzzy FMEA techniques are described in detail. Fourthly, PROMETHEE and Fuzzy PROMETHEE techniques are introduced step by step. Fifthly, application of this study is realized. Finally, conclusion is given.

FAILURE MODE AND EFFECTS ANALYSIS

Nowadays, Firms have to improve the quality of the final product in order to compete in the existing markets. Final product quality level is closely related to the risks of the production system and failures caused by risks. Therefore, the investigation and diagnosis of potential risks that reduce the reliability and performance of the production systems is a major problem. This problem necessitates the analysis of the production system in detail. FMEA is one of the most common methods used in many industries to overcome this problem. FMEA is also named as a quality improvement technique which aims to prevent errors at the early stages of the production process and evaluate the potential causes of errors at the beginning of the design process. This method focuses on the types of errors resulting from inadequate product manufacturing processes (Eryürek & Tanyaş, 2003, p. 33).

FMEA was first used in the USA for controlling of flight systems in the 1950s. It was used in the automobile industry in the 1970s and later became part of the total quality management (Akkurt, 2002, p. 307). One of the unchanged rules of total quality management is continuous improvement. Error prevention is a basic concept which is used to achieve continuous improvement in total quality management (Devadasan, Muthu, Samson, & Sankaran, 2003, p. 551). Therefore, FMEA is widely used in total quality management applications. In this method occurrence, severity, and detection values of every failure type are determined. There are four basic questions to analyze occurrence, severity, and detection of a failure type;

- What are the errors in the systems?
- What is the frequency of these errors?
- What can cause these errors?
- What will be the effect of these errors?

Occurrence expresses the frequency of a failure or likelihood of a failure. The severity factor shows how much effect a failure will generate. Also, severity is the situation which faced by customer when the product or process failure occurs. Detection is the noticeability degree of a failure before it occurs. Also, possibility of defective items not reaching the customers or noticing of defective items by producer

Table 1. Occurrence evaluation criteria

Rating	Probability of Failure Occurrence	Failure Rate
9,10	Very High	>1 in 2 1 in 3
7,8	High	1 in8 1 in 20
4,5,6	Moderate	1 in 80 1 in 400 1 in 2000
2,3	Low	1 in 15,000 1 in 150,000
1	Remote	<1 in 1,500,000

before not reaching the customer. The risk priority number is obtained by multiplying these three values. It can be stated as,

$$RPN= O \times S \times D \quad (1)$$

The value of the RPN ensures that the types of errors in the process are ordered from top to bottom. Also, RPN number indicates the relative importance of errors and determines the priority in the recovery activities. Thus, it can help producers to reduce internal and external failure costs by taking corrective action. (Vahdani, Salimi, & Charkhchian, 2015, p. 358). In traditional FMEA, Occurrence, severity, and detection are evaluated using 10-point scale showed in Table 1, 2, and 3 (Wang, Chin, Poon, & Yang, 2009, p.1196). Higher RPN values indicate that the failure type is more important than the others. Therefore, companies should prioritize failure type with higher RPN value and take corrective action for this failure type (Tay &Lİm, 2006, 1049).

The traditional FMEA procedure is composed of 12 steps (Chanamool & Naenna, 2016, p. 442):

Table 2. Severity evaluation criteria

Rating	Effect	Severity
10	Hazardous no warning	Very high severity, failure occurs without warning
9	Hazardous with warning	Very high severity, failure occurs with warning
8	Very high	System inoperable with destructive failure
7	High	System inoperable with equipment damage
6	Moderate	System inoperable with minor damage
5	Low	System inoperable without damage
4	Very low	System operable with some degradation of performance
3	Minor	System operable with some degradation of performance
2	Very minor	System operable with minimal intervention
1	None	No effect

Table 3. Detection evaluation criteria

Rating	Effect	Probability of Detection by Design Control
10	Absolute uncertainty	Potential failure cause cannot be detected by design control
9	Very remote	Potential failure cause can be detected with very remote chance
8	Remote	Potential failure cause can be detected with remote chance
7	Very low	Potential failure cause can be detected with very low chance
6	Low	Potential failure cause can be detected with low chance
5	Moderate	Potential failure cause can be detected with moderate chance
4	Moderately high	Potential failure cause can be detected with moderately high chance
3	High	Potential failure cause can be detected with high chance
2	Very high	Potential failure cause can be detected with very high chance
1	Almost certain	Potential failure cause can be detected precisely

1. Determine the scale table for occurrence severity, and detection
2. Choose the process
3. Study on the process and collect information about the process
4. Determine the potential failure types.
5. Determine the possibility degree or frequency of each failure type
6. Determine the potential effect of each failure type
7. Determine the detectability degree of each failure type
8. Evaluate Occurrence for each failure type
9. Evaluate the efficiency of control or prevention
10. Evaluate the effect for each failure type
11. Calculate the RPN of each failure type
12. Decide whether corrective action needs to be taken according to the RPN. The answer is yes, back to step 3, otherwise the process is end.

Traditional FMEA procedure is summarized with a flowchart which is showed in Figure 1.

FUZZY FMEA

The traditional FMEA has been criticized in many study in the literature (Garcia, Schirru, & Emelo 2005, Chen, 2007, Yang, Bonsall, & Wang 2008, Abdelgawad & Fayek, 2010, Liu, Liu, & Li, 2014, Kutlu & Ekmekçioğlu, 2012, Gargama & Chaturverdi 2011, Mandal & Maiti, 2014) causes several drawbacks. There are four major drawbacks which are mentioned by the authors:

1. The degree of importance among risk factors is not considered. It is accepted that all risk factors have equal importance degree.
2. It is difficult to evaluate risk factors precisely. Most of the information collected for FMEA is expressed in linguistically, such as 'very low', 'important' or 'very high' etc.

Figure 1. Traditional FMEA flowchart

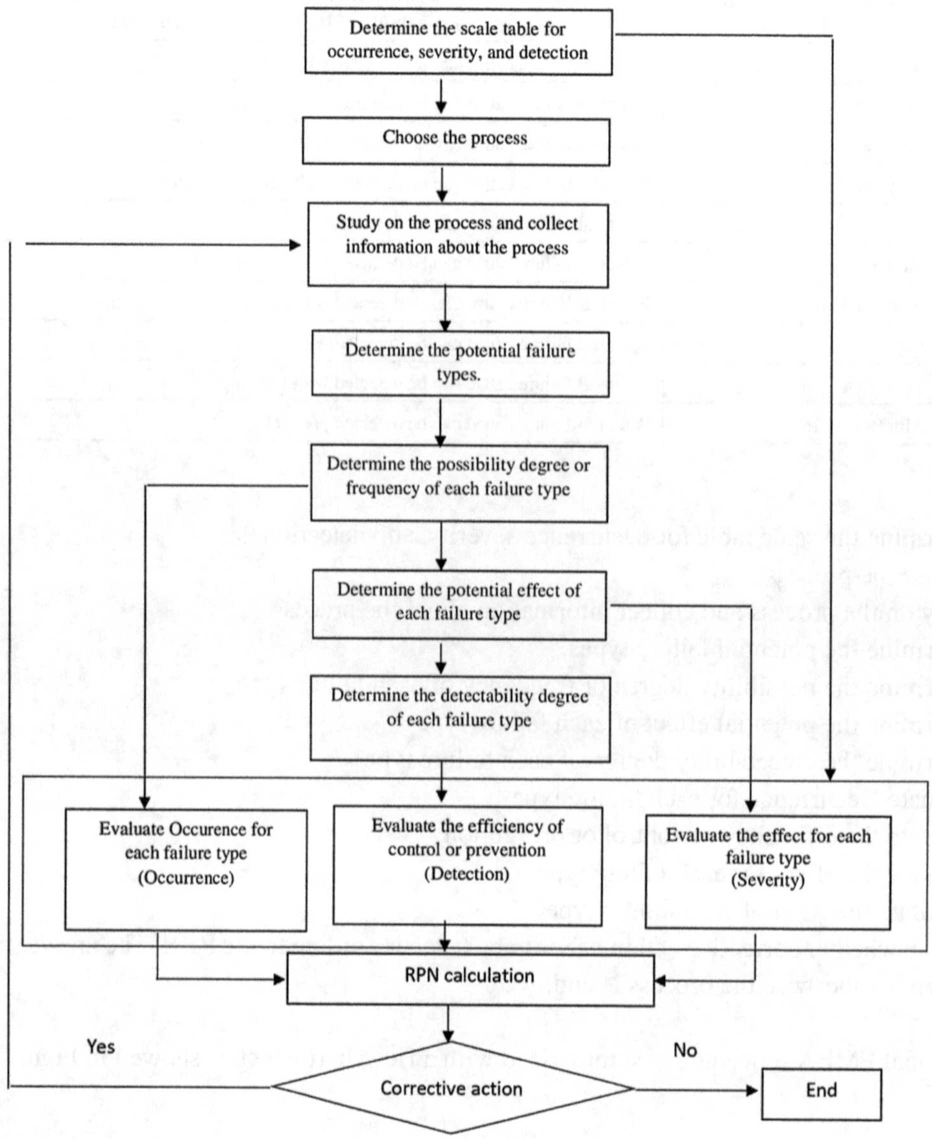

3. Different combination of risk factors can give the same RPN value. Their hidden risks may be different in total.
4. Mathematical calculation of RPN value is debatable. Small changes can make a big difference on RPN because of the strong sensitivity.

A great number of studies have carried out for overcoming shortcomings of traditional FMEA and increasing the efficiency of FMEA by using fuzzy logic. While some studies have recommended to use fuzzy system in calculation of RPN value which is named as Fuzzy FMEA, the others have recommended to use fuzzy FMEA with the fuzzy multicriteria decision making methods. Some of the examples about

Figure 2.

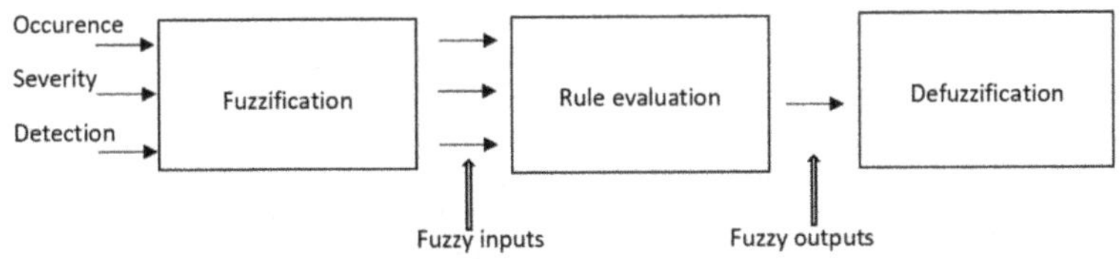

combination of FMEA and fuzzy multicriteria decision making methods were given in the introduction part of this study.

Firstly, fuzzy FMEA was proposed by Bowles and Pelaez in 1995.Researchers presented the risk factors in fuzzy set and evaluated them min-max inferencing, then defuzzified the fuzzy number to prioritize the failure types. Guimarães & Lapa, 2004 proposed a fuzzy FMEA method for volume control system. Chin et al., 2008 tried to apply fuzzy FMEA on product design system. Kumru & Kumru, 2013 used fuzzy FMEA to increase performance of purchasing process of a hospital. Mandal & Maiti, 2014 combined fuzzy FMEA with possibility theory and applied the model on Wang's data set to obtain more efficient system. Chanamool & Naenna, 2016 used fuzzy FMEA in a hospital's emergency department to improve decision making process.

Fuzzy FMEA studies in the literature is generally related to the fuzzy rule base method which contains three basic phases. These phases are described as follows:

- **Fuzzification phase:** linguistic expressions are used for three risk factors O, S, and D to transform fuzzy system. Fuzzy input factors of fuzzy FMEA is obtained from this phase (Dinmohammadi & Shafiee, 2013).Table 4 represents linguistic terms interpretations for risk factors O, S, and D to develop fuzzy rule system. Table 4 has been created combining Guimarães & Lapa, 2007 and Mandal & Maiti, 2014.
- **Rule evaluation phase:** Experts knowledge is collected about failure types in linguistic terms and constructed if-then rules. At the end of this phase fuzzy RPN numbers are obtained. These are named as fuzzy outputs.
- **Defuzzification phase:** Fuzzy RPN numbers is transformed to crisp data. Several methods are recommended for defuzzification process; center of gravity (COG) method, weighted average method, min-max method, Yager index method.

Fuzzy FMEA is summarized with a flowchart in Figure 2.

PROMETHEE AND FUZZY PROMETHEE

The PROMETHEE method was developed by Brans and firstly introduced in 1982 at a Canadian conference. PROMETHEE, which is an effective and easy method to apply, has been implemented successfully in various fields of production and service sector. PROMETHEE has been developed to assist the decision makers for most appropriate selection and ranking in multi-criteria decision making problems. In the other words, the basic aim of this method is prioritization. Alternatives which can create a solution for the multicriteria problem are compared pairwise with respect to each criterion (Ömürbek & Eren,

Table 4. Interpretations of risk factors to develop fuzzy system

Linguistic Term	Occurrence	Severity	Detection
Remote	A failure type's occurrence probability is extremely unlikely	It is not noticeable by the operators, because of the fact that this failure type doesn't show any effect on system performance	Root cause of failure type cannot be detected, failure type has almost uncertainty
Low	A failure type's occurrence probability is low, few failures	A failure type which doesn't cause deterioration on system performance, but it can create small changes on the product	Root cause of failure type can be detected with very low chance
Moderate	A failure type's occurrence probability is moderate, occasional failures	A failure type which causes slight damage on system performance, also it creates dissatisfaction for customer or operator in terms of the product	Root cause of failure type can be detected with moderate chance when the inspection or test is carried out
High	A failure type's occurrence probability is high, repeated failures	A failure type which causes important deterioration on system performance, it can create major impacts on the product	Root cause of failure type can be detected with high chance when the inspection or test is carried out
Very high	A failure type's occurrence probability is certain, it is almost inevitable	A failure type which seriously affects the ability to complete a task of the process, destructive failure	Root cause of failure type be detected almost certainly when the inspection or test is carried out

2016, p.178, Senvar et al., 2014, p.27). Pairwise comparison is carried out according to the preference functions explained by Brans.

Decision makers need two different information before applying the PROMETHEE method ((Dağdeviren, 2008, p. 400):

1. The PROMETHEE method doesn't have an ability to give weights of criteria. This information can be set by the decision makers or obtained from the other methods. AHP is one of the most commonly used methods for determining weights. if criterion weights determined by decision-makers are of equal importance, all weights are taken equally. The weights given to the criteria are a positive number changing from 0 to 1. The importance of criteria is directly proportional to the size of weights.
2. Information about preference function. Preference function is used by decision makers when comparing the contribution of the alternatives in terms of every single criterion.

The PROMETHEE method represents both advantages and disadvantages for users (Ulengin, Topçu & Şahin, 2001, p. 186):

1. The PROMETHEE method is easy to use
2. The PROMETHEE method allow both partial and total ranking of alternatives
3. The PROMETHEE method shows better performance than the other multicriteria decision making methods like AHP and ELECTRE

Table 5. Evaluation matrix

Alternatives /Criteria	k_1	k_2	k_3	.....
A	$k_1(a)$	$k_2(a)$	$k_3(a)$	.....
B	$k_1(b)$	$k_2(b)$	$k_3(b)$	.....
C	$k_1(c)$	$k_2(c)$	$k_3(c)$	.....
....	...	....	....	

The PROMETHEE procedure is composed of seven steps. The steps are briefly given below (Greco, Figueira, & Ehrgott, 2005, pp. 170-174).

Step 1: The decision points (alternatives) and the evaluation criteria that will influence the decision-making of the decision-maker are determined. Each alternative is then evaluated by the experts on the basis of each criterion. At the end of this process an evaluation matrix is obtained. There is no obligation to normalize the weights of criteria. Table 5 represents the example of evaluation matrix.

Step 2: The preference function must be specified for each criterion. The degree of preference for the best alternative is designated using preference function in the pairwise comparison. The result of this pairwise comparison can be explained in terms of preferences while comparing two alternatives such as a and b. Therefore, a preference function should be chosen for every single criterion (Kabadayı & Dağ, 2017, p. 248). These preference functions describe the difference between decision points such as a and b which can take positive number between 0 and 1. Brans & Vincke in 1985 identified six different preference functions (linear type, U type, V type, level type, usual type and Gaussian type) to facilitate decision makers' decision process.

The PROMETHEE method requires to determine threshold values according to the preference function type chosen by decision makers:

q: indifference value
p: strict preference
s: value between p and q

Indifference value (q) is the largest value that is considered as negligible in the comparison of two alternatives.

strict preference value (p) is minimum difference value which create a precise preference by the decision maker.

Function type most preferred is specified as linear type according to the research result obtain from the literature. Equation 2 is a set to represent the linear type function calculation.

$$P(a,b) = 0, d \leq q$$

$$P(a,b) = \frac{d-q}{p-q}, q \leq d \leq p \quad (2)$$

$P(a,b) = 1, d \geq p$

d is the difference between performance of alternatives like a and b for a criterion.

Step 3: Common preference function Pj (a,b) is determined to compare alternatives. All alternatives are compared in terms of each criterion. Equation (3) is the general representation of the preference function used in the comparison alternatives.

$$P(a,b) = \begin{cases} 0 & f(a) \leq f(b) \\ p\left[f(a) - f(b)\right] & f(a) > f(b) \end{cases} \tag{3}$$

Step 4: In this step, preference indexes are computed for every pair of alternatives in terms of a particular criterion. Preference degree ranging from 0 to 1. Preference indexes are computed by using Equations (4) and (5).w_j is the weight of criterion j. k shows the criterion number.

$$\pi(a,b) = \sum_{j}^{k} P_j(a,b).w_j \tag{4}$$

$$\pi(b,a) = \sum_{j}^{k} P_j(b,a).w_j \tag{5}$$

$\pi\left(a,b\right)$ indicates the superiority of alternative a over b for each criterion
$\pi\left(b,a\right)$ indicates the superiority of alternative b over a for each criterion

Step 5: Positive preference flow (φ^{+}) and negative preference flow (φ^{-}) are computed to rank the alternatives. These are shown in equation (6) and (7) respectively. n is the number of alternatives.

$$\varphi^{+}(a) = \frac{1}{n-1}\Sigma(a,x); x = (b,c,d.....,) \tag{6}$$

$$\varphi^{-}(a) = \frac{1}{n-1}\Sigma(x,a); x = (b,c,d.....,) \tag{7}$$

Positive preference flow identifies the superiority measure of alternative a over other alternatives and the negative preference flow indicates weakness of a. The alternative with the higher positive preference flow is superior to the other alternatives. The alternative with the higher negative preference flow is inferior to the other alternatives. An alternative is a better choice than the other alternatives for decision makers when the negative preference flow is low.

Step 6: Partial ordering of alternatives is performed with PROMETHEE I, after determining positive and negative preference flows. By this means, the quality of relations between alternatives is determined. Evaluations at this stage are expressed as superiority (P), equality (I) and incomparable (R). (P^+, I^+) and (P^-, I^-) values are determined and positive and negative values are compared. The following considerations are taken into account in this comparison.

1. Alternative a is preferred to alternative b, when one of the elements of Equation (8) is satisfied.

$$\varphi^+(a) > \varphi^+(b)\, and\, \varphi^-(a) < \varphi^-$$

$$\varphi^+(a) > \varphi^+(b)\, and\, \varphi^-(a) = \varphi^-(b) \tag{8}$$

$$\varphi^+(a) = \varphi^+(b)\, and\, \varphi^-(a) < \varphi^-(b)$$

2. Two alternatives a and b have the same positive preference flow and negative preference flow. This situation is represented by Equation (9).

$$\varphi^+(a) = \varphi^+(b)\, and\, \varphi^-(a) = \varphi^-(b) \tag{9}$$

3. Two alternatives a and b are considered incomparable. This situation is represented by Equation (10).

$$\varphi^+(a) > \varphi^+(b)\, and\, \varphi^-(a) > \varphi^-(b) \tag{10}$$

$$\varphi^+(a) < \varphi^+(b)\, and\, \varphi^-(a) < \varphi^-(b)$$

Step 7: PROMETHEE II provides complete ranking of alternatives.Net priority values (φ^{net}) should be obtained to find complete ranking of alternatives. Net priority values are calculated by the difference between positive and negative preference flows. Equation (11) represents the net priority calculation.

$$\varphi^{net}(a) = \varphi^+(a) - \varphi^-(a) \tag{11}$$

There are two decisions, when comparing net priority values of the two alternatives:

1. If $\varphi^{net}(a) > \varphi^{net}(b)$, alternative a preferred to alternative b.
2. If $\varphi^{net}(a) = \varphi^{net}(b)$ alternative a and b are the same.

PROMETHEE method has been applied successfully in many industrial areas. However, the method can give the wrong results because of the fact that, inputs used in the method are based on decision makers' personal opinions.

Fuzzy PROMETHEE method has been advised which is composed of combining fuzzy set theory and PROMETHEE method to prevent wrong and uncertain result. The method was first proposed by Lé Teno and Mareschal in 1998.The aim of the method is to achieve more precise and more sensitive results. Fuzzy PROMETHEE method has been applied in various MCDM studies successfully in the literature. PROMETHEE method. Geldermann Spengler, T., & Rentz (2000) applied the fuzzy PROMETHEE method in iron and steel making company. Bilsel, Büyüközkan & Ruan (2006) ranked web sites of Turkish hospitals using fuzzy. Aloini, Dulmi, & Mininno (2009) applied a hybrid fuzzy PROMETHEE method to select the best logistic service provider. Li and Li (2010) applied a new PROMETHEE method by considering generalized fuzzy numbers. Chen, Wang, &Wu (2011) proposed the fuzzy PROMETHEE method to find most suitable suppliers for a company which works in the field of information systems. Tuzkaya et. al (2011) investigated the best material handling system which has important effects on production performance by using fuzzy PROMETHEE method. Elevli (2014) used the fuzzy PROMETHEE method to choose most convenient location among the potential logistic centers. Ozsahin et al. (2017) evaluated the common nuclear medicine imaging devices using fuzzy PROMETHEE to help manufacturers, hospitals, and radiologists. Gul, Celik, Gumus, &Guneri (2018) recommended the fuzzy PROMETHEE method based on trapezoidal fuzzy numbers to solve material selection problem in automotive company.

Fuzzification operation is applied in three steps of PROMETHEE method. The first step is identifying the weights of criteria. The second step is evaluating of every alternative based on each criterion and the last step is calculating of the preference function. Table 6 represents the linguistic variables and corresponding fuzzy numbers used in this study (Li, 1999, p. 96).

In this study, linear preference function which has two threshold values (q and p) to be identified is preferred by decision makers to evaluate each criterion. Linear preference function is converted to the fuzzy numbers using Equation (12).

$$P(a,b) = 0, n - c \leq q$$

Table 6. Linguistic variables and corresponding fuzzy numbers

Linguistic Variables	Fuzzy Number
Remote (R)	(0;0;0,25)
Low (L)	(0;0,25;0,50)
Moderate (M)	(0,25;0,50;0,75)
High(H)	(0,50; 0,75;1,00)
Very high (VH)	(0,75;1,00;1,00)

$$P(a,b) = \frac{d-q}{p-q}, q \leq n-c \, and \, n+d \leq p \tag{12}$$

$$P(a,b) = 1, n+d \geq p$$

In equation (12), q and p values are crisp numbers. The membership functions are adjusted accordingly so that n-c >=0 and n+d<=1. d value is expressed as (n, c, d) in the fuzzy system and (n,c,d) is a triangular fuzzy number which represents the difference between a and b (Yılmaz & Dağdeviren, 2010, p. 816).

Yager (1981) proposed the useful method to compare fuzzy numbers. According to the Yager's index, a triangular fuzzy number's magnitude is represented by center of the triangle and can be shown as in Equation (13) (Senvar vd., 2014: 29).

F=(n-c, n, n+ d)= (3n-c+d)/3 (13)

SOLUTION METHODOLOGY

This study includes the integration of Fuzzy FMEA with the Fuzzy PROMETHEE method. Firstly, weight of the risk factors is determined using Fuzzy system. For this process, the importance degrees of risk factors are evaluated by three different decision makers. Then, these evaluations are aggregated using geometric mean. Yager index is used to obtain crisp value of the risk factors. Secondly, Fuzzy PROMETHEE method is used to obtain risk priority ranking of each failure type. In this process, every failure type is evaluated by four decision makers using triangular fuzzy numbers according to the risk factors. These evaluations are aggregated using geometric mean. Then, Fuzzy PROMERTHEE steps are applied respectively. Positive, negative and net flow values are computed. Net flow values are converted to crisp numbers with the Yager index. Lastly, failure types are ranked according to the net flow value.

APPLICATION

This study has performed a real life application in a pharmaceutical firm in Turkey. The company is a worldwide enterprise that has been manufacturing for over 100 years. In this study, the most manufactured product in the company was handled. The manufacturing process of the product consists of 11 different steps. The production steps are raw material transfer, raw material sampling, raw material weighing, mixture preparing, elimination, last mixture, transfer for printing, printing, packaging, stability, and holding of the product respectively. The printing process of the product is carried out in another production company because of the fact that there is not enough machinery and manpower that can meet the increasing demand. Eleven majorfailure types have been detected by decision makers which is composed of production manager, quality control manager, and supervisors in this production process. Table7 represents the failure types (FT) and their definitions.

Figure 3.

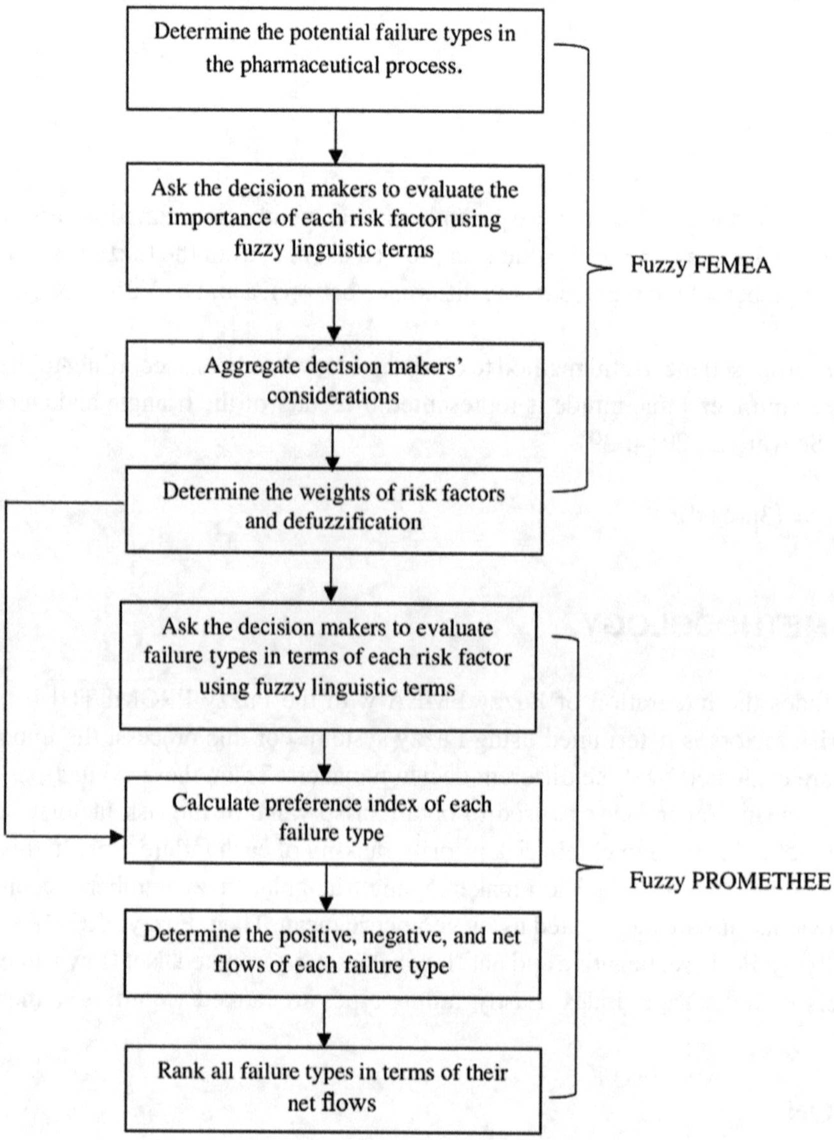

In this study, the researcher has investigated FT's of this production process with the managers by using FMEA. After the determining of risk types, the researcher applied the fuzzy PROMETHEE method to obtain the priority order of risk types.

The application procedure is summarized with a flowchart which is showed in Figure 3.

First of all, weights of risk factors (O,S, and D)are designated by decision makers. Decision makers team is composed of four experts which have extensive information about the related pharmaceutical production process. Decision makers team is asked to evaluate importance of each criterion. For the evaluation process, fuzzy linguistic scale given in Table 4 is used by decision makers team. Then the linguistic evaluations are converted to the triangular fuzzy number using Table 6. The geometric mean

Table 7. Failure types (FT)

Code	Failure Type
FT 1	Deterioration of raw material because of the high temperature
FT 2	Deterioration of raw material because of the sun light
FT 3	Not obtaining the homogeny last mixture
FT 4	Foreign particles during elimination
FT 5	Not suitable particle size
FT 6	Mixing the particles with an another product particles
FT 7	Deviation from specifications during the pressing
FT 8	Not suitable product images
FT 9	Humidity
FT 10	Fragility problem
FT 11	Not suitable impermeability test results

Table 8. The weight of risk factors

Decision maker		DM 1	DM 2	DM 3	DM 4	Fuzzy Weight
Risk Factors	O	VH	VH	H	H	(0.61,0.86,1)
	S	H	H	VH	H	(0.55,0.80,1)
	D	M	M	VH	H	(0.39,0.65,0.86)

Table 9. Expert's evaluation results for each failure type

Decision Maker		Risk Factor											
		O				S				D			
		DM1	DM2	DM3	DM4	DM1	DM2	DM3	DM4	DM1	DM2	DM3	DM4
Failure Type	FT 1	L	R	L	L	H	H	M	M	VH	H	VH	VH
	FT 2	H	M	M	M	H	H	VH	M	VH	VH	H	VH
	FT 3	L	R	R	M	VH	VH	H	H	VH	H	H	H
	FT 4	M	M	M	L	VH	VH	VH	H	VH	VH	H	VH
	FT 5	L	M	M	M	H	M	H	H	H	H	H	VH
	FT 6	M	R	L	R	VH	VH	VH	VH	M	H	M	H
	FT 7	L	L	R	R	VH	VH	VH	VH	VH	H	H	H
	FT 8	R	R	R	L	M	M	H	M	VH	VH	H	H
	FT 9	M	H	H	M	H	H	H	VH	M	M	H	M
	FT 10	M	L	L	L	VH	H	H	H	M	L	M	M
	FT 11	L	R	R	R	H	VH	VH	VH	M	L	L	L

is used to aggregate decision makers' considerations. Table 8 represents the decision makers' thoughts about the weights of risk factors.

Then, Crisp values are calculated by using Equation (14). The weights of risk factors are obtained as follows: O-0.38, S-0.36, D-0,26. After the determining of risk factor weights, eleven failure types are evaluated in terms of each risk factor. Each expert is asked to evaluate failure types considering each risk factor. Table 9 represents the expert's evaluation results for each failure type. For this evaluation, fuzzy linguistic scale given in Table 4 is used. The linguistic evaluations are converted to the triangular fuzzy number using Table 6.The geometric mean is used for aggregating the experts' evaluation. The aggregated fuzzy numbers are presented in Table 10. Then, the fuzzy PROMETHEE method is adopted to identify risk priority of the failure types.

After decision makers team research, the preference function for all risk factors is determined as linear. Also, they have accepted the indifference value q as 0 and the strict value p as 0.60 for all risk factors. According to the equation (4), fuzzy preference functions are calculated for all the failure types. Table 11 represents the fuzzy preference function of failure type 1 as an example.

Preference indexes are obtained by using Equation (5)-(6). Then, defuzzification is made with the Yager index. Table 12 shows the crisp number of failure type's preference index 1 as an example.

In the last step positive- negative preference flows of alternatives and net flows of alternatives are calculated by using Equation (7), (8) and (12) respectively. Table 13 summarizes all flows of the alternatives.

All failure types are ranked in terms of the descending order of their net outranking flow. Table 14 shows the outranking graph of complete order. It is shown in Table 14Fthat, FT 10 has the highest net flow value and is followed by FT 11and FT 9 respectively. Besides, FT 8 has the lowest net flow value and is followed by FT 1. The failure type with the highest net flow value is identified as the most critical. It can be said that 'fragility problem' is the most critical failure type and 'not suitable product image' is the least critical failure type for the company. The company should focus on the failure types with higher net flow value and observe them frequently. In this pharmaceutical production process, corrective action need to be taken for the FT 10 which has high risk.

Table 10. Aggregated evaluation of failure types in fuzzy number

Failure Type	Risk Factor		
	Occurrence	Severity	Detection
FT 1	(0,0, 0.35)	(0.35, 0.61, 0.87)	(0, 0.3, 0.3)
FT 2	(0.3, 0.55, 0.80)	(0.47, 0.73, 0.93)	(0, 0.42, 0.3)
FT 3	(0, 0, 0.51)	(0.61, 0.87, 1)	(0,0,0.42)
FT 4	(0, 0.42, 0.68)	(0.68, 0.93, 1)	(0, 0.3, 0.3)
FT 5	(0, 0.42, 0.68)	(0.42, 0.68, 0.93)	(0,0,0.42)
FT 6	(0, 0, 0.51)	(0.75, 1, 1)	(0,0, 0.51)
FT 7	(0, 0, 0.35)	(0.75, 1, 1)	(0,0,0.42)
FT 8	(0, 0, 0.30)	(0.30, 0.55, 0.80)	(0,0 0.35)
FT 9	(0.35, 0.61, 0.87)	(0.55, 0.80, 1)	(0, 0.42, 0.67)
FT 10	(0, 0.30, 0.55)	(0.55, 0.80, 1)	(0.3, 0.55, 0.8)
FT 11	(0, 0, 0.30)	(0.68, 0.93, 1)	(0.42, 0.67, 0.93)

Table 11. The fuzzy preference function

P(a, x)	Risk Factor		
	Occurrence	Severity	Detection
P(1-2)	(-0.3, 0.8, 0.9)	(-0.12, 1.54, 1.6)	(0, 0.3,0.3)
P(1-3)	(0, 0.51, 0.35)	(-0,26, 1.61, 1.74)	(0, 0.42,0.3)
P(1-4)	(0, 0.68, 0.77)	(-0.33, 1.61, 1.8)	(0,0, 0.3)
P(1-5)	(0, 0.68, 0.77)	(-0.07, 1.54, 1.55)	(0, 0.42,0.3)
P(1-6)	(0, 0.51, 0.35)	(-0.4, 1.61, 1.87)	(0, 0.51, 0,3)
P(1-7)	(0, 0.35, 0.35)	(-0.4, 1.61, 1.87)	(0, 0.42,0.3)
P(1-8)	(0, 0.3,0.35)	(0.05, 1.41, 1.42)	(0, 0.3,0.3)
P(1-9)	(-0.35, 0.87,0.96)	(-0.2, 1.61, 1.67)	(0, 0.67, 0.72)
P(1-10)	(0, 0.55, 0.65)	(-0.2, 1.61, 1.67)	(-0.3, 0.8, 0.85)
P1-11)	(0, 0.3,0.35)	(-0.33, 1.61, 1.8)	(-0.42, 0.93, 0.97)

Table 12. Preference indexes of failure type 1

π(a,x)	Value	π(x, a)	Value
π (1-2)	0.000	π (1-2)	0.229
π (1-3)	0.000	π (1-3)	0.181
π (1-4)	0.019	π (1-4)	0.160
π (1-5)	0.019	π (1-5)	0.057
π (1-6)	0.000	π (1-6)	0.252
π (1-7)	0.000	π (1-7)	0.205
π (1-8)	0.043	π (1-8)	0.007
π (1-9)	0.007	π (1-9)	0.311
π (1-10)	0.021	π (1-10)	0.231
π (1-11)	0.011	π (1-11)	0.336

CONCLUSION

The purposes of this study is to present a systematic approach about risk prioritization using a multicriteria decision making method. The researcher utilizes the PROMETHEE method to obtain risk priorities of failure types in the pharmaceutical production process. Fuzzy system is integrated in both FMEA and the PROMETHEE method to get rid of the subjectivity and vagueness. Thus, the proposed method is able to specify the weights of risk factors and risk priority of failure types objectively. According to results of the study, fragility is the main problem of this production process. This problem has the priority of taking corrective action by the company, since the fragility of the drugs causes the patient to not take the required dose. It is significant point that, the company should focus on this failure types with the highest risk in order to enhance quality level.

Table 13. All flows of the alternatives

Failure Type	φ^{+}	φ^{-}	φ^{net}
FT 1	0.012	0.196	-0.184
FT 2	0.153	0.104	0.049
FT 3	0.090	0.261	-0.171
FT 4	0.072	0.101	-0.029
FT 5	0.020	0.160	-0.140
FT 6	0.051	0.054	-0.003
FT 7	0.113	0.072	0.041
FT 8	0.010	0.230	-0.221
FT 9	0.224	0.075	0.149
FT10	0.511	0.093	0.418
FT 11	0.229	0.050	0.179

Table 14. Complete outranking flow of alternatives

Ranking	Failure Type
1	FT 10
2	FT 11
3	FT 9
4	FT 2
5	FT 7
6	FT 4
7	FT 6
8	FT 5
9	FT 3
10	FT 1
11	FT 8

There are several causes in order to apply FMEA method in a production process. It enables closer observation of risks in the production process. Closer observation provides continuous improvement. Continuous improvement is required to obtain quality product. Quality product gives companies competitive power in the market. Competitiveness ensures the profitability and continuity of the firm.

In the future research, different multicriteria decision making methods can be used to evaluate priority of failure types. Besides, hybrid methods can be tried to obtain more effective results.

REFERENCES

Abdelgawad, M., & Fayek, A. R. (2010). Risk management in the construction industry using combined fuzzy FMEA and fuzzy AHP. *Journal of Construction Engineering and Management*, *136*(9), 1028–1036. doi:10.1061/(ASCE)CO.1943-7862.0000210

Akkurt, M. (2002). *Kalite kontrol excel destekli*. İstanbul/Türkiye: Birsen Yayınevi.

Aloini, D., Dulmin, R., & Mininno, V. (2010). A hybrid fuzzy-PROMETHEE method for logistics service selection: Design of a decision support tool. *International Journal of Uncertainty, Fuzziness, and Knowledge-based Systems*, *18*(04), 345–369. doi:10.1142/S0218488510006593

Bao, J., Johansson, J., & Zhang, J. (2017). An occupational disease assessment of the mining industry's occupational health and safety management system based on FMEA and an improved AHP model. *Sustainability*, *9*(1), 94. doi:10.3390u9010094

Bilsel, R. U., Büyüközkan, G., & Ruan, D. (2006). A fuzzy preference-ranking model for a quality evaluation of hospital web sites. *International Journal of Intelligent Systems*, *21*(11), 1181–1197. doi:10.1002/int.20177

Bowles, J. B., & Peláez, C. E. (1995). Fuzzy logic prioritization of failures in a system failure mode, effects and criticality analysis. *Reliability Engineering & System Safety*, *50*(2), 203–213. doi:10.1016/0951-8320(95)00068-D

Braglia, M. (2000). MAFMA: Multi-attribute failure mode analysis. *International Journal of Quality & Reliability Management*, *17*(9), 1017–1033. doi:10.1108/02656710010353885

Braglia, M., Frosolini, M., & Montanari, R. (2003). Fuzzy TOPSIS approach for failure mode, effects and criticality analysis. *Quality and Reliability Engineering International*, *19*(5), 425–443. doi:10.1002/qre.528

Brans, J. P., & Vincke, P. (1985). Note—A Preference Ranking Organisation Method: (The PROMETHEE Method for Multiple Criteria Decision-Making). *Management Science*, *31*(6), 647–656. doi:10.1287/mnsc.31.6.647

Chanamool, N., & Naenna, T. (2016). Fuzzy FMEA application to improve decision-making process in an emergency department. *Applied Soft Computing*, *43*, 441–453. doi:10.1016/j.asoc.2016.01.007

Chang, K. H. (2015). A novel general risk assessment method using the soft TOPSIS approach. *Journal of Industrial and Production Engineering*, *32*(6), 408–421. doi:10.1080/21681015.2015.1070375

Chen, J. K. (2007). Utility priority number evaluation for FMEA. *Journal of Failure Analysis and Prevention*, *7*(5), 321–328. doi:10.100711668-007-9060-2

Chen, Y. H., Wang, T. C., & Wu, C. Y. (2011). Strategic decisions using the fuzzy PROMETHEE for IS outsourcing. *Expert Systems with Applications*, *38*(10), 13216–13222. doi:10.1016/j.eswa.2011.04.137

Cheraghi, M., Karbassi, A., Monavari, S. M., & Baghvand, A. (2018). Environmental risk management associated with the development one of oil fields in southwestern Iran using AHP and FMEA methods. *Anthropocentric Pollution Journal, 2*(2), 33-40. *Fakültesi Dergisi, 29*(4).

Chin, K. S., Chan, A., & Ya, J. B. (2008). Development of a fuzzy FMEA based product design system. *International Journal of Advanced Manufacturing Technology*, *36*(7-8), 633–649. doi:10.100700170-006-0898-3

Dağdeviren, M. (2008). Decision making in equipment selection: An integrated approach with AHP and PROMETHEE. *Journal of Intelligent Manufacturing*, *19*(4), 397–406. doi:10.100710845-008-0091-7

Devadasan, S. R., Muthu, S., Samson, R. N., & Sankaran, R. A. (2003). Design of total failure mode and effects analysis programme. *International Journal of Quality & Reliability Management*, *20*(5), 551–568. doi:10.1108/02656710310476525

Dinmohammadi, F., & Shafiee, M. (2013). A fuzzy-FMEA risk assessment approach for offshore wind turbines. *International Journal of Prognostics and Health Management*, *4*(13), 59–68.

Ekmekçioğlu, M., & Can Kutlu, A. (2012). A fuzzy hybrid approach for fuzzy process FMEA: An application to a spindle manufacturing process. *International Journal of Computational Intelligence Systems*, *5*(4), 611–626. doi:10.1080/18756891.2012.718104

El Mokrini, A., Dafaoui, E., Berrado, A., & El Mhamedi, A. (2016). An approach to risk assessment for outsourcing logistics: Case of pharmaceutical industry. *IFAC-PapersOnLine*, *49*(12), 1239–1244. doi:10.1016/j.ifacol.2016.07.681

Elevli, B. (2014). Logistics freight center locations decision by using Fuzzy-PROMETHEE. *Transport*, *29*(4), 412–418. doi:10.3846/16484142.2014.983966

Emovon, I. (2016). Failure mode and effects analysis of ship systems using an integrated Dempster Shafer theory and Electre method. *Journal of Advanced Manufacturing Technology (JAMT)*, *10*(1), 45-60, *31*(5), 761-772.

Emovon, I., Norman, R. A., Alan, J. M., & Pazouki, K. (2015). An integrated multicriteria decision making methodology using compromise solution methods for prioritising risk of marine machinery systems. *Ocean Engineering*, *105*, 92–103. doi:10.1016/j.oceaneng.2015.06.005

Eryürek, Ö. F. (2003). *Hata Türü Ve Etkileri Analizinde Yeni Bir Karar Verme Modeli* (Doctoral dissertation, Fen Bilimleri Enstitüsü).

Figueira, J., Greco, S., & Ehrgott, M. (Eds.). (2005). *Multiple criteria decision analysis: state of the art surveys* (Vol. 78). Springer Science & Business Media. doi:10.1007/b100605

Garcia, P., Schirru, R., Frutuoso E. Melo, P. F. (2005). A fuzzy data environment analysis approach for FMEA. *Progress in Nuclear Energy*, *46*(3-4), 359–373. doi:10.1016/j.pnucene.2005.03.016

Gargama, H., & Chaturvedi, S. K. (2011). Criticality assessment models for failure mode effects and criticality analysis using fuzzy logic. *IEEE Transactions on Reliability*, *60*(1), 102–110. doi:10.1109/TR.2010.2103672

Geldermann, J., Spengler, T., & Rentz, O. (2000). Fuzzy outranking for environmental assessment. Case study: Iron and steel making industry. *Fuzzy Sets and Systems*, *115*(1), 45–65. doi:10.1016/S0165-0114(99)00021-4

Guimarães, A. C. F., & Lapa, C. M. F. (2007). Fuzzy inference to risk assessment on nuclear engineering systems. *Applied Soft Computing*, *7*(1), 17–28. doi:10.1016/j.asoc.2005.06.002

Gul, M., Celik, E., Gumus, A. T., & Guneri, A. F. (2018). A fuzzy logic based PROMETHEE method for material selection problems. *Beni-Suef University Journal of Basic and Applied Sciences*, *7*(1), 68–79. doi:10.1016/j.bjbas.2017.07.002

Helvacioglu, S., & Ozen, E. (2014). Fuzzy based failure modes and effect analysis for yacht system design. *Ocean Engineering*, *79*, 131–141. doi:10.1016/j.oceaneng.2013.12.015

Ilangkumaran, M., Shanmugam, P., Sakthivel, G., & Visagavel, K. (2014). Failure mode and effect analysis using fuzzy analytic hierarchy process. *International Journal of Productivity and Quality Management*, *14*(3), 296–313. doi:10.1504/IJPQM.2014.064807

Kabadayı, N., & Dag, S. (2017). Bulanik Dematel ve bulanik Promethee yöntemleri ile kablo üretiminde makine seçimi (Machine Selection in a Cable Manufacturing with Using Fuzzy Dematel and Fuzzy Promethee). *Karadeniz Teknik Üniversitesi Sosyal Bilimler Enstitüsü Sosyal Bilimler Dergisi*, *7*(1), 239–260.

Kumru, M., & Kumru, P. Y. (2013). Fuzzy FMEA application to improve purchasing process in a public hospital. *Applied Soft Computing*, *13*(1), 721–733. doi:10.1016/j.asoc.2012.08.007

Lapa-Guimaraes, J., & Pickova, J. (2004). New solvent systems for thin-layer chromatographic determination of nine biogenic amines in fish and squid. *Journal of Chromatography. A*, *1045*(1-2), 223–232. doi:10.1016/j.chroma.2004.06.014 PMID:15378899

Le Téno, J. F., & Mareschal, B. (1998). An interval version of PROMETHEE for the comparison of building products' design with ill-defined data on environmental quality. *European Journal of Operational Research*, *109*(2), 522–529. doi:10.1016/S0377-2217(98)00074-5

Liu, H. C., Li, P., You, J. X., & Chen, Y. Z. (2015). A novel approach for FMEA: Combination of interval 2-tuple linguistic variables and gray relational analysis. *Quality and Reliability Engineering International*, *31*(5), 761–772. doi:10.1002/qre.1633

Liu, H. C., Li, Z., Song, W., & Su, Q. (2017). Failure mode and effect analysis using cloud model theory and PROMETHEE method. *IEEE Transactions on Reliability*, *66*(4), 1058–1072. doi:10.1109/TR.2017.2754642

Liu, H. C., Liu, L., & Li, P. (2014). Failure mode and effects analysis using intuitionistic fuzzy hybrid weighted Euclidean distance operator. *International Journal of Systems Science*, *45*(10), 2012–2030. doi:10.1080/00207721.2012.760669

Liu, H. C., Liu, L., Liu, N., & Mao, L. X. (2012). Risk evaluation in failure mode and effects analysis with extended VIKOR method under fuzzy environment. *Expert Systems with Applications*, *39*(17), 12926–12934. doi:10.1016/j.eswa.2012.05.031

Lolli, F., Ishizaka, A., Gamberini, R., Rimini, B., & Messori, M. (2015). FlowSort-GDSS–A novel group multi-criteria decision support system for sorting problems with application to FMEA. *Expert Systems with Applications*, *42*(17-18), 6342–6349. doi:10.1016/j.eswa.2015.04.028

Mandal, S., & Maiti, J. (2014). Risk analysis using FMEA: Fuzzy similarity value and possibility theory-based approach. *Expert Systems with Applications*, *41*(7), 3527–3537. doi:10.1016/j.eswa.2013.10.058

Mangeli, M., Shahraki, A., & Saljooghi, F. H. (2019). Improvement of risk assessment in the FMEA using nonlinear model, revised fuzzy TOPSIS, and support vector machine. *International Journal of Industrial Ergonomics*, *69*, 209–216. doi:10.1016/j.ergon.2018.11.004

Ömürbek, N., & Eren, H. (2016). Promethee, Moora ve Copras yöntemleri ile oran analizi sonuçlarinin değerlendirilmesi: Bir uygulama. *Mehmet Akif Ersoy Üniversitesi Sosyal Bilimler Enstitüsü Dergisi*, *8*(16), 174–187. doi:10.20875b.69615

Ozfirat, P. M. (2014). Bulanik önceliklendirme metodu ve hata türü ve etkileri analizini birleştiren yeni bir risk analizi yöntemi. *Gazi Üniversitesi Mühendislik-Mimarlık Fakültesi Dergisi*, *29*(4), 755–768.

Ozsahin, D. U., Uzun, B., Musa, M. S., Şentürk, N., Nurçin, F. V., & Ozsahin, I. (2017). Evaluating nuclear medicine imaging devices using fuzzy PROMETHEE method. *Procedia Computer Science*, *120*, 699–705. doi:10.1016/j.procs.2017.11.298

Sachdeva, A., Kumar, D., & Kumar, P. (2009). Multi-factor failure mode critically analysis using TOPSIS. *Journal of Industrial Engineering International*, *5*(8), 1–9.

Senvar, O., Tuzkaya, G., & Kahraman, C. (2014). Multi criteria supplier selection using fuzzy PROMETHEE method. In *Supply chain management under fuzziness* (pp. 21–34). Berlin, Germany: Springer. doi:10.1007/978-3-642-53939-8_2

Shahrabi, M., & Shojaei, A. A. (2014). Application of FMEA and AHP in Lean Maintenance. *International Journal of Modern Engineering Sciences*, *3*(1), 61–73.

Silvia, C., Antonella, C., & Enea, M. (2018). The ELECTRE I method to support the FMECA. *IFAC-PapersOnLine*, *51*(11), 459–464. doi:10.1016/j.ifacol.2018.08.361

Simşir, F., Demir, H. İ., & Azdemir, S. (n.d.). Demir çelik sektöründe hibrid DEMATEL ve TOPSIS-ELECTRE yöntemleri ile hata türleri ve etkileri analizi. *Akademik Platform Mühendislik ve Fen Bilimleri Dergisi*, *6*(3), 22-34.

Sisman, B. (2017). Hata türü ve etkileri analizinde bulanik AHP ve bulanik VIKOR yöntemleri ile otomotiv sektöründe risk değerlendirmesi-risk evaluating by fuzzy ahp and fuzzy vikor methods in failure mode and effects analysis for automotive sector. *Mehmet Akif Ersoy Üniversitesi Sosyal Bilimler Enstitüsü Dergisi*, *9*(18), 234–250.

Tay, K. M., & Lim, C. P. (2006). Application of fuzzy inference techniques to FMEA. In *Applied soft computing technologies: The challenge of complexity* (pp. 161–171). Berlin, Germany: Springer. doi:10.1007/3-540-31662-0_13

Torra, V. (2010). Hesitant fuzzy sets. *International Journal of Intelligent Systems*, *25*(6), 529–539.

Tuzkaya, G., Ozgen, D., & Gulsun, B. (2011). Malzeme taşıma sistemi alternatiflerinin değerlendirilmesinde bulanık-Promethee yaklaşımı. *Doğuş Üniversitesi Dergisi*, *12*(1), 144–155. doi:10.31671/dogus.2019.157

Ulengin, F., Topcu, Y. I., & Sahin, S. Ö. (2001). An integrated decision aid system for Bosphorus water-crossing problem. *European Journal of Operational Research, 134*(1), 179–192. doi:10.1016/S0377-2217(00)00247-2

Vahdani, B., Salimi, M., & Charkhchian, M. (2015). A new FMEA method by integrating fuzzy belief structure and TOPSIS to improve risk evaluation process. *International Journal of Advanced Manufacturing Technology, 77*(1-4), 357–368. doi:10.100700170-014-6466-3

Wang, Y. M., Chin, K. S., Poon, G. K. K., & Yang, J. B. (2009). Risk evaluation in failure mode and effects analysis using fuzzy weighted geometric mean. *Expert Systems with Applications, 36*(2), 1195–1207. doi:10.1016/j.eswa.2007.11.028

Yang, Z., Bonsall, S., & Wang, J. (2008). Fuzzy rule-based Bayesian reasoning approach for prioritization of failures in FMEA. *IEEE Transactions on Reliability, 57*(3), 517–528. doi:10.1109/TR.2008.928208

Yerlikaya, M. A., Burak, E. F. E., & Efe, O. F. (2016). İş Güvenliğinde Bulanık Promethee Yöntemiyle Hata Türleri ve Etkilerinin Analizi: Bir İnşaat Firmasında Uygulama. *Gümüşhane Üniversitesi Fen Bilimleri Enstitüsü Dergisi, 6*(2), 126–137. doi:10.17714/gufbed.2016.06.012

ADDITIONAL READING

Arikan, R., Dağdeviren, M., & Kurt, M. (2013). A fuzzy multi-attribute decision making model for strategic risk assessment. *International Journal of Computational Intelligence Systems, 6*(3), 487–502. doi:10.1080/18756891.2013.781334

De Smet, Y. (2019). Beyond Multicriteria Ranking Problems: The Case of PROMETHEE. In *New Perspectives in Multiple Criteria Decision Making* (pp. 95–114). Cham: Springer. doi:10.1007/978-3-030-11482-4_3

Gilchrist, W. (1993). Modelling failure modes and effects analysis. *International Journal of Quality & Reliability Management, 10*(5), 02656719310040105. doi:10.1108/02656719310040105

Inoue, H., & Yamada, S. (2010). Failure mode and effects analysis in pharmaceutical research. *International Journal of Quality and Service Sciences, 2*(3), 369–382. doi:10.1108/17566691011090080

Liao, H., & Xu, Z. (2014). Multi-criteria decision making with intuitionistic fuzzy PROMETHEE. *Journal of Intelligent & Fuzzy Systems, 27*(4), 1703–1717. doi:10.3233/IFS-141137

Liu, H. C., Liu, L., & Liu, N. (2013). Risk evaluation approaches in failure mode and effects analysis: A literature review. *Expert systems with applications, 40*(2), 828-838. Stamatis, D. H. (2003). *Failure mode and effect analysis: FMEA from theory to execution.* ASQ Quality press.

Maheswaran, K., & Loganathan, T. (2013). A Novel Approach for Prioritization of Failure modes in FMEA using MCDM. *International Journal of Engineering Research and Applications, 3*(4), 733–739.

Zhang, K., Kluck, C., & Achari, G. (2009). A comparative approach for ranking contaminated sites based on the risk assessment paradigm using fuzzy PROMETHEE. *Environmental Management*, *44*(5), 952–967. doi:10.100700267-009-9368-7 PMID:19763684

KEY TERMS AND DEFINITIONS

Defuzzyfication: It is an operation to convert fuzzy number into crisp number.

Fuzzyfication: It is an operation to convert crisp number into fuzzy number.

Fuzzy Logic: It is a form of multi-valued logic obtained from fuzzy set theory to deal with reasoning that is approximate rather than precise.

Multicriteria-Decision Making: To select best alternative.

Quality: It is the degree to which a system meets specified requirements.

Risk: The possibility of something failure happening.

Risk Priority Number: It is a measure for evaluating risk in a process.

Chapter 14
Nudge Theory and Decision Making:
Enabling People to Make Better Choices

Vikramsinh Amarsinh Patil
Symbiosis International University, India

ABSTRACT

This chapter examines the theoretical underpinnings of nudge theory and makes a case for incorporating nudging into the decision-making process in corporate contexts. Nudging and more broadly behavioural economics have become buzzwords on account of the seminal work that has been done by economists and highly publicized interventions employed by governments to support national priorities. Firms are not to be left behind, however. What follows is extensive documentation of such firms that have successfully employed nudging techniques. The examples are segmented by the nudge recipient, namely - managers, employees, and consumers. Firms can guide managers to become better leaders, employees to become more productive, and consumers to stay loyal. However, nudging is not without its pitfalls. It can be used towards nefarious ends and be notoriously difficult to implement and execute. Therefore, nudges should be rigorously tested via experimentation and should be ethically sound.

INTRODUCTION

Decision-making is an integral part of modern management. It involves the selection of a course of action from two or more possible alternatives to arrive at a solution for a given problem. These decisions affect people and are implicitly geared towards altering people's choices or courses of action. However, the success of such decisions would crucially depend on the behavioral response of the affected individuals. Behavioral economics, which explicitly models how people will behave when one relaxes the classical assumption of rationality, could provide a sound theoretical base for assessing and evaluating such behavioral response. In fact while pioneered by policymakers to support national priorities, behavioural economics (and 'nudging' in particular) has been attracting significant interest from business leaders, for quite some time now, who wish to take their decision-making to the next level.

DOI: 10.4018/978-1-7998-2216-5.ch014

Contrary to popular notion, behavioral economics is a fairly old genre of economic theory. One could say that the field originated with the publication of *Theory of Moral Sentiments'* by Adam Smith in 1759 (which predates *Wealth of Nations* published in 1776) since Smith argues in the former that human beings' actions are influenced by the interplay of 'passions' and the 'impartial spectator' (Ashraf, Camerer & Loewenstein, 2005)[1]. This was a far cry from the rational '*homo economicus'* that featured prominently in his later work and would subsequently serve as the bedrock of classical economic theory.

It is unclear why the *Theory of Moral Sentiments* did not catch on with the general academic discourse. Nonetheless, behavioral economics received a major fillip during the 1970s when psychologists Amos Tversky and Daniel Kahneman published a series of iconoclastic papers that formalized something that was fairly obvious in actual practice - human beings are not rational and their decision making is influenced by a multitude of biases, mental short-cuts and emotions. Since then, the field has become a highly influential one with prominent economists such as Matthew Rabin, Andrei Shleifer, Richard Thaler, Cass Sunstein and Dan Ariely making landmark contributions and making the field accessible to the general public through popular novels such as '*Thinking Fast and Slow'* and '*Predictably Irrational'*[2]

However, the one behavioral economics book which has arguably had the most profound impact on public policy and the corporate world is '*Nudge: Improving Decisions About Health, Wealth and Happiness*' ('Nudge') - written by Richard Thaler and Cass R. Sunstein. As explained by Thaler, 'nudges' refer to small, discreet changes that affect an individual's choice-making process without his knowledge and without interfering with his options. Stated differently, a 'nudge' is a technique that inconspicuously alters the choice architecture of consumers such that an individual ends up choosing the option which is the most suitable or beneficial to him without his knowledge.

Sunstein and Thaler's book outlined multiple examples drawn from the fields of finance, health and public policy where nudge type interventions had been administered and provided policy directions that governments could follow for more effective governance. Crucial to the moral justification for using nudges is the concept of 'libertarian paternalism'. People do not always make the most rational choices as per societal norms or by keeping in mind what is best for them. The choice architect however can subliminally guide the individual to take that decision that works best for them[3]. In other words, people can be made to choose something without actually robbing them of their agency to refuse such choice. Another key point worth highlighting is that the logical base for nudges lies in the dual system framework propounded by Kahneman and Tversky[4]. Essentially, there are two systems in the human mind - 'System 1' which makes fast, automatic decisions subject to influences and 'System 2' which makes slow, reflective and goal-oriented decisions. Thaler and Sunstein believe that with the proper nudge it is possible to take advantage of the System 1's decision-making skills to ultimately make the right choice[5]

Nudging has taken over major industries, especially the marketing world, where nudges are incorporated to induce a consumer to buy the product. However, it was first pioneered by institutions and governments, notably in the UK and the USA. Prominent proponents of nudging include former US President Barack Obama who exhorted government departments to adopt behavioural economics to support national priorities, such as enabling Americans to find better jobs or lead healthier lives (Legett, 2014). Other countries such as Germany, Australia and United Kingdom have also set up dedicated nudge units within their governments. In fact, the recent Economic Survey of India of 2019 talks about the power of nudges to promote gender equity and cleanliness and advocates the setting up of a nudge unit for India as well (Department of Economic Affairs, 2019). When applied to organisations, nudges can be used as a powerful tool to build the leadership muscle and trigger productivity boosts through change initiatives. Major Silicon Valley companies are applying the novel concept of 'Nudge Management' in their organisation that applies insights from behavioural sciences to optimise the decisions of employees in alignment with the goal of the organisation.

Although the advantages of nudge theory are many, it would not be incorrect to state that nudges can prove to be a menace if misused. Nudges can often tend to manipulate consumers and companies can certainly take advantage of the judgement heuristics of human beings. A classic example would be that of Uber, where the drivers are nudged into working longer hours by informing them of the next fare opportunity even before the current ride is over. Netflix uses the same algorithm when it streams the next episode of a series before the current one is over, thereby making it convenient for the person to binge-watch all the episodes at one go. These dark nudges exist in all sectors, be it telecom industry or finance or entertainment. Dark nudges can lead to a great loss of welfare and even cause consumers to be divested of their ability to choose freely. They have been used to maximise profits for the companies rather than maximise welfare for the consumers.

However, while the less benevolent uses of nudge theory do exist in the society, the right application of nudges can improve the decision-making skills of people. When properly utilised, nudge theory has a wide array of benefits right from improving aim at men's urinals to eating healthier food items to organ donation and to the recycling of waste for protection of the environment. Moreover, as this chapter will argue, when nudges are employed by companies in an ethical and transparent manner, the benefits of efficient management and workforce along with positive customer response can also be unlocked.

This chapter has a twofold aim - one is to familiarize readers with the basic theoretical underpinning of nudge theory and second, to provide a panoramic view of the various ways in which nudges have been employed by companies in various sectors The focus on nudging by companies is informed by the focus on public policy applications - that is, while nudges have been taken up by various governments with great gusto and policies implemented by government nudge units are well-known and publicized, the same applications for companies tend to recede in the background or are not well-known. The chapter provide a description of the various known examples of company nudging with the aim that nudging and behavioral economics becomes more accessible to companies who may be contemplating the use of nudge-like interventions but are unsure of where to start or what has worked or not worked.

The chapter will proceed as follows - Background provides a brief sketch of literature, Main Focus reiterates the chapter's prerogative of focusing on corporate nudging examples, Issues exhaustively describes such examples (segmented by applications to company managers, employees and customers) as well as the potential drawbacks and limitations of nudging, Solutions and Recommendations provides answers to overcome previously mentioned limitations and implementation advice followed lastly by the Conclusion.

BACKGROUND

The Two Waves of Behavioral Economics

While behavioral economics did exist as a construct, with its theoretical rudiments even predating the classical economics revolution, the field came into the limelight and was formally addressed by that name much later when research straddling psychology and economics started garnering mainstream attention from the seventies onwards. Legett (2014) identifies two 'waves' in the behavioral economics field.

The first wave began with the influential concept of 'bounded rationality' as propounded by Herbert Simon ('Human rationality is very limited, very much bounded by the situation and by human computational powers" (Simon, 1990)). From the 1960s, early proponents became interested in how restricted rationality would impact the assumptions and conclusions of traditional economic theory using mathematical simulations and models (Sent, 2004). However, they were so keen on creating a distinct paradigm that their work was never properly assimilated into the mainstream (Sent, 2004). The second wave as identified by Legett (2014) and more rigorously by Sent (2004) began with the work of Tversky and Kahneman. Also known as 'new behavioral economics' (NBE), it was not as radical as it predecessor since it did not want to replace mainstream economics. It was still concerned with the deviations of human behaviour from rationality assumptions and relied crucially on experimentation and explicitly including insights from Psychology (which had been a cause for controversy in the previous period). This new behavioral economics is an undisputed section of mainstream economics for now and is appreciated for the nuance it provides to standard classical economics[6]. Thaler who gave nudge theory to the world is described as a proponent and contributor to the NBE paradigm.

What Constitutes a Nudge?

To know formally what nudges are, it is best one refers to the definitions provided by the theorists themselves. Thaler and Sunstein (2009) define a nudge in their eponymous book as -

"A nudge, as we will use the term, is any aspect of the choice architecture that alters people's behaviour in a predictable way without forbidding any options or significantly changing their economic incentives. To count as a mere nudge, the intervention must be cheap and easy to avoid. Nudges are not mandates. Putting fruit at eye level [hoping that people then choose fruit over unhealthy alternatives] counts as a nudge. Banning junk food does not" (p.6).

A nudge is therefore a 'gentle' push towards 'something'. This 'something' as described by Van Der Heijden and Kosters (2015) can be one of two things - a choice which is in the interest of the person being nudged (Type 1 nudges) or a choice which ensures a collectively beneficial outcome (Type 2 nudges). Type 1 nudges could include automatically enrolling employees into a pension savings scheme while Type 2 nudges could include promoting environment -friendly behaviour which would benefit the entire community even though the action performed by the nudged would be an individual one (Heijden & Kosters, 2015). In sum this means, that nudges can be used to incentivize positive behaviour (saving more) and/ or disincentivize negative behaviour (pollution)

There are several mechanisms through which nudges operate while acting against some well-documented behavioral bias. Again turning to the theorists themselves, Sunstein (2014) provides a crisp overview of ten such mechanisms. The most prominent perhaps is that of the 'default option'. A famous example of this is the 'Save More Tomorrow' (SMT) program described in Thaler and Benartzi (2001) which essentially involved automatic enrolment in a retirement savings scheme of employees at a company and committing them to a particular savings rate which increased with their pay. The plan was immensely successful with most of program participants tripling their savings rate. The SMT program's ingenuity lay in its ability to use people's inertia (they know that they must save for their twilight years but are reluctant or lazy to act on that initiative) to its advantage - majority people who were enrolled in the program did not opt-out. Default option techniques have been used widely to increase pension enrolment and savings rate in a wide array of countries such as the United Kingdom, Italy, New Zealand and Chile (Vats, 2016)[7].

Others nudging technique that has had beneficial implications is the use of social norms. These have found application in the field of taxation. The United Kingdom, for example, increased its tax collections by sending letters to tardy payers informing them that their neighbours had already paid their taxes and the benefits that would accrue to all if taxes were paid. Others include - 'increasing ease of convenience', 'simplification', 'warning', 'pre-commitment strategies', 'reminders', 'eliciting implementation intentions', 'informing people of the nature and consequences of their past choices' (Sunstein, 2014).

Areas of Application

Nudge theory assumes significance from its vast applications in guiding choices for decision-making, which extend over numerous spheres — health, education, employment, and so forth. Arno & Thomas (2016) discuss how nudge has the potential in framing public health plan to tackle obesity. It was observed from their studies conducted in wealthy countries, particularly United States, that nudges led to an average 15.3% surge in improving dietary or alimentary choices, as gauged by an alteration in frequency of healthy choices or a change in general caloric consumption.

Hausman & Welch (2010) have attempted to clarify nudges from the standpoint of "libertarian paternalism," which may seem akin to an "oxymoron, but it is both possible and legitimate for private and public institutions to affect behaviour while also respecting freedom of choice" (Sunstein & Thaler, 2003). Consumers most often fail to make welfare maximising choices (Abdukadirov, 2016). Libertarian paternalism can thus be illustrated with an example of a father attempting to negotiate the best deal between two sons fighting for a larger share of an apple. When a father is faced with a situation of a single apple to be evenly distributed among his two sons — each grappling for a bigger chunk — he can let one cut the apple and let the other choose a piece. Here, cutting the apple unevenly may result in unfair distribution as the one who has the freedom to choose may end up picking the larger piece. Thus, the father spearheads the right choice and leads the one responsible for slicing the fruit to do so evenly. Examples of libertarian paternalism include "command and control" or "cap and trade" where emissions ought to be controlled to avoid taxes; "sin taxes" levied on demerit goods; banning ad campaigns of liquor and tobacco; etc. Policy makers essentially envisage that —regardless of societal intricacy and an individualised citizenry — the only means to tackle awful challenges such as obesity or climate change is to motivate citizens to act of their own accord through nudges (Leggett, 2014). Nevertheless, Shove (2010) disparages 'sneaky' governmental efforts to employ seemingly banal, mundane solutions for bringing about a change in group norms with respect to environmental concerns.

The implications of nudges are evident in organizational behaviour too. Nudges can be a guiding force to overcome the limitations of bounded rationality in an organization. Managers dedicate considerable efforts to arrive at suitable organizational decisions (Al-Tarawneh, 2011). Hall-Ellis (2015) explains how skilled managers can apply nudging to impel decisions that subordinate and entrench the exercise within the institution as a learning organization. Embracing a nudge transforms the workspace setting, such that individuals make choices serving their best interests with respect to job satisfaction and climbing up the professional ladder, thus contributing to organizational growth. Nudging has definite ramifications that lead to rising productivity, self-esteem and reduced outlays.

With respect to consumer behaviour, studies indicate that nudging can lead to healthier choices. Romero & Biswas (2016), on the basis of seven studies, evidently validate that exhibiting healthy/nutritious/nourishing items to the left and unhealthy/unwholesome items to the right, boosts penchant for the healthy alternatives. Additionally, the quantity of consumption of a healthy item is greater when placed to the left (vs. right) of the unhealthy item. The authors thereby suggest that a "healthy-left, unhealthy-right" lateral exhibitory pattern is analogous to consumers' psychological arrangement of foodstuff that differs in healthfulness, which augments restraint and self-discipline, thereby guiding healthy alternatives.

However, a great deal of literature on nudging is tangled up with its public policy applications (Halpern, 2015; Johnson & Goldstein, 2003; Johnson et al., 2012; Larrick & Soll, 2008; Ly, Mazar, Zhao, & Soman, 2013; Sunstein, 2013; Thaler & Sunstein, 2008; The World Bank, 2015 *as quoted in* Benartzi et al. (2017)). Van Deun, Van Acker, Fobe and Brans (2019) provide an extensive analysis of the literature available on public policy applications of nudging. They find that most literature is focused on health and environmental policy but other areas also include law, social security, transportation and education. This interest in nudging for government is exciting on account of its low cost implications (Sunstein, 2014; Benartzi et al. 2018). It is this dense availability of literature on public policy and nudges and relative discreetness of corporate applications that has motivated the present chapter to focus on examples of nudging in the corporate sector.

MAIN FOCUS

Insights from the field of Psychology have influenced management and company policies for some time now, as discussed by McKinsey (2018). One can easily see how marketing, for example would require knowledge of what influences a consumer's decision to buy something and design of incentive plans by the Human Resources would require knowledge on what motivates people to work. Reliance on basic behavioral norms such as 'more money means better work' or 'discounts mean more buyers' is not unfounded. But one could argue that obvious incentives that often tend to be framed in monetary terms pre-suppose rational individuals who will never become inured to the positive incentive or resentful of the negative[8]. Nudging, is a refreshing contrast to on-the-nose (dis)incentives since they embed themselves sub-consciously and make it easier for people to do the right thing without any compulsion or restrictions, As such, they can provide exciting possibilities for companies to incorporate into their employee management or sales functions.

Companies are run by multiple individuals and are made or broken by the decisions that these individuals make. A firm according to standard economic theory may want to maximize profits and/or have other objectives be it sales maximization, employee satisfaction etc. Intuitively, the achievement of these goals would require that management consistently take well fleshed out decisions, employees be productive and customers readily buy the goods and services made by the firm. Managers, employees and customers are in the end humans and prone to all sorts of biases that can lead to actions or decisions that impede the achievement of the firm's goals. A well-designed nudge could help streamline operations, increase the efficiency of human resources and augment sales and customer retention - all of which are naturally desirable actions from a firm's viewpoint.

While a lot of ink has been spilt on how governments have used or can use nudges to support national priorities such as health and taxation, somewhere companies and their usage of behavioral economics has tended to remain discreet - perhaps because companies have been reluctant to divulge the solutions that have worked for them. Nevertheless, nudging is no less important for companies and central premise of this chapter is to underscore the power of nudges in overhauling decision making processes and driving organizational change specifically within corporate contexts.

NUDGING IN THE CORPORATE CONTEXT

This section provides an extensive overview of the various ways through which nudges have been employed by companies and will also highlight certain pitfalls in the application of nudges.

Nudges for Managers

Managers preside over employees and have the responsibility of ensuring that work flow proceeds smoothly, subordinates are encouraged to contribute constructive inputs, and to be a good team player. Often, managers know what their duties are. They after all mostly have a business school education that has ingrained in them the traits and practices of a desirable leader. But, their knowledge often does not translate into actions. This is the famous 'Knowledge-Doing' Gap problem.

Pfeffer and Sutton (2000) postulate several plausible reasons for this gap. One is "the tendency to equate talking about something with actually doing something about it". Managers may come out with lofty mission statements promising to uphold certain values or achieve certain objectives and then actually don't do anything about it. The mission statements are heavily publicized through various forms of communication be it emails to employees or placards hung at prominent places. However, once the initial momentum has petered out, the statement remains a piece of nicely worded text. Another is that memory supersedes original thinking. When confronted with a problem, managers may resort to conventions and standard operating procedures due to deadline pressure, fatigue or treading in unknown environments. This puts the manager in a condition where she is unable to process the information that indicates that a new solution is required. Such reliance on convention may not always gel with the unique specifics of the problem under consideration (Pfeffer & Sutton, 2000).

It could also be that managers attend corporate training sessions and leave with new ideas. Once at work, however, they end up slipping into their old ways. To counter this exact problem, Dhar et al. (2019) cite the example of a major multinational energy company that leveraged 'digital nudges' and 'peer influence' to encourage executives to actually practice some training they had received on being more connected to the organization's workforce. Executives were made to set small, weekly goals related to improving their leadership capabilities. They were then asked to share weekly updates on their progress on a WhatsApp group message thread. Reminder messages from the change management team nudged around 40-50% of the executives to carry out the weekly updates. The rest fell in line simply from viewing their peer's progress reports (Dhar et al., 2019).

Another prerogative of managers is to ensure a healthy working culture. Dhar et al. (2019) cite the example of Boston Consulting Group's in-house email system that is designed to subtly remind managers to let their employees peacefully spend their time-off from work. If an executive happens to be sending a mail after hours to a colleague, she would see a pop-up message that would ask whether the mail could be marked as 'low priority', if sending could be deferred to the next business day or if the mail should still be sent anyway. A small pop-up message is all that is required to let managers know that they might not be acting as a reasonable team player by compelling their colleagues to focus on work while at home. Executives can therefore think twice before sending a mail that can actually wait until the next day. Moreover, like all good nudges, the pop-up does not preclude the manager from sending the mail anyway.

Biases that permeate managers' thinking can often lead to costly missteps as well. The case of German electric utility RWE is particularly informative. RWE spent ten billion euros in the last half of the 2000's on massive investment projects related to power generation. However, technological progress in renewable energy and increasing popular antagonism towards the polluting nature of conventional power generation started hampering the viability of RWE's proposed projects and inflicted heavy losses. A post-mortem analysis revealed that while external factors had played their part, the company's decision-makers had fallen prey to a multitude of cognitive biases. Managers had assumed things would continue to be the same as always (status quo bias) and had heavily invested in one single area only. Moreover, they had been excessively optimistic about their ability to deliver despite there being a lack of managerial experience in how to deal with large investments (McKinsey, 2017).

In its overhaul of operations, RWE started appointing 'devil's advocates' who are senior personnel and completely independent of the project under consideration. They propose the negative counter-argument to all that the boardroom people present and bring about more debate and discussion rather than mute and blind approval (McKinsey, 2017). The presence of a dissenting opinion, someone who consistently brings up the worst case scenario nudges the managers to think from all sides of the issue and thereby temper any exaggerated belief they may have in the viability of the project.

While the above examples revolve around nudges that can be applied to managers, Ebert and Freibichler (2017) provide multiple examples where managers can use nudging to make their subordinates deliver better results. One relates to increasing the efficiency of meetings. Managers may end up calling for multiple meetings which stretch for long due to an 'information bias' or a tendency to collect more information without actually acting on it. This reduces actual working and productivity hours of workers. Instead, the default duration for meetings on business software could be reduced from one hour to half an hour thereby re-biasing workers to believe that this reduced duration is now the 'standard'. Employees will therefore spend less time in the board room and more time at their desks. Managers could also start a practice of 'no meeting days' to ensure that their subordinates have a distraction-free day which enables them to whole-heartedly concentrate on their projects at hand.These are small steps that managers can implement in their workplace to ensure that their team is making the best use of their time (Ebert & Freibichler, 2017).

Nudges for Employees

"Planning fallacy" as proposed by Kahneman and Tversky (1979) refers to the tendency of individuals to underestimate the time that may be required for the completion of a task. Very often this translates into people thinking that there is enough time to work on a project and thereby rushing to complete the task hurriedly just before the deadline elapses due to improper planning allocation of work over the preceding days. In other words, people procrastinate - especially when the task at hand is onerous. When employees procrastinate, it can have pointedly adverse consequences for the company in terms of the lost time and productivity.

This was exactly the problem that was faced by Bancamia, a Colombian bank whose loan officers were putting off credit disbursal and sourcing new clients towards the last two weeks of the month. Ideally, they were supposed to do so during the first two weeks so as to devote enough attention to resolving delinquent accounts at month-end. This procrastination was leading to sub-optimal timing of cash flows and heightened cash management costs for Bancamia along with reported high levels of stress and job dissatisfaction due to pressures to achieve new loan goals. The bank was worried that such stress could affect the soundness of the credit decisions taken by the officers (Cadena, Cristea, Delgado-Medrano & Schoar, 2011).

Cadena et al., (2011) then document how an experiment called the 'Madrugador Program' was implemented with the express objective of getting loan officers to allocate their responsibilities more evenly throughout the month. In the intervention, small positive incentives (such as gift certificates, movie tickets etc) were offered on a weekly basis to employees for timely achievement of goals pertaining to allocating a certain percentage (8-37%) of sourcing work to the first two weeks. Crucially, employees were provided weekly reminders of their goals and were sent copies of the 'Madrugador Bulletin' a newsletter that mentioned the three best performers of the month, the top performer in each branch and contained reminders of the grand prizes that were to be won for consistent performance throughout the duration of the program. Further, halfway through the first and second weeks, the Branch Manager would periodically meet with the loan officers and have a chat about the work accomplished so far and remind them of what was left to be achieved.

The results of the experiment were very compelling. There was a 30% of improvement in goal achievement and an 18% increase in new loan sourcing of the first two weeks of the month. While the quantum of monthly loan disbursal did not change, there was better temporal allocation by workers and no significant change in credit quality. Perhaps, most importantly, loan officers reported feeling less stressed and more satisfied with their work. What is particularly noteworthy is that the researcher's results turned significant when the branch managers started interacting with the loan officers and providing friendly reminders of time-management goals. The Madrugador Program is therefore a very powerful example of nudges working wonders to combat employee irrationality. The weekly prizes were non-monetary and were akin to positive reminders of goals. These were complemented by the non-intrusive re-enforcement from the bulletin and branch manager discussions. Even the name of the program may have worked as a nudge since 'Madrugador' in Spanish means 'early-riser' and its frequent usage and appearance in the newsletter would have strengthened the notion that those who started off early in the month would be rewarded (Cadena et al., 2019).

Another major example of nudging employees to adopt desirable behavior comes from a study conducted at Virgin Atlantic. Gosnell, List & Metcalfe (2016) carried out an experiment to test how nudges could be leveraged to make Virgin Atlantic's pilots more efficient in using fuel during pre-flight, in-flight and post-touchdown operations. Over the course of eight months, three treatment groups received accurate feedback on their monthly fuel usage in three different ways - one group received printed feedback reports that provided information on the fuel savings achieved in the previous month. The second group received the same report along with positive encouragement to achieve certain pre-set targets (if targets were achieved, captains would be praised with statements such as 'Well done!'). Lastly, the third group in addition to reports and targets were offered a 'pro-social incentive' where if targets were achieved a donation would be made to a charity of the pilot's choice on their behalf. The feedback reports would contain the potential donations that could result if pilots remained committed to achieving their goals.

The results were highly encouraging. All three treatment effects resulted in pilots becoming more conservative in their fuel usage. Cumulative fuel savings from the treatments amounted to 2.5 -7 thousand kg. While there was a significant difference between the effects of receiving just feedback and the other two treatments, there was not much significant difference between the targets treatment and the pro-social treatment. However, the pro-social incentive did induce a significant reduction in flight time (Gosnell,

List & Metcalfe, 2011). The most important take-away from this study is that when firms generate negative externalities, an alternative to penal laws targeting firms, is to make employees more conscious of the effect of their work. Similar to the Madrugador Program, the fuel efficiency reports and targets served as gentle, non-intrusive reminders to pilots to curb their tendency to go overboard on fuel usage.

Another avenue, where employees' irrationality could deliver sub-optimal outcomes is in the much-researched area of savings and retirement plans. Google, for one, found that its employees were not taking enough advantage of its 401(k) matching program. It collaborated with a group of researchers to examine how the wording of reminder emails sent to employees could be tweaked to increase more contribution to retirement savings. Choi, Haisley, Kurkowski & Massey (2012) adopted close to nine different linguistic nudges in their treatment emails and while their experimental design is complex and beyond the scope of this chapter, an interesting tactic used was that of 'anchoring'.

Choi et al., (2012) describe that employees in the 'anchoring' treatment group received one of four emails each of which were identical to each other and the control email (the one that Google normally sent to its employees) except that the treatment mails contained an additional one-two sentences that gave an example of by how much an employee's contribution rate could be increased (anchors) so as to avail more of the benefits for which they were eligible. The different anchor cues were - 1%, 3% 10% and 20%. Care was taken to ensure that the wording and the example given were arbitrary and not suggestive of what an employee should do.

The experiment's results revealed that one year from receiving the mail both low and high anchors had caused a change in employees' savings rate. While 1% example mails had actually caused savings rate to decline against that of the control group participants, the other three all resulted in an increase in savings rate with the 10% example resulting in an increase in "contribution rates by up to 1.9% of income" (Choi et al., 2012). One could therefore say that these small, innocuous sentences were enough to get employees thinking about their savings behavior with higher numerical cues leading to greater increases in savings rates.

On a similar theme, Blumenstock, Callen & Ghani (2018) detail an experiment that was conducted in Afghanistan where they tested the effects of various versions of a mobile money savings account called 'M-Pasandaz'. Employees were randomly assigned one of two products with different default contribution rates - 0% and 5%. The results showed that those who were assigned the 5% default account were 40% more likely to make contributions to their account as compared to the 0% group. The researchers found that once the experiment was over and all financial incentives had been removed, close to half still wished to continue contributing. This experiment has highly positive implications for how companies operating in environments as extreme as Afghanistan can also promote financially prudent behavior in their employees.

Nudging Customers

A company could employ nudging techniques to increase sales of their products. Marketing campaigns have a naturally strong relationship with nudging since the former are designed with the objective of increasing footfalls and sales and using the latter could ensure greater impact by embedding their message into the sub-conscience of consumers. In fact, McKinsey (2018) argues that techniques similar to nudging have been used by marketers for quite some time now. A simple but well-known example is that of supermarkets which stock candies and chocolates near check-out counters. Customers often tend to wait for a long time for their turn - this boredom coupled with easy visibility of a sweet treat can easily cause shoppers to impulse buy those chocolates.

However, there could be other areas in which companies could nudge their customers. An example from Google can help substantiate this point. AdWords is a service by which small businesses can get Google to show advertisements relating to their products and services in the 'Search Results'. AdWords customers on average start seeing results after 3 months. But many are not that patient enough. They want immediate results not realizing that their ads need to be finetuned multiple times before they start leading to footfalls ("Google: The behavioral economics behind crafting Google's AdWords campaign I Irrational Labs I Behavioral Economics", 2019).

To prevent customers from quitting before the three-month window, Irrational Labs carried out an experiment in which a random sample of calls made to Google's call centre by first time customers were informed of a "My 3 Month Expert Access Program". Call centre representatives used the word 'three words' often and would question the advertisers about their longterm goals. Further, the representative scheduled a series of five future calls where they would discuss other aspects of AdWords with the concerned customer. The customer in turn committed to the future dates on the first call itself. These measures helped enforce the idea that AdWords was a longterm investment for the business owner. Another innovative tactic was that customers were sent an email that contained the image of the fruit tree. The tree functioned as a visual metaphor: initial efforts, given time will yield great results ("Google: The behavioral economics behind crafting Google's AdWords campaign I Irrational Labs I Behavioral Economics", 2019).

The experiment was successful. Irrational Labs found a 14% increase in customer retention rate for customers who were subject to the aforementioned communication as compared to others who were not. Here, the nudges were used via 'framing' - in this case, the call centre representatives were conscientious enough to repeatedly present AdWords as a longterm investment for the business owner and not some quick fix.

For another example, many hotels ask customers to re-use their towels in order to minimize profligate water use. Goldstein, Griskevicius & Cialdini (2011) detail an experiment in which three types of messages exhorting customers to re-use their towels were printed on signs found in the bathroom. The messages read as follows - "Help Save the Environment", "Partner with us To Help Save the Environment" and "We're Doing Our Part for the Environment, Can We Count on You? The second message stated that if customers chose to re-use their towels, then the hotel would donate a part of the energy savings to an environmental non-profit. Conversely, the third message read, that the hotel had made a contribution on behalf of its guests and was requesting towel re-use as a way to recover the expense.

The researchers found that close to half (45%) of those who received the third message participated in the program as opposed to 35% for the first message and 30% for the second message. The researchers pin it down to hotel guests feeling a sense of heightened obligation to return the favor that the hotel had done something for them on their behalf for a third party (the environment) (Goldstein, Griskevicius & Cialdini, 2011). The third message functioned as a nudge in that customers felt more compelled to re-use their towel due to the personalized nature of that message.

Special Examples

In the area of finance, one finds examples where companies have used nudges to induce positive habits into their customers. The 'Credit Card Accountability, Responsibility and Disclosure Act' (CARD) (2009) is a noteworthy example. The CARD Act mandated that credit card companies should prominently display and differentiate between the time and interest expenses of paying the minimum amount required to stay current and the amount that would be required to meet the credit card debt within a period of three years. The latter option results in considerable savings as opposed to the former. Therefore, the customer may be nudged towards paying off the debt quickly by making a larger payment (the size of the payment being negated by the savings in interest and time). Agarwal, Chomsisengphet, Mahoney and Stroebel (2013) find that this disclosure requirement enabled a plausible maximum of $ 71 million in interest savings per year. Positive effects of this disclosure are further supported by Jones, Loibl and Tennyson (2015).

Another example is the Acorns App which greatly simplifies financial decisions for its customers. It offers two products - Acorns Core which is a micro-investing account where as little as one dollar may be diverted from the paycheck amount to a well-diversified portfolio selected by the app for the customer. Another is Acorns Later which helps customers save for their retirement by automatically selecting an Individual Retirement Account (IRA) based on lifestyle and other characteristics. The significance of this app lies in its suitability for those who work in the gig economy and don't have access to formal retirement saving plans from their employers (Benartzi, 2017). The name of the app itself is a nudge since it brings to mind a squirrel burying a small acorn which later grows up to be a tree.

A last example is that of the Personal Capital App. The app aggregates all accounts of a customer and provides easy to access information on savings and expenses and the allocation of spending. Benartzi (2017) notes that while the app provides the same information as was available on one's desktop, the easy availability on a mobile app helped people make wiser spending decisions. In fact, the average user decreased their spending by 15.7% and that too spending in the discretionary category (Benartzi, 2017).

Reality Checks: Pitfalls of Nudging

Nudges can be used to dupe and deceive too. Perhaps, this ability of nudges to be used for deception stems from its inherent discreetness. Nudges that have a sinister edge are commonly referred to as 'dark nudges'. Dark nudges have largely cropped up in areas where companies interact with their consumers. The following examples fundamentally differ from those aforementioned on grounds that while the former were explicitly designed towards inculcating positive traits or benefitting the nudged individual, the upcoming ones are designed to create a win-loss situation for implementer and the nudged respectively.

The most (in) famous example of dark nudges would be that of Uber. In a sensational expose published in the New York Times, it was revealed that Uber was using nudges to insidiously egg their drivers into staying on the road for longer intervals of time. Uber's drivers can go off the streets whenever they please. However, in situations of high demand it would be in Uber's interest to ensure that there as many drivers as possible on the road. To get drivers to stay, Uber drivers are reminded of previous day's earnings and are awarded meaningless badges on meeting certain targets. Further, drivers are notified of their next fare opportunity and the possible associated earnings even before the current ride is over (Gino, 2017). These nudges have the effect of robbing the drivers off their personal agency. The point of a nudge is to simply make something easier without making anything off-limits. 'Nudges' that veer on silent compulsion often arise from the abuse of default options by online retailers.

For example, online ticket booking sites such as Livenation and TicketMaster are known to automatically add magazine subscription fees to tickets that have already been lined up for purchase at the time for check-out. Customers need to opt-out of these subscriptions by ticking a small, inconspicuous box. This means that the purchase is automatically made for you unless you select 'no'. Customers usually realize they have purchased these subscriptions when it's too late - after they have paid. To receive a rebate, customers must print out a form, fill it by hand and send it by post to the company (Brignull, 2019).

Richard Thaler himself documented a similar experience he had with the Times of London. Thaler who wished to read a review of his book, encountered a paywall on the paper's website. He decided to go for a one-month trial subscription which with the intent of cancelling the subscription after reading the article. However, the cancellation procedure was particularly onerous. A 15 days notice had to be given (which meant the trial was only good for two weeks) and one had to personally call the London office during British business hours and pay international calling charges (Thaler, 2015). The excessively difficult cancellation procedure insidiously nudges consumers to simply stay put with a purchase that they did not intend to make.

A second controversy is to do with the choice architect. Critics question why one should consider the choice architect's opinion of what should be right for the individual to actually be valid. Looking at the aforementioned examples, this concern does seem valid. Livenation and Times of London created nudges that did not actually benefit the consumer, it benefitted the company. In a similar vein, Dholakia (2016) points out that nudges can be condescending. Companies, by implementing nudges are implicitly telling their customers that they are weak-willed and cannot take a well fleshed-out decision for themselves. Unless this nudge is employed, the individual will never be better off.

Further, they are incredibly difficult to get right or can have unintended effects if not designed properly. A compelling example comes from Costa & Kahn (2010) who examine the effect of political ideology on energy conservation nudges. They take the example of a Californian utility that sends out Home Energy Reports (HERs) to its customers along with the power bill. These HERs provide information on the recipient's power usage pattern for that month and provide a comparison with the usage pattern of a typical household in their community. This is an example of 'Social Proofing'. However, while the HERs led to more sustainable power usage, the reduction in consumption varied according to political ideology of the receiver - liberals were much more conscientious while conservatives were more likely to opt out of receiving these HERs and reported disliking them (Costa & Kahn, 2010).

RECOMMENDATIONS AND SOLUTIONS

For a company questioning whether its nudges are ethical or not or even for the general individual who wishes to be aware of how she may unknowingly duped - Thaler's principles for ethical usage of nudges should be helpful. They are -

1. Transparency: Nudges should be clear in their intentions. They should not have any covert motives or result in misleading the nudged
2. Easy Opting Out: One of the fundamental characteristics of a nudge is that it does not restrict any actions or choices. Stated differently, they should be easily avoidable.
3. Welfare Improving: There should be a compelling reason to believe that the effect that would be produced by the nudge would benefit the nudged (Thaler, 2015).

If we consider LiveNation, one sees that the subscription fees are added surreptitiously. Removal of such subscription charges is cumbersome and in general results in inconvenience to the concerned person. Similarly, Thaler's experience with Times of London shows that while the subscription model may have been transparent in terms of pricing and duration, it was inconvenient to cancel and not welfare - improving. They fail to meet most or all of Thaler's criteria.

Conversely, Boston Consulting Group's in-house email system has no hidden intentions. It's clearly to signal managers to re-consider their decisions. Since it provides the option to send the mail anyway, it does not preclude any medium of action and ensures emergency communication can take place. And in general it is welfare improving since managers get a chance to re-evaluate their decisions and not position themselves as inconsiderate team players while employees too can be stress-free away from work. Thaler's criteria is, therefore, a very useful way to benchmark any nudge type of intervention that a company or government may think of implementing. An entity would only bolster its ethical credentials by abiding to these tenets which in turn would have further positive effects.

Designing and implementing a nudge is a very difficult process as aforementioned. Companies often take the help of management consultancy firms to design appropriate and customized solutions for problems they may be facing. What is important is that these solutions should be suited to the specifics of the situation or problem faced. Further, the choice architect must be crystal clear on the exact nature of the problem, the desired outcomes from the nudge and must account for all possible variations in behavioral response. The experiment with the Californian utility suggests that idiosyncratic factors such as political ideology could have pronounced impacts on a nudge. The lesson is that nudges have to be more 'targeted' in their approach as voiced by Costa & Kahn (2010).

Additionally, it is crucial to test out a nudge by way of experimentation before rolling it out completely. It is perhaps no co-incidence that most of the examples cited in this chapter come from experiments that were conducted in a wide variety of settings. These types of experiments are commonly referred to as 'Randomized Controlled Trials' (RCTs). RCTs involve having the treatment group(s) to which a particular variation of the nudge is applied and a control group which receives no treatment. The presence of the control helps eliminate any common impact and arrive at the true, unique effect of the intervention. This in turn helps establish causality between the nudge and the observed behavioral response.

Checking whether the effects that prevailed during the experiment persist after the experimental is also another test of the effectiveness of the nudge. For example, the Madrugador Project that was discussed above, Cadena et al., (2011) note that the improved time management performance observed in loan officers did not survive once the intervention was terminated. This helps one conclude that whatever effects were observed were solely due to the presence of those friendly reminders and not some innate change in the loan officers. In fact, the authors note that Bancamia is in process of re-starting the scheme on its own due to the high positive response (Cadena et al., 2011).

FUTURE RESEARCH DIRECTIONS

This chapter briefly touched upon the concept of 'Digital Nudges'. Given the increasing digitization of the mediums through which companies interact with their customers, future research could focus on the design and implementation strategies for digital nudges and discussing novel areas in which they could be applied. More research is also required on the prevalence of dark nudges. Dark nudges take advantage of their implicit discreetness to dupe and deceive. Further research could try to answer whether companies found using dark nudges should be disciplined in any way and whether this requires a commitment from the company itself or an external regulatory response.

CONCLUSION

This chapter set out to cover the theoretical underpinnings of nudge theory. Fundamentally, behavioral economics recognizes that humans are well - only humans. They have biases, make errors of judgement and rely on heuristics. It is this explicit acknowledgement of human nature that makes behavioral economics so appealing and powerful in its implications.

Multiple examples were taken up to understand how nudging could be employed to affect the behaviour of managers, employees and consumers. Managers could be made better team players, employees can be made more productive and consumers can be led towards to staying committed to a company and also undertake beneficial actions. At the same time, nudging can have potential adverse consequences. When used to cheat or dupe, they cease to lead the recipients to better outcomes thereby defeating the original purpose of nudging altogether. Nudging should be ethical and create win-win situations. Nudges should also be tested extensively through rigorous experimentation before being rolled out and be designed keeping in mind the unique circumstances of the problem faced.

In sum, nudging has a plethora of positive applications for decision-making and should be explored by any entity wishing to make its processes more efficient. The field of nudging and broadly behavioral economics research is still evolving and it will be exciting to see the new insights that will eventually emerge.

REFERENCES

Abdukadirov, S. (2016). *Nudge Theory in Action: Behavioral Design in Policy and Markets*. Basingstoke, UK: Springer. doi:10.1007/978-3-319-31319-1

Agarwal, S., Chomsisengphet, S., Mahoney, N., & Stroebel, J. (2013). Regulating Consumer Financial Products: Evidence from Credit Cards. *The Quarterly Journal of Economics*, *130*(1), 111–164. doi:10.1093/qje/qju037

Al-Tarawneh, H. A. (2011). The Main Factors beyond Decision Making. *Journal of Management Research*, *4*(1). doi:10.5296/jmr.v4i1.1184

Arno, A., & Thomas, S. (2016). The efficacy of nudge theory strategies in influencing adult dietary behaviour: A systematic review and meta-analysis. *BMC Public Health*, *16*(1), 676. doi:10.118612889-016-3272-x PMID:27475752

Benartzi, S. (2017). How Digital Tools and Behavioral Economics Will Save Retirement. Retrieved September 30, 2019, from https://hbr.org/2017/12/how-digital-tools-and-behavioral-economics-will-save-retirement

Benartzi, S., Beshears, J., Milkman, K., Sunstein, C., Thaler, R., Shankar, M., ... Galing, S. (2017). Should Governments Invest More in Nudging? *Psychological Science*, *28*(8), 1041–1055. doi:10.1177/0956797617702501 PMID:28581899

Blumenstock, J., Callen, M., & Ghani, T. (2018). Why Do Defaults Affect Behavior? Experimental Evidence from Afghanistan. *The American Economic Review*, *108*(10), 2868–2901. doi:10.1257/aer.20171676

Bonner, S., & Sprinkle, G. (2002). The effects of monetary incentives on effort and task performance: Theories, evidence, and a framework for research. *Accounting, Organizations, and Society*, *27*(4-5), 303–345. doi:10.1016/S0361-3682(01)00052-6

Brignull, H. (2019). Dark Patterns - Types of Dark Pattern. Retrieved August 31, 2019, from https://www.darkpatterns.org/types-of-dark-pattern

Cadena, X., Schoar, A., Cristea, A., & Delgado-Medrano, H. (2019). *Fighting Procrastination in the Workplace: An Experiment.* NBER Working Paper 16944. Cambridge. National Bureau of Economic Research. Retrieved from https://www.nber.org/papers/w16944

Choi, J., Haisley, E., Kurkoski, J., & Massey, C. (2012). *Small Cues Change Savings Choices*. SSRN Electronic Journal; doi:10.3386/w17843

Costa, D., & Kahn, M. (2013). Energy Conservation "Nudges" and Environmentalist Ideology: Evidence from A Randomized Residential Electricity Field Experiment. *Journal of the European Economic Association*, *11*(3), 680–702. doi:10.1111/jeea.12011

Department of Economic Affairs. (2019). *Economic Survey*, *2018-19*, 29–56.

Dhar, J., Bailey, A., Mingardon, S., & Tankersley, J. (2019). The Persuasive Power of the Digital Nudge. Retrieved 30 August 2019, from https://www.bcg.com/publications/2017/people-organization-operations-persuasive-power-digital-nudge.aspx

Dholakia, U. (2016). Why Nudging Your Customers Can Backfire. Retrieved August 31, 2019, from https://hbr.org/2016/04/why-nudging-your-customers-can-backfire

Ebert, P., & Freibichler, W. (2017). Nudge management: Applying behavioural science to increase knowledge worker productivity. *Journal of Organization Design*, *6*(1), 4. doi:10.118641469-017-0014-1

Gino, F. (2017). Uber Shows How Not to Apply Behavioral Economics. Retrieved August 31, 2019, from https://hbr.org/2017/04/uber-shows-how-not-to-apply-behavioral-economics

Goldstein, N., Griskevicius, V., & Cialdini, R. (2011). Reciprocity by Proxy. *Administrative Science Quarterly*, *56*(3), 441–473. doi:10.1177/0001839211435904

Google. The behavioral economics behind crafting Google's AdWords campaign | Irrational Labs | Behavioral Economics. (2019). Retrieved August 31, 2019, from https://irrationallabs.org/work/behavioral-science-behind-crafting-googles-adwords-campaign/

Gosnell, G., List, J., & Metcalfe, R. (2016). *A New Approach to an Old-Age Problem: Solving Externalities by Incenting Workers Directly. NBER Working Paper 22316*. Cambridge, UK: National Bureau of Economic Research; Retrieved from https://www.nber.org/papers/w22316 doi:10.3386/w22316

Hall-Ellis, S. D. (2015). Nudges and decision making: A winning combination. *The Bottom Line (New York, N.Y.)*, *28*(4), 133–136. doi:10.1108/BL-07-2015-0015

Hausman, D. M., & Welch, B. (2010). Debate: To Nudge or Not to Nudge*. *Journal of Political Philosophy*, *18*(1), 123–136. doi:10.1111/j.1467-9760.2009.00351.x

Jones, L., Loibl, C., & Tennyson, S. (2015). Effects of informational nudges on consumer debt repayment behaviours. *Journal of Economic Psychology*, *51*, 16–33. doi:10.1016/j.joep.2015.06.009

Kosters, M., & Van der Heijden, J. (2015). From mechanism to virtue: Evaluating Nudge theory. *Evaluation*, *21*(3), 276–291. doi:10.1177/1356389015590218

Leggett, W. (2014). The politics of behaviour change: Nudge, neoliberalism and the state. *Policy and Politics*, *42*(1), 3–19. doi:10.1332/030557312X655576

McKinsey. (2018). Behavioral science in business: Nudging, debiasing, and managing the irrational mind [Podcast]. Retrieved August 31, 2019, from https://www.mckinsey.com/business-functions/organization/our-insights/behavioral-science-in-business-nudging-debiasing-and-managing-the-irrational-mind

Romero, M., & Biswas, D. (2016). Healthy-Left, Unhealthy-Right: Can Displaying Healthy Items to the Left (versus Right) of Unhealthy Items Nudge Healthier Choices? *The Journal of Consumer Research*, *43*(1), 103–112. doi:10.1093/jcr/ucw008

Samson, A. (2014). The Behavioral Economics Guide 2014 (1st ed.).

Sent, E. (2004). Behavioral Economics: How Psychology Made Its (Limited) Way Back Into Economics. *History of Political Economy*, *36*(4), 735–760. doi:10.1215/00182702-36-4-735

Shove, E. (2010). Beyond the ABC: Climate Change Policy and Theories of Social Change. *Environment and Planning A. Economy and Space*, *42*(6), 1273–1285. doi:10.1068/a42282

Simon, H. (1990). *Reason in Human Affairs*. Redwood City, CA: Stanford University Press.

Sunstein, C. (2014). *Nudging: A Very Short Guide*. SSRN Electronic Journal; doi:10.2139srn.2499658

Sunstein, C. R., & Thaler, R. H. (2003). *Libertarian Paternalism Is Not An Oxymoron*. SSRN Electronic Journal; doi:10.2139srn.405940

Thaler, R., Sunstein, C., & Balz, J. (2012). Choice Architecture. In E. Sharif, *The Behavioral Foundations of Public Policy*. Retrieved from https://papers.ssrn.com/sol3/papers.cfm?abstract_id=2536504

Thaler, R. H. (2015). The Power of Nudges, for Good and Bad. *The New York Times*.

Thaler, R. H., & Benartzi, S. (2004). Save More Tomorrow™: Using Behavioral Economics to Increase Employee Saving. *Journal of Political Economy*, *112*(S1), S164–S187. doi:10.1086/380085

Thaler, R. H., & Sunstein, C. R. (2009). *Nudge: Improving Decisions about Health, Wealth, and Happiness*. Penguin Books.

Tversky, A., & Kahneman, D. (1979). Intuitive Prediction: Biases and Corrective Procedures. *TIMS Studies In Management Science*, *12*, 313–327.

Van Der Heijden, J., & Kosters, M. (2019). From mechanism to virtue: evaluating Nudge-theory. Retrieved 29 September 2019, from https://openresearch-repository.anu.edu.au/bitstream/1885/71637/8/01_Kosters_From_Mechanism_to_Virtue_2015.pdf

Van Deun, H., Van Acker, W., Fobe, E., & Brans, M. (2019). Nudging in Public Policy and Public Management: A scoping review of the literature. Retrieved 30 September 2019, from https://www.psa.ac.uk/sites/default/files/conference/papers/2018/VanDeun_vanAcker_Fob%C3%A9_Br

Vats, A. (2019). Concept Note on Auto Enrolment for increase in pension coverage in India. Retrieved September 29, 2019, from https://www.pfrda.org.in/writereaddata/links/enrolment12348adc6a2-38d3-417f-aaa5-6dbe40a0769b.pdf

ADDITIONAL READING

AlMarshedi, A., Wanick, V., Wills, G. B., & Ranchhod, A. (2016). Gamification and Behaviour. *Progress in IS*, 19-29. doi:10.1007/978-3-319-45557-0_2

Binns, C., & Low, W. Y. (2017). Nobel Prizes, Nudge Theory, and Public Health. *Asia-Pacific Journal of Public Health, 29*(8), 632–634. doi:10.1177/1010539517743630 PMID:29145732

Bolton, G., Dimant, E., & Schmidt, U. (2018). *When a Nudge Backfires: Using Observation with Social and Economic Incentives to Promote Pro-Social Behavior*. SSRN Electronic Journal; doi:10.2139srn.3294375

John, P., Cotterill, S., Richardson, L., Moseley, A., Stoker, G., Smith, G., ... Nomura, H. (2013). *Nudge, Nudge, Think, Think: Experimenting with Ways to Change Civic Behaviour*. London, United Kingdom: A&C Black.

Lin, Y., Osman, M., & Ashcroft, R. (2017). Nudge: Concept, Effectiveness, and Ethics. *Basic and Applied Social Psychology, 39*(6), 293–306. doi:10.1080/01973533.2017.1356304

Marjanovic, Z. (2017). The Fruitless Pursuit of Nudging Healthy Behavior: Comment on Lin, Osman, and Ashcroft. *Basic and Applied Social Psychology, 39*(6), 309–310. doi:10.1080/01973533.2017.1369413

Mongin, P., & Cozic, M. (2018). Rethinking nudge: Not one but three concepts. *Behavioural Public Policy, 2*(1), 107–124. doi:10.1017/bpp.2016.16

Murakami, M., Nomura, S., & Tsubokura, M. (2018). Call for a new epidemiological approach to disaster response. *Journal of Epidemiology and Community Health*, jech-2017-210397. doi:10.1136/jech-2017-210397

Pedwell, C. (2017). Habit and the Politics of Social Change. *Body & Society, 23*(4), 59–94. doi:10.1177/1357034X17734619

Reijula, S., Kuorikoski, J., Ehrig, T., Katsikopoulos, K., & Sunder, S. (2018). Nudge, Boost, or Design? Limitations of behaviorally informed policy under social interaction. doi:10.31235/osf.io/zh3qw

Sunstein, C. R., & Reisch, L. A. (2017). *The Economics of Nudge: Critical Concepts in Economics.*

Tan, H., Lv, X., Liu, X., & Gursoy, D. (2018). Evaluation nudge: Effect of evaluation mode of online customer reviews on consumers' preferences. *Tourism Management, 65*, 29–40. doi:10.1016/j.tourman.2017.09.011

KEY TERMS AND DEFINITIONS

Anchoring: An often arbitrary numerical cue that significantly influences individual thought processes. Subsequent answers to questions or decisions could be based around the information provided by the anchor.

Choice Architect: The individual or organization that is in a position to alter aspects of the choice architecture and thereby affect the behaviour of individuals.

Choice Architecture: The socio-political environment or context in which individuals take decisions.

Dark Nudges: Nudges that are employed for nefarious purposes, usually to trick and deceive others. They end up creating zero sum situations and do not contribute to the welfare of the recipient.

Default Option: The option that automatically gets chosen for an individual if no active step or decision is taken.

Framing: The notion that the same piece of information when worded differently or introduced in different settings and situations will lead to different conclusions or choices.

Homo Economicus: A fundamental assumption in traditional economic theory that presumes individuals to be rational in all that they do. Rational means that individuals are completely objective; they analyze all available data to weigh pros and cons before taking a decision and are concerned with their self-interest only.

Libertarian Paternalism: This refers to the notion of nudges guiding individuals towards self-benefitting decisions without explicitly interfering into personal choice or violating freedom of action.

Planning Fallacy: The tendency to under-estimate the time required and over- estimate one's ability to execute a task.

Social Proofing: The influence of other's actions on one's own actions.

ENDNOTES

1 The paper provides a cogent overview of the issues that Adam Smith touched upon in his *Theory of Moral Sentiments* and how they relate to topics studied today as a formal part of behavioral economics.

2 Samson (2014) provides a comprehensive sketch of the evolution of behavioral economics as a sub-field of economics.

3 The choice architect is the person or institution (such as the government) who creates an environment in which individuals take decisions and who can therefore modify the features of that environment to influence individual decision - making. Refer to Thaler, Sunstein and Balz (2010).

4 Many thanks to the anonymous reviewer who pointed this out.

5 The dual system framework can be compared with Smith's dichotomy presented in his Theory of Moral Sentiments and ultimately with the Freudian Personality Theory which argues that an individual's personality is shaped by the conflict between the 'id' and the 'conscious' parts of the brain.

6 A comprehensive evaluation of how Psychology and Economics have intersected and informed each other over the years is beyond the scope of this chapter. Sent (2004) does an excellent work of the same. Legett (2004) also provides a limited but cogent analysis of the same and provides direction to various other references that touch on the same.

7 Vats (2019) provides a brief sketch of automatic enrollment pension plans in these countries and also suggests how the same could be implemented in India.

8 Of course, this is a over-simplification of the issue. The point here is to contrast how nudges which are less overt can provide a more efficient alternative to monetary incentives. Bonner and Sprinkle (2002) provide a through overview of the literature on monetary incentives.

Chapter 15
Data Analysis on Global Stratification

Kirti Raj Bhatele
Rustamji Institute of Technology, India & BSF Academy, Gwalior, India

Stuti Singhal
Rustamji Institute of Technology, India & BSF Academy, Tekanpur, India

Muktasha R. Mithora
Rustamji Institute of Technology, India & BSF Academy, Gwalior, India

Sneha Sharma
Rustamji Institute of Technology, India & BSF Academy, Tekanpur, India

ABSTRACT

This chapter will guide you through the modeling, uses, and trends in data analysis and data science. The authors focus on the importance of pictorial data in replacement of numeric data. In most situations, graphical representation of data can present the information more distinctly, informative, and in less space than the same information requires in sentence form. This chapter provides a brief knowledge about representing data to more understandable form such that any person whether layman or not can understand it without any difficulty. This chapter also deals with the software Tableau which we use to convert the table data into graphical data. This Chapter contains 11 heat maps related to the world economies and their detailed study on several different topics. It will also give light on the basics of Python Language and its various algorithm studies to compare all the world economies based on their development.

INTRODUCTION

In old times, with lower population and low invention in technologies, humans did not have much idea about data and its uses. They don't keep it safely, does not understand its need and importance. Unknowingly, they share it with other peoples and their relatives. But as soon as technology grown, people

DOI: 10.4018/978-1-7998-2216-5.ch015

understand its importance. With the increase in technology and intelligence, people start collecting the data and try to keep it safely. As per the increase in the volume of the data with change in time, there is an emerging need for the professionals working in the field, sorting the data, analysing it and drawing out various trends from it. By the use of results from the analysis, different predictions are done and different measures are being taken in order to have the best possible solution. The various advantages of data analysis and data science are being studied in the following chapter. In this chapter, we are going to give an example of Global Stratification, which will be going to base on different measures. We will be learning about different data collection techniques from various resources present online. Then we will be briefing about the software that we are going to use in order to visualize the data collected by us. We will be doing this for making it easier for the layman to understand in his or her language. The chapter focuses on the topics like: Health, Political Freedom, Public Sector, Work and Life, Violence Rights, Energy Issues, etc. The countries will be classified on these factors and its result will be used to categorize them in different categories.

DATA ANALYSIS: AN INTRODUCTION

The data analysis takes place when event is repeated over a period to many numbers of times. It can be detected statistically or graphically. The data can be of many forms and can be collected from various sources such as survey on internet, previous records of associated data to be analysed. The data which have been collected are known as raw data. The requirement of data analysis is that to predict the possibility for future of an event. For example- Let a day be selected for predicting the possibility of rain, to predict the possibility by analysing the whole record of rain for that day and by making algorithm, the probability of the rain for that day will be resulted. This is how the prediction occurs. The data analysis is using widely by the different websites and also in different fields. The data analysis is used in different fields such as education, weather, business intelligence, construction, digital marketing, risk analysis, software analysis etc. The data analysis is also done by cleaning and modelling of the data and helps in supporting to the resulted data. The data refining is one of the main procedures for data analysis. The raw data should be appropriate for data analysis (Said & Torra, 2019).

History

Herman Hollerith invented Tabulating Machine in 1890. This machine was based on punch cards. The data scientist came in need when data was gathering in large amount and handling the data became difficult. The data handling was also a part of data analysis. The data analysis has given many benefits such as to manage and store the data and to use that data for the prediction of an event. It was important to use that data that was stored in machine because it helped to understand and improve the business processes and economic growth for a country and saved the time and money. Every company got the benefit. Before analysis the data it is necessary that for whom and for which purpose the analysis is going to be conducting. That became the main step of data analysis which helps the people to make decisions. Historical analytics is also a term which defines the analysis of an activity and the data from the past to recognize the patterns, correlations and other statistical relationships. Business Evolution was the main reason to build a field of data analysis (Miyazaki, M. 2015).

Current Scenario

The average salary for data scientist is $113,346 as per Glass door. There are different types of data handling i.e. qualitative and quantitative. The Quality data is the data taken within no numerical value, colors, gender etc. The quantitative data are also divided into two types i.e. countable or discrete and measurable or continuous data. Covering all fields of business analytics and industrial economics, there are highlights of them such as Finance, Sales, Marketing, Social Media, SEO, Consumer Data, e-Commerce, Human Resources etc. The working process of data analytics is based on automated inputs and user inputs which gave result. Mainly Google Analytics were introduced in 2005. It is one of the biggest companies in the field of Data Analytics.

Future Aspects

There are different future aspects of data analytics such as Real-time analytics which defined as data collection and reporting of data in real time. Big Data which collects large amounts of historical data which is easily accessible in real time cloud and expansion of business become forward, Predictive Analytics is basically based on study of previous trends and predictive analysis which deals with big data to forecast the future actions, Automated Analytics which requires small numbers of inputs by which the data gets analyzed itself in different ways was that optimize the business system and growth of business etc. (Guerzhoy, M., 2019).

As the country is growing, Data analytics is also improving its techniques and methods for making strategies to get the maximum profit to business and improving the career of the individual person. Data Analytics has become a good career option in India which increases the employment in India. It simply not totally depends on the programming skills of the person who is applying for the job. It depends on the analysis and results to which the companies can get maximum profit and increases their business.

Uses of Data Analysis

Some of different applications of the data analysis are as follows:-

1. Data Analysis finds the pattern of the data.
2. It also contributes the relationships among the data.
3. Focuses on understanding of non numerical data such as text, images, audio and video etc.
4. It identifies the relevant data sets which will need analytics applications.
5. It works with others to collect, integrate and prepare the data for analysis.
6. It develops the models and assesses for finding their relevant data.
7. It communicates the result to the business executives and other end users.

Trends in Data Analysis

There are top 10 trends of data analysis are as follows (Durcevic, S., 2018): -

1. It is used for data governance and trust.
2. It is also used to empower the artificial intelligence.

3. It helps the chief data officer and chief analytics officer.
4. It helps in data discovery.
5. It helps in connecting the clouds.
6. It works on the predictive and prescriptive analytics tools.
7. It helps in security.
8. It produces collaborative business intelligence.
9. It stores the consumer experience.
10. It maintains the quality and data management.

DATA SCIENCE: AN INTRODUCTION

Data Science is done by the help of data analysis. By data analysis, when the data is collected then it goes towards the pattern formation and goes under the making of predictions and algorithms. It is good field to give an idea to the computer to take decision along with the artificial intelligence. Many different fields come under the data science like Data Handling, Mining of data, and Data Warehousing and many more. Different tools that are used by the data scientist are SAS, Apache Spark, BigML, MATLAB, Tableau etc. Data Scientist also includes Maths, Stats, Algorithms, Software Engineering, and Data Communication etc. Mainly it does not require high level coding of employee but employees should have a little knowledge of Python Coding. Hadoop is also a platform for Data Scientist. Data Scientist has a good scope for job. The data science field is newly discovered not much older than the website creation platform and increasing the data by different types of users and events are handled by data science. This field has an ability to tackle all types of problems. The data science is managing with clouds and storage of distributed computing. Market relevant strategies are also improving and business intelligence strategy is also increasing to develop our country and economic growth. Employment level is also increasing in our country. (Rouse M., 2019)

History of Data Science

Journey of data science was begun in 1962 when John W. Tukey who was a mathematician, predicted the effect of modern-day electronic computing. Data Science was becoming in market in 2001. Data Science helped the people to data handling and other fields. It was then pushed by the people as per their needs. Claude is also known as the father of data science or information theory. The term data scientist was mentioned in 2008 a Google search engine is a good example for describing the basics of data science. Google is the company where data scientists are evaluating and improving their products more than other companies. Data were earlier collecting in a spreadsheet in Excel which is in numeric form and complex form which cannot be easily explainable.

Current Scenario

Data Scientist is not only for business analysis, they are also contributing in building the data products and software platforms. The value of data science has increased in the United States, United Kingdom, Germany, France, Sweden, Australia etc. The data scientists are still in demand for virtually growth of every industry, from retail to manufacturing, collecting data from different customers and implement those data into the algorithms. There are multiple approaches towards a problem, with data science; one can find the best or easy way to solve the problem. By different software such as tableau, different languages such as python, R Language, Power BI etc. application of data to find the pattern becomes easy. Data visualization is become easy. Online shopping websites such as amazon.com/in are good examples for the application of data science, data handling, data analysis and big data. Data Science is not involving only in finding the results by the data but also involving in building the data products and software platform, with visualization and machine learning algorithms.

Future Aspects

The data science helps in growth of internet of things i.e. IoT and Artificial Intelligence. The organization and pattern making problems can be solved with data science. It can select the correct data sets and variables. With data science, the employment will increase more in rest of the countries. Data Science is moving forward to handle the complex data and to implement the work in different fields of work such as in statistics, computation etc. Data Science is a technology which will save time and space for the data by combining with the cloud technology. The increasing amount of data, better computing resources and improving machine learning algorithm with move data science forward and its applications in different fields (Venkat, T., 2014).

Uses of Data Science

There are many uses of data science are as follows: -

1. Data Research becomes east by the data science.
2. It increases the visualization by applications of different software or tools.
3. Data Science also helps in improving the e-Commerce experience, Increasing Customer experience, Improving Searches, Music Recommendation etc.

Trends of Data Science

Some of the trends in data science are:

1. Rapidly growing IoT networks
2. Accessible Artificial Intelligence
3. The rise of predictive analysis
4. Dark data migration to the cloud
5. Quantum Computing
6. Open source solution
7. Edge Computing
8. Smarter Chat bots (Gupta, A. et al., 2018)

COUNTRIES AND VARIOUS FIELDS OVER WHICH EVALUATION IS DONE

Past Visualization

In the past few decades we can see according to the data collected by UNFAO (United Nation Food and Agriculture Organization), IEA (International Energy Agency) that many countries were facing the problem such as the number of people accessing the technology, electricity, and food. What is the status of government? Is the government is able to fulfil the resources given to its citizens? Some of the countries were developed at that time and this can be seen by the development they are doing in every field. For example, in the field of technology, they made technology so far to be reached by the citizens of developing or under developing countries. Not only the technology but also the happiness index of the population of the country also matters. The ways people tackle with personal and professional life also count. The important thing is that at what rate the countries are growing (growth rate) and number of literate youth which will help in growing the country's development. So the literacy rate of the country is very important in terms of further development of the country in future (Hirve, S. et al. 2019).

It has been recorded since past 200 years' that people living in different countries of the world achieved a constant progress in health issues that has been directly led to increases in life expectancy. Life expectancy in the UK becomes more than 80 years, showing a major leap in improvement. In the late 1960s, another country named Japan, surpassed UK in health facilities and surprised the world with its life rates. The world got amazed again when South Korea comes up with the life rate even greater than the one possessed by the UK and Japan. It was a slow but steady improvement.

Current Issues

At today's date business of all sizes uses analytics for the best result. For example, if you ask a shopkeeper why he stopped delivering at a particular road he will tell you that its residents try to bargain a lot and hence he loses money and interest, but on the street next to that he has some great customers for whom he provides excellent service. This is the heart of analytics. The shopkeeper tested delivering that street and realized that he is losing money – the next one month he stopped delivering to the residents of that street. All the factors are important to increase the growth rate of business or overall country growth rate. The main factor of growth is GDP produced by each country. As it is clearly visible that the present scenario of some countries that comes under the category of Developed countries are the countries that has stable economy and shows advancement in technological infrastructure comparative to the ones that are among the less industrialized nations. Generally, the criteria of developed countries depend on the Gross Domestic Product (GDP) and industrial base of that nation. The estimates come from the International Centre for Tax and Development, and are represented as the prominent share in GDP.

As we can directly infer from the most updated data recently, it is surprisingly to know that at one end of the spectrum we have countries such as Cuba, Sweden, France, Norway and Denmark, where total tax revenues by citizens are higher than 30% whereas at the other end, we do have countries such as Libya and Saudi Arabia, where taxes account for less than 2% of national gross income. The countries with high GDPs are Australia, Germany, Czech Republic, Canada, Austria, Belgium, Cyprus, Denmark, Finland, etc.

Now, the countries with low GDP (Gross Domestic Product) are come under the category of developing countries. The developing countries are the nation that has less industrial base and relatively low

GDP than developed once. The developing countries are those which are trying to be fully developed day by day by maintaining their resources.

The countries with low GDP are Afghanistan, Albania, Algeria, Angola, China, Colombia, India, Iran, Kuwait, Malaysia, Qatar, etc. The above countries with low GDP rates indicate that the financial condition of the country is weaker than the countries with higher GDP.

Future Prediction

According to our survey of all the countries in the world, the countries Afghanistan, Angola, Bangladesh, Burkina Faso, Burundi, etc. are the countries which are underdeveloped, according to the score generated by our project out of 100 (the countries with a score of 65 or below 65 are rated under developing countries on the various 10 factors). The countries above 65 are rated as developing countries as their all 10 factors have an average greater than 65.

The above countries have to work on technology; another important factor is the population of a country. Population of a country matters a lot in terms of sharing resources for example, if a country has a limited resources and population is high in that country than the total share of the resources will decrease per person and this will eventually decrease the total rate of development in that country.

In future the problem of big data will occur on a large scale and the technicians have to manage it so there is a huge scope in data science to work and develop their own country. The citizens of the country have to be literate so that they can make their country progress in each field. The overall growth of the country will depend on the nourishment, literacy rate, etc.

After a remarkable growth in 2017 and early 2018, global economic activity get slowed down notably in the second half of last year, which creates a huge loss to the world forum. It is reflecting a confluence of factors affecting major economies. China's growth declined following a combination of needed regulatory tightening to read shadow banking and thus increasing in trade tension with the United States.

According to a study by US banking group Citi, India will soon be the world's largest economy within 39 years. It has been predicted that Indian GDP in 2050, measured by purchasing power parity (PPP), will be $85.97 trillion. China, in second place, will run at a GDP of $ 80.02 trillion and the US at an average of $ 39.07 trillion.

Energy (Percent of Population Having Access to Electricity)

In today's world, where everything runs from electricity, it seems to be one of the important social and economic factors to mark a country's development. "Access to electricity" does not have any specific meaning that is accepted by all. However, most people infer from the term is the fastest delivery of electricity, safe cooking facilities and a required minimum level of consumption. According to the International Energy Agency (IEA) the term denotes more than just the delivery to the household. It motivates the rural as well as urban households to use the minimum amount of electricity based on their needs. The information shows that the minimum threshold for rural household is 250 kilowatt-hours per annum and for urban household it counts for 500 kilowatt-hours per annum.

A steady increase has been seen at a global level in accessing the electricity from the last few decades. The data measures 85 percent in 2014 which is 12 percent more than the record marked in 1990 in having reach to electricity by the global population.

Food (Percent of Undernourished Population)

The percent of the population being undernourished in a country comes up as a prominent factor in the indication of hunger used by the UN Food and Agriculture Organization. It is used in measuring the share of the population which has an insufficient caloric (dietary energy) intake which is the minimum energy requirements defined as necessary for a given population. The data which has been collected shows the prevalence of undernourishment by world region. It focuses on the countries having high rates of undernourishment over the last two decades.

Growth and Inequality (GDP per Person)

The Gross Domestic Product widely known as GDP of an economy is an important factor to show its development. It is the measurement of total production in a country in a specified period of time. Also, here by total production it means is, the total monetary value of all the services and good produced within the economy of a country. The estimation is done in an approx value which is also a very tedious job for everyone to calculate. But, the chances of mistakes is minimised with the rise in technology. It becomes very tough in comparing such values across borders of nations as the price and value of a single commodity also differs to a great extent. Hence, a standard currency value is used to grant it some uniformity. From the last studies it is found that, the higher the GDP rate comes out for a country, the more developed it ought to come up in. The prosperity for an economic nation is measured via GDP per capita, the value of all services and goods produced by a nation in an annum divided by the population within a country. A country's development is also marked by its GDP over the years.

Health (Expenditure on Health Issues)

Health is Wealth for an individual as well as for a nation. If the residents of a nation will be healthy enough than half of the problem seems to be solved automatically in an economy. Those nations whose people know how to take care of themselves are the ones whose population cares for the environment too. And the government who takes care of the health of its population seems the one who know its responsibility well enough. With the discovery of powerful new ways of treatments, the expenditure of health remedies comes up to be the costliest ones. It is not in the budget for the people who live below poverty. So, they have no choice other than living without treatments. But, the problem can be solved when a government approve appropriate budget annually for the ones who cannot afford such costly treatments. There are various policies running in almost every nation of the world, ensuring a good health to the citizens, but the budget granted varies according to the annual income of the nation. So, this field have been taken in the research to mark how much a government spend on the health facilities of its citizens and care for them.

Politics (Countries Living in Democracies)

Democracy is the power of the citizen to express their feelings and to choose the one who is going to make rules for them. It keeps a fear within authorities that if they will not work properly; there is a fair chance with the voters to change them. The fairer the process of choosing makes that political score of a country higher. Many of the country found out to be the Anocracies ones which mean that they fall in between the spectrum of being democratic and non-democratic and are not fully democratic as well as not fully autocratic. The autocratic country does not give at least minimum rights to its citizens.

Population (Life Expectancy)

The life expectancy has increased in recent years due to increase in health facilities and advancement in medical fields. But, now it seems to decrease in the future, due to adverse environment conditions and the style of living. It has been seen that the life expectancy of underdeveloped countries are very less and people won't live much in such nations. This can be the result of various things like less medical facilities, harsh surroundings, desire to die early, depression and lack of bonding between people. If the example of Japan, is taken then, it seems that living for a longer number of years also does not ensure steady rate of development because now the country is facing the problem of an old population. It is the developing one but no one can ensure its certainty. Hence, this field is added as the factor to decide a country's classification.

Public Sector (Share of Tax in GDP)

In an economy, it is important to notice the different ways used to raise and spend revenue because it has a major impact on social and economic development of nations. In this field of public sector, we mainly focus on the data which contain the source of government revenue: taxation. The latest estimate from the International Centre for Tax and Development shows that half of the countries generate 80 percent of government revenues from tax collection. Also, has been seen that, almost all the countries in the world collect more than 50 percent of revenue in the form of taxes. Studies show that the extent of collecting revenue from its citizens marks the growth of government as one of the economic features.

The gap between the developed and developing countries can be clearly seen from the way they collect taxes from its citizens. As a pattern, it has been traced that developing countries impose heavy amount of trade tax and consumption tax on its citizens.

It has been surprisingly seen that developed countries collect a large amount of tax in comparison to the one collected by the developing ones. This clearly shows that the efficient mechanism of tax collection process took place in the leadership of developed countries and is not adapted by the developing ones.

Technology (Share of Population Using the Internet)

With the spread of web technology from the 20th century, it is one of the important factors that are considered in classifying a country in a specified category of underdeveloped or developing. Use of the internet by a citizen of a country is marked as the status symbol nowadays in almost every country. It has brought together the world at a single place. In this field, we collected the data of countries' population having access to internet facility from the last two decades. All the relevant sources have been searched on to collect the most reliable data for the project.

Violence and Rights (Human Right Protection)

Fundamental rights are the basic thing that a government should ensure for its citizens. In a democracy, it becomes even more important one. Every citizen can accept from government to fulfil their basic right and need. It can include anything from the right to speak, right to express, right to work in a healthy environment to the right to get an education.

Development of a nation can be marked from its extent of protecting basic human rights. It is not given that much importance in economy to ensure development but bureaucrats generally forget that it is the basic rule of ensuring development. We do accept the reason that it is hard enough to keep track of such things but there is a solution to everything always. The united nation keeps a track of all the countries following human rights but the situation does not seem to be good at the present time.

Work and Life (Happiness Index)

Everyone desires to live a happy and satisfied life in the time span and for that they do work, earn a living and also spread happiness. But all of these things are going in very less countries. It is sad to see that most of us are not satisfied with the way we are living in. It all comes out to be very personal questions and the remedy is only with a particular individual to get out from this.

Researchers have been asking to change the measure of development from numeric data of GDP to subjective and important measure of happiness. This field shows how satisfied and happy an individual is from his workspace environment, government policies and health facilities provided by the government of a country. People are spread on a wide spectrum of happiness level within a country as well as inter countries. The data contains a glimpse of the same.

Reports shows that the countries which are economically well established and stable are the one whose residents are the happiest ones in comparison to the one which is little economic unstable. From such reports, we can conclude that, life satisfaction and income tend to go together.

TABLEAU

The founders of Tableau are Chris Stolte, Pat Hanrahan and Christian Chabot. These founders studied from Stanford University, USA in 2003. This software helps to make the data more interactive and comprehensive. Its market revenue was US $877 million in 2017 and in 2016 its US $827 million. The total income of Tableau for 2014 was US $5,873,000. There are 4,181 employees (counted till May 2019) are working in Tableau. The Headquarters of Tableau Industry is in Seattle, United States, Washington. Important people are Adam Selipsky, the CEO, Christian Chabot, the Co-founder and Chris Stolte, the Chairman of the Board, Andrew Beers, the Co-founder and Technical Advisor, CDO Pat Hanrahan, the Chief Scientist and Co-founder of the company.

Software Products include in Tableau are Tableau Desktop for both Personal and Professional Editions, Tableau Server, Tableau Online, Tableau Prep Builder which was released in 2018, Tableau Vizable which is a Consumer data visualization mobile app released in 2015, Tableau Public which is absolutely free to use, Tableau Reader which is also free to use.

The best elements of Tableau are blending of data, Data Collaboration and Real Time Analysis. It does not require any technical or any kind of programming skills. The Tableau is one of the fastest growing and spreading software and powerful visualization tool which is highly used by business companies. The tableau is for single user and can be accessed to different devices such as laptop, computer, tablet, etc. It is easy to use. One can publish their resulted data graphs and data in excel format to tableau public and one can open it without any login id or password of the user. Some people are also investing in tableau because it has good visualization, powerful computation, user experience and quick insights. Users are downloading tableau large in numbers. Increase in numbers of user's increases in invested money.

In May 2013, revenue of the tableau reached $234.44 million and in 2012 showed a growth of 82% over $128 million. Revenue of $34.2 million was generated in 2010. It grew from $34.2 million to $64.2 million in 2011 and $127.7 million in 2012. The increase in marketing makes investors to invest money in tableau. On 10 Jun 2019, Salesforce.com announced that they would be occupying tableau in 15.7-billion-dollar deal.

Working

Tableau has a platform which helps to pull the data from any platform and extract it such as pdf, excel a database in the cloud such as Amazon web services; complex database like Oracle, Other Cloud SQL sources can be extracted. When Tableau was launched, it gives the reliability to customers to connect the database to any other database. The data connects and gives the valuable and customized result to the customer and gives a beautiful visual representation of the result such as Pie Chart, Statistics, Heat Map etc. are some representative graphs of Tableau.

The data can be published to the Tableau Server from Tableau Desktop. Experience increases at a high rate at the end users' side by the help of Tableau Server in accessing the files and data in different forms. Tableau is an enterprise platform where collaboration of works, classification of data, governance works, and security model implementation, automation features are also supported in it. The Tableau is platform where the Data User can access the data in graphical representation form by using the profile in Tableau Public which is free of cost and can save their data in their profile. User's data can be accessed be access from all locations and in any device such as Desktop, Mobile or email. The built-in function in tableau software access the maps, geographical positions, access positions by area code, postal codes, airports, administrative places such as Country, State/Province, District etc. These positions are mapped automatically in resulted graphs (Jena, B., 2019).

Application

Some Applications of Tableau are as follows: -

1. Tableau arranges the visualization tools used for analysis.
2. It is easy to access the data by easy representation and helps resolving the big data issues.
3. It has a good performance and enhance the progress.
4. It can be used without coding.
5. It is good for big data.
6. It integrates over 250 applications.
7. It can blend the data.
8. It can define the data in different variations.
9. It can secure the data.
10. It can arrange the data.
11. It has also an option for real time analysis.
12. It has a feature of collaboration of data.
13. Make representation of big data a quick and easy process

14. It bundled with the MS Office tools.
15. Web servers such as Google Chrome, Safari, Firefox and Internet Explorer supports tableau server.

LANGUAGE-R

In the World with different growing technologies in every field, computer science is too not excluded. With the change in time, from the dark ages of computers where human themselves has to do tedious jobs of performing lengthy repetitive calculations with no security of being absolutely correct to the rise in the modern age which makes works on fingertips and allow people to frequently update the data and keep a security check in it. It has crossed the stage of those enormous, large- space consuming computers that were better than the manual calculations but still need lots of time for calculation along with various numbers of resources. But now we are in the modern age of mobile computers that has made the work a task as easy as blinking the eyes. As it is known worldwide that this change is not at all spontaneous rather is a gradually increasing process, we develop new technologies, make use of it, find the problems of it, and improve it for a better version of it. Now, we are in the time of various options for a particular technology. The task in today's technical world has been easier due to the presence of different already developed software in every possible field. This software is built with the help of language that used to develop them. Languages are there for the human to easily code things into abstract form that gets converted in binary language that a machine can understand easily. There are various forms of language each for a different purpose.

Language R is one such language in the varieties of language present for coding works. The developer of R is Ross Ihaka and Robert Gentleman, in 1993, at the University of Auckland. It is an extension for the S programming language. R possesses an elaborated catalogue of statistical and graphical methods. It is free software environment. It has shown its presence to a great extent, for developing statistical software, reporting and data analysis and graphical representation by the data miners and statisticians. C, Fortran and R itself primarily forms the GNU package, source code for R software. The fundamental of R is an interpreted computer language which allows modular programming, looping as well as branching using libraries and functions. It is a language that offers different function to take input and display outputs. It also supports a variety of data types of the variable as R-objects to store information like character, lists, vectors, matrices, data frames, etc. There are various built in functions available in the language R to make coding easier enough. R allows us to import datasets from different software like Microsoft Excel, Microsoft Access, SQL, etc. R-Studio is one of the most well-known Integrated Development Environment (IDE) for R. The R Journal can be openly access, for statistical computing the journal of the R project is generally referred. It consists of articles on the applications and improvements of R, consisting programming tips, packages and foundation news (Kaya, E. et al. 2019).

R is a simple, well-developed and effective programming language that includes loops, conditional, input and output facilities and user-defined recursive functions. It provides a range of calculations on arrays, lists, vectors, matrices, etc. With the presence of vast libraries and vast collection of advanced tools for data analysing and result storing, it is one of the prominent languages in the analysis world. It provides a graphical representation for data analysis and allows a user to display the result either on a computer screen or a print on paper. It uses various forms of graphical representation for a data analysis result like pie charts, bar graphs, box plots, histograms, line graphs, scatter plot, etc. Language R can import data from various file formats such as CSV file formats, Excel file formats, Binary file formats,

XML file formats, JSON file format, Web Data file format and Database file formats. (Vries, A. & Meys, J., 2015) R has a power to do various calculations in a single step with the help of vector data type which requires a loop code in other languages for its implementation and execution. It is still one of the powerful tools for performing virtually any statistical computation. R is an interpreted language, which can interpret the code provided directly and then the code runs, making the development cycle an easy to go process. One of the prominent features of R programming is that it has a distributed computing- an open source, high performance platform which split the tasks between the multiple processing nodes to minimize execution time and make the analysis of large datasets an easier process.

Applications

R has shown a wide range of working applications in the Computer Science world from the time of its origin. The most advanced issues in the fields running from extensive marketing to computational science has been tackled by millions of data researchers and analysts by the use of R programming language, round the world. R Programming applications includes the universe from computational statistics, hypothetical and the hard sciences, for example, astronomy, genomics and chemistry to practical applications in business, drug advancement, medicine, health care, finance, marketing and much more. (Dataflair Team, 2019) Language R has spread its branches over the fields like banking, e-commerce, finance, social-media, Healthcare and many more. Since R has a collection of 5,000 packages (libraries of functions) big portions of which are dedicatedly devoted to specific applications, you can directly make use of the already developed ones instead of developing of yours own. R is a primarily instrument used by many of the quantitative analysts in the field of finance. When you explore the features of R, it is found that it is capable for every process from importing the data to its cleaning, exploring it to visualizing it, doing kind of statistics and analyses, all of the approach up to trading concurrently and buying of production and function selling, depending on what type of process you are working for. R Programming has brought major changes in Big Data Analytics and other aspects of data science and data analytics. (Agrawal, V. 2016) R has shown its wide use for descriptive statistics, which summarizes the main features of the data in the form of central tendency, skewness, finding kurtosis. It is also used for exploratory data analysis.

DATA VISUALIZATION

Data Visualization is a graphical representation of information and data by different visualization tools. Our eyes have a greater adaptability to different colors and shapes rather than numeric or textual data. When a data scientist is designing an advanced predictive model or a machine learning algorithm, it is easy to visualize the output as the intended one rather than the numeric form of the result. Here, the researchers, has given a brief on each of the graph form after a deep study on each of the topic taken as a measure to stratify the world.

Energy

The field energy states the percent of population within a country having access to electricity in their daily routine. It is visualized in a format of tree maps. As shown in the figure, country represented with

Figure 1. The energy graph depicting percentage of population within a country having access to electricity in their daily lives

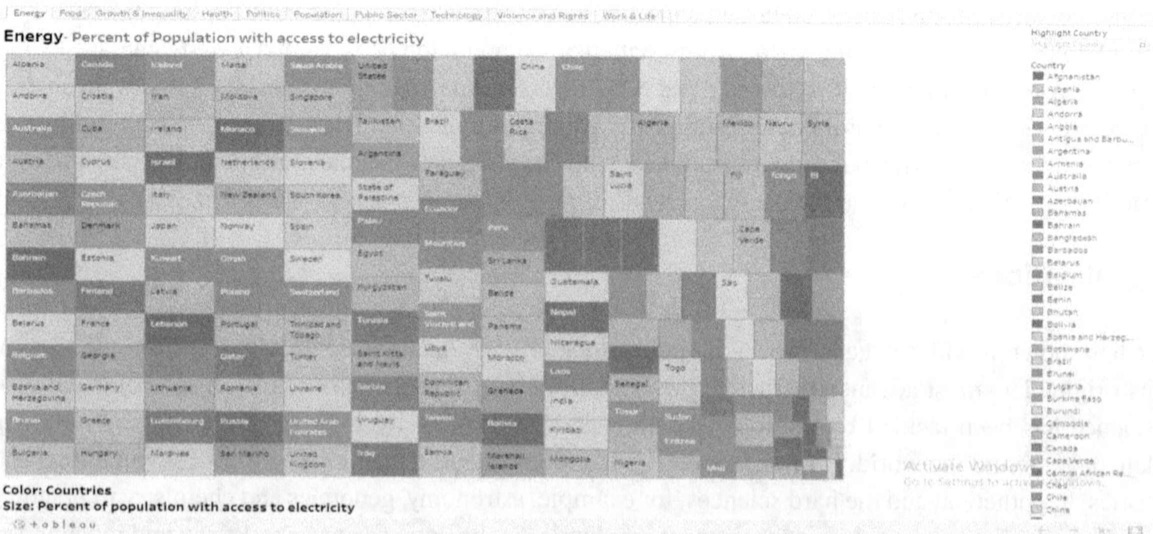

the biggest size rectangular box denotes the maximum percent of population having access to electricity over the tenure of the last two decades. The smallest size of rectangular box shows that electricity is still a dream come true for the residents of that particular country that is Chad.The energy graph is illustrated with the help of Figure 1 given above

Figure 2. The food graph depicting states the percent of undernourished population within a country

Food

The field food states the percent of undernourished population within a country. It is visualized as a word cloud (text size and colour) format graphs. As, it is clear from the figure, that the country whose name is written in the largest text size denotes the highest percent of undernourished people in the state. This generally includes the countries from the African continent which has a high rate of food scarcity and measures have to be taken soon in order to transform the situations for the betterment of the lives of the people. The Food graph is illustrated with the help of Figure 2 given above.

Growth and Inequality

The field growth & Inequality shows the GDP per capita value for a country. It is represented with the help of continuous line graph which is scaled with the value on the y-axis showing the range in International Dollars. The x-axis denotes the countries name. The higher the point in the visualization shows the country with the highest GDP value. Here, the countries are arranged in the ascending order of their names and has a range of GDP values. Monaco shows the highest GDP per capita and is the first preference as a residential place of richest people in the World.The growth and Inequality graph is illustrated with the help of Figure 3given above

Health

The field health shows the total healthcare expenditure as a share of GDP in the annual budget by a particular country's government. Here, in the graph, the x-axis denotes the countries with y-axis showing the percent of GDP share by the government. It is studied by the researchers that developed countries give large share of GDP as health expenditure for it citizens and developing countries focuses more on infrastructure and basic needs rather than health issues. The viewer can scroll horizontally to know about

Figure 3. The growth and inequality graph depicting the GDP per capita value for a country

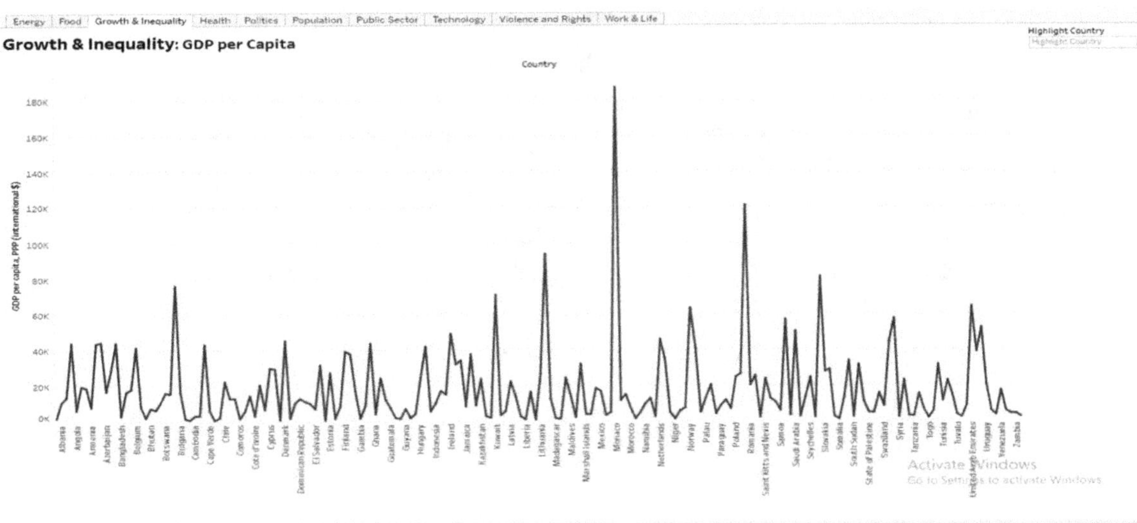

Figure 4. The Health graph depicting the total healthcare expenditure as a share of GDP in the annual budget by a particular country's government

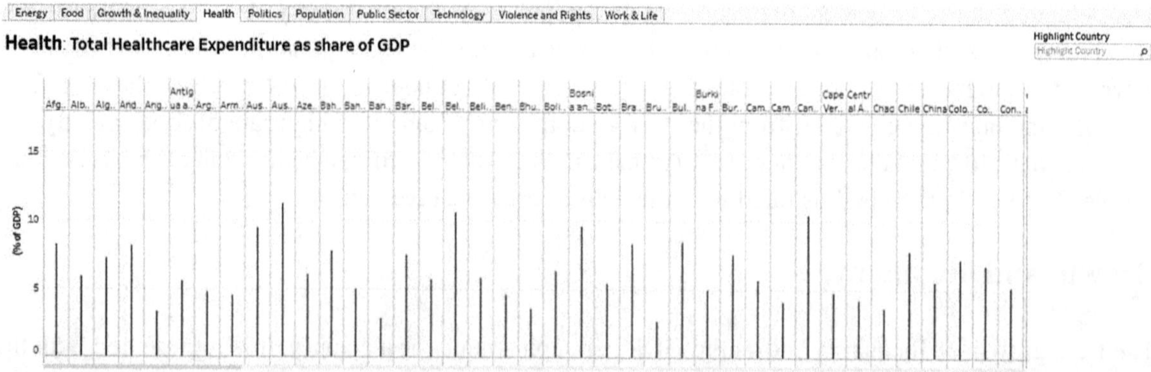

different countries. By rolling the cursor on the desired bar, one can easily get to know about the exact share of GDP in health situations. The Health graph is illustrated with the help of Figure 4 given above.

Politics

Politics show up the political regime of a country. It gives them a democratic score that states how much democracy is running or following by the particular governance of the country. It gives a score from -10 to 10 where, -10 show a dictator country and +10 is given to democratic constituency. In the graph, bar below the axis denote a negative score and above the axis denote a positive score. Here, also the x-axis denotes the country tab and y-axis shows the political regime score. The graph is termed as bar chart. The Politics graph is illustrated with the help of Figure 5given above.

Figure 5. The politics graph depicting the political regime of a country

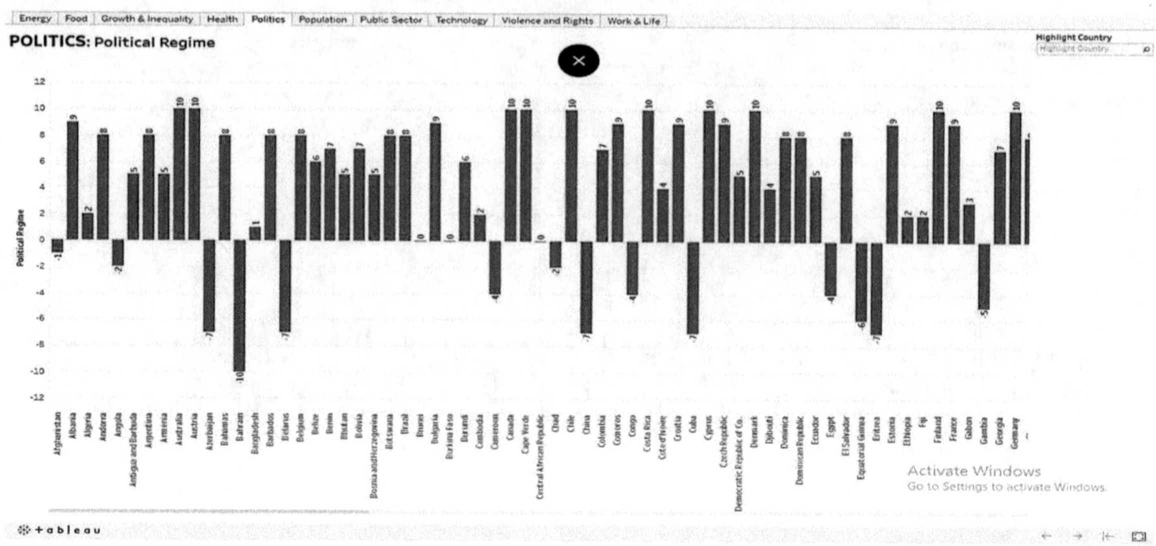

Figure 6. The population graph shows the average life expectancy of an individual residing within a country

Population

The field population shows the average life expectancy of an individual living within a country. It is represented with the help of heat map denoting the location of each country and the average life of its individual. The darker the shade shows the residents are long lived and get ill less in comparison with other countries. The average life expectancy varies from 50 years to 90 years for an individual of a country. The developed countries have shown a large life expectancy due to the latest medical facilities and cleanliness of the surrounding environment in comparison to the developing ones.The Population graph is illustrated with the help of Figure 6 given above.

Figure 7. The public sector graph depicting the share of total tax in the GDP of a country

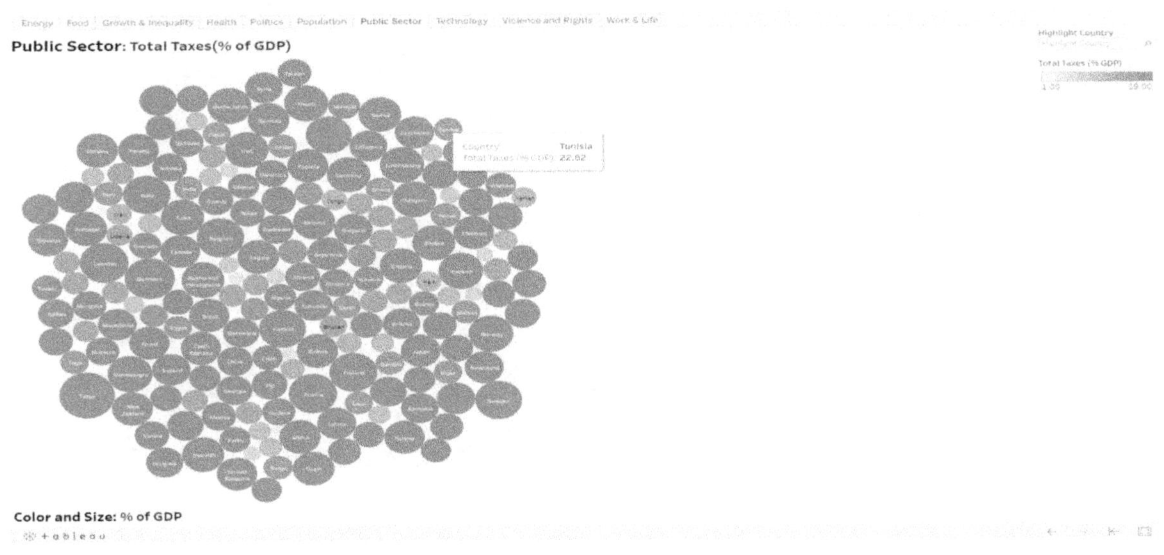

Public Sector

Public Sector denotes the share of total tax in the GDP of a country. It means how much amount a person pays as a tax contribute to the GDP of a governance. It is visualized with the help of packed bubble chart. The larger the size of bubble and darker the shade denotes the high share of GDP as tax. It makes the visualization easier and simple to analyse and study. The researchers found that developed countries take more tax from its residents than the one taken by the developing ones. The Public sector graph is illustrated with the help of Figure 7 given above.

Technology

Technology field represent the share of the population of a country having reach to the internet facility of the world. It is represented by the continuous area chart that shows the peak points showing the exact percent of population. The x-axis shows the countries name and y-axis shows the percentage share. One can again scroll horizontally to look up the details for the desired country. Astonishingly, researchers found that in the 21st century too, some countries have given a zero access to internet facilities to its citizens. It is surprising that a country having low basic needs have a great access to such luxurious facilities. The Technology graph is illustrated with the help of Figure 8 given above.

Violence and Rights

Violence and right field shows whether the basic human right that is the fundamental right of every living being is given or not by the government of countries to its citizens. It ranges from a negative score of -5 to a positive score of +5. Studies have shown that even the most developed countries are not able to fulfil the fundamental rights of its citizens, which is an alarming issue. Every year various social

Figure 8. The technology graph represents the share of population of a country having access to the internet facility of the world

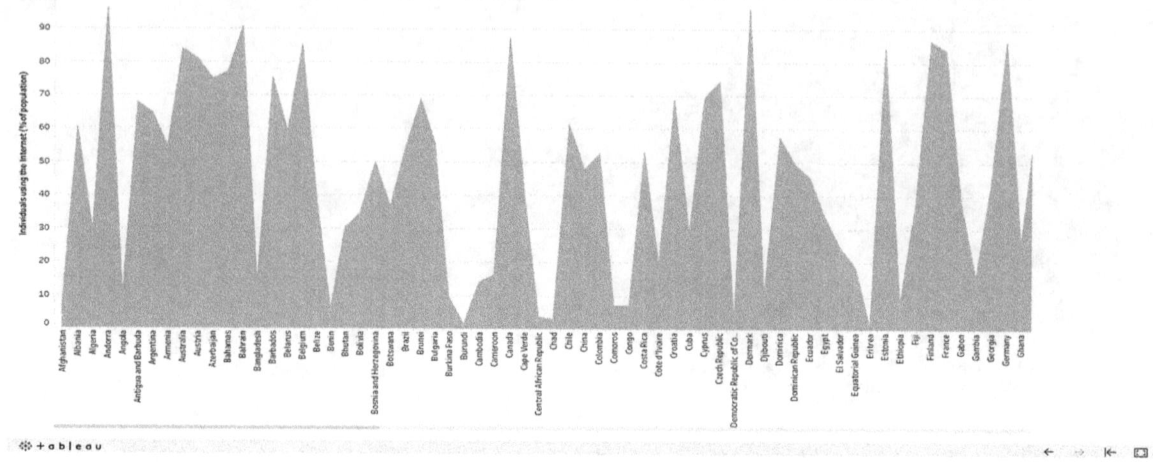

Figure 9. The violence and right graph shows that whether the basic human right that is the fundamental right of every living being is given or not by the government of countries to its citizens

organizations take out the report indicating the score for the same. The visualization is done with the help of a heat map. The Violence and Rights graph is illustrated with the help of Figure 9 given above.

Work and Life

Work and life field shows the world happiness index of a particular country's residents. It shows how happy and satisfies the population of the country. It is visualized by the pie chart with varies in colors. The range of the index varied from 0 to 10. Finland continuously has been the happiest country in the world today. Rolling the cursor over the pie chart will show you exact score of the country's happiness population. Researchers found that the country with all the basic facilities to most of the citizens is happier than the one who is struggling in doing so.The Work and Life graph is illustrated with the help of Figure 10 given above.

Figure 10. The work and life graph shows the world happiness index of a particular country's residents

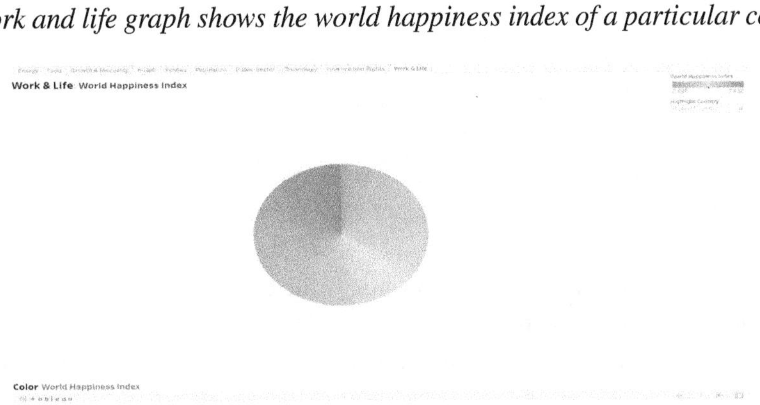

RESULT

The result of the above study done on various countries' government policies for their citizens is analysed by studying the data of the country over the last two decades. This result is also termed as data analysis on various fields. Data analysis is the process of developing answers to questions through the examination and interpretation of data. The output of data analysis is presented in such a manner and communicated to the world that the need of raw statistic does not found to be useful anymore. Researchers directly look for the conclusion of a dataset (if present) rather than studying it and deriving the result again and again. Analysis is an important tool for obtaining information from the data. To present an effective result of an analysis, analysts look for the current as well as future aspects of the data and represent the most widely informative version of the dataset.

While writing this chapter, a detailed study is carried out on the various topics that seems to be the most important one in deciding a nation's growth and economy. They show the strength of the government and welfare policies that a particular country's government is applying on its citizens. Different fields that were studied in deciding the criteria of a country being developing or underdeveloped are:

- Energy (Percent of population having access to electricity)
- Food (Percent of undernourished population)
- Growth & Inequality (GDP per person)
- Health (Expenditure on health issues)
- Politics (Countries living in democracies)
- Population (Life expectancy)
- Public Sector (Share of tax in GDP)
- Technology (Share of population using the internet)
- Violence and Rights (Human Right Protection)
- Work and life (Happiness Index)

The authentic data of all the fields for all the country's present in the world is collected over the last two decades and cleaned. After, the collection of data, different graphs is formed using the platform Tableau software that pictorially represents the dataset studied. It is an online web based application that allows us to look for our graphical form of data anywhere, anytime. We connected the dataset present in excel sheets to the Tableau platform that makes work an easy going process. After the formation of graphs, came one of the most important parts of the project that is calculating the result of the effect of the government's policies on a country's status symbol. It is seen that countries having larger technical amenities are at the top then the ones with less new technologies. Language R is chosen to analyse the dataset collected and declares the overall result of the study. Library "DPYLR" is used in order to calculate the details of the datasets extract information from the same and produce the desired result or the possible outcome. An algorithm is developed to determine the growth rate of a country based on the multiple factors that were taken in order to reach out for a result. Based on the learning and consultancy of the scholars in the field a final parameter that is "Score" is set up to classify the countries based on the parameters collected and studied. This score value is the one that is used to classify the countries as either the underdeveloped or developing one.

According to studies and author's concern there is no country that should come under the category of developed ones, because there is always a chance of improvement for the better version in the eco-

Figure 11. Graph depicting the result in which 50 countries among 195 countries being underdeveloped and 145 are under the category of being the developing ones

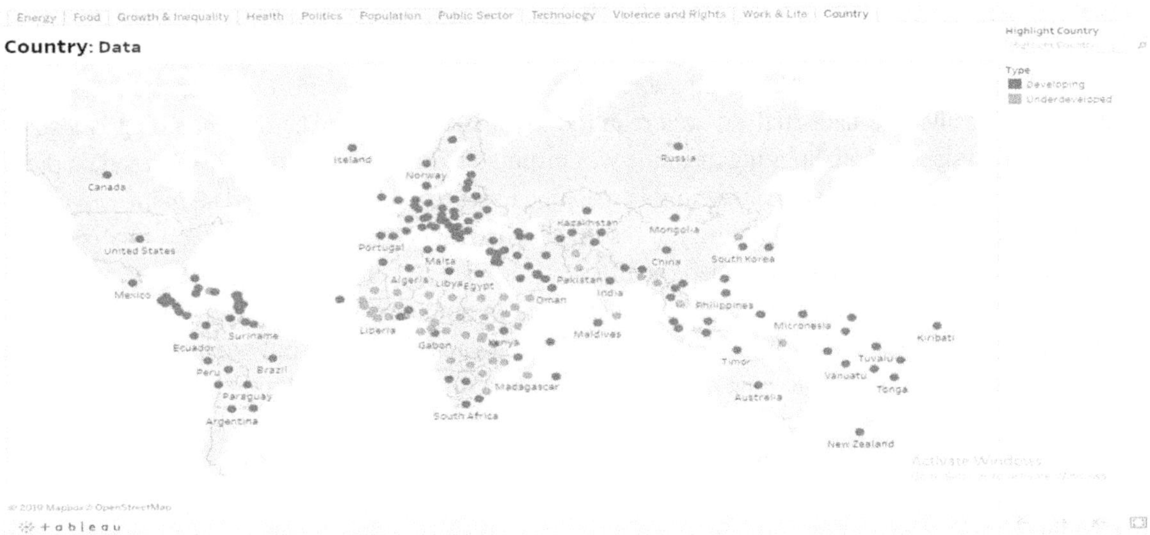

system. Hence, the countries in the study are just fall among the category of being underdeveloped or developing ones.

The country which satisfy maximum of the basic needs of its citizens, give them enough liberty to live their life the way they desire for, low crime rates, let them using their fundamental right to democracy, giving them good healthcare services, access to electricity, giving them enough food to enable their survival and protecting the rights that were stated by the UN for every individual in the world is considered to be at the top profile than the one who are not able to do so. The Graph depicting the result of 195 countries is illustrated with the help of Figure 11 given below:

With this the result comes up to be approx. 50 countries among 195 countries being underdeveloped and 145 are under the category of being the developing ones. It has been seen during the studies that countries located in the African continent seems to be the worst affected than anywhere else in the world. Among fifty countries more than three-fourth are being the part of African continent. It has been also seen that the countries among the developing ones that has a high GDP rate collects a large part of it from the revenue taxes by its citizens. Many more interesting facts come to light, after a detailed study of such an awesome project. One being that North Korea has zero percent of population using the internet services. Somewhere, the percent of population having access to electricity is 100% whereas somewhere it is just about being 7%. Another interesting fact seen is that on a scale of 10, 7 is the highest happiness index among 195 countries. No country has exceeded it till now.

So, at the end of this study, authors realized that the world is full of various interesting facts and there are many of the things one can do to make this world a better place to live in either with the help of new technologies and new ideas to reform the culture of living practices.

CONCLUSION

The data is the set of variables, numbers, symbols etc. which makes information. In data science, the data analysis done before making the data algorithm and then analysis occur by it. The data analysis is having the main objective to make the data more arrange able, pattern able etc. by which the users access the data more easily. The data analysis was required to handle the data. The data handling is also the part of data analysis. As the tabulating machine was invented Herman Hollerith in 1890 based on punch cards. Earlier, the data was used to store in this machine to save time and money. The main step of data analysis is to take decision by predicting the result. The data analysis is used to make visualization of the data which are arranged and patterned by different software's such as tableau, excel sheets etc. The data analyst and data scientist jobs are highly increasing in numbers which increases the employment and develops the economic growth of the country. The data analysis is not only depending on coding, it is depending on the analysis and the result by which the companies will get maximum profit in business field. There are many applications of data analysis such as it develops the models and finding their relevant data, communicates the result to business executive and other users, helps in security of data, store the data in the cloud etc. Data science is done by the help of the data analysis. The data science was begun in 1962. The application of data science is to make the prediction by using algorithm. Many different fields are coming under data science such as data handling, data analysis, big data, data mining etc. data science requires a little knowledge of python language for using Hadoop platform. The data science is used in online shopping websites, in the web browsing etc. There are many types of applications combining the data analysis and data science, one of the applications is explained in this chapter. The Global Stratification is the analysis by the data of different countries in different fields such as Energy (Percent of population having access to electricity), Food (Percent of undernourished population), Growth and Inequality (GDP per person), Health (Expenditure on health issues), Politics (Countries living in democracies), Population (Life Expectancy), Public Sector (Share of tax in GDP), Technology (Share of population using the internet), Violence and Rights (Human Right Protection), Work and Life (Happiness Index) by which these data are implemented in algorithm by using R-Language which comes under data science. By the help of algorithm, the prediction of underdeveloped and developing countries becomes easy. R programming is the programming language which was developed in 1993 in New Zealand. It is an implementation of the S programming language. It allows to import the data from different platforms such as MS Excel, Microsoft Access, SQL etc. Mainly is used in IDE named as R-Studio. As the data visualization is also required to represent the data graphically interactive and give information as the user required. Tableau is the software that is used to visualise the data of countries on different fields and to give the creative representation to the data and explains the graph in different forms such as pie chart, heat map, statistically etc. The different fields which was used for global stratification are described in this chapter. The scores are generated by the help of the algorithm and programme which run on R-Studio supporting R-language. The scores decide that which countries are developing and which countries are under-developed. The prediction was came for different fields for 195 countries that the 50 of these countries are underdeveloped, 145 countries are developing and one of them is India. The countries some has 100% electricity access to the population while some countries did not have global internet such as North Korea. Some countries have more taxes rate taken from the citizens of the country as for development of that country. Globally the stratification becomes easy with the help of the data analysis, data science, tableau, R- Programming etc.

REFERENCES

Agrawal, V. (2016). Applications of R Programming In Real World. Retrieved from https://elearningindustry.com/applications-r-programming-r-eal-world

Data Analysis. Retrieved from https://en.wikipedia.org/wiki/Data_analysis

Data science. Retrieved from https://en.wikipedia.org/wiki/Data_science

Dataflair Team. (2019). Uncover the R Applications – Why Top Companies are using R Programming. Retrieved from https://data-flair.training/blogs/r-applications

Durcevic, S. (2018). Top 10 Analytics And Business Intelligence Trends for 2019. Retrieved from https://www.datapine.com/blog/business-intelligence-trends/

Guerzhoy, M. (2019). Introduction to Data Science as a Pathway to Further Study in Computing. In *Proceedings of the 2019 ACM Conference on International Computing Education Research (ICER '19)*. Toronto, Canada: ACM. 10.1145/3291279.3341203

Gupta, A., Deokar, A., Iyer, L., Sharda, R., & Schrader, D. (2018). Big Data & Analytics for Societal Impact: Recent Research and Trends. *Information Systems Frontiers*, *20*(2), 185–194. doi:10.100710796-018-9846-7

Hirve, S., & Reddy, C. H. (2019). A Survey on Visualization Techniques Used for Big Data Analytics. *Advances in Intelligent Systems and Computing, Springer*, *924*, 447–459. doi:10.1007/978-981-13-6861-5_39

History of Tableau. Retrieved from https://www.javatpoint.com/history-of-tableau

Introduction of R language. Retrieved from https://www.slideshare.net/humzarajput/history-of-computer-16571911

Jena, B. (2019). An Approach for Forecast Prediction in Data Analytics Field by Tableau Software, *International Journal of Information Engineering and Electronic Business. MECS, Hong Kong*, *11*, 19–26.

Kaya, E., Agca, M., Adiguzel, F., & Cetin, M. (2019). *Spatial data analysis with R programming for environment. Human and Ecological Risk Assessment: An International Journal* (Vol. 19). Taylor & Francis.

Miyazaki, M. (2015). A Brief History of Data Analysis. Retrieved from https://www.flydata.com/blog/a-brief-history-of-data-analysis/

Overview of the R language. Retrieved from https://www.guru99.com/r-programming-introduction-basics.html

R - Binary Files. Retrieved from https://www.tutorialspoint.com/r/r_binary_files.htm

Rouse, M. (2019). Data analytics (DA). Retrieved from https://searchdatamanagement.techtarget.com/definition/data-analytics

Said, A., & Torra, V. (2019). Data Science: An Introduction. In A. Said, & V. Torra (Eds.), *Data Science in Practice. Studies in Big Data* (Vol. 46). Cham, Switzerland: Springer. doi:10.1007/978-3-319-97556-6_1

Tableau Software. Retrieved from https://en.wikipedia.org/wiki/Tableau_Software

The History of the Evolution of Business Analytics. (2018). Retrieved from https://www.cyfe.com/blog/history-evolution-business-analytics/

Venkat, T. (2014). What is the future of data science? Retrieved from https://www.quora.com/What-is-the-future-of-data-science-1

Vries, A. & Meys, J. (2015). R for Dummies. *Wiley publication.*

What is Tableau? Uses and Applications. Retrieved from https://www.guru99.com/what-is-tableau.html

ADDITIONAL READING

Gallup, J., & Sachs, J. (1999). Geography and economic development. Centre for International Development, Harvard University, Working Paper 1, http://www.cid.harvard.edu/

Howse, R. (2004). The WHO/WTO study on trade and public health: A critical assessment. *Risk Analysis, 24*(2), 501–507. doi:10.1111/j.0272-4332.2004.00448.x PMID:15078321

Kennelly, B., O'Shea, E., & Garvey, E. (2003). Social, capital, life expectancy and mortality: A cross-national examination. *Social Science & Medicine, 56*(12), 2367–2377. doi:10.1016/S0277-9536(02)00241-1 PMID:12742601

Kim, S., & Shin, E.-H. (2002). A longitudinal analysis of globalization and regionalization in international trade: A social network approach. *Social Forces, 81*(2), 445–468. doi:10.1353of.2003.0014

Knoke, D. (1990). *Political networks.* Cambridge: Cambridge University Press. doi:10.1017/CBO9780511527548

KEY TERMS AND DEFINITIONS

Data Analysis: Data Analysis is a process of gathering and extracting information from the data already present in different ways and order to study the pattern occurs.

Data Science: Data Science is the branch of science that uses technologies to predict the upcoming nature of different things such as a market or weather conditions. It shows a wide usage in today's world.

Data Visualization: Data Visualization is a way of representing the data collected in the form of figures and diagrams like tables, charts, graphs in order to make the data for common man more easily understandable.

Language R: Language R is a programming language developed in 1993 for the graphics and statistical computing. It is useful for Statisticians and those who deal with number chunks.

Tableau Software: Tableau software is a virtual platform for conversion of numbers into graphs and charts form. It simplifies the process of conversion and visualization.

Compilation of References

Abdallah, L. (2005). EverCare Nurse Practitioner Practice Activities: Similarities and Differences across Five Sites. *Journal of the American Academy of Nurse Practitioners*, *17*(9), 355–362. doi:10.1111/j.1745-7599.2005.00063.x PMID:16115114

Abdel-Basset, M., Manogaran, G., Gamal, A., & Smarandache, F. (2019). A Group Decision Making Framework Based on Neutrosophic TOPSIS Approach for Smart Medical Device Selection. *Journal of Medical Systems*, *43*(2), 38. doi:10.100710916-019-1156-1 PMID:30627801

Abdelgawad, M., & Fayek, A. R. (2010). Risk management in the construction industry using combined fuzzy FMEA and fuzzy AHP. *Journal of Construction Engineering and Management*, *136*(9), 1028–1036. doi:10.1061/(ASCE)CO.1943-7862.0000210

Abdukadirov, S. (2016). *Nudge Theory in Action: Behavioral Design in Policy and Markets*. Basingstoke, UK: Springer. doi:10.1007/978-3-319-31319-1

Adalı, E., Işık, A., & Kundakcı, K. (2016). An alternative approach based on Fuzzy PROMETHEE method for the supplier selection problem. *Uncertain Supply Chain Management*, *4*(3), 183–194. doi:10.5267/j.uscm.2016.2.002

Agarwal, A., Shankar, R., & Tiwari, M. K. (2007). Modeling agility of supply chain. *Industrial Marketing Management*, *36*(4), 443–457. doi:10.1016/j.indmarman.2005.12.004

Agarwal, P., Sahai, M., Mishra, V., Bag, M., & Singh, V. (2011). A review of multi-criteria decision-making techniques for supplier evaluation and selection. *International Journal of Industrial Engineering Computations*, *2*(4), 801–810. doi:10.5267/j.ijiec.2011.06.004

Agarwal, S., Chomsisengphet, S., Mahoney, N., & Stroebel, J. (2013). Regulating Consumer Financial Products: Evidence from Credit Cards. *The Quarterly Journal of Economics*, *130*(1), 111–164. doi:10.1093/qje/qju037

Aghalaya, S. N., Elias, A. A., & Pati, R. K. (2012). Analysing reverse logistics in the Indian pharmaceuticals industry: A systems approach. In 26th Australian and New Zealand Academy of Management (ANZAM) Conference 2012.

Agrawal, V. (2016). Applications of R Programming In Real World. Retrieved from https://elearningindustry.com/applications-r-programming-r-eal-world

Aguarón-Joven, J., Escobar-Urmeneta, M. T., García-Alcaraz, J. L., Moreno-Jiménez, J. M., & Vega-Bonilla, A. (2015). A new synthesis procedure for TOPSIS based on AHP. *Dyna (Bilbao)*, *82*(191), 11–19. doi:10.15446/dyna.v82n191.51140

Ahmad, N., Usman Awan, M., Raouf, A., & Sparks, L. (2009). Development of a service quality scale for pharmaceutical SCs. *International Journal of Pharmaceutical and Healthcare Marketing*, *3*(1), 26–45. doi:10.1108/17506120910948494

Ahuja, R., Sawhney, A., & Arif, M. (2017). Prioritising BIM Capabilities of an Organisation: An Interpretive Structural Modeling Analysis. *Procedia Engineering, 86*, 2–10. doi:10.1016/j.proeng.2017.07.166

Aikhuele, D. O., & Turan, F. B. M. (2016). An Interval Fuzzy-Valued M-TOPSIS Model for Design Concept Selection. *The National Conference for Postgraduate Research 2016*, Universiti Malaysia Pahang, 374–384.

Aikhuele, D. O., & Odofin, S. (2017). A Generalized Triangular Intuitionistic Fuzzy Geometric Averaging Operator for Decision-Making in Engineering and Management. *Information, 8*(3), 1–17. doi:10.3390/info8030078

Aikhuele, D. O., Sorooshian, S., Ansah, R. H., & Turan, F. M. (2017). Application of intuitionistic fuzzy topsis model for troubleshooting an offshore patrol boat engine. *Polish Maritime Research, 24*(94), 68–76. doi:10.1515/pomr-2017-0051

Aikhuele, D. O., & Turan, F. B. M. (2017). An integrated fuzzy dephi and interval-valued intuitionistic fuzzy M-Topsis model for design concept selection. *Pakistan Journal of Statistics and Operation Research, 13*(2), 425. doi:10.18187/pjsor.v13i2.1413

Aikhuele, D. O., & Turan, F. M. (2017). An Intuitionistic Fuzzy Multi-Criteria Decision-Making Method Based on an Exponential-Related Function. *International Journal of Fuzzy System Applications, 6*(4), 33–46. doi:10.4018/IJFSA.2017100103

Aikhuele, D. O., & Turan, F. M. (2017b). Extended TOPSIS model for solving multi-attribute decision making problems in engineering. *Decision Science Letters, 6*, 365–376. doi:10.5267/j.dsl.2017.2.002

Aikhuele, D. O., & Turan, F. M. (2018). A modified exponential score function for troubleshooting an improved locally made Offshore Patrol Boat engine. *Journal of Marine Engineering & Technology, 17*(1), 52–58. doi:10.1080/20464177.2017.1286841

Akıncılar, A., & Dağdeviren, M. (2014). A hybrid multi-criteria decision-making model to evaluate hotel websites. *International Journal of Hospitality Management, 36*, 263–271. doi:10.1016/j.ijhm.2013.10.002

Akkurt, M. (2002). *Kalite kontrol excel destekli*. İstanbul/Türkiye: Birsen Yayınevi.

Alarcin, F., Balin, A., & Demirel, H. (2014). Fuzzy AHP and Fuzzy TOPSIS integrated hybrid method for auxiliary systems of ship main engines. *Journal of Marine Engineering & Technology, 13*(1), 3–11. doi:10.1080/20464177.2014.11020288

Alawamleh, M., & Popplewell, K. (2011). Interpretive Structural Modelling of Risk Sources in a Virtual Organisation. *International Journal of Production Research, 49*(20), 6041–6063. doi:10.1080/00207543.2010.519735

Albadvi, A., Chaharsooghi, S. K., & Esfahanipour, A. (2007). Decision making in stock trading: An application of PROMETHEE. *European Journal of Operational Research, 177*(2), 673–683. doi:10.1016/j.ejor.2005.11.022

Alencar, L. H., de Almeida, A. T., & Mota, C. M. de M. (2007). Sistemática proposta para seleção de fornecedores em gestão de projetos. *Gestão & Produção, 14*(3), 477–487. doi:10.1590/S0104-530X2007000300005

Almeida, A. T. (2011). O conhecimento e o uso de métodos multicritério de apoio a decisão. Recife: Editora Universitária Da UFPE., 232.

Almeida, A. T. de, & Costa, A. P. C. S. (2002). Modelo de decisão multicritério para priorização de sistemas de informação com base no método PROMETHEE. *Gestão & Produção, 9*(2), 201–214. doi:10.1590/S0104-530X2002000200007

Aloini, D., Dulmin, R., & Mininno, V. (2010). A hybrid fuzzy-PROMETHEE method for logistics service selection: Design of a decision support tool. *International Journal of Uncertainty, Fuzziness, and Knowledge-based Systems, 18*(04), 345–369. doi:10.1142/S0218488510006593

Al-Rashdan, D., Al-Kloub, B., Dean, A., & Al-Shemmeri, T. (1999). Environmental impact assessment and ranking the environmental projects in Jordan. *European Journal of Operational Research*, *118*(1), 30–45. doi:10.1016/S0377-2217(97)00079-9

Al-Tarawneh, H. A. (2011). The Main Factors beyond Decision Making. *Journal of Management Research*, *4*(1). doi:10.5296/jmr.v4i1.1184

Anandan, V., & Uthra, G. (2017). Extension of TOPSIS using L1 Family of Distance Measures. Advances in Fuzzy Mathematics, 12, 4 (pp. 897–908). Research India Publications; Retrieved from http://www.ripublication.com

Anantatmula, V., & Kanungo, S. (2008). Role of IT and KM in improving project management performance. *Vine*, *38*(3), 357–369. doi:10.1108/03055720810904862

Anderson, D. R., Sweeney, D. J., & Williams, T. A. (2004). *Quantitative methods for business. Mason/Ohio*. Thomson South-Western.

Anderson, D. R., Sweeney, D. J., Williams, T. A., Camm, J. D., & Martin, R. K. (2011). *An Introduction to Management Science: Quantitative Approaches to Decision Making* (13th ed.). Cengage Learning.

Ansari, M. F., Kharb, R. K., Luthra, S., Shimmi, S. L., & Chatterji, S. (2013). Analysis of Barriers to Implement Solar Power Installations in India Using Interpretive Structural Modeling Technique. *Renewable & Sustainable Energy Reviews*, *27*, 163–174. doi:10.1016/j.rser.2013.07.002

Anukul, M., & Deshmukh, S. G. (1994). Vendor selection using interpretive structural modelling (ISM). *International Journal of Operations & Production Management*, *14*(6), 52–59. doi:10.1108/01443579410062086

Aoki, S., Saga, R., Ichinotsubo, T., Niu, W., & Tsuji, H. (2013). Dependency Extraction from Growth Trajectory using Sequential Pattern. *13th International Conference on Knowledge Management and Knowledge Technologies*, (pp. 1-6). 10.1145/2494188.2494197

Apan, M., Öztel, A., & İslamoğlu, M. (2018). Comparative empirical analysis of financial failures of enterprises with Altman z-score and VIKOR methods: BIST food sector application. *AABFJ*, *12*(1), 77–101. doi:10.14453/aabfj.v12i1.6

Araz, O. U. (2005, December). A simulation based multi-criteria scheduling approach of dual-resource constrained manufacturing systems with neural networks. In *Australasian Joint Conference on Artificial Intelligence* (pp. 1047-1052). Berlin, Germany: Springer. 10.1007/11589990_138

Arce, M. E., Saavedra, A., Míguez, J. L., & Granada, E. (2015). The use of grey-based methods in multi-criteria decision analysis for the evaluation of sustainable energy systems: A review. *Renewable & Sustainable Energy Reviews*, *47*, 924–932. doi:10.1016/j.rser.2015.03.010

Arno, A., & Thomas, S. (2016). The efficacy of nudge theory strategies in influencing adult dietary behaviour: A systematic review and meta-analysis. *BMC Public Health*, *16*(1), 676. doi:10.118612889-016-3272-x PMID:27475752

Atanassov, K. T. (1986). Intuitionistic fuzzy sets. *Fuzzy Sets and Systems*, *20*(1), 87–96. doi:10.1016/S0165-0114(86)80034-3

Atanassov, K. T. (1994). New operations defined over the intuitionistic fuzzy sets. *Fuzzy Sets and Systems*, *61*(2), 137–142. doi:10.1016/0165-0114(94)90229-1

Attri, R., Dev, N., & Sharma, V. (2013). Interpretive Structural Modelling (ISM) Approach: An Overview. *Research Journal of Management Sciences*, 3-8.

Attri, R., Grover, S., Dev, N., & Kumar, D. (2013). An ISM approach for modelling the enablers in the implementation of total productive maintenance (TPM). *International Journal of System Assurance Engineering and Management, 4*(4), 313–326. doi:10.100713198-012-0088-7

Ayağ, Z. (2005). A fuzzy AHP-based simulation approach to concept evaluation in an NPD environment. *IIE Transactions, 37*(9), 827–842. doi:10.1080/07408170590969852

Azadfallah, M. (2016). Supplier Selection using MADM Method Under Uncertainty. *Journal of Supply Chain Management Systems, 5*(3), 1–8. doi:10.21863/jscms/2016.5.3.034

Azevedo, S., Carvalho, H., & Cruz-Machado, V. (2013). Using interpretive structural modelling to identify and rank performance measures: An application in the automotive supply chain. *Baltic Journal of Management, 8*(2), 208–230. doi:10.1108/17465261311310027

Bag, S. (2016). Green strategy, supplier relationship building and supply chain performance: Total interpretive structural modelling approach. *International Journal of Procurement Management, 9*(4), 398–426. doi:10.1504/IJPM.2016.077702

Bana e Costa, C., & Vansnick, J. (2008). A critical analysis of the eigenvalue method used to derive priorities in AHP. *European Journal of Operational Research, 187*(3), 1422–1428. doi:10.1016/j.ejor.2006.09.022

Bankacılık Düzenleme ve Denetleme Kurumu. (2017). Retrieved from http://www.bddk.org.tr/WebSitesi/default.aspx

Bao, J., Johansson, J., & Zhang, J. (2017). An occupational disease assessment of the mining industry's occupational health and safety management system based on FMEA and an improved AHP model. *Sustainability, 9*(1), 94. doi:10.3390u9010094

Başkaya, Z., & Öztürk, B. (2011). Evaluation of salesperson candidate's with fuzzy TOPSIS. *Business and Economics Research Journal, 2*(2), 77–100.

Bass, S. J., & Kwakernaak, H. (1977). Rating and ranking of multi-aspects alternatives using fuzzy sets. *Automatica, 13*(1), 47–58. doi:10.1016/0005-1098(77)90008-5

Behl, A., & Pal, A. (2016). Analysing the barriers towards sustainable financial inclusion using mobile banking in rural India. *Indian Journal of Science and Technology, 9*(15), 1–7. doi:10.17485/ijst/2016/v9i15/92100

Behl, A., & Pal, A. (2019). Sustainability of environmentally sound technologies using interpretive structural modelling. *International Journal of Innovation and Sustainable Development, 13*(1), 1–19. doi:10.1504/IJISD.2019.096702

Behl, A., Pal, A., & Roy, K. K. (2016). Integrated framework for governance of cooperative: An Interpretive Structural Modeling approach. *Indian Journal of Economics and Development, 4*, 2.

Behl, A., Rathi, P., & Kumar, V. A. (2018). Sustainability of the Indian auto rickshaw sector: Identification of enablers and their interrelationship using TISM. *International Journal of Services and Operations Management, 31*(2), 137–168. doi:10.1504/IJSOM.2018.094750

Behl, A., Singh, M., & Venkatesh, V. G. (2016). Enablers and barriers of mobile banking opportunities in rural India: A strategic analysis. *International Journal of Business Excellence, 10*(2), 209–239. doi:10.1504/IJBEX.2016.077999

Behzadian, M., Kazemzadeh, R. B., Albadvi, A., & Aghdasi, M. (2010). PROMETHEE: A comprehensive literature review on methodologies and applications. *European Journal of Operational Research, 200*(1), 198–215. doi:10.1016/j.ejor.2009.01.021

Behzadian, M., Otaghsara, K., Yazdani, M., & Ignatius, J. (2012). A state of the art survey of TOPSIS applications. *Expert Systems with Applications, 39*(17), 13051–13069. doi:10.1016/j.eswa.2012.05.056

Beikkhakhian, Y., Javanmardi, M., Karbasian, M., & Khayambashi, B. (2015). The application of ISM model in evaluating agile suppliers selection criteria and ranking suppliers using fuzzy TOPSIS-AHP methods. *Expert Systems with Applications*, *42*(15-16), 6224–6236. doi:10.1016/j.eswa.2015.02.035

Beliakov, G., Pradera, A., & Calvo, T. (2007). *Aggregation Functions: A Guide for Practitioners. Soft Computing* (Vol. 18). doi:10.1007/3-540-32367-8_3

Belton, V., & Gear, T. (1983). On a short-coming of Saaty's method of analytic hierarchies. *Omega*, *11*(3), 228–230. doi:10.1016/0305-0483(83)90047-6

Benartzi, S. (2017). How Digital Tools and Behavioral Economics Will Save Retirement. Retrieved September 30, 2019, from https://hbr.org/2017/12/how-digital-tools-and-behavioral-economics-will-save-retirement

Benartzi, S., Beshears, J., Milkman, K., Sunstein, C., Thaler, R., Shankar, M., ... Galing, S. (2017). Should Governments Invest More in Nudging? *Psychological Science*, *28*(8), 1041–1055. doi:10.1177/0956797617702501 PMID:28581899

Bernroider, E. W. N., & Stix, V. (2003). The Evaluation of ERP Systems Using Data Envelopment Analysis. *The Proceedings CD of IRMA 2003- Information Resources Management Association International Conference*, pp. 283-386.

Beynon, M. J., & Wells, P. (2008). The lean improvement of the chemical emissions of motor vehicles based on preference ranking: A PROMETHEE uncertainty analysis. *Omega*, *36*(3), 384–394. doi:10.1016/j.omega.2006.04.015

Bhaumik, S. K., Driffield, N., & Pal, S. (2010). Does ownership structure of emerging-market firms affect their outward FDI? The case of the Indian automotive and pharmaceutical sectors. *Journal of International Business Studies*, *41*(3), 437–450. doi:10.1057/jibs.2009.52

Bilsel, R. U., Büyüközkan, G., & Ruan, D. (2006). A fuzzy preference-ranking model for a quality evaluation of hospital web sites. *International Journal of Intelligent Systems*, *21*(11), 1181–1197. doi:10.1002/int.20177

Biswas, P. (2017). Modeling Reconfigurability in Supply Chains Using Total Interpretive Structural Modeling. *Journal of Advanced in Management Research*, *14*(2), 194–221. doi:10.1108/JAMR-09-2016-0071

Biswas, P., Pramanik, S., & Giri, B. C. (2016). TOPSIS method for multi-attribute group decision-making under single-valued neutrosophic environment. *Neural Computing & Applications*, *27*(3), 727–737. doi:10.100700521-015-1891-2

Biswas, P., Pramanik, S., & Giri, B. C. (2016b). Value and ambiguity index based ranking method of single-valued trapezoidal neutrosophic numbers and its application to multi-attribute decision making. *Neutrosophic Sets and Systems*, *12*(July), 127–138.

Blumenstock, J., Callen, M., & Ghani, T. (2018). Why Do Defaults Affect Behavior? Experimental Evidence from Afghanistan. *The American Economic Review*, *108*(10), 2868–2901. doi:10.1257/aer.20171676

Bolaños, R., Fontela, E., Nenclares, A., & Pastor, P. (2005). Using interpretive structural modelling in strategic decision-making groups. *Management Decision*, *43*(6), 877–895. doi:10.1108/00251740510603619

Bonner, S., & Sprinkle, G. (2002). The effects of monetary incentives on effort and task performance: Theories, evidence, and a framework for research. *Accounting, Organizations, and Society*, *27*(4-5), 303–345. doi:10.1016/S0361-3682(01)00052-6

Boran, F. E., Genc, S., Kurt, M., & Akay, D. (2009). A multi-criteria intuitionistic fuzzy group decision making for supplier selection with TOPSIS method. *Expert Systems with Applications*, *36*(8), 11363–11368. doi:10.1016/j.eswa.2009.03.039

Boult, C., Karm, L., & Groves, C. (2008). Improving Chronic Care: The "Guided Care" Model. *The Permanente Journal*, 50–54. Retrieved from https://www.ncbi.nlm.nih.gov/pmc/articles/PMC3042340 PMID:21369513

Bouwmeester, C. (2012). The PACE Program: Home-Based Long-Term Care. *The Consultant Pharmacist*, *27*(1), 24–30. doi:10.4140/TCP.n.2012.24 PMID:22231995

Bouzon, M., Govindan, K., & Rodriguez, C. M. T. (2015). Reducing the extraction of minerals: Reverse logistics in the machinery manufacturing industry sector in Brazil using ISM approach. *Resources Policy*, *46*, 27–36. doi:10.1016/j.resourpol.2015.02.001

Bowen, J., Stevens, D., Sixta, C., Provost, L., Johnson, J., Woods, D., & Wagner, E. (2010). Developing measures of educational change for academic health care teams implementing the chronic care model in teaching practices. *Journal of General Internal Medicine*, *25*(S4), 586–592. doi:10.100711606-010-1358-1 PMID:20737234

Bowles, J. B., & Peláez, C. E. (1995). Fuzzy logic prioritization of failures in a system failure mode, effects and criticality analysis. *Reliability Engineering & System Safety*, *50*(2), 203–213. doi:10.1016/0951-8320(95)00068-D

Boyd, C., Reider, L., Frey, K., Scharfstein, D., Leff, B., Wolff, J., ... Boult, C. (2010). The Effects of Guided Care on the Perceived Quality of Health Care for Multi-morbid Older Persons: 18-Month Outcomes from a Cluster-Randomized Controlled Trial. *Journal of General Internal Medicine*, *25*(3), 235–242. doi:10.100711606-009-1192-5 PMID:20033622

Braglia, M., Frosolini, M., & Montanari, R. (2003). Fuzzy TOPSIS approach for failure mode, effects and criticality analysis. *Quality and Reliability Engineering International, 19*(5), 425–443.

Braglia, M. (2000). MAFMA: Multi-attribute failure mode analysis. *International Journal of Quality & Reliability Management, 17*(9), 1017–1033. doi:10.1108/02656710010353885

Braglia, M., Frosolini, M., & Montanari, R. (2003). Fuzzy TOPSIS approach for failure mode, effects and criticality analysis. *Quality and Reliability Engineering International*, *19*(5), 425–443. doi:10.1002/qre.528

Brans, J.-P., & De Smet, Y. (2016). PROMETHEE Methods (pp. 187–219). doi:10.1007/978-1-4939-3094-4_6

Brans, J. P., & Mareschal, B. (1992). PROMETHEE V: MCDM problems with segmentation constraints. *INFOR*, *30*(2), 85–96. doi:10.1080/03155986.1992.11732186

Brans, J. P., & Mareschal, B. (1995). The PROMETHEE VI procedure: How to differentiate hard from soft multicriteria problems. *Journal of Decision Systems*, *4*(3), 213–223. doi:10.1080/12460125.1995.10511652

Brans, J. P., Mareschal, B., & Vincke, Ph. (1984). PROMITHEE: A new family of outranking methods in MCDM. *Operations Research*, *84*, 477–490.

Brans, J. P., & Vincke, P. (1985). Note—A Preference Ranking Organisation Method: (The PROMETHEE Method for Multiple Criteria Decision-Making). *Management Science*, *31*(6), 647–656. doi:10.1287/mnsc.31.6.647

Brans, J.-P., & Mareschal, B. (2005). Promethee Methods. In *Multiple Criteria Decision Analysis: State of the Art Surveys* (pp. 163–186). New York: Springer-Verlag; doi:10.1007/0-387-23081-5_5

Briggs, T., Kunsch, P. L., & Mareschal, B. (1990). Nuclear waste management: An application of the multicriteria PROMETHEE methods. *European Journal of Operational Research*, *44*(1), 1–10. doi:10.1016/0377-2217(90)90308-X

Brignull, H. (2019). Dark Patterns - Types of Dark Pattern. Retrieved August 31, 2019, from https://www.darkpatterns.org/types-of-dark-pattern

Bruin, S., Versnel, N., Lemmens, L., Molema, C., Schellevis, F., Nijpels, G., & Baan, C. (2012). Comprehensive care programs for patients with multiple chronic conditions: A systematic literature review. *Health Policy (Amsterdam)*, *107*(2-3), 108–145. doi:10.1016/j.healthpol.2012.06.006 PMID:22884086

Bruno, G., Esposito, E., Genovese, A., & Passaro, R. (2009). *The Analytic Hierarchy Process in the Supplier Selection Problem.*

Büyüközkan, G., & Güleryüz, S. (2016). Lojistik firma web sitelerinin performanslarının çok kriterli değerlendirilmesi. *Journal of the Faculty of Engineering and Architecture of Gazi University, 31*(4), 889–902.

Cables, E., García-Cascales, M. S., & Lamata, M. T. (2012). The LTOPSIS: An alternative to TOPSIS decision-making approach for linguistic variables. *Expert Systems with Applications, 39*(2), 2119–2126. doi:10.1016/j.eswa.2011.07.119

Cadena, X., Schoar, A., Cristea, A., & Delgado-Medrano, H. (2019). *Fighting Procrastination in the Workplace: An Experiment.* NBER Working Paper 16944. Cambridge. National Bureau of Economic Research. Retrieved from https://www.nber.org/papers/w16944

Cai, T. (2011). *A conceptual framework for value creation management in the lean product development process (Unpublished master's thesis).* University of Calgary, Calgary, AB. doi:10.11575/PRISM/4026.

Carmo, B. B. T. do, Neto, J. F. B., & Dutra, N. G. da S. (2011). Análise do impacto nos custos de transporte de um modelo de seleção de fornecedores baseado em variáveis socioambientais e de competitividade, *21*(3), 466–483. doi:10.1590/S0103-65132011005000013

Castillo, O., & Melin, P. (2008). Type-2 Fuzzy Logic: Theory and Applications. Berlin, Germany: Springer-Verlag. doi:10.1007/978-3-540-76284-3

Çebi, S. (2013). A quality evaluation model for the design quality of online shopping websites. *Electronic Commerce Research and Applications, 12*(2), 124–135. doi:10.1016/j.elerap.2012.12.001

Çelebi Demirarslan, P., Küçükönder, H., & Kıngır, S. (2019). Entropi tabanlı TOPSIS ve VIKOR yaklaşımı ile akademisyenler üzerinde duygusal performans değerlendirme: Bartın örneği. *Elektronik Sosyal Bilimler Dergisi, 18*(69), 232–251.

CEN national Members. (2001). [*COMITÉ EUROPÉEN DE NORMALISATION.*]. *EUROPEAN STANDARD EN, 10202*, 2001.

Chaira, T. (2001). A novel intuitionistic fuzzy C means clustering algorithm and its application to medical images. *Applied Soft Computing, 11*(2), 1711–1717. doi:10.1016/j.asoc.2010.05.005

Chanamool, N., & Naenna, T. (2016). Fuzzy FMEA application to improve decision-making process in an emergency department. *Applied Soft Computing, 43*, 441–453. doi:10.1016/j.asoc.2016.01.007

Chand, M., Raj, T., & Shankar, R. (2014). Analysing the operational risks in SC by using weighted interpretive structure modelling technique. *International Journal of Services and Operations Management, 18*(4), 378–403. doi:10.1504/IJSOM.2014.063242

Chan, F. T. S. (2002). Design of material handling equipment selection system: An integration of expert system with analytic hierarchy process approach. *Integrated Manufacturing Systems, 13*(1), 58–68. doi:10.1108/09576060210411512

Chan, F. T. S., Ip, R. W. L., & Lau, H. (2001). Integration of expert system with analytic hierarchy process for the design of material handling equipment selection system. *Journal of Materials Processing Technology, 116*(2–3), 137–145. doi:10.1016/S0924-0136(01)01038-X

Chang, D. Y. (1996). Applications of the extent analysis method on fuzzy AHP. *European Journal of Operational Research, 95*(3), 649–655. doi:10.1016/0377-2217(95)00300-2

Chang, K. H. (2015). A novel general risk assessment method using the soft TOPSIS approach. *Journal of Industrial and Production Engineering, 32*(6), 408–421. doi:10.1080/21681015.2015.1070375

Charan, P., Shankar, R., & Baisya, R. K. (2008). Analysis of interactions among the variables of supply chain performance measurement system implementation. *Business Process Management Journal, 14*(4), 512–529. doi:10.1108/14637150810888055

Cha, S. H. (2007). Comprehensive Survey on Distance/Similarity Measures between Probability Density Functions. *International Journal of Mathematical Models and Methods in Applied Sciences, 1*(4), 300–307.

Chen, P., & Wang, J. (2009). Application of a fuzzy AHP method to risk assessment of international construction projects, In 2009 International Conference on Electronic Commerce and Business Intelligence, (pp. 459-462). IEEE.

Chen, C.-T. (2000). Extensions of the TOPSIS for group decision-making under fuzzy environment. *Fuzzy Sets and Systems, 114*(1), 1–9. doi:10.1016/S0165-0114(97)00377-1

Chen, C.-T., Lin, C.-T., & Huang, S.-F. (2006). A fuzzy approach for supplier evaluation and selection in supply chain management. *International Journal of Production Economics, 102*(2), 289–301. doi:10.1016/j.ijpe.2005.03.009

Chen, J. K. (2007). Utility priority number evaluation for FMEA. *Journal of Failure Analysis and Prevention, 7*(5), 321–328. doi:10.100711668-007-9060-2

Chen, J. K., & Chen, S. (2010). A Pro-Performance Appraisal System for The University. *Expert Systems with Applications, 37*(3), 2108–2116. doi:10.1016/j.eswa.2009.07.063

Chen, J. K., & Chen, S. (2010). Using A Novel Conjunctive MCDM Approach Based On DEMATEL, Fuzzy Anp, And TOPSIS As An Innovation Support System For Taiwanese Higher Education. *Expert Systems with Applications, 37*(3), 1981–1990. doi:10.1016/j.eswa.2009.06.079

Chen, S. J., Hwang, C. L., & Hwang, F. P. (1992). *Fuzzy multiple attribute decision making (methods and applications).* Lecture Notes in Economics and Mathematical Systems. doi:10.1007/978-3-642-46768-4

Chen, S.-M., & Lee, L.-W. (2010). Fuzzy multiple attributes group decision-making based on the interval type-2 TOPSIS method. *Expert Systems with Applications, 37*(4), 2790–2798. doi:10.1016/j.eswa.2009.09.012

Chen, T. Y., & Tsao, C. Y. (2008). The interval-valued fuzzy TOPSIS method and experimental analysis. *Fuzzy Sets and Systems, 159*(11), 1410–1428. doi:10.1016/j.fss.2007.11.004

Chen, Y. H., Wang, T. C., & Wu, C. Y. (2011). Strategic decisions using the fuzzy PROMETHEE for IS outsourcing. *Expert Systems with Applications, 38*(10), 13216–13222. doi:10.1016/j.eswa.2011.04.137

Cheraghi, M., Karbassi, A., Monavari, S. M., & Baghvand, A. (2018). Environmental risk management associated with the development one of oil fields in southwestern Iran using AHP and FMEA methods. *Anthropocentric Pollution Journal, 2*(2), 33-40. *Fakültesi Dergisi, 29*(4).

Cherrafi, A., Elfezazi, S., Garza-Reyes, J. A., Benhida, K., & Mokhlis, A. (2017). Barriers in Green Lean implementation: A combined systematic literature review and interpretive structural modelling approach. *Production Planning and Control, 28*(10), 829–842. doi:10.1080/09537287.2017.1324184

Chien, M. K., & Shih, L. H. (2007). An empirical study of the implementation of green supply chain management practices in the electrical and electronic industry and their relation to organizational performances. *International Journal of Environmental Science and Technology, 4*(3), 383–394.

Chin, K. S., Chan, A., & Ya, J. B. (2008). Development of a fuzzy FMEA based product design system. *International Journal of Advanced Manufacturing Technology, 36*(7-8), 633–649. doi:10.100700170-006-0898-3

Chittoor, R., Sarkar, M. B., Ray, S., & Aulakh, P. S. (2009). Third-world copycats to emerging multinationals: Institutional changes and organizational transformation in the Indian pharmaceutical industry. *Organization Science*, *20*(1), 187–205. doi:10.1287/orsc.1080.0377

Choi, J., Haisley, E., Kurkoski, J., & Massey, C. (2012). *Small Cues Change Savings Choices*. SSRN Electronic Journal; doi:10.3386/w17843

Chou, W. C., & Cheng, Y. P. (2012). A hybrid fuzzy MCDM approach for evaluating website quality of Professional accounting firms. *Expert Systems with Applications*, *39*(3), 2783–2793. doi:10.1016/j.eswa.2011.08.138

Chung, Y. F., Liu, S. H., Wang, C.H. & Pang, C. T. (2015). Applying fuzzy MCDM methods to the evaluation on portal website service quality. *The SIJ Transactions on Computer Science Engineering & its Applications (CSEA)*, *3*(1), 8-15.

Chun-ho, C. (2019). A New Multi-Criteria Assessment Model Combining GRA Techniques with Intuitionistic Fuzzy Entropy-Based TOPSIS Method for Sustainable Building Materials Supplier Selection. *Sustainability*, *11*(2265).

Churchman, C. W., Ackoff, R. L., & Arnoff, E. L. (1957). *Introduction to operations research*. New York: John Wiley & Sons.

Chu, T. C. (2002). Selecting plant location via a fuzzy TOPSIS approach. *International Journal of Advanced Manufacturing Technology*, *20*(11), 859–864. doi:10.1007001700200227

Coleman, K., Austin, B., Brach, C., & Wagner, E. (2009). Evidence On The Chronic Care Model In The New Millennium. *Health Affairs*, *28*(1), 75–85. doi:10.1377/hlthaff.28.1.75 PMID:19124857

Cooper, M. C., Lambert, D. M., & Pagh, J. D. (1997). SC management: More than a new name for logistics. *International Journal of Logistics Management*, *8*(1), 1–14. doi:10.1108/09574099710805556

Costa, D., & Kahn, M. (2013). Energy Conservation "Nudges" and Environmentalist Ideology: Evidence from A Randomized Residential Electricity Field Experiment. *Journal of the European Economic Association*, *11*(3), 680–702. doi:10.1111/jeea.12011

Costa, J. F. da S., Brazil, C. H. A., & De Oliveira, M. B. (2003). Metodologia multicritério e ECR: Utilização no mercado varejista. *Revista Produção*, *13*(2), 114–122. doi:10.1590/S0103-65132003000200011

Cunha, S. M. A. (2008). *Selecção de Fornecedores – Estudo de Caso*. Universidade de Aveiro.

Dağdeviren, M. (2008). Decision making in equipment selection: An integrated approach with AHP and PROMETHEE. *Journal of Intelligent Manufacturing*, *19*(4), 397–406. doi:10.100710845-008-0091-7

Dagdeviren, M., Yavuz, S., & Kılınç, N. (2009). Weapon selection using the AHP and TOPSIS methods under fuzzy environment. *Expert Systems with Applications*, *36*(4), 8143–8151. doi:10.1016/j.eswa.2008.10.016

Dagdeviren, M., & Yüksel, İ. (2008). Developing a fuzzy analytic hierarchy process (AHP) model for behavior-based safety management. *Information Sciences*, *178*(6), 1717–1733. doi:10.1016/j.ins.2007.10.016

Dalvi-Esfahani, M., Ramayah, T., & Nilashi, M. (2017). Modelling Upper Echelons' Behavioural Drivers of Green IT/IS Adoption Using an Integrated Interpretive Structural Modelling–Analytic Network Process Approach. *Telematics and Informatics*, *34*(2), 583–603. doi:10.1016/j.tele.2016.10.002

Daneshvar Rouyendegh, B., Yildizbasi, A., & Arikan, Ü. Z. B. (2018). Using Intuitionistic Fuzzy TOPSIS in Site Selection of Wind Power Plants in Turkey. *Advances in Fuzzy Systems*, *2018*, 1–14. doi:10.1155/2018/6703798

Daneshvar, B., Erdebilli, R. B., Yildizbasi, A., & Arikan, Ü. Z. B. (2018). Using Intuitionistic Fuzzy TOPSIS in Site Selection of Wind Power Plants in Turkey. *Advances in Fuzzy Systems*, *2018*(Mcdm), 1–14.

Darko, A., Chan, A. P. C., Ameyaw, E. E., Owusu, E. K., Parn, E., & Edwards, D. J. (2019). Review of application of analytic hierarchy process (AHP) in construction. *International Journal Construction Management, 19*(5), 436–452. doi:10.1080/15623599.2018.1452098

Data Analysis. Retrieved from https://en.wikipedia.org/wiki/Data_analysis

Data science. Retrieved from https://en.wikipedia.org/wiki/Data_science

Dataflair Team. (2019). Uncover the R Applications – Why Top Companies are using R Programming. Retrieved from https://data-flair.training/blogs/r-applications

De Boer, L., Labro, E., & Morlacchi, P. (2001). A review of methods supporting supplier selection. *European Journal of Purchasing & Supply Management, 7*(2), 75-89.

de Boer, L., Labro, E., & Morlacchi, P. (2001). A review of methods supporting supplier selection. *European Journal of Purchasing and Supply Management, 7*(2), 75–89. doi:10.1016/S0969-7012(00)00028-9

De Keyser, W., & Peeters, P. (1996). A note on the use of PROMETHEE multicriteria methods. *European Journal of Operational Research, 89*(3), 457–461. doi:10.1016/0377-2217(94)00307-6

de Santis, R. B., Golliat, L., & de Aguiar, E. P. (2017). Multi-Criteria Supplier Selection Using Fuzzy Analytic Hierarchy Process: Case Study from a Brazilian Railway Operator. *Brazilian Journal of Operations & Production Management, 14*(3), 428–437. doi:10.14488/BJOPM.2017.v14.n3.a15

Deng, H. (2007). A Similarity-Based Approach to Ranking Multicriteria Alternatives. *International Conference on Intelligent Computing ICIC 2007: Advanced Intelligent Computing Theories and Applications with Aspects of Artificial Intelligence*, pp. 253-262. 10.1007/978-3-540-74205-0_28

Deng, H., Yeh, C. H., & Willis, R. J. (2000). Inter-company comparison using modified TOPSIS with objective weights. *Computers & Operations Research, 27*(10), 963–973. doi:10.1016/S0305-0548(99)00069-6

Department of Economic Affairs. (2019). *Economic Survey, 2018-19*, 29–56.

Deschrijver, G., & Kerre, E. E. (2007). On the position of intuitionistic fuzzy set theory in the framework of theories modelling imprecision. *Information Sciences, 177*(8), 1860–1866. doi:10.1016/j.ins.2006.11.005

Despeisse, M., Mbaye, F., Ball, P. D., & Levers, A. (2012). The emergence of sustainable manufacturing practices. *Production Planning and Control, 23*(5), 354–376. doi:10.1080/09537287.2011.555425

Despic, O., & Simonovic, S. P. (2000). Aggregation operators for soft decision making in water resources. *Fuzzy Sets and Systems, 115*(1), 11–33. doi:10.1016/S0165-0114(99)00030-5

Devadasan, S. R., Muthu, S., Samson, R. N., & Sankaran, R. A. (2003). Design of total failure mode and effects analysis programme. *International Journal of Quality & Reliability Management, 20*(5), 551–568. doi:10.1108/02656710310476525

Devi, P. U. M., Rao, B. S., & Shekhar, B. R. (2017). Service quality in the pharmaceutical SC: A case study with reference to a major Indian pharmaceutical company. *International Journal of Services Sciences, 6*(2), 147–161. doi:10.1504/IJSSCI.2017.088753

Dewangan, D. K., Agrawal, R., & Sharma, V. (2015). Enablers for competitiveness of Indian manufacturing sector: An ISM-fuzzy MICMAC analysis. *Procedia: Social and Behavioral Sciences, 189*, 416–432. doi:10.1016/j.sbspro.2015.03.200

Dhar, J., Bailey, A., Mingardon, S., & Tankersley, J. (2019). The Persuasive Power of the Digital Nudge. Retrieved 30 August 2019, from https://www.bcg.com/publications/2017/people-organization-operations-persuasive-power-digital-nudge.aspx

Dholakia, U. (2016). Why Nudging Your Customers Can Backfire. Retrieved August 31, 2019, from https://hbr.org/2016/04/why-nudging-your-customers-can-backfire

Diabat, A., Khreishah, A., Kannan, G., Panikar, V., & Gunasekaran, A. (2013). Benchmarking the interactions among barriers in third-party logistics implementation: An ISM approach. *Benchmarking: An International Journal*, *20*(6), 805–824. doi:10.1108/BIJ-04-2013-0039

Dias, E. M. P. da S. (2015). *Modelo de apoio à decisão multicritério para selecção de fornecedores de azeite*. Faculdade de Economia do Porto.

Ding, J. F. (2011). An integrated fuzzy topsis method for ranking alternatives and its application. *Journal of Marine Science and Technology*, *19*(4), 341–352.

Dinmohammadi, F., & Shafiee, M. (2013). A fuzzy-FMEA risk assessment approach for offshore wind turbines. *International Journal of Prognostics and Health Management*, *4*(13), 59–68.

Dorr, D., Wilcox, A., Burns, L., Brunker, C., Narus, S., & Clayton, P. (2006). Implementing a Multidisease Chronic Care Model in Primary Care Using People and Technology. *Disease Management*, *9*(1), 1–15. doi:10.1089/dis.2006.9.1 PMID:16466338

Dozic, S., Lutovac, T., & Kalic, M. (2018). Fuzzy AHP approach to passenger aircraft type selection. *Journal of Air Transport Management*, *68*, 165–175. doi:10.1016/j.jairtraman.2017.08.003

Dubey, E., Gunasekaran, A., Sushil, A., & Singh, T. (2015). Building Theory of Sustainable Manufacturing Using Total Interpretive Structural Modelling. *International Journal of Systems Science: Operations & Logistics*, *2*(4), 231–247.

Dubey, R., & Ali, S. S. (2014). Identification of flexible manufacturing system dimensions and their interrelationship using total interpretive structural modelling and fuzzy MICMAC analysis. *Global Journal of Flexible Systems Management*, *15*(2), 131–143. doi:10.100740171-014-0058-9

Dubois, D., & Prade, H. (2004). On the use of aggregation operations in information fusion processes. *Fuzzy Sets and Systems*, *142*(1), 143–161. doi:10.1016/j.fss.2003.10.038

Durcevic, S. (2018). Top 10 Analytics And Business Intelligence Trends for 2019. Retrieved from https://www.datapine.com/blog/business-intelligence-trends/

Durmuş, M., & Tayyar, N. (2017). AHP ve TOPSIS ile farklı kriter ağırlıklandırma yöntemlerinin kullanılması ve karar verici görüşleriyle karşılaştırılması. *Eskişehir Osmangazi Üniversitesi İİBF Dergisi*, *12*(3), 65–80.

Dursun, M., & Karsak, E. (2010). A fuzzy MDCM approach for personnel selection. *Expert Systems with Applications*, *37*(6), 4324–4330. doi:10.1016/j.eswa.2009.11.067

e Costa, C. A. B., & Vansnick, J. C. (1999). The MACBETH Approach: Basic Ideas, Software, and an Application. In N. Meskens, & M. Roubens (Eds.), Advances in Decision Analysis. Mathematical Modelling: Theory and Applications (pp. 131-157). The Netherlands: Springer. doi:10.1007/978-94-017-0647-6_9

e Costa, C. A. B., & Vansnick, JEnsslin, C., & Corrêa, L., C. (1999). Decision support systems in action: Integrated application in a multicriteria decision aid process. *European Journal of Operational Research*, *113*(2), 315–335. doi:10.1016/S0377-2217(98)00219-7

e Costa, C. A. B., & Vansnick, J. C. (1995). General Overview of the Macbeth Approach. In P. Pardalos, Y. Siskos, & C. Zopounidis (Eds.), *Advances in Multicriteria Analysis. Nonconvex Optimization and Its Applications* (pp. 93–100). Boston, MA: Springer; doi:10.1007/978-1-4757-2383-0_6

Ebert, P., & Freibichler, W. (2017). Nudge management: Applying behavioural science to increase knowledge worker productivity. *Journal of Organization Design*, *6*(1), 4. doi:10.118641469-017-0014-1

Efe, B. (2016). An integrated fuzzy multi criteria group decision making approach for ERP system selection. *Applied Soft Computing*, *38*, 106–117. doi:10.1016/j.asoc.2015.09.037

Efe, B., & Efe, Ö. F. (2018). Intuitionistic fuzzy number-based group decision making approach for personnel selection. *Uludağ University Journal of The Faculty of Engineering*, *23*(3), 11–26. doi:10.17482/uumfd.338406

Efe, B., Kurt, M., & Efe, Ö. F. (2017). An integrated intuitionistic fuzzy set and mathematical programming approach for an occupational health and safety policy. *Gazi University Journal of Science*, *30*(2), 73–95.

Ekmekçioğlu, M., & Can Kutlu, A. (2012). A fuzzy hybrid approach for fuzzy process FMEA: An application to a spindle manufacturing process. *International Journal of Computational Intelligence Systems*, *5*(4), 611–626. doi:10.1080/18756891.2012.718104

Eko Saputro, T., & Daneshvar Rouyendegh, B. (2016). A hybrid approach for selecting material handling equipment in a warehouse. *International Journal of Management Science and Engineering Management*, *11*(1), 34–48. doi:10.1080/17509653.2015.1042535

El Mokrini, A., Dafaoui, E., Berrado, A., & El Mhamedi, A. (2016). An approach to risk assessment for outsourcing logistics: Case of pharmaceutical industry. *IFAC-PapersOnLine*, *49*(12), 1239–1244. doi:10.1016/j.ifacol.2016.07.681

Elevli, B. (2014). Logistics freight center locations decision by using Fuzzy-PROMETHEE. *Transport*, *29*(4), 412–418. doi:10.3846/16484142.2014.983966

Elissen, A., Steuten, L., Lemmens, L., Drewes, H., Lemmens, K., Meeuwissen, J., ... Vrijhoef, H. (2013). Meta-analysis of the effectiveness of chronic care management for diabetes: Investigating heterogeneity in outcomes. *Journal of Evaluation in Clinical Practice*, 753–762. doi:10.1111/j.1365-2753.2012.01817.x PMID:22372830

El-Santawy, M. F. (2012). A VIKOR method for solving personnel training selection problem. *International Journal of Computational Science*, *1*(2), 9–12.

Emovon, I. (2016). Failure mode and effects analysis of ship systems using an integrated Dempster Shafer theory and Electre method. *Journal of Advanced Manufacturing Technology (JAMT)*, *10*(1), 45-60, *31*(5), 761-772.

Emovon, I., Norman, R. A., Alan, J. M., & Pazouki, K. (2015). An integrated multicriteria decision making methodology using compromise solution methods for prioritising risk of marine machinery systems. *Ocean Engineering*, *105*, 92–103. doi:10.1016/j.oceaneng.2015.06.005

Ensslin, L., Giffhorn, E., Ensslin, S. R., Petri, S. M., & Vianna, W. B. (2010). Avaliação do desempenho de empresas terceirizadas com o uso da metodologia multicritério de apoio à decisão - construtivista. *Pesquisa Operacional*, *30*(1), 125–152. doi:10.1590/S0101-74382010000100007

Enyinda, C. I. (2009). *Modeling risk management in the pharmaceutical industry global SC logistics using analytic hierarchy process model*. North Dakota State University.

Ertuğrul, I., & Karakasoğlu, N. (2008). Comparison of fuzzy AHP and fuzzy TOPSIS methods for facility location selection. *International Journal of Advanced Manufacturing Technology*, *39*(7-8), 783–795. doi:10.100700170-007-1249-8

Eryürek, Ö. F. (2003). *Hata Türü Ve Etkileri Analizinde Yeni Bir Karar Verme Modeli* (Doctoral dissertation, Fen Bilimleri Enstitüsü).

Faisal, M. N. (2010). Analysing the Barriers to Corporate Social Responsibility in Supply Chains: An Interpretive Structural Modelling Approach. *International Journal of Logistics: Research and Applications*, *13*(3), 179–195. doi:10.1080/13675560903264968

Farris, D. R., & Sage, A. P. (1975). On the Use of Interpretive Structural Modelling for Worth Assessment. *Computers & Electrical Engineering*, *2*(2-3), 149–174. doi:10.1016/0045-7906(75)90004-X

Felder, R., Alwan, M., & Zhang, M. (2008). *Systems Engineering Approach to Medical Automation*. Norwood, MA: Artech House.

Figueira, J., Mousseau, V., & Roy, B. (2005). ELECTRE methods. In Multiple criteria decision analysis: State of the art surveys, 133-153, Springer New York. doi:10.1007/0-387-23081-5_4

Figueira, J., de Smet, I., & Brans, J. P. (2004). *MCDA methods for sorting and clustering problems: PROMETHEE TRI and PROMETHEE CLUSTER. Université Libre de Bruxelles*. Service de Mathématiques de la Gestion.

Figueira, J., Greco, S., & Ehrgott, M. (2004). *Multiple criteria decision analysis; state of the art surveys*. New York: Springer.

Figueira, J., Greco, S., & Ehrogott, M. (2005). *Multiple Criteria Decision Analysis: State of the Art Surveys*. New York: Springer; doi:10.1007/b100605

Forman, E. H., & Gass, S. I. (2001). The Analytic Hierarchy Process—An Exposition. *Operations Research*, *49*(4), 469–486. doi:10.1287/opre.49.4.469.11231

Forman, E. H., & Selly, M. A. (2002). *Decision by objectives: How to convince others that you are right*. Pittsburgh, PA: Scientific Pub Co.

Forsberg, K., Mooz, H., & Cotterman, H. (2005). *Visualizing project management: models and frameworks for mastering complex systems*. Wiley.

Fraser, A., Howard, M., Alder, J., Boobier, S., Burke, V., & Chambers, J. (2005). Across cultures implementing the Evercare model. 16-19. doi:10.7748/nop2005.10.17.7.16.c2388

Freeman, S., Edwards, R., & Schroder, B. (2006). How smaller born-global firms use networks and alliances to overcome constraints to rapid internationalization. *Journal of International Marketing*, *14*(3), 33–63. doi:10.1509/jimk.14.3.33

Gan, J., & Luo, L. (2017). Using DEMATEL and Intuitionistic Fuzzy Sets to Identify Critical Factors Influencing the Recycling Rate of End-Of-Life Vehicles in China. *Sustainability*, *9*(1873), 1–22. doi:10.3390u9101873

Ganga, G. M. D., & Carpinetti, L. C. R. (2011). A fuzzy logic approach to supply chain performance management. *International Journal of Production Economics*, *134*(1), 177–187. doi:10.1016/j.ijpe.2011.06.011

Ganguly, A., Chatterjee, D., & Talukdar, A. (2019). Knowledge Sharing Barriers Affecting Pharmaceutical SC Performance. In Global SCs in the Pharmaceutical Industry (pp. 269–291). Hershey, PA: IGI Global.

Garcia, P. , Schirru, R., Frutuoso E. Melo, P. F. (2005). A fuzzy data environment analysis approach for FMEA. *Progress in Nuclear Energy*, *46*(3-4), 359–373. doi:10.1016/j.pnucene.2005.03.016

Gardas, B. B., Raut, R. D., & Narkhede, B. E. (2017). A state-of the-art survey of interpretive structural modelling methodologies and applications. *International Journal of Business Excellence*, *11*(4), 505–560. doi:10.1504/IJBEX.2017.082576

Gargama, H., & Chaturvedi, S. K. (2011). Criticality assessment models for failure mode effects and criticality analysis using fuzzy logic. *IEEE Transactions on Reliability*, *60*(1), 102–110. doi:10.1109/TR.2010.2103672

Geldermann, J., & Rentz, O. (2005). Multi-criteria Analysis for Technique Assessment: Case Study from Industrial Coating. *Journal of Industrial Ecology*, *9*(3), 127–142. doi:10.1162/1088198054821591

Geldermann, J., Spengler, T., & Rentz, O. (2000). Fuzzy outranking for environmental assessment. Case study: Iron and steel making industry. *Fuzzy Sets and Systems*, *115*(1), 45–65. doi:10.1016/S0165-0114(99)00021-4

Ghazanfari, M., Rouhani, S., & Jafari, M. (2014). A fuzzy TOPSIS model to evaluate the Business Intelligence competencies of Port Community Systems. *Polish Maritime Research*, *21*(2), 86–96. doi:10.2478/pomr-2014-0023

Gino, F. (2017). Uber Shows How Not to Apply Behavioral Economics. Retrieved August 31, 2019, from https://hbr.org/2017/04/uber-shows-how-not-to-apply-behavioral-economics

Goh, M., Prakash, S., & Yeo, R. (2007). Resource-based approach to IT shared services in a manufacturing firm. *Industrial Management & Data Systems*, *107*(2), 251–270. doi:10.1108/02635570710723831

Gök-kısa, A. C., & Perçin, S. (2018). Bütünleşik entropi ağırlık-VIKOR yöntemi ile bilişim teknolojisi sektöründe performans ölçümü. *Ekonomik ve Sosyal Araştırmalar Dergisi*, *14*(1), 1–13.

Goldstein, N., Griskevicius, V., & Cialdini, R. (2011). Reciprocity by Proxy. *Administrative Science Quarterly*, *56*(3), 441–473. doi:10.1177/0001839211435904

Gomes, E. G., Pereira, M., & Lins, E. (2002). Integrating Geographical Information Systems and Multi-Criteria Methods: A Case Study. *Annals of Operations Research*, *116*(1/4), 243–269. doi:10.1023/A:1021344700828

Google PageSpeed Insights (PSI). (2019). *About PageSpeed Insights.* Retrieved from https://developers.google.com/speed/docs/insights/v5/about?hl=trTR&utm_source=PSI&utm_medium=incoming-link&utm_campaign=PSI

Google. The behavioral economics behind crafting Google's AdWords campaign | Irrational Labs | Behavioral Economics. (2019). Retrieved August 31, 2019, from https://irrationallabs.org/work/behavioral-science-behind-crafting-googles-adwords-campaign/

Gorane, S. J., & Kant, R. (2013). Modelling the SCM enablers: An integrated ISM-fuzzy MICMAC approach. *Asia Pacific Journal of Marketing and Logistics*, *25*(2), 263–286. doi:10.1108/13555851311314059

Gosnell, G., List, J., & Metcalfe, R. (2016). *A New Approach to an Old-Age Problem: Solving Externalities by Incenting Workers Directly. NBER Working Paper 22316.* Cambridge, UK: National Bureau of Economic Research; Retrieved from https://www.nber.org/papers/w22316 doi:10.3386/w22316

Govindan, K., Kannan, D., Mathiyazhagan, K., Jabbour, A. B., & Jabbour, C. J. (2013). Analysing Green Supply Chain Management Practices in Brazil's Electrical/Electornics Industry Using Interpretive Structural Modelling. *The International Journal of Environmental Studies*, *70*(4), 477–493. doi:10.1080/00207233.2013.798494

Govindan, K., Soleimani, H., & Kannan, D. (2015). Reverse logistics and closed-loop SC: A comprehensive review to explore the future. *European Journal of Operational Research*, *240*(3), 603–626. doi:10.1016/j.ejor.2014.07.012

Goyal, G., Samalia, H. V., & Verma, P. (2017). Interpretive structural modeling for integrating quality management in manufacturing and service counterparts. *International Journal of Quality & Reliability Management*, *34*(9), 1568–1591. doi:10.1108/IJQRM-11-2015-0169

greenfacts. (n.d.). Retrieved from https://www.greenfacts.org/glossary/index.htm

Guerzhoy, M. (2019). Introduction to Data Science as a Pathway to Further Study in Computing. In *Proceedings of the 2019 ACM Conference on International Computing Education Research (ICER '19)*. Toronto, Canada: ACM. 10.1145/3291279.3341203

Guimarães, A. C. F., & Lapa, C. M. F. (2007). Fuzzy inference to risk assessment on nuclear engineering systems. *Applied Soft Computing*, *7*(1), 17–28. doi:10.1016/j.asoc.2005.06.002

Gul, M., Celik, E., Gumus, A. T., & Guneri, A. F. (2018). A fuzzy logic based PROMETHEE method for material selection problems. *Beni-Suef University Journal of Basic and Applied Sciences*, *7*(1), 68–79. doi:10.1016/j.bjbas.2017.07.002

Gümüş, S., & Bali, O. (2017). Dynamic Aggregation Operators Based on Intuitionistic Fuzzy Tools and Einstein Operations. *Fuzzy Information and Engineering*, *9*(1), 45–65. doi:10.1016/j.fiae.2017.03.003

Gunasekaran, A., Lai, K. H., & Cheng, T. E. (2008). Responsive SC: A competitive strategy in a networked economy. *Omega*, *36*(4), 549–564. doi:10.1016/j.omega.2006.12.002

Güngör, Z., Gürkan, K., & Saadettin, E. (2009). A fuzzy AHP approach to personnel selection problem. *Applied Soft Computing*, *9*(2), 641–646. doi:10.1016/j.asoc.2008.09.003

Gupta, A., Deokar, A., Iyer, L., Sharda, R., & Schrader, D. (2018). Big Data & Analytics for Societal Impact: Recent Research and Trends. *Information Systems Frontiers*, *20*(2), 185–194. doi:10.100710796-018-9846-7

Gupta, H., & Barua, M. K. (2017). Supplier selection among SMEs on the basis of their green innovation ability using BWM and fuzzy TOPSIS. *Journal of Cleaner Production*, *152*, 242–258. doi:10.1016/j.jclepro.2017.03.125

Gupta, V., Acharya, P., & Patwardhan, M. (2013). A strategic and operational approach to assess the lean performance in radial tyre manufacturing in India: A case-based study. *International Journal of Productivity and Performance Management*, *62*(6), 634–651. doi:10.1108/IJPPM-Jun-2012-0057

Gürcan, H. İ. (2003). Haber sitelerinde içerik ve tasarıma yönelik değerlendirme ölçütlerine bir yaklaşım. *Selçuk İletişim Dergisi*, *2*(4), 90–99.

Hababou, M., & Martel, J. M. (1998). A multicriteria approach for selecting a portfolio manager. *INFOR*, *36*(3), 161–176. doi:10.1080/03155986.1998.11732354

Haleem, A., Sushil, Qadri, M. A., & Kumar, S. (2012). Analysis of critical success factors of world-class manufacturing practices: An application of interpretative structural modelling and interpretative ranking process. *Production Planning and Control*, *23*(10-11), 722–734. doi:10.1080/09537287.2011.642134

Hall-Ellis, S. D. (2015). Nudges and decision making: A winning combination. *The Bottom Line (New York, N.Y.)*, *28*(4), 133–136. doi:10.1108/BL-07-2015-0015

Hansen, J. V., McKell, L. J., & Heitger, L. E. (1979). ISMS: Computer-aided analysis for design of decision-support systems. *Management Science*, *25*(11), 1069–1081. doi:10.1287/mnsc.25.11.1069

Hashemi, H., Mousavi, S. M., & Zavadskas, E. K. (2018). A New Group Decision Model Based on Grey-Intuitionistic Fuzzy-ELECTRE and VIKOR for Contractor Assessment Problem. *Sustainability*, *10*(1635), 1–19. doi:10.3390u10051635 PMID:30607262

Hatcher, M. (2008). Asset Evaluation and Selection Using The Analytic Hierarchy Process. *International Journal of Business Research*, *8*(3), 118–124.

Hausman, D. M., & Welch, B. (2010). Debate: To Nudge or Not to Nudge*. *Journal of Political Philosophy*, *18*(1), 123–136. doi:10.1111/j.1467-9760.2009.00351.x

Hawthorne, R. W., & Sage, A. P. (1975). On applications of interpretive structural modeling to higher education program planning. *Socio-Economic Planning Sciences*, *9*(1), 31–43. doi:10.1016/0038-0121(75)90039-7

Helvacioglu, S., & Ozen, E. (2014). Fuzzy based failure modes and effect analysis for yacht system design. *Ocean Engineering*, *79*, 131–141. doi:10.1016/j.oceaneng.2013.12.015

Hirth, V., Baskins, J., & Dever-Bumba, M. (2009). Program of all-inclusive care (PACE): Past, present, and future. *Journal of the American Medical Directors Association*, *10*(3), 155–160. doi:10.1016/j.jamda.2008.12.002 PMID:19233054

Hirve, S., & Reddy, C. H. (2019). A Survey on Visualization Techniques Used for Big Data Analytics. *Advances in Intelligent Systems and Computing, Springer*, *924*, 447–459. doi:10.1007/978-981-13-6861-5_39

History of Tableau. Retrieved from https://www.javatpoint.com/history-of-tableau

Ho, W., Xu, X., & Dey, P. K. (2010). Multi-criteria decision-making approaches for supplier evaluation and selection: A literature review. *European Journal of Operational Research*, *202*(1), 16–24. doi:10.1016/j.ejor.2009.05.009

Hughes, D. L., Dwivedi, Y. K., Rana, N. P., & Simintiras, A. (2016). Information Systems Project Failure-Analysis of Causal Links Using Interpretive Structural Modelling. *Production Planning and Control*, *27*(16), 1313–1333. doi:10.1080/09537287.2016.1217571

Hughes, D. L., Rana, N. P., & Dwivedi, Y. K. (2019). Elucidation of IS project success factors: An interpretive structural modelling approach. *Annals of Operations Research*, 1–32.

Hu, J., Du, Y., Mo, H., Wei, D., & Deng, Y. (2016). A modified weighted TOPSIS to identify influential nodes in complex networks. *Physica A*, *444*, 73–85. doi:10.1016/j.physa.2015.09.028

Human Development Reports. (n.d.). Retrieved from http://hdr.undp.org/en/humandev

Hung, C.-C., & Chen, L.-H. (2009). A Fuzzy TOPSIS Decision Making Model with Entropy Weight under Intuitionistic Fuzzy Environment. *Proceedings of the International MultiConference of Engineers and Computer Scientists IMECS 2009, Hong Kong, I*, 18–21.

Huq, F., Pawar, K. S., & Rogers, H. (2016). SC configuration conundrum: How does the pharmaceutical industry mitigate disturbance factors? *Production Planning and Control*, *27*(14), 1206–1220.

Husain, A. A. F., Hasan, W. Z. W., Shafie, S., Hamidon, M. N., & Pandey, S. S. (2018). A review of transparent solar photovoltaic technologies. *Renewable & Sustainable Energy Reviews*, *94*(3), 779–791. doi:10.1016/j.rser.2018.06.031

Hwang, C. L., & Yoon, K. (1981). *Multiple attributes decision making methods and applications*. Berlin, Germany: Springer-Verlag. doi:10.1007/978-3-642-48318-9

Hwang, C.-L., & Yoon, K. (1981). *Multiple attribute decision making, methods and applications. Lecture Notes in Economics and Mathematical Systems* (Vol. 186). New York: Springer-Verlag.

Ilangkumaran, M., Shanmugam, P., Sakthivel, G., & Visagavel, K. (2014). Failure mode and effect analysis using fuzzy analytic hierarchy process. *International Journal of Productivity and Quality Management*, *14*(3), 296–313. doi:10.1504/IJPQM.2014.064807

Introduction of R language. Retrieved from https://www.slideshare.net/humzarajput/history-of-computer-16571911

Isern, D., Marin, L., Valls, A., & Moreno, A. (2010). The Unbalanced Linguistic Ordered Weighted Averaging operator. *International Conference on Fuzzy Systems* (pp. 1-8). Barcelona, Spain: IEEE. 10.1109/FUZZY.2010.5584199

Ishizaka, A., & Nemery, P. (2013). Multi-criteria decision analysis methods and software, Wiley & Sons, Atrium, Southern Gate, Chichester, UK.

Ishizaka, A., & Labib, A. (2011). Review of the main developments in the analytic hierarchy process. *Expert Systems with Applications*. doi:10.1016/j.eswa.2011.04.143

Jadhav, J. R., Mantha, S. S., & Rane, S. B. (2014). Development of framework for sustainable Lean implementation: An ISM approach. *Journal of Industrial Engineering International, 10*(3), 72. doi:10.100740092-014-0072-8

Jafarnejad, A., & Shahaei, B. (2007). *Introduction to organizational agility and agile manufacturing* (pp. 25–79). Iran: Nashre Mehraban.

Jambulingam, T., Kathuria, R., & Nevin, J. R. (2009). How fairness garners loyalty in the pharmaceutical SC: Role of trust in the wholesaler-pharmacy relationship. *International Journal of Pharmaceutical and Healthcare Marketing, 3*(4), 305–322. doi:10.1108/17506120911006029

Janes, F. R. (1988). Interpretive structural modelling: A methodology for structuring complex issues. *Transactions of the Institute of Measurement and Control, 10*(3), 145–154. doi:10.1177/014233128801000306

Jang, J. S. R., & Sun, C. T. (1995). Neuro-fuzzy modeling and control. *Proceedings of the IEEE, 83*(3), 378–406. doi:10.1109/5.364486

Jayalakshmi, B., & Pramod, V. R. (2015). Total Interpretive Structural Modeling (TISM) of the Enablers of a Flexible Control System for Industry. *Global Journal of Flexible Systems Management, 16*(1), 63–85. doi:10.100740171-014-0080-y

Jedlicka, A. (1980). Interpretive Structural Modeling: Cross Cultural Uses.

Jee, D.-H., & Kang, K.-J. (2000). A method for optimal material selection aided with decision making theory. *Materials & Design, 21*(3), 199–206. doi:10.1016/S0261-3069(99)00066-7

Jena, B. (2019). An Approach for Forecast Prediction in Data Analytics Field by Tableau Software, *International Journal of Information Engineering and Electronic Business. MECS, Hong Kong, 11*, 19–26.

Jena, J., Sidharth, S., Thakur, L. S., Kumar Pathak, D., & Pandey, V. C. (2017). Total Interpretive Structural Modeling (TISM): Approach and Application. *Journal of Advances in Management Research, 14*(2), 162–181. doi:10.1108/JAMR-10-2016-0087

Jharkharia, S., & Shankar, R. (2004). IT enablement of supply chains: Modeling the enablers. *International Journal of Productivity and Performance Management, 53*(8), 700–712. doi:10.1108/17410400410569116

Jharkharia, S., & Shankar, R. (2004). Supply chain management: Some insights from Indian manufacturing companies. *Asian Academy of Management Journal, 9*(1), 79–98.

Jharkharia, S., & Shankar, R. (2005). IT-enablement of supply chains: Understanding the barriers. *Journal of Enterprise Information Management, 18*(1), 11–27. doi:10.1108/17410390510571466

Jolhe, D. A., & Subhash Babu, A. (2014). Modifications in Interpretive Structural Modelling Methodology to Enhance its Applicability in Group Decision Process and Power of Discrimination. *International Journal of Business Excellence, 7*(3), 281–348. doi:10.1504/IJBEX.2014.060779

Jones, L., Loibl, C., & Tennyson, S. (2015). Effects of informational nudges on consumer debt repayment behaviours. *Journal of Economic Psychology, 51*, 16–33. doi:10.1016/j.joep.2015.06.009

Jornocode. (2019). *Similarity and distance in data: Part 1*. Retrieved from http://journocode.com/2016/03/10/ similarity-and-distance-part-1/

Jose-M, M. L., & Montserrat, C. R. (2010). The Generalized Hybrid Averaging Operator and its Application in Decision Making. *REVISTA DE METODOS CUANTITATIVOS PARA LA ECONOMIA Y LA EMPRESA*, (9), 69–84.

Joshi, D., & Kumar, S. (2014). Intuitionistic fuzzy entropy and distance measure based TOPSIS method for multi-criteria decision making. *Egyptian Informatics Journal*, *15*(2), 97–104. doi:10.1016/j.eij.2014.03.002

Jovane, F., Yoshikawa, H., Alting, L., Boer, C. R., Westkamper, E., Williams, D., ... Paci, A. M. (2008). The incoming global technological and industrial revolution towards competitive sustainable manufacturing. *CIRP Annals*, *57*(2), 641–659. doi:10.1016/j.cirp.2008.09.010

Junior, F. R. L., Osiro, L., & Carpinetti, L. C. R. (2014). A comparison between Fuzzy AHP and Fuzzy TOPSIS methods to supplier selection. *Applied Soft Computing*, *21*, 194–209. doi:10.1016/j.asoc.2014.03.014

Jyoti, B., Banwet, D. K., & Deshmukh, S. G. (2010). Modelling the success factors for national R&D organizations: A case of India. *Journal of Modelling in Management*, *5*(2), 158–175. doi:10.1108/17465661011061005

Kabadayı, N., & Dag, S. (2017). Bulanik Dematel ve bulanik Promethee yöntemleri ile kablo üretiminde makine seçimi (Machine Selection in a Cable Manufacturing with Using Fuzzy Dematel and Fuzzy Promethee). *Karadeniz Teknik Üniversitesi Sosyal Bilimler Enstitüsü Sosyal Bilimler Dergisi*, *7*(1), 239–260.

Kabak, M., Özceylan, E., Dağdeviren, M., & Genç, T. (2017). Evaluation of distance education websites: A hybrid multicriteria approach. *Turkish Journal of Electrical Engineering and Computer Sciences*, *25*, 2809–2819. doi:10.3906/elk-1512-271

Kahraman, C., Keshavarz Ghorabaee, M., Zavadskas, E. K., Cevik Onar, S., Yazdani, M., & Oztaysi, B. (2017). Intuitionistic fuzzy EDAS method: an application to solid waste disposal site selection. *Journal of Environmental Engineering and Landscape Management, 25*(1).

Kahraman, C. (Ed.). (2006). *Fuzzy applications in industrial engineering* (Vol. 201). Berlin, Germany: Springer. doi:10.1007/3-540-33517-X

Kale, D., & Little, S. (2007). From imitation to innovation: The evolution of R&D capabilities and learning processes in the Indian pharmaceutical industry. *Technology Analysis and Strategic Management*, *19*(5), 589–609. doi:10.1080/09537320701521317

Kaluarachchi, K. A. S. P. (2010). Organizational culture and total quality management practices: A Sri Lankan case. *The TQM Journal*, *22*(1), 41–55. doi:10.1108/17542731011009612

Kanda, A., & Deshmukh, S. G. (2008). SC coordination: Perspectives, empirical studies and research directions. *International Journal of Production Economics*, *115*(2), 316–335. doi:10.1016/j.ijpe.2008.05.011

Kannan, G., Pokharel, S., Sasi Kumar, P. (2009). A hybrid approach using ISM and fuzzy TOPSIS for the selection of reverse logistics provider. Resources, Conservation, and Recycling 54, pp. 28-36.

Kara, S., Ibbotson, S., & Kayis, B. (2014). Sustainable product development in practice: An international survey. *Journal of Manufacturing Technology Management*, *25*(6), 848–872. doi:10.1108/JMTM-09-2012-0082

Kaya, E., Agca, M., Adiguzel, F., & Cetin, M. (2019). *Spatial data analysis with R programming for environment. Human and Ecological Risk Assessment: An International Journal* (Vol. 19). Taylor & Francis.

Kelemenis, A., & Askounis, D. (2010). A new TOPSIS-based multi-criteria approach to personnel selection. *Expert Systems with Applications*, *37*(7), 4999–5008. doi:10.1016/j.eswa.2009.12.013

Kelle, P., Woosley, J., & Schneider, H. (2012). Pharmaceutical supply chain specifics and inventory solutions for a hospital case. *Operations Research for Health Care*, *1*(2-3), 54–63. doi:10.1016/j.orhc.2012.07.001

Khan, U., & Haleem, A. (2012). Smart Organisations: Modelling of Enablers Using an Integrated ISM and Fuzzy-MICMAC Approach. *International Journal of Intelligent Enterprise*, *1*(3-4), 248–269. doi:10.1504/IJIE.2012.052556

Kiker, G. A., Bridges, T. S., Varghese, A., Seager, T. P., & Linkov, I. (2005). Application of multicriteria decision analysis in environmental decision making. *Integrated Environmental Assessment and Management: An International Journal*, *1*(2), 95–108. doi:10.1897/IEAM_2004a-015.1 PMID:16639891

Klauer, B., Drechsler, M., & Messner, F. (2006). Multicriteria analysis under uncertainty with IANUS—Method and empirical results. *Environment and Planning. C, Government & Policy*, *24*(2), 235–256. doi:10.1068/c03102s

Kosters, M., & Van der Heijden, J. (2015). From mechanism to virtue: Evaluating Nudge theory. *Evaluation*, *21*(3), 276–291. doi:10.1177/1356389015590218

Krmac, E., & Djordjević, B. (2018). An evaluation of indicators of railway intelligent transportation systems using the group analytic hierarchy process. *Electronics Science Technology and Application*, *4*(2), 15–22. doi:10.18686/esta.v4i2.57

Kulak, O. (2005). A decision support system for fuzzy multi-attribute selection of material handling equipments. *Expert Systems with Applications*, *29*(2), 310–319. doi:10.1016/j.eswa.2005.04.004

Kulatilaka, N. (1988). Valuing the flexibility of flexible manufacturing systems. *IEEE Transactions on Engineering Management*, *35*(4), 250–257. doi:10.1109/17.7447

Kumar, A., Sah, B., Singh, A. R., Deng, Y., He, X., Kumar, P., & Bansal, R. C. (2017). A review of multi criteria decision making (MCDM) towards sustainable renewable energy development. *Renewable & Sustainable Energy Reviews*, *69*, 596–609. doi:10.1016/j.rser.2016.11.191

Kumar, A., Zavadskas, E. K., Mangla, S. K., Agrawal, V., Sharma, K., & Gupta, D. (2018). When risks need attention: Adoption of green SC initiatives in the pharmaceutical industry. *International Journal of Production Research*, 1–23.

Kumar, D., Goyal, P., & Kumar, V. (2019). Modeling and classification of enablers of CSR in Indian firms. *Journal of Modelling in Management*, *14*(2), 456–475. doi:10.1108/JM2-07-2018-0100

Kumar, N., Kumar, S., Haleem, A., & Gahlot, P. (2013). Implementing lean manufacturing system: ISM approach. [JIEM]. *Journal of Industrial Engineering and Management*, *6*(4), 996–1012. doi:10.3926/jiem.508

Kumar, P., Singh, R. K., & Kumar, R. (2017). An integrated framework of interpretive structural modeling and graph theory matrix approach to fix the agility index of an automobile manufacturing organization. *International Journal of System Assurance Engineering and Management*, *8*(1), 342–352. doi:10.100713198-015-0350-x

Kumar, S., Dieveney, E., & Dieveney, A. (2009). Reverse logistic process control measures for the pharmaceutical industry supply chain. *International Journal of Productivity and Performance Management*, *58*(2), 188–204. doi:10.1108/17410400910928761

Kumar, S., Luthra, S., Govindan, K., Kumar, N., & Haleem, A. (2016). Barriers in green lean six sigma product development process: An ISM approach. *Production Planning and Control*, *27*(7-8), 604–620.

Kumlu, K. B., & Tüdeş, Ş. (2018). Multi criteria decision making techniques in urban planning and geology. In N. Ceryan (Ed.), *Handbook of Research on Trends and Digital Advances in Engineering Geology* (pp. 530–568). Hershey, PA: IGI Global; doi:10.4018/978-1-5225-2709-1.ch015

Kumru, M., & Kumru, P. Y. (2013). Fuzzy FMEA application to improve purchasing process in a public hospital. *Applied Soft Computing*, *13*(1), 721–733. doi:10.1016/j.asoc.2012.08.007

Kureshi, N., Qureshi, F., & Sajid, A. (2010). Current health of quality management practices in service sector SME: A case study of Pakistan. *The TQM Journal*, *22*(3), 317–329. doi:10.1108/17542731011035541

Kusumawardani, R. P., & Agintiara, M. (2015). Application of fuzzy AHP-TOPSIS method for decision making in human resource manager selection process. *Procedia Computer Science*, *72*, 638–646. doi:10.1016/j.procs.2015.12.173

Kutlu, A. C., & Ekmekçioğlu, M. (2012). Fuzzy failure modes and effects analysis by using fuzzy TOPSIS-based fuzzy AHP. *Expert Systems with Applications*, *39*(1), 61–67. doi:10.1016/j.eswa.2011.06.044

Lai, F., Zhao, X., & Wang, Q. (2006). The impact of information technology on the competitive advantage of logistics firms in China. *Industrial Management & Data Systems*, *106*(9), 1249–1271. doi:10.1108/02635570610712564

Lai, Y. J., Liu, T. Y., & Hwang, C. L. (1994). TOPSIS for MODM. *European Journal of Operational Research*, *76*(3), 486–500. doi:10.1016/0377-2217(94)90282-8

Lapa-Guimaraes, J., & Pickova, J. (2004). New solvent systems for thin-layer chromatographic determination of nine biogenic amines in fish and squid. *Journal of Chromatography. A*, *1045*(1-2), 223–232. doi:10.1016/j.chroma.2004.06.014 PMID:15378899

Le Téno, J. F., & Mareschal, B. (1998). An interval version of PROMETHEE for the comparison of building products' design with ill-defined data on environmental quality. *European Journal of Operational Research*, *109*(2), 522–529. doi:10.1016/S0377-2217(98)00074-5

Lee, C. C., & Tseng, H. C. (2018). Integrating fuzzy membership function, entropy method and VIKOR to select qualified and stable employee. *2018 International Conference on Information Management and Processing* (vol. 1, pp. 26-31). Global: IEEE Press. 10.1109/ICIMP1.2018.8325836

Lee, L.-W., & Chen, S.-M. (2008a). Fuzzy interpolative reasoning using interval Type-2 fuzzy sets. In *Proceedings of the International Conference on Industrial, Engineering, and Other Applications of Applied Intelligent Systems* (pp. 92-101). Berlin, Germany: Springer. 10.1007/978-3-540-69052-8_10

Lee, A. H. I. (2009). A fuzzy supplier selection model with the consideration of benefits opportunities, costs and risks. *Expert Systems with Applications*, *36*(2), 2879–2893. doi:10.1016/j.eswa.2008.01.045

Lee, A. H., Wang, W., & Lin, T. (2010). An Evaluation Framework for Technology Transfer of New Equipment in High Technology Industry. *Technological Forecasting and Social Change*, *77*(1), 135–150. doi:10.1016/j.techfore.2009.06.002

Lee, H. L., & Ng, S. M. (1997). Introduction to the special issue on global SC management. *Production and Operations Management*, *6*(3), 191–192. doi:10.1111/j.1937-5956.1997.tb00425.x

Lee, L.-W., & Chen, S.-M. (2008b). Fuzzy multiple attributes group decision-making based on the extension of TOPSIS method and interval type-2 fuzzy sets. In *Proceedings of the 2008 International Conference on Machine Learning and Cybernetics* 6, pp. 3260-3265. IEEE 10.1109/ICMLC.2008.4620968

Leggett, W. (2014). The politics of behaviour change: Nudge, neoliberalism and the state. *Policy and Politics*, *42*(1), 3–19. doi:10.1332/030557312X655576

Lemmens, K., Lemmens, L., Boom, J., Drewes, H., Meeuwissen, J., Steuten, L., ... Baan, C. (2013). Chronic care management for patients with COPD: A critical review of available evidence. *Journal of Evaluation in Clinical Practice*, 734–752. doi:10.1111/j.1365-2753.2011.01805.x PMID:22133473

Leonardi, G. (2016). A Fuzzy Model for a Railway-Planning Problem. *Applied Mathematical Sciences*, *10*(27), 1333–1342. doi:10.12988/ams.2016.63106

Lewis, M. A. (2000). Lean production and sustainable competitive advantage. *International Journal of Operations & Production Management*, *20*(8), 959–978. doi:10.1108/01443570010332971

Lim, M. K., Tseng, M. L., Tan, K. H., & Bui, T. D. (2017). Knowledge Management in Sustainable Supply Chain Management: Improving Performance through an Interpretive Structural Modelling Approach. *Journal of Cleaner Production*, *62*, 806–816. doi:10.1016/j.jclepro.2017.06.056

Lin, M. C., Wang, C. C., & Chen, T. C. (2006). A strategy for managing customer-oriented product design. *Concurrent Engineering*, *14*(3), 231–244. doi:10.1177/1063293X06068390

Lin, Y. T., Lin, C. L., Yu, H. C., & Tzeng, G. H. (2011). Utilisation of interpretive structural modelling method in the analysis of interrelationship of vendor performance factors. *International Journal of Business Performance Management*, *12*(3), 260–275. doi:10.1504/IJBPM.2011.039890

Liu, P., & Zhang, L. (2014). *The Extended VIKOR Method for Multiple Criteria Decision Making Problem Based on Neutrosophic Hesitant Fuzzy Set.*

Liu, H. C., Li, P., You, J. X., & Chen, Y. Z. (2015). A novel approach for FMEA: Combination of interval 2-tuple linguistic variables and gray relational analysis. *Quality and Reliability Engineering International*, *31*(5), 761–772. doi:10.1002/qre.1633

Liu, H. C., Li, Z., Song, W., & Su, Q. (2017). Failure mode and effect analysis using cloud model theory and PROMETHEE method. *IEEE Transactions on Reliability*, *66*(4), 1058–1072. doi:10.1109/TR.2017.2754642

Liu, H.-C., Liu, L., & Li, P. (2014). Failure mode and effects analysis using intuitionistic fuzzy hybrid weighted Euclidean distance operator. *International Journal of Systems Science*, *45*(10), 2012–2030. doi:10.1080/00207721.2012.760669

Liu, H.-C., Liu, L., & Li, P. (2015). Failure mode and effects analysis using intuitionistic fuzzy hybrid TOPSIS approach. *Soft Computing*, *19*(4), 1085–1098. doi:10.100700500-014-1321-x

Liu, H.-C., Liu, L., Liu, N., & Mao, L.-X. (2012). Risk evaluation in failure mode and effects analysis with extended VIKOR method under fuzzy environment. *Expert Systems with Applications*, *39*(17), 12926–12934. doi:10.1016/j.eswa.2012.05.031

Liu, H.-C., You, J.-X., Lin, Q.-L., & Li, H. (2014). Risk assessment in system FMEA combining fuzzy weighted average with fuzzy decision-making trial and evaluation laboratory. *International Journal of Computer Integrated Manufacturing*, *28*(7), 701–714. doi:10.1080/0951192X.2014.900865

Liu, P., Li, Q., Bian, J., Song, L., & Xiahou, X. (2018). Using interpretative structural modeling to identify critical success factors for safety management in subway construction: A china study. *International Journal of Environmental Research and Public Health*, *15*(7), 1359. doi:10.3390/ijerph15071359 PMID:29958438

Li, X., Wang, K., Liu, L., Xin, J., Yang, H., & Gao, C. (2011). Application of the entropy weight and TOPSIS method in safety evaluation of coal mines. *Procedia Engineering*, *26*, 2085–2091. doi:10.1016/j.proeng.2011.11.2410

Lolli, F., Ishizaka, A., Gamberini, R., Rimini, B., & Messori, M. (2015). FlowSort-GDSS–A novel group multi-criteria decision support system for sorting problems with application to FMEA. *Expert Systems with Applications*, *42*(17-18), 6342–6349. doi:10.1016/j.eswa.2015.04.028

Lootsma, F. A. (2007). *Multi-criteria decision analysis via ratio and difference judgement* (Vol. 29). Springer Science and Business Media.

Lootsma, F. A. (2007). *Multi-criteria decision analysis via ratio and difference judgement. Science and Business Media* (Vol. 29). Springer.

Lozano-Minguez, E., Kolios, A. J., & Brennan, F. (2011). Multi-criteria assessment of offshore wind turbine support structures. *Renewable Energy, 36*(11), 2831–2837. doi:10.1016/j.renene.2011.04.020

Luthra, S., Garg, D., & Haleem, A. (2014). Greening the SC using SAP-LAP analysis: A case study of an auto ancillary company in India. *International Journal of Business Excellence*, *7*(6), 724–746. doi:10.1504/IJBEX.2014.065505

Luthra, S., Kumar, V., Kumar, S., & Haleem, A. (2011). Barriers to implement green supply chain management in automobile industry using interpretive structural modeling technique: An Indian perspective. [JIEM]. *Journal of Industrial Engineering and Management*, *4*(2), 231–257. doi:10.3926/jiem.2011.v4n2.p231-257

Macuzic, I., Tadic, D., Aleksic, A., & Stefanovic, M. (2016). A two-step fuzzy model for the assessment and ranking of organizational resilience factors in the process industry. *Journal of Loss Prevention in the Process Industries*, *40*, 122–130. doi:10.1016/j.jlp.2015.12.013

Madlener, R., & Sunak, Y. (2011). Impacts of urbanization on urban structures and energy demand: What can we learn for urban energy planning and urbanization management? *Sustainable Cities and Society*, *1*(1), 45–53. doi:10.1016/j.scs.2010.08.006

Mahajan, V., Nauriyal, D. K., & Singh, S. P. (2015). Trade performance and revealed comparative advantage of Indian pharmaceutical industry in new IPR regime. *International Journal of Pharmaceutical and Healthcare Marketing*, *9*(1), 56–73. doi:10.1108/IJPHM-05-2013-0030

Mahmoodzadeh, S., Shahrabi, J., Pariazar, M., & Zaeri, M. S. (2007). Project selection by using fuzzy AHP and TOPSIS technique. *International Journal of Humanities and Social Science*, *1*(3), 135–140.

Malekian, A., & Azarnivand, A. (2016). Application of integrated Shannon's entropy and VIKOR techniques in prioritization of flood risk in the Shemshak Watershed, Iran. *Water Resources Management*, *30*(1), 409–425. doi:10.100711269-015-1169-6

Malone, D. W. (1975). An introduction to the application of interpretive structural modeling. *Proceedings of the IEEE*, *63*(3), 397–404. doi:10.1109/PROC.1975.9765

Mandal, S., & Maiti, J. (2014). Risk analysis using FMEA: Fuzzy similarity value and possibility theory-based approach. *Expert Systems with Applications*, *41*(7), 3527–3537. doi:10.1016/j.eswa.2013.10.058

Mangeli, M., Shahraki, A., & Saljooghi, F. H. (2019). Improvement of risk assessment in the FMEA using nonlinear model, revised fuzzy TOPSIS, and support vector machine. *International Journal of Industrial Ergonomics*, *69*, 209–216. doi:10.1016/j.ergon.2018.11.004

Mangla, S., Madaan, J., Sarma, P. R., & Gupta, M. P. (2014). Multi-Objective Decision Modelling Using Interpretive Structural Modelling for Green Supply Chains. *International Journal of Logistics Systems and Management*, *17*(2), 125–142. doi:10.1504/IJLSM.2014.059113

Mangle, L., Phillips, P., Pitts, M., & Laver-Bradbury, C. (2014). Implementation of Independent Nurse Prescribing in UK Mental Health Settings: Focus on Attention-Deficit/Hyperactivity Disorder. *ADHD Attention Deficit and Hyperactivity Disorders*, *6*(4), 269–279. doi:10.100712402-014-0138-x PMID:24744052

Mani, V., Agarwal, R., Gunasekaran, A., Papadopoulos, T., Dubey, R., & Childe, S. J. (2016). Social sustainability in the SC: Construct development and measurement validation. *Ecological Indicators*, *71*, 270–279. doi:10.1016/j.ecolind.2016.07.007

Maniya, K. D., & Bhatt, M. G. (2011). A multi-attribute selection of automated guided vehicle using the AHP/M-GRA technique. *International Journal of Production Research*, *49*(20), 6107–6124. doi:10.1080/00207543.2010.518988

Marafon, A., Ensslin, L., Oliveira, R., & Ensslin, S. (2015). The effectiveness of multi-criteria decision aid methodology. *European Journal of Innovation Management*, *18*(1), 86–109. doi:10.1108/EJIM-10-2013-0106

Mareschal, B. (1986). Stochastic multicriteria decision making and uncertainty. *European Journal of Operational Research*, *26*(1), 58–64. doi:10.1016/0377-2217(86)90159-1

MareschalB. (2013). *Visual PROMETHEE.*

Martin, J. M., Fajardo, W., Blanco, A., & Requena, I. (2003). Constructing linguistic versions for the multicriteria decision support systems preference ranking organization method for enrichment evaluation I and II. *International Journal of Intelligent Systems*, *18*(7), 711–731. doi:10.1002/int.10112

Mathiyazhagan, K., Govindan, K., NoorulHaq, A., & Geng, Y. (2013). An ISM approach for the barrier analysis in implementing green supply chain management. *Journal of Cleaner Production*, *47*, 283–297. doi:10.1016/j.jclepro.2012.10.042

Matsuo, Y., Yanagisawa, A., & Yamashita, Y. (2013). A global energy outlook to 2035 with strategic considerations for Asia and Middle East energy supply and demand interdependencies. *Energy Strategy Reviews*, *2*(1), 79–91. doi:10.1016/j.esr.2013.04.002

McKinsey. (2018). Behavioral science in business: Nudging, debiasing, and managing the irrational mind [Podcast]. Retrieved August 31, 2019, from https://www.mckinsey.com/business-functions/organization/our-insights/behavioral-science-in-business-nudging-debiasing-and-managing-the-irrational-mind

Mehralian, G., Zarenezhad, F., & Rajabzadeh Ghatari, A. (2015). Developing a model for an agile SC in pharmaceutical industry. *International Journal of Pharmaceutical and Healthcare Marketing*, *9*(1), 74–91. doi:10.1108/IJPHM-09-2013-0050

Mendes, L. P. L. (2013). *Análise dos métodos de seleção de fornecedores*. Instituto Superior de Engenharia do Porto.

Mishra, R. K. (2012). Measuring SC efficiency: A DEA approach. *Journal of Operations and SC Management*, *5*(1), 45–69.

Mitkova, V., Mlynarovic, V., & Tus, B. (2007). A performance and risk analysis on the Slovak private pension funds market. *Ekonomický časopis. Journal of Economics*, *3*(55), 232–249.

Miyazaki, M. (2015). A Brief History of Data Analysis. Retrieved from https://www.flydata.com/blog/a-brief-history-of-data-analysis/

Moffett, A., & Sarkar, S. (2006). Incorporating multiple criteria into the design of conservation area networks: A minireview with recommendations. *Diversity & Distributions*, *12*(2), 125–137. doi:10.1111/j.1366-9516.2005.00202.x

Mohammed, I. R., Shankar, R., & Banwet, D. K. (2008). Creating flex-lean-agile value chain by outsourcing: An ISM-based interventional roadmap. *Business Process Management Journal*, *14*(3), 338–389. doi:10.1108/14637150810876670

Mohsen, O., & Fereshteh, N. (2017). An extended VIKOR method based on entropy measure for the failure modes risk assessment – A case study of the geothermal power plant (GPP). *Safety Science*, *92*, 160–172. doi:10.1016/j.ssci.2016.10.006

Morte, R. C. G. (2013). *Modelo De Apoio À Decisão Multicritério Para a Avaliação De Desempenho De Motoristas Numa Empresa Portuguesa De Transporte Rodoviário*. Faculdade de Economia do Porto.

Müller, M., & Seuring, S. (2007). Reducing information technology-based transaction costs in supply chains. *Industrial Management & Data Systems*, *107*(4), 484–500. doi:10.1108/02635570710740652

Muruganantham, G., Vinodh, S., Arun, C. S., & Ramesh, K. (2018). Application of interpretive structural modelling for analysing barriers to total quality management practices implementation in the automotive sector. *Total Quality Management & Business Excellence*, *29*(5-6), 524–545. doi:10.1080/14783363.2016.1213627

Nabeeh, N. A., Smarandache, F., Abdel-Basset, M., El-Ghareeb, H. A., & Aboelfetouh, A. (2019). An Integrated Neutrosophic-TOPSIS Approach and Its Application to Personnel Selection: A New Trend in Brain Processing and Analysis. *IEEE Access: Practical Innovations, Open Solutions*, *7*, 29734–29744. doi:10.1109/ACCESS.2019.2899841

Narayana, A., S., A. Elias, A., & K. Pati, R. (2014). Reverse logistics in the pharmaceuticals industry: A systemic analysis. *International Journal of Logistics Management*, *25*(2), 379–398. doi:10.1108/IJLM-08-2012-0073

Narayana, S. A., Pati, R. K., & Vrat, P. (2012). Research on management issues in the pharmaceutical industry: A literature review. *International Journal of Pharmaceutical and Healthcare Marketing*, *6*(4), 351–375. doi:10.1108/17506121211283235

Nguyen, H.-T., Md Dawal, S. Z., Nukman, Y., Rifai, A., & Aoyama, H. (2016). An Integrated MCDM Model for Conveyor Equipment Evaluation and Selection in an FMC Based on a Fuzzy AHP and Fuzzy ARAS in the Presence of Vagueness. *PLOS ONE*, *11*(4). . pone.0153222 doi:10.1371/journal

Nishat Faisal, M. (2010). Sustainable supply chains: A study of interaction among the enablers. *Business Process Management Journal*, *16*(3), 508–529. doi:10.1108/14637151011049476

Nishat Faisal, M., Banwet, D. K., & Shankar, R. (2006). Supply chain risk mitigation: Modeling the enablers. *Business Process Management Journal*, *12*(4), 535–552. doi:10.1108/14637150610678113

Norman, R. Z. (1965). Structural models: An introduction to the theory of directed graphs.

Nuño, R. (2009). Atención innovadora a las condiciones crónicas: más necesaria que nunca. Revista de Innovación Sanitaria y Atención Integrada, 1-8. Retrieved from https://www.researchgate.net/publication/33544067_Atencion_innovadora_a_las_condiciones_cronicas_mas_necesaria_que_nunca

Ohno, T. (1997). O sistema Toyota de produção: além da produção em larga escala. (Bookman, Ed.). Bookman.

Olson, D. L. (2004). Comparison of weights in TOPSIS models. *Mathematical and Computer Modelling*, *40*(7), 721–727. doi:10.1016/j.mcm.2004.10.003

Ömürbek, N., Eren, H., & Dağ, O. (2017). Entropi-Aras ve Entropi-Moosra yöntemleri ile yaşam kalitesi açısından AB ülkelerinin değerlendirilmesi. *Ömer Halisdemir Üniversitesi İktisadi ve İdari Bilimler Fakültesi Dergisi*, *10*(2), 29-48.

Ömürbek, N., & Eren, H. (2016). Promethee, Moora ve Copras yöntemleri ile oran analizi sonuçlarinin değerlendirilmesi: Bir uygulama. *Mehmet Akif Ersoy Üniversitesi Sosyal Bilimler Enstitüsü Dergisi*, *8*(16), 174–187. doi:10.20875b.69615

Onder, G., & Onder, E. (2015). *Çok kriterli karar verme yöntemleri, Analitik hiyerarşi süreci* (pp. 21–74). Bursa, Turkey: Dora Press.

Opricovic, S. (1998). Multicriteria optimization of civil engineering systems. Faculty of Civil Engineering, Belgrade, 2(1), 5-21.

Opricovic, S. (1998). *Multi-criteria optimization of civil engineering systems*. Belgrade, Serbia: Faculty of Civil Engineering.

Opricovic, S., & Tzeng, G. H. (2004). Compromise solution by MCDM methods: A comparative analysis of VIKOR and TOPSIS. *European Journal of Operational Research*, *156*(2), 445–455. doi:10.1016/S0377-2217(03)00020-1

Opricovic, S., & Tzeng, G. H. (2007). Extended VIKOR Method in Comparison With Other Outranking Methods. *European Journal of Operational Research*, *178*(2), 514–529. doi:10.1016/j.ejor.2006.01.020

Orhan, S., Ozkan, E., & Uysal, S. (2017). Outsourcing of health and safety service case from Turkey a case study joint health and safety units's efficiency. *Journal of Business Science*, *5*(3), 207–234. doi:10.22139/jobs.358810

Ortiz-Barrios, M. A., Kucukaltan, B., Carvajal-Tinoco, D., Neira-Rodado, D., & Jiménez, G. (2017). Strategic hybrid approach for selecting suppliers of high-density polyethylene. *Journal of Multi-Criteria Decision Analysis, 24*(5/6), 296–316. doi:10.1002/mcda.1617

Overview of the R language. Retrieved from https://www.guru99.com/r-programming-introduction-basics.html

Ozfirat, P. M. (2014). Bulanik önceliklendirme metodu ve hata türü ve etkileri analizini birleştiren yeni bir risk analizi yöntemi. *Gazi Üniversitesi Mühendislik-Mimarlık Fakültesi Dergisi, 29*(4), 755–768.

Ozkok, B. A., & Pappalardo, E. (2013). Fuzzy analytic hierarchy process and its application to e-marketplace selection. In P. Papajorgji, A. Guimarães, & M. Guarracino (Eds.), *Enterprise Business Modeling, Optimization Techniques, and Flexible Information Systems* (pp. 26–44). Hershey, PA: IGI Global; doi:10.4018/978-1-4666-3946-1.ch003

Ozsahin, D. U., Uzun, B., Musa, M. S., Şentürk, N., Nurçin, F. V., & Ozsahin, I. (2017). Evaluating nuclear medicine imaging devices using fuzzy PROMETHEE method. *Procedia Computer Science, 120*, 699–705. doi:10.1016/j.procs.2017.11.298

Paksoy, S. (2015). Assessment of Country Indicators with VIKOR Method. *The International Journal of Economic and Social Research, 11*(11), 2.

Panda, B., & Thakur, H. P. (2016). Decentralization and health system performance - a focused review of dimensions, difficulties, and derivatives in India. *BMC Health Services Research*, 1–14. doi:10.118612913-016-1784-9 PMID:28185593

Papageorgiou, L. G., Rotstein, G. E., & Shah, N. (2001). Strategic supply chain optimization for the pharmaceutical industries. *Industrial & Engineering Chemistry Research, 40*(1), 275–286. doi:10.1021/ie990870t

Park, J. H., Gwak, M. G., & Kwun, Y. C. (2011). Linguistic harmonic mean operators and their applications to group decision making. *International Journal of Advanced Manufacturing Technology, 57*(1–4), 411–419. doi:10.100700170-011-3295-5

Park, J. H., Kwun, Y. C., & Koo, J. H. (2011). Dynamic uncertain linguistic weighted harmonic mean operators applied to decision making. In *Proceedings 2011 International Conference on System Science and Engineering, ICSSE 2011* (pp. 101–106). 10.1109/ICSSE.2011.5961882

Parvathi, R., & Malathi, C. (2012). Intuitionistic fuzzy linear optimization. *Notes on Intuitionistic Fuzzy Sets, 18*(1), 48–56.

Patil, S. K., & Kant, R. (2014). A fuzzy AHP-TOPSIS framework for ranking the solutions of knowledge management adoption in supply chain to overcome its barriers. *Expert Systems with Applications, 41*(2), 679–693. doi:10.1016/j.eswa.2013.07.093

Pérez-Domínguez, L., Alvarado-Iniesta, A., Rodríguez-Borbón, I., & Vergara-Villegas, O. (2015). Intuitionistic Fuzzy MOORA for Supplier Selection. *Dyna (Bilbao), 82*(191), 34–41. doi:10.15446/dyna.v82n191.51143

Pfohl, H. C., Gallus, P., & Thomas, D. (2011). Interpretive Structural Modeling of Supply Chain Risks. *International Journal of Physical Distribution & Logistics Management, 41*(9), 839–859. doi:10.1108/09600031111175816

Pinter, U., & Pšunder, I. (2013). Evaluating construction project success with use of the M-TOPSIS method. *Journal of Civil Engineering and Management, 19*(1), 16–23. doi:10.3846/13923730.2012.734849

Poduval, P. S., & Pramod, V. R. (2015). Interpretive Structural Modeling (ISM) and its application in analyzing factors inhibiting implementation of Total Productive Maintenance (TPM). *International Journal of Quality & Reliability Management, 32*(3), 308–331. doi:10.1108/IJQRM-06-2013-0090

Podvezko, V. (2009). Application of AHP technique. *Journal of Business Economics and Management*, *10*(2), 181–189. doi:10.3846/1611-1699.2009.10.181-189

Prakash, C., & Barua, M. K. (2016). A combined MCDM approach for evaluation and selection of third-party reverse logistics partner for Indian electronics industry. *Sustainable Production and Consumption*, *7*, 66–78. doi:10.1016/j.spc.2016.04.001

Promentilla, M. A. B., Janairo, J. I. B., Yu, D. E. C., Pausta, C. M. J., Beltran, A. B., Huelgas-Orbecido, A. P., ... Tan, R. R. (2018). A stochastic fuzzy multicriteria decision-making model for optimal selection of clean technologies. *Journal of Cleaner Production*, *183*, 1289–1299. doi:10.1016/j.jclepro.2018.02.183

Punniyamoorthy, M., Thamaraiselvan, N., & Manikandan, L. (2013). Assessment of SC risk: Scale development and validation. Benchmarking. *International Journal (Toronto, Ont.)*, *20*(1), 79–105.

Puri, J., & Prasad Yadav, S. (2015). Intuitionistic fuzzy data envelopment analysis: An application to the banking sector in India. *Expert Systems with Applications*, *42*(11), 4982–4998. doi:10.1016/j.eswa.2015.02.014

Purohit, J. K., Mittal, M. L., Mittal, S., & Sharma, M. K. (2016). Interpretive structural modeling-based framework for mass customisation enablers: An Indian footwear case. *Production Planning and Control*, *27*(9), 774–786. doi:10.1080/09537287.2016.1166275

Queiruga, D., Walther, G., Gonzalez-Benito, J., & Spengler, T. (2008). Evaluation of sites for the location of WEEE recycling plants in Spain. *Waste Management (New York, N.Y.)*, *28*(1), 181–190. doi:10.1016/j.wasman.2006.11.001 PMID:17198752

Qureshi, M. N., Kumar, D., & Kumar, P. (2007). Modeling the logistics outsourcing relationship variables to enhance shippers' productivity and competitiveness in logistical supply chain. *International Journal of Productivity and Performance Management*, *56*(8), 689–714. doi:10.1108/17410400710833001

R - Binary Files. Retrieved from https://www.tutorialspoint.com/r/r_binary_files.htm

Raj, T., & Attri, R. (2010). Quantifying barriers to implementing total quality management (TQM). *European Journal of Industrial Engineering*, *4*(3), 308–335. doi:10.1504/EJIE.2010.033333

Raj, T., Shankar, R., & Suhaib, M. (2007). An ISM Approach for Modelling the Enablers of Flexible Manufacturing System: The Case for India. *International Journal of Production Research*, *46*(24), 1–30.

Raj, T., Shankar, R., & Suhaib, M. (2008). An ISM approach for modelling the enablers of flexible manufacturing system: The case for India. *International Journal of Production Research*, *46*(24), 6883–6912. doi:10.1080/00207540701429926

Rantanen, J., & Fedotov, I. A. (1995). *ILO Standards, principles and approaches in occupational health services*. Retrieved from https://www.ilo.org/safework/info/publications/WCMS_110439/lang--en/index.htm

Rao, D. A., Sai, V. N., & Babu, K. P. (2017). An Integrated approach using VIKOR and Entropy methods for a Supplier selection problem. [IJIET]. *International Journal of Innovations in Engineering and Technology*, *8*(3), 1–9.

Ravikumar, M. M., Marimuthu, K., & Parthiban, P. (2015). Evaluating lean implementation performance in Indian MSMEs using ISM and AHP models. *International Journal of Services and Operations Management*, *22*(1), 21–39. doi:10.1504/IJSOM.2015.070881

Ravi, V., & Shankar, R. (2005). Analysis of interactions among the barriers of reverse logistics. *Technological Forecasting and Social Change*, *72*(8), 1011–1029. doi:10.1016/j.techfore.2004.07.002

Ravi, V., Shankar, R., & Tiwari, M. K. (2005). Productivity improvement of a computer hardware supply chain. *International Journal of Productivity and Performance Management*, *54*(4), 239–255. doi:10.1108/17410400510593802

Reddy, M. R. S., Jigeesh, N., & Kumar, P. (2017). The Integration of Project Management with SC Management in Indian Pharmaceutical Projects. *IUP Journal of SC Management*, *14*(4), 61–71.

Rezaei-kelidbari, H. R., Homayounfar, M., & Foumani, S. F. A. (2016). A Combined Group EA-PROMETHEE Method for a Supplier Selection Problem. *Iranian Journal of Optimization*, *8*(2), 87–100.

Rich, M. (1999). The PACE model: Description and impressions of a capitated model of long-term care for the elderly. *Care Management Journals*, *1*(1), 62–70. doi:10.1891/1521-0987.1.1.62 PMID:10835798

Rodrigues Lima-Junior, F., & Ribeiro Carpinetti, L. C. (2016). A multicriteria approach based on fuzzy QFD for choosing criteria for supplier selection. *Computers & Industrial Engineering*, *101*, 269–285. doi:10.1016/j.cie.2016.09.014

Romero, M., & Biswas, D. (2016). Healthy-Left, Unhealthy-Right: Can Displaying Healthy Items to the Left (versus Right) of Unhealthy Items Nudge Healthier Choices? *The Journal of Consumer Research*, *43*(1), 103–112. doi:10.1093/jcr/ucw008

Rostampour, S. (2012). An application of TOPSIS for ranking internet web browsers. *Decision Science Letters*, *1*(2), 53–58. doi:10.5267/j.dsl.2012.09.001

Roszkowska, E. (2013). Rank ordering criteria weighting methods – a comparative overview. *Optimum Studia Ekonomiczne Nr*, *5*(65), 14–33. doi:10.15290/ose.2013.05.65.02

Rouse, M. (2019). Data analytics (DA). Retrieved from https://searchdatamanagement.techtarget.com/definition/data-analytics

Rouyendegh, B. D. (2018). The Intuitionistic Fuzzy ELECTRE model The Intuitionistic Fuzzy ELECTRE model. *International Journal of Management Science and Engineering Management*, (September 2017), 1–7. doi:10.1080/17509653.2017.1349625

Roy, B. (1989). *The outranking approach and the foundations of ELECTRE methods*. University of Paris-Dauphine, Document Du Lamsade.

Roy, B. (1991). The outranking approach and the foundations of ELECTRE methods. *Theory and Decision*, *31*(1), 49–73. doi:10.1007/BF00134132

Roy, B., & Vincke, P. (1981). Multicriteria analysis: Survey and new directions. *European Journal of Operational Research*, *8*(3), 207–218. doi:10.1016/0377-2217(81)90168-5

Roy, T., & Dutta, R. K. (2019). Integrated fuzzy AHP and fuzzy TOPSIS methods for multi-objective optimization of electro discharge machining process. *Soft Computing*, *23*(13), 5053–5063. doi:10.100700500-018-3173-2

Saaty, R. W. (1987). The analytic hierarchy process—What it is and how it is used. *Mathematical Modelling*, *9*(3–5), 161–176. doi:10.1016/0270-0255(87)90473-8

Saaty, T. L. (1980). *The analytic hierarchy process*. New York: McGraw Hill.

Saaty, T. L. (1980). *The Analytic Hierarchy Process*. New York: McGraw-Hill.

Saaty, T. L. (1986). Axiomatic foundation of the analytic hierarchy process. *Management Science*, *32*(7), 841–855. doi:10.1287/mnsc.32.7.841

Saaty, T. L. (1990). How to make a decision: The analytic hierarchy process. *European Journal of Operational Research, 48*(1), 9–26. doi:10.1016/0377-2217(90)90057-I

Saaty, T. L. (1991). *Método de Análise Hierárquica. Tradução e Revisão por Wainer da Silveira e Silva.* São Paulo, Brazil: McGraw-Hill.

Saaty, T. L. (2000). *Fundamentals of decision making and priority theory with the analytic hierarchy process* (Vol. 6). RWS Publications.

Saaty, T. L. (2008). Decision making with the analytic hierarchy process. *International Journal of Services Sciences, 1*(1), 83. doi:10.1504/IJSSCI.2008.017590

Sachdeva, A., Kumar, D., & Kumar, P. (2009). Multi-factor failure mode critically analysis using TOPSIS. *Journal of Industrial Engineering International, 5*(8), 1–9.

Saeedi, S., & Malek, M. R. (2008). An intuitionistic fuzzy analytic network process for parking site selection Intuitionistic Fuzzy Analytical Network Process (IF-ANP) for Spatial Multi Criteria Decision Making under Uncertainty, (August 2015). doi:10.1142/9789812799470

Sahney, S. (2008). Critical success factors in online retail–an application of quality function deployment and interpretive structural modeling. *International Journal of Business and Information, 3*(1).

Sahney, S., Banwet, D. K., & Karunes, S. (2008). An integrated framework of indices for quality management in education: A faculty perspective. *The TQM Journal, 20*(5), 502–519. doi:10.1108/17542730810898467

Said, A., & Torra, V. (2019). Data Science: An Introduction. In A. Said, & V. Torra (Eds.), *Data Science in Practice. Studies in Big Data* (Vol. 46). Cham, Switzerland: Springer. doi:10.1007/978-3-319-97556-6_1

Salimifard, K., Abbaszadeh, M. A., & Ghorbangpur, A. (2010). Interpretive Structural Modeling of Critical Success Factors in Banking Process Re-Engineering. *International Journal of Business Research Papers, 6*(2), 95–103.

Samantra, C., Datta, S., & Mahapatra, S. S. (2017). A Risk-based decision support framework for selection of appropriate safety measure system for underground coal mines. *International Journal of Injury Control and Safety Promotion, 24*(1), 54–68. doi:10.1080/17457300.2015.1061561 PMID:26176824

Samson, A. (2014). The Behavioral Economics Guide 2014 (1st ed.).

Sarhan, J. G., Hu, X., & Xia, B. (2016, December). An overview of the application of Interpretive Structural Modeling (ISM) in construction management research. In *Proceedings of the International Conference on Sustainable Built Environment SBE16* (pp. 316-319).

Sarkar, S., Pratihar, D. K., & Sarkar, B. (2018). An integrated fuzzy multiple criteria supplier selection approach and its application in a welding company. *Journal of Manufacturing Systems, 46*, 163–178. doi:10.1016/j.jmsy.2017.12.004

Sawant, V. B., Mohite, S. S., & Patil, R. (2011). *A Decision-Making Methodology for Automated Guided Vehicle Selection Problem Using a Preference Selection Index Method.* 176–181. Berlin, Germany: Springer-Verlag.

Saxena, J. P., Sushil, & Vrat, P. (2006). Policy and strategy formulation: An application of flexible systems methodology. GIFT Pub.

Saxena, D., Singh, S., & Verma, K. (2010). Application of computational intelligence in emerging power systems. *International Journal of Engineering Science and Technology, 2*(3), 1–7. doi:10.4314/ijest.v2i3.59166

Saxena, J. P., & Vrat, P. (1990). Impact of indirect relationships in classification of variables—A micmac analysis for energy conservation. *Systems Research, 7*(4), 245–253. doi:10.1002res.3850070404

Schinasi, G. J. (2004). Defining Financial Stability.

Selevan, J., Kindermann, D., Pines, J., & Fields, W. (2015). What Accountable Care Organizations Can Learn from Kaiser Permanente California's Acute Care Strategy. *Population Health Management, 233-236.* doi:10.1089/pop.2014.0157 PMID:25856631

Şengül, Ü., & Eren, M. (2016). Selection of digital marketing tools using fuzzy AHP-fuzzy TOPSIS. In A. Kumar, & M. Dash (Eds.), *Fuzzy optimization and multi-criteria decision making in digital marketing* (pp. 97–126). Hershey, PA: IGI Global; doi:10.4018/978-1-4666-8808-7.ch005

Sent, E. (2004). Behavioral Economics: How Psychology Made Its (Limited) Way Back Into Economics. *History of Political Economy, 36*(4), 735–760. doi:10.1215/00182702-36-4-735

Senvar, O., Tuzkaya, G., & Kahraman, C. (2014). Multi criteria supplier selection using fuzzy PROMETHEE method. In *Supply chain management under fuzziness* (pp. 21–34). Berlin, Germany: Springer. doi:10.1007/978-3-642-53939-8_2

Seow, Y., & Rahimifard, S. (2011). A framework for modelling energy consumption within manufacturing systems. *CIRP Journal of Manufacturing Science and Technology, 4*(3), 258–264. doi:10.1016/j.cirpj.2011.03.007

Shahabadkar, P. (2012). Deployment of Interpretive Stuctural Modelling Methodology in Supply Chain Management- An Overview. *International Journal of Industrial Engineering & Production Research, 23*(3), 195–205.

Shah, N. (2004). Pharmaceutical supply chains: Key issues and strategies for optimisation. *Computers & Chemical Engineering, 28*(6-7), 929–941. doi:10.1016/j.compchemeng.2003.09.022

Shahrabi, M., & Shojaei, A. A. (2014). Application of FMEA and AHP in Lean Maintenance. *International Journal of Modern Engineering Sciences, 3*(1), 61–73.

Shanian, A., & Savadogo, O. (2006). TOPSIS multiple-criteria decision support analysis for material selection of metallic bipolar plates for polymer electrolyte fuel cell. *Journal of Power Sources, 159*(2), 1095–1104. doi:10.1016/j.jpowsour.2005.12.092

Shannon, E. (1948). A mathematical theory of communication. *The Bell System Technical Journal, 27*(3), 379–423. doi:10.1002/j.1538-7305.1948.tb01338.x

Sharma, H. D., Gupta, A. D., & Sushil. (1995). The objectives of waste management in India: A futures inquiry. *Technological Forecasting and Social Change, 48*(3), 285–309. doi:10.1016/0040-1625(94)00066-6

Sharma, M., Tiwari, P., & Chaubey, D. S. (2016). Summarizing factors of customer experience and building a structural model using total interpretive structural modelling technology. *Global Business Review, 17*(3), 730–741. doi:10.1177/0972150916630825

Sharma, R., & Garg, S. (2010). Interpretive structural modelling of enablers for improving the performance of automobile service centre. *International Journal of Services Operations and Informatics, 5*(4), 351–372. doi:10.1504/IJSOI.2010.037003

Sharma, V., Dixit, A. R., & Qadri, M. A. (2016). Modeling lean implementation for manufacturing sector. *Journal of Modelling in Management, 11*(2), 405–426. doi:10.1108/JM2-05-2014-0040

Sharma, V., Dixit, A. R., Qadri, M. A., & Kumar, S. (2015). An interpretive hierarchical model for lean implementation in machine tool sector. *International Journal of Productivity and Quality Management, 15*(3), 381–406. doi:10.1504/IJPQM.2015.068475

Shaverdi, M., Ramezani, I., & Rostamy, A. A. (2016). Multi-criteria decision-making models for sustainable and green supply chain management based on fuzzy approach. In A. Kumar, & M. Dash (Eds.), *Fuzzy optimization and multi-criteria decision making in digital marketing* (pp. 291–307). Hershey, PA: IGI Global; doi:10.4018/978-1-4666-8808-7.ch013

Shemshadi, A., Shirazi, H., Toreihi, M., & Tarokh, M. J. (2011). A fuzzy VIKOR method for supplier selection based on entropy measure for objective weighting. *Expert Systems with Applications*, *38*(10), 12160–12167. doi:10.1016/j.eswa.2011.03.027

Shih, H. S., Shyur, H. J., & Lee, E. S. (2007). An extension of TOPSIS for group decision making. *Mathematical and Computer Modelling*, *45*(7), 801–813. doi:10.1016/j.mcm.2006.03.023

Shiraz, S. E., Şengül, Ü., & Eren, M. (2013). Ranking of Countries According to Their Level of Development with the Vikor and Topsis Using Entropy. *6th International Conference of Iranian Operations Research Society, Research Center of Operations Research.*

Shove, E. (2010). Beyond the ABC: Climate Change Policy and Theories of Social Change. *Environment and Planning A. Economy and Space*, *42*(6), 1273–1285. doi:10.1068/a42282

Siemens, A. G. (2012). *Power Engineering Guide*. Siemens; doi:10.100710342-012-0675-9

Silvia, C., Antonella, C., & Enea, M. (2018). The ELECTRE I method to support the FMECA. *IFAC-PapersOnLine*, *51*(11), 459–464. doi:10.1016/j.ifacol.2018.08.361

SimilarWeb. (2019). Retrieved from https://www.similarweb.com/website/

Simon, H. (1990). *Reason in Human Affairs*. Redwood City, CA: Stanford University Press.

Simşir, F., Demir, H. İ., & Azdemir, S. (n.d.). Demir çelik sektöründe hibrid DEMATEL ve TOPSIS-ELECTRE yöntemleri ile hata türleri ve etkileri analizi. *Akademik Platform Mühendislik ve Fen Bilimleri Dergisi, 6*(3), 22-34.

Singh, K., & Misra, S. (2018). Theory of Constraints for Managing Downstream SC in Indian FMCG Sector: A Literature Review. *Journal of SC Management Systems*, *7*(1).

Singh, M. D., & Kant, R. (2008). Knowledge management barriers: An interpretive structural modeling approach. *International Journal of Management Science and Engineering Management*, *3*(2), 141–150. doi:10.1080/17509653.2008.10671042

Singh, M. D., Shankar, R., Narain, R., & Agarwal, A. (2003). An interpretive structural modeling of knowledge management in engineering industries. *Journal of Advances in Management Research*, *1*(1), 28–40. doi:10.1108/97279810380000356

Singh, R. K., Garg, S. K., & Deshmukh, S. G. (2007). Interpretive structural modelling of factors for improving competitiveness of SMEs. *International Journal of Productivity and Quality Management*, *2*(4), 423–440. doi:10.1504/IJPQM.2007.013336

Singh, R. K., Garg, S. K., Deshmukh, S. G., & Kumar, M. (2007). Modelling of critical success factors for implementation of AMTs. *Journal of Modelling in Management*, *2*(3), 232–250. doi:10.1108/17465660710834444

Singh, R. K., Gunasekaran, A., & Kumar, P. (2018). Third party logistics (3PL) selection for cold chain management: A fuzzy AHP and fuzzy TOPSIS approach. *Annals of Operations Research*, *267*(1-2), 531–553. doi:10.100710479-017-2591-3

Singh, R. K., Sharma, H. O., & Garg, S. K. (2010). Interpretive Structural Modelling for Selection of Best Supply Chain Practices. *International Journal of Business Performance and Supply Chain Modelling*, *2*(3-4), 237–257. doi:10.1504/IJBPSCM.2010.036201

Sisman, B. (2017). Hata türü ve etkileri analizinde bulanik AHP ve bulanik VIKOR yöntemleri ile otomotiv sektöründe risk değerlendirmesi-risk evaluating by fuzzy ahp and fuzzy vikor methods in failure mode and effects analysis for automotive sector. *Mehmet Akif Ersoy Üniversitesi Sosyal Bilimler Enstitüsü Dergisi*, *9*(18), 234–250.

Sivaprakasam, R., Selladurai, V., & Sasikumar, P. (2015). Implementation of interpretive structural modelling methodology as a strategic decision-making tool in a Green Supply Chain Context. *Annals of Operations Research*, *233*(1), 423–448. doi:10.100710479-013-1516-z

Sivilevicius, H. (2011). Application of expert evaluation method to determine the importance of operating asphalt mixing plant quality criteria rank correlation. *The Baltic Journal of Road and Bridge Engineering*, *6*(1), 48–58. doi:10.3846/bjrbe.2011.07

Snoddon, J. (2010). *Case management of long-term conditions. Principles and practice for nurses*. Oxford, UK: Wiley-Blackwell. doi:10.1002/9781444319866

Song, W., Ming, X., Wu, Z., & Zhu, B. (2013). Failure modes and effects analysis using integrated weight-based fuzzy TOPSIS. *International Journal of Computer Integrated Manufacturing*, *26*(12), 1172–1186. doi:10.1080/0951192X.2013.785027

Sonmez, M. (2006). *A review and critique of supplier selection process and practices*. Loughborough University.

Soto, C. M. A., Liern, V., & Pérez-Gladish, B. (2018). Normalization in TOPSIS-based approaches with data of different nature: Application to the ranking of mathematical videos. *Annals of Operations Research. Springer, 2018*. doi:10.100710479-018-2945-5

Strandberg, C. (2009). *The role of human resource management in corporate social responsibility issue brief and roadmap. Report for Industry Canada*. Burnaby, BC: Strandberg Consulting.

Suh, Y., Park, Y., & Kang, D. (2019). Evaluating mobile services using integrated weighting approach and fuzzy VIKOR. *PLoS One*, *14*(9). doi:10.1371/journal.pone.0222312 PMID:31487317

Sunstein, C. (2014). *Nudging: A Very Short Guide*. SSRN Electronic Journal; doi:10.2139srn.2499658

Sunstein, C. R., & Thaler, R. H. (2003). *Libertarian Paternalism Is Not An Oxymoron*. SSRN Electronic Journal; doi:10.2139srn.405940

Susarla, N., & Karimi, I. A. (2012). Integrated supply chain planning for multinational pharmaceutical enterprises. *Computers & Chemical Engineering*, *42*, 168–177. doi:10.1016/j.compchemeng.2012.03.002

Sushil, A. (2012). Interpreting the Interpretive Structural Model. *Global Journal of Flexible Systems Management*, *13*(2), 87–106. doi:10.100740171-012-0008-3

Tableau Software. Retrieved from https://en.wikipedia.org/wiki/Tableau_Software

Tae, P., Lee, W., & Yang, Z. (2018). *Multi Criteria Decision Making in Maritime Studies and Logistics*. Springer.

Taha, H. A. (1997). *Operations Research*. Fayetteville: Pearson Education.

Talib, F., Rahman, Z., & Qureshi, M. N. (2011). Analysis of interaction among the barriers to total quality management implementation using interpretive structural modeling approach. Benchmarking. *International Journal (Toronto, Ont.)*, *18*(4), 563–587.

Talib, F., Rahman, Z., & Qureshi, M. N. (2011). Analysis of interaction among the barriers to total quality management implementation using interpretive structural modeling approach. *Benchmarking: An International Journal*, *18*(4), 563–587. doi:10.1108/14635771111147641

Tan, Y., Shen, L., Langston, C., & Liu, Y. (2010). Construction project selection using fuzzy TOPSIS approach. *Journal of Modelling in Management*, *5*(3), 302–315. doi:10.1108/17465661011092669

Taşabat, E. S., Cinemre, N., & Şen, S. (2015). Financial Performance Evaluation of Turkish Deposit Banks By Application of Different Weighting Techniques in Multi-Criteria Decision Making Methods. *Social Sciences Research Journal*, 4(2), 96-110 (June 2015).

Taşabat, S. E., Cinemre, N., & Şen, S. (2005). Farklı Ağırlıklandırma Tekniklerinin Denendiği Çok Kriterli Karar Verme Yöntemleri İle Türkiye'deki Mevduat Bankalarının Mali Performanslarının Değerlendirilmesi. *Social Sciences Research Journal*, *4*(2), 96-110.

Taşabat, E. S. (2019). A novel Multi Criteri Decision Making Method: DSC TOPSIS. *Mathematical Problems in Engineering*.

Taşabat, E. S. (2019). A Novel Multi Criteria Decision Making Method: DSC TOPSIS. *Mathematical Problems in Engineering*, *2019*.

Taşabat, E. S., Aydın, O., & Sayi, H. (2018). *Multi Criteria Decision Making Methods*. Gece Akademi Press.

Tay, K. M., & Lim, C. P. (2006). Application of fuzzy inference techniques to FMEA. In *Applied soft computing technologies: The challenge of complexity* (pp. 161–171). Berlin, Germany: Springer. doi:10.1007/3-540-31662-0_13

Taylan, O., Bafail, A. O., Abdulaal, R. M. S., & Kabli, M. R. (2014). Construction projects selection and risk assessment by fuzzy AHP and fuzzy TOPSIS methodologies. *Applied Soft Computing*, *17*, 105–116. doi:10.1016/j.asoc.2014.01.003

Temucin, T., Tozan, H., Vayvay, O., Valiček, J., & Harničarova, M. (2014). A fuzzy-based decision model for nontraditional machining process selection. *International Journal of Advanced Manufacturing Technology*, *70*(9-12), 2275–2282. doi:10.100700170-013-5474-z

Terrientes, L. M. D. V. (2015). *Hierarchical outranking methods for multi-criteria decision aiding*. Universitat Rovira i Virgili.

Thakkar, J., Deshmukh, S. G., Gupta, A. D., & Shankar, R. (2005, January). Selection of third-party logistics (3PL): A hybrid approach using interpretive structural modeling (ISM) and analytic network process (ANP). In *Supply Chain Forum*. Taylor & Francis. *International Journal (Toronto, Ont.)*, *6*(1), 32–46.

Thakkar, J., Deshmukh, S. G., Gupta, A. D., & Shankar, R. (2007). Development of a balanced scorecard. *International Journal of Productivity and Performance Management*.

Thakkar, J., Kanda, A., & Deshmukh, S. G. (2008). Interpretuve Structural Modelling (ISM) of IT-Enablers for Indian Manufacturing SMEs. *Information Management & Computer Security*, *16*(2), 113–136. doi:10.1108/09685220810879609

Thakkar, J., Kanda, A., & Deshmukh, S. G. (2013). SC issues in SMEs: Select insights from cases of Indian origin. *Production Planning and Control*, *24*(1), 47–71. doi:10.1080/09537287.2011.599119

Thaler, R. H. (2015). The Power of Nudges, for Good and Bad. *The New York Times*.

Thaler, R., Sunstein, C., & Balz, J. (2012). Choice Architecture. In E. Sharif, *The Behavioral Foundations of Public Policy*. Retrieved from https://papers.ssrn.com/sol3/papers.cfm?abstract_id=2536504

Thaler, R. H., & Benartzi, S. (2004). Save More Tomorrow™: Using Behavioral Economics to Increase Employee Saving. *Journal of Political Economy*, *112*(S1), S164–S187. doi:10.1086/380085

Thaler, R. H., & Sunstein, C. R. (2009). *Nudge: Improving Decisions about Health, Wealth, and Happiness*. Penguin Books.

Thanki, S., Govindan, K., & Thakkar, J. (2016). An investigation on lean-green implementation practices in indian SMEs using analytical hierarchy process (AHP) Approach. *Journal of Cleaner Production, 135*, 284–295. doi:10.1016/j.jclepro.2016.06.105

The History of the Evolution of Business Analytics. (2018). Retrieved from https://www.cyfe.com/blog/history-evolution-business-analytics/

Thirupathi, R. M., & Vinodh, S. (2016). Application of interpretive structural modelling and structural equation modelling for analysis of sustainable manufacturing factors in Indian automotive component sector. *International Journal of Production Research, 54*(22), 6661–6682. doi:10.1080/00207543.2015.1126372

Tian, G., Zhang, H., Feng, Y., Jia, H., Zhang, C., Jiang, Z., ... Li, P. (2017). Operation patterns analysis of automotive components remanufacturing industry development in China. *Journal of Cleaner Production, 164*, 1363–1375. doi:10.1016/j.jclepro.2017.07.028

Ting, K. (2017, July 1). A modified TOPSIS with a different ranking index. *European Journal of Operational Research, 260*(1), 152–160. doi:10.1016/j.ejor.2016.11.052

Torra, V. (2000). The WOWA operator and the interpolation function W*: Chen and Otto's interpolation method revisited. *Fuzzy Sets and Systems, 113*(3), 389–396. doi:10.1016/S0165-0114(98)00040-2

Torra, V. (2010). Hesitant fuzzy sets. *International Journal of Intelligent Systems, 25*(6), 529–539.

Tripathy, S., Sahu, S., & Ray, P. K. (2013). Interpretive Structural Modelling for Critical Success Factors of R&D Performance in Indian Manufacturing Firms. *Journal of Modelling in Management, 8*(2), 212–240. doi:10.1108/JM2-11-2011-0061

Tsaura, S. H., Chang, T. Y., & Yen, C. H. (2002). The evaluation of airline service quality by fuzzy MCDM. *Tourism Management, 23*(2), 107–115. doi:10.1016/S0261-5177(01)00050-4

Türkiye Bankalar Birliği Seçilmiş Rasyolar 2016 Raporu. (2017, December 1). Retrieved from http://www.tbb.org.tr/Content/Upload/istatistiki raporlar/tumu/903/Secilmis_Rasyolar-2016.zip

Tuzkaya, G., Ozgen, D., & Gulsun, B. (2011). Malzeme taşıma sistemi alternatiflerinin değerlendirilmesinde bulanık-Promethee yaklaşımı. *Doğuş Üniversitesi Dergisi, 12*(1), 144–155. doi:10.31671/dogus.2019.157

Tversky, A., & Kahneman, D. (1979). Intuitive Prediction: Biases and Corrective Procedures. *TIMS Studies In Management Science, 12*, 313–327.

Tzeng, G.-H., & Huang, J.-J. (2011). *Multiple Attribute Decision Making: Methods and Applications*. Chapman and Hall/CRC. doi:10.1201/b11032

Ulengin, F., Topcu, Y. I., & Sahin, S. Ö. (2001). An integrated decision aid system for Bosphorus water-crossing problem. *European Journal of Operational Research, 134*(1), 179–192. doi:10.1016/S0377-2217(00)00247-2

Vahdani, B., Salimi, M., & Charkhchian, M. (2015). A new FMEA method by integrating fuzzy belief structure and TOPSIS to improve risk evaluation process. *International Journal of Advanced Manufacturing Technology, 77*(1-4), 357–368. doi:10.100700170-014-6466-3

Vaidya, O. S., & Kumar, S. (2006). Analytic hierarchy process: An overview of applications. *European Journal of Operational Research, 169*(1), 1–29. doi:10.1016/j.ejor.2004.04.028

Vaillancourt, K., & Waaub, J. P. (2004). Equity in international greenhouse gases abatement scenarios: A multicriteria approach. *European Journal of Operational Research, 153*(2), 489–505. doi:10.1016/S0377-2217(03)00170-X

Valipour Parkouhi, S., & Safaei Ghadikolaei, A. (2017). A resilience approach for supplier selection: Using Fuzzy Analytic Network Process and grey VIKOR techniques. *Journal of Cleaner Production, 161*, 431–451. doi:10.1016/j.jclepro.2017.04.175

Van Der Heijden, J., & Kosters, M. (2019). From mechanism to virtue: evaluating Nudge-theory. Retrieved 29 September 2019, from https://openresearch-repository.anu.edu.au/bitstream/1885/71637/8/01_Kosters_From_Mechanism_to_Virtue_2015.pdf

Van Deun, H., Van Acker, W., Fobe, E., & Brans, M. (2019). Nudging in Public Policy and Public Management: A scoping review of the literature. Retrieved 30 September 2019, from https://www.psa.ac.uk/sites/default/files/conference/papers/2018/VanDeun_vanAcker_Fob%C3%A9_Br

Vats, A. (2019). Concept Note on Auto Enrolment for increase in pension coverage in India. Retrieved September 29, 2019, from https://www.pfrda.org.in/writereaddata/links/enrolment12348adc6a2-38d3-417f-aaa5-6dbe40a0769b.pdf

Venkat, T. (2014). What is the future of data science? Retrieved from https://www.quora.com/What-is-the-future-of-data-science-1

Verma, A., Seth, N., & Singhal, N. (2011). Enablers of Supply Chain Competitiveness: An Interpretve Structural Modelling Approach. *International Journal of Value Chain Management, 5*(3-4), 212–231. doi:10.1504/IJVCM.2011.043227

Verma, A., Seth, N., & Singhal, N. (2018). Application of Interpretive Structural Modelling to establish Interrelationships among the Enablers of Supply Chain Competitiveness. *Materials Today: Proceedings, 5*(2), 4818–4823.

Vishwakarma, V., Prakash, C., & Barua, M. K. (2016). Modeling the barriers of Indian Pharmaceutical SC using fuzzy AHP. *International Journal of Operational Research.*

Vommi, V. B. (2017). TOPSIS with statistical distances: A new approach to MADM. *Decision Science Letters, 6*, 49–66. doi:10.5267/j.dsl.2016.8.001

Vries, A. & Meys, J. (2015). R for Dummies. *Wiley publication.*

Wagner, E. H. (2011). Counterpoint: chronic illness and primary care. Medical care, 49(11), 973-975.

Wagner, E. H. (2019). Organizing Care for Patients With Chronic Illness Revisited. Milbank Quarterly Classics, 659-664. doi:10.1111/1468-0009.12416

Walker, H., Di Sisto, L., & McBain, D. (2008). Drivers and barriers to environmental supply chain management practices: Lessons from the public and private sectors. *Journal of Purchasing and Supply Management, 14*(1), 69–85. doi:10.1016/j.pursup.2008.01.007

Wallace, P. (2005a). The Care Management Institute: Making the Right Thing Easier to Do. *The Permanente Journal*, 56-57. doi:10.7812/TPP/05-026

Wallace, P. (2005). Physician involvement in disease management as part of the CCM. *Health Care Financing Review*, 19–31. Retrieved from https://www.ncbi.nlm.nih.gov/pmc/articles/PMC4194903/ PMID:17288075

Waller, R. J. (1980). Contextual relations and mathematical relations in interpretive structural modeling. *IEEE Transactions on Systems, Man, and Cybernetics, 10*(3), 143–145. doi:10.1109/TSMC.1980.4308451

Wang, J. J., Jing, Y. Y., Zhang, C. F., & Zhao, J. H. (2009). Review on multi-criteria decision analysis aid in sustainable energy decision-making. *Renewable & Sustainable Energy Reviews, 13*(9), 2263–2278. doi:10.1016/j.rser.2009.06.021

Wang, J. W., Cheng, C. H., & Huang, K. C. (2009). Fuzzy hierarchical TOPSIS for supplier selection. *Applied Soft Computing, 9*(1), 377–386. doi:10.1016/j.asoc.2008.04.014

Wang, T. C., & Lee, H. D. (2009). Developing a fuzzy TOPSIS approach based on subjective weights and objective weights. *Expert Systems with Applications*, *36*(5), 8980–8985. doi:10.1016/j.eswa.2008.11.035

Wang, W. P. (2010). A fuzzy linguistic computing approach to supplier evaluation. *Applied Mathematical Modelling*, *34*(10), 3130–3141. doi:10.1016/j.apm.2010.02.002

Wang, Y. M., Chin, K. S., Poon, G. K. K., & Yang, J. B. (2009). Risk evaluation in failure mode and effects analysis using fuzzy weighted geometric mean. *Expert Systems with Applications*, *36*(2), 1195–1207. doi:10.1016/j.eswa.2007.11.028

Wan, S. P., Wang, Q. Y., & Dong, J. Y. (2013). The extended VIKOR method for multi-attribute group decision making with triangular intuitionistic fuzzy numbers. *Knowledge-Based Systems*, *52*, 65–77. doi:10.1016/j.knosys.2013.06.019

Warfield, J. N. (1974). Developing interconnection matrices in structural modeling. *IEEE Transactions on Systems, Man, and Cybernetics*, *SMC-4*(1), 81–87. doi:10.1109/TSMC.1974.5408524

Warfield, J. N. (1974). Developing subsystem matrices in structural modeling. *IEEE Transactions on Systems, Man, and Cybernetics*, *SMC-4*(1), 74–80. doi:10.1109/TSMC.1974.5408523

Warfield, J. N. (1974). *Structuring Complex Systems. Monograph No. 4*. Columbus, OH: Battelle Memorial Institute.

Warfield, J. N. (1976). *Societal systems*. Planning, Policy, and Complexity.

Warfield, J. N. (1994). *Science of generic design: managing complexity through systems design*. Iowa State Press.

Warfield, J. N. (2003). *The mathematics of structure*. AJAR Publishing.

Warfield, J. N., & Staley, S. M. (1996). Structural thinking: Organizing complexity through disciplined activity. *Systems Research*, *13*(1), 47–67. doi:10.1002/(SICI)1099-1735(199603)13:1<47::AID-SRES27>3.0.CO;2-A

Watson, R. (1978). Interpretive Structural Modelling-A Useful Tool for Worth Assessment? *Technological Forecasting and Social Change*, *11*(2), 165–185. doi:10.1016/0040-1625(78)90028-8

Wei, G.-W. (2011). Gray relational analysis method for intuitionistic fuzzy multiple attribute decision making. *Expert Systems with Applications*, *38*(9), 11671–11677. doi:10.1016/j.eswa.2011.03.048

Wetzstein, A., Hartmann, E., Benton, W. C. Jr, & Hohenstein, N.-O. (2016). A systematic assessment of supplier selection literature – State-of-the-art and future scope. *International Journal of Production Economics*, *182*, 304–323. doi:10.1016/j.ijpe.2016.06.022

What is Tableau? Uses and Applications. Retrieved from https://www.guru99.com/what-is-tableau.html

Womack, J. P., & Jones, D. T. (1994). From lean production to the lean enterprise. *Harvard Business Review*, *72*(2), 93–103.

World Development Indicators. The Story. (n.d.). Retrieved from http://datatopics.worldbank.org/world-development-indicators/stories/world-development-indicators-the-story.html

World Health Organization - WHO. (2007). Decentralization in health care. Strategies and outcomes. New York: McGraw-Hill. Retrieved from http://www.euro.who.int/en/publications/abstracts/decentralization-in-health-care.-strategies-and-outcomes-2007

Wu, H., & Niu, D. (2017). Study on influence factors of electric vehicles charging station location based on ISM and FMICMAC. *Sustainability*, *9*(4), 484. doi:10.3390u9040484

Wu, J., Sun, J., Liang, L., & Zha, Y. (2011). Determination of weights for ultimate cross efficiency using Shannon Entropy. *Expert Systems with Applications*, *38*(5), 5162–5165. doi:10.1016/j.eswa.2010.10.046

Xu, Z. (2013). *Linguistic Decision Making: Theory and Methods*. Beijing, China: Science Press Beijing; doi:10.1007/978-3-642-29440-2

Xu, Z. S., & Da, Q. L. (2002). The ordered weighted geometric averaging operators. *International Journal of Intelligent Systems*, *17*(7), 709–716. doi:10.1002/int.10045

Yadav, D. K., & Barve, A. (2015). Analysis of critical success factors of humanitarian supply chain: An application of Interpretive Structural Modeling. *International Journal of Disaster Risk Reduction*, *12*, 213–225. doi:10.1016/j.ijdrr.2015.01.008

Yager, R. R. (1988). On ordered weighted averaging aggregation operators in multi criteria decision making. *IEEE Transactions on Systems, Man, and Cybernetics*, *18*(1), 183–190. doi:10.1109/21.87068

Yager, R. R., & Xu, Z. (2006). The continuous ordered weighted geometric operator and its application to decision making. *Fuzzy Sets and Systems*, *157*(10), 1393–1402. doi:10.1016/j.fss.2005.12.001

Yalçın, N., & Ünlü, U. (2018). A multi-criteria performance analysis of initial public offering (IPO) firms using CRITIC and VIKOR methods. *Technological and Economic Development of Economy*, *24*(2), 534–560. doi:10.3846/20294913.2016.1213201

Yang, J. L., Chiu, H. N., Tzeng, G. H., & Yeh, R. H. (2009). Vendor selection by integrated fuzzy MCDM techniques with independent and interdependent relationships. *Information Sciences*, *178*(21), 4166–4183. doi:10.1016/j.ins.2008.06.003

Yang, M. G. M., Hong, P., & Modi, S. B. (2011). Impact of lean manufacturing and environmental management on business performance: An empirical study of manufacturing firms. *International Journal of Production Economics*, *129*(2), 251–261. doi:10.1016/j.ijpe.2010.10.017

Yang, Z., Bonsall, S., & Wang, J. (2008). Fuzzy rule-based Bayesian reasoning approach for prioritization of failures in FMEA. *IEEE Transactions on Reliability*, *57*(3), 517–528. doi:10.1109/TR.2008.928208

Yazdani, M. (2015). New intuitionistic fuzzy approach with multi-objective optimisation on the basis of ratio analysis method. *International Journal of Business and Systems Research*, *9*(4), 355–374. doi:10.1504/IJBSR.2015.072584

Yeh, C. H. (2002). A Problem Based Selection of Multi-Attribute Decision-Making Methods. *International Transactions in Operational Research*, *9*(2), 169–181. doi:10.1111/1475-3995.00348

Yeravdekar, A., & Behl, A. (2018). The unprecedented commercialisation of Indian cricket: A study using total interpretive structural modelling. *International Journal of Services and Operations Management*, *31*(3), 277–302. doi:10.1504/IJSOM.2018.095558

Yeravdekar, S., & Behl, A. (2017). Benchmarking model for management education in India: A total interpretive structural modeling approach. Benchmarking. *International Journal (Toronto, Ont.)*, *24*(3), 666–693.

Yeravdekar, S., & Behl, A. (2017). Benchmarking model for management education in India: A total interpretive structural modeling approach. *Benchmarking: An International Journal*, *24*(3), 666–693. doi:10.1108/BIJ-06-2016-0082

Yerlikaya, M. A., Burak, E. F. E., & Efe, O. F. (2016). İş Güvenliğinde Bulanık Promethee Yöntemiyle Hata Türleri ve Etkilerinin Analizi: Bir İnşaat Firmasında Uygulama. *Gümüşhane Üniversitesi Fen Bilimleri Enstitüsü Dergisi*, *6*(2), 126–137. doi:10.17714/gufbed.2016.06.012

Yin, P. Y., & Guo, Y. M. (2013). Optimization of multi-criteria website structure based on enhanced tabu search and web usage mining. *Applied Mathematics and Computation*, *219*(24), 11082–11095. doi:10.1016/j.amc.2013.05.033

Yüce, G., & Temiz, İ. (2017). Multi Criteria Decision Making Methods Approach to Asynchronous Electric. *The Journal of Operations Research, Statistics, Econometrics, and Management Information Systems*, *5*(2), 171–190. doi:10.17093/alphanumeric.313270

Yudatama, U., Hidayanto, A. N., & Nazief, B. A. (2018). Approach Using Interpretive Structural Model (ISM) to Determine Key Sub-Factors at Factors: Benefits, Risk Reductions, Opportunities and Obstacles in Awareness IT Governance. *Journal of Theoretical and Applied Information Technology*, *96*(16), 5536–5549.

Yu, P. L. (1973). A class of solutions for group decision problems. *Management Science*, *19*(8), 936–946. doi:10.1287/mnsc.19.8.936

Yurdakul, M., & İç, Y. T. (2005). Development of a performance measurement model for manufacturing companies using the AHP and TOPSIS approaches. *International Journal of Production Research*, *43*(21), 4609–4641. doi:10.1080/00207540500161746

Zadeh, L. A. (1965). Fuzzy sets. *Information and Control*, *8*(3), 338–353. doi:10.1016/S0019-9958(65)90241-X

Zeleny, M. (1982). *Multiple criteria decision making*. New York: McGraw-Hill.

Zhang, M. S., Pawar, K., Shah, J., & Mehta, P. (2013). Evaluating outsourcing partners' capability: A case study from the pharmaceutical SC. *Journal of Manufacturing Technology Management*, *24*(8), 1080–1101. doi:10.1108/JMTM-02-2012-0023

Zhou, L., & Chen, H. (2014). Generalized Ordered Weighted Proportional Averaging Operator and Its Application to Group Decision Making. *Informatica*, *25*(2), 327–360. doi:10.15388/Informatica.2014.17

Zhou, X., Ding, Y., & Lu, M. (2018). Study on bond selection under intuitionistic fuzzy conditions. *Journal of Algorithms & Computational Technology*, *12*(4), 376–386. doi:10.1177/1748301818791505

Zopounidis, C., & Doumpos, M. (2002). Multi-criteria decision aid in financial decision making: Methodologies and literature review. *Journal of Multi-Criteria Decision Analysis*, *11*(4-5), 167–186. doi:10.1002/mcda.333

About the Contributors

Abhishek Behl is a PhD scholar at Shailesh J. Mehta School of Management, Indian Institute of Technology Bombay, Mumbai, India. He is pursuing his second PhD in the area of Decision Sciences and Business Analytics at IIT (B); he has successfully completed his first PhD in the area of Financial Inclusion and Rural Development from Symbiosis International University in 2015. He has also enjoyed the honor of being 'Emerald Research Scholar' awarded by Emerald Publishing House, UK, and Symbiosis International University, for notable contribution in research (2014-2016). He has served as a Resource Person for renowned educational institutions in India and conducted numerous Management Development Programmes in India and overseas. He has published several papers in journals indexed in prominent indices. He has also presented papers at a number of national and international conferences. His research interests are primarily focused on actionable inquiries and exploration mostly in the area of management with stems in Information Technology, Business Analytics, and Decision Science.

* * *

Daniel Aikhuele lectures at the College of Engineering, Bells University of Technology, Ota, Nigeria. He holds a PhD degree in Manufacturing Engineering from the Universiti Malaysia Pahang, Pekan, Malaysia. An MS.c degree in Advanced Manufacturing Systems from the Teesside University, Middlesbrough, United Kingdom and a B.Eng degree in Materials and Production Engineering from the Ambrose Alli University, Ekpoma, Nigeria. His research areas include, reliability management, product development and evaluation, energy and fuzzy multi-criteria analysis in engineering. He is a seasoned researcher and educator, he has published more than 30 international journal articles in top-class journal outlets.

Aastha Behl is an Assistant Professor in the Department of Management at PSIT, Kanpur. Academically, she is a Company Secretary and Masters in Commerce. She has also qualified UGC-NET and teaches Law and Finance related subjects. She also holds research interest in law related areas and has published papers in the same.

Kirti Bhatele is working as an Assistant professor in the Dept. of CSE in Rustamji Institute of technology BSF Academy Gwalior. He has received Bachelor's degree in Information Technology in 2010 from Rajiv Gandhi Technical University, Bhopal, India and Master of Technology (M.Tech) degree (Information Technology) in 2012 from Rajiv Gandhi Technical University, Bhopal, India. Currently he is pursuing P h.D from the Rajiv Gandhi Technical University, Bhopal, India. He has published more than ten research papers in International journal and Conferences. He has also published eight Book

Chapters. He has received three Government research fellowships from the Madhya Pradesh Council of Science and Technology, Bhopal, M.P, India. His Research Interest lies in Image Processing, Medical Image Processing, Machine learning, etc.

William Alberto Cruz Castañeda is working as a collaborating Assistant Professor in the Department of Computer Sciences at the Universidade do Estado de Santa Catarina - UDESC Joinville Center for Technological Sciences. In 2006, he received the B.Sc. degree in computer sciences from the Benemerita Universidad Autonoma de Puebla, México. In 2008 it was certified by Mexican Standard NMX-I-059/02-NYCE-2005 MOPROSOFT for software development, maintenance and evaluation. In 2010 he received the M.S. degree, and in 2016 he received the PhD degree both in electrical engineering focused on biomedical engineering from the Universidade Federal de Santa Catarina - UFSC, Brazil. His research interests include ubiquitous computing, internet of things, wearable devices, ubiquitous health, machine learning, multi-criteria decision-analysis, healthcare technology management, home care, chronic disease management, and digital assistive technologies. It includes the design, development and implementation of computational solutions that facilitate the acquisition, processing, transmission and management of heterogeneous data.

Sündüs Dağ is an assistant professor within the Department Operations Management/Business School at the Istanbul University. Before joining Istanbul University, Dr. DAǦ worked in several sectors including pharmaceutical. Dr. DAǦ is extensively involved in research regarding quality control, quality management systems, multicriteria decision making.

Pankaj Dutta is an Associate Professor in the field of Decision Sciences and Operations Research. Before joining SJMSOM, he has served as a Lecturer at BITS Pilani, Rajasthan. He has also worked as Postdoctoral fellow at EPFL, Swiss Federal Institute of Technology, Switzerland and Visiting Fellow at Karlsruhe Institute of Technology, Germany and Humboldt University of Berlin, Germany. His current areas of research interest include Data Analytics, Supply Chain Modeling and Optimization, E-commerce, Production Planning and Retail Inventory Management, Reverse Logistics, Project Scheduling, Mathematical Finance and Decision-Making under Risk and Uncertainty. He is also interested in System Simulation, Fuzzy set theory and its application to Industrial Engineering & Management. He pioneered the concept of fuzzy random demand in the field of Inventory Systems. He has publications in international journals like European Journal of Operational Research, International Journal of Production Research, Journal of Cleaner Production, Annals of Operations Research, International Journal of Systems Science, Computers and Industrial Engineering, Computers and Mathematics with Applications and International Journal of Advanced Manufacturing Technology.

Ömer Faruk Efe graduated from Selçuk University, Department of Industrial Engineering in 2008. He received the M.Sc. degree in Industrial Engineering from Selçuk University. He received Ph.D. degree in Industrial Engineering from Sakarya University. His research interests are Multi-criteria decision making, fuzzy logic, lean production, ergonomics, occupational health and safety. He has been working as an Assistant Professor in Afyon Kocatepe University.

Ana Paula Lopes has a Ph.D. in Mathematics. She is professor at the Accounting and Administration Institute of the Porto Polytechnic (ISCAP/P.PORTO) since 2000. She is the author of several peer-reviewed publications on the subject. She has been coordinator of several Projects related with the Use of Technology and Pedagogical Innovation in Distance Education. In 2015, she received the Award for Pedagogical Innovation in Distance Education. She has been Member of Scientific Committee of several International Conferences and is a Member of the Scientific Board of Hyperion Economic Journal (HEJ). She also serves as a regular reviewer as a member of the program committee for several International Conferences. She is a researcher at Communication and Education Research Centre (CEOS.PP) and researcher at Research Centre for the Study of Population, Economics and Society (CEPESE). Her main research interests focus are LMS supports platforms, information technologies in education, E-learning teaching, teaching/learning education paradigm, Decision Making.

Muktasha Mithora is an engineering graduate and Teaching Assistant from the Rustamji Institute of Technology, BSF Academy, Tekanpur an institute run by the Border Security Force. She has work on various projects related to Data Analysis such as "Global Stratification" and IoT.

Tuğba Kıral Özkan received her undergraduate degree at the Department of Econometrics, Faculty of Economics and Administrative Sciences, Uludağ University. She completed her Master's degree at Marmara University, Institute of Social Sciences, Department of Management and Organization. She received her Ph.D. from Operations Research at Marmara University, Institute of Social Sciences. Currently, she is the Deputy Dricetor of the Graduate School of Educational Sciences is the Deputy Director of Educational Sciences at Bahcesehir University (BAU). She has experience in projects as researcher founded by Erasmus+. Also she is the researcher of Erasmus+ KA2 on "Up to Youth Promoting Future Digital Social Entrepreneurs, No: 2018-1-TR01-KA205-057895, 2018." Her current research interests include measurement and evaluation, optimization methods, multi criteria decision making. She offers research methods and statistical data analysis courses in undergraduate and graduate programs at BAU.

Burcu Avcı Öztürk graduated from Uludag University, Department of Business Administration in 2001. She holds her Master (2004) and Doctorate (2011) degrees in the field of Quantitative Methods at Social Sciences Institute of Uludag University. She has been working as an Assistant Professor in Department of Business Administration/Quantitative Methods at Uludag University since 2015. Her research interests are Optimization, Multi-criteria decision making (MCDM), Fuzzy optimization, Fuzzy MCDM, Data envelopment analysis and Sustainability performance evaluation.

Vikramsinh Patil is a Third Year BSc. (Hons) Economics student at Symbiosis School of Economics, Symbiosis International (Deemed) University, Pune. His research interests lie in the domain of financial economics, specifically corporate finance and its intersection with policymaking.

Rafaela Pinho is a planner of several production lines in a multinational in the north of Portugal, where she is responsible for high level planning, managing the resources for the production lines, as well as the production itself. She started the Customer Service function, Demand Planner, having been invited to take part in a high-level planning function, Previously, Rafaela worked in a shoe company where she was responsible for managing orders, giving customer support and managing stocks. Rafaela is based in a degree in Economics from the Faculty of Economics of Porto, continuing in the Polytechnic

Institute of Porto with a master's degree in Logistics, having distinguished herself as the best student of the course. Rafaela is ambitious, persistent and focused. She loves animals and likes to enjoy her free time to play sports and enjoy every moment with her family.

Sneha Sharma is an engineering graduate and teaching Assistant from the Rustamji Institute of Technology, BSF Academy Tekanpur, an institute run by the Border Security. She has work on various projects related to Data Analysis such as "Global Stratification". She has written various articles and Blogs on Computer Programming and Big Data Science.

Stuti Singhal is an engineering graduate and Teaching Assistant from the Rustamji Institute of Technology, BSF Academy Tekanpur, an institute run by the Border Security. She has work on various projects related to Data Analysis such as "Global Stratification" and represented college in the National Level competitions like Hackathon. She has written various articles and Blogs on Computer Programming and Big Data Science.

Shilpi Swati is an alumnus of Shailesh J Mehta School of Management and has finished her MBA. She understands and applies management practices in the real world through her innovative thought process.

Semra Erpolat Taşabat completed undergraduate education at Hacettepe University Faculty of Science, Department of Statistics in 1999 and her postgraduate education in 2002 at Hacettepe University Institute of Science in Statistics Department. She received Ph.D education in 2007 at the Institute of Statistics of Mimar Sinan Fine Arts University and in 2010 from Marmara University Social Sciences Institute, Department of Operational Research. In 2013, she was appointed as Associate Professor in Quantitative Decision Methods. In 2004, she started to work as a research assistant in the Department of Statistics in the Faculty of Arts and Sciences at Mimar Sinan Fine Arts University. She worked as an assistant professor in the same department in 2007, as an associate professor in 2013 and as a professor in 2019. She is still working as a full-time lecturer in the same department and a part time lecturer at Bahçeşehir University.

Merve Cengiz Toklu is an Assistant Professor at the Sakarya University in the Department of Industrial Engineering. She received the M.Sc. and the Ph.D. degree in Industrial Engineering from the Sakarya University, Sakarya, Turkey in 2010 and 2016, respectively. Her main areas of research interest are performance management, strategic management, multi-criteria decision making, and fuzzy logic. She has worked as a production planning consultant in a manufacturing SME for four years. She has been working at Sakarya University since 2011.

Index

(A+) 77, 174, 188

A

AHP 21, 33, 45, 62-67, 71-73, 78, 84, 111-112, 114-115, 117-118, 123-125, 127, 134, 140, 174, 190, 226-227, 253, 280, 297, 306, 311-313
Alternative (A) 84
AMOS 21, 26, 336
Analytic Hierarchy Process (AHP) 33, 45, 62, 65, 84, 112, 117, 140, 174, 280, 297, 311
Anchoring 344, 353
ANP 21, 78, 114, 253, 280, 297
Application 1-2, 19, 28-32, 34, 36, 63, 66, 68, 71, 100, 112, 118, 123-125, 127, 134, 140, 170, 173, 175-176, 181, 190, 200, 227, 260, 276, 283, 286, 312-313, 323-324, 337, 339, 341, 359, 365, 374, 376
Average Visit Duration 280

B

Banking 189, 192, 198, 203, 210, 361, 367
Behavioural Economics 335-336
Bounce Rate 280

C

Case Study 13, 111, 171, 189, 203, 225, 232, 251, 286
Category Traffic Rank 280
CC 188
Choice Architecture 336, 338, 347-348, 353
Confirmatory Factor Analysis (CFA) 21, 26
Corporate Nudging 337
Corporate Social Responsibility 13
Correlation 45, 191, 239, 241, 244, 286
Country Traffic Rank 280
Criteria (C) 27, 30-31, 45, 62-68, 71-72, 75-79, 84-86, 90-91, 94, 96-97, 99, 111-116, 118-127, 129-132, 134-135, 139-140, 142, 147-149, 151, 160, 163-164, 168-170, 174-175, 179-180, 189-193, 198-201, 203, 210, 214, 225-230, 233-234, 244, 251-263, 266, 268, 276-277, 281-289, 291, 297-298, 300, 305-306, 309, 312, 322, 348, 360, 374

D

Dark Nudges 337, 346, 348, 353
Data Analysis 355-359, 366-367, 374, 376, 378
Data Science 355-356, 358-359, 361, 367, 376, 378
Data Visualization 359, 364, 367, 376, 378
Decentralized Healthcare Service 94, 109
Decision Making 33, 51, 62-63, 84, 86-87, 112-115, 134-135, 163, 170, 174-175, 189, 199, 214, 225-226, 238, 244, 252, 280-281, 284-285, 306, 316-317, 327-328, 335-336, 341
Decision Process 175, 191, 276
Decision-Maker 65, 91, 97, 112, 114-115, 118, 122-123, 127, 131, 134, 143, 168, 175, 191, 287-288, 295, 297, 304-305, 319
Default Options 346
Defuzzyfication 334
Delphi Technique 2, 26
DEMATEL 170, 253, 280
Development 30, 34, 36, 47, 50-51, 86, 89, 95-96, 142, 189-190, 225-227, 232-233, 236, 241, 244, 256, 285, 310, 355, 360-364, 366-367, 376
Driving and Dependence Power 26, 46-47, 53, 58
Dynamic Operator 174, 181

E

Estimated Input Latency (EIL) 280
Euclidean Distance 174, 189-190, 192, 196, 198, 214, 227, 229, 312
Exploratory Factor Analysis 21, 26

F

Financial Performance 189, 198, 210, 214
First Contentful Paint (FCP) 280
First Meaningful Paint (FMP) 281
FMEA 254, 310-317, 323-324, 327-328
Framing 10, 16, 339, 345, 353
Fuzzy Logic 62-63, 66, 139-142, 164, 168, 253, 310, 316, 334
Fuzzy MICMAC 46-47, 51, 54-55, 58
Fuzzy number 141, 170-172, 281, 317, 323-324, 326, 334
Fuzzy Set 55, 64-65, 78, 84, 94, 141-142, 169, 171-172, 174, 187-188, 192, 253, 312, 317, 322, 334
Fuzzyfication 334

G

Global Traffic Rank 281
Graph Theory 29

H

HDI 225, 227, 232-233, 239-241, 244
Healthcare 48-49, 85-87, 89, 94, 96-97, 100, 102, 104, 106, 109-110, 367, 369-370, 375
Healthcare Service Assessment 110
Healthcare Service Management 110
Home Care 97, 110
Homo Economicus 336, 353

I

Importance Weight 63, 143, 168, 277
Interoperable Decision-Making 104
Interpretive Structural Modelling 28-29, 35-36, 46-47
Intuitionistic Fuzzy Set 142, 169, 171-172, 174, 192
ISM 1-3, 6, 8, 10-13, 15-19, 21, 28-36, 47-48, 51, 54, 58

J

Joint Health Safety Unit (JHSU) 63, 84

L

L1 Distance Family 214
Language R 366-367, 374, 378
Level of Development 226-227, 233
Libertarian Paternalism 336, 339, 353
Logistics 30-31, 46-49, 51, 55, 58
Lq Distance Family 214

M

Manufacturing 28-33, 35-36, 47, 50, 147-148, 164, 178, 284, 286, 311, 313, 323, 358
Measuring Attractiveness 90
Medical Device 110
Medical Equipment 95, 97-98, 110
MICMAC Analysis 1, 11-12, 18-19, 21, 46-47, 54, 58
Modelling 21, 26-29, 31, 35-36, 45-47, 58, 356
Multi Criteria Decision Analysis (MCDA) 27
Multi-Criteria Decision Making (MCDM) 62, 84, 112, 114, 189, 199, 225, 252, 281, 285, 309, 317, 334
Multi-criteria Group Decision-making (MCGDM) 170

N

NP 277, 281
Nudging 335-337, 339-344, 346, 349

O

Occupational Health and Safety (OHS) 78, 84, 312
Occupational Safety Services 62

P

Page Views/Visit 281
Patient Safety 86, 100, 106
Performance score (PS) 281
Pharmaceutical Process 311
Pharmaceutical Supply Chain 46-47, 313
Planning Fallacy 342, 353
Preference Ranking Organization Method for Enrichment Evaluation (PROMETHEE) 112, 121, 282-283, 309, 312
Prioritization 253, 317, 327

Q

Quality Improvement 85-87, 310-311, 313

R

Renewable Power Plants 169
Risk Priority Number 311, 314, 334

S

Services Effectiveness 106
Social Proofing 347, 353
Speed Index (SI) 281

Structural Equation Modelling (SEM) 26-27, 45, 58
Supplier 31, 63, 68, 111-113, 123-125, 127-128, 130-132, 134-135, 139-140, 170, 254, 286, 297

T

Tableau 355, 358-359, 364-365, 374, 376, 378
Tableau Software 365, 374, 378
Technique for Order Preference by Similarity to Ideal Solution (TOPSIS) 33, 45, 84, 139-140, 170, 174-175, 281, 312
Technology Reliability 86, 100, 106
The Time to Interactive (TTI) 281

U

Unbalanced Linguistic 90, 93

V

VIKOR 64, 78, 170, 174, 180-181, 190, 225-227, 230, 236, 238-241, 244, 251-254, 256-257, 259-260, 267, 276-277, 312

W

Website Performance Evaluation 253
World Wide Web 251, 281

X

XMCDA 104-105, 110
μA 169, 171-172, 187
υA 169, 172, 188
*L*1 Family Distance 198

www.ingramcontent.com/pod-product-compliance
Lightning Source LLC
LaVergne TN
LVHW060359300926
849162LV00006B/1305